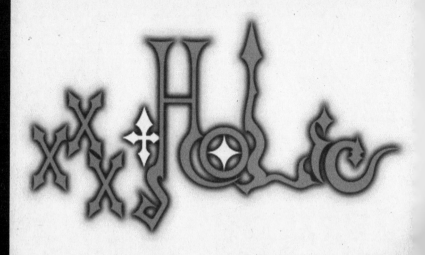

CLAMP

TRANSLATED AND ADAPTED BY

William Flanagan

LETTERED BY

Dana Hayward

KC
KODANSHA
COMICS

[9]

xxxHOLiC Omnibus volume 7 is a work of fiction. Names, characters, places, and incidents are the products of the author's imagination or are used fictitiously. Any resemblance to actual events, locales, or persons, living or dead, is entirely coincidental.

A Kodansha Comics Trade Paperback Original.

Published in the United States by Kodansha Comics, an imprint of
Kodansha USA Publishing, LLC, New York.

Publication rights for this English edition arranged through
Kodansha Ltd., Tokyo.

First published in Japan in 2010-2011 by Kodansha Ltd., Tokyo, as
xxxHOLiC, volumes 18 and 19.

ISBN 978-1-63236-120-2

Printed in the United States of America.

www.kodanshacomics.com

9 8 7 6 5 4 3 2 1

Translator: William Flanagan
Lettering: North Market Street Graphics
Kodansha Comics edition cover design: Phil Balsman

xxxHOLiC crosses over with *Tsubasa*. Although it isn't necessary to read *Tsubasa* to understand the events in *xxxHOLiC*, you'll get to see the same events from different perspectives if you read both series!

Contents

Honorifics Explained

Throughout the Kodansha Comics books, you will find Japanese honorifics left intact in the translations. For those not familiar with how the Japanese use honorifics and, more important, how they differ from American honorifics, we present this brief overview.

Politeness has always been a critical facet of Japanese culture. Ever since the feudal era, when Japan was a highly stratified society, use of honorifics—which can be defined as polite speech that indicates relationship or status—has played an essential role in the Japanese language. When addressing someone in Japanese, an honorific usually takes the form of a suffix attached to one's name (example: "Asuna-san"), is used as a title at the end of one's name, or appears in place of the name itself (example: "Negi-sensei," or simply "Sensei!").

Honorifics can be expressions of respect or endearment. In the context of manga and anime, honorifics give insight into the nature of the relationship between characters. Many English translations leave out these important honorifics and therefore distort the feel of the original Japanese. Because Japanese honorifics contain nuances that English honorifics lack, it is our policy at Kodansha Comics not to translate them. Here, instead, is a guide to some of the honorifics you may encounter in Kodansha Comics books.

-san: This is the most common honorific and is equivalent to Mr., Miss, Ms., or Mrs. It is the all-purpose honorific and can be used in any situation where politeness is required.

-sama: This is one level higher than "-san" and is used to confer great respect.

-dono: This comes from the word "tono," which means "lord." It is an even higher level than "-sama" and confers utmost respect.

-kun: This suffix is used at the end of boys' names to express familiarity or endearment. It is also sometimes used by men among friends, or when addressing someone younger or of a lower station.

-chan: This is used to express endearment, mostly toward girls. It is also used for little boys, pets, and even among lovers. It gives a sense of childish cuteness.

Bozu: This is an informal way to refer to a boy, similar to the English terms "kid" and "squirt."

Sempai/
Senpai: This title suggests that the addressee is one's senior in a group or organization. It is most often used in a school setting, where underclassmen refer to their upperclassmen as "sempai." It can also be used in the workplace, such as when a newer employee addresses an employee who has seniority in the company.

Kohai: This is the opposite of "sempai" and is used toward underclassmen in school or newcomers in the workplace. It connotes that the addressee is of a lower station.

Sensei: Literally meaning "one who has come before," this title is used for teachers, doctors, or masters of any profession or art.

-[blank]: This is usually forgotten in these lists, but it is perhaps the most significant difference between Japanese and English. The lack of honorific means that the speaker has permission to address the person in a very intimate way. Usually, only family, spouses, or very close friends have this kind of permission. Known as yobisute, it can be gratifying when someone who has earned the intimacy starts to call one by one's name without an honorific. But when that intimacy hasn't been earned, it can be very insulting.

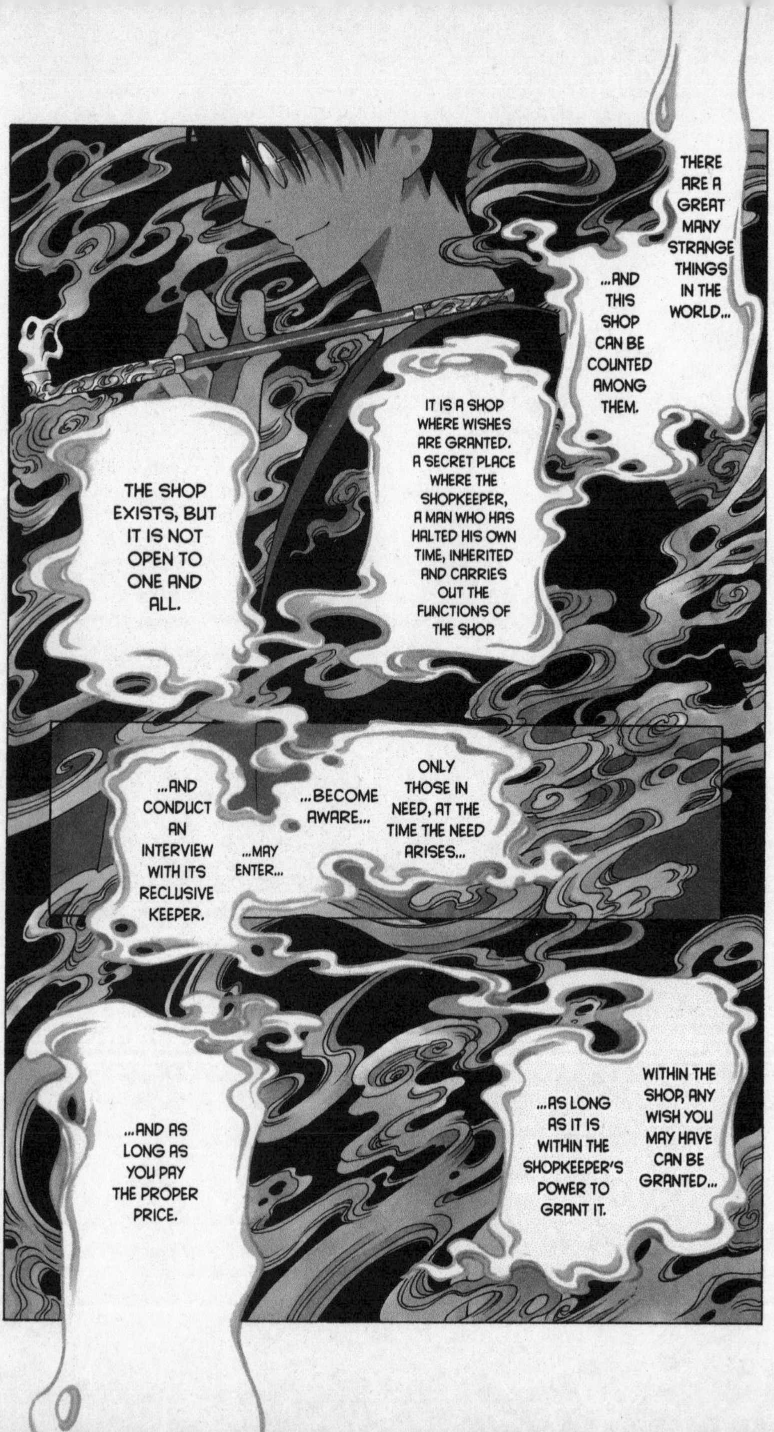
THERE ARE A GREAT MANY STRANGE THINGS IN THE WORLD...
...AND THIS SHOP CAN BE COUNTED AMONG THEM.
IT IS A SHOP WHERE WISHES ARE GRANTED. A SECRET PLACE WHERE THE SHOPKEEPER, A MAN WHO HAS HALTED HIS OWN TIME, INHERITED AND CARRIES OUT THE FUNCTIONS OF THE SHOP.
THE SHOP EXISTS, BUT IT IS NOT OPEN TO ONE AND ALL.
ONLY THOSE IN NEED, AT THE TIME THE NEED ARISES...
...BECOME AWARE...
...MAY ENTER...
...AND CONDUCT AN INTERVIEW WITH ITS RECLUSIVE KEEPER.
WITHIN THE SHOP, ANY WISH YOU MAY HAVE CAN BE GRANTED...
...AS LONG AS IT IS WITHIN THE SHOPKEEPER'S POWER TO GRANT IT.
...AND AS LONG AS YOU PAY THE PROPER PRICE.

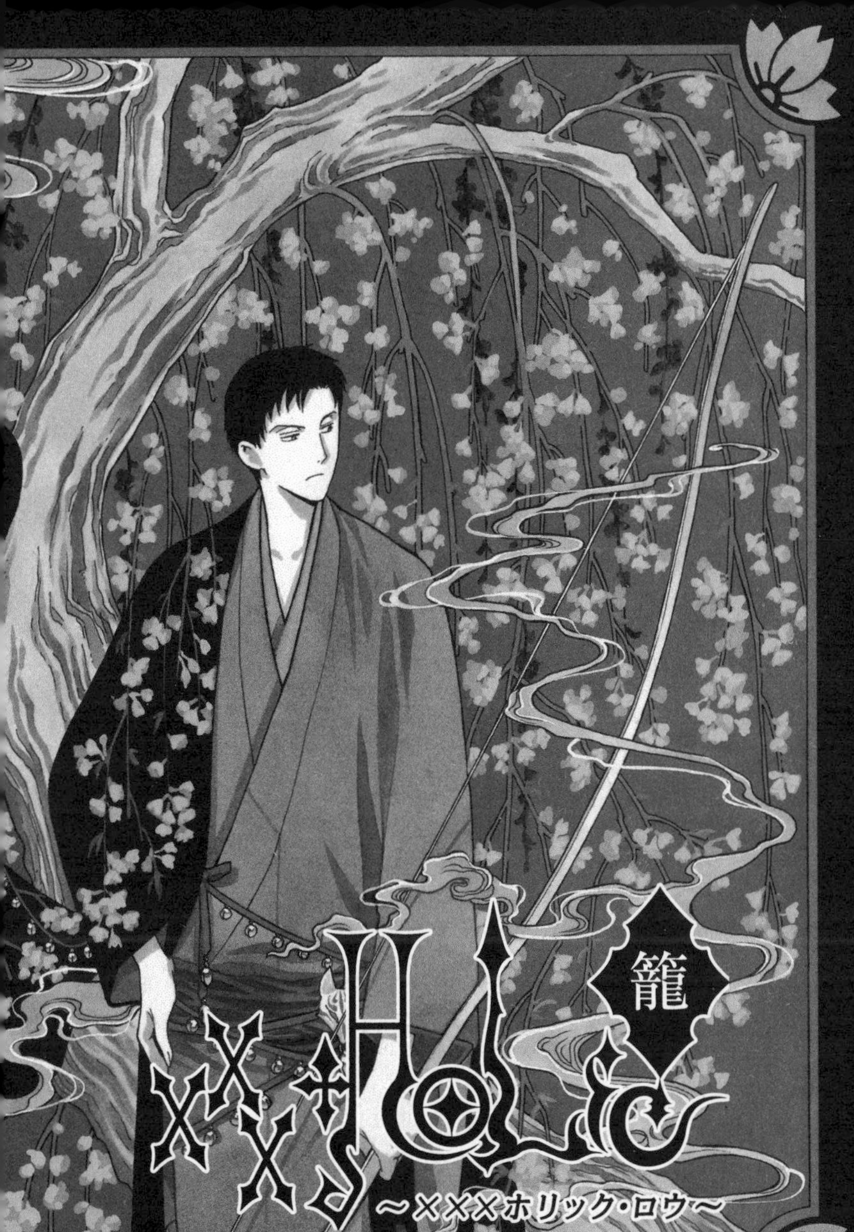

xxxHOLiC
籠
~×××ホリック·ロウ~

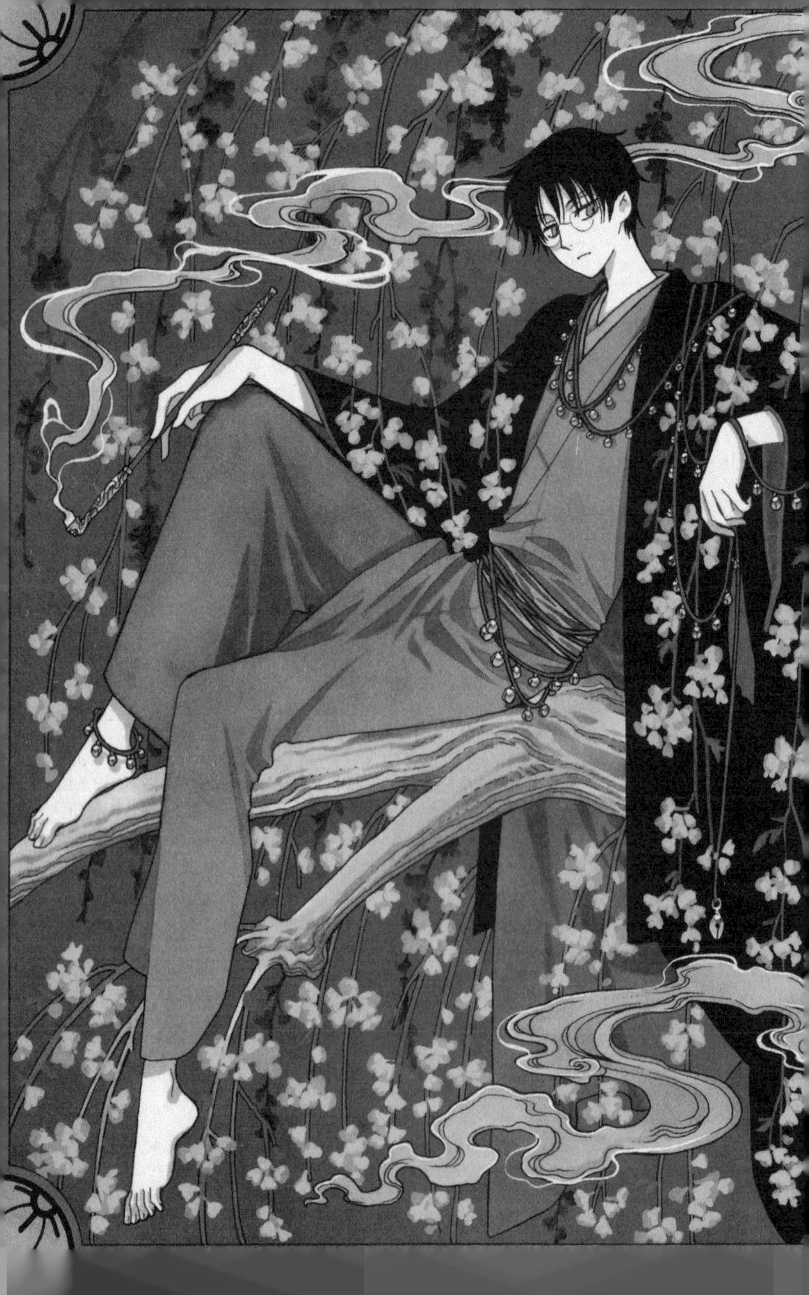

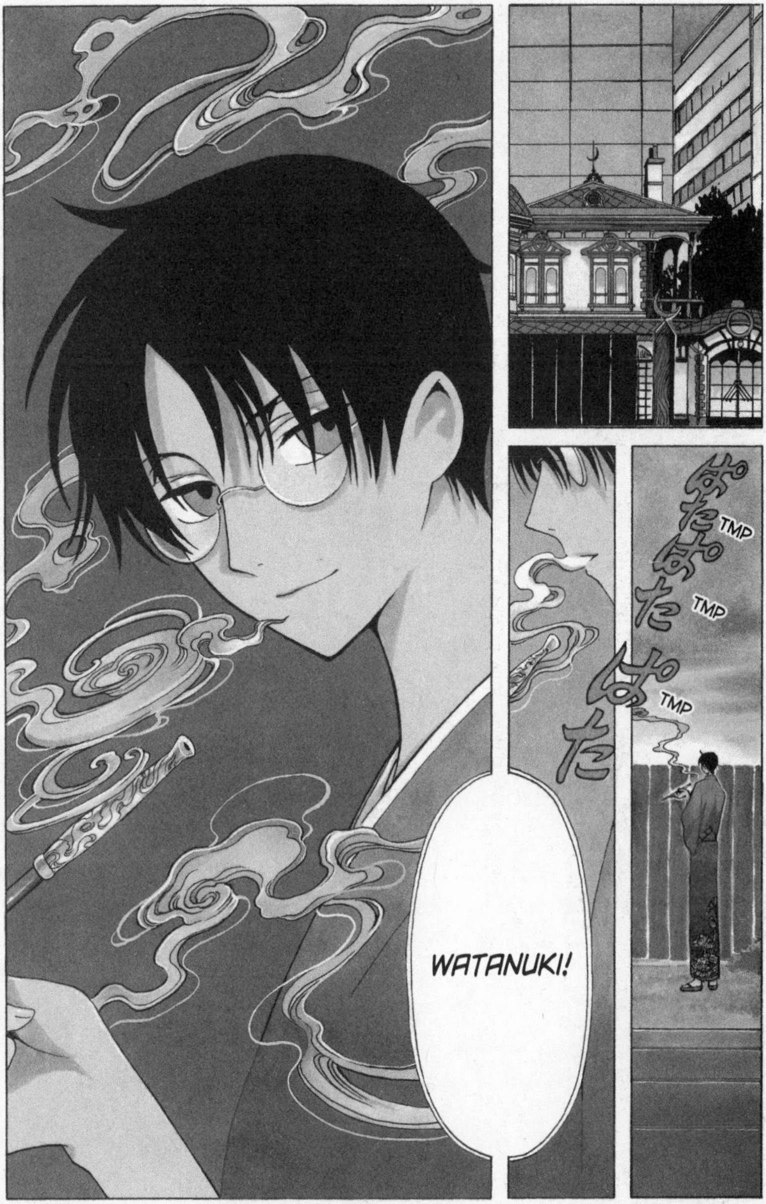
ぱたぱたぱた
TMP
TMP
TMP
WATANUKI!

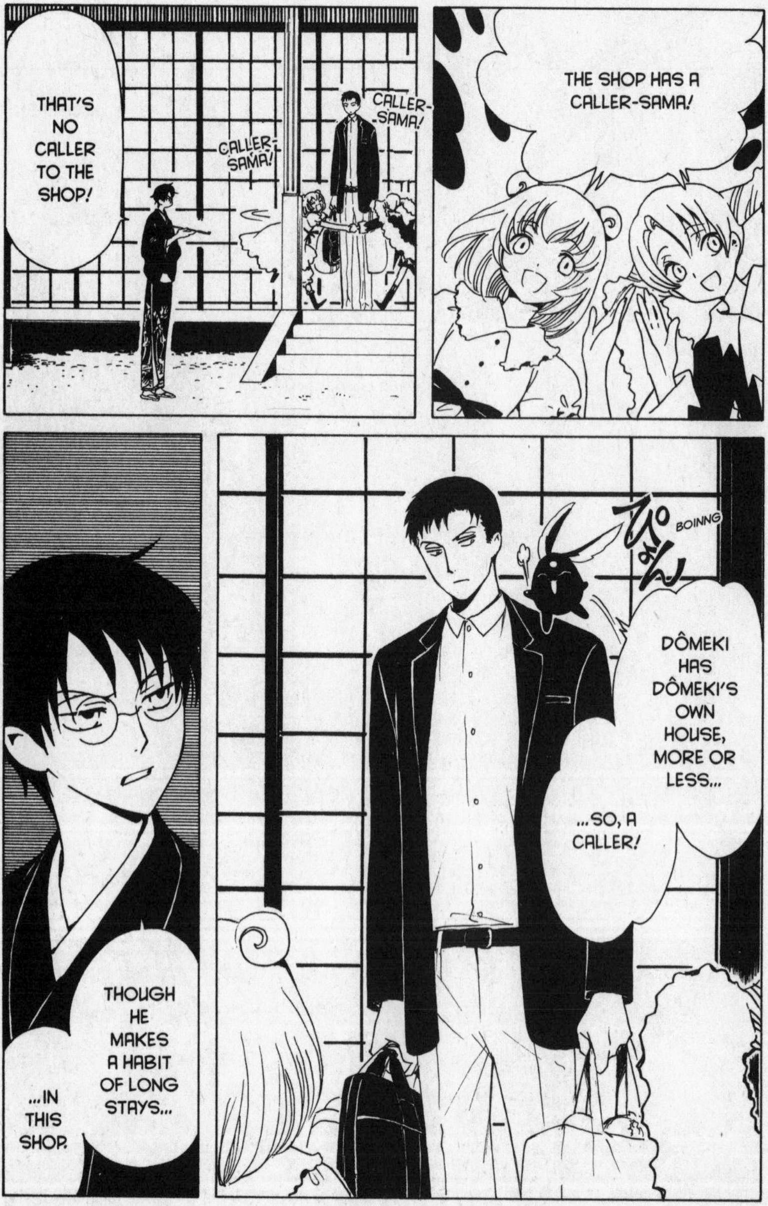
THE SHOP HAS A CALLER-SAMA!
CALLER-SAMA!
CALLER-SAMA!
THAT'S NO CALLER TO THE SHOP!
ぴょん
BOINNG
DÔMEKI HAS DÔMEKI'S OWN HOUSE, MORE OR LESS...
...SO, A CALLER!
THOUGH HE MAKES A HABIT OF LONG STAYS...
...IN THIS SHOP.

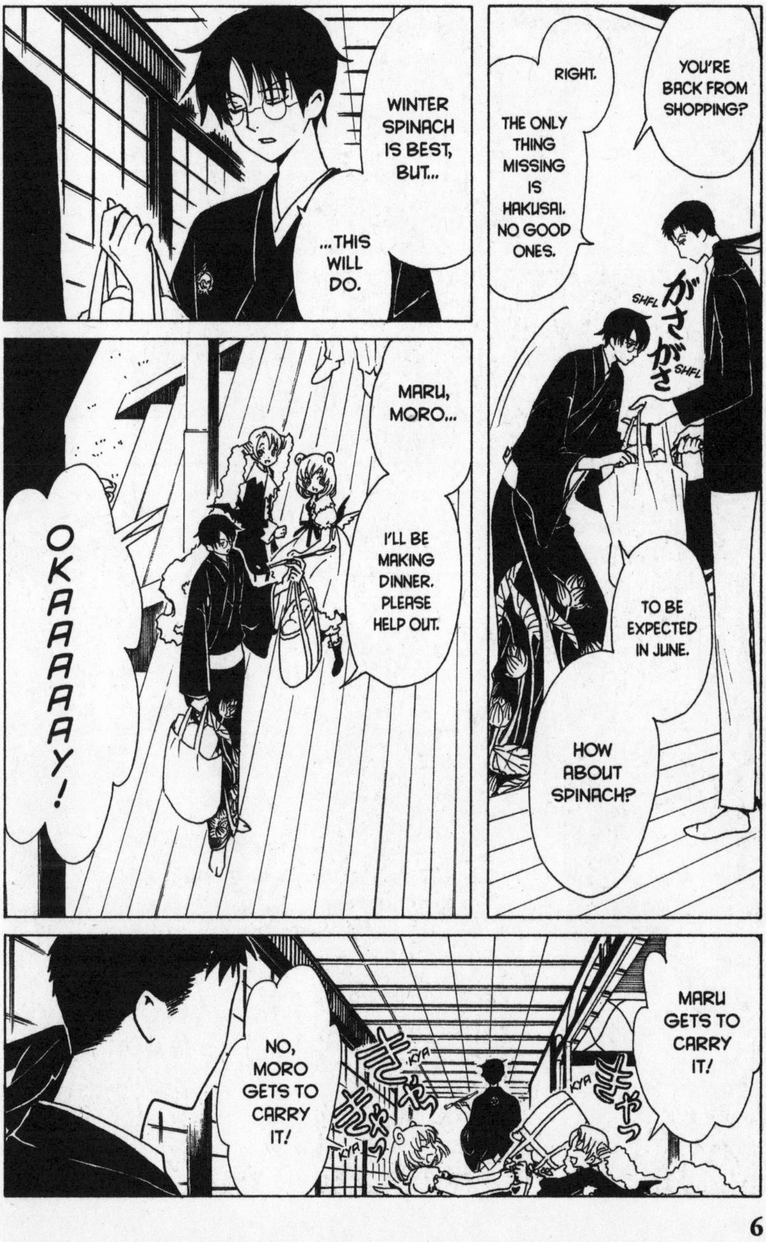
YOU'RE BACK FROM SHOPPING?
RIGHT.
THE ONLY THING MISSING IS HAKUSAI. NO GOOD ONES.
WINTER SPINACH IS BEST, BUT...
...THIS WILL DO.
がさがさ
SHFL
SHFL
TO BE EXPECTED IN JUNE.
HOW ABOUT SPINACH?
MARU, MORO...
I'LL BE MAKING DINNER. PLEASE HELP OUT.
OKAAAAAAY!
MARU GETS TO CARRY IT!
きゃっ
KYA
NO, MORO GETS TO CARRY IT!
きゃっ
KYA
きゃっ
KYA

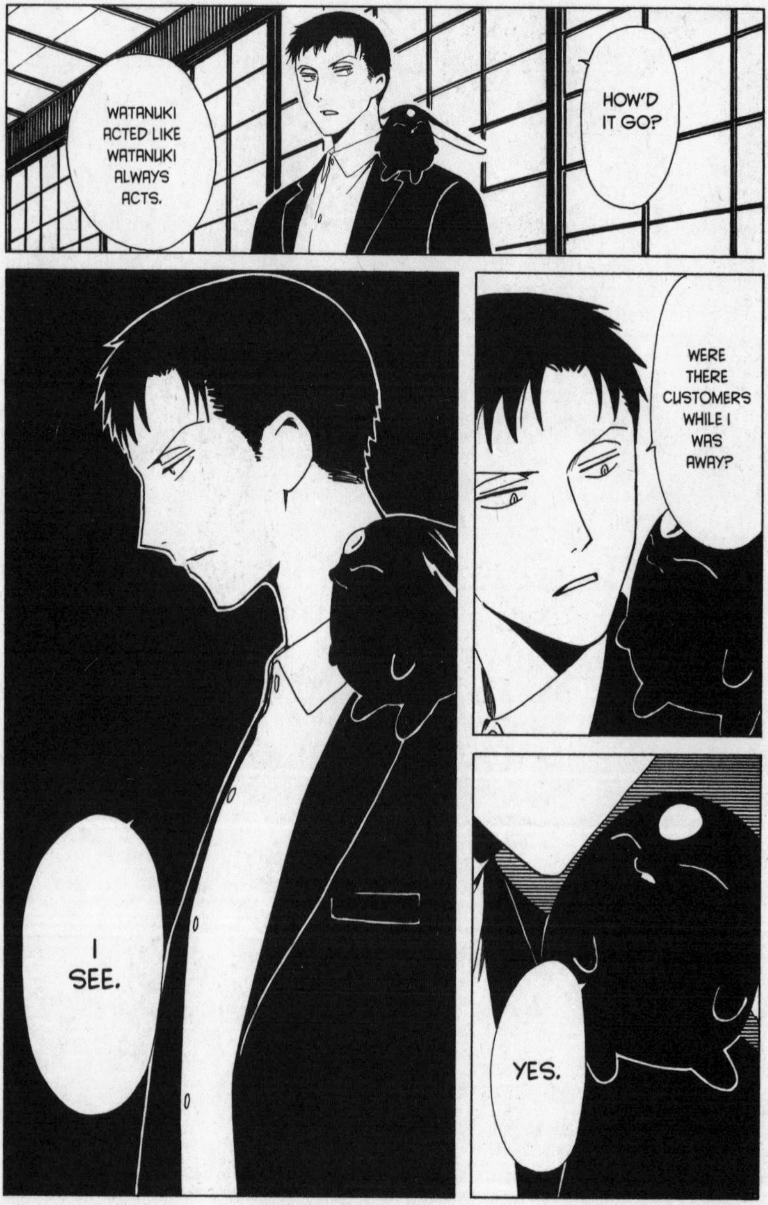
HOW'D IT GO?
WATANUKI ACTED LIKE WATANUKI ALWAYS ACTS.
WERE THERE CUSTOMERS WHILE I WAS AWAY?
YES.
I SEE.

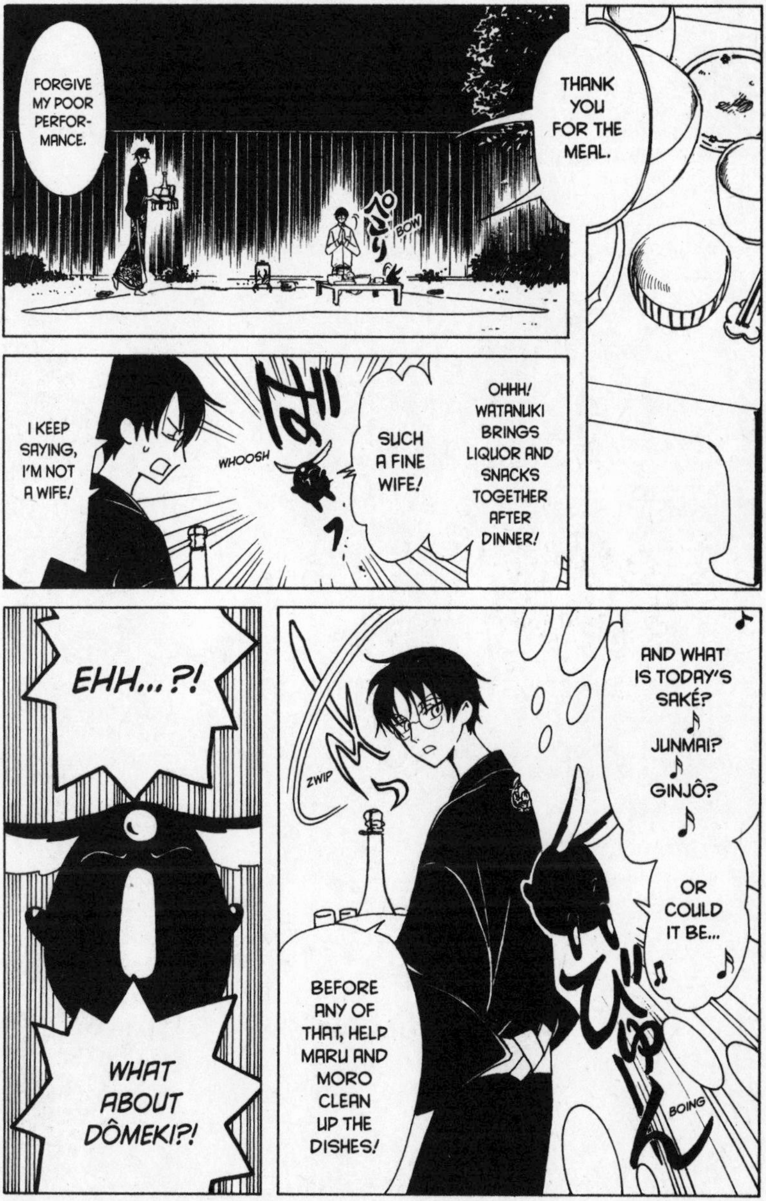
THANK YOU FOR THE MEAL.
BOW
FORGIVE MY POOR PERFORMANCE.
OHHH! WATANUKI BRINGS LIQUOR AND SNACKS TOGETHER AFTER DINNER!
SUCH A FINE WIFE!
WHOOSH
I KEEP SAYING, I'M NOT A WIFE!
AND WHAT IS TODAY'S SAKÉ? ♪ JUNMAI? ♪ GINJÔ? ♪
OR COULD IT BE... ♪
BOING
ZWIP
BEFORE ANY OF THAT, HELP MARU AND MORO CLEAN UP THE DISHES!
EHH...?!
WHAT ABOUT DÔMEKI?!

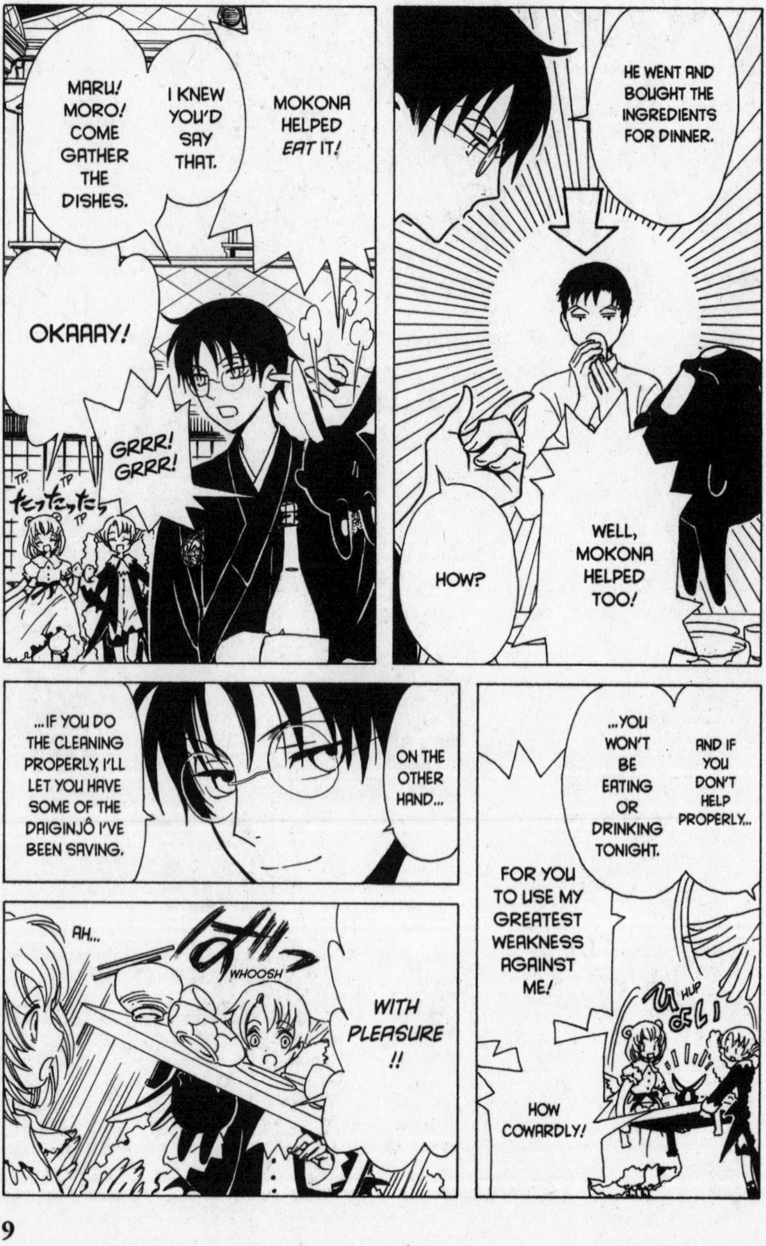
HE WENT AND BOUGHT THE INGREDIENTS FOR DINNER.
WELL, MOKONA HELPED TOO!
HOW?
MOKONA HELPED *EAT* IT!
I KNEW YOU'D SAY THAT.
MARU! MORO! COME GATHER THE DISHES.
OKAAAY!
GRRR! GRRR!
TP. TP TP
たったった
AND IF YOU DON'T HELP PROPERLY...
...YOU WON'T BE EATING OR DRINKING TONIGHT.
FOR YOU TO USE MY GREATEST WEAKNESS AGAINST ME!
ひょい HUP
HOW COWARDLY!
ON THE OTHER HAND...
...IF YOU DO THE CLEANING PROPERLY, I'LL LET YOU HAVE SOME OF THE DAIGINJÔ I'VE BEEN SAVING.
WITH PLEASURE !!
はっ WHOOSH
AH...

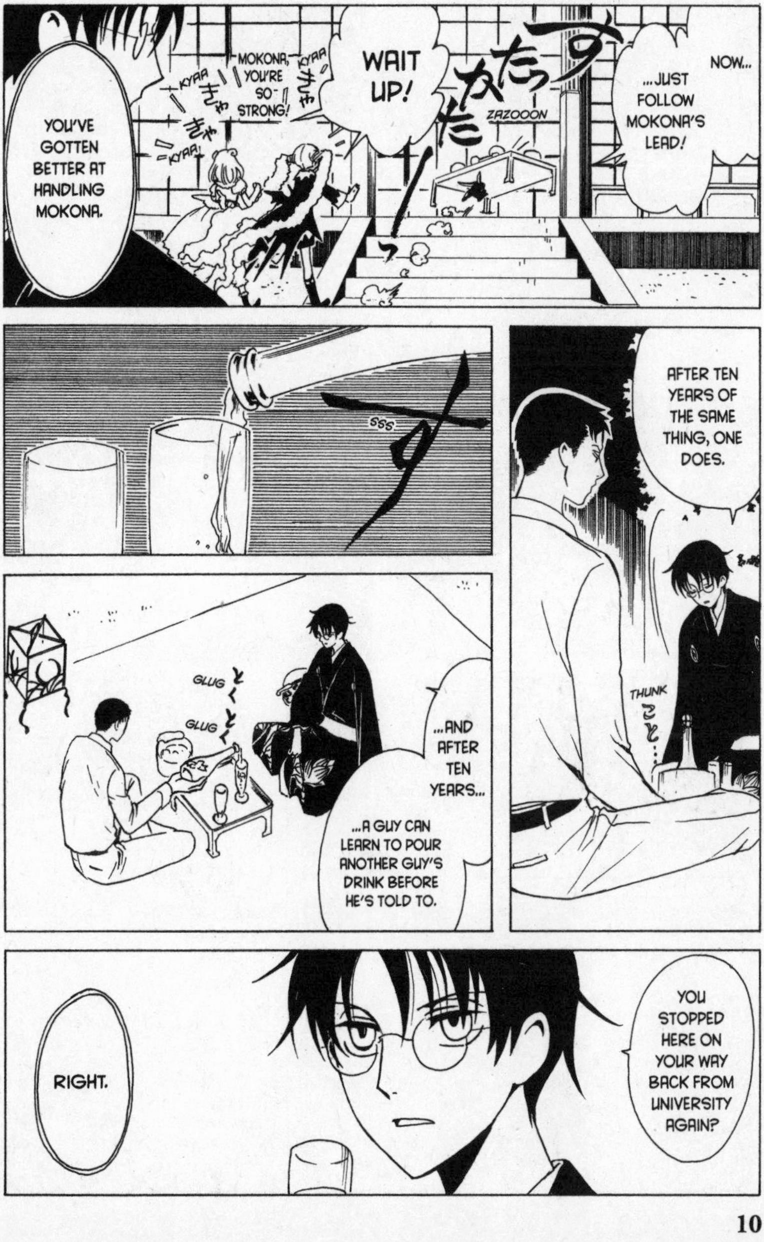
NOW...
...JUST FOLLOW MOKONA'S LEAD!
ZAZOOON
WAIT UP!
KYAA
MOKONA, YOU'RE SO STRONG!
KYAA
KYAA!
YOU'VE GOTTEN BETTER AT HANDLING MOKONA.
AFTER TEN YEARS OF THE SAME THING, ONE DOES.
THUNK
SSS
...AND AFTER TEN YEARS...
...A GUY CAN LEARN TO POUR ANOTHER GUY'S DRINK BEFORE HE'S TOLD TO.
GLUG
GLUG
YOU STOPPED HERE ON YOUR WAY BACK FROM UNIVERSITY AGAIN?
RIGHT.

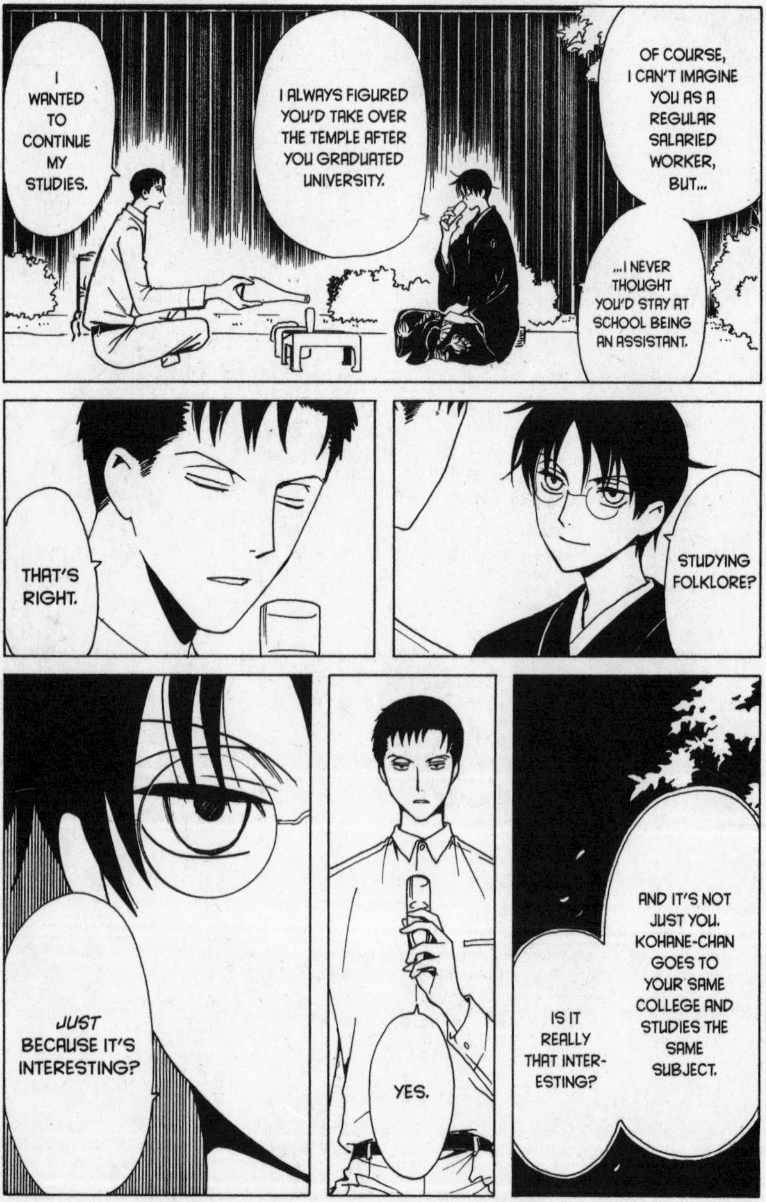
OF COURSE, I CAN'T IMAGINE YOU AS A REGULAR SALARIED WORKER, BUT...
...I NEVER THOUGHT YOU'D STAY AT SCHOOL BEING AN ASSISTANT.
I ALWAYS FIGURED YOU'D TAKE OVER THE TEMPLE AFTER YOU GRADUATED UNIVERSITY.
I WANTED TO CONTINUE MY STUDIES.
STUDYING FOLKLORE?
THAT'S RIGHT.
AND IT'S NOT JUST YOU. KOHANE-CHAN GOES TO YOUR SAME COLLEGE AND STUDIES THE SAME SUBJECT.
IS IT REALLY THAT INTER-ESTING?
YES.
JUST BECAUSE IT'S INTERESTING?

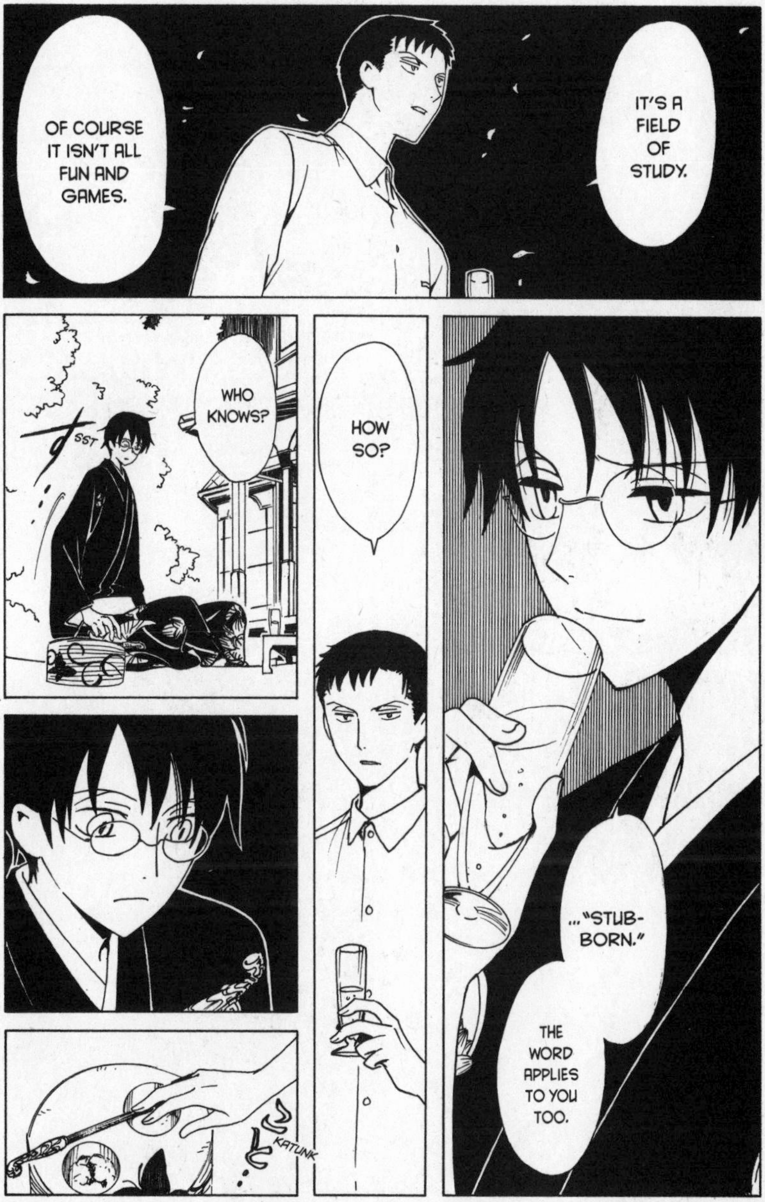

IT'S A FIELD OF STUDY.
OF COURSE IT ISN'T ALL FUN AND GAMES.
..."STUB-BORN."
THE WORD APPLIES TO YOU TOO.
HOW SO?
WHO KNOWS?
SST
KATUNK

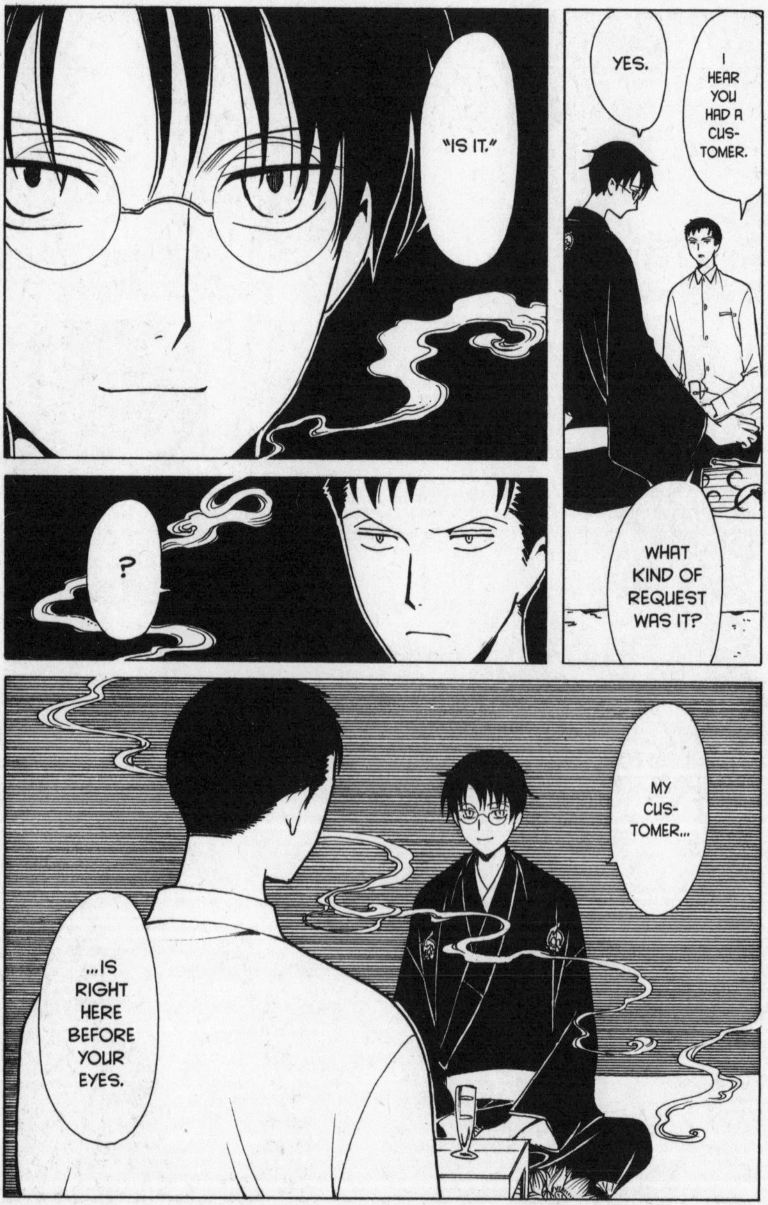
I HEAR YOU HAD A CUS-TOMER.
YES.
WHAT KIND OF REQUEST WAS IT?
"IS IT."
?
MY CUS-TOMER...
...IS RIGHT HERE BEFORE YOUR EYES.

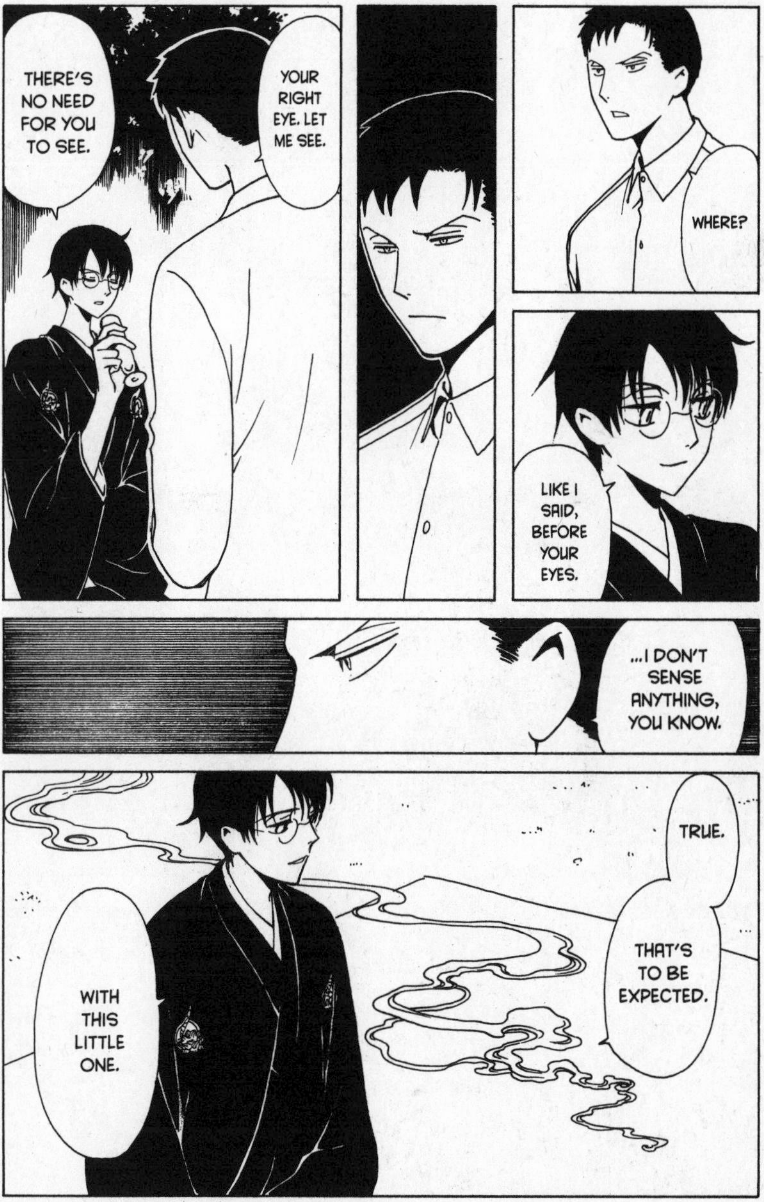
WHERE?
LIKE I SAID, BEFORE YOUR EYES.
YOUR RIGHT EYE. LET ME SEE.
THERE'S NO NEED FOR YOU TO SEE.
...I DON'T SENSE ANYTHING, YOU KNOW.
TRUE.
THAT'S TO BE EXPECTED.
WITH THIS LITTLE ONE.

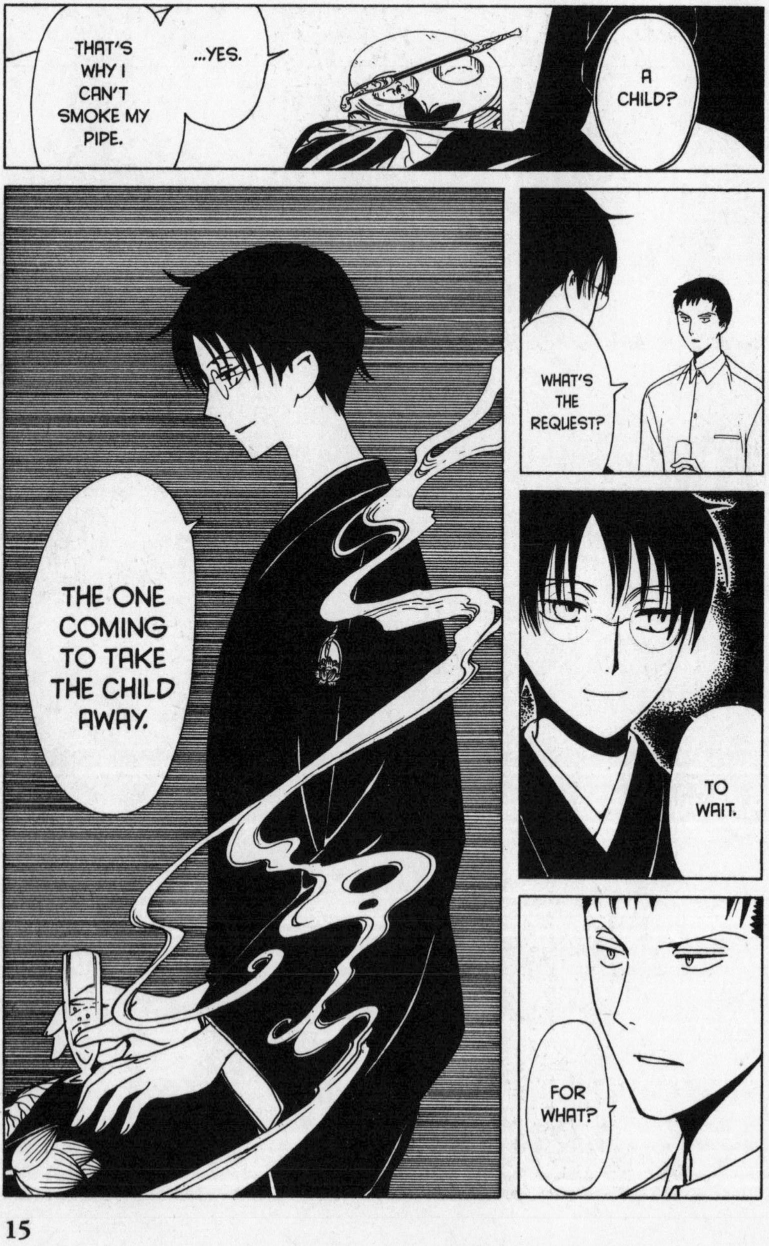
A CHILD?
...YES.
THAT'S WHY I CAN'T SMOKE MY PIPE.
WHAT'S THE REQUEST?
TO WAIT.
FOR WHAT?
THE ONE COMING TO TAKE THE CHILD AWAY.

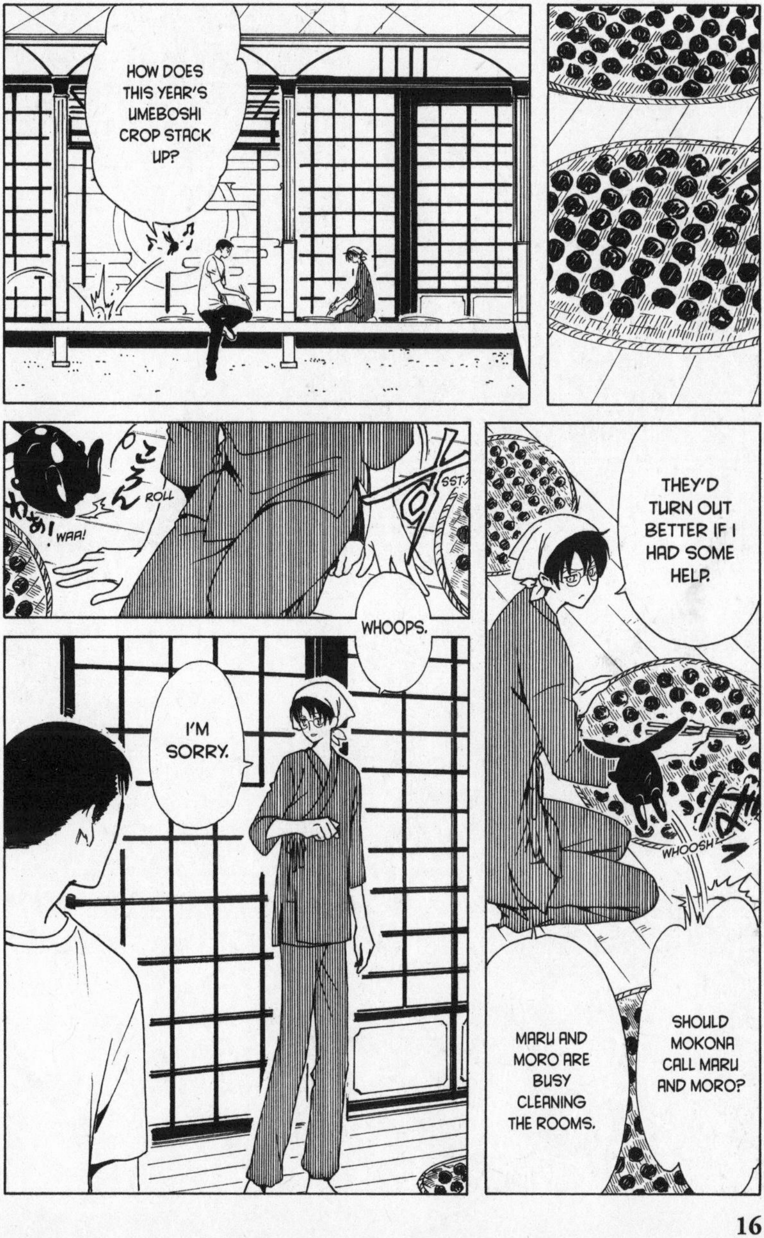
HOW DOES THIS YEAR'S UMEBOSHI CROP STACK UP?
THEY'D TURN OUT BETTER IF I HAD SOME HELP.
WHOOSH
SHOULD MOKONA CALL MARU AND MORO?
MARU AND MORO ARE BUSY CLEANING THE ROOMS.
SST
ころん ROLL
わあ! WAA!
WHOOPS.
I'M SORRY.

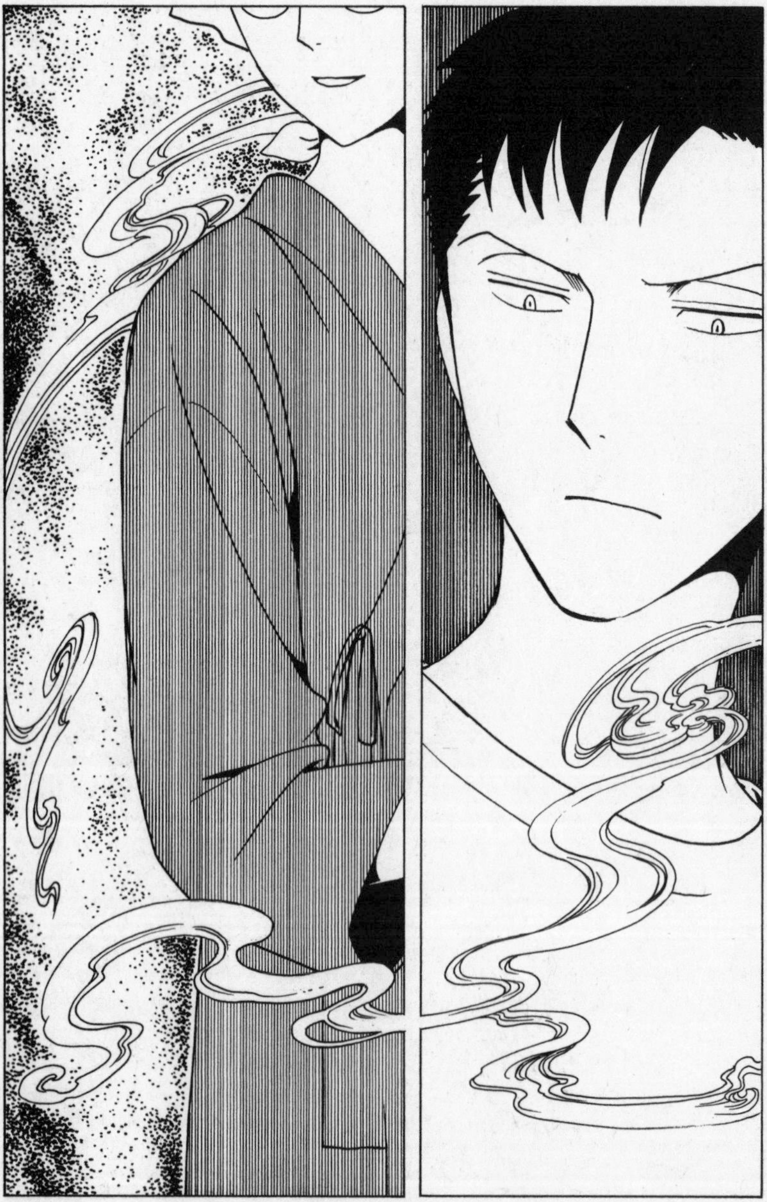

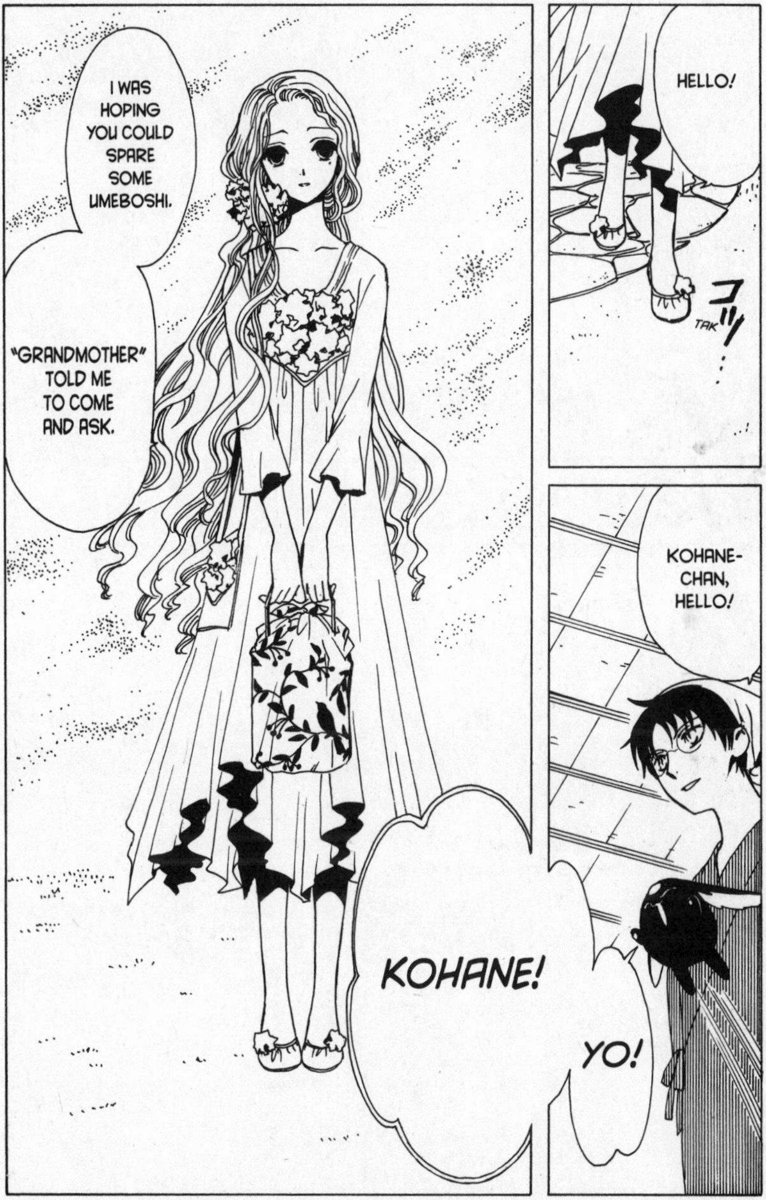
HELLO!
TAK
KOHANE-CHAN, HELLO!
YO!
KOHANE!
I WAS HOPING YOU COULD SPARE SOME UMEBOSHI.
"GRANDMOTHER" TOLD ME TO COME AND ASK.

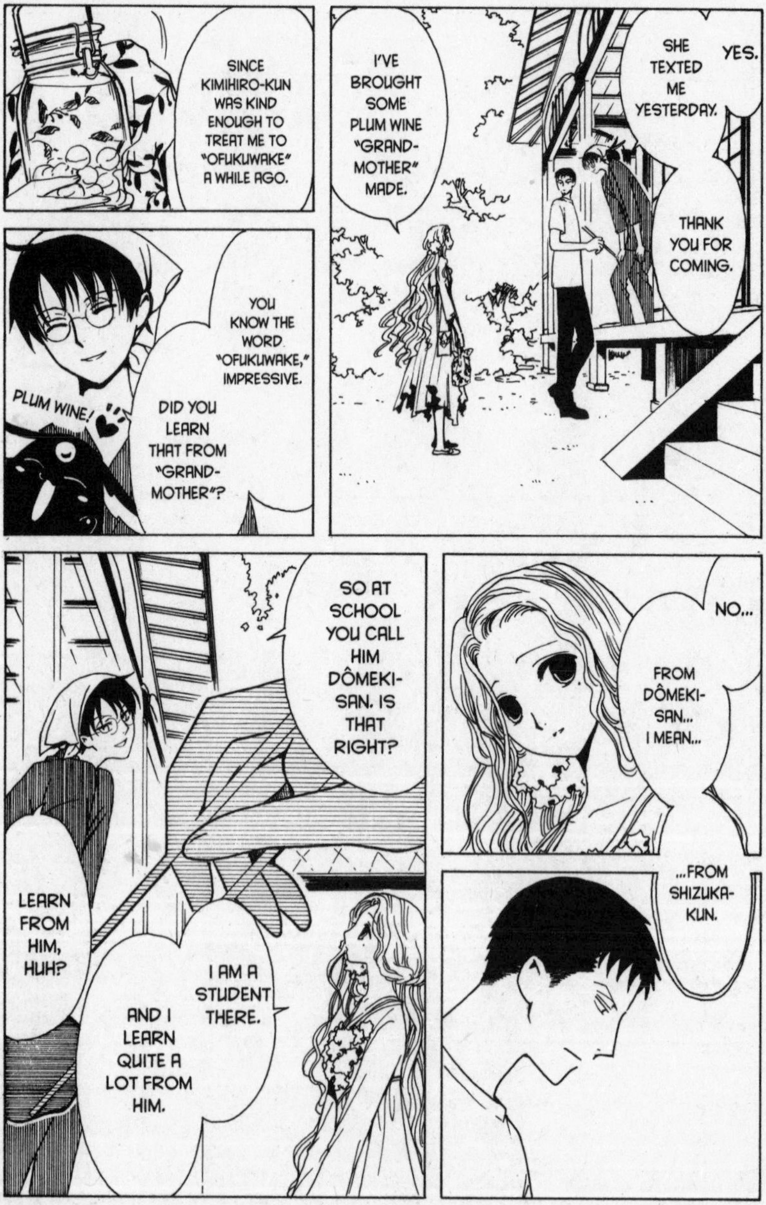
YES.
SHE TEXTED ME YESTERDAY.
THANK YOU FOR COMING.
I'VE BROUGHT SOME PLUM WINE "GRANDMOTHER" MADE.
SINCE KIMIHIRO-KUN WAS KIND ENOUGH TO TREAT ME TO "OFUKUWAKE" A WHILE AGO.
PLUM WINE!
YOU KNOW THE WORD "OFUKUWAKE," IMPRESSIVE.
DID YOU LEARN THAT FROM "GRANDMOTHER"?
NO...
FROM DÔMEKI-SAN... I MEAN...
...FROM SHIZUKA-KUN.
SO AT SCHOOL YOU CALL HIM DÔMEKI-SAN. IS THAT RIGHT?
I AM A STUDENT THERE.
AND I LEARN QUITE A LOT FROM HIM.
LEARN FROM HIM, HUH?

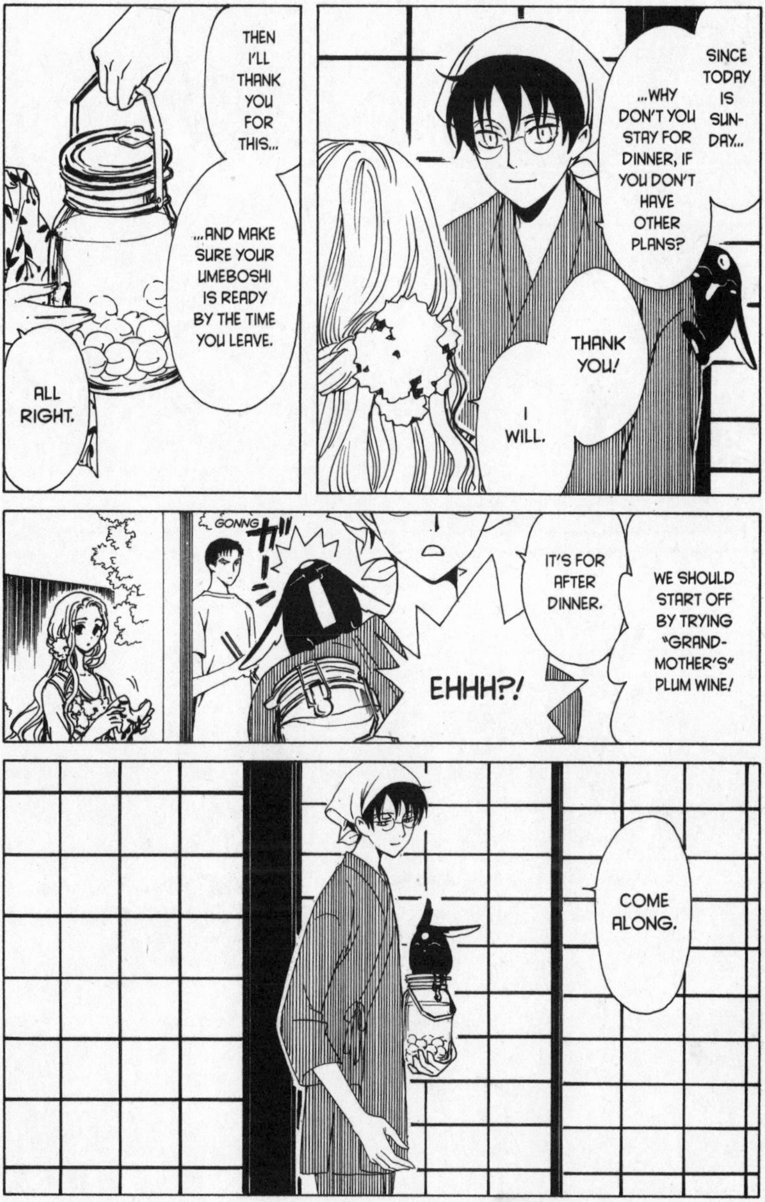
SINCE TODAY IS SUN-DAY...
...WHY DON'T YOU STAY FOR DINNER, IF YOU DON'T HAVE OTHER PLANS?
THANK YOU!
I WILL.
THEN I'LL THANK YOU FOR THIS...
...AND MAKE SURE YOUR UMEBOSHI IS READY BY THE TIME YOU LEAVE.
ALL RIGHT.
WE SHOULD START OFF BY TRYING "GRAND-MOTHER'S" PLUM WINE!
IT'S FOR AFTER DINNER.
EHHH?!
GONNG
COME ALONG.

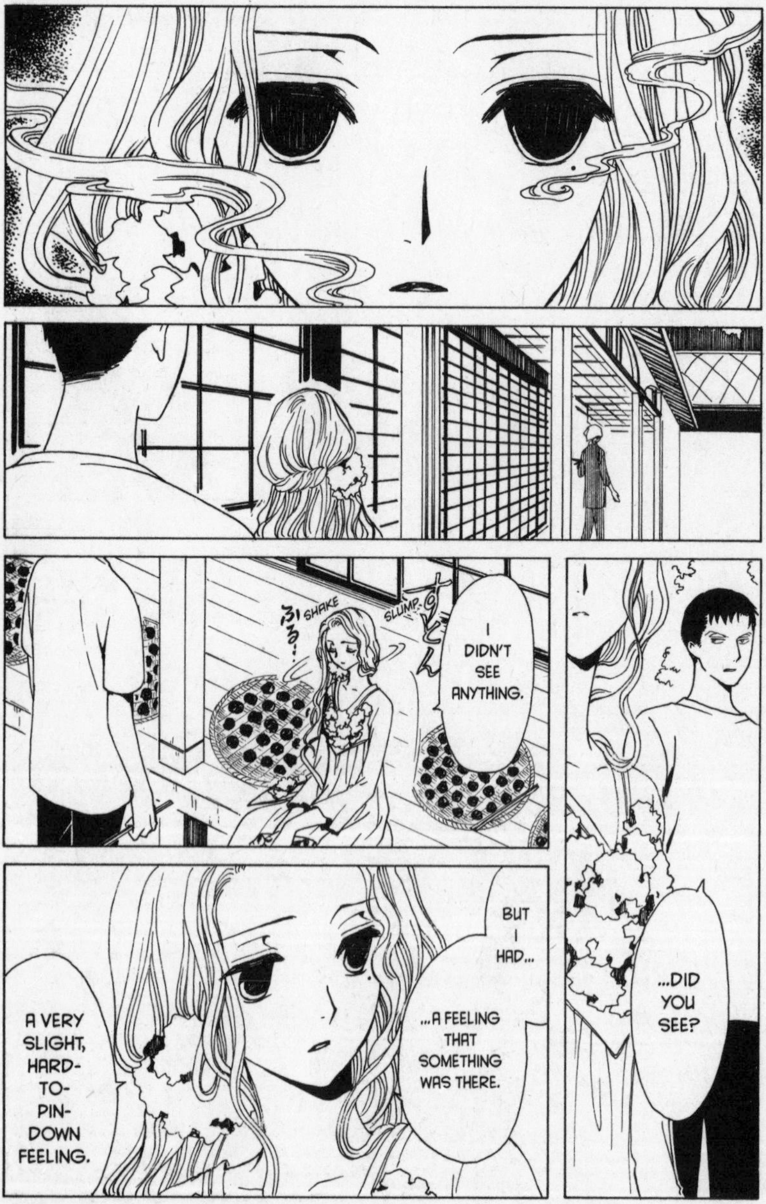
...DID YOU SEE?
I DIDN'T SEE ANYTHING.
すとん SLUMP
ふる SHAKE
BUT I HAD...
...A FEELING THAT SOMETHING WAS THERE.
A VERY SLIGHT, HARD-TO-PIN-DOWN FEELING.

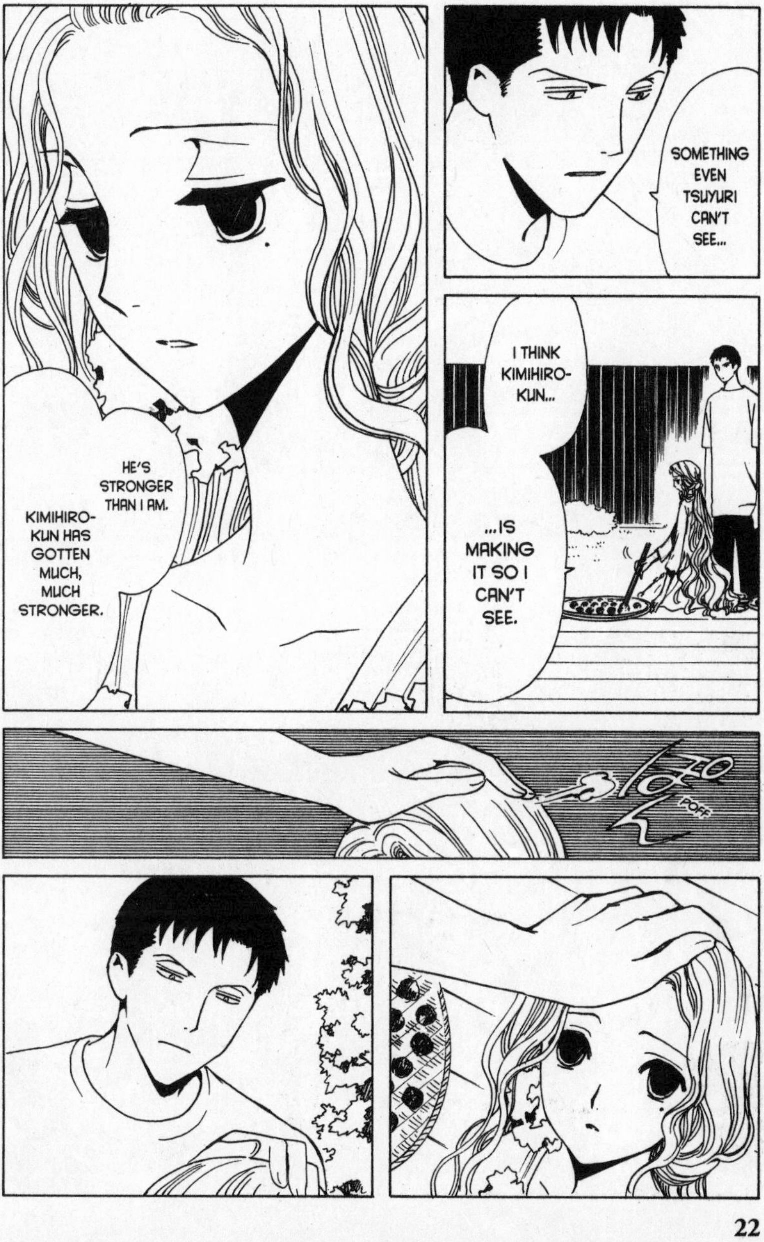
SOMETHING EVEN TSUYURI CAN'T SEE...
I THINK KIMIHIRO-KUN...
...IS MAKING IT SO I CAN'T SEE.
HE'S STRONGER THAN I AM.
KIMIHIRO-KUN HAS GOTTEN MUCH, MUCH STRONGER.
POFF

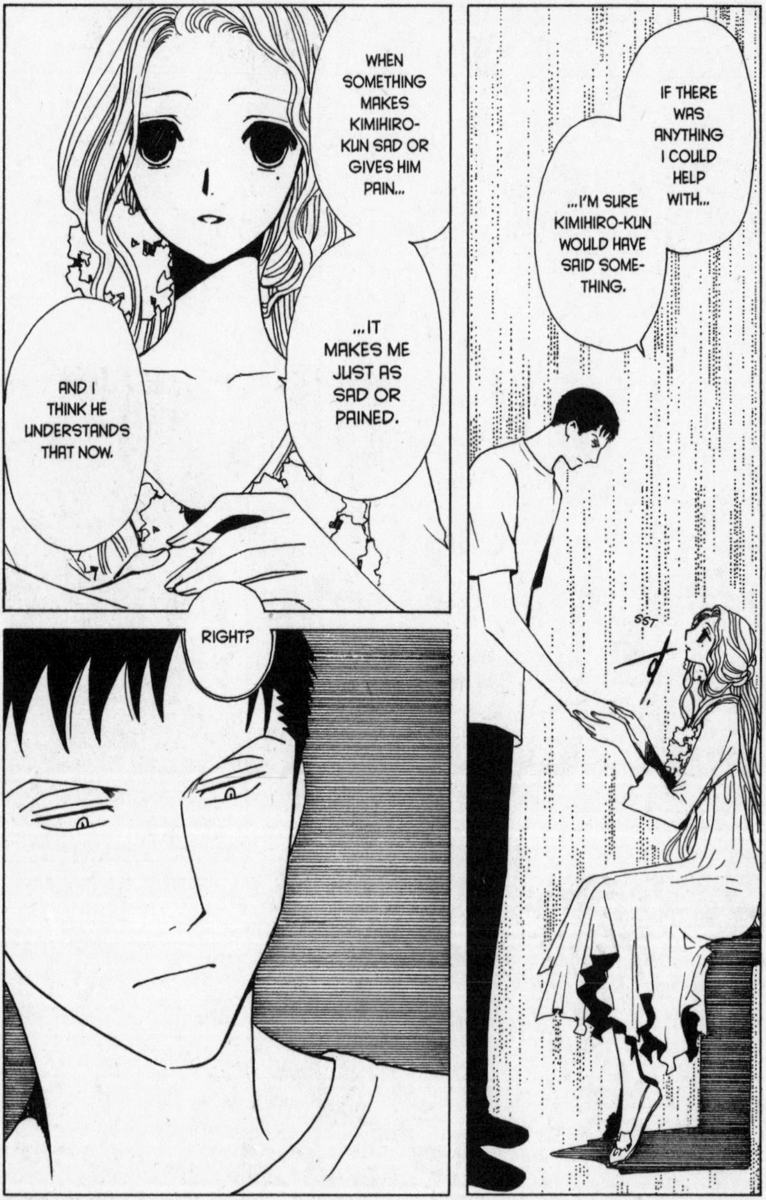
IF THERE WAS ANYTHING I COULD HELP WITH...
...I'M SURE KIMIHIRO-KUN WOULD HAVE SAID SOMETHING.
SST
WHEN SOMETHING MAKES KIMIHIRO-KUN SAD OR GIVES HIM PAIN...
...IT MAKES ME JUST AS SAD OR PAINED.
AND I THINK HE UNDERSTANDS THAT NOW.
RIGHT?

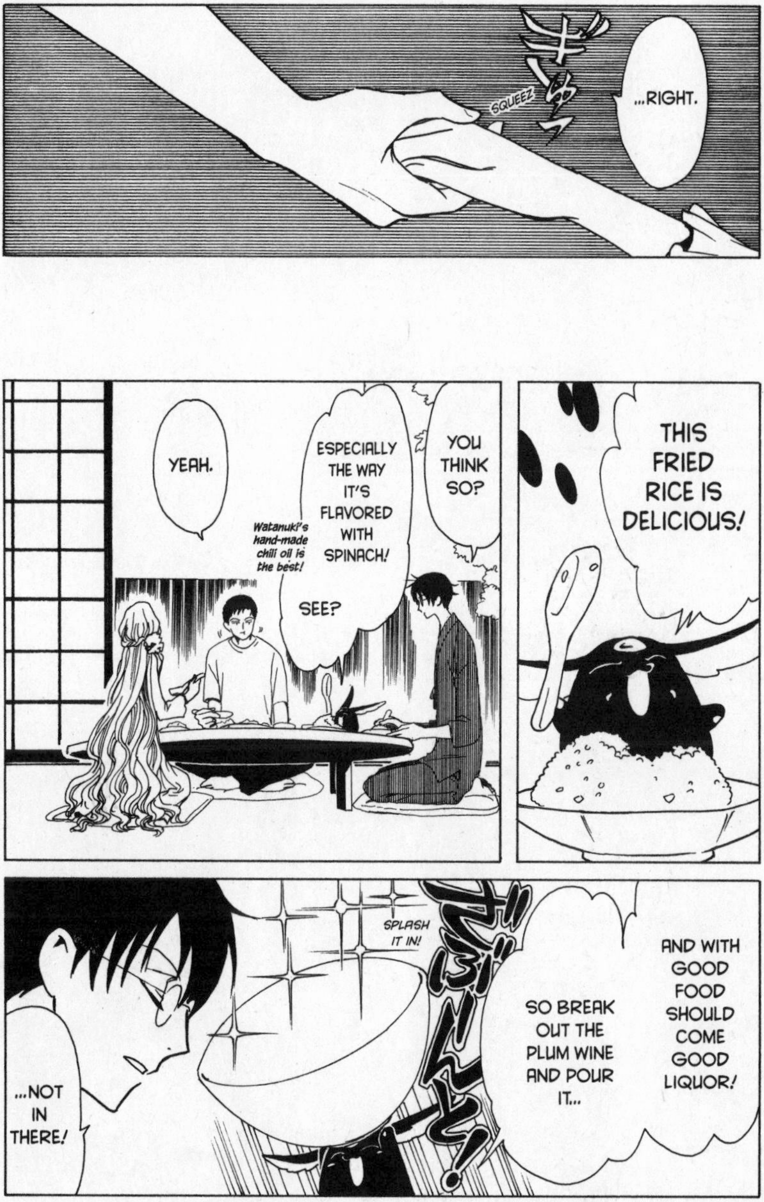
SQUEEZ
...RIGHT.
THIS FRIED RICE IS DELICIOUS!
YOU THINK SO?
ESPECIALLY THE WAY IT'S FLAVORED WITH SPINACH!
YEAH.
Watanuki's hand-made chili oil is the best!
SEE?
AND WITH GOOD FOOD SHOULD COME GOOD LIQUOR!
SO BREAK OUT THE PLUM WINE AND POUR IT...
SPLASH IT IN!
...NOT IN THERE!

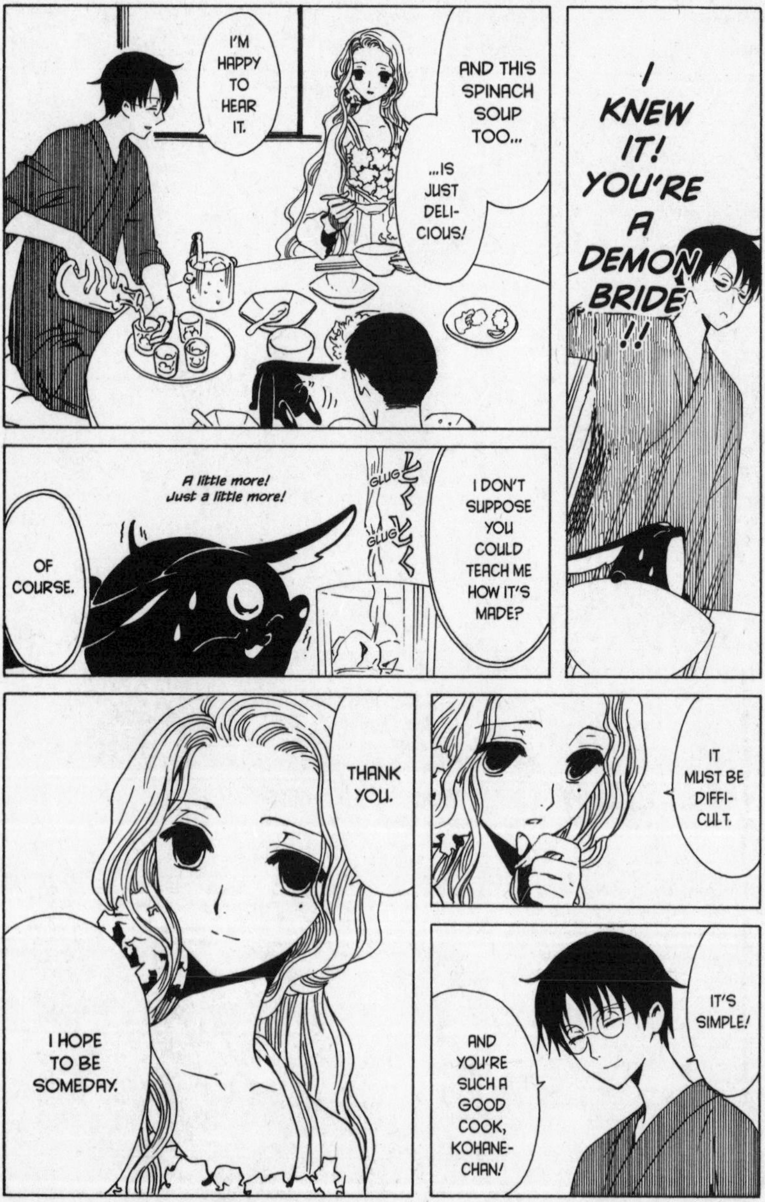
I KNEW IT! YOU'RE A DEMON BRIDE!!
AND THIS SPINACH SOUP TOO...
...IS JUST DELICIOUS!
I'M HAPPY TO HEAR IT.
I DON'T SUPPOSE YOU COULD TEACH ME HOW IT'S MADE?
GLUG
GLUG
A little more! Just a little more!
OF COURSE.
IT MUST BE DIFFICULT.
IT'S SIMPLE!
AND YOU'RE SUCH A GOOD COOK, KOHANE-CHAN!
THANK YOU.
I HOPE TO BE SOMEDAY.

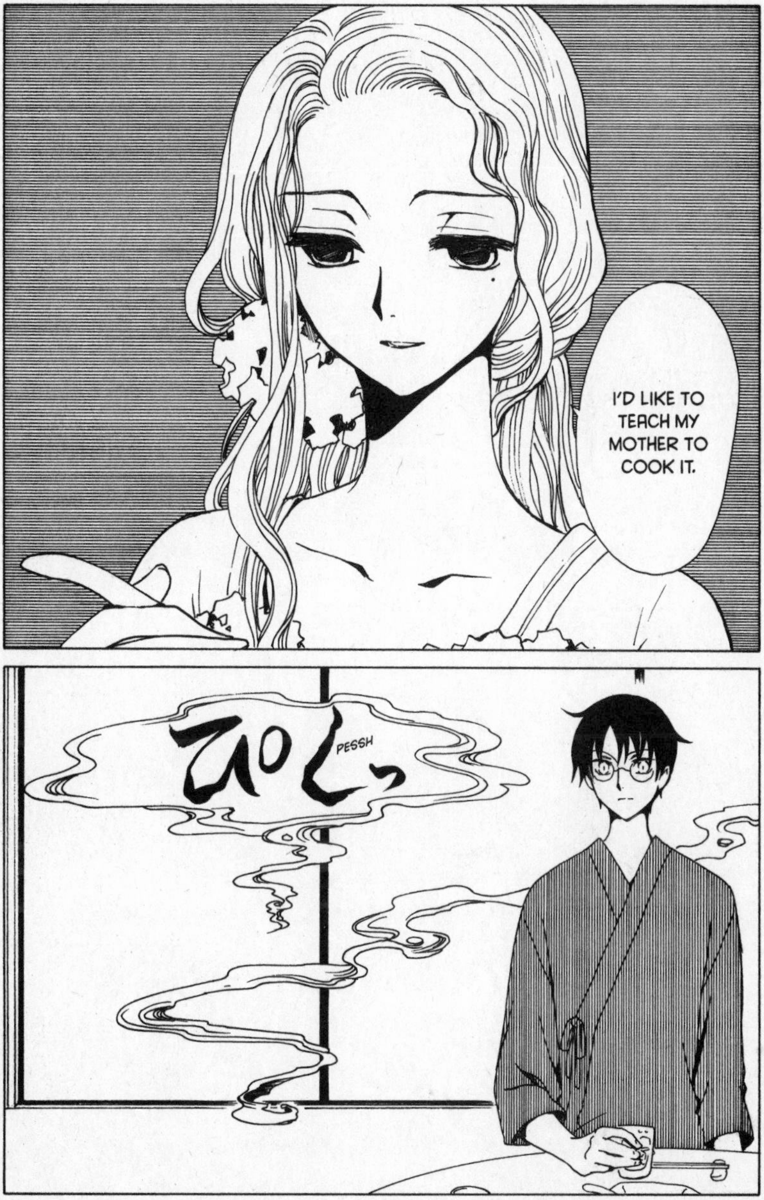
I'D LIKE TO TEACH MY MOTHER TO COOK IT.
ぴしっ
PESSH

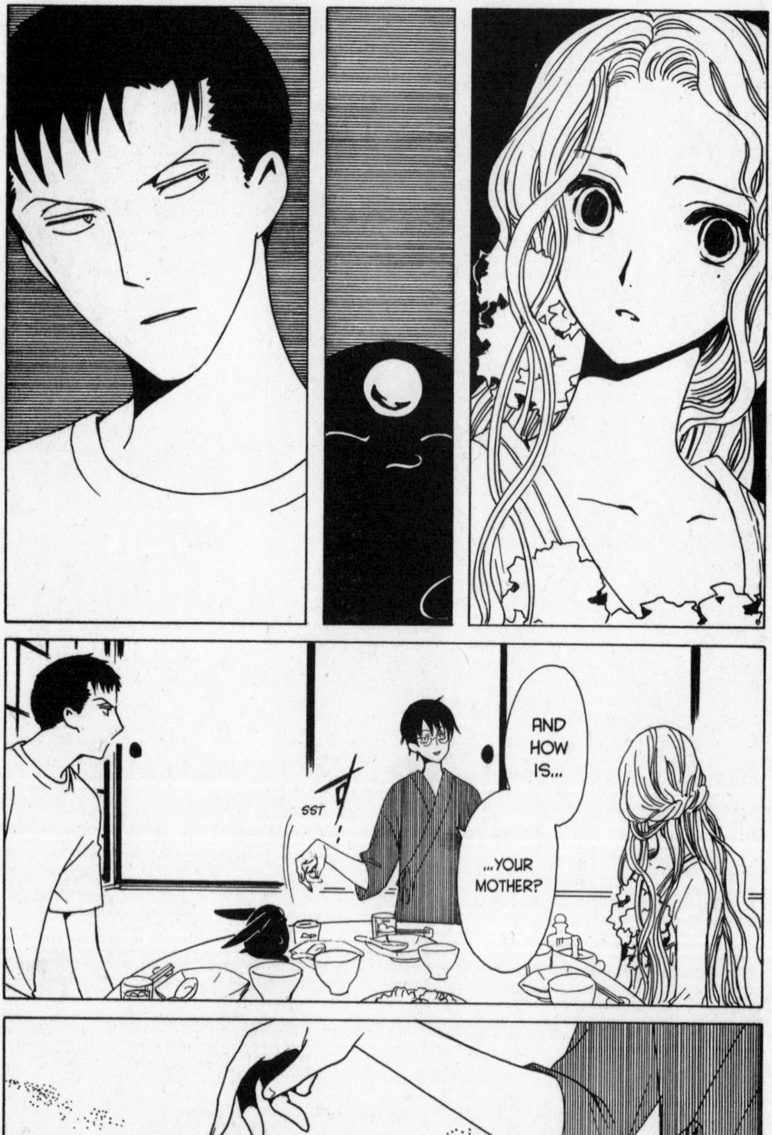
AND HOW IS...
...YOUR MOTHER?
SST

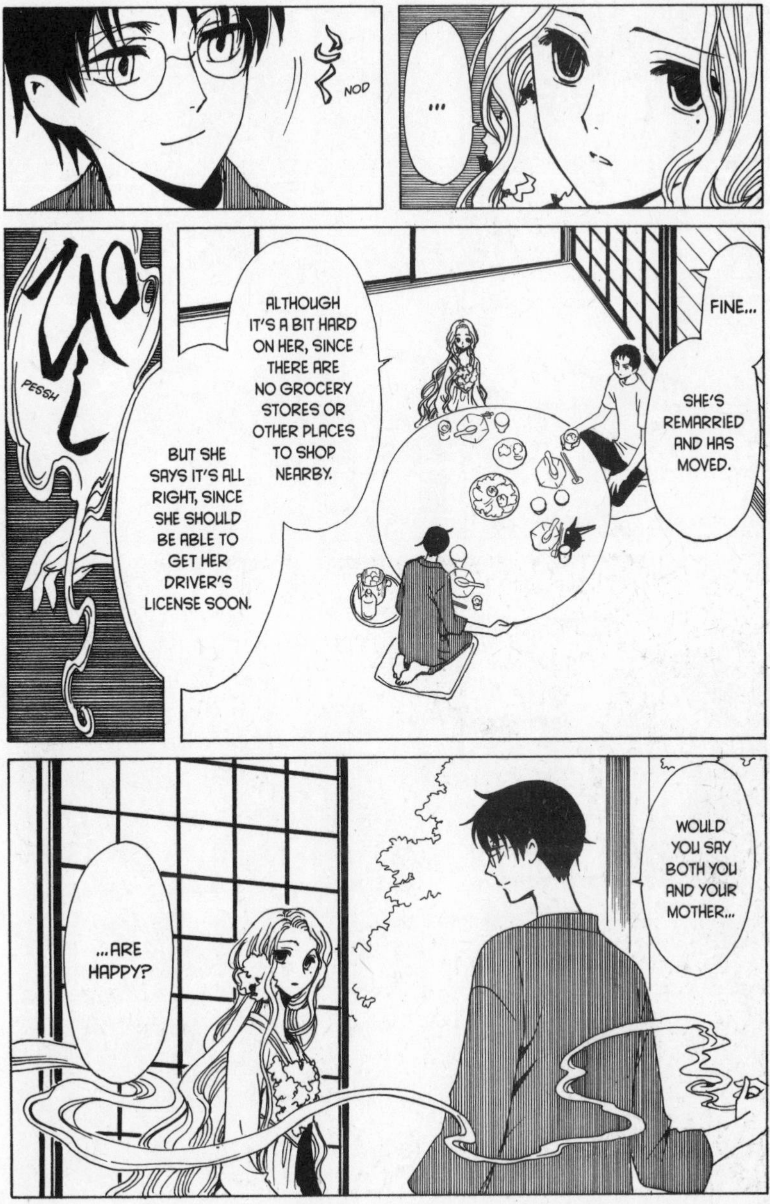
...
NOD
FINE...
SHE'S REMARRIED AND HAS MOVED.
ALTHOUGH IT'S A BIT HARD ON HER, SINCE THERE ARE NO GROCERY STORES OR OTHER PLACES TO SHOP NEARBY.
BUT SHE SAYS IT'S ALL RIGHT, SINCE SHE SHOULD BE ABLE TO GET HER DRIVER'S LICENSE SOON.
PESSH
WOULD YOU SAY BOTH YOU AND YOUR MOTHER...
...ARE HAPPY?

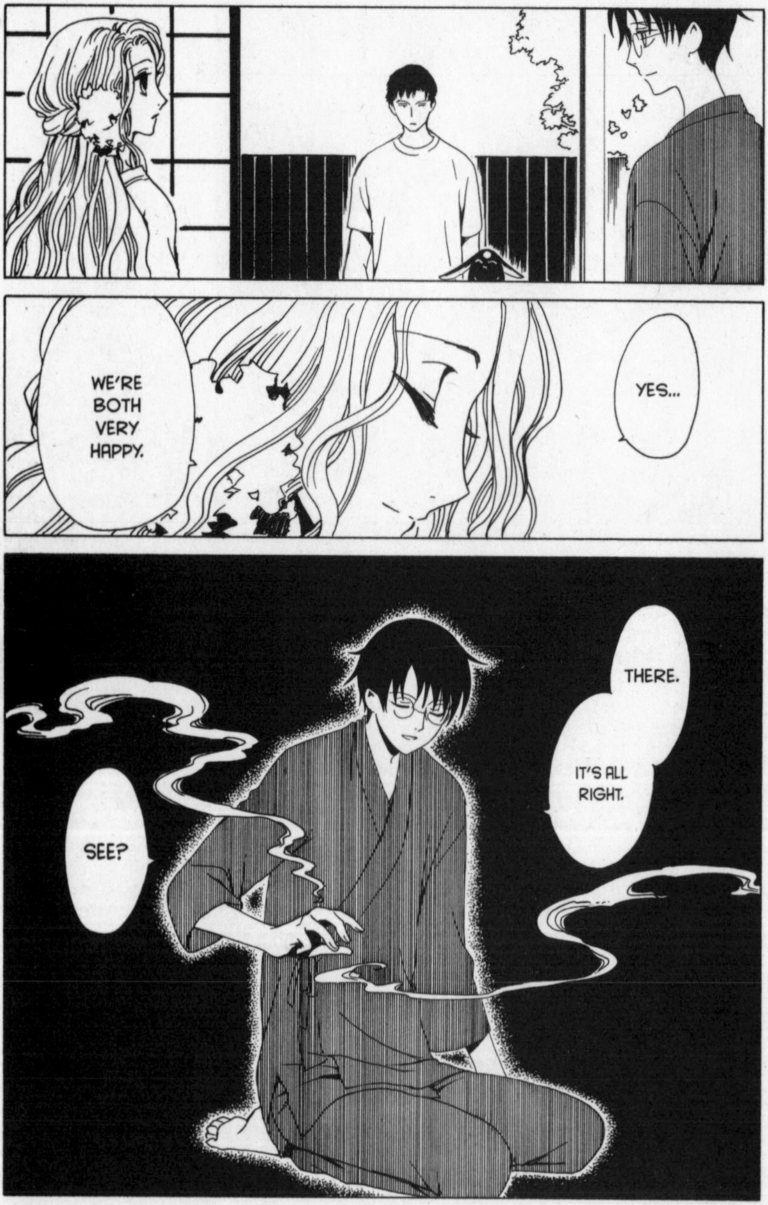
YES...
WE'RE BOTH VERY HAPPY.
THERE.
IT'S ALL RIGHT.
SEE?

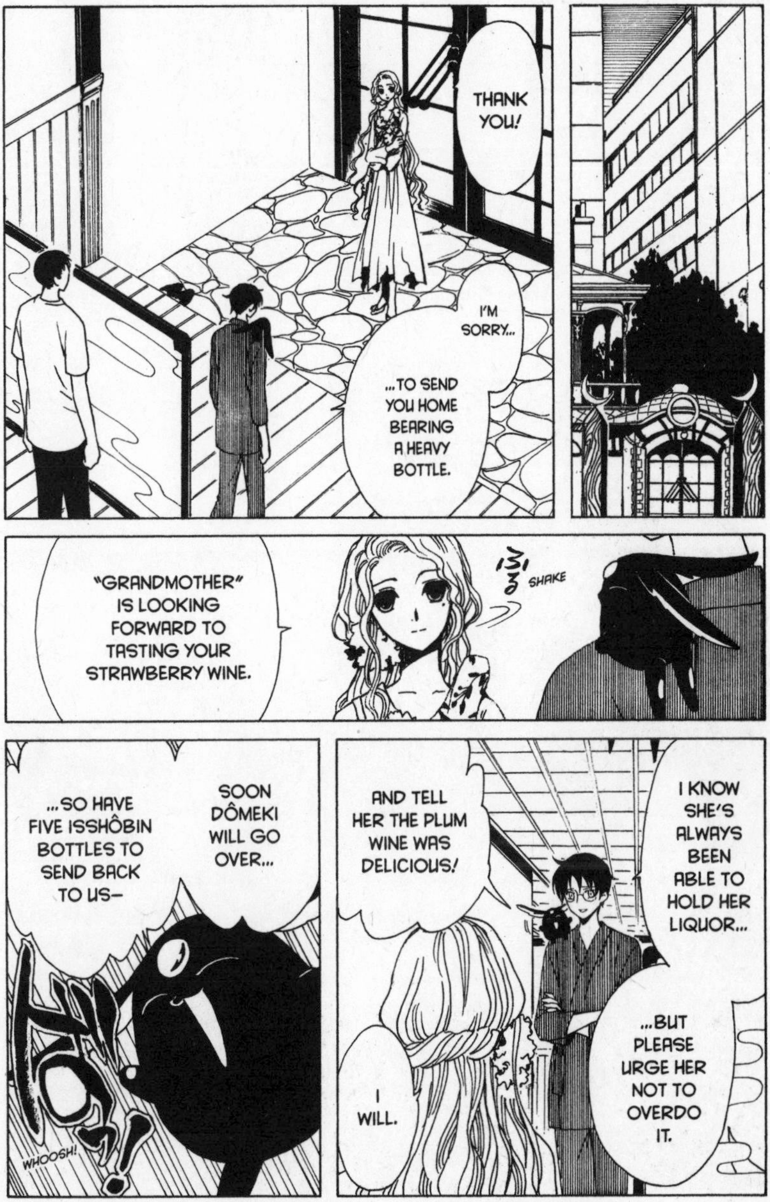
THANK YOU!
I'M SORRY...
...TO SEND YOU HOME BEARING A HEAVY BOTTLE.
SHAKE
"GRANDMOTHER" IS LOOKING FORWARD TO TASTING YOUR STRAWBERRY WINE.
I KNOW SHE'S ALWAYS BEEN ABLE TO HOLD HER LIQUOR...
...BUT PLEASE URGE HER NOT TO OVERDO IT.
AND TELL HER THE PLUM WINE WAS DELICIOUS!
I WILL.
SOON DÔMEKI WILL GO OVER...
...SO HAVE FIVE ISSHÔBIN BOTTLES TO SEND BACK TO US—
WHOOSH!

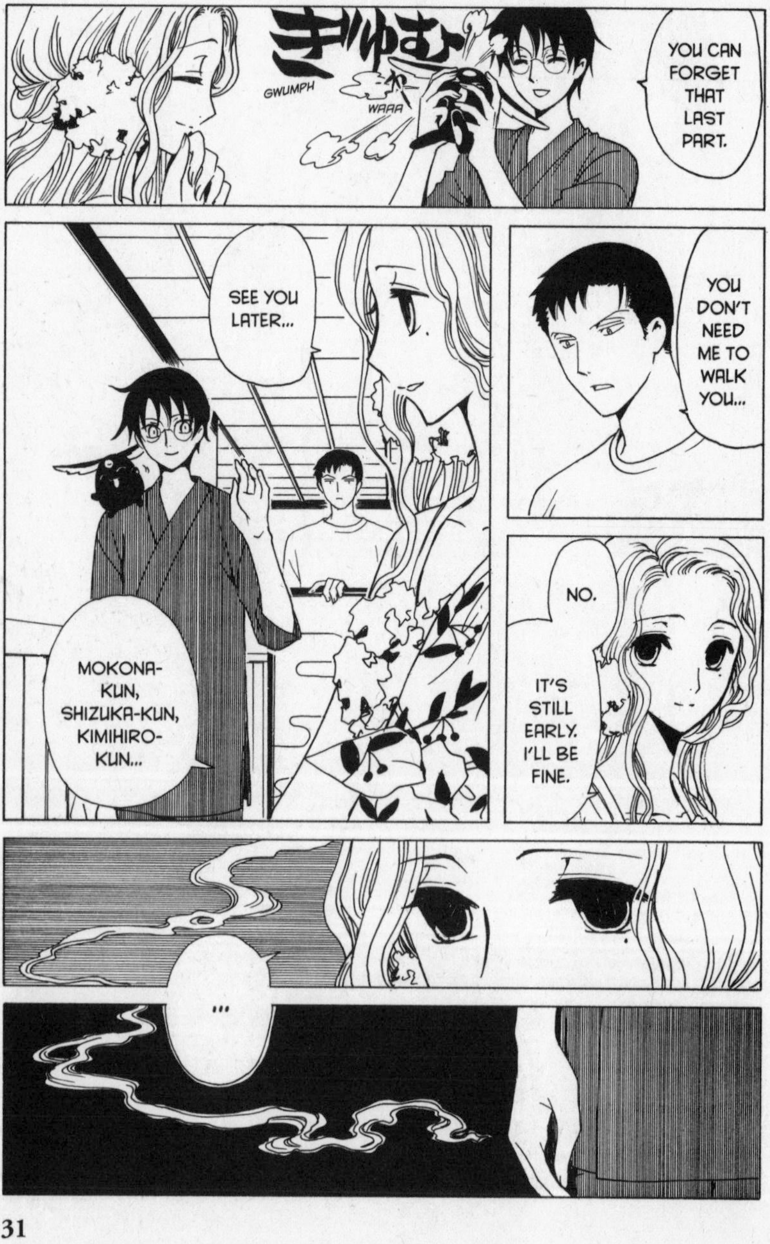
YOU CAN FORGET THAT LAST PART.
GWUMPH
WAAA
YOU DON'T NEED ME TO WALK YOU...
NO.
IT'S STILL EARLY. I'LL BE FINE.
SEE YOU LATER...
MOKONA-KUN, SHIZUKA-KUN, KIMIHIRO-KUN...
...

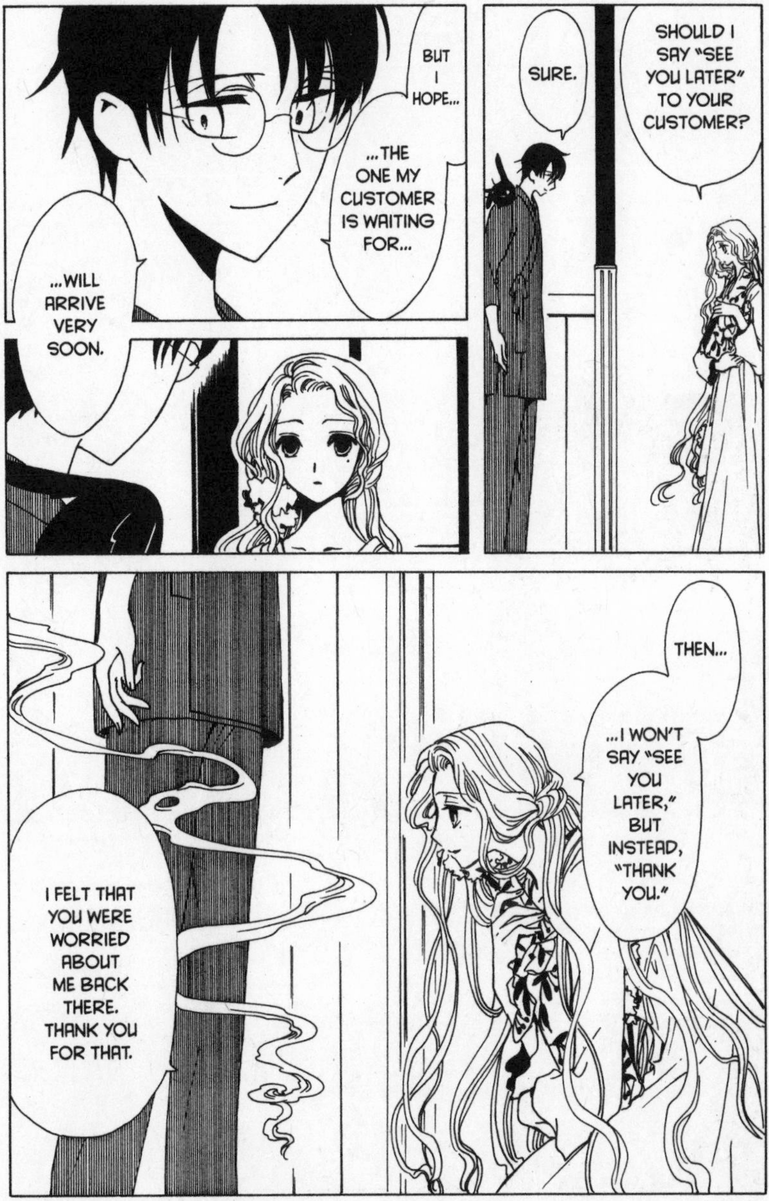
SHOULD I SAY "SEE YOU LATER" TO YOUR CUSTOMER?
SURE.
BUT I HOPE...
...THE ONE MY CUSTOMER IS WAITING FOR...
...WILL ARRIVE VERY SOON.
THEN...
...I WON'T SAY "SEE YOU LATER," BUT INSTEAD, "THANK YOU."
I FELT THAT YOU WERE WORRIED ABOUT ME BACK THERE. THANK YOU FOR THAT.

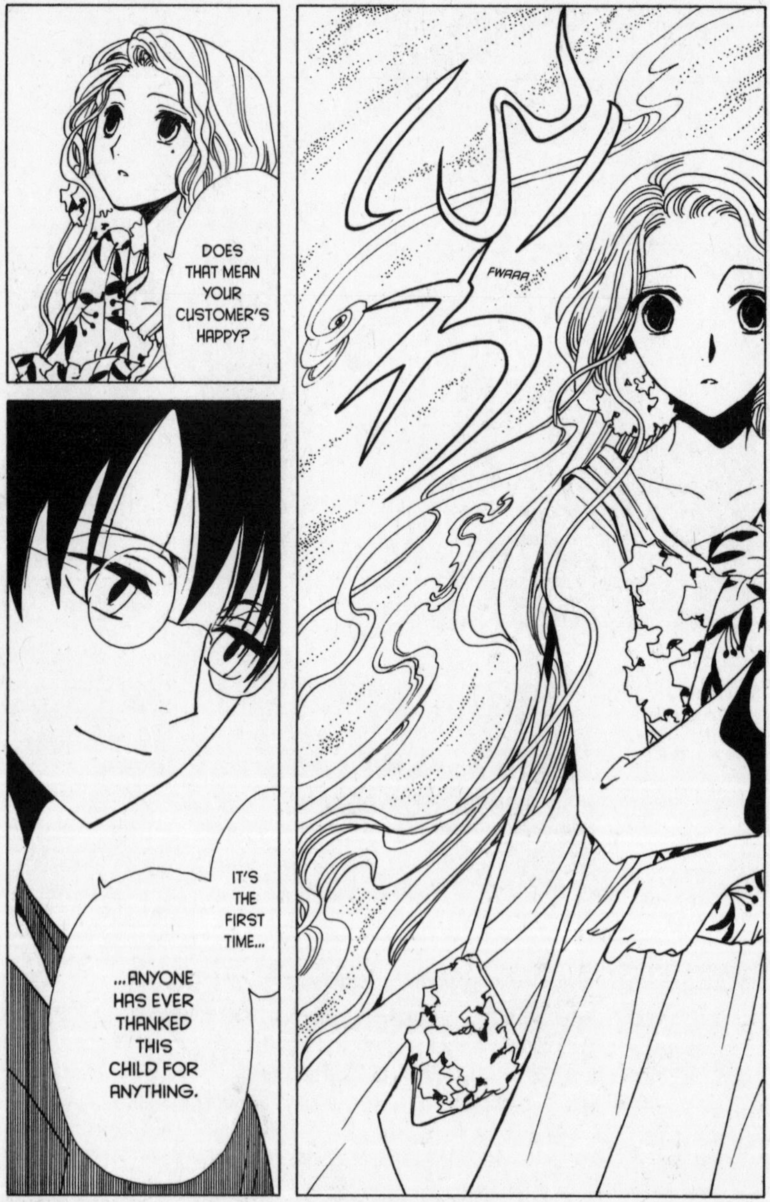
FWAAA
DOES THAT MEAN YOUR CUSTOMER'S HAPPY?
IT'S THE FIRST TIME...
...ANYONE HAS EVER THANKED THIS CHILD FOR ANYTHING.

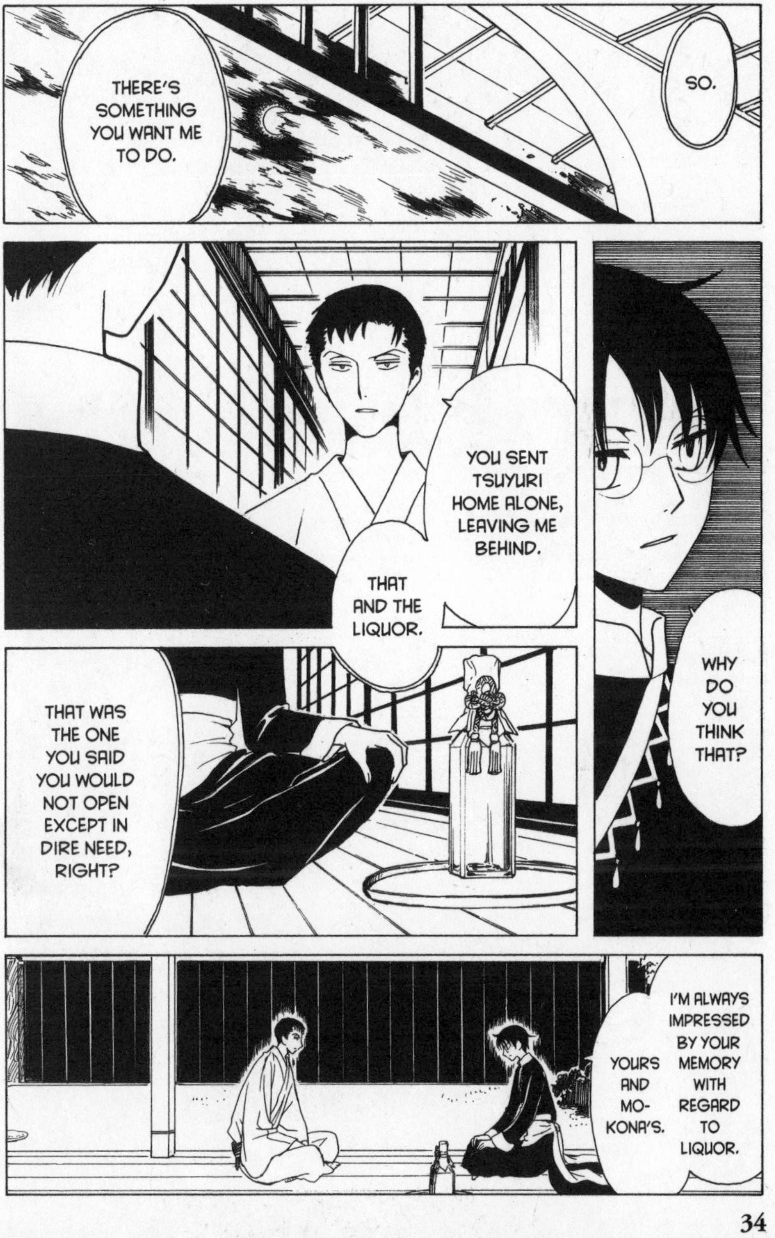
SO.
THERE'S SOMETHING YOU WANT ME TO DO.
WHY DO YOU THINK THAT?
YOU SENT TSUYURI HOME ALONE, LEAVING ME BEHIND.
THAT AND THE LIQUOR.
THAT WAS THE ONE YOU SAID YOU WOULD NOT OPEN EXCEPT IN DIRE NEED, RIGHT?
I'M ALWAYS IMPRESSED BY YOUR MEMORY WITH REGARD TO LIQUOR.
YOURS AND MO-KONA'S.

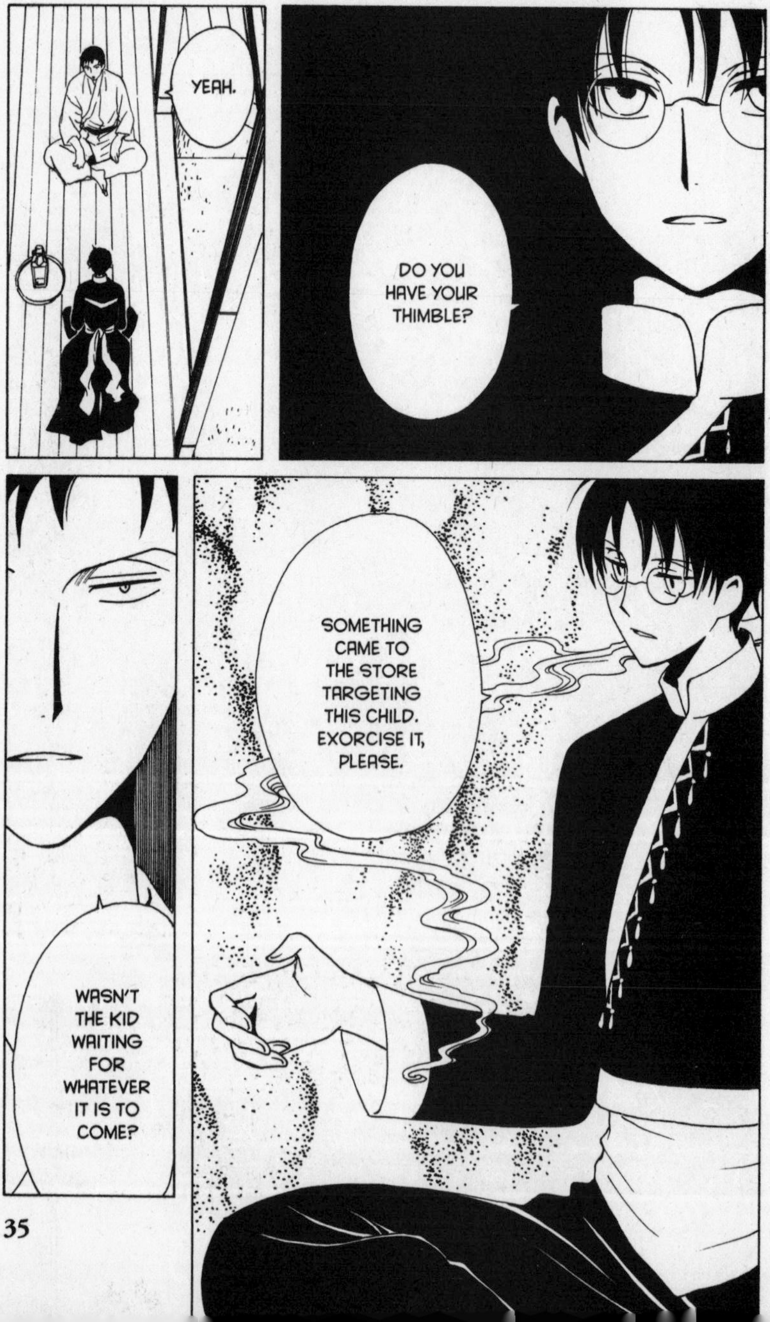
DO YOU HAVE YOUR THIMBLE?
YEAH.
SOMETHING CAME TO THE STORE TARGETING THIS CHILD. EXORCISE IT, PLEASE.
WASN'T THE KID WAITING FOR WHATEVER IT IS TO COME?

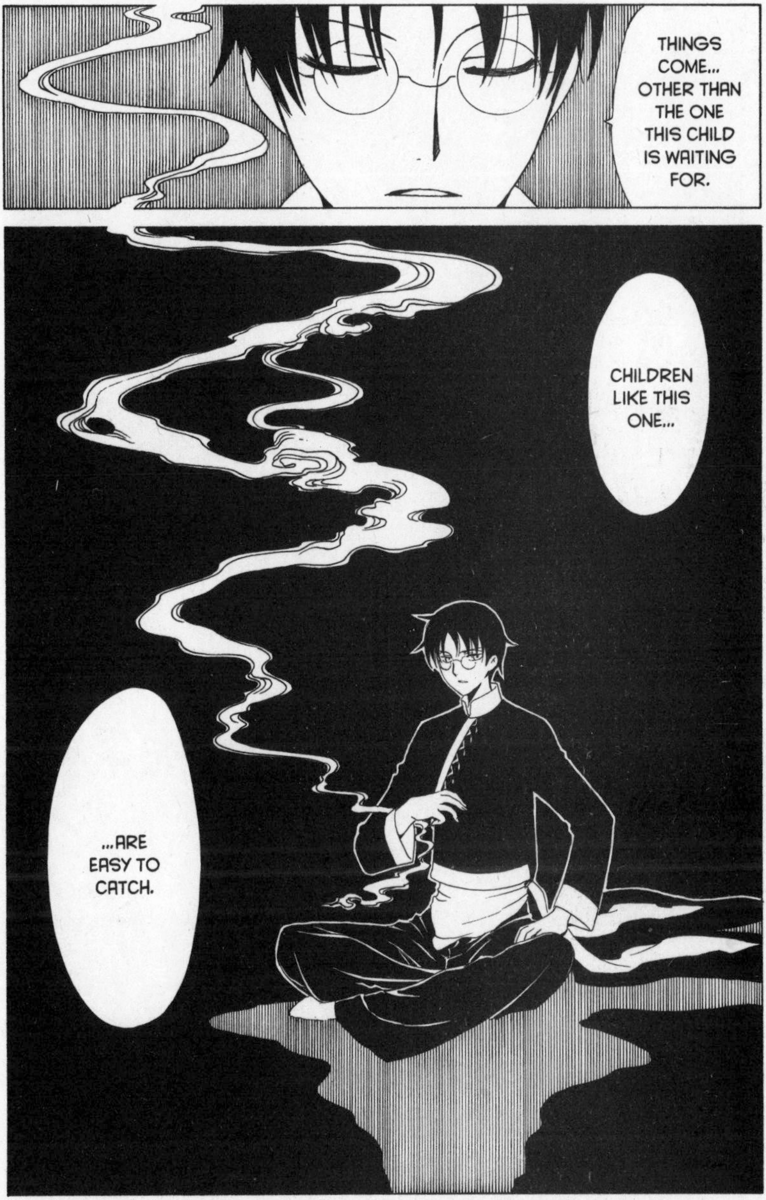
THINGS COME... OTHER THAN THE ONE THIS CHILD IS WAITING FOR.
CHILDREN LIKE THIS ONE...
...ARE EASY TO CATCH.

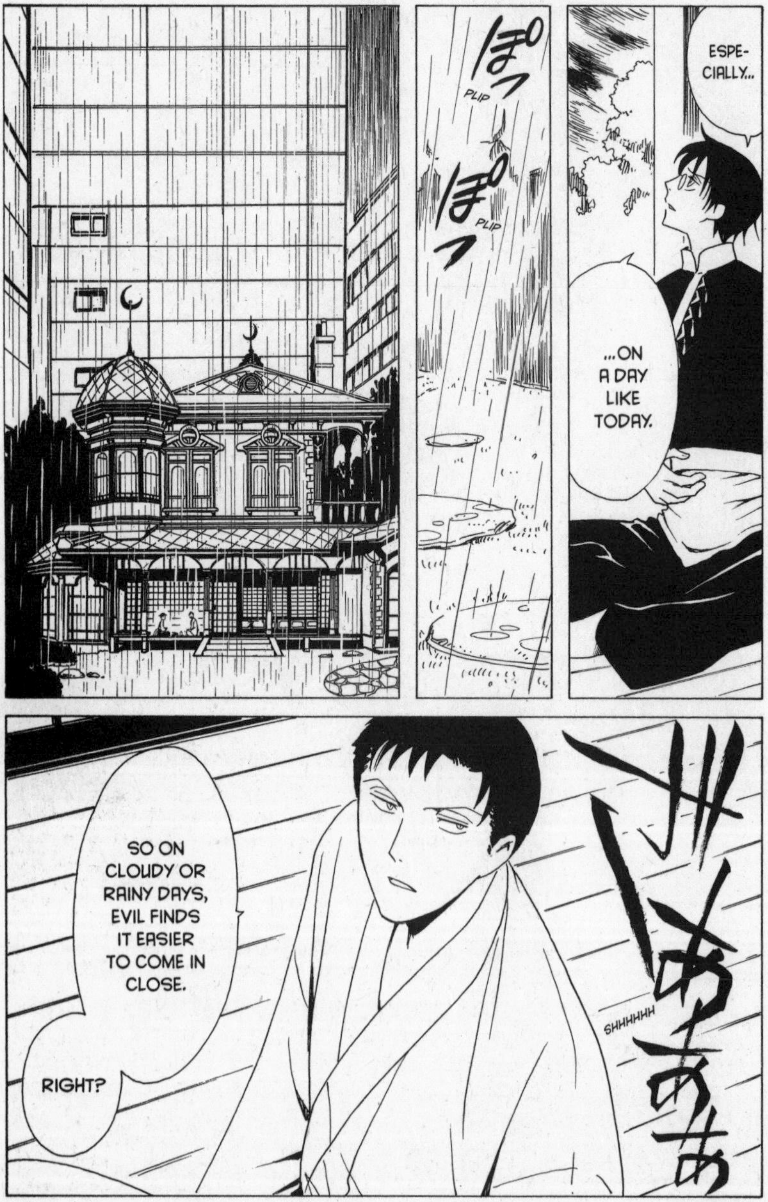
ESPE-CIALLY...
...ON A DAY LIKE TODAY.
ぽっ
PLIP
ぽっ
PLIP
ザーあああ
SHHHHHH
SO ON CLOUDY OR RAINY DAYS, EVIL FINDS IT EASIER TO COME IN CLOSE.
RIGHT?

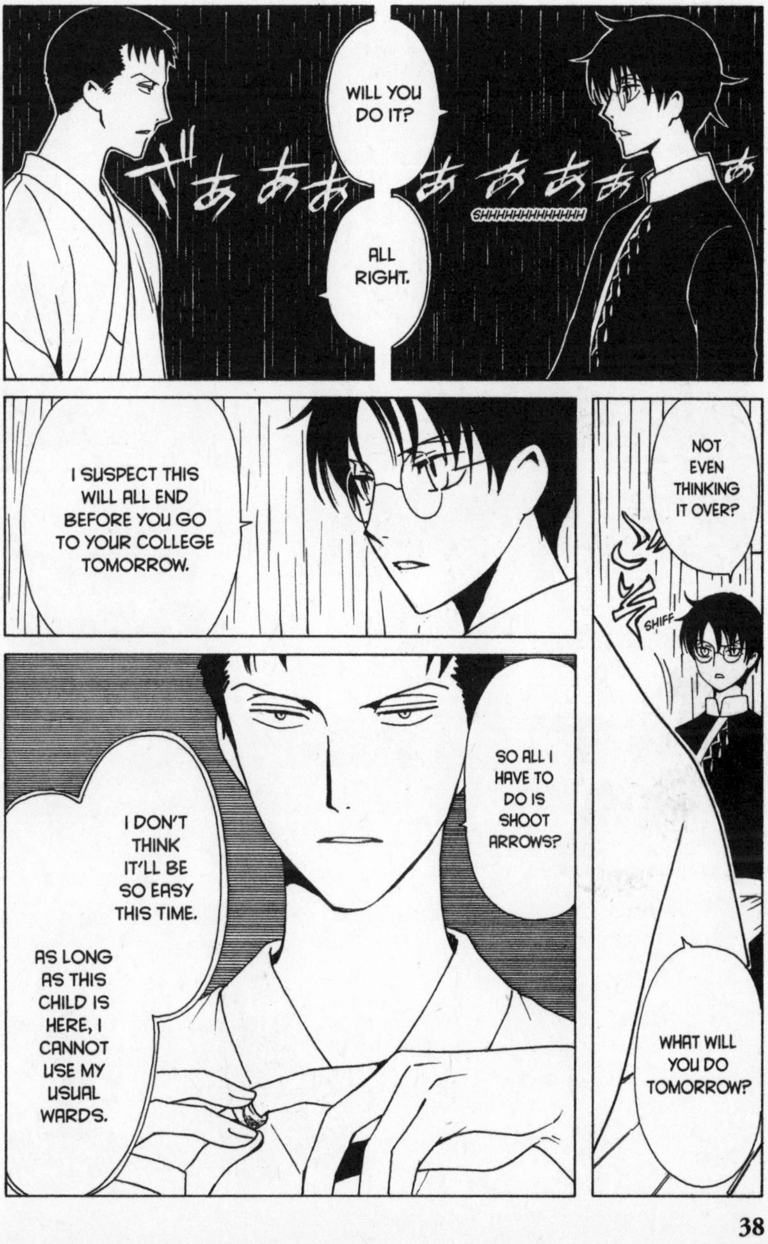
WILL YOU DO IT?
ALL RIGHT.
ザあああ あああああ
SHHHHHHHHHHHHH
NOT EVEN THINKING IT OVER?
SHIFF
WHAT WILL YOU DO TOMORROW?
I SUSPECT THIS WILL ALL END BEFORE YOU GO TO YOUR COLLEGE TOMORROW.
SO ALL I HAVE TO DO IS SHOOT ARROWS?
I DON'T THINK IT'LL BE SO EASY THIS TIME.
AS LONG AS THIS CHILD IS HERE, I CANNOT USE MY USUAL WARDS.

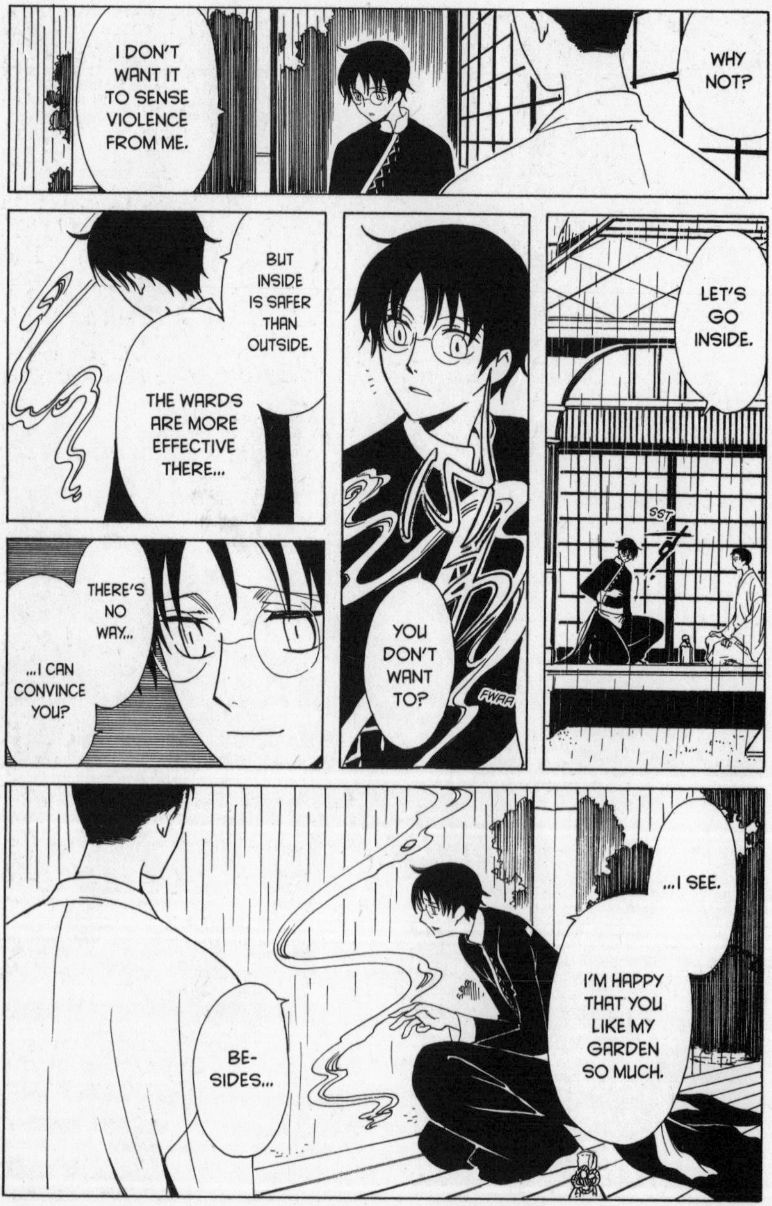
WHY NOT?
I DON'T WANT IT TO SENSE VIOLENCE FROM ME.
LET'S GO INSIDE.
SST
YOU DON'T WANT TO?
FWAA
BUT INSIDE IS SAFER THAN OUTSIDE.
THE WARDS ARE MORE EFFECTIVE THERE...
THERE'S NO WAY...
...I CAN CONVINCE YOU?
...I SEE.
I'M HAPPY THAT YOU LIKE MY GARDEN SO MUCH.
BE-SIDES...

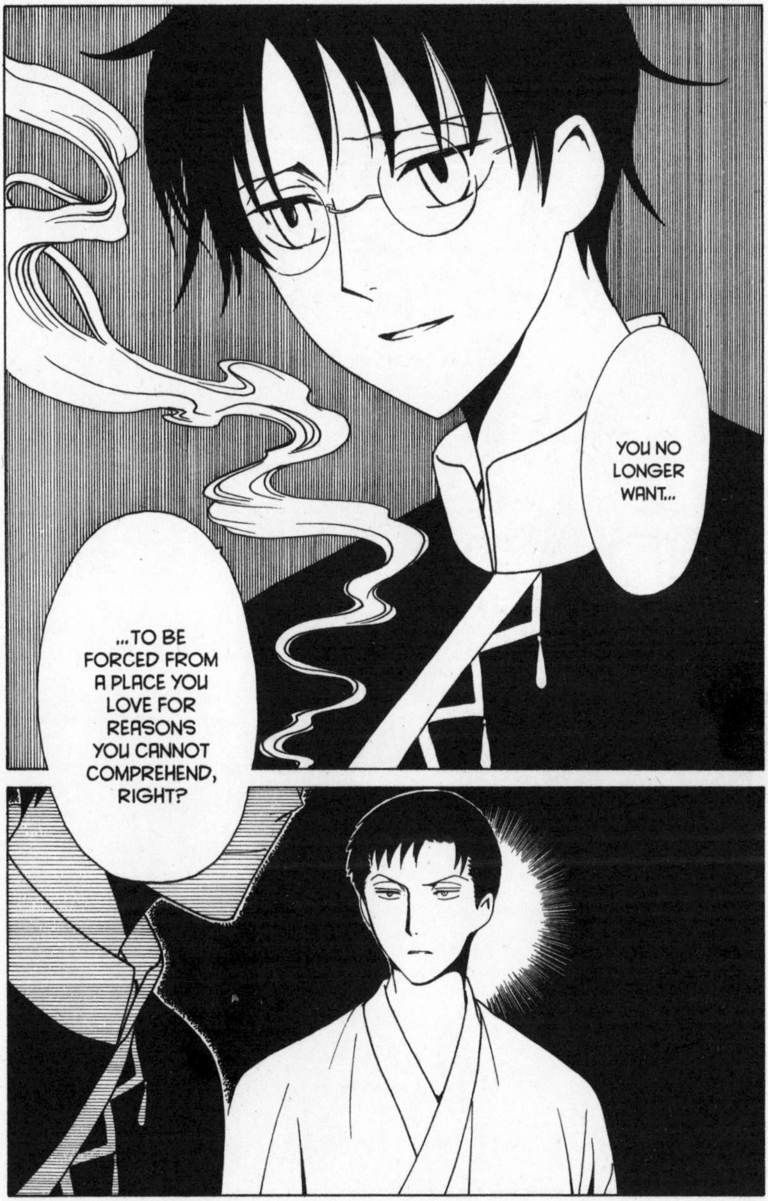
YOU NO LONGER WANT...
...TO BE FORCED FROM A PLACE YOU LOVE FOR REASONS YOU CANNOT COMPREHEND, RIGHT?

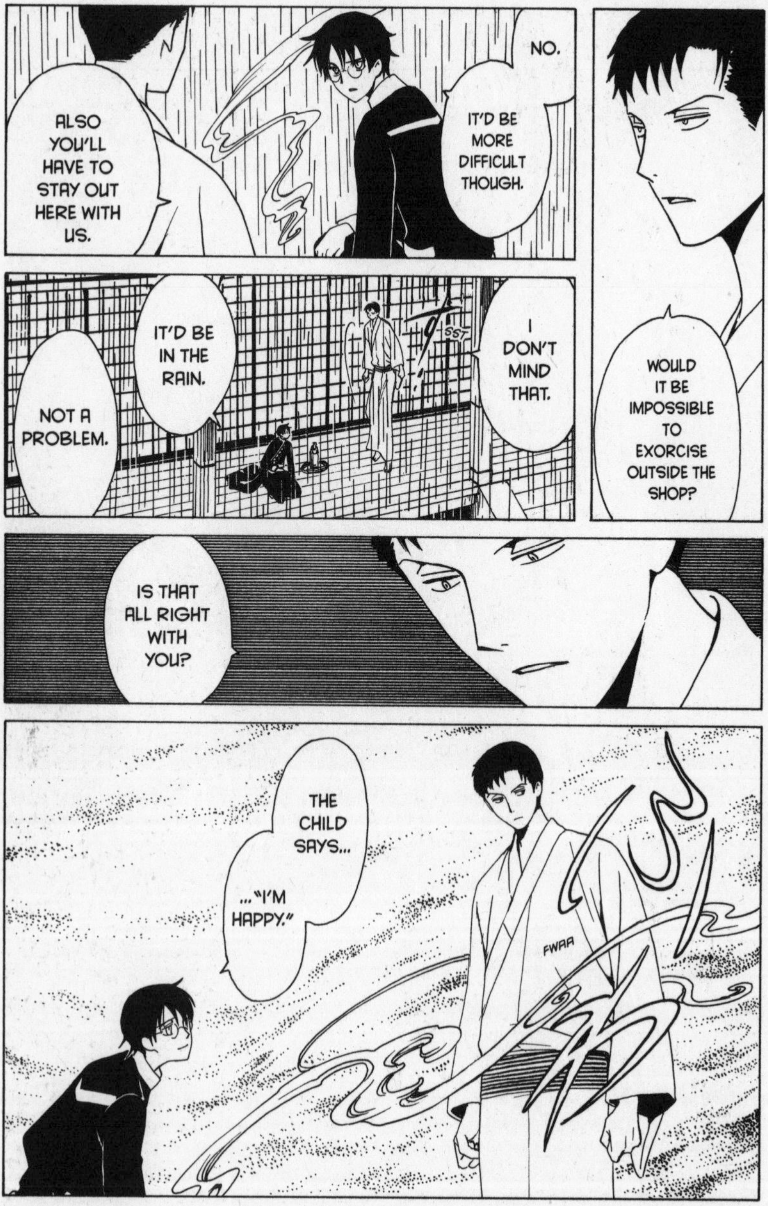
WOULD IT BE IMPOSSIBLE TO EXORCISE OUTSIDE THE SHOP?
NO.
IT'D BE MORE DIFFICULT THOUGH.
ALSO YOU'LL HAVE TO STAY OUT HERE WITH US.
I DON'T MIND THAT.
SST
IT'D BE IN THE RAIN.
NOT A PROBLEM.
IS THAT ALL RIGHT WITH YOU?
THE CHILD SAYS...
..."I'M HAPPY."
FWAA

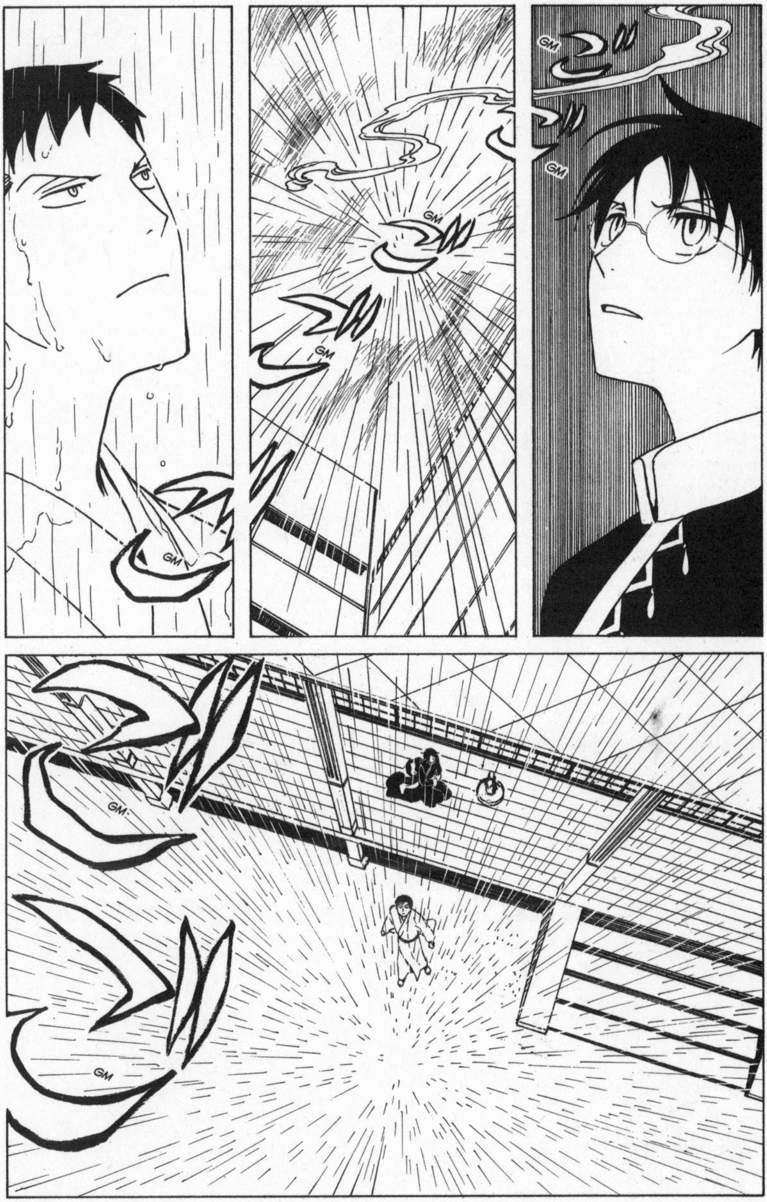
GM
GM
GM
GM
GM
GM
GM

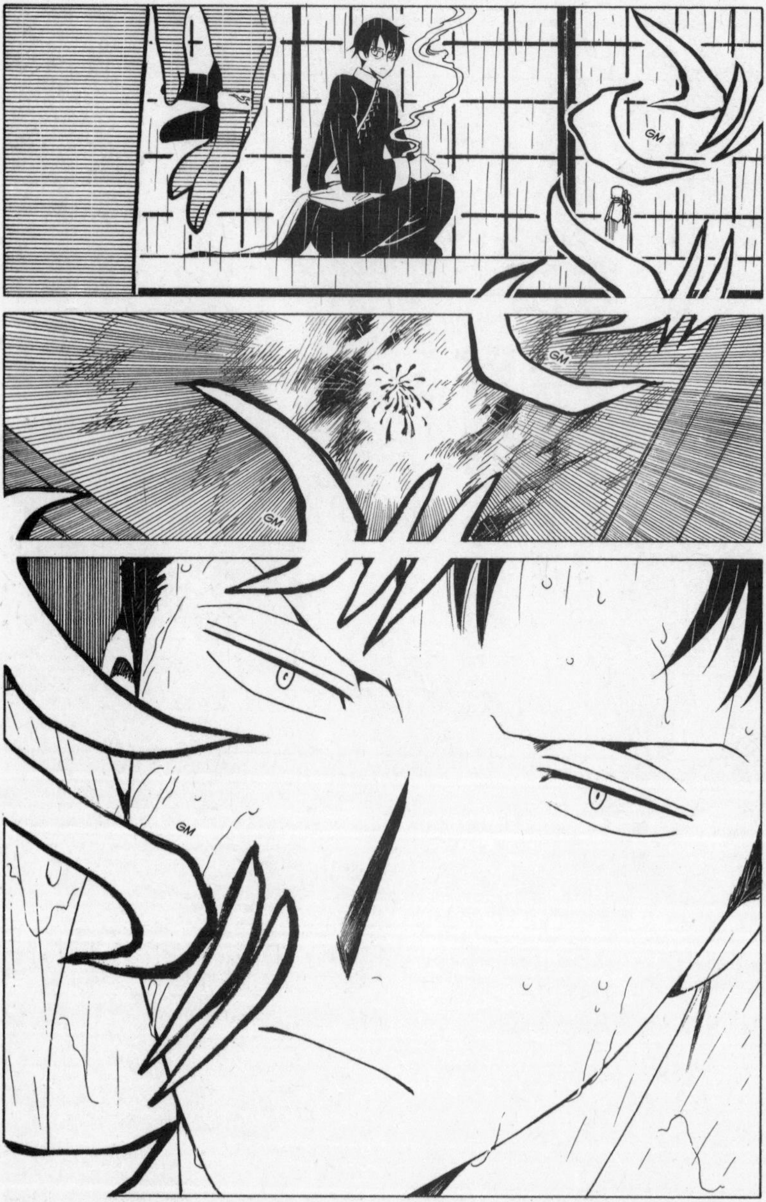
GM
GM
GM
GM

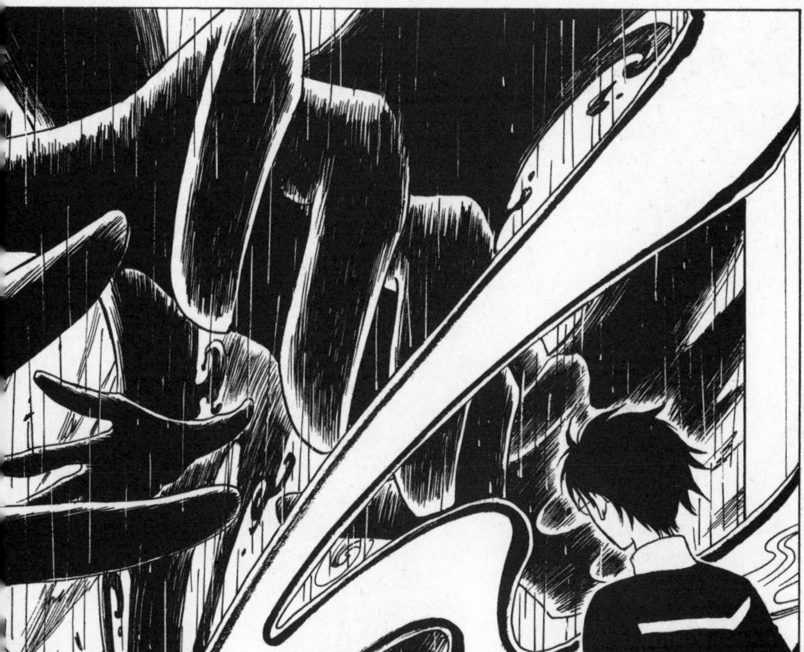
OOM

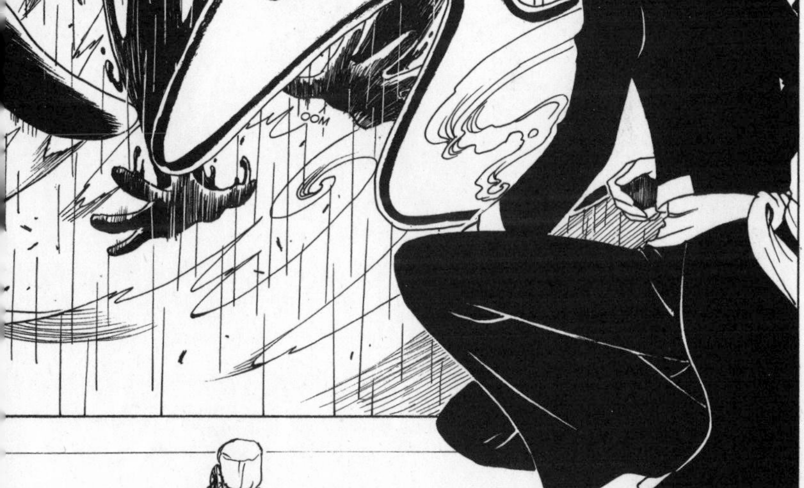

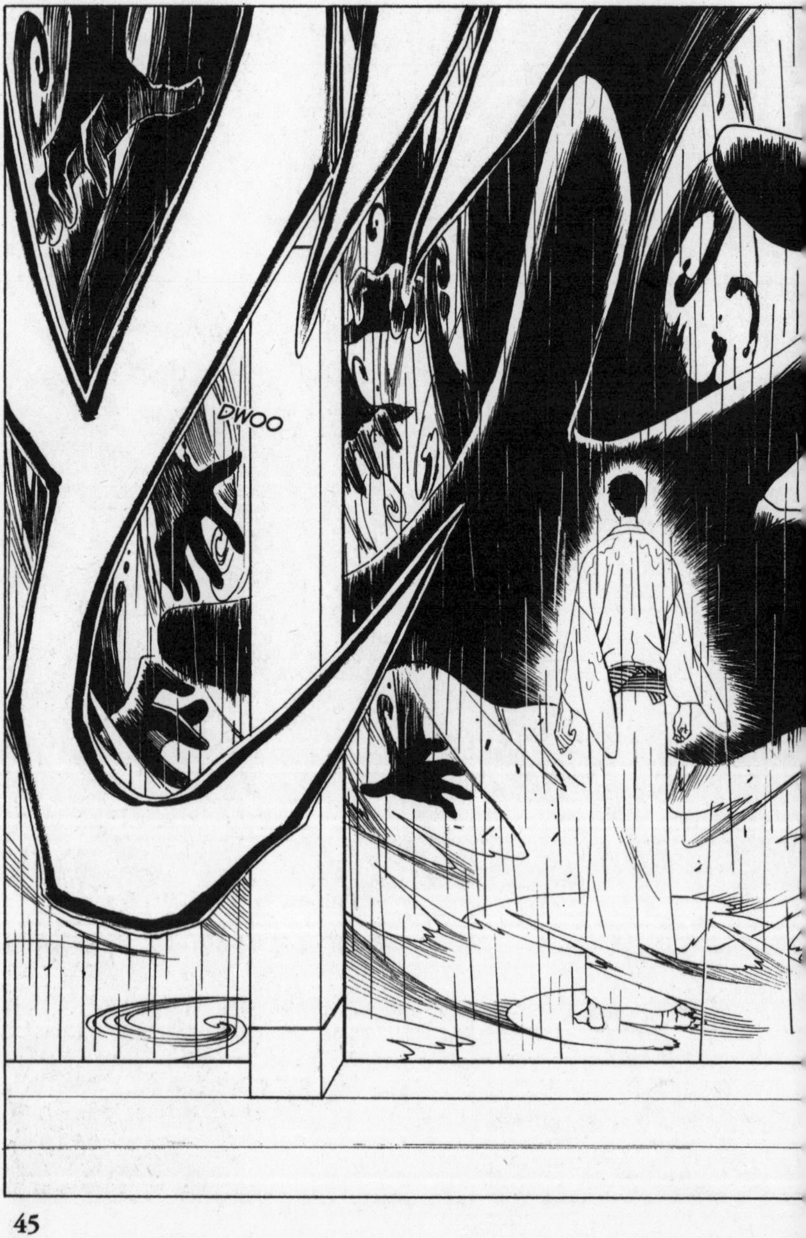
DWOO

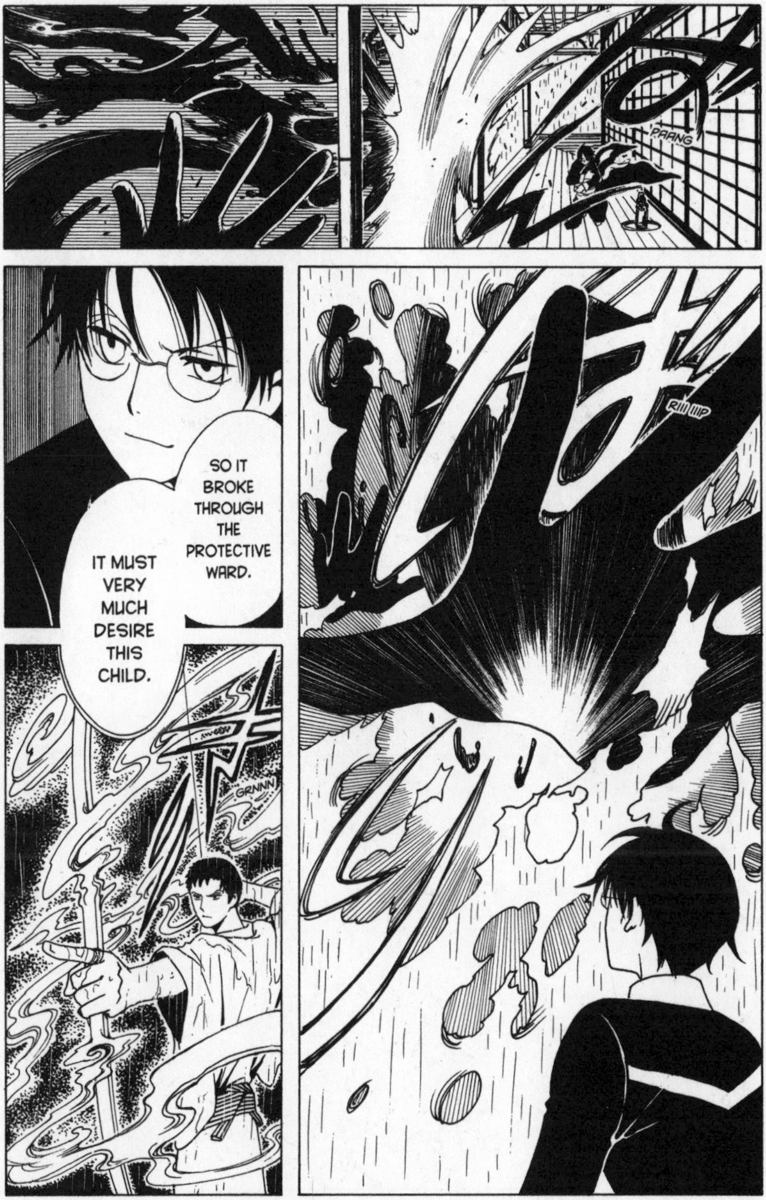
PAANG
RIIIIIP
SO IT BROKE THROUGH THE PROTECTIVE WARD.
IT MUST VERY MUCH DESIRE THIS CHILD.
GRNNN

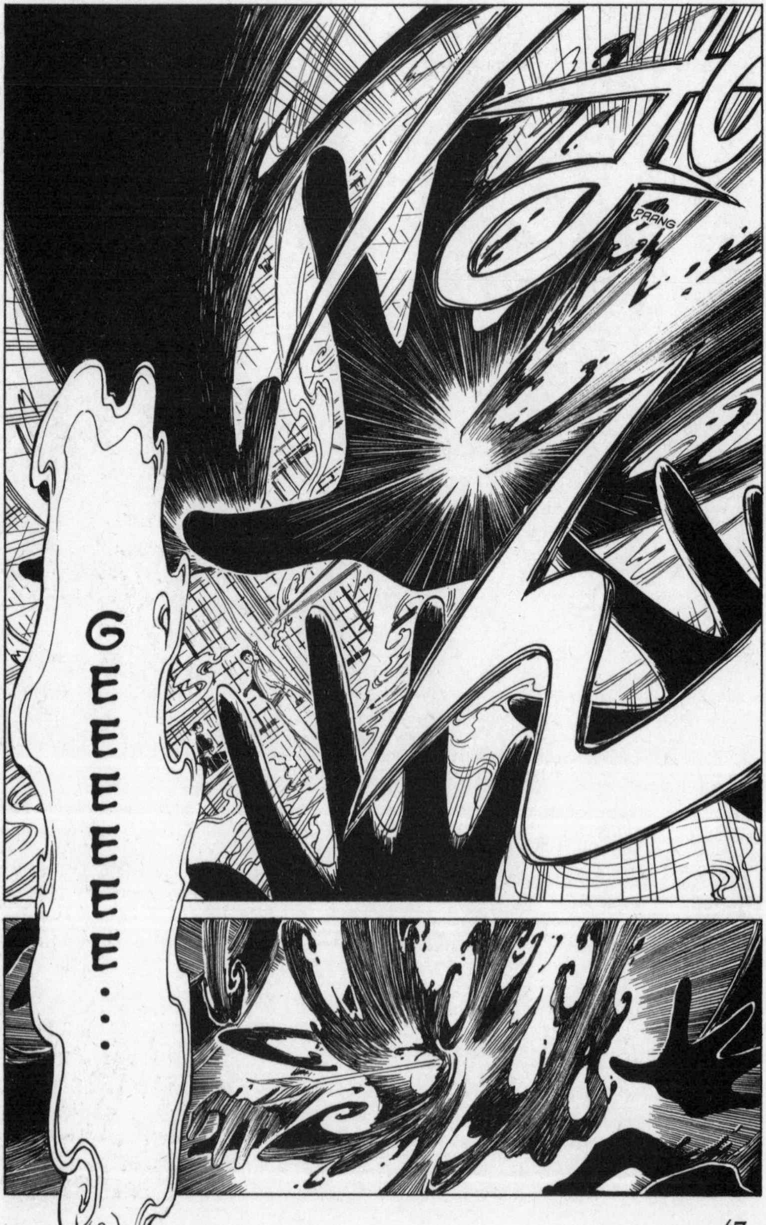
PRANG
GEEEEEEE...

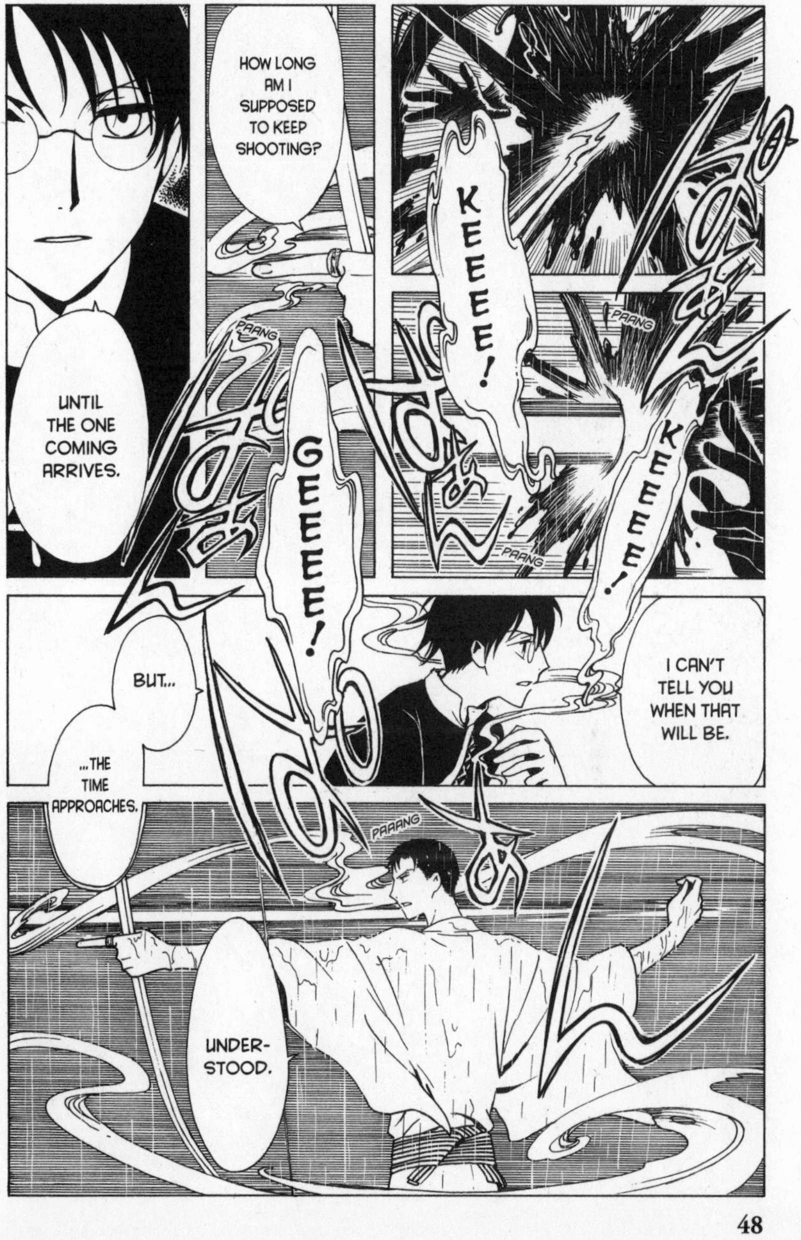
KEEEE!
PAAANG
KEEEE!
PAAANG
HOW LONG AM I SUPPOSED TO KEEP SHOOTING?
PAAANG
GEEEE!
UNTIL THE ONE COMING ARRIVES.
I CAN'T TELL YOU WHEN THAT WILL BE.
BUT...
...THE TIME APPROACHES.
PAAANG
UNDER-STOOD.

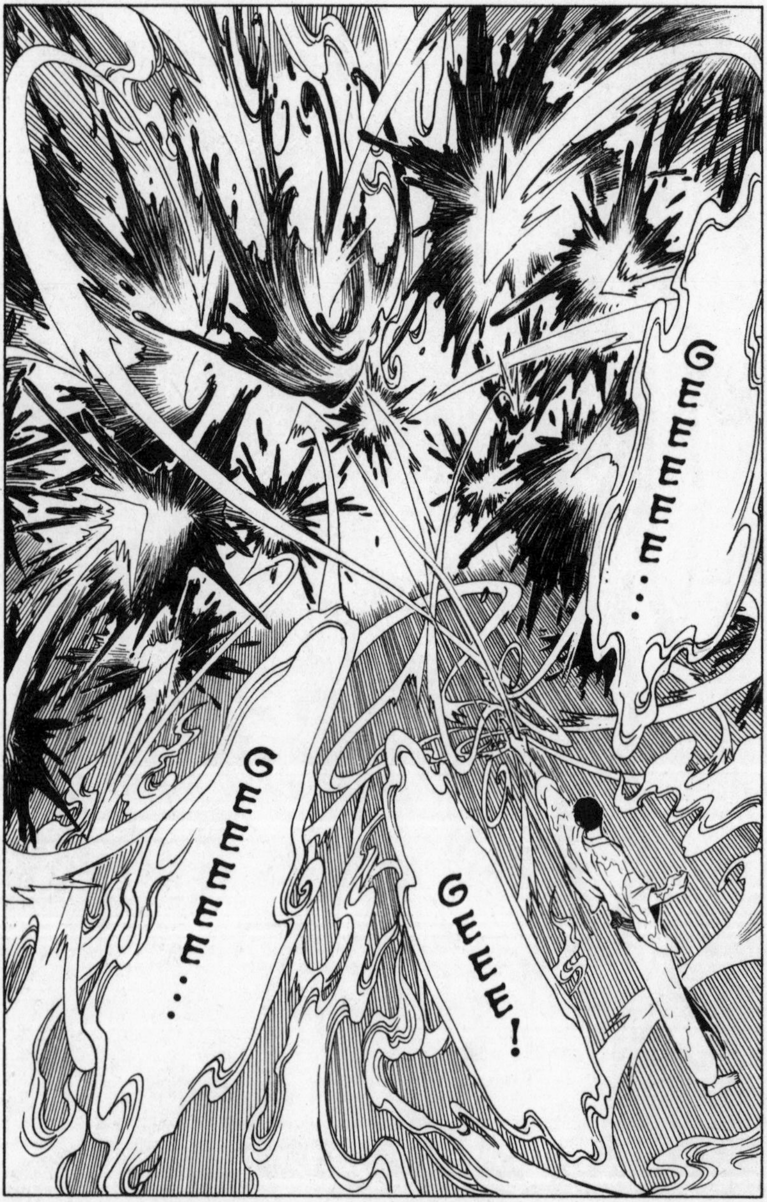
GEEEEEE...
GEEEE!
GEEEEEE...

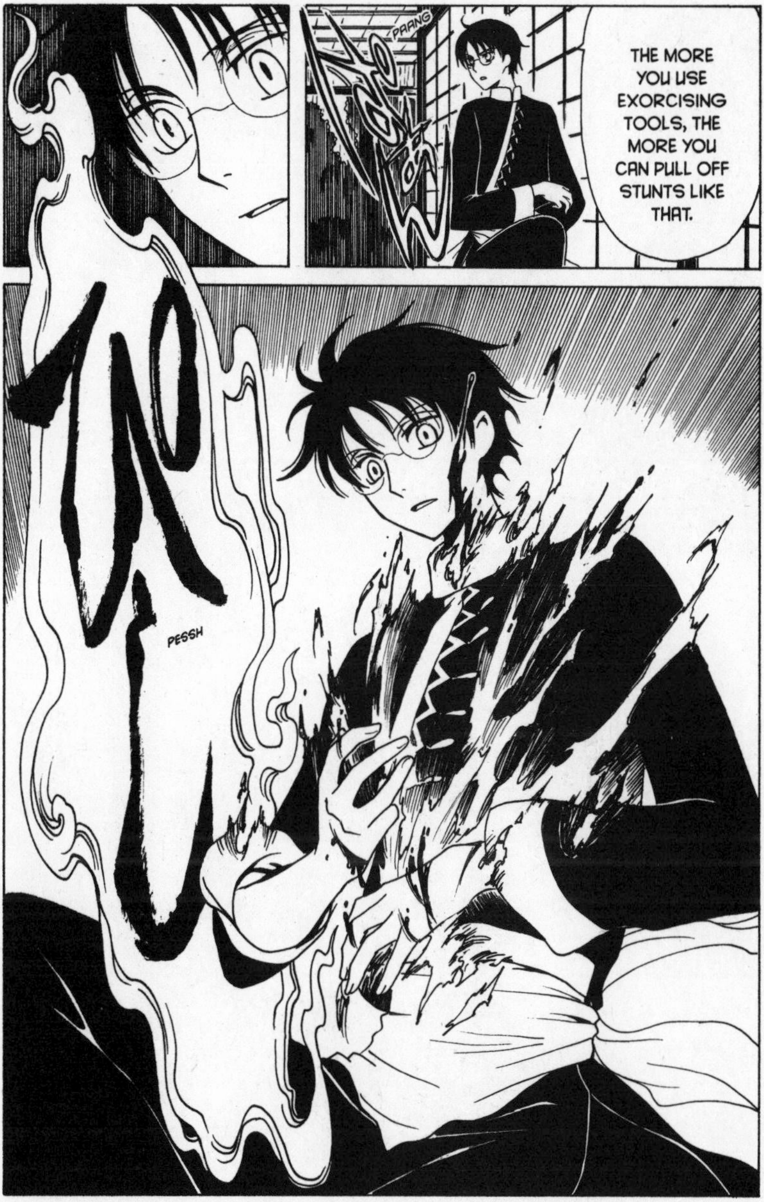
THE MORE YOU USE EXORCISING TOOLS, THE MORE YOU CAN PULL OFF STUNTS LIKE THAT.
PAANG
PESSH

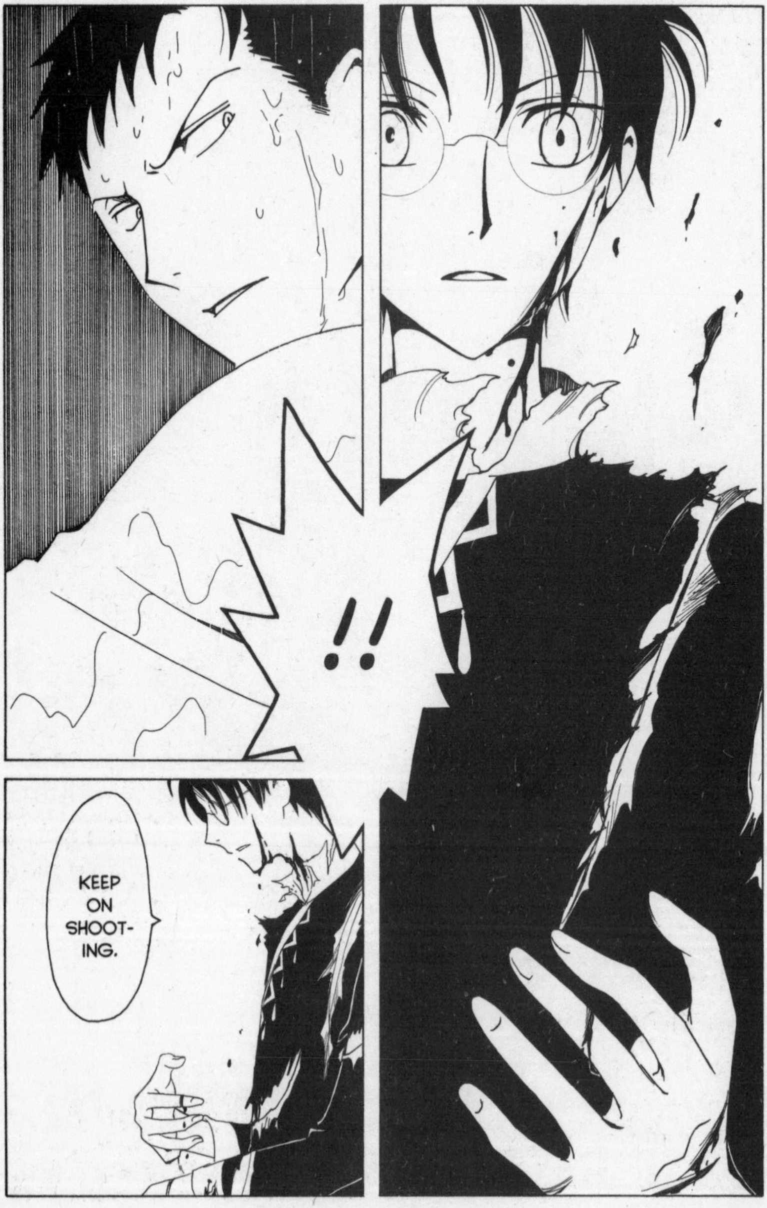
!!
KEEP ON SHOOT- ING.

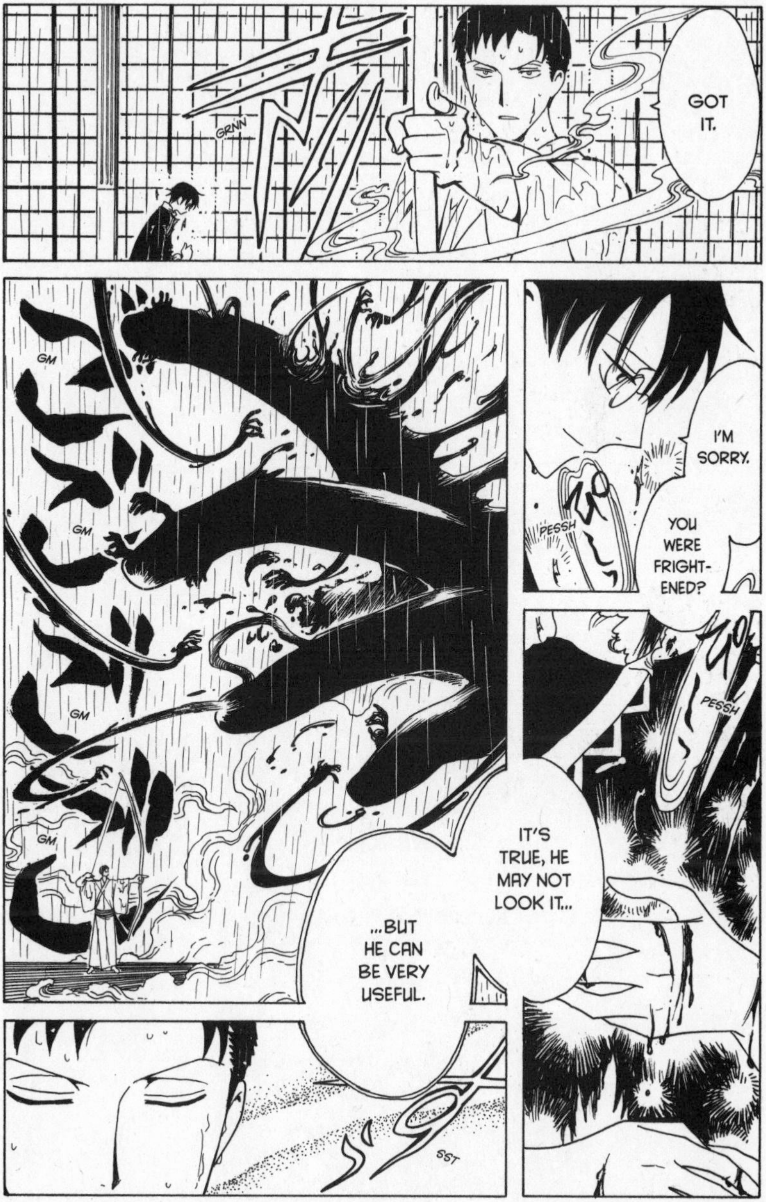
GOT IT.
GRNN
I'M SORRY.
YOU WERE FRIGHT-ENED?
PESSH
PESSH
IT'S TRUE, HE MAY NOT LOOK IT...
GM
GM
GM
GM
...BUT HE CAN BE VERY USEFUL.
SST

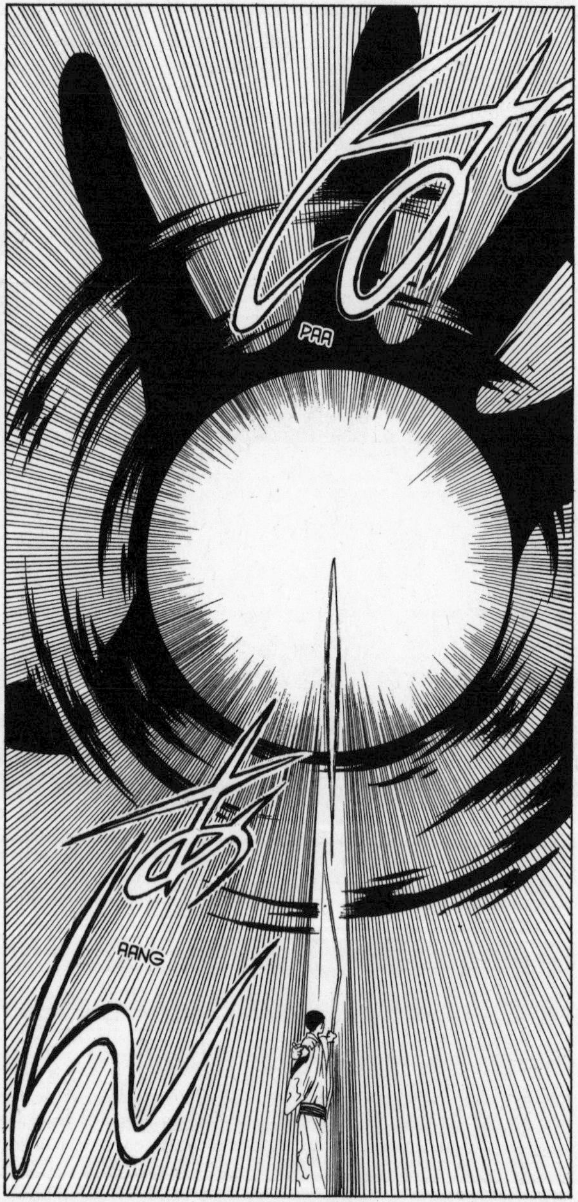
PAA
RANG
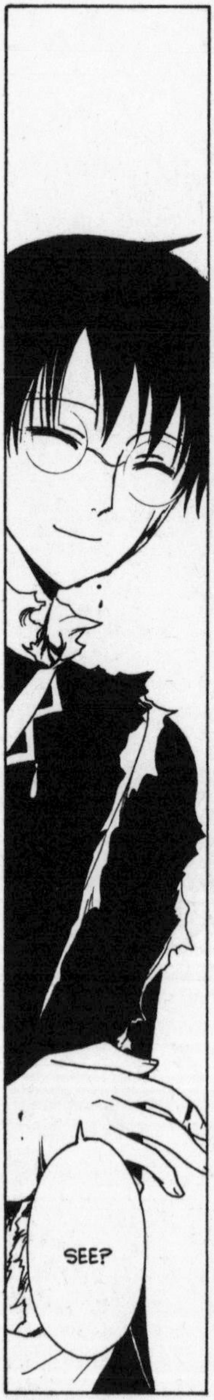
SEE?

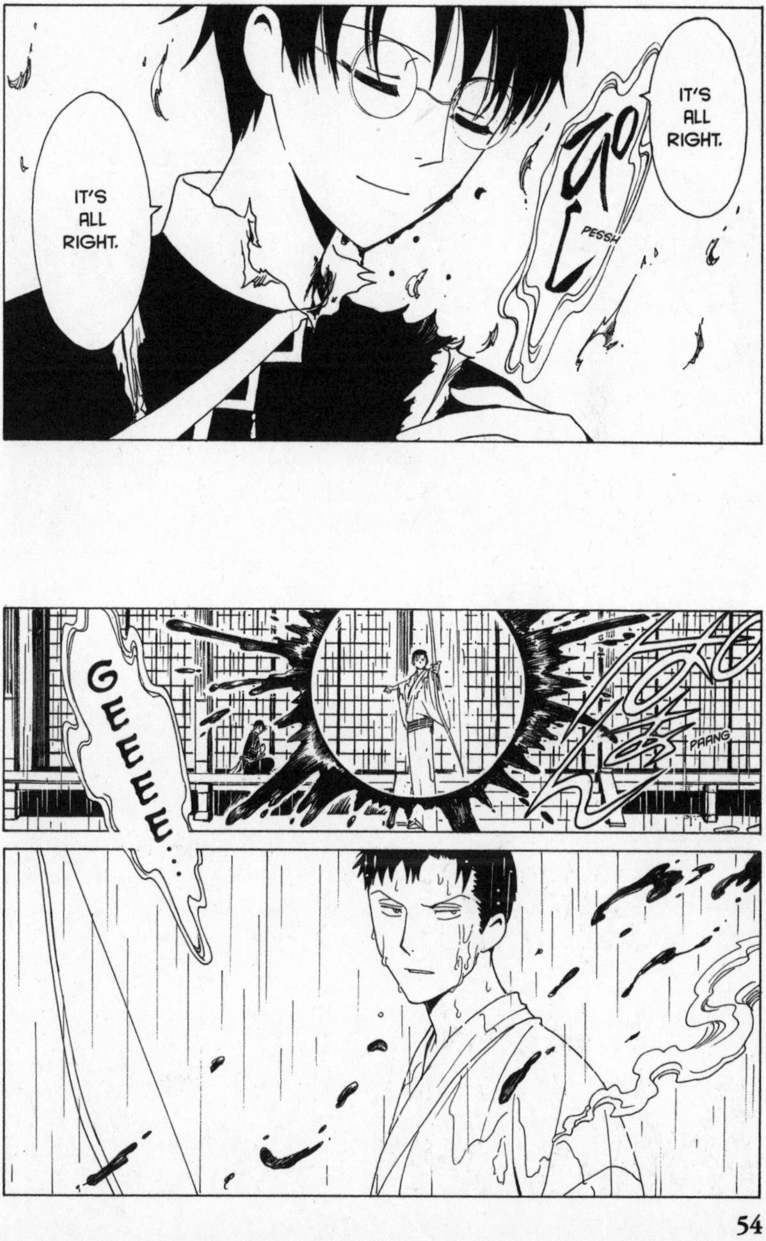
IT'S ALL RIGHT.
PESSH
IT'S ALL RIGHT.
PAANG
GEEEE...

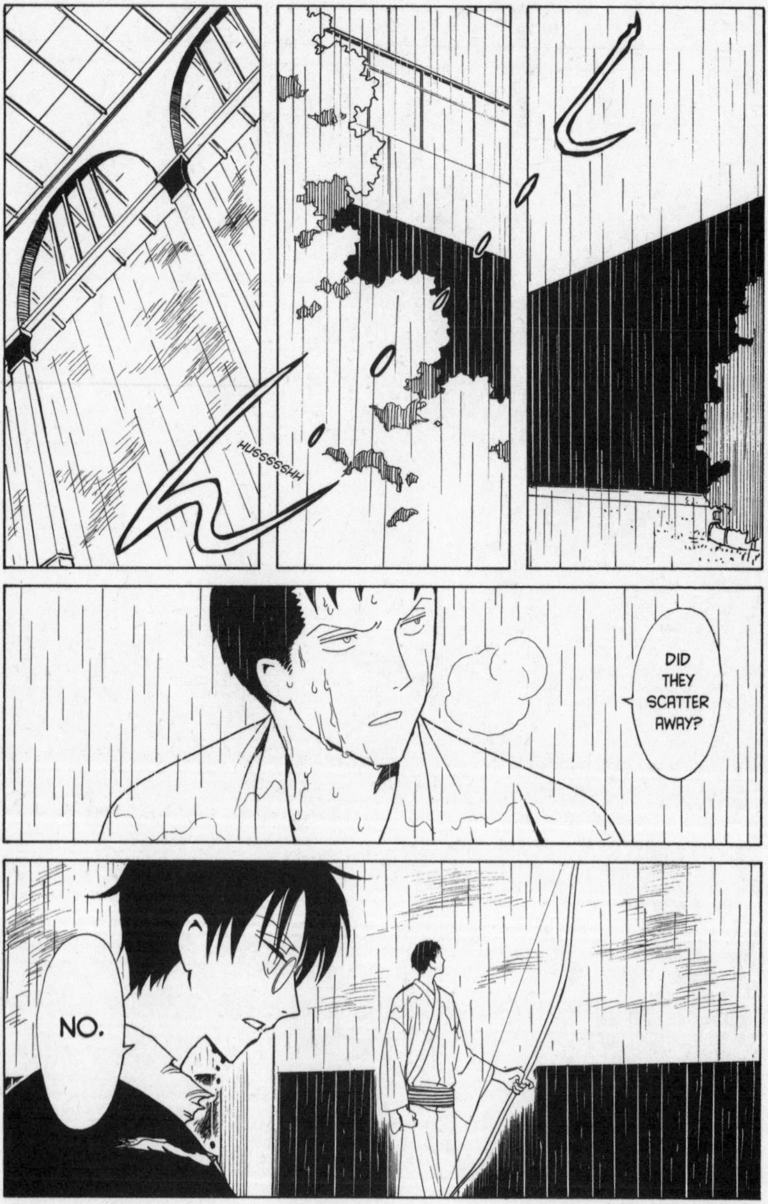
HUSSSSSHH
DID THEY SCATTER AWAY?
NO.

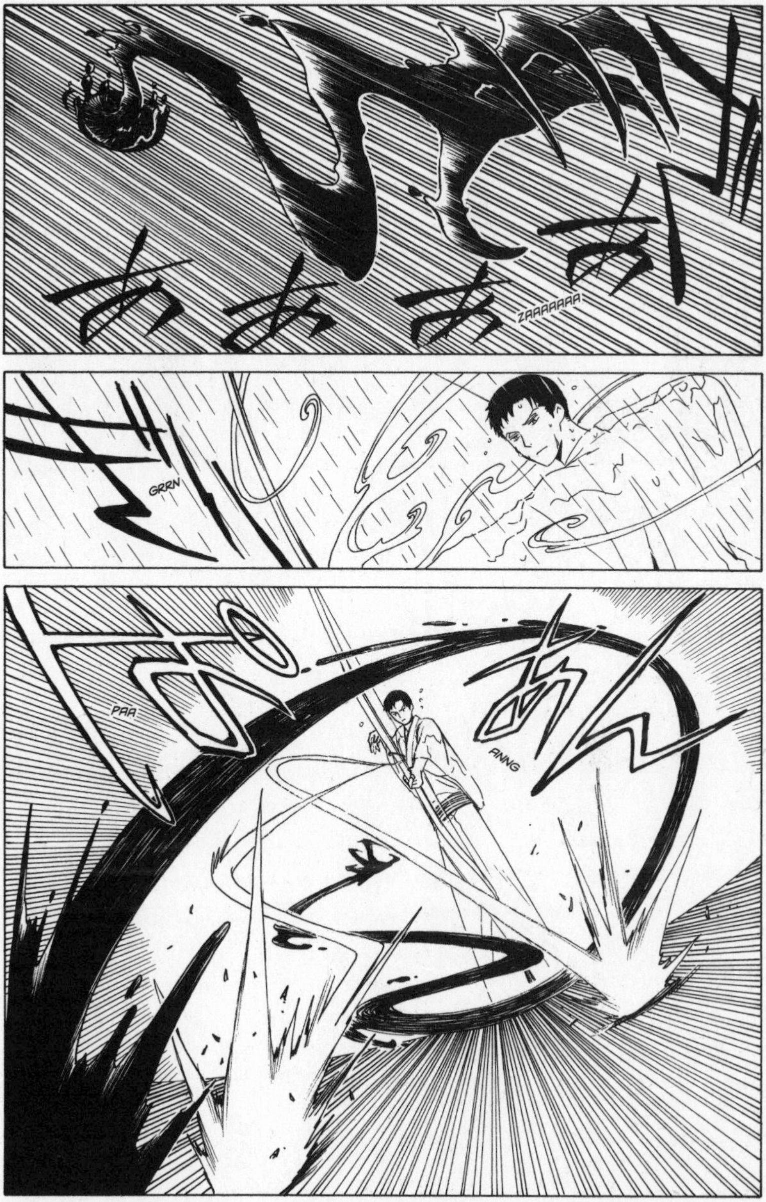
ZAAAAAAA
GRRN
ANNG
PAA

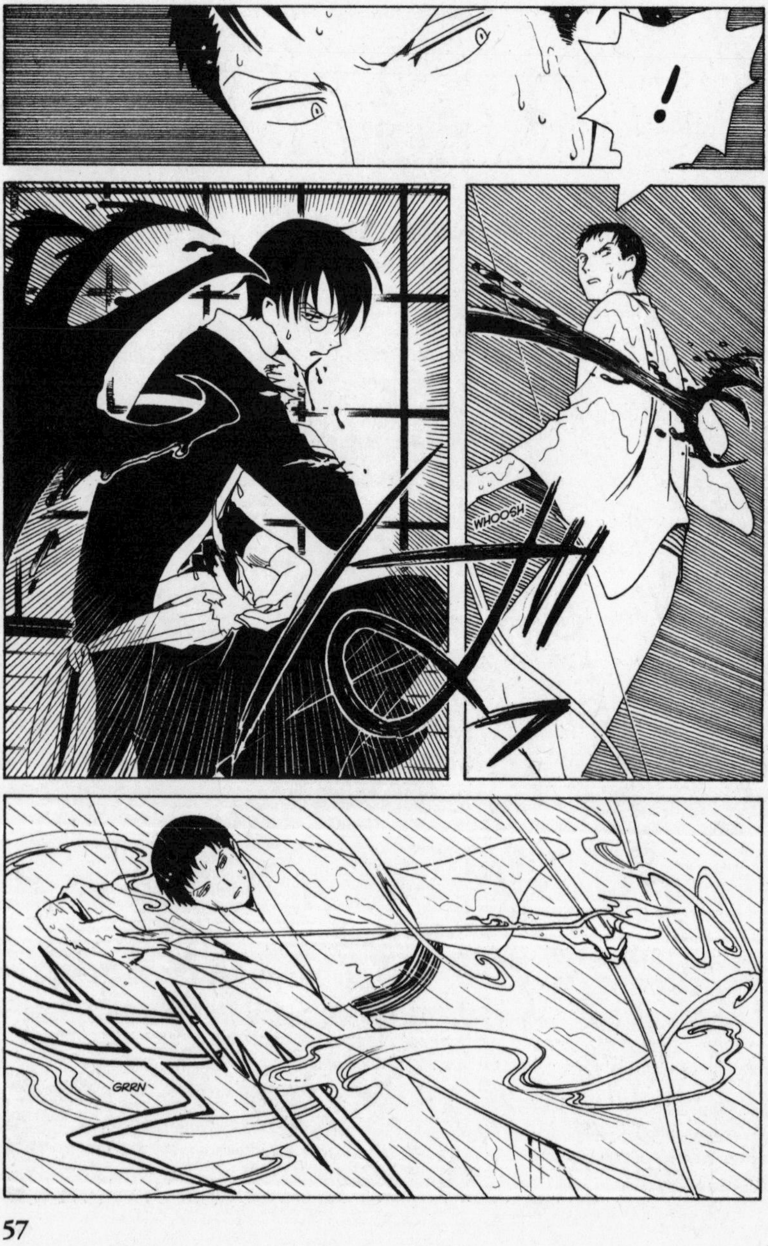
!
WHOOSH
GRRN

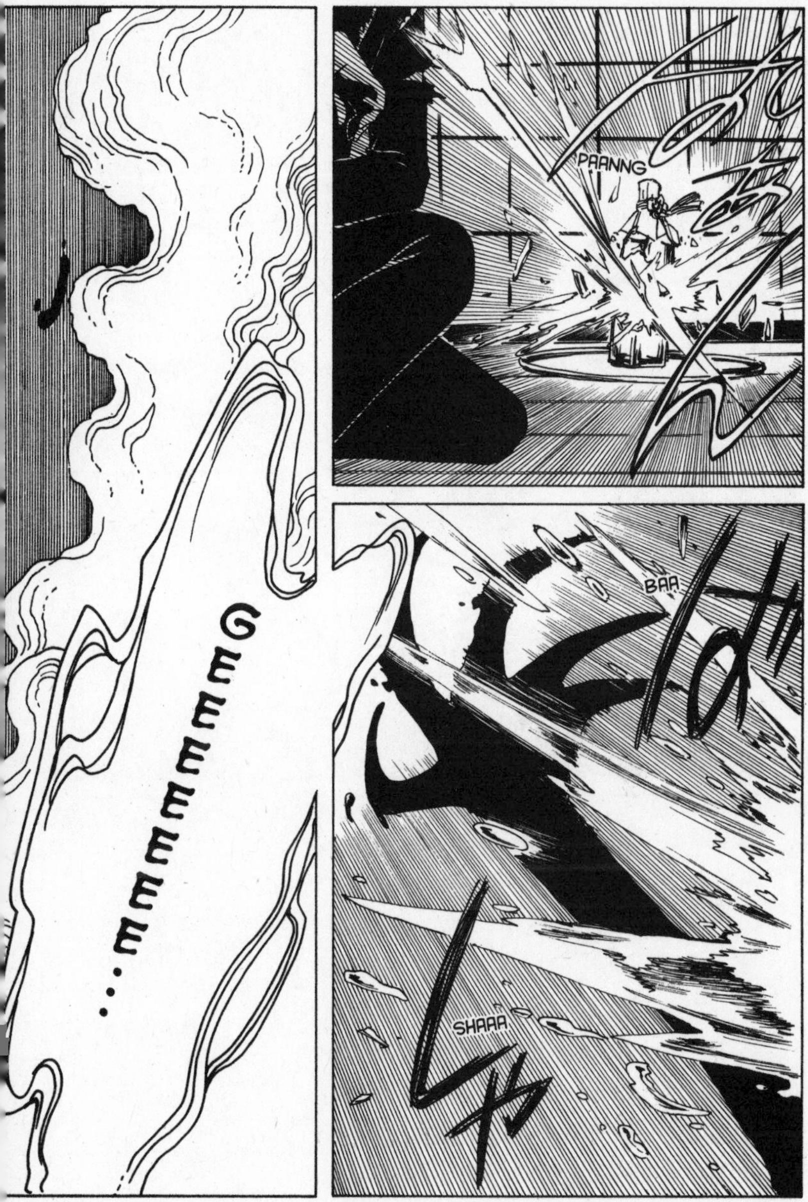
PRANNG
BAA
SHAAA
GEEEEEEE...

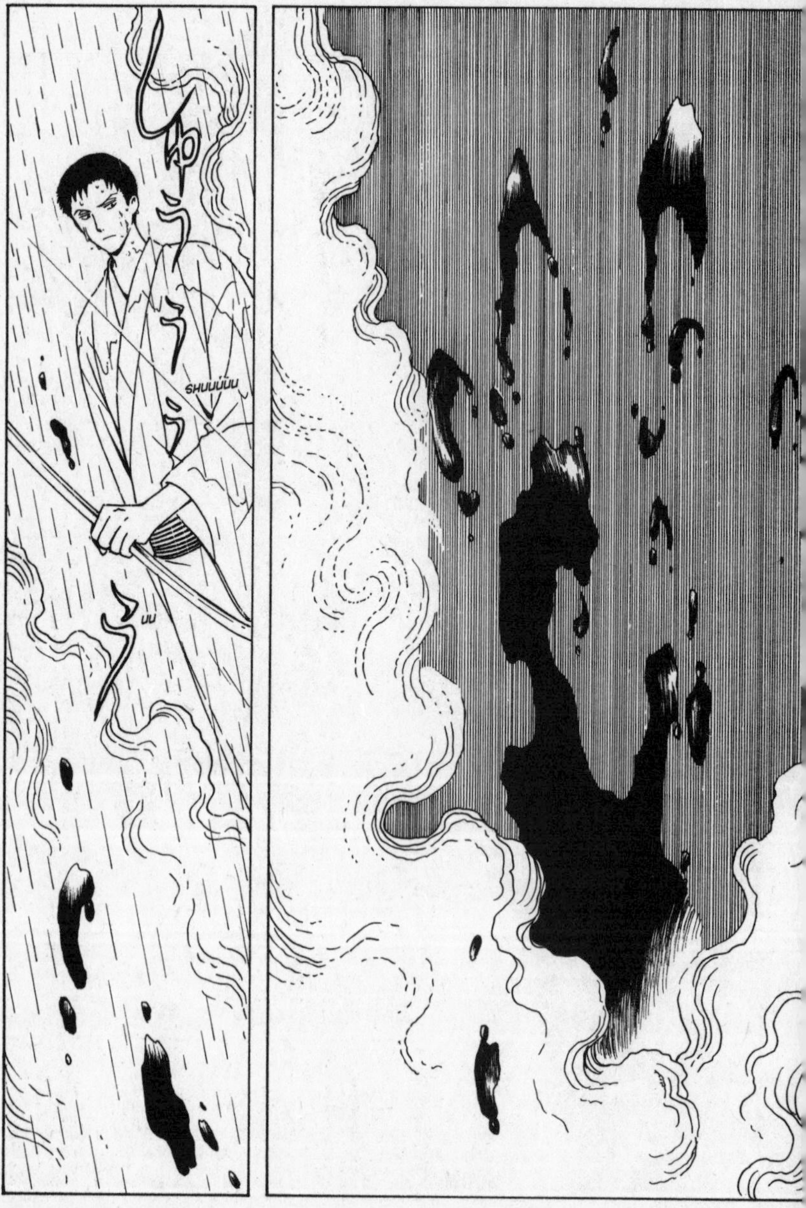
しゅううう
SHUUUUU
UU

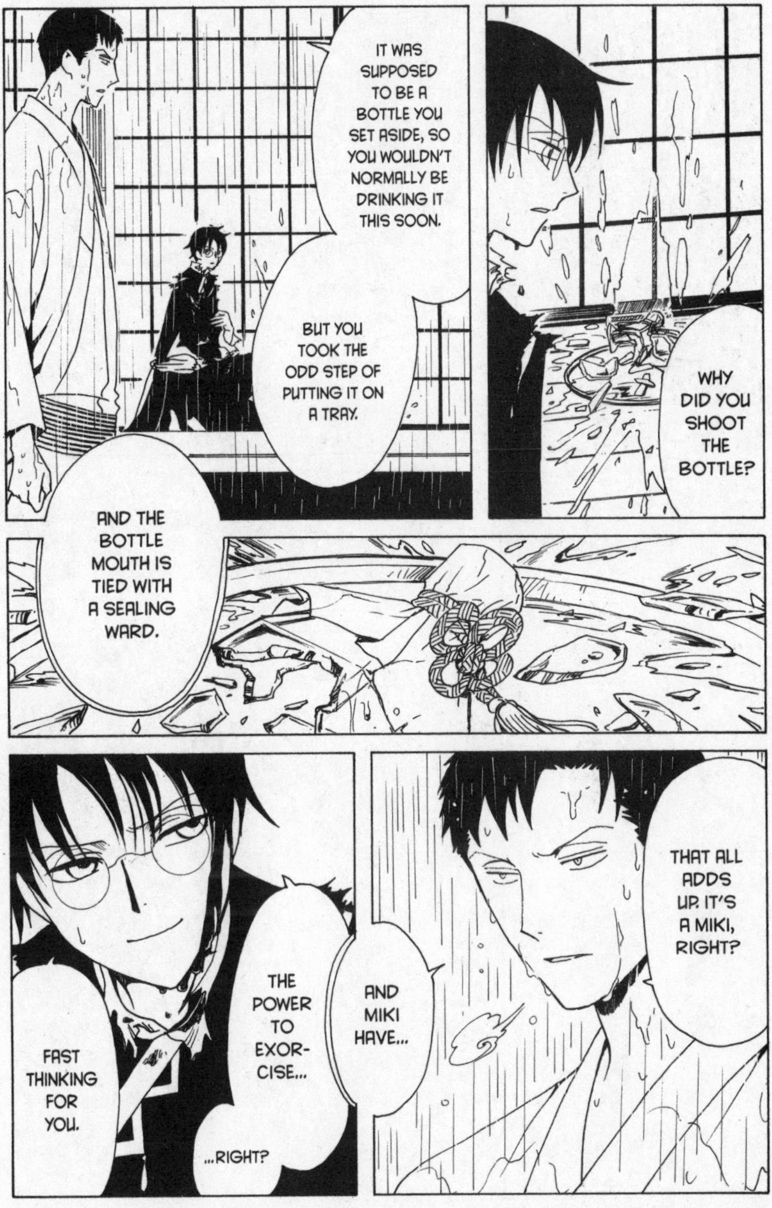
WHY DID YOU SHOOT THE BOTTLE?
IT WAS SUPPOSED TO BE A BOTTLE YOU SET ASIDE, SO YOU WOULDN'T NORMALLY BE DRINKING IT THIS SOON.
BUT YOU TOOK THE ODD STEP OF PUTTING IT ON A TRAY.
AND THE BOTTLE MOUTH IS TIED WITH A SEALING WARD.
THAT ALL ADDS UP. IT'S A MIKI, RIGHT?
AND MIKI HAVE...
THE POWER TO EXORCISE...
...RIGHT?
FAST THINKING FOR YOU.

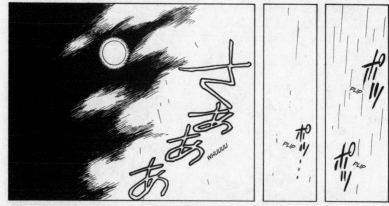

WHUUUU

PLIP PLIP

PLIP PLIP

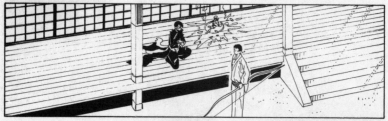

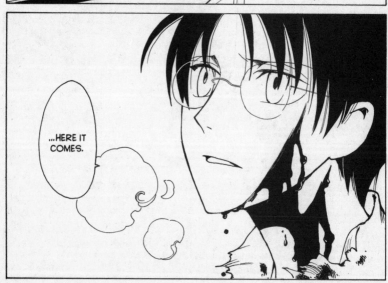

...HERE IT COMES.

61

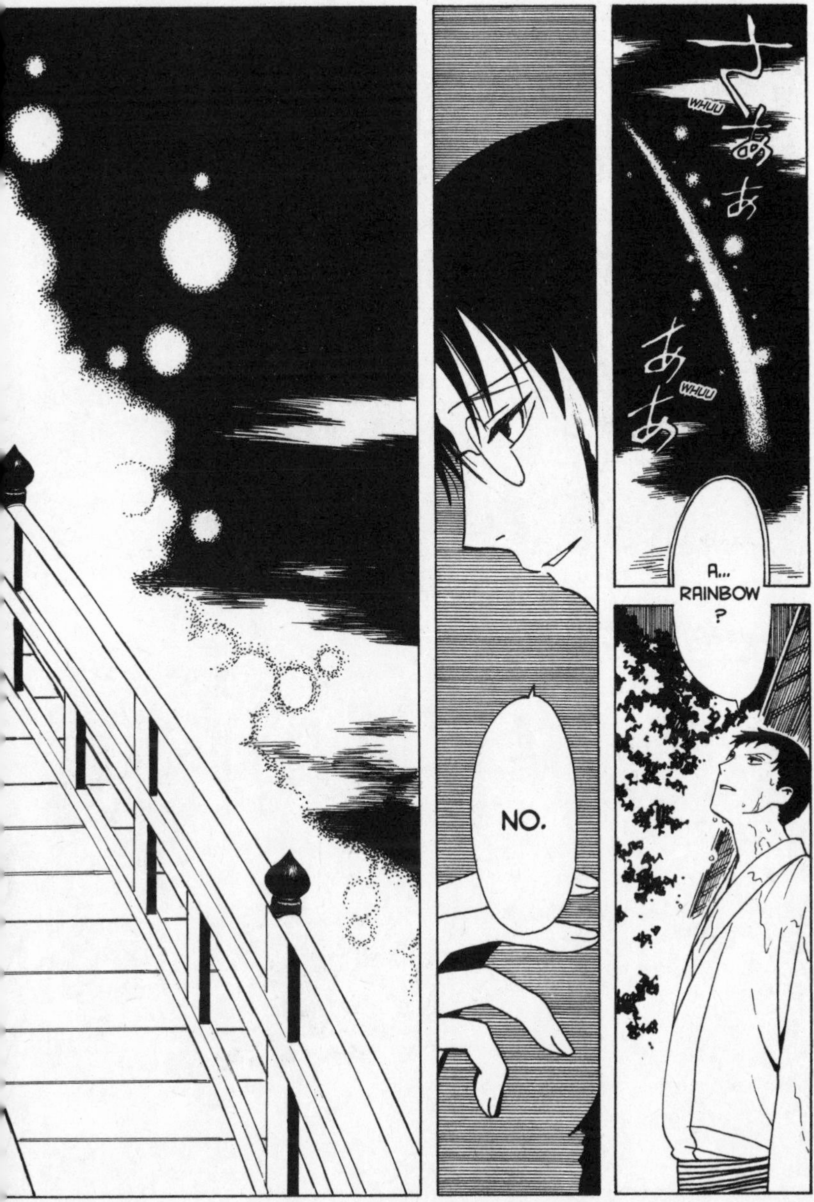
WHUU
WHUU
A... RAINBOW ?
NO.

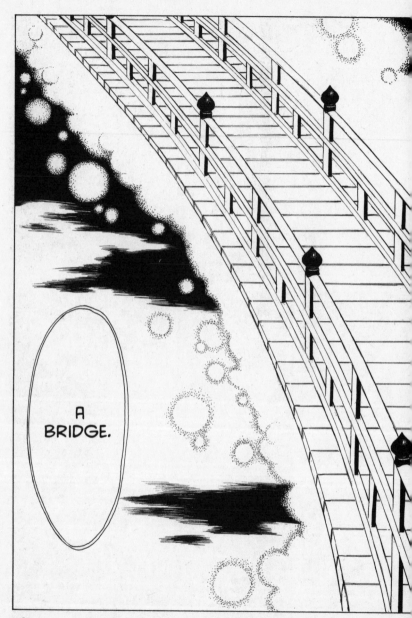

A
BRIDGE.

63

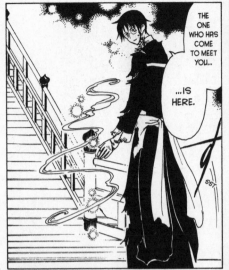

THE ONE WHO HAS COME TO MEET YOU...

...IS HERE.

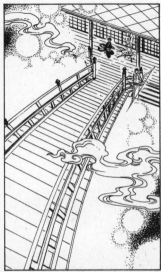

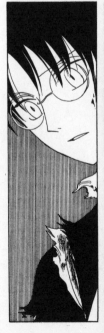

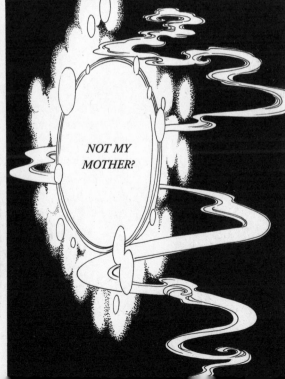

NOT MY MOTHER?

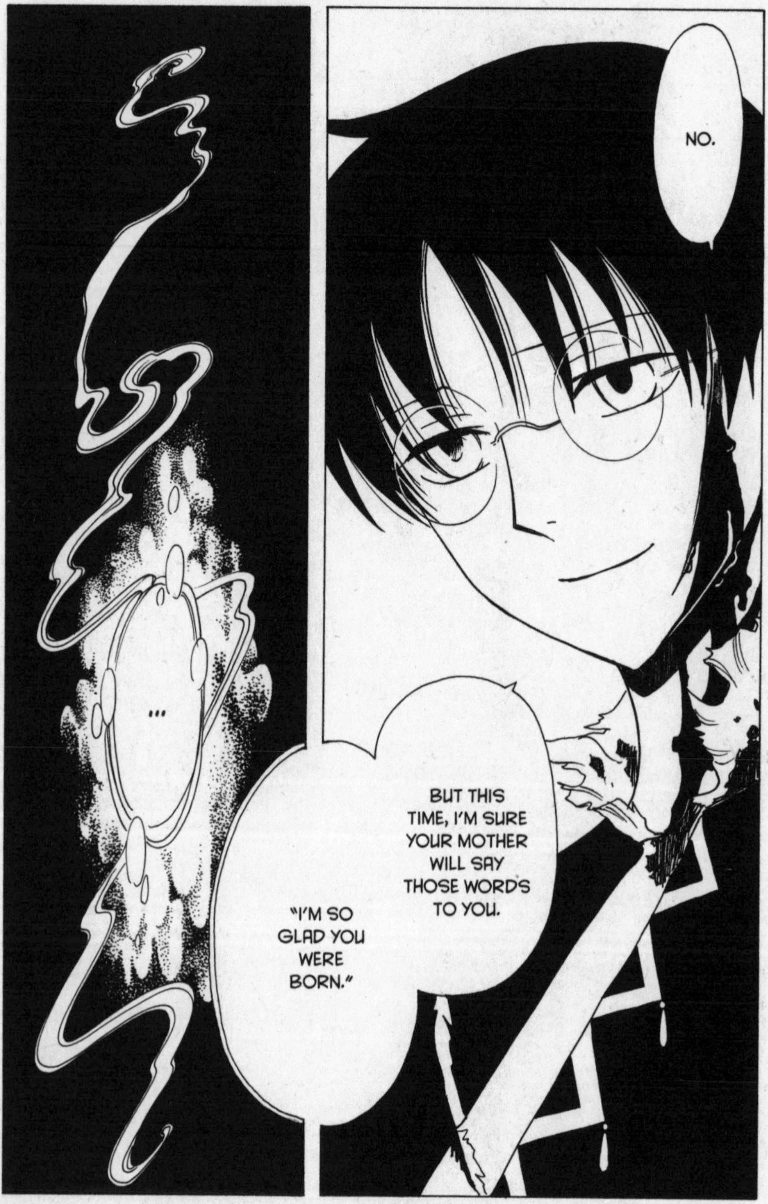
NO.
BUT THIS TIME, I'M SURE YOUR MOTHER WILL SAY THOSE WORDS TO YOU.
"I'M SO GLAD YOU WERE BORN."
...

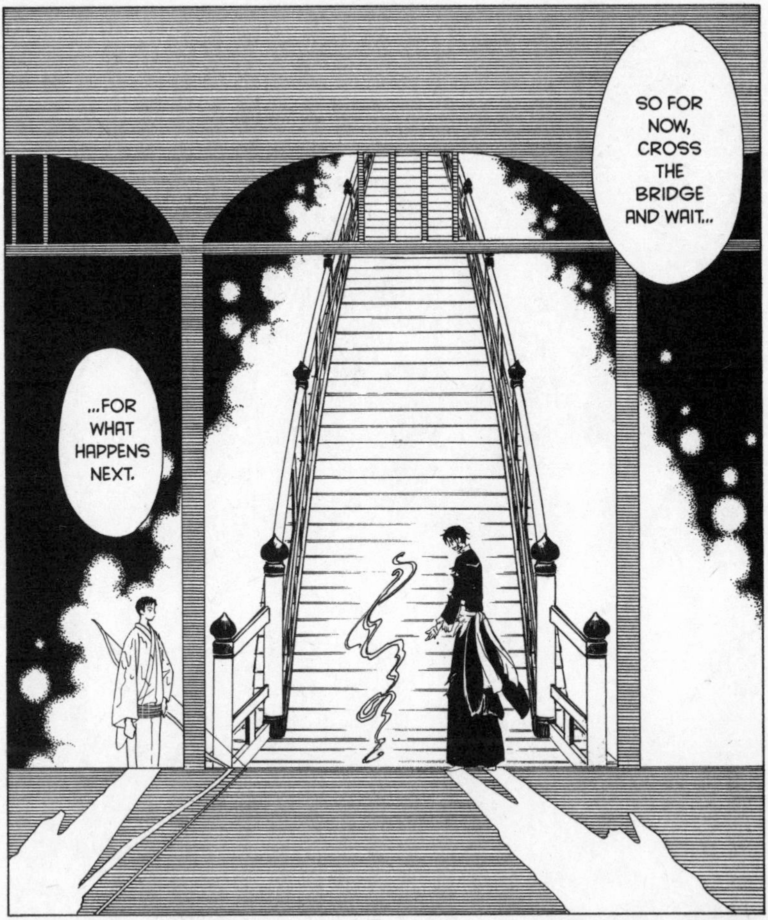
SO FOR NOW, CROSS THE BRIDGE AND WAIT...
...FOR WHAT HAPPENS NEXT.
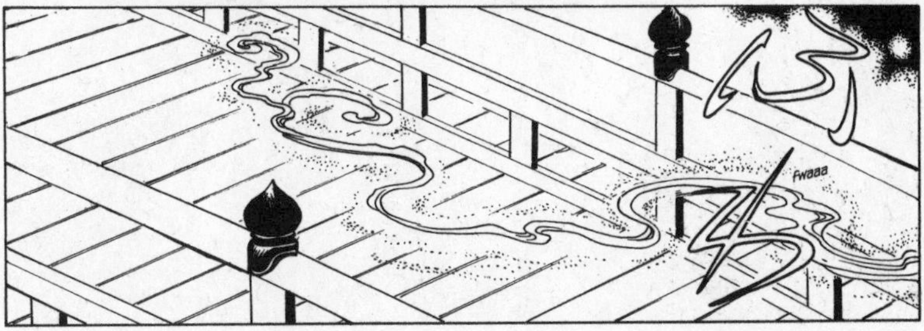
fwaaa

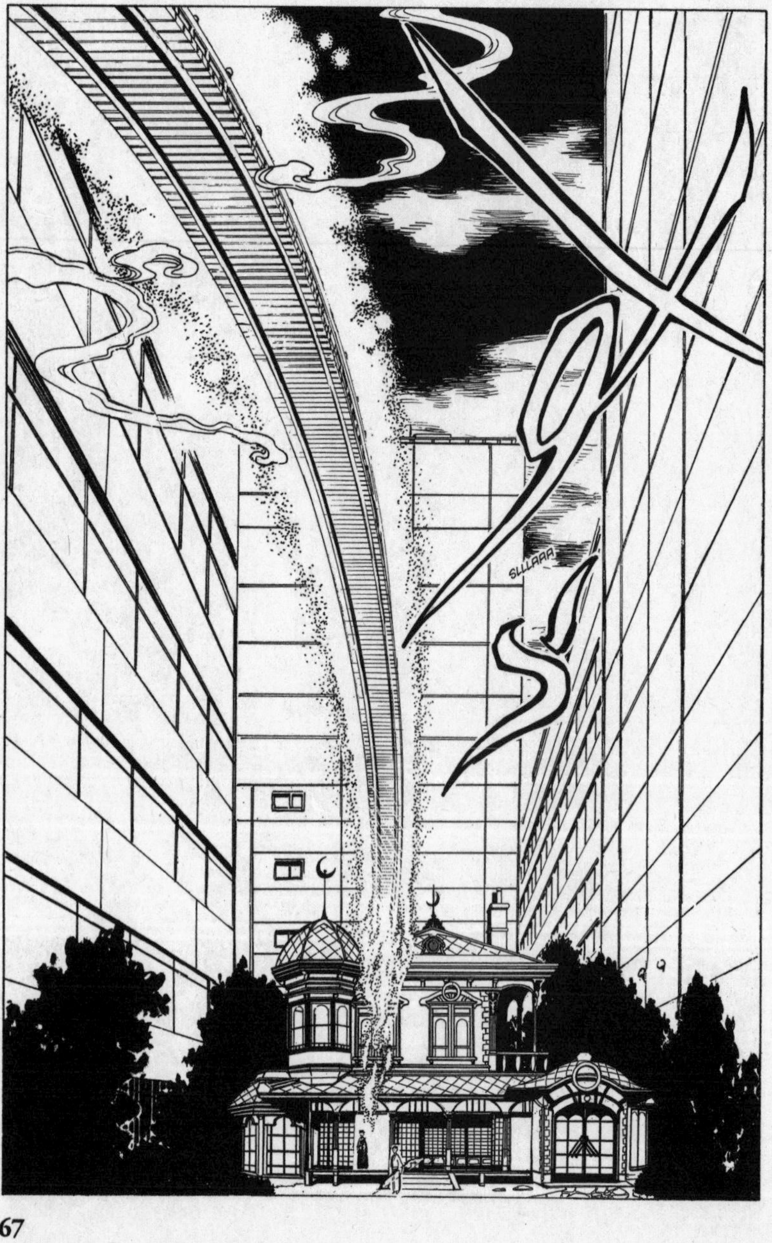
SLLLAAA

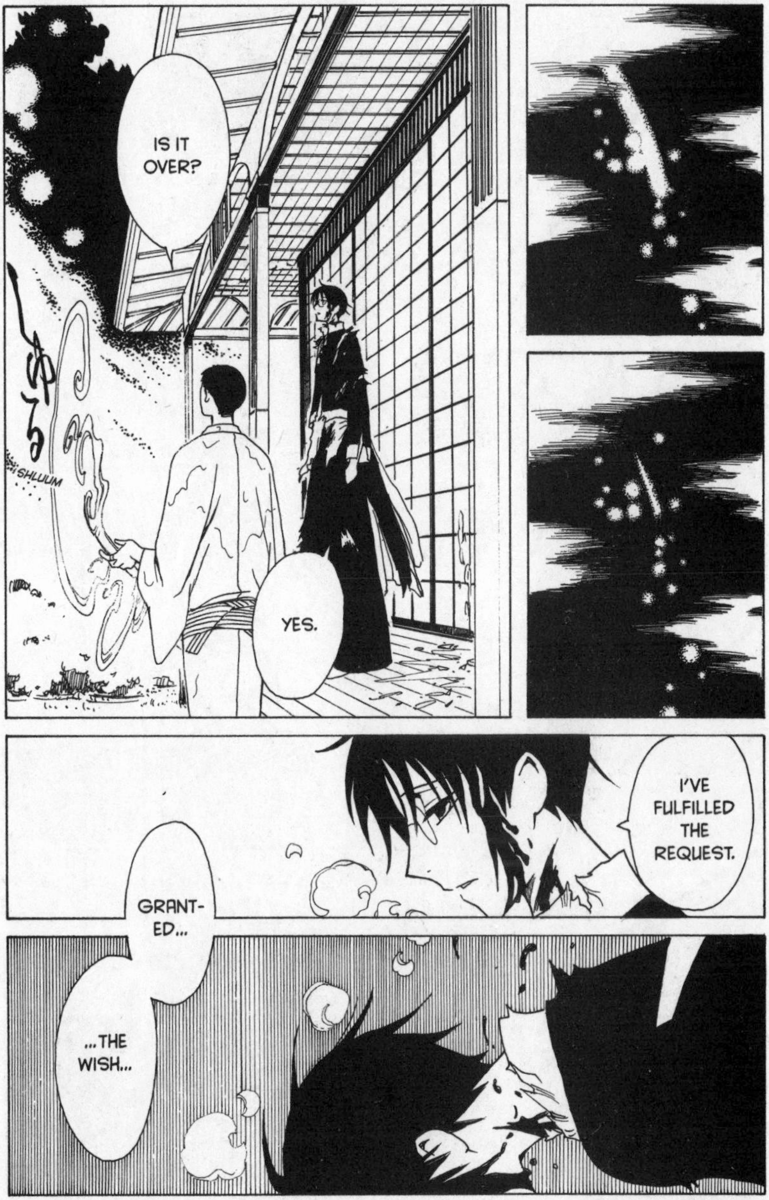
IS IT OVER?
しゅる
SHLUUM
YES.
I'VE FULFILLED THE REQUEST.
GRANT-ED...
...THE WISH...

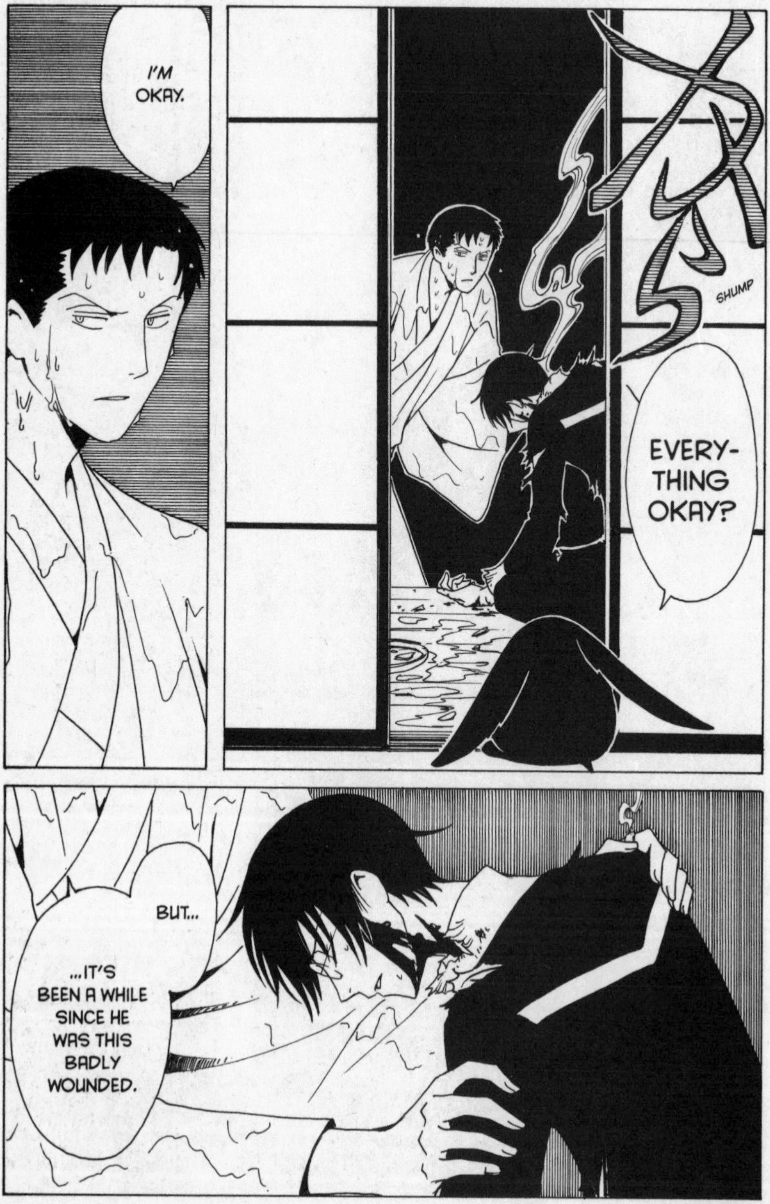
SHUMP
EVERY-THING OKAY?
I'M OKAY.
BUT...
...IT'S BEEN A WHILE SINCE HE WAS THIS BADLY WOUNDED.

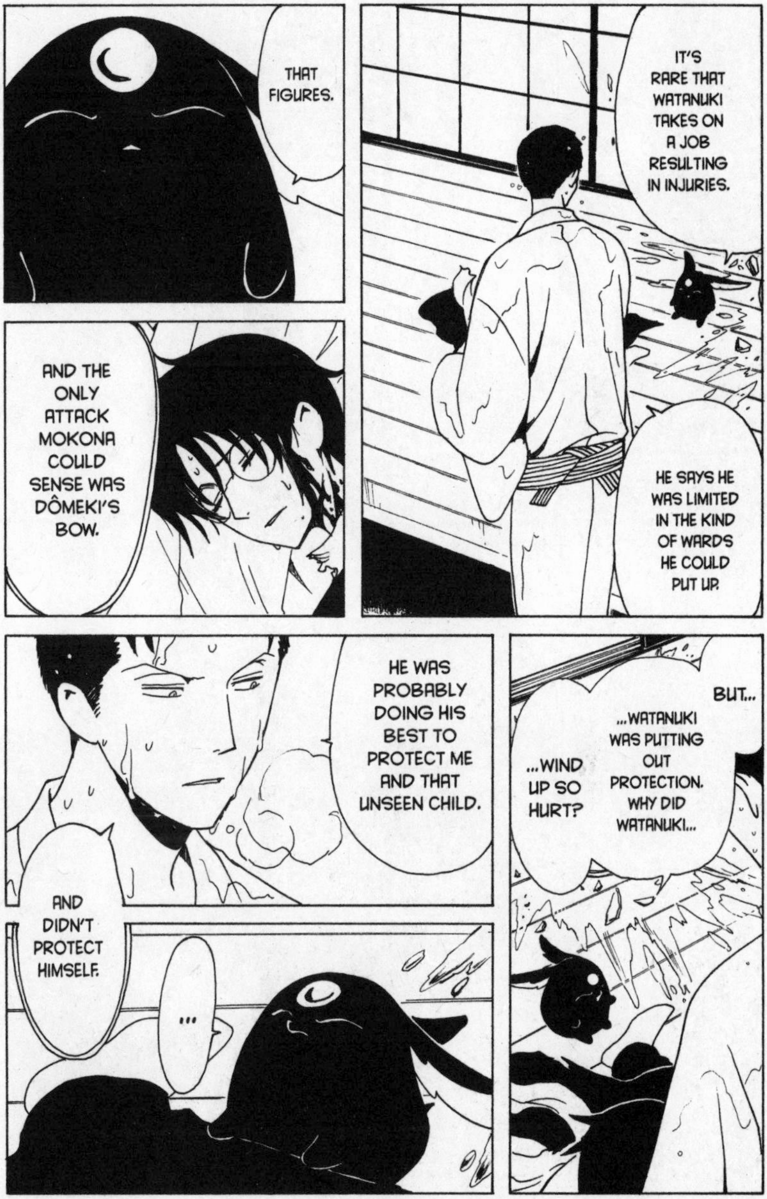
IT'S RARE THAT WATANUKI TAKES ON A JOB RESULTING IN INJURIES.
HE SAYS HE WAS LIMITED IN THE KIND OF WARDS HE COULD PUT UP.
THAT FIGURES.
AND THE ONLY ATTACK MOKONA COULD SENSE WAS DÔMEKI'S BOW.
BUT...
...WATANUKI WAS PUTTING OUT PROTECTION. WHY DID WATANUKI...
...WIND UP SO HURT?
HE WAS PROBABLY DOING HIS BEST TO PROTECT ME AND THAT UNSEEN CHILD.
AND DIDN'T PROTECT HIMSELF.
...

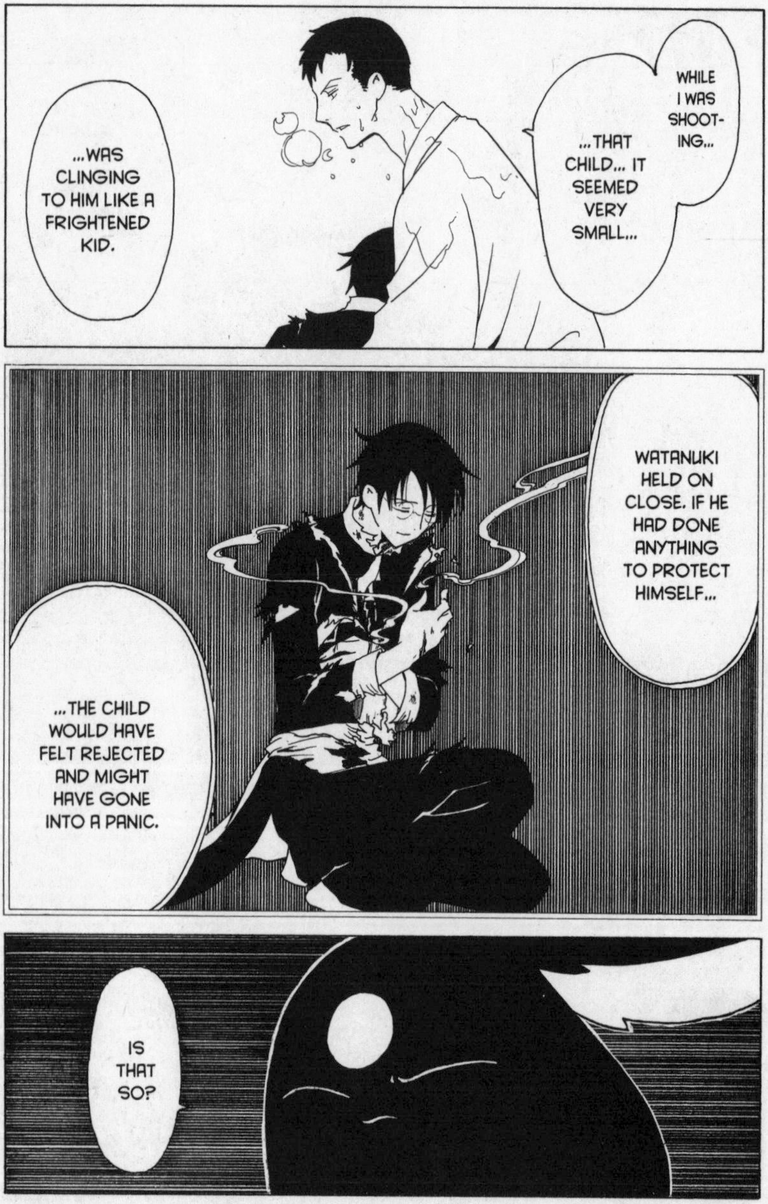
WHILE I WAS SHOOT- ING...
...THAT CHILD... IT SEEMED VERY SMALL...
...WAS CLINGING TO HIM LIKE A FRIGHTENED KID.
WATANUKI HELD ON CLOSE. IF HE HAD DONE ANYTHING TO PROTECT HIMSELF...
...THE CHILD WOULD HAVE FELT REJECTED AND MIGHT HAVE GONE INTO A PANIC.
IS THAT SO?

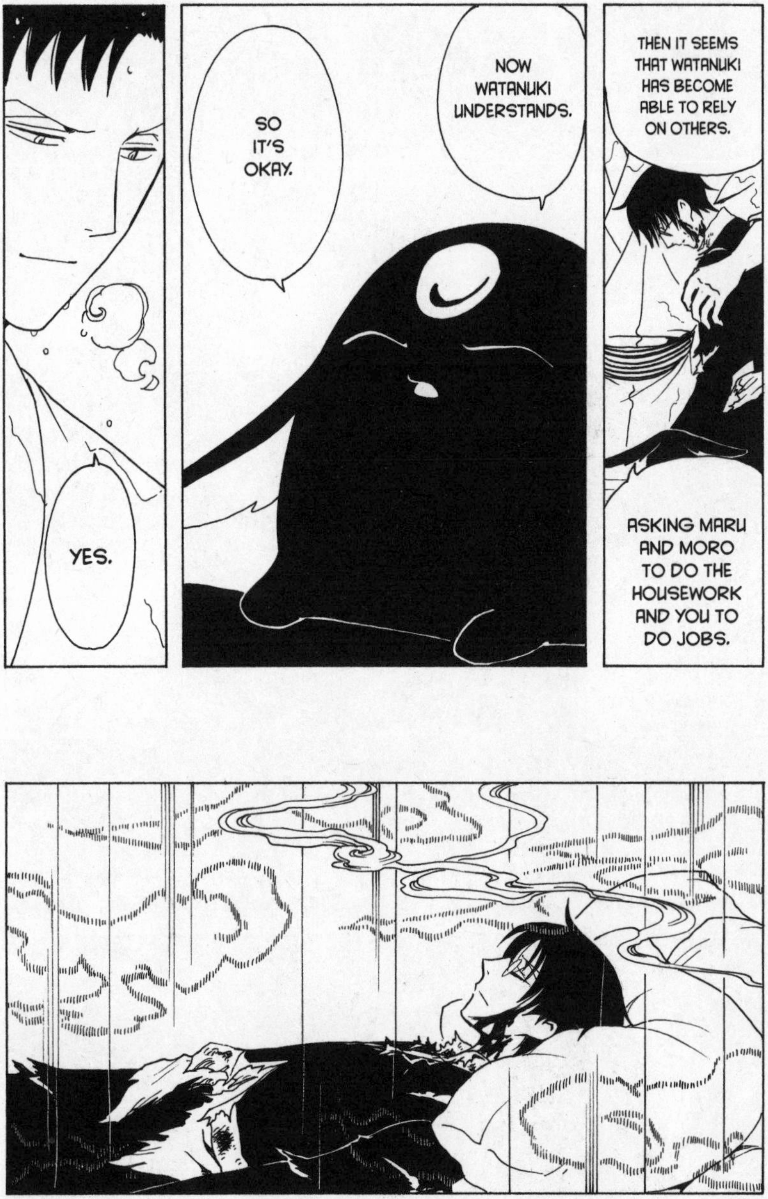
THEN IT SEEMS THAT WATANUKI HAS BECOME ABLE TO RELY ON OTHERS.
ASKING MARU AND MORO TO DO THE HOUSEWORK AND YOU TO DO JOBS.
NOW WATANUKI UNDERSTANDS.
SO IT'S OKAY.
YES.

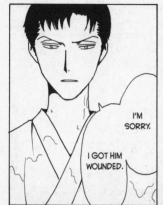

I'M SORRY.

I GOT HIM WOUNDED.

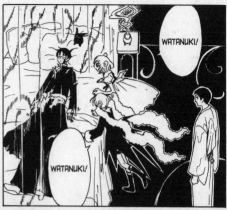

WATANUKI!

WATANUKI!

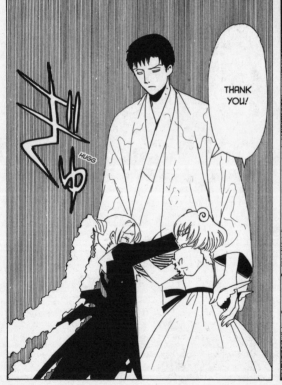

THANK YOU!

HUGG

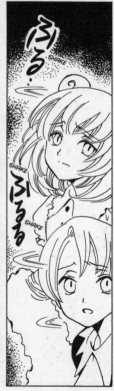

SHAKE

SHAKE

SHAKE

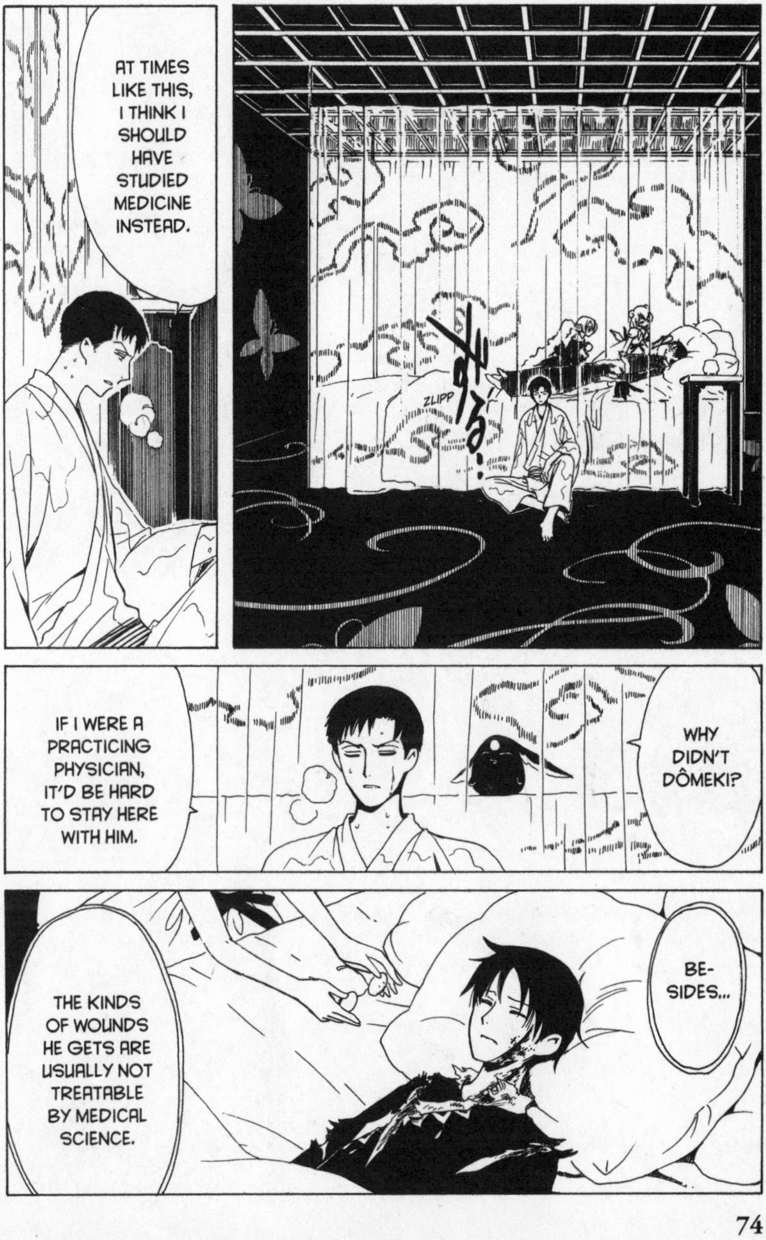
ZLIPP
AT TIMES LIKE THIS, I THINK I SHOULD HAVE STUDIED MEDICINE INSTEAD.
WHY DIDN'T DÔMEKI?
IF I WERE A PRACTICING PHYSICIAN, IT'D BE HARD TO STAY HERE WITH HIM.
BE-SIDES...
THE KINDS OF WOUNDS HE GETS ARE USUALLY NOT TREATABLE BY MEDICAL SCIENCE.

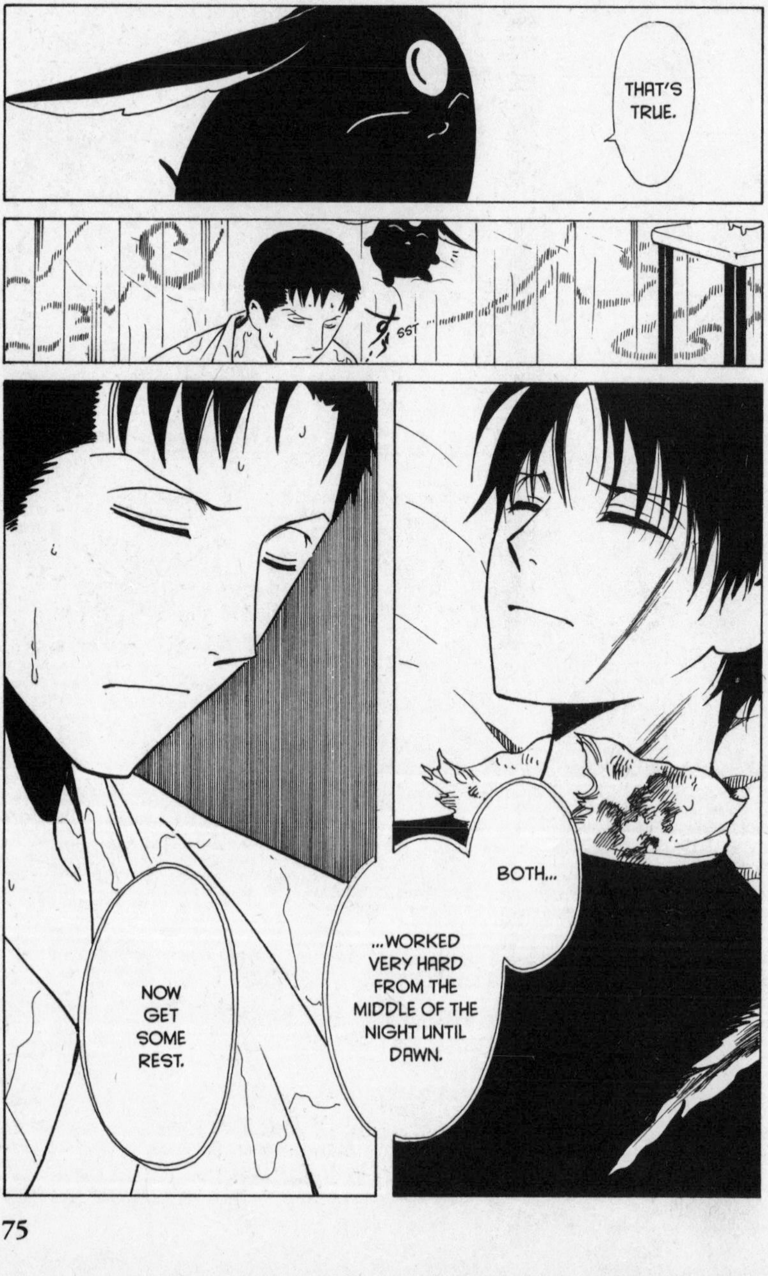
THAT'S TRUE.
SST
BOTH...
...WORKED VERY HARD FROM THE MIDDLE OF THE NIGHT UNTIL DAWN.
NOW GET SOME REST.

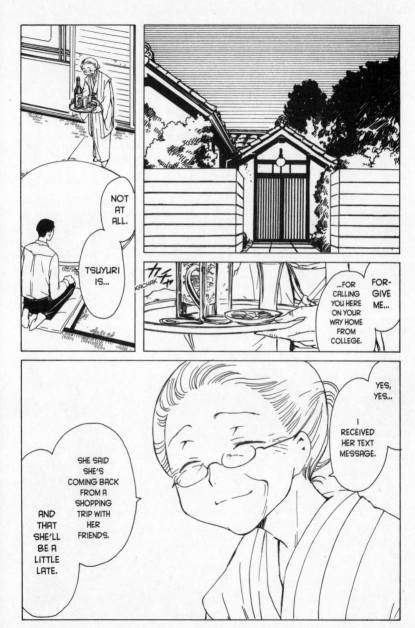

NOT AT ALL.

TSUYURI IS...

KACHAK

FOR-GIVE ME...

...FOR CALLING YOU HERE ON YOUR WAY HOME FROM COLLEGE.

YES, YES...

I RECEIVED HER TEXT MESSAGE.

SHE SAID SHE'S COMING BACK FROM A SHOPPING TRIP WITH HER FRIENDS.

AND THAT SHE'LL BE A LITTLE LATE.

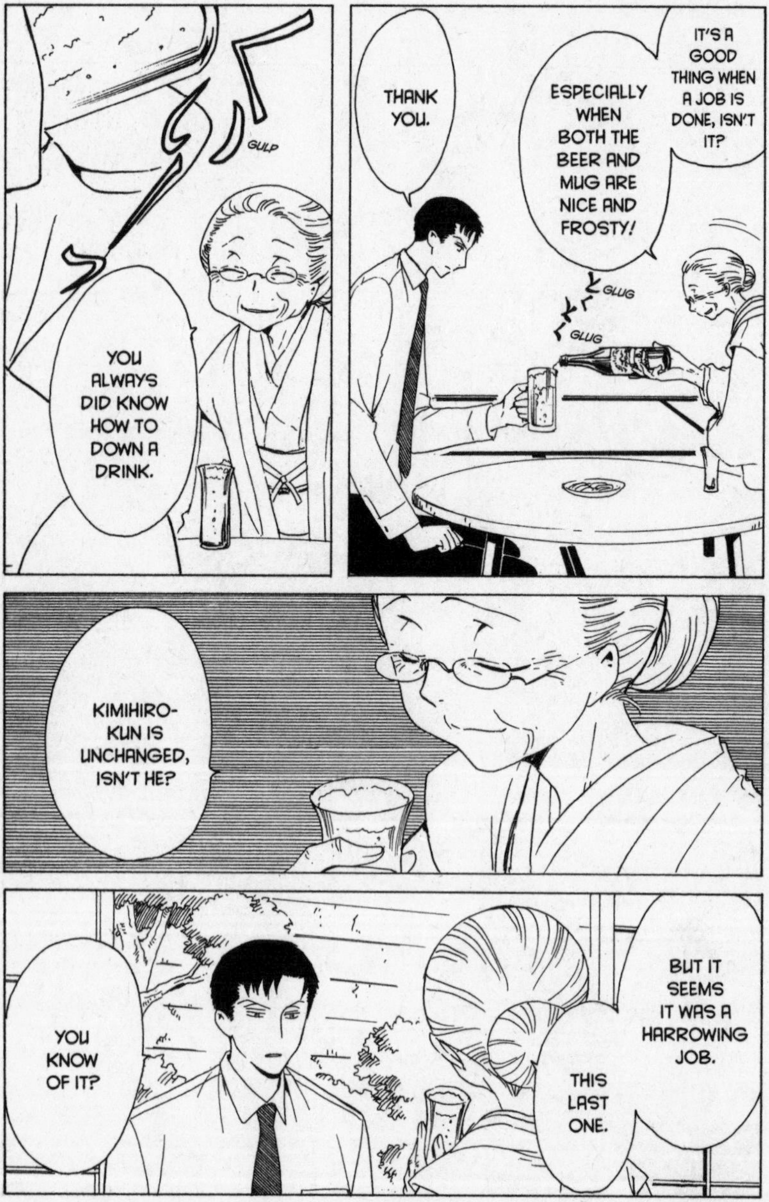
IT'S A GOOD THING WHEN A JOB IS DONE, ISN'T IT?
ESPECIALLY WHEN BOTH THE BEER AND MUG ARE NICE AND FROSTY!
GLUG
GLUG
THANK YOU.
GULP
YOU ALWAYS DID KNOW HOW TO DOWN A DRINK.
KIMIHIRO-KUN IS UNCHANGED, ISN'T HE?
BUT IT SEEMS IT WAS A HARROWING JOB.
THIS LAST ONE.
YOU KNOW OF IT?

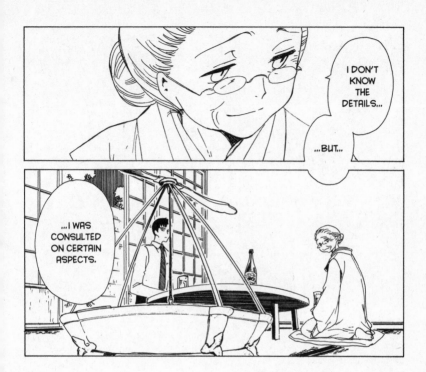

I DON'T KNOW THE DETAILS...
...BUT...
...I WAS CONSULTED ON CERTAIN ASPECTS.
SO...
THAT IS WHAT THIS WAS ABOUT...
IT WAS AN ORDEAL, WASN'T IT?
FOR BOTH YOURSELF AND KIMIHIRO-KUN.

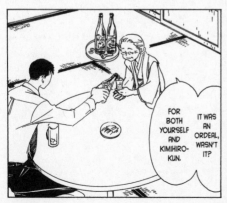

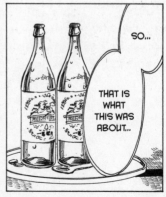

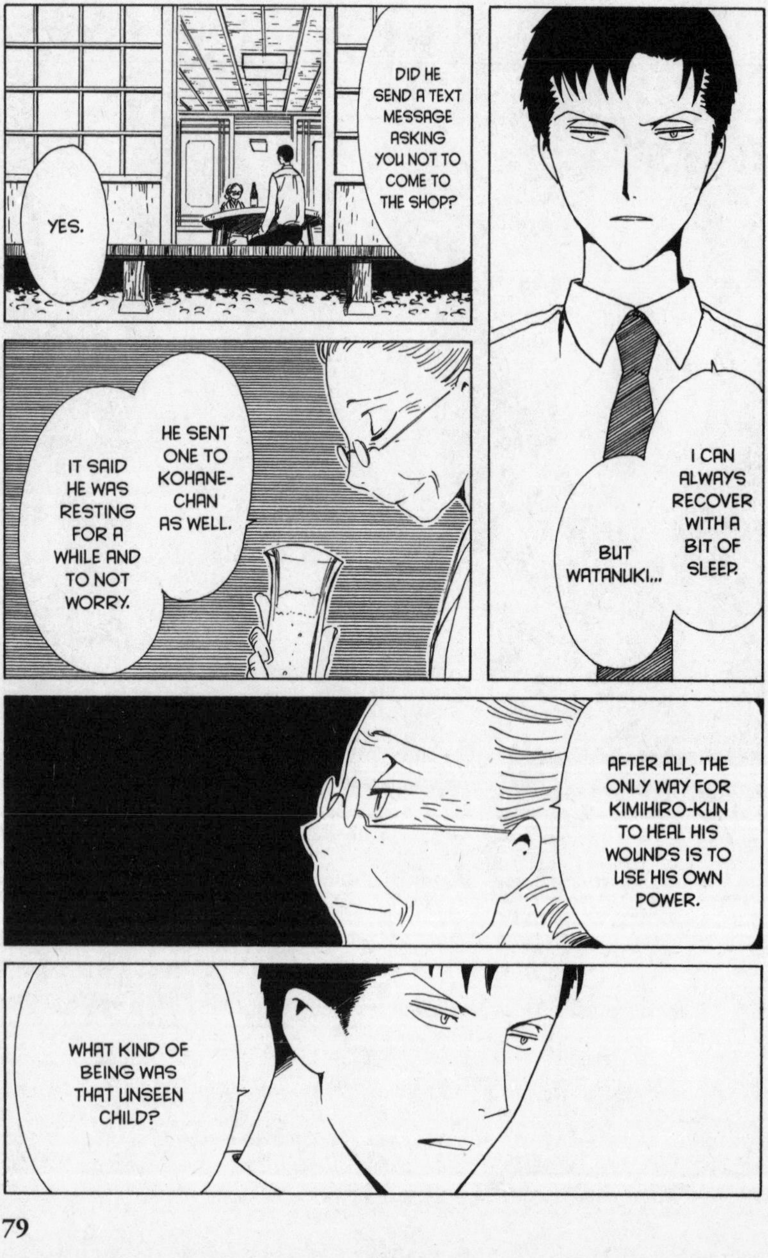
I CAN ALWAYS RECOVER WITH A BIT OF SLEEP.
BUT WATANUKI...
DID HE SEND A TEXT MESSAGE ASKING YOU NOT TO COME TO THE SHOP?
YES.
HE SENT ONE TO KOHANE-CHAN AS WELL.
IT SAID HE WAS RESTING FOR A WHILE AND TO NOT WORRY.
AFTER ALL, THE ONLY WAY FOR KIMIHIRO-KUN TO HEAL HIS WOUNDS IS TO USE HIS OWN POWER.
WHAT KIND OF BEING WAS THAT UNSEEN CHILD?

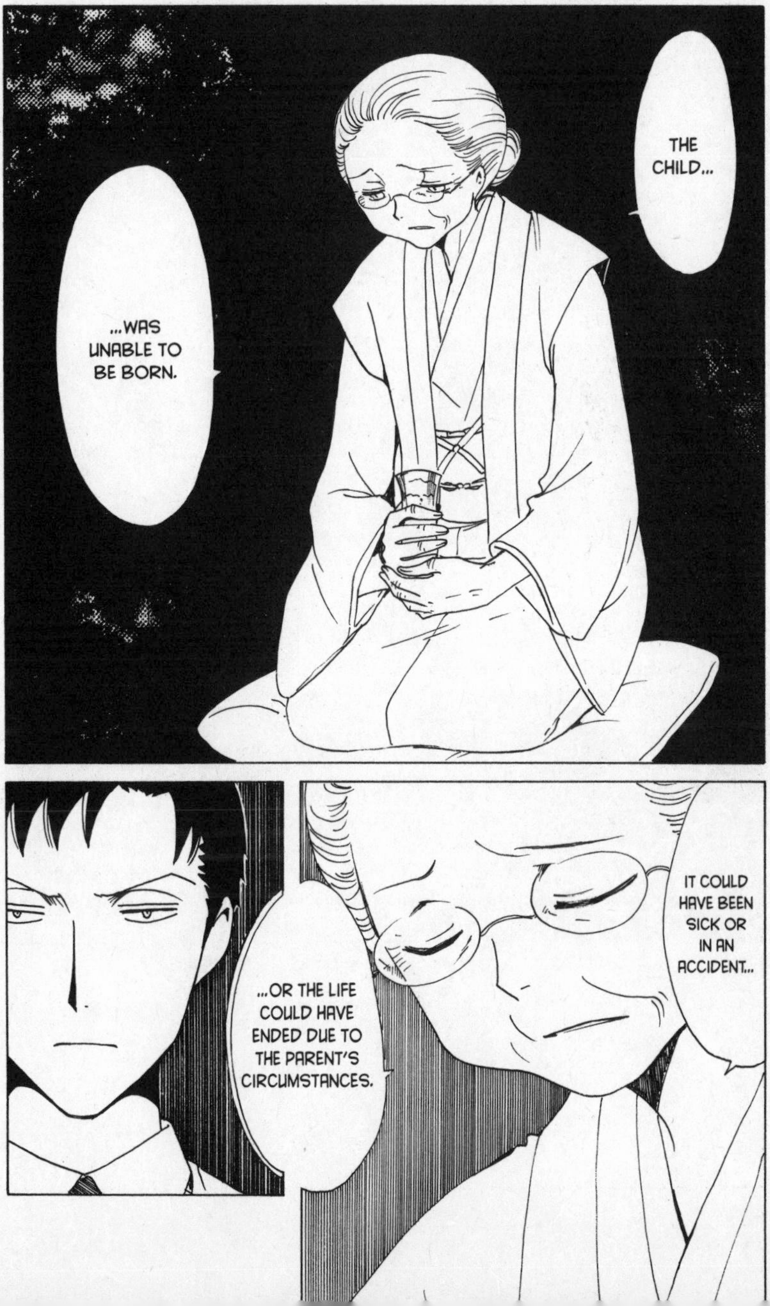
THE CHILD...
...WAS UNABLE TO BE BORN.
IT COULD HAVE BEEN SICK OR IN AN ACCIDENT...
...OR THE LIFE COULD HAVE ENDED DUE TO THE PARENT'S CIRCUMSTANCES.

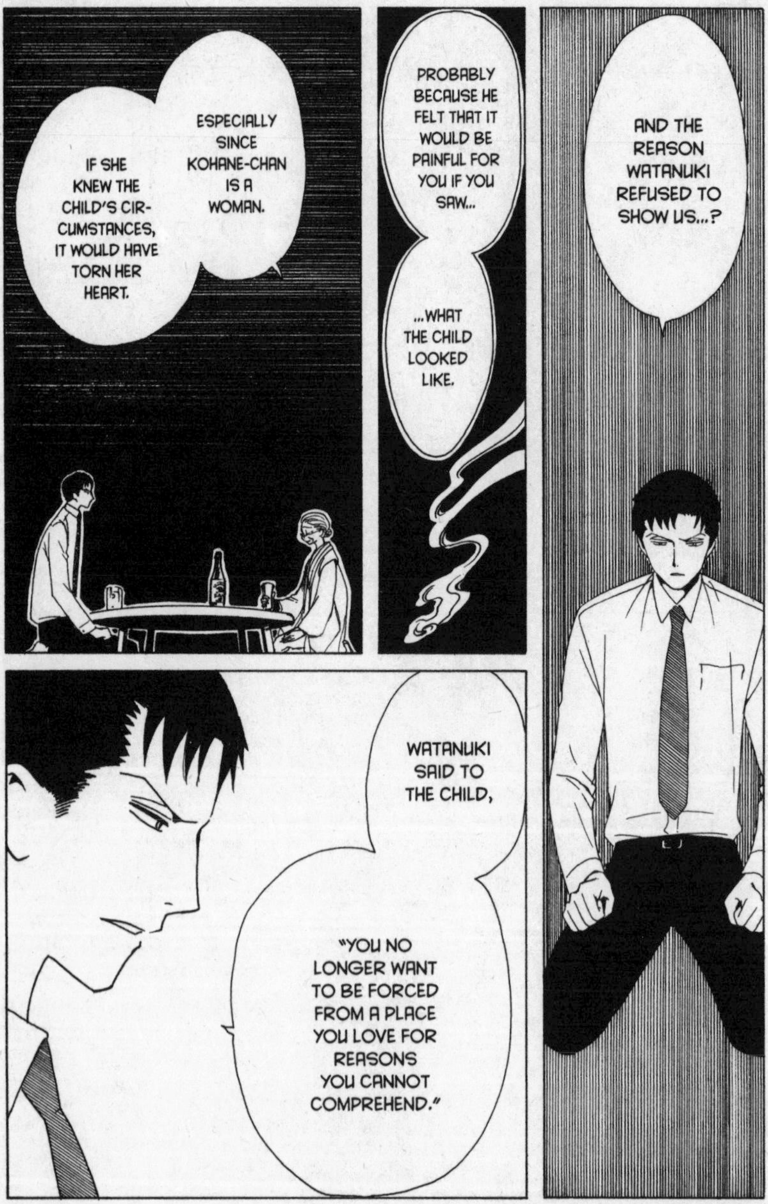
AND THE REASON WATANUKI REFUSED TO SHOW US...?
PROBABLY BECAUSE HE FELT THAT IT WOULD BE PAINFUL FOR YOU IF YOU SAW...
...WHAT THE CHILD LOOKED LIKE.
IF SHE KNEW THE CHILD'S CIR-CUMSTANCES, IT WOULD HAVE TORN HER HEART.
ESPECIALLY SINCE KOHANE-CHAN IS A WOMAN.
WATANUKI SAID TO THE CHILD,
"YOU NO LONGER WANT TO BE FORCED FROM A PLACE YOU LOVE FOR REASONS YOU CANNOT COMPREHEND."

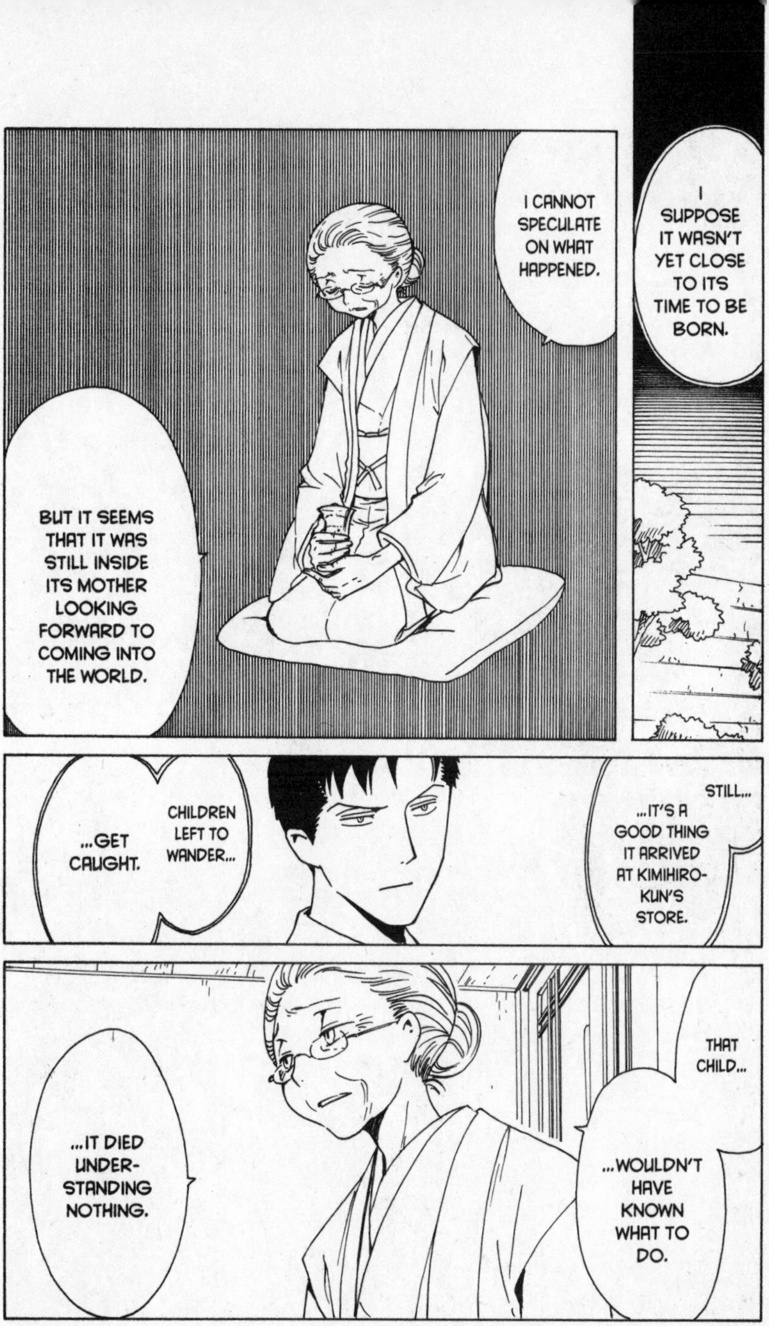
I SUPPOSE IT WASN'T YET CLOSE TO ITS TIME TO BE BORN.
I CANNOT SPECULATE ON WHAT HAPPENED.
BUT IT SEEMS THAT IT WAS STILL INSIDE ITS MOTHER LOOKING FORWARD TO COMING INTO THE WORLD.
STILL...
...IT'S A GOOD THING IT ARRIVED AT KIMIHIRO-KUN'S STORE.
CHILDREN LEFT TO WANDER...
...GET CAUGHT.
THAT CHILD...
...WOULDN'T HAVE KNOWN WHAT TO DO.
...IT DIED UNDER-STANDING NOTHING.

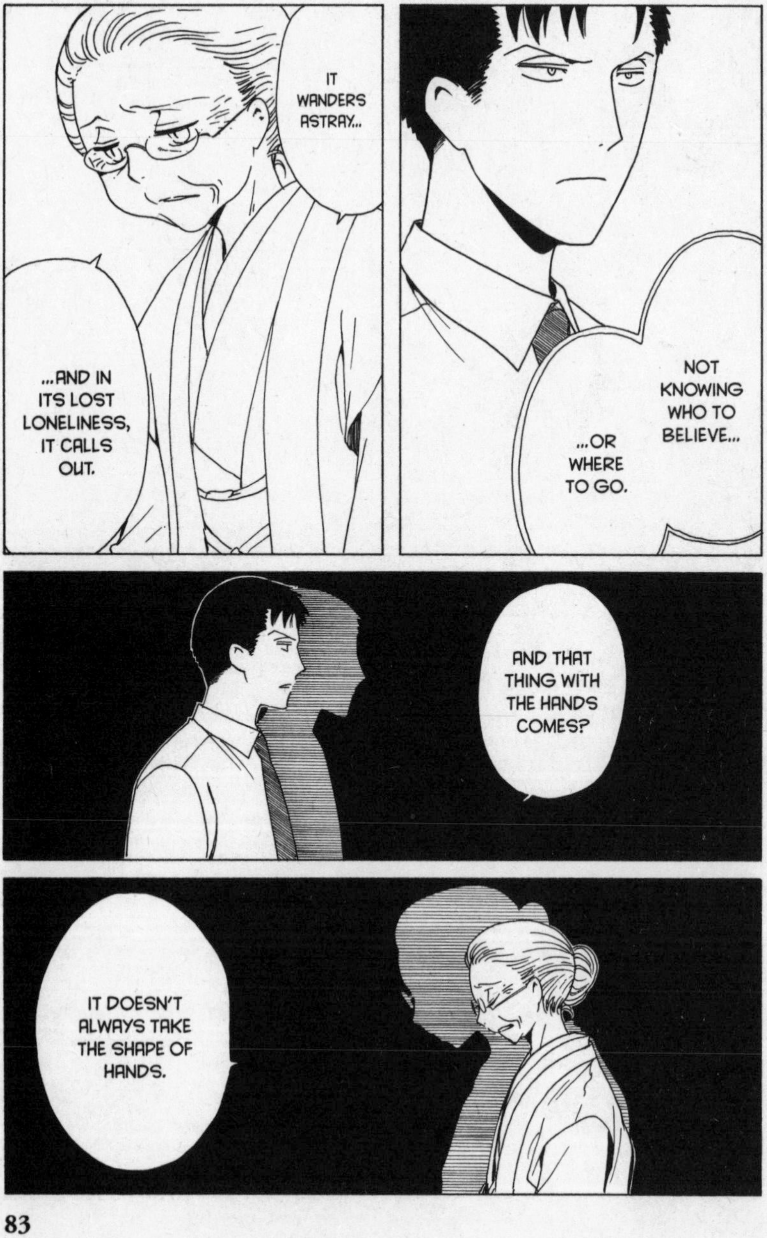
NOT KNOWING WHO TO BELIEVE...
...OR WHERE TO GO.
IT WANDERS ASTRAY...
...AND IN ITS LOST LONELINESS, IT CALLS OUT.
AND THAT THING WITH THE HANDS COMES?
IT DOESN'T ALWAYS TAKE THE SHAPE OF HANDS.

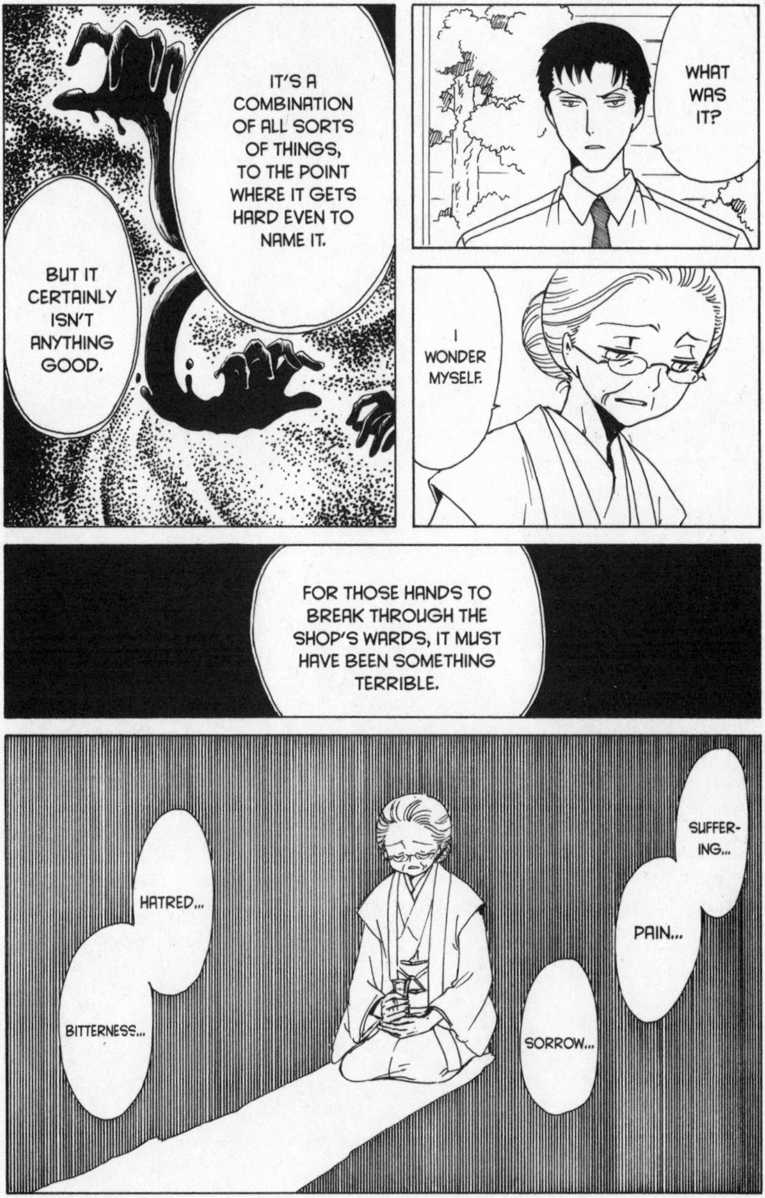
WHAT WAS IT?
I WONDER MYSELF.
IT'S A COMBINATION OF ALL SORTS OF THINGS, TO THE POINT WHERE IT GETS HARD EVEN TO NAME IT.
BUT IT CERTAINLY ISN'T ANYTHING GOOD.
FOR THOSE HANDS TO BREAK THROUGH THE SHOP'S WARDS, IT MUST HAVE BEEN SOMETHING TERRIBLE.
SUFFERING...
PAIN...
SORROW...
HATRED...
BITTERNESS...

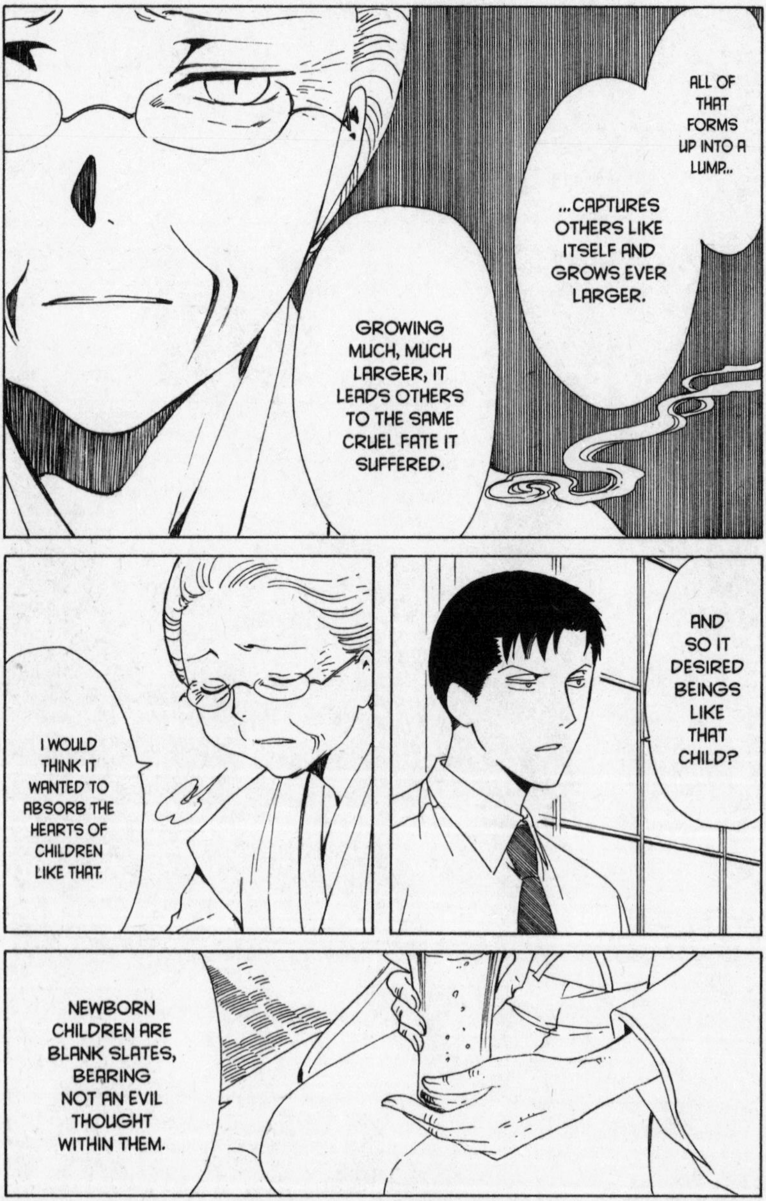
ALL OF THAT FORMS UP INTO A LUMP...
...CAPTURES OTHERS LIKE ITSELF AND GROWS EVER LARGER.
GROWING MUCH, MUCH LARGER, IT LEADS OTHERS TO THE SAME CRUEL FATE IT SUFFERED.
AND SO IT DESIRED BEINGS LIKE THAT CHILD?
I WOULD THINK IT WANTED TO ABSORB THE HEARTS OF CHILDREN LIKE THAT.
NEWBORN CHILDREN ARE BLANK SLATES, BEARING NOT AN EVIL THOUGHT WITHIN THEM.

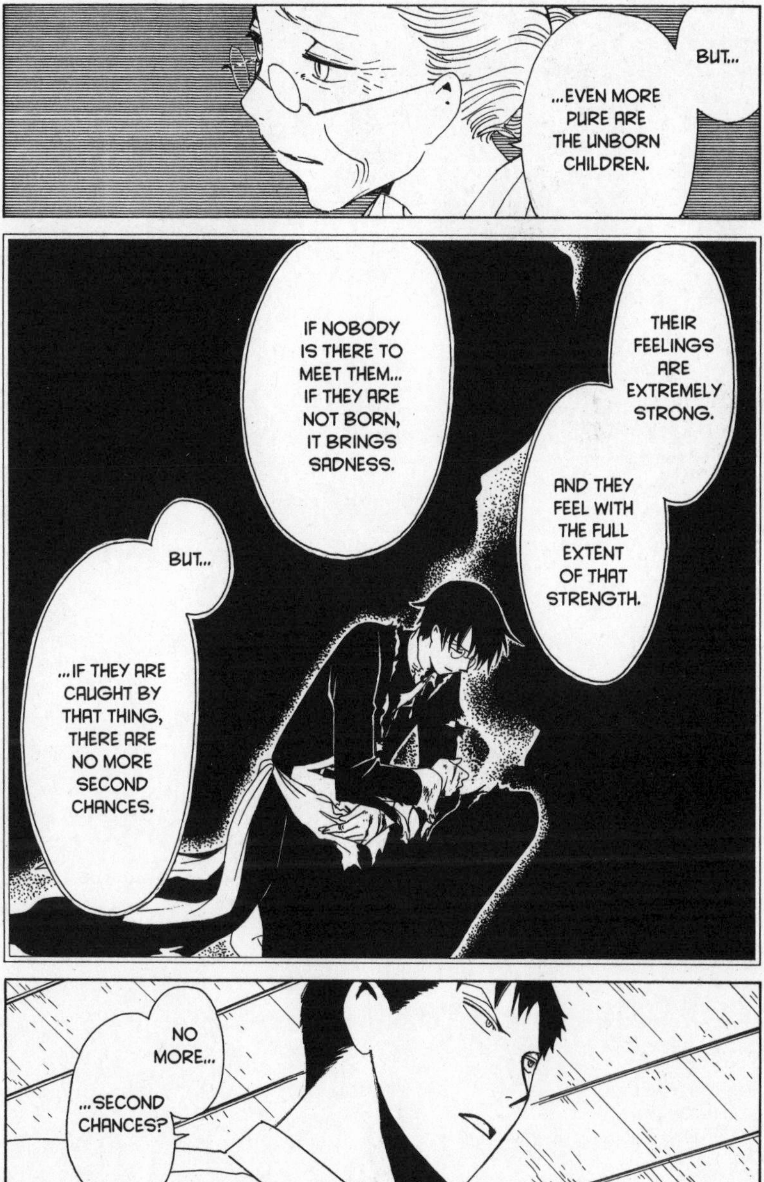
BUT...
...EVEN MORE PURE ARE THE UNBORN CHILDREN.
THEIR FEELINGS ARE EXTREMELY STRONG.
AND THEY FEEL WITH THE FULL EXTENT OF THAT STRENGTH.
IF NOBODY IS THERE TO MEET THEM... IF THEY ARE NOT BORN, IT BRINGS SADNESS.
BUT...
...IF THEY ARE CAUGHT BY THAT THING, THERE ARE NO MORE SECOND CHANCES.
NO MORE...
...SECOND CHANCES?

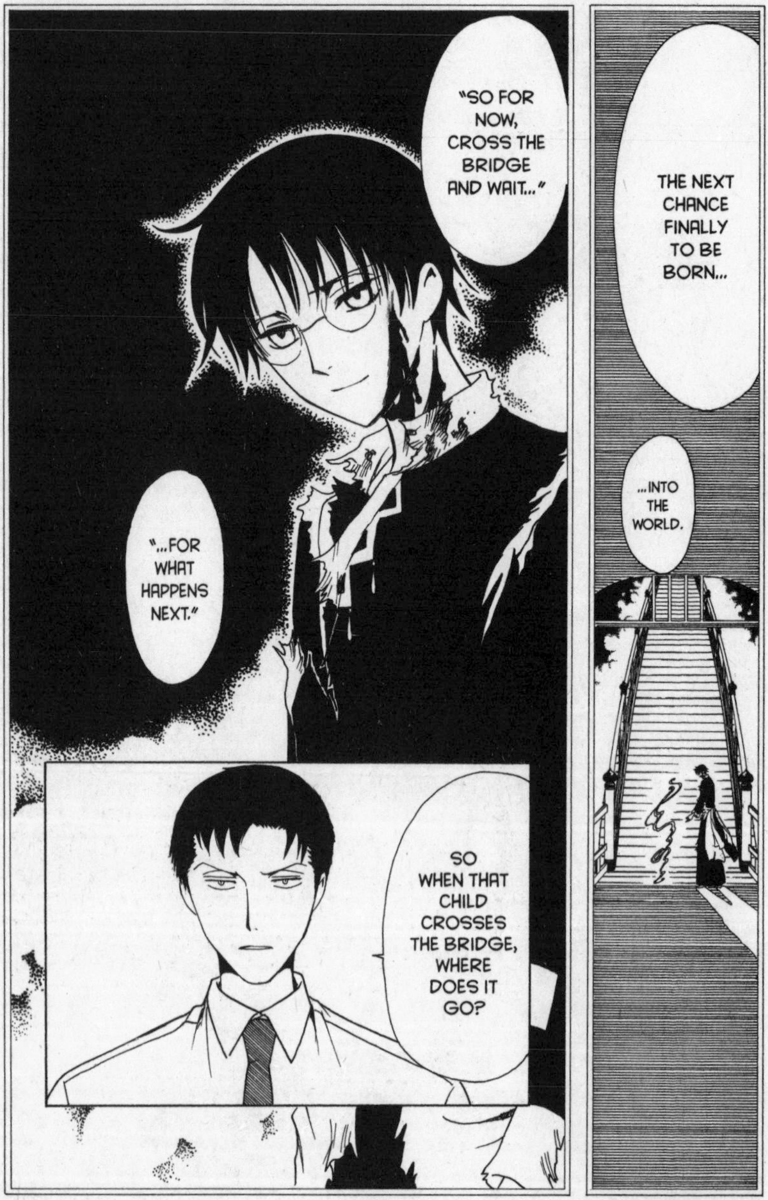
THE NEXT CHANCE FINALLY TO BE BORN...
...INTO THE WORLD.
"SO FOR NOW, CROSS THE BRIDGE AND WAIT..."
"...FOR WHAT HAPPENS NEXT."
SO WHEN THAT CHILD CROSSES THE BRIDGE, WHERE DOES IT GO?

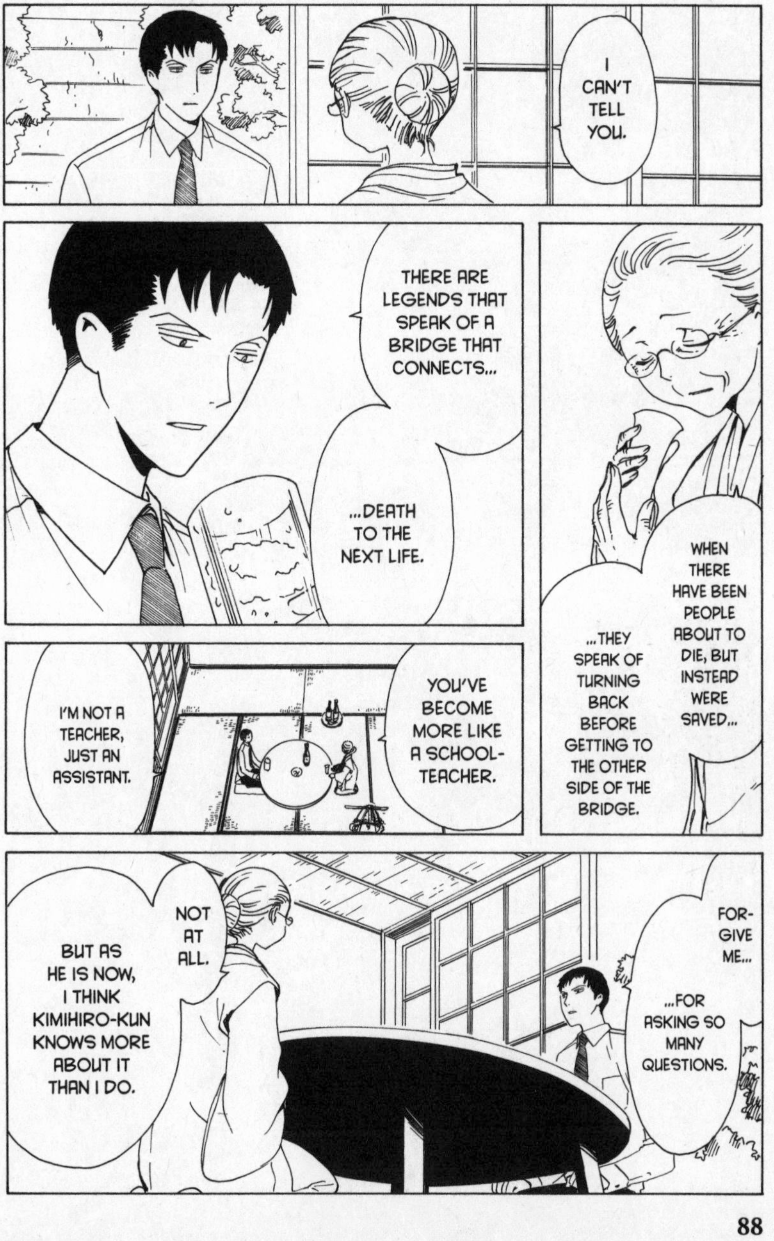

I CAN'T TELL YOU.
WHEN THERE HAVE BEEN PEOPLE ABOUT TO DIE, BUT INSTEAD WERE SAVED...
...THEY SPEAK OF TURNING BACK BEFORE GETTING TO THE OTHER SIDE OF THE BRIDGE.
THERE ARE LEGENDS THAT SPEAK OF A BRIDGE THAT CONNECTS...
...DEATH TO THE NEXT LIFE.
YOU'VE BECOME MORE LIKE A SCHOOL-TEACHER.
I'M NOT A TEACHER, JUST AN ASSISTANT.
FOR-GIVE ME...
...FOR ASKING SO MANY QUESTIONS.
NOT AT ALL.
BUT AS HE IS NOW, I THINK KIMIHIRO-KUN KNOWS MORE ABOUT IT THAN I DO.

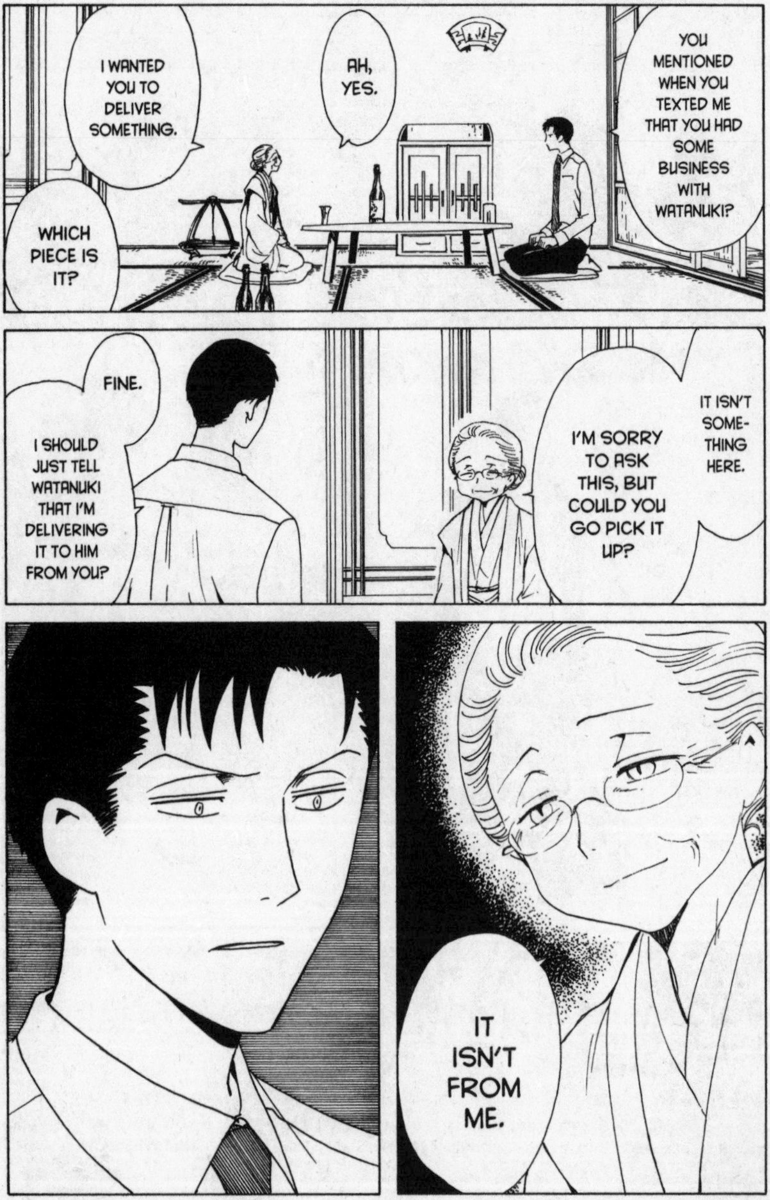
YOU MENTIONED WHEN YOU TEXTED ME THAT YOU HAD SOME BUSINESS WITH WATANUKI?
AH, YES.
I WANTED YOU TO DELIVER SOMETHING.
WHICH PIECE IS IT?
IT ISN'T SOMETHING HERE.
I'M SORRY TO ASK THIS, BUT COULD YOU GO PICK IT UP?
FINE.
I SHOULD JUST TELL WATANUKI THAT I'M DELIVERING IT TO HIM FROM YOU?
IT ISN'T FROM ME.

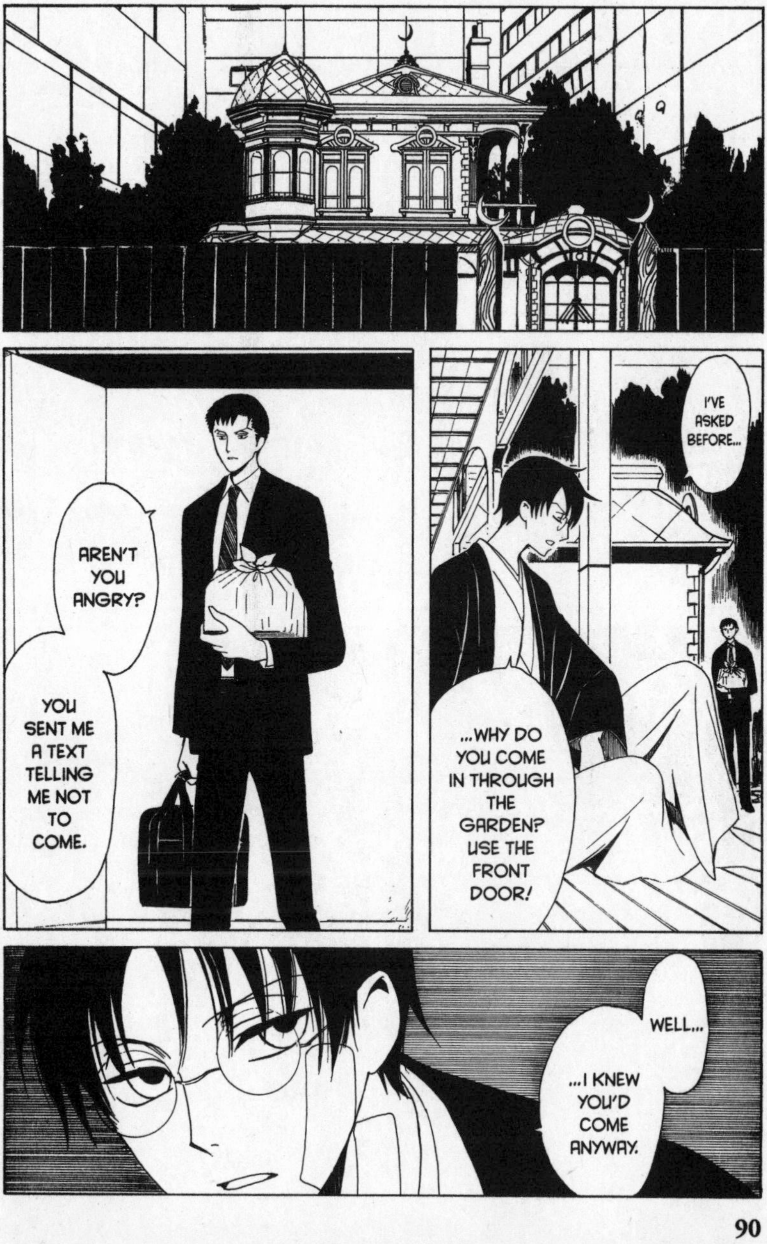
I'VE ASKED BEFORE...
...WHY DO YOU COME IN THROUGH THE GARDEN? USE THE FRONT DOOR!
AREN'T YOU ANGRY?
YOU SENT ME A TEXT TELLING ME NOT TO COME.
WELL...
...I KNEW YOU'D COME ANYWAY.

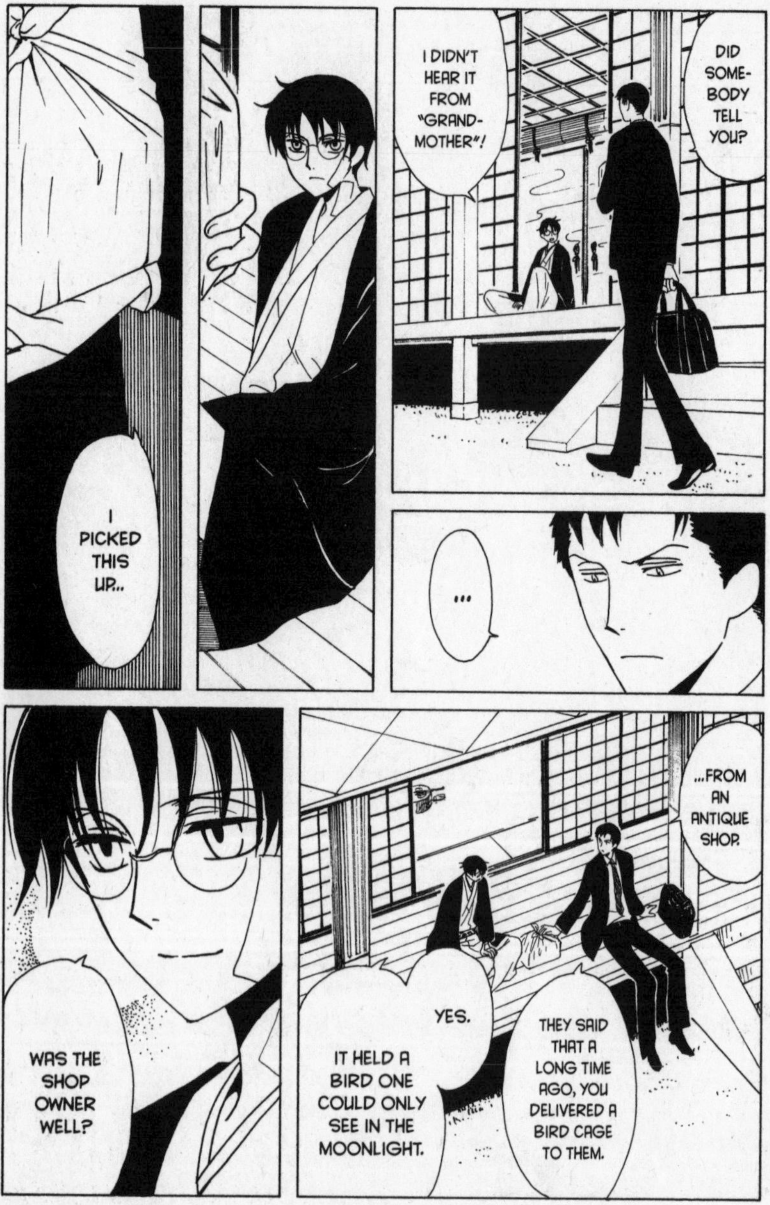
DID SOME-BODY TELL YOU?
I DIDN'T HEAR IT FROM "GRAND-MOTHER"!
...
I PICKED THIS UP...
...FROM AN ANTIQUE SHOP.
THEY SAID THAT A LONG TIME AGO, YOU DELIVERED A BIRD CAGE TO THEM.
YES.
IT HELD A BIRD ONE COULD ONLY SEE IN THE MOONLIGHT.
WAS THE SHOP OWNER WELL?

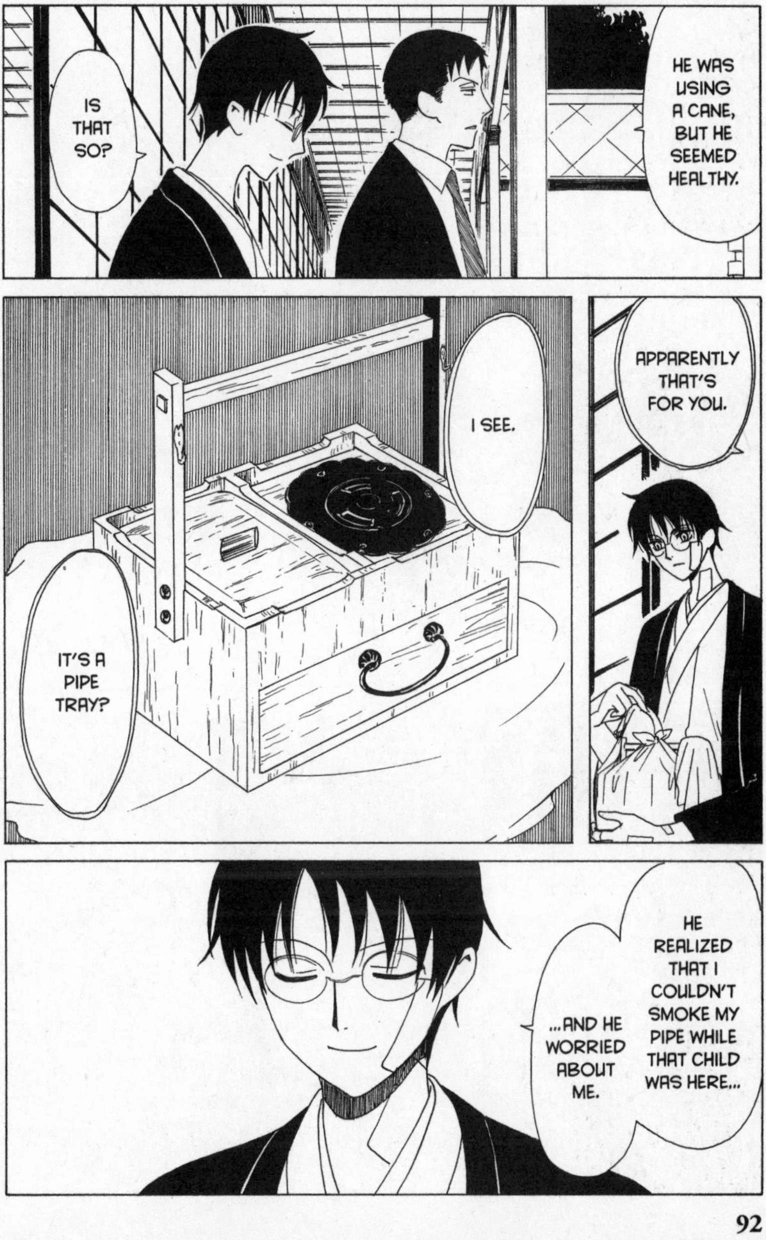
HE WAS USING A CANE, BUT HE SEEMED HEALTHY.
IS THAT SO?
APPARENTLY THAT'S FOR YOU.
I SEE.
IT'S A PIPE TRAY?
HE REALIZED THAT I COULDN'T SMOKE MY PIPE WHILE THAT CHILD WAS HERE...
...AND HE WORRIED ABOUT ME.

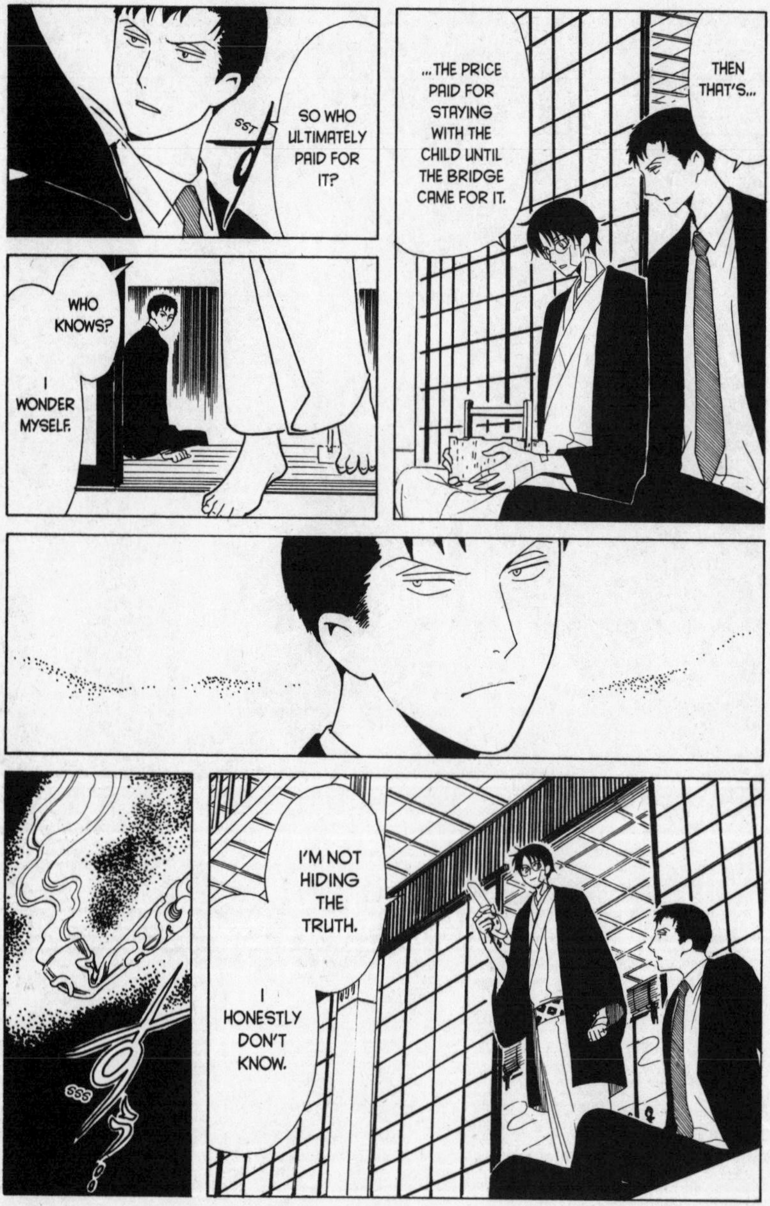
THEN THAT'S...
...THE PRICE PAID FOR STAYING WITH THE CHILD UNTIL THE BRIDGE CAME FOR IT.
SO WHO ULTIMATELY PAID FOR IT?
SST
WHO KNOWS?
I WONDER MYSELF.
I'M NOT HIDING THE TRUTH.
I HONESTLY DON'T KNOW.
SSS

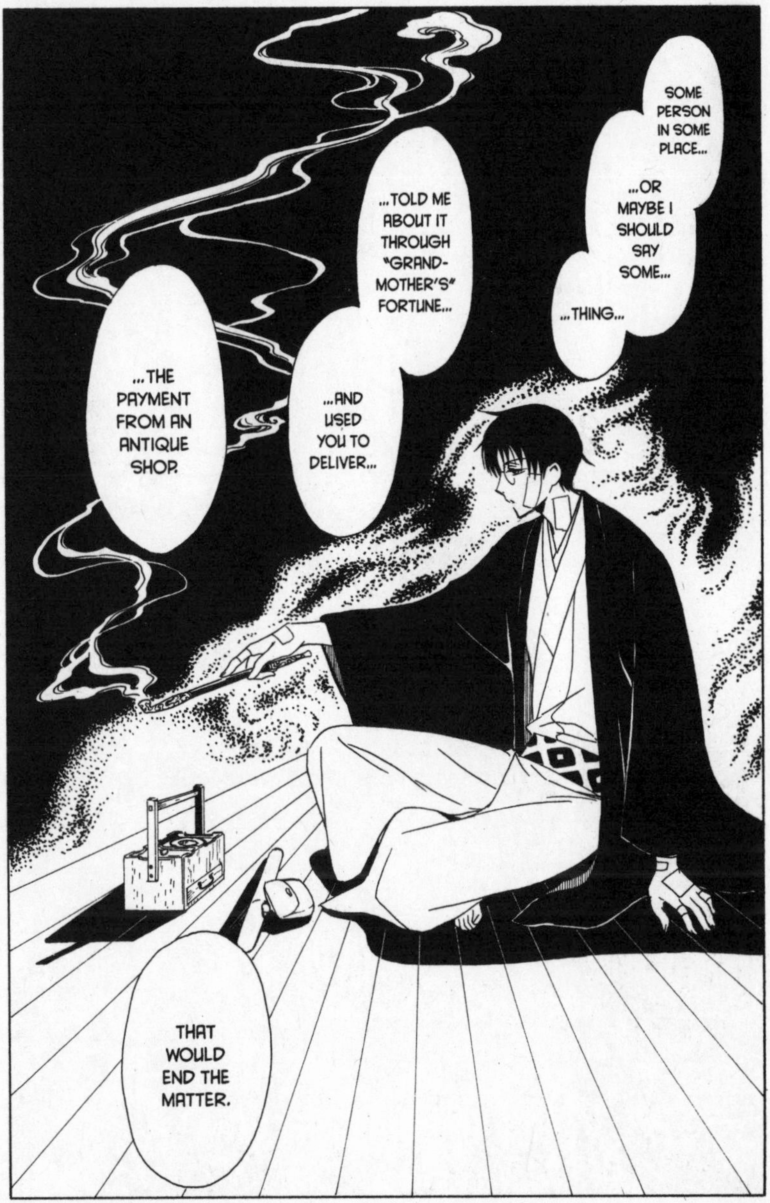
SOME PERSON IN SOME PLACE...
...OR MAYBE I SHOULD SAY SOME...
...THING...
...TOLD ME ABOUT IT THROUGH "GRAND-MOTHER'S" FORTUNE...
...AND USED YOU TO DELIVER...
...THE PAYMENT FROM AN ANTIQUE SHOP.
THAT WOULD END THE MATTER.

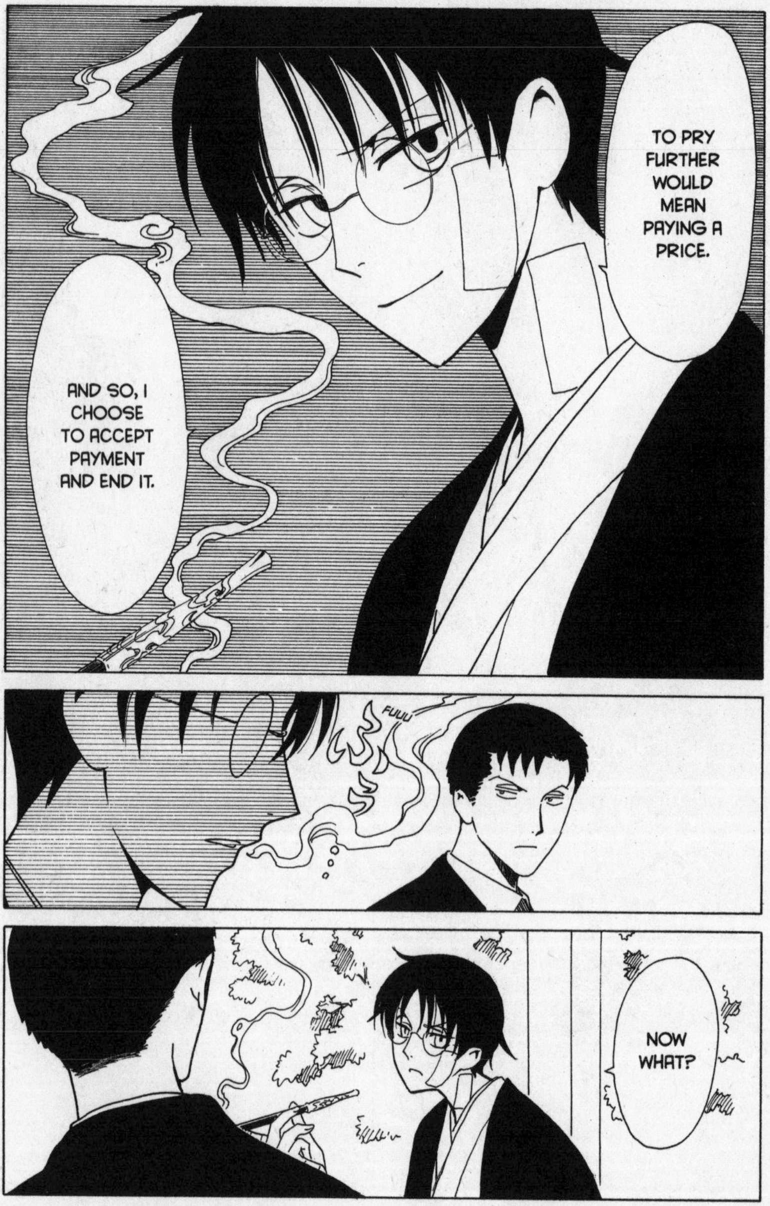
TO PRY FURTHER WOULD MEAN PAYING A PRICE.
AND SO, I CHOOSE TO ACCEPT PAYMENT AND END IT.
FUUU
NOW WHAT?

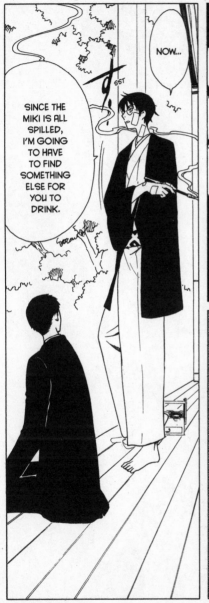

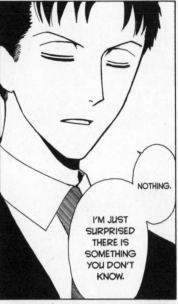

NOTHING.
I'M JUST SURPRISED THERE IS SOMETHING YOU DON'T KNOW.
THAT'S ONLY NATURAL, RIGHT?
NOW...
SST
SINCE THE MIKI IS ALL SPILLED, I'M GOING TO HAVE TO FIND SOMETHING ELSE FOR YOU TO DRINK.

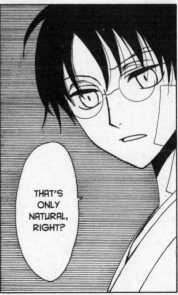

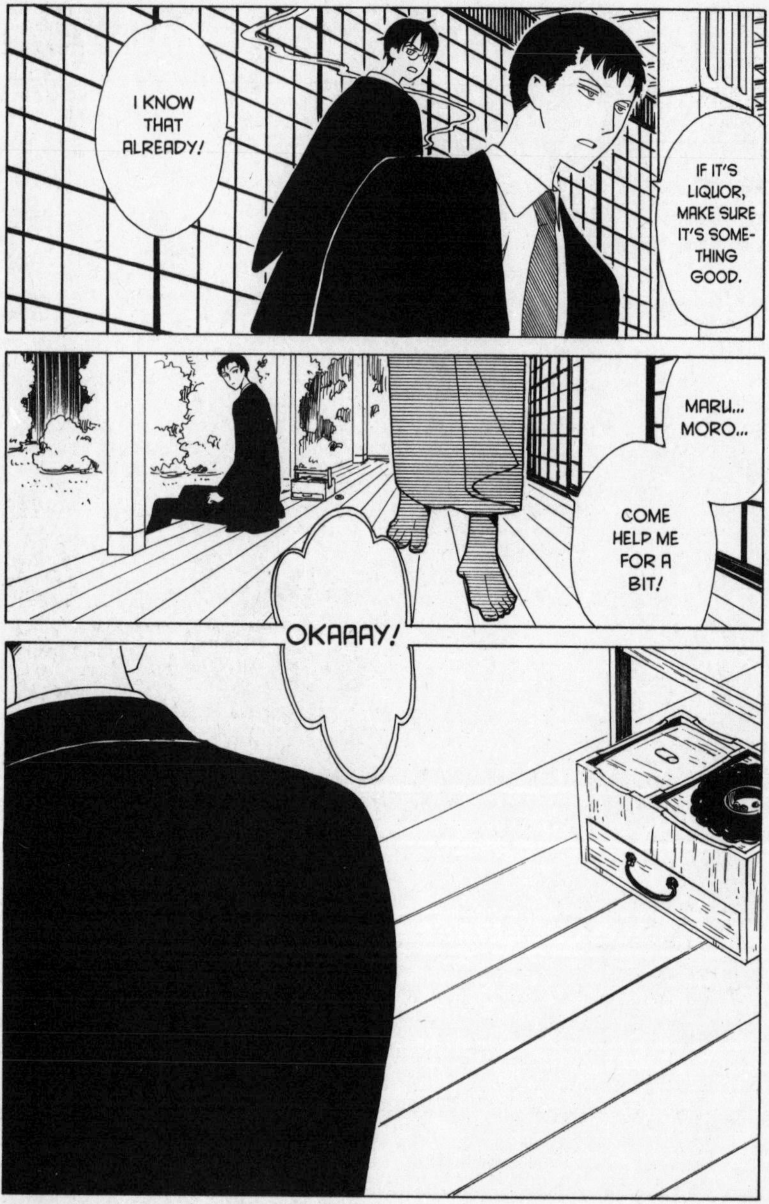

IF IT'S LIQUOR, MAKE SURE IT'S SOME-THING GOOD.
I KNOW THAT ALREADY!
MARU... MORO...
COME HELP ME FOR A BIT!
OKAAAY!

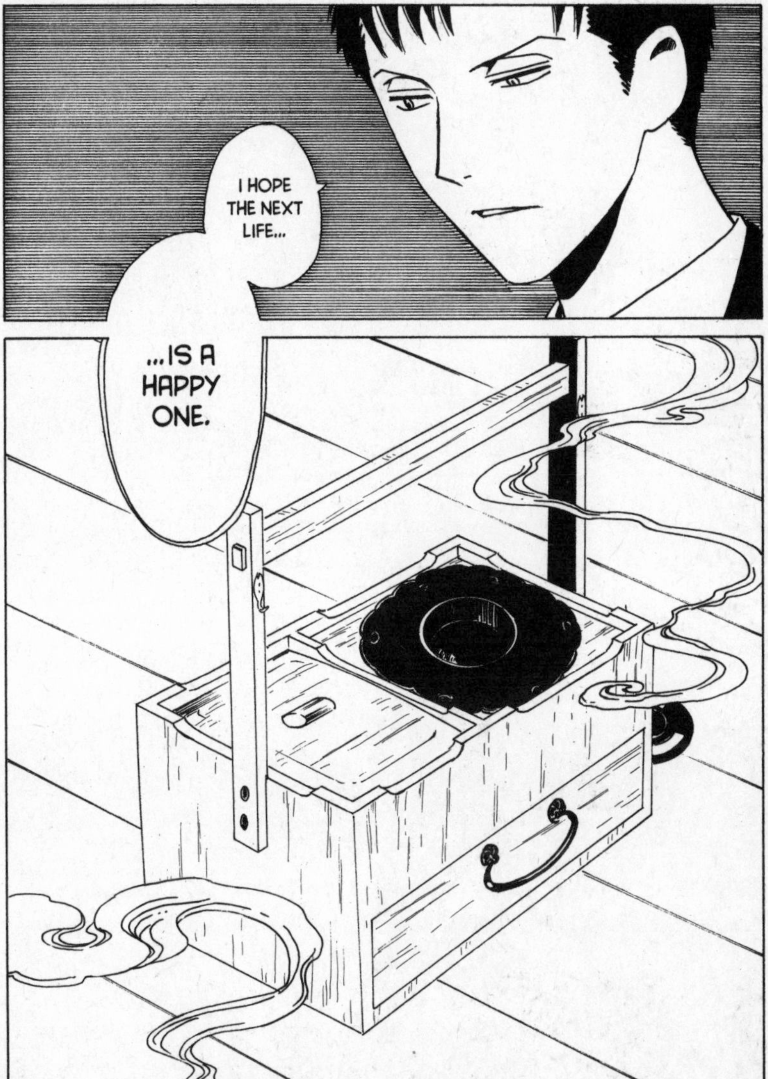
I HOPE THE NEXT LIFE...
...IS A HAPPY ONE.

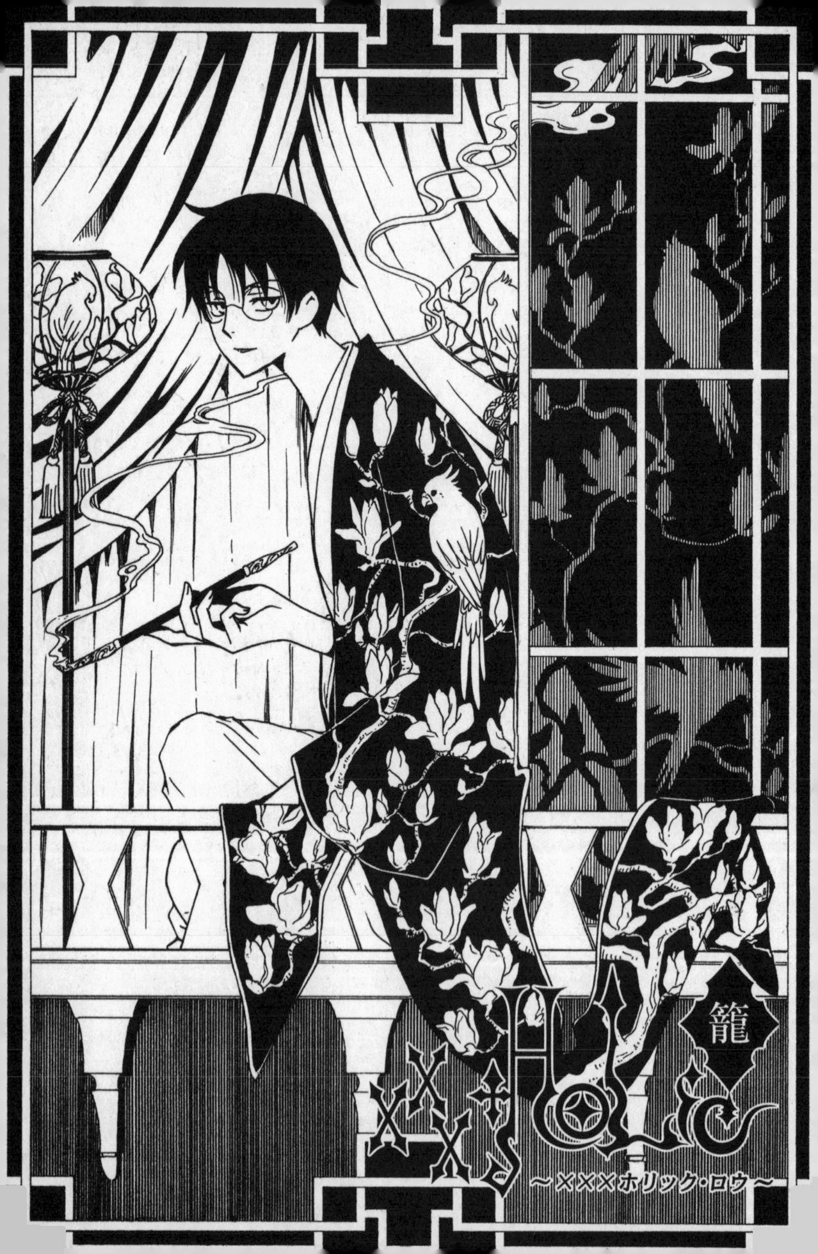
籠
xxxHOLiC
~×××ホリック・ロウ~

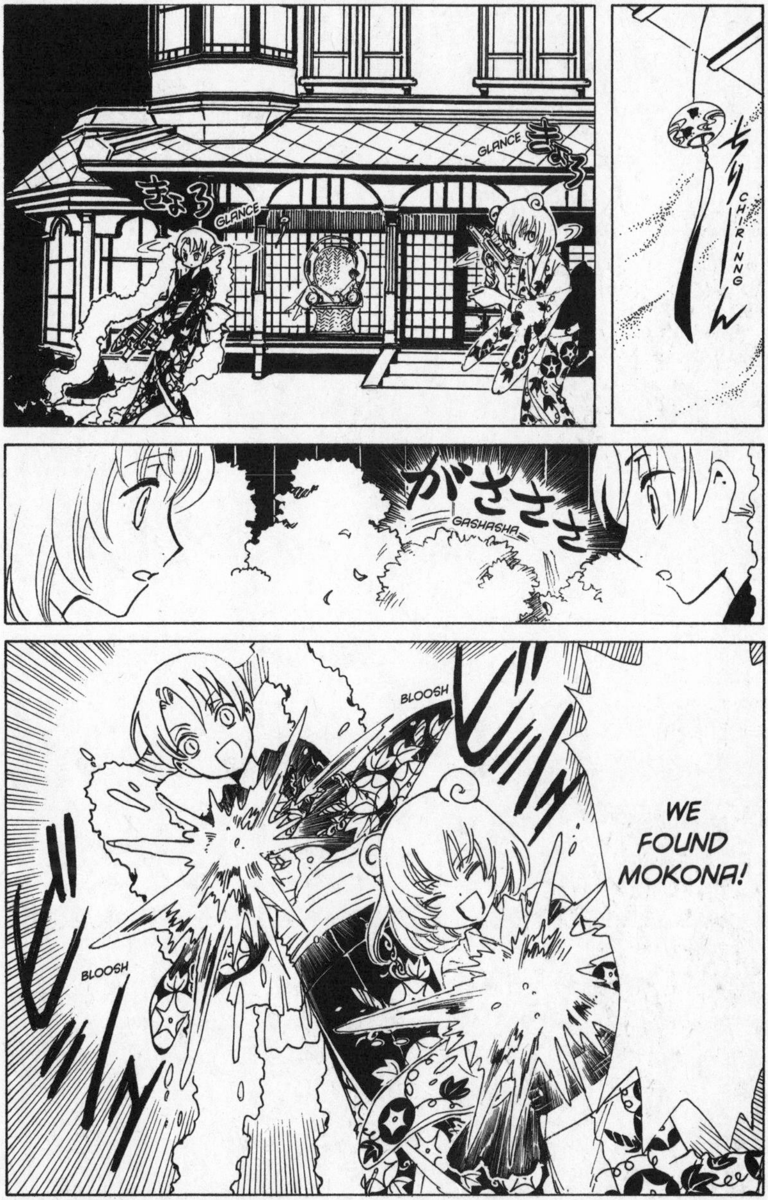
ちりん
CHIRINNG
きょろ
GLANCE
きょろ
GLANCE
がさささ
GASHASHA
WE FOUND MOKONA!
BLOOSH
BLOOSH

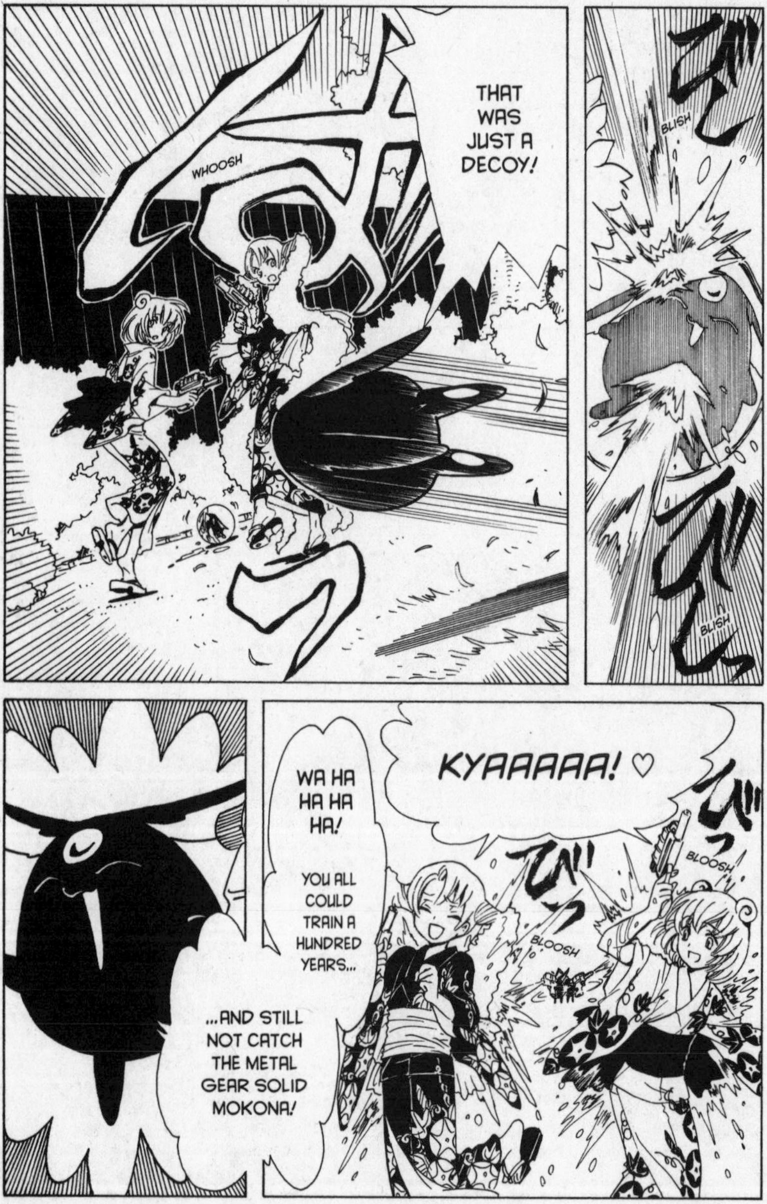
BLISH
BLISH
THAT WAS JUST A DECOY!
WHOOSH
KYAAAAA! ♡
BLOOSH
WA HA HA HA HA!
YOU ALL COULD TRAIN A HUNDRED YEARS...
BLOOSH
...AND STILL NOT CATCH THE METAL GEAR SOLID MOKONA!

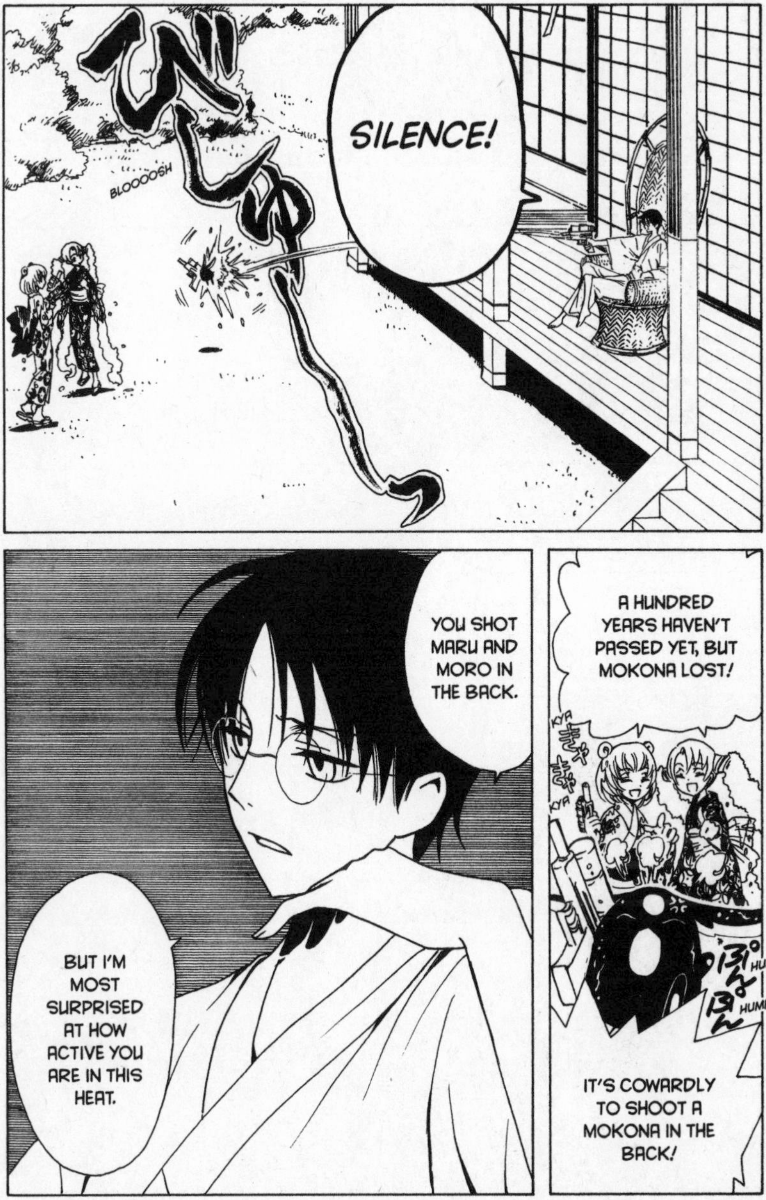
SILENCE!
BLOOOOSH
A HUNDRED YEARS HAVEN'T PASSED YET, BUT MOKONA LOST!
KYA
KYA
HUMPH
HUMPH
IT'S COWARDLY TO SHOOT A MOKONA IN THE BACK!
YOU SHOT MARU AND MORO IN THE BACK.
BUT I'M MOST SURPRISED AT HOW ACTIVE YOU ARE IN THIS HEAT.

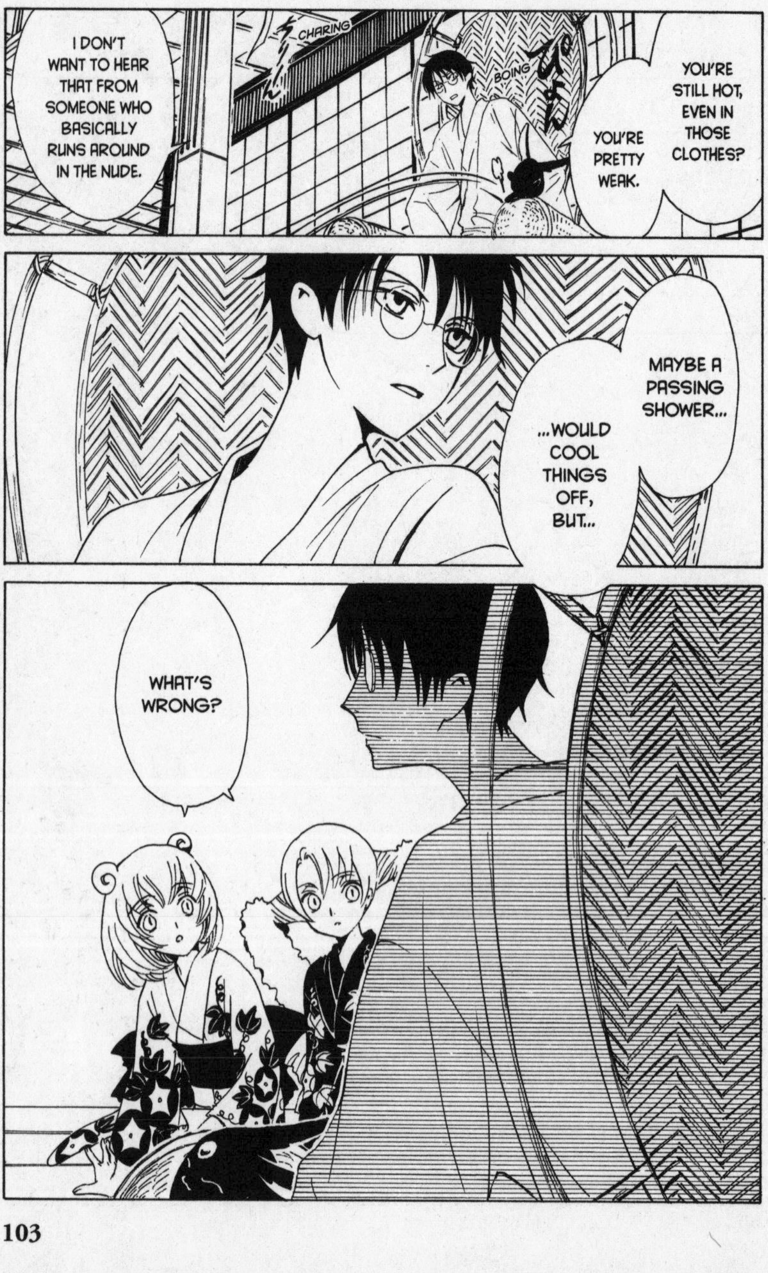
YOU'RE STILL HOT, EVEN IN THOSE CLOTHES?
YOU'RE PRETTY WEAK.
BOING
CHARING
I DON'T WANT TO HEAR THAT FROM SOMEONE WHO BASICALLY RUNS AROUND IN THE NUDE.
MAYBE A PASSING SHOWER...
...WOULD COOL THINGS OFF, BUT...
WHAT'S WRONG?

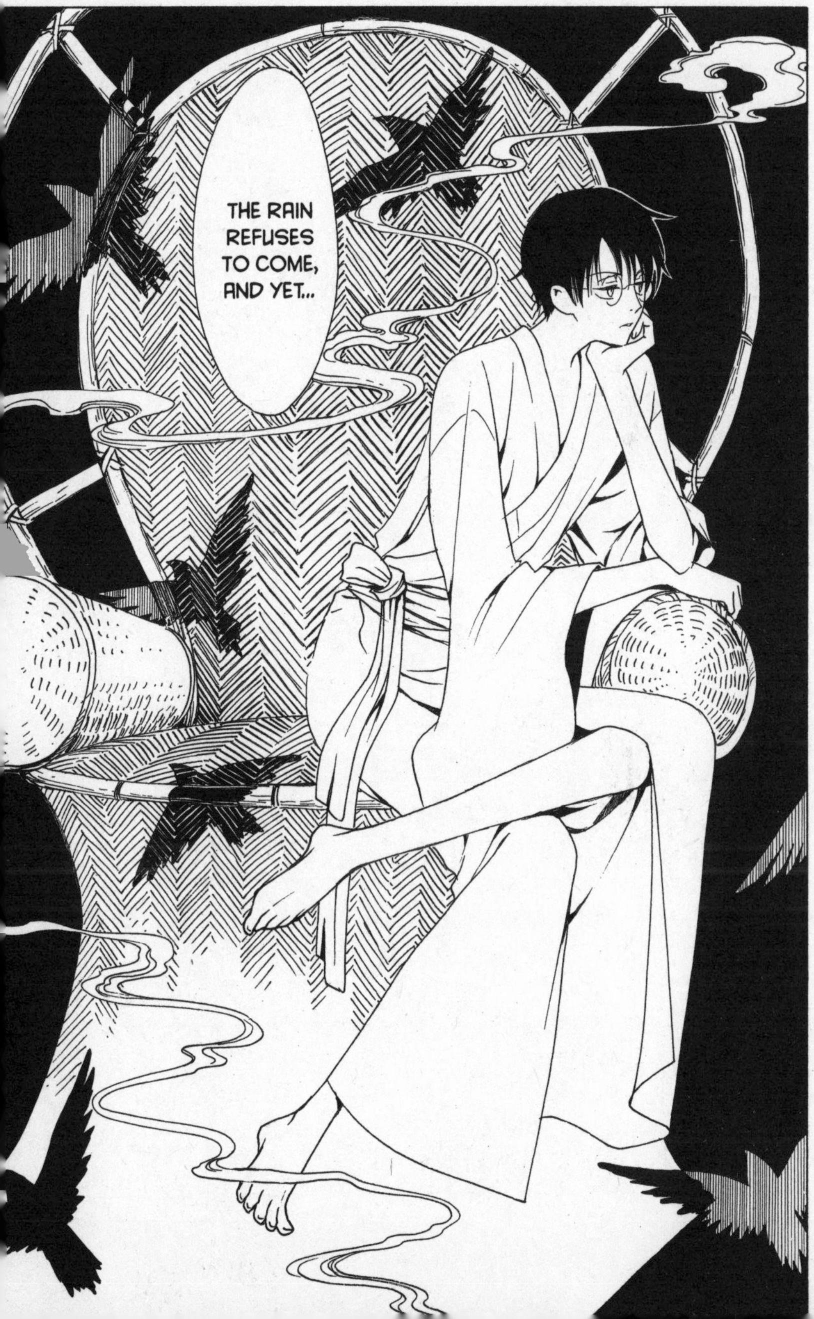
THE RAIN REFUSES TO COME, AND YET...

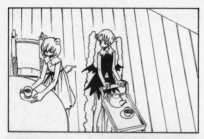

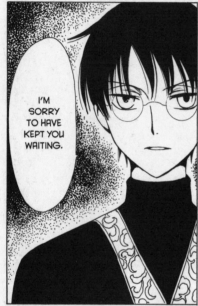

I'M SORRY TO HAVE KEPT YOU WAITING.

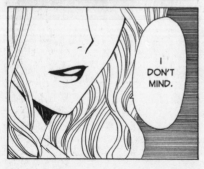

I DON'T MIND.

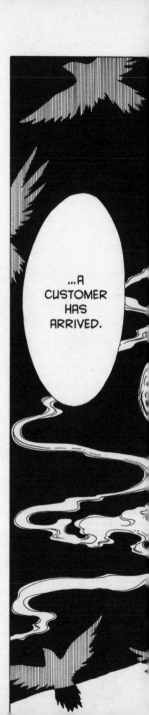

...A CUSTOMER HAS ARRIVED.

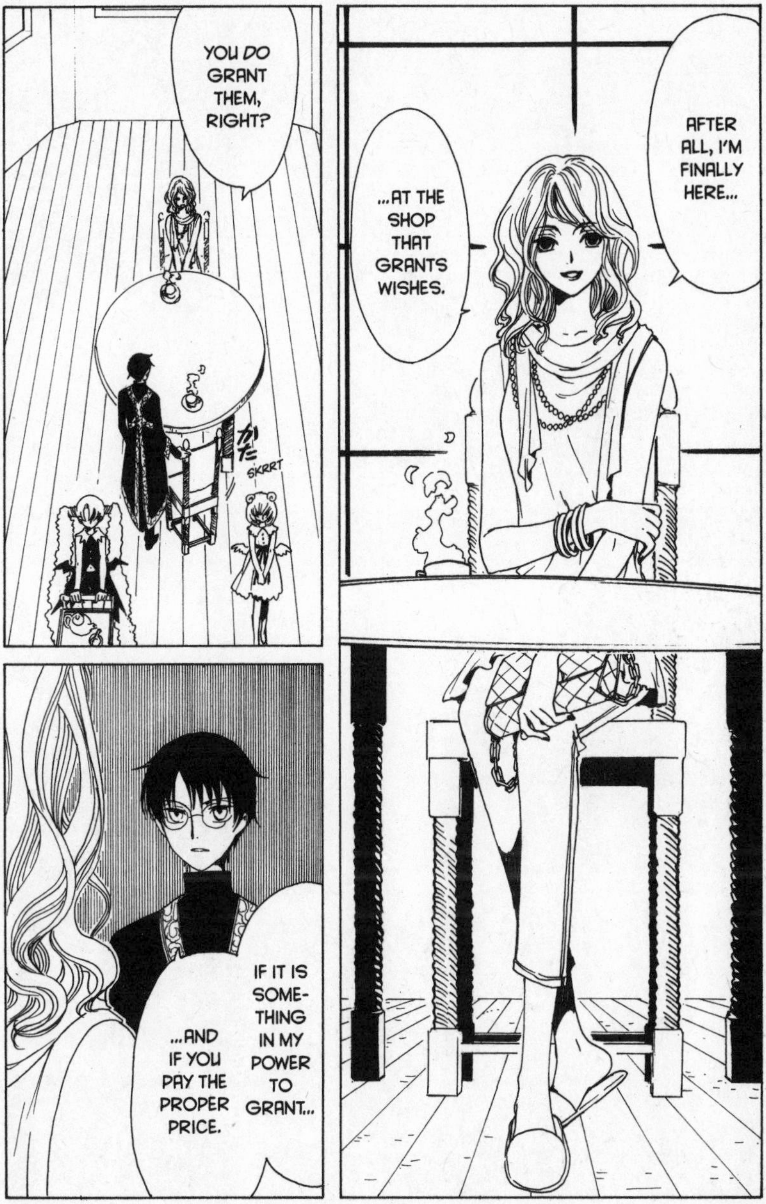
AFTER ALL, I'M FINALLY HERE...
...AT THE SHOP THAT GRANTS WISHES.
YOU DO GRANT THEM, RIGHT?
SKRRT
IF IT IS SOME-THING IN MY POWER TO GRANT...
...AND IF YOU PAY THE PROPER PRICE.

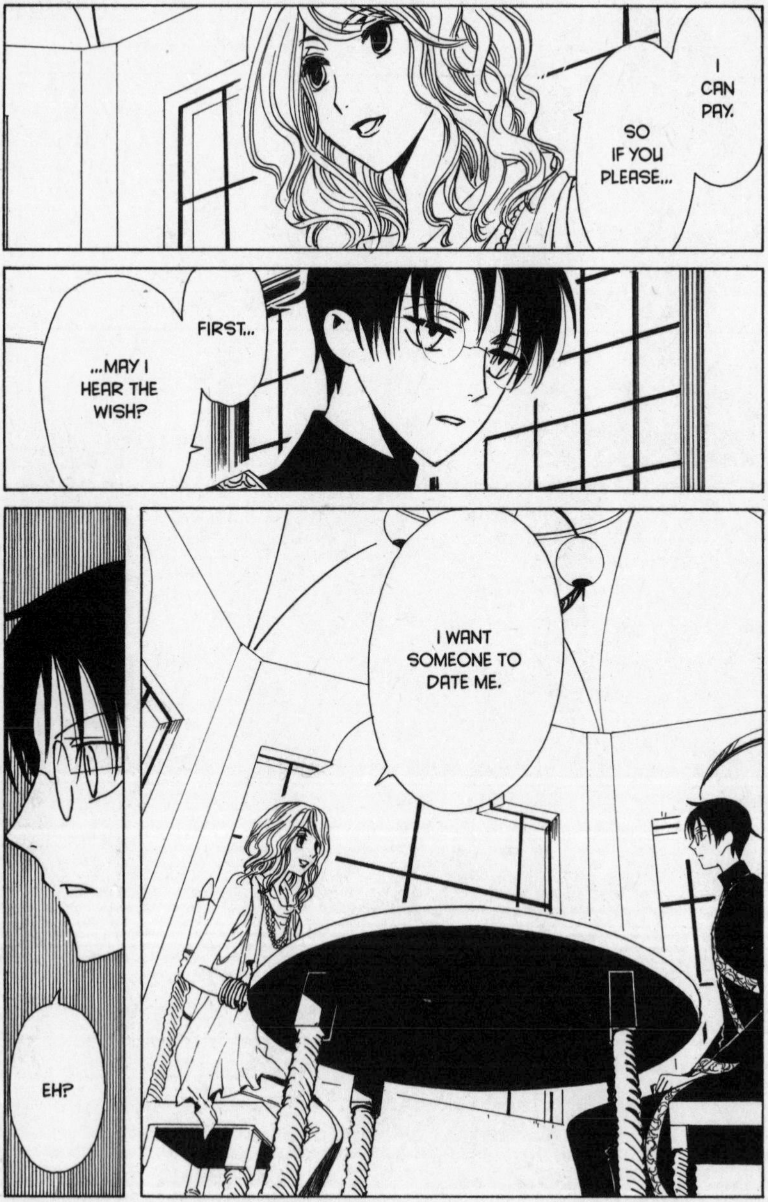
I CAN PAY.
SO IF YOU PLEASE...
FIRST...
...MAY I HEAR THE WISH?
I WANT SOMEONE TO DATE ME.
EH?

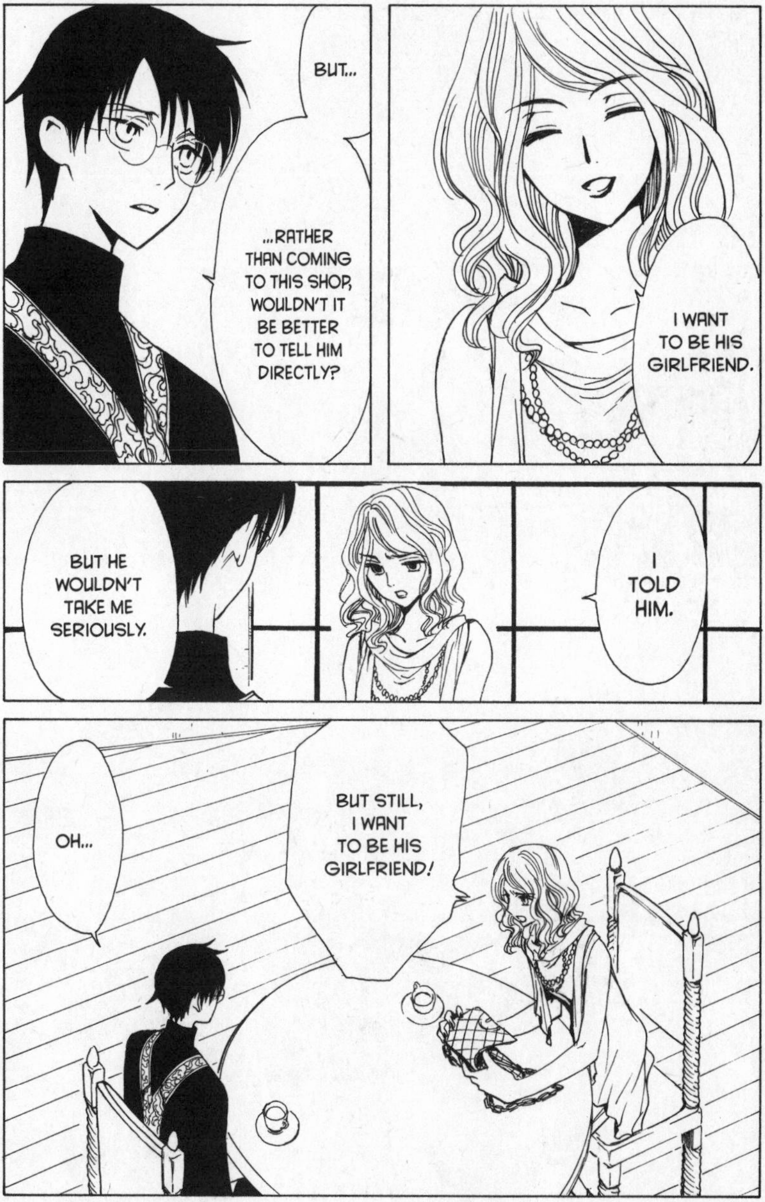
I WANT TO BE HIS GIRLFRIEND.
BUT...
...RATHER THAN COMING TO THIS SHOP, WOULDN'T IT BE BETTER TO TELL HIM DIRECTLY?
I TOLD HIM.
BUT HE WOULDN'T TAKE ME SERIOUSLY.
BUT STILL, I WANT TO BE HIS GIRLFRIEND!
OH...

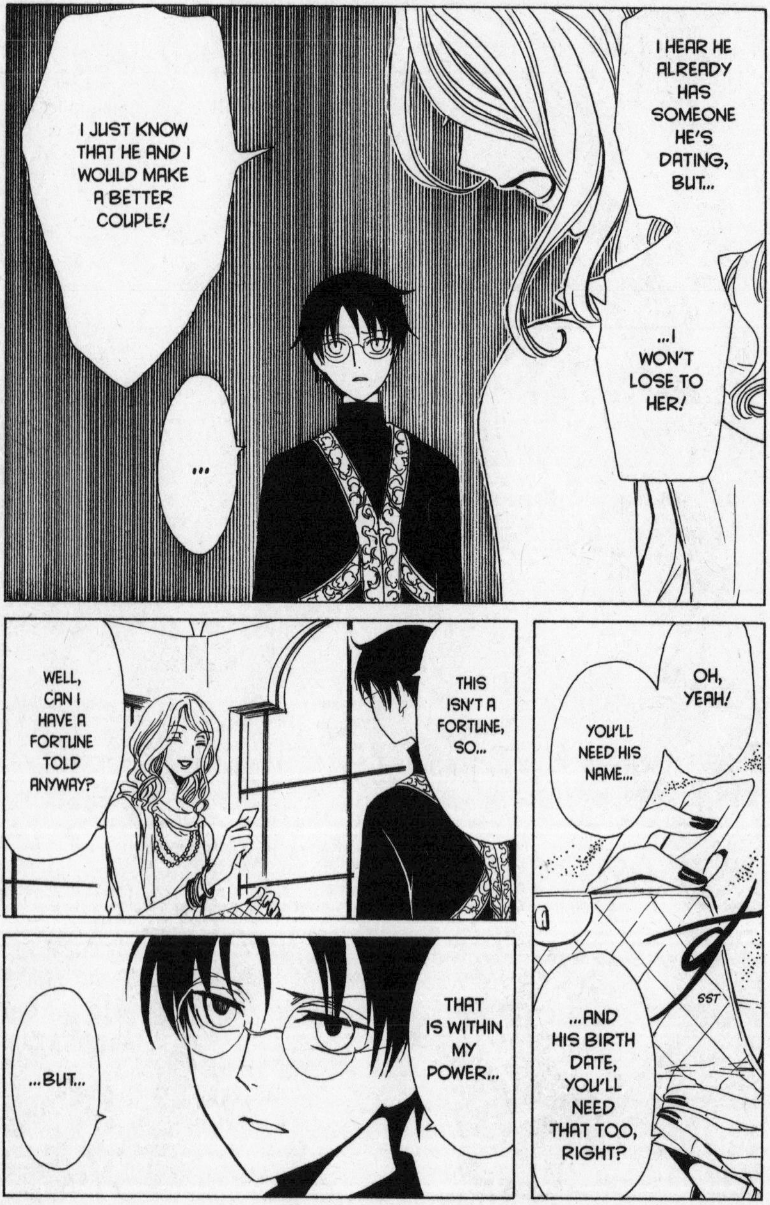
I HEAR HE ALREADY HAS SOMEONE HE'S DATING, BUT...
...I WON'T LOSE TO HER!
I JUST KNOW THAT HE AND I WOULD MAKE A BETTER COUPLE!
...
OH, YEAH!
YOU'LL NEED HIS NAME...
SST
...AND HIS BIRTH DATE, YOU'LL NEED THAT TOO, RIGHT?
THIS ISN'T A FORTUNE, SO...
WELL, CAN I HAVE A FORTUNE TOLD ANYWAY?
THAT IS WITHIN MY POWER...
...BUT...

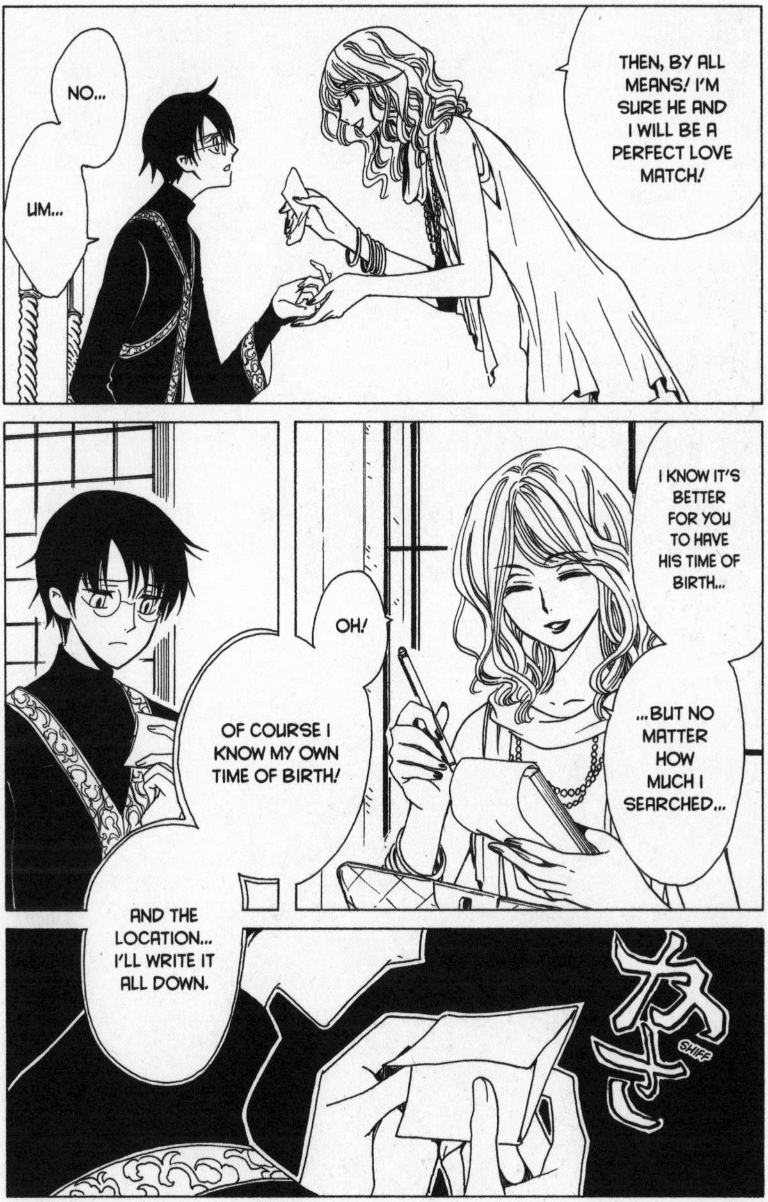
THEN, BY ALL MEANS! I'M SURE HE AND I WILL BE A PERFECT LOVE MATCH!
NO...
UM...
I KNOW IT'S BETTER FOR YOU TO HAVE HIS TIME OF BIRTH...
...BUT NO MATTER HOW MUCH I SEARCHED...
OH!
OF COURSE I KNOW MY OWN TIME OF BIRTH!
カサ
SHIFF
AND THE LOCATION... I'LL WRITE IT ALL DOWN.

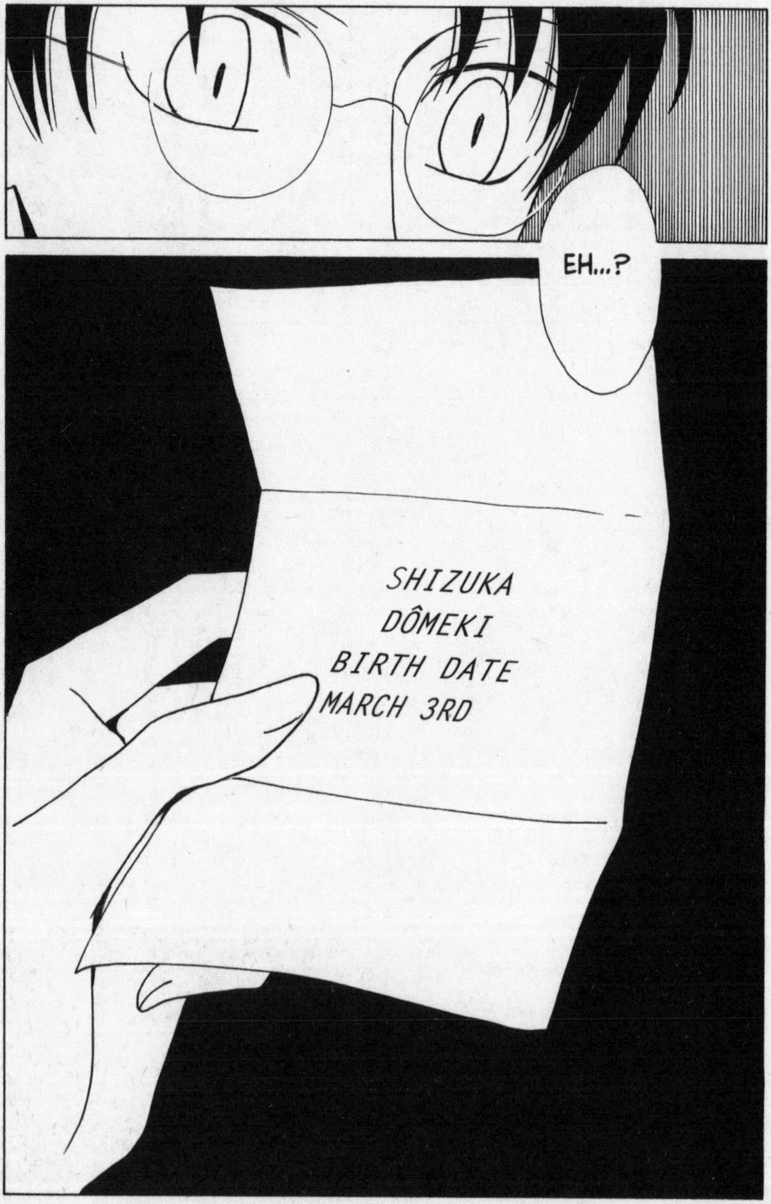
EH...?
SHIZUKA
DÔMEKI
BIRTH DATE
MARCH 3RD

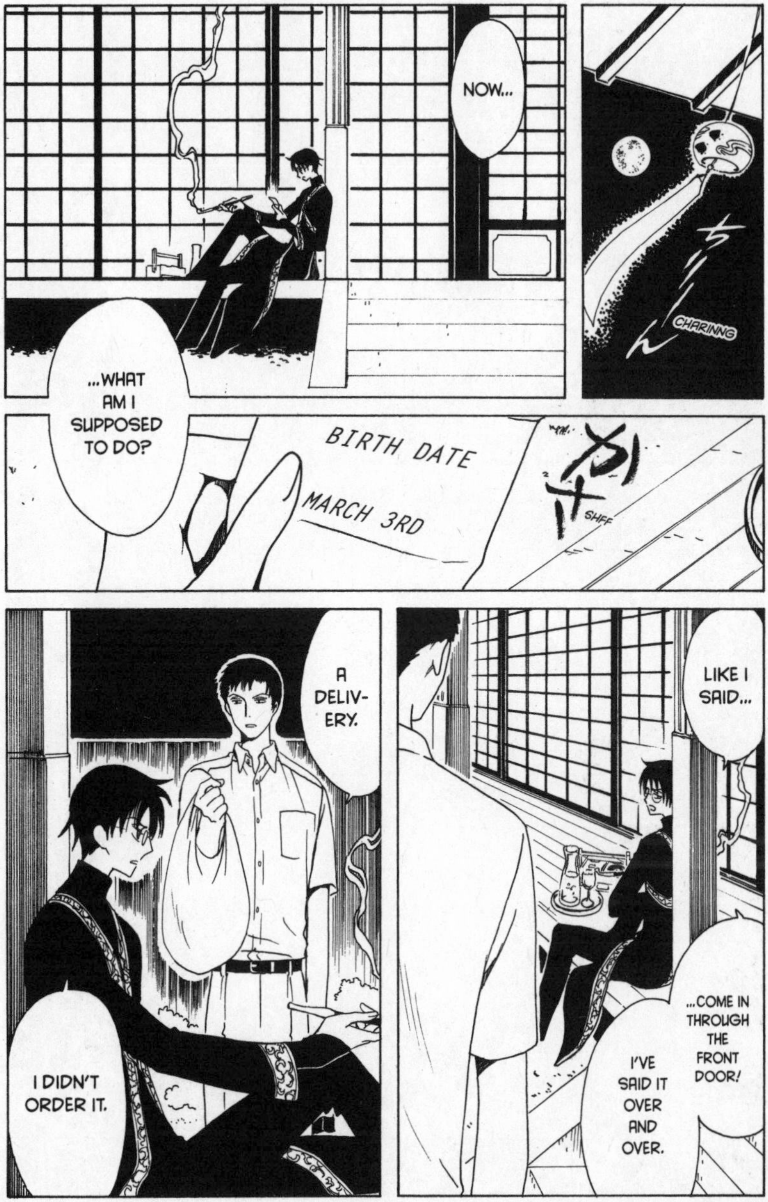
CHARINNG
NOW...
...WHAT AM I SUPPOSED TO DO?
SHFF
BIRTH DATE
MARCH 3RD
LIKE I SAID...
...COME IN THROUGH THE FRONT DOOR!
I'VE SAID IT OVER AND OVER.
A DELIVERY.
I DIDN'T ORDER IT.

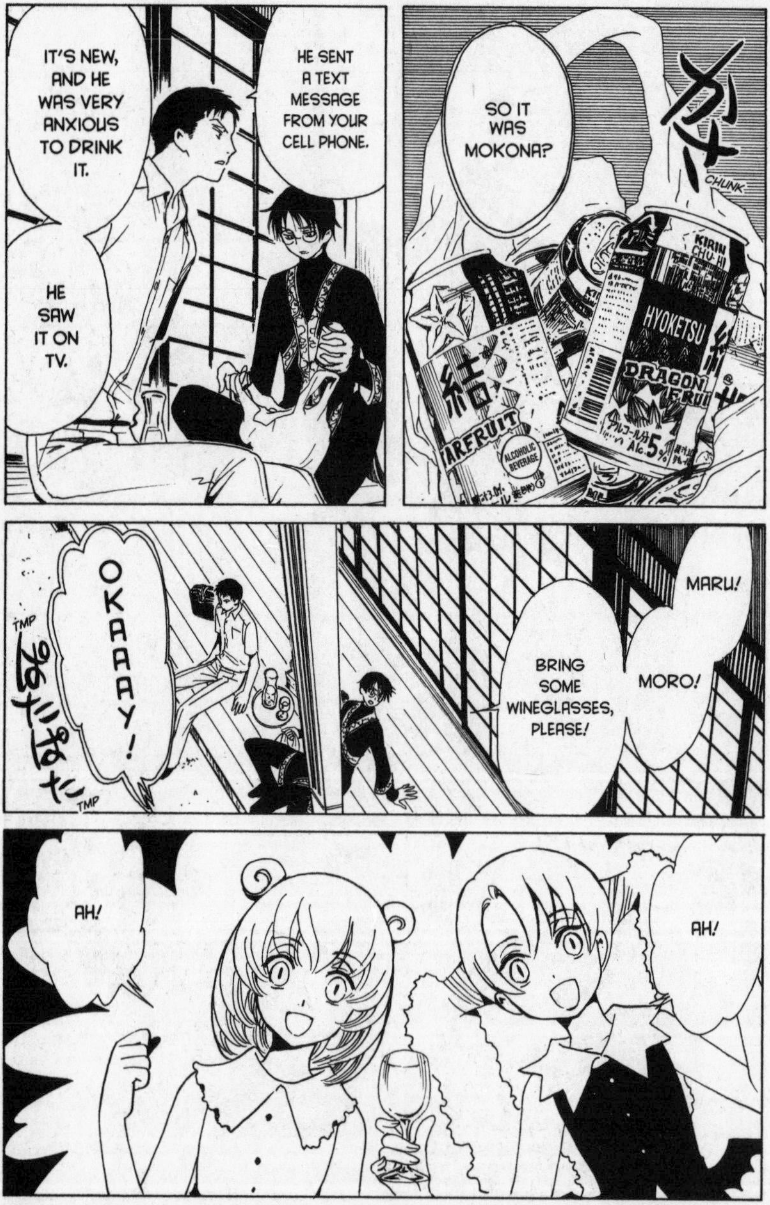
SO IT WAS MOKONA?
カタ
CHUNK
KIRIN CHU-HI
HYOKETSU
DRAGON FRUIT
Alc. 5%
ALCOHOLIC BEVERAGE
HE SENT A TEXT MESSAGE FROM YOUR CELL PHONE.
IT'S NEW, AND HE WAS VERY ANXIOUS TO DRINK IT.
HE SAW IT ON TV.
MARU!
MORO!
BRING SOME WINEGLASSES, PLEASE!
OKAAAY!
TMP
ぱたぱた
TMP
AH!
AH!

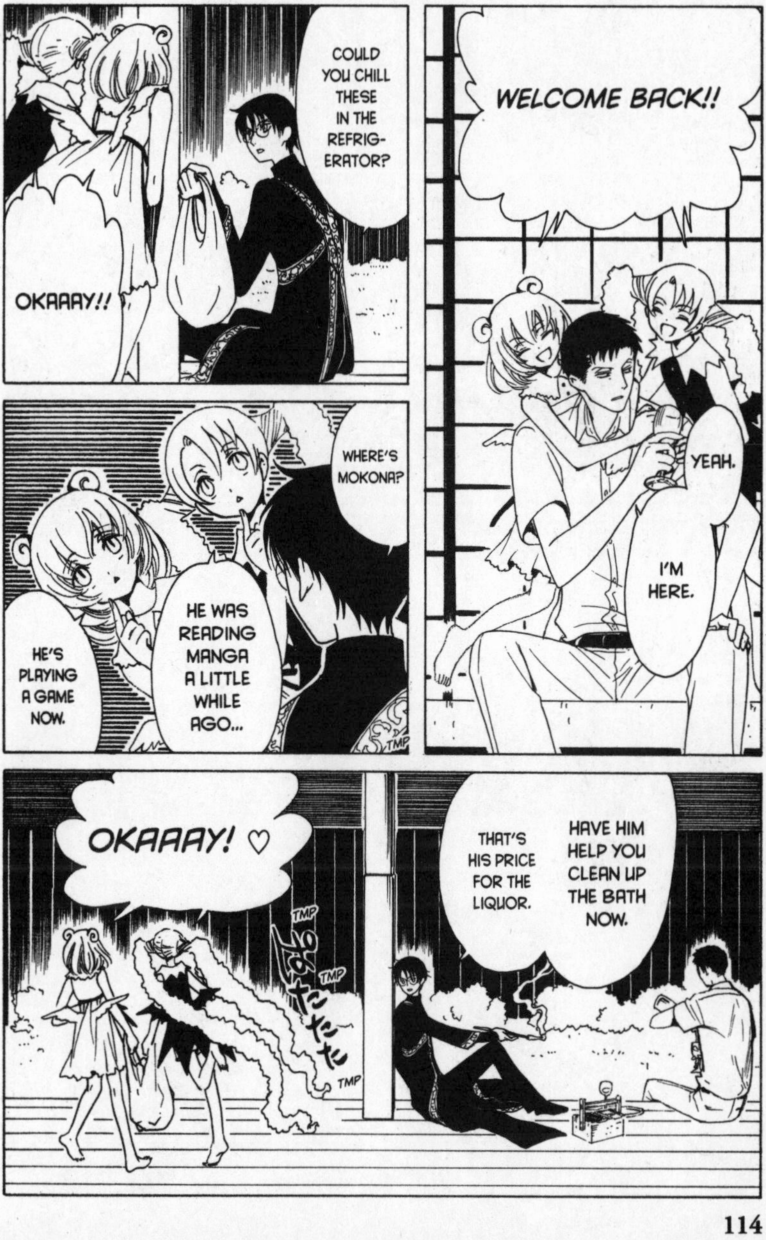
WELCOME BACK!!
YEAH.
I'M HERE.
COULD YOU CHILL THESE IN THE REFRIGERATOR?
OKAAAY!!
WHERE'S MOKONA?
HE WAS READING MANGA A LITTLE WHILE AGO...
HE'S PLAYING A GAME NOW.
TMP
HAVE HIM HELP YOU CLEAN UP THE BATH NOW.
THAT'S HIS PRICE FOR THE LIQUOR.
OKAAAY! ♡
TMP
TMP
TMP

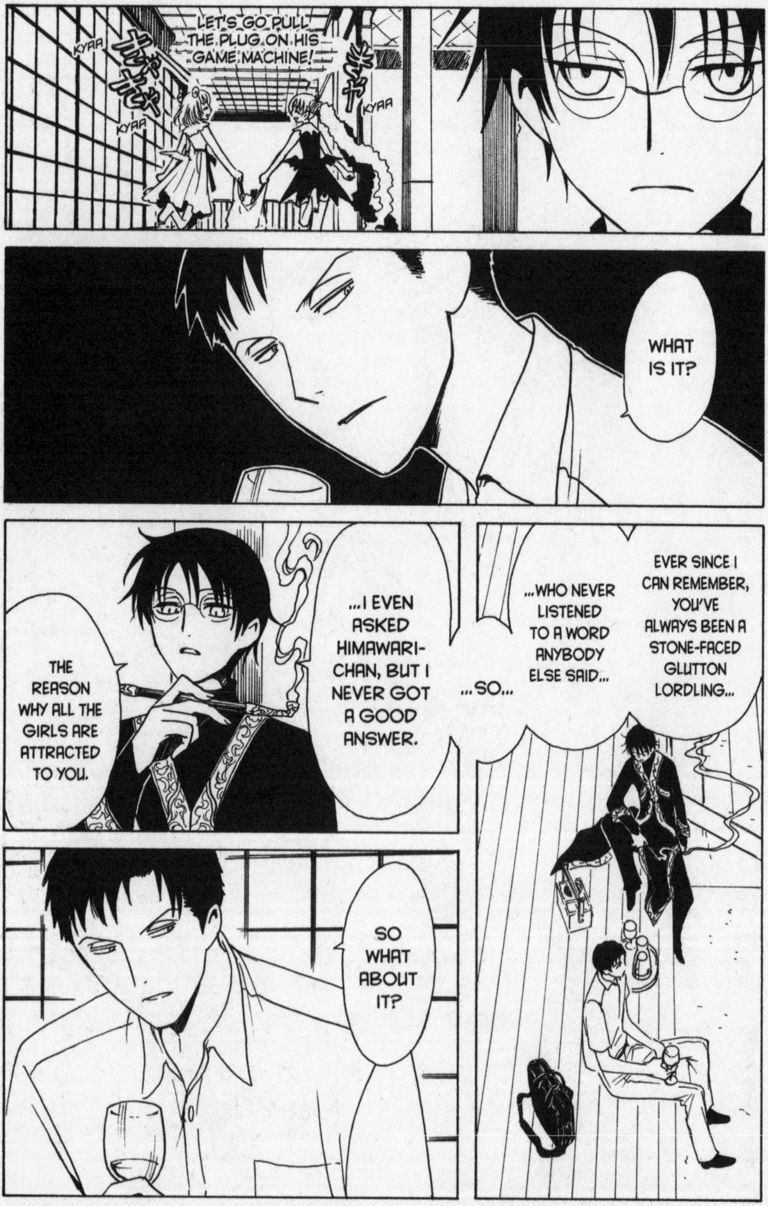
LET'S GO PULL THE PLUG ON HIS GAME MACHINE!
KYAA
KYAA
KYAA
WHAT IS IT?
EVER SINCE I CAN REMEMBER, YOU'VE ALWAYS BEEN A STONE-FACED GLUTTON LORDLING...
...WHO NEVER LISTENED TO A WORD ANYBODY ELSE SAID...
...SO...
...I EVEN ASKED HIMAWARI-CHAN, BUT I NEVER GOT A GOOD ANSWER.
THE REASON WHY ALL THE GIRLS ARE ATTRACTED TO YOU.
SO WHAT ABOUT IT?

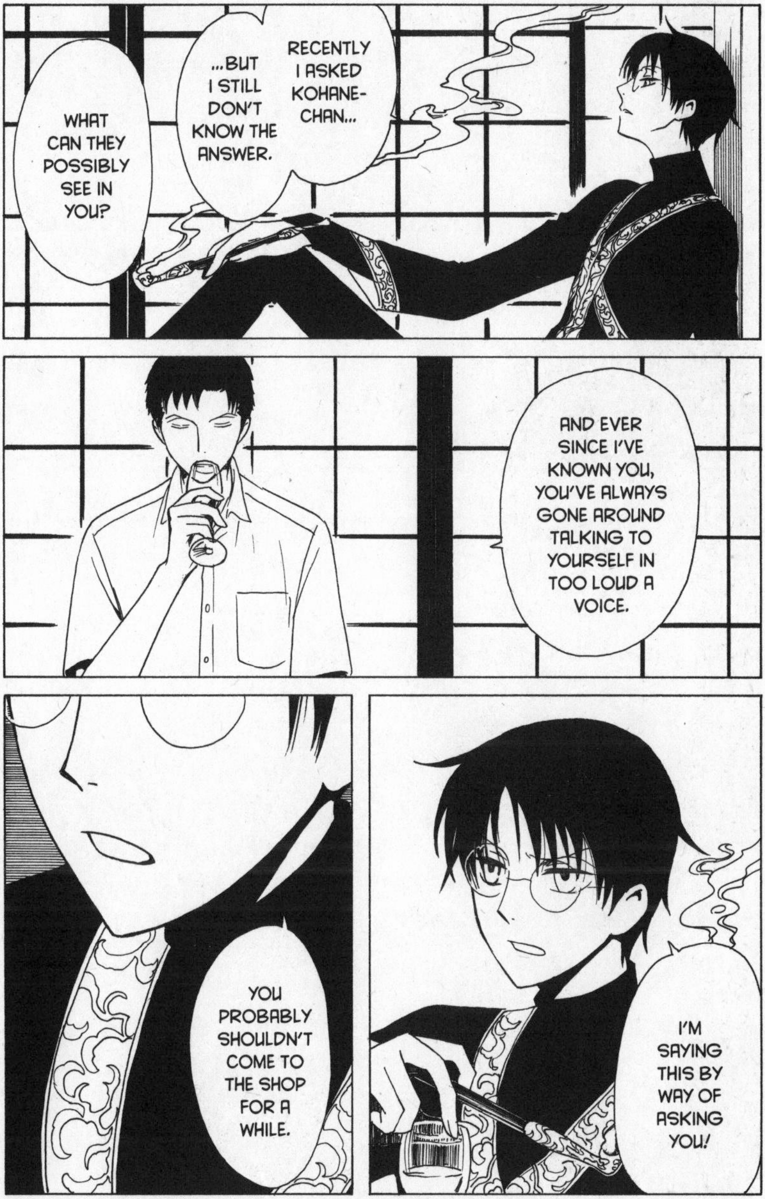
RECENTLY I ASKED KOHANE-CHAN...
...BUT I STILL DON'T KNOW THE ANSWER.
WHAT CAN THEY POSSIBLY SEE IN YOU?
AND EVER SINCE I'VE KNOWN YOU, YOU'VE ALWAYS GONE AROUND TALKING TO YOURSELF IN TOO LOUD A VOICE.
I'M SAYING THIS BY WAY OF ASKING YOU!
YOU PROBABLY SHOULDN'T COME TO THE SHOP FOR A WHILE.

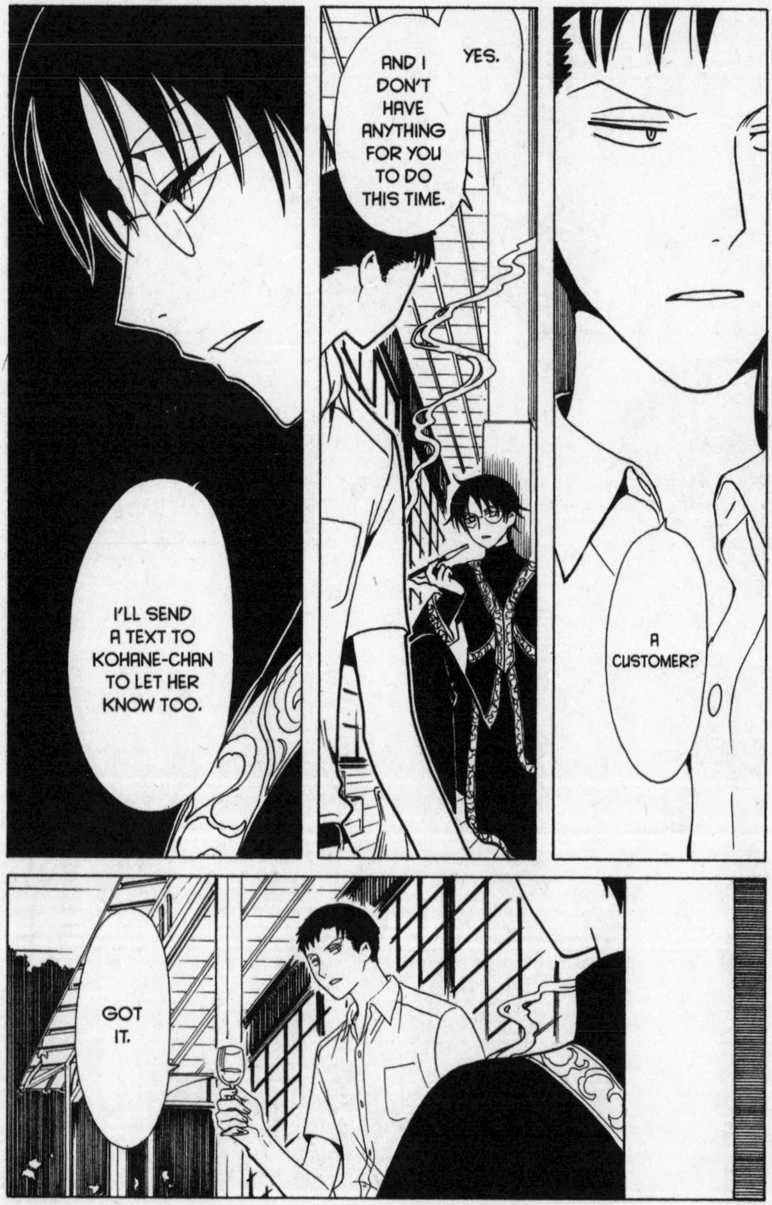
A CUSTOMER?
YES.
AND I DON'T HAVE ANYTHING FOR YOU TO DO THIS TIME.
I'LL SEND A TEXT TO KOHANE-CHAN TO LET HER KNOW TOO.
GOT IT.

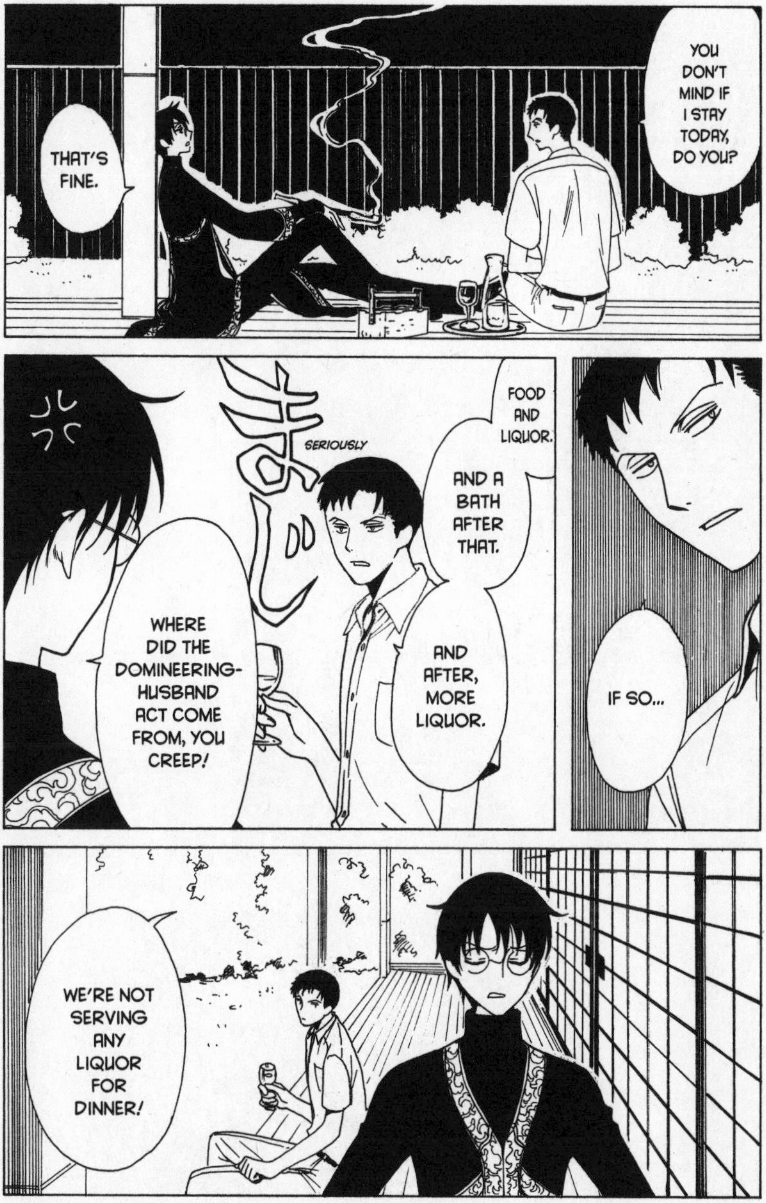
YOU DON'T MIND IF I STAY TODAY, DO YOU?
THAT'S FINE.
IF SO...
FOOD AND LIQUOR.
AND A BATH AFTER THAT.
AND AFTER, MORE LIQUOR.
SERIOUSLY
WHERE DID THE DOMINEERING-HUSBAND ACT COME FROM, YOU CREEP!
WE'RE NOT SERVING ANY LIQUOR FOR DINNER!

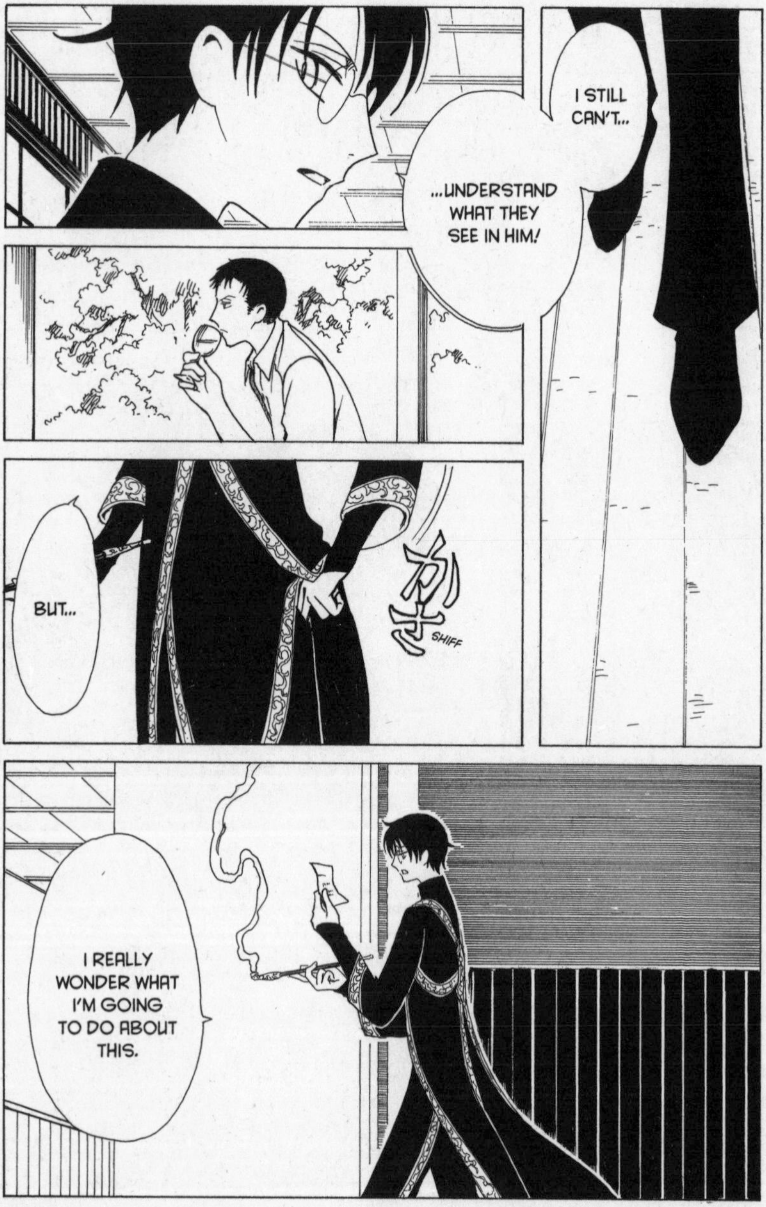
I STILL CAN'T...
...UNDERSTAND WHAT THEY SEE IN HIM!
BUT...
カキ
SHIFF
I REALLY WONDER WHAT I'M GOING TO DO ABOUT THIS.

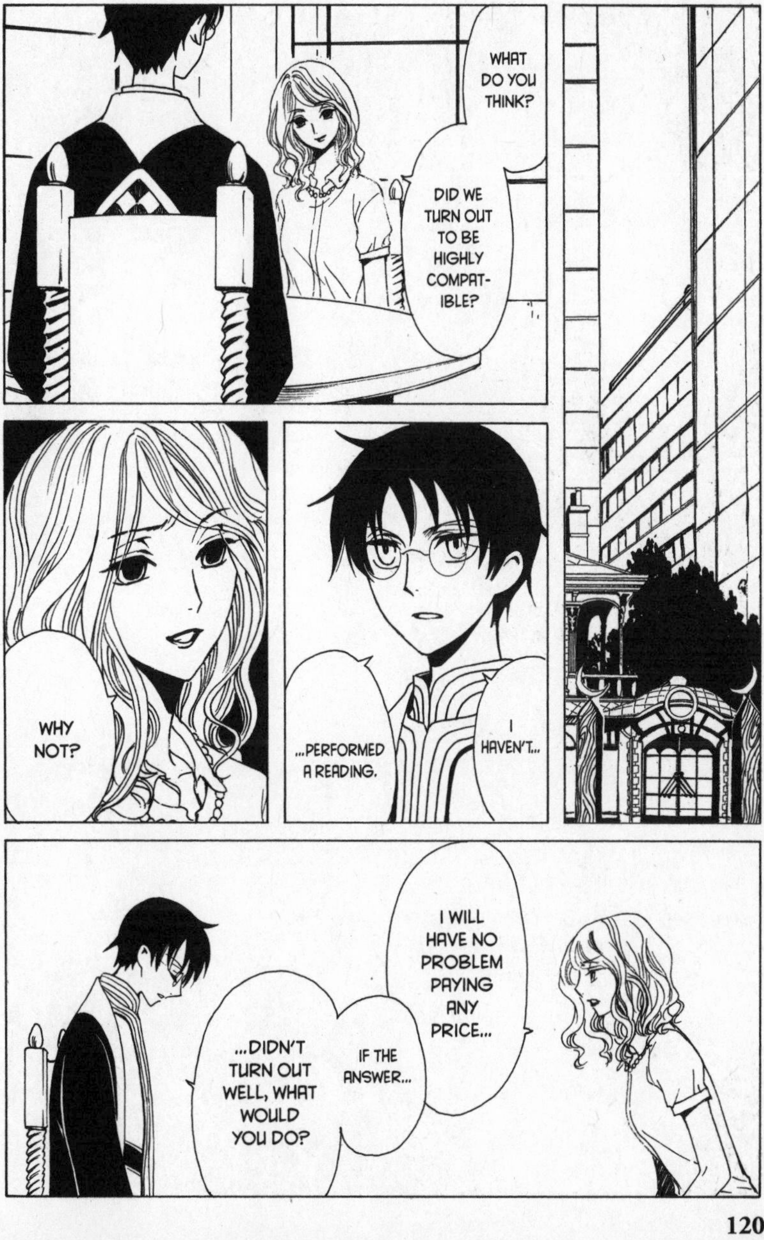
WHAT DO YOU THINK?
DID WE TURN OUT TO BE HIGHLY COMPAT-IBLE?
I HAVEN'T...
...PERFORMED A READING.
WHY NOT?
I WILL HAVE NO PROBLEM PAYING ANY PRICE...
IF THE ANSWER...
...DIDN'T TURN OUT WELL, WHAT WOULD YOU DO?

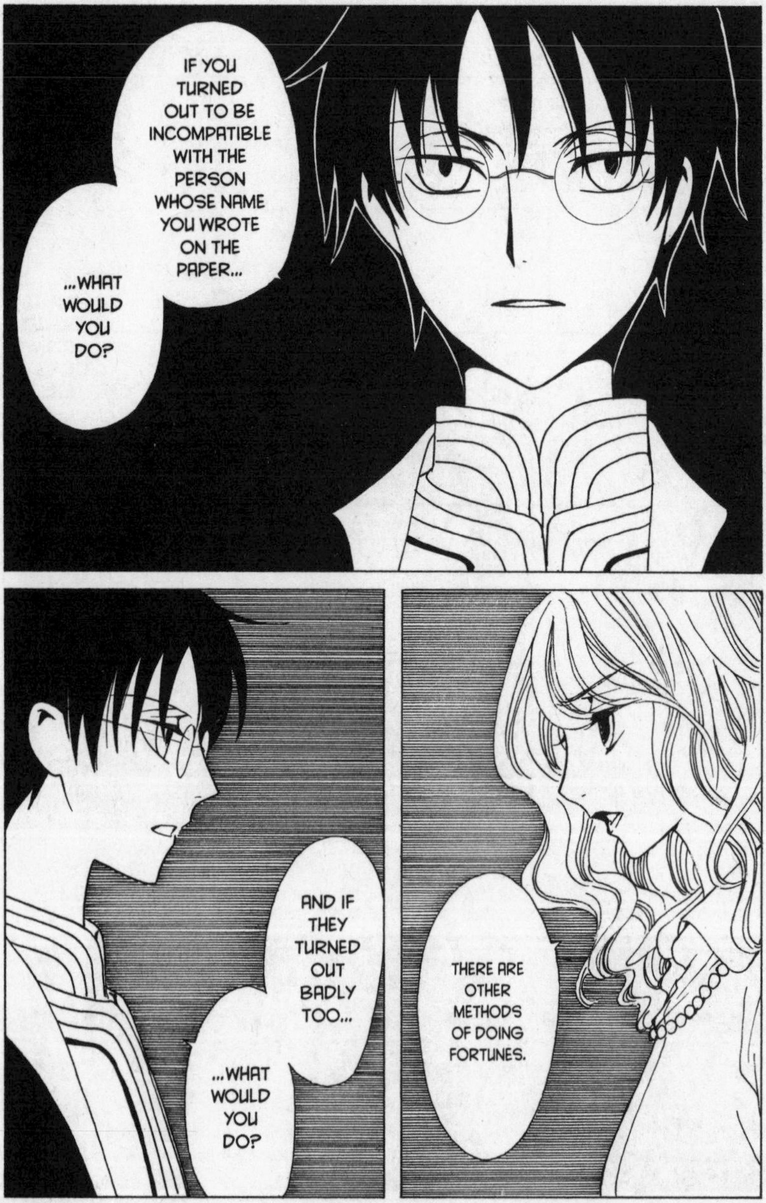
IF YOU TURNED OUT TO BE INCOMPATIBLE WITH THE PERSON WHOSE NAME YOU WROTE ON THE PAPER...
...WHAT WOULD YOU DO?
THERE ARE OTHER METHODS OF DOING FORTUNES.
AND IF THEY TURNED OUT BADLY TOO...
...WHAT WOULD YOU DO?

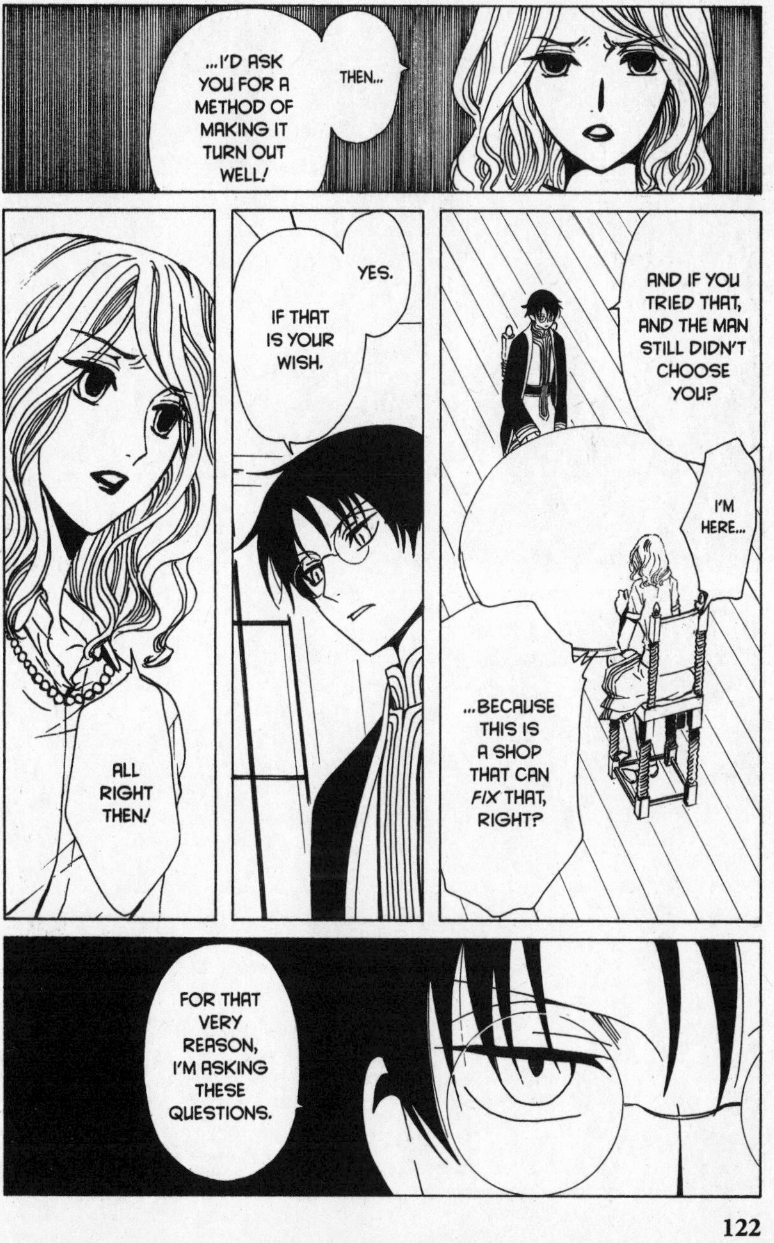
THEN...
...I'D ASK YOU FOR A METHOD OF MAKING IT TURN OUT WELL!
AND IF YOU TRIED THAT, AND THE MAN STILL DIDN'T CHOOSE YOU?
I'M HERE...
...BECAUSE THIS IS A SHOP THAT CAN *FIX* THAT, RIGHT?
YES.
IF THAT IS YOUR WISH.
ALL RIGHT THEN!
FOR THAT VERY REASON, I'M ASKING THESE QUESTIONS.

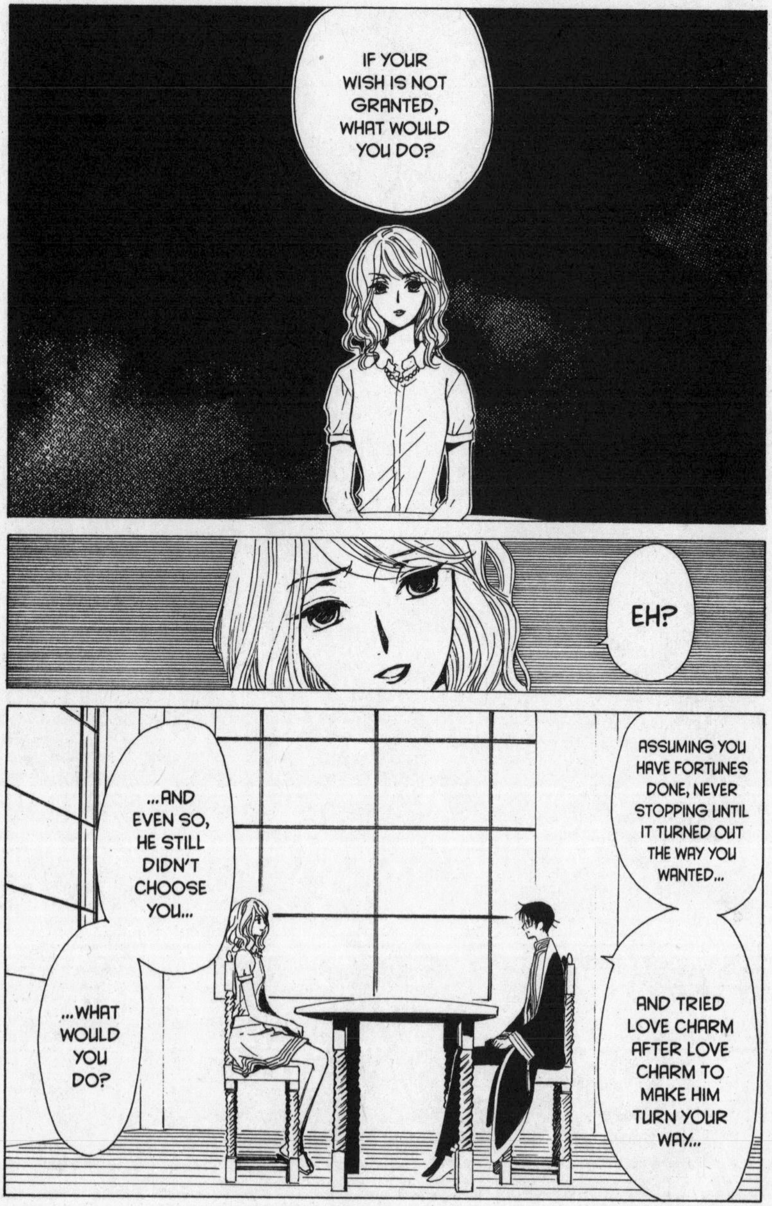
IF YOUR WISH IS NOT GRANTED, WHAT WOULD YOU DO?
EH?
ASSUMING YOU HAVE FORTUNES DONE, NEVER STOPPING UNTIL IT TURNED OUT THE WAY YOU WANTED...
AND TRIED LOVE CHARM AFTER LOVE CHARM TO MAKE HIM TURN YOUR WAY...
...AND EVEN SO, HE STILL DIDN'T CHOOSE YOU...
...WHAT WOULD YOU DO?

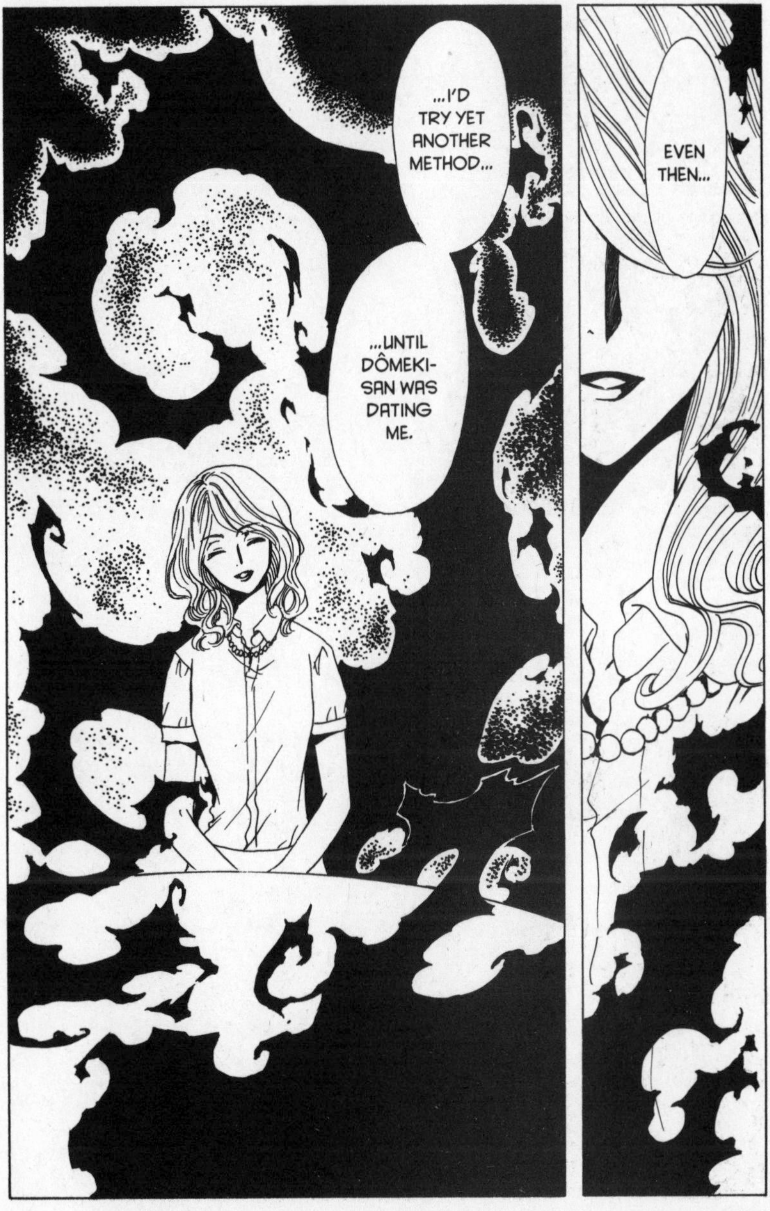
EVEN THEN...
...I'D TRY YET ANOTHER METHOD...
...UNTIL DÔMEKI-SAN WAS DATING ME.

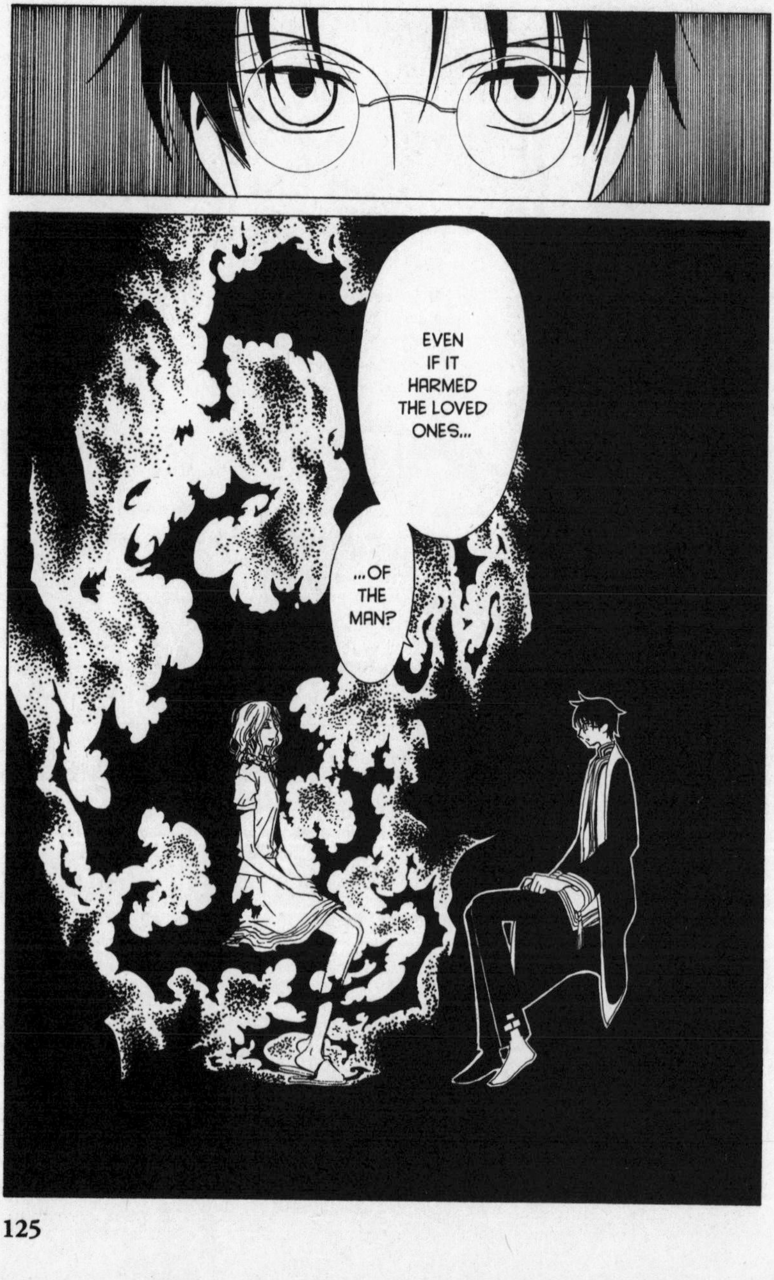
EVEN IF IT HARMED THE LOVED ONES...
...OF THE MAN?

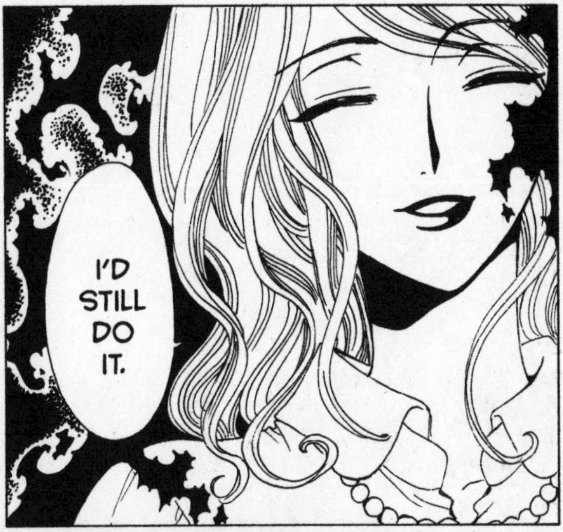
I'D STILL DO IT.

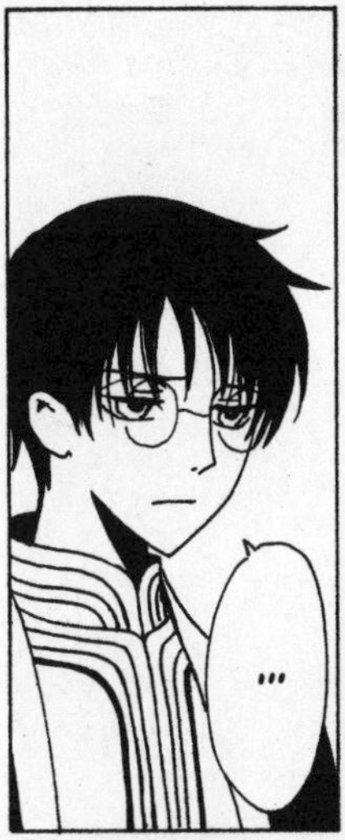
...

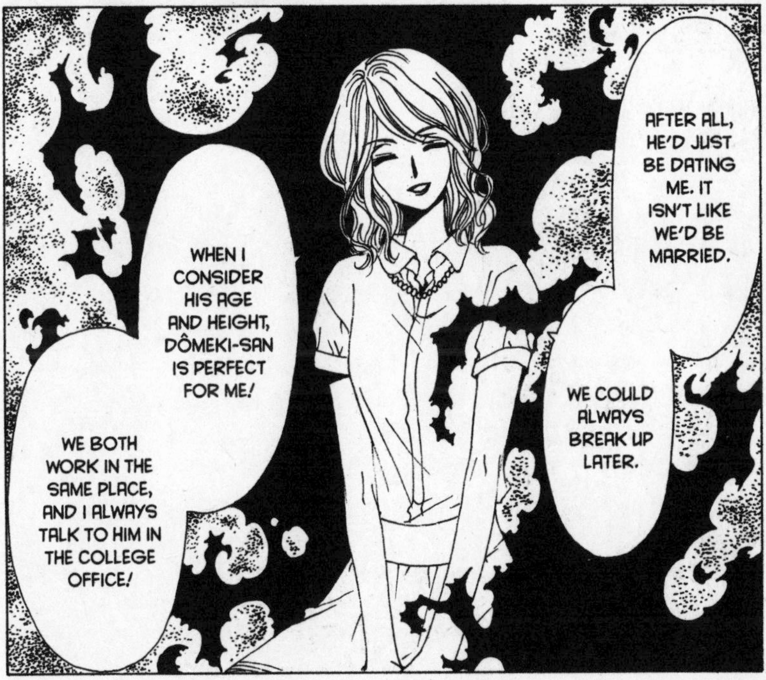
AFTER ALL, HE'D JUST BE DATING ME. IT ISN'T LIKE WE'D BE MARRIED.
WE COULD ALWAYS BREAK UP LATER.
WHEN I CONSIDER HIS AGE AND HEIGHT, DÔMEKI-SAN IS PERFECT FOR ME!
WE BOTH WORK IN THE SAME PLACE, AND I ALWAYS TALK TO HIM IN THE COLLEGE OFFICE!

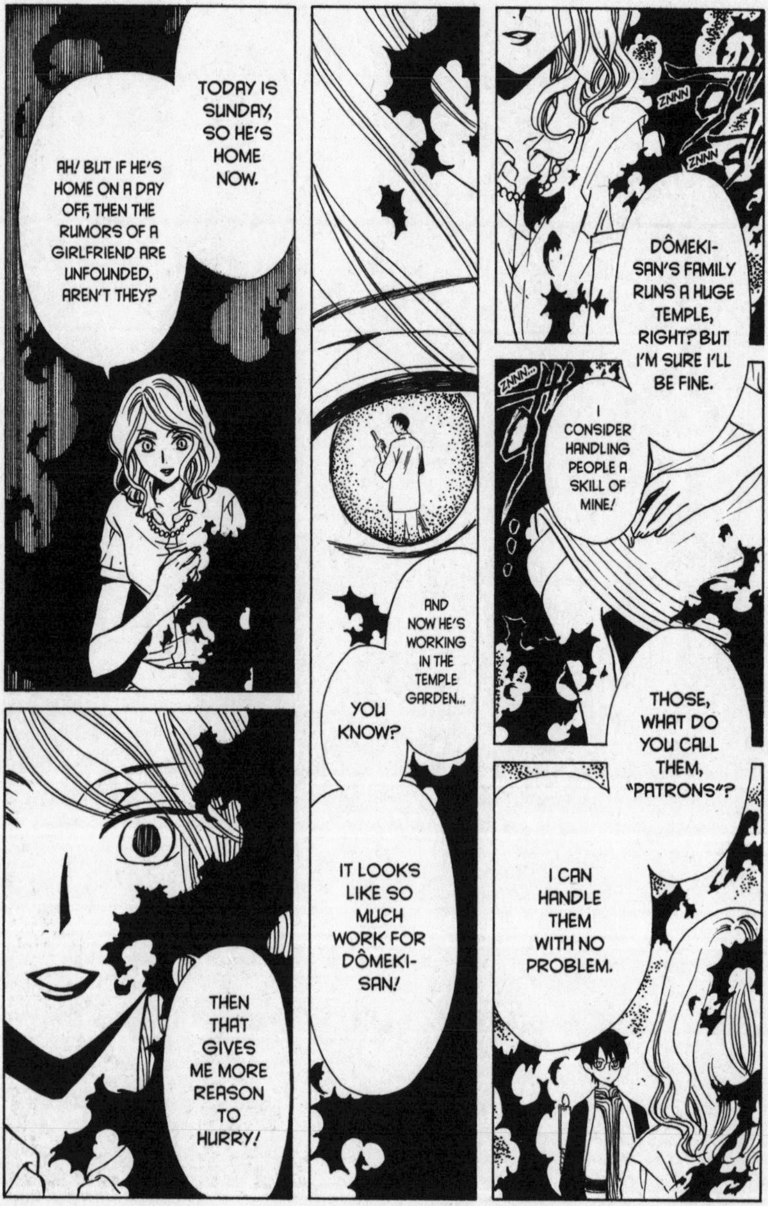
ZNNN
ZNNN
DÔMEKI-SAN'S FAMILY RUNS A HUGE TEMPLE, RIGHT? BUT I'M SURE I'LL BE FINE.
ZNNN...
I CONSIDER HANDLING PEOPLE A SKILL OF MINE!
THOSE, WHAT DO YOU CALL THEM, "PATRONS"?
I CAN HANDLE THEM WITH NO PROBLEM.
AND NOW HE'S WORKING IN THE TEMPLE GARDEN...
YOU KNOW?
IT LOOKS LIKE SO MUCH WORK FOR DÔMEKI-SAN!
TODAY IS SUNDAY, SO HE'S HOME NOW.
AH! BUT IF HE'S HOME ON A DAY OFF, THEN THE RUMORS OF A GIRLFRIEND ARE UNFOUNDED, AREN'T THEY?
THEN THAT GIVES ME MORE REASON TO HURRY!

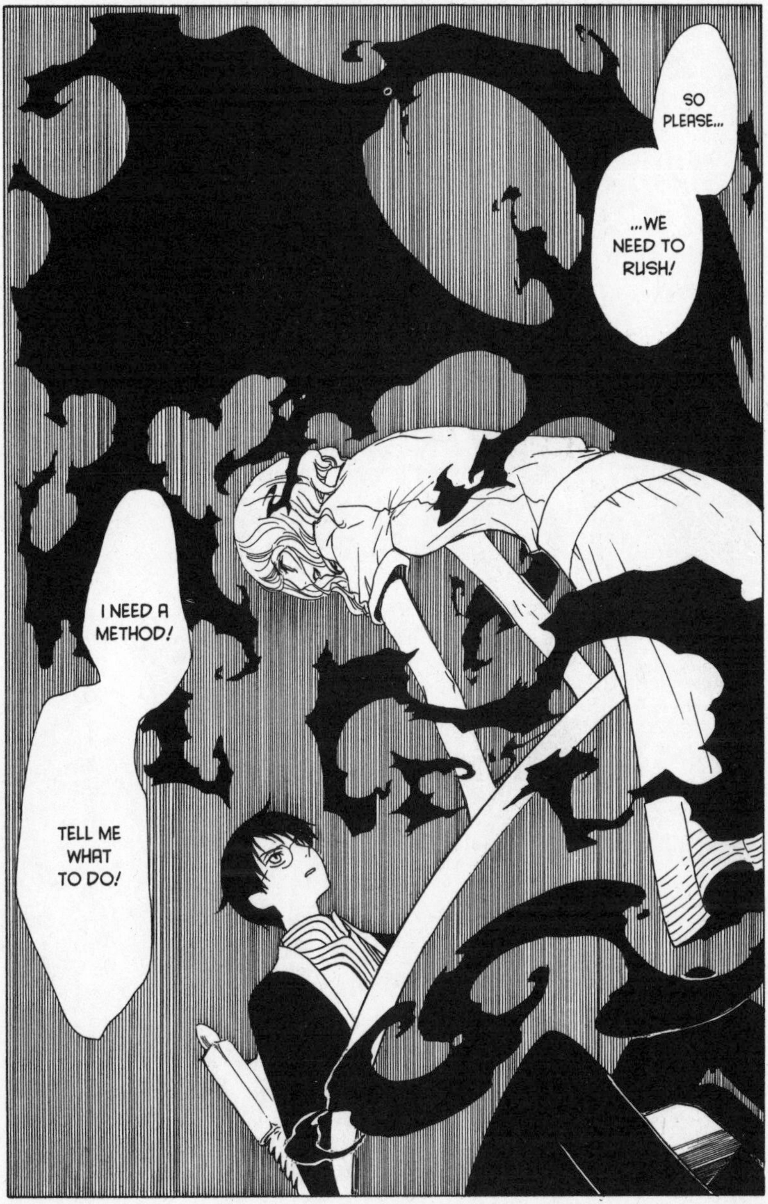
SO PLEASE...
...WE NEED TO RUSH!
I NEED A METHOD!
TELL ME WHAT TO DO!

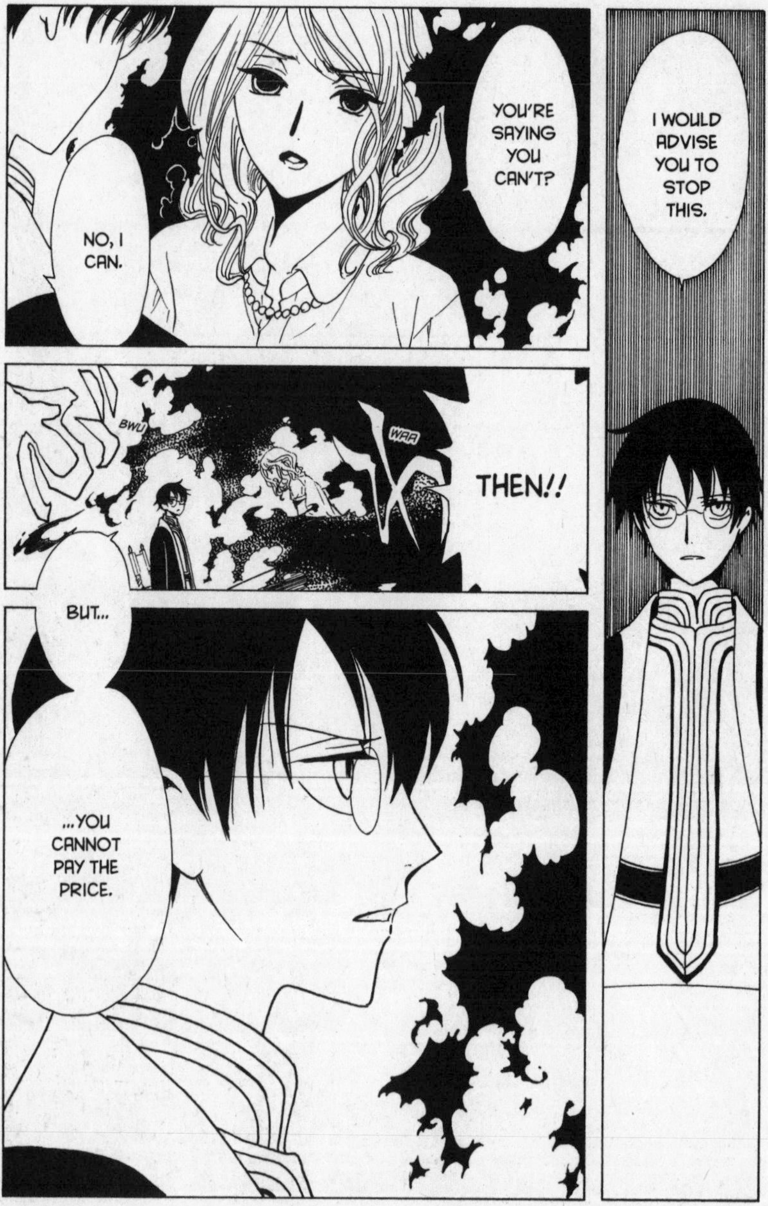
I WOULD ADVISE YOU TO STOP THIS.
YOU'RE SAYING YOU CAN'T?
NO, I CAN.
THEN!!
WAA
BWU
BUT...
...YOU CANNOT PAY THE PRICE.

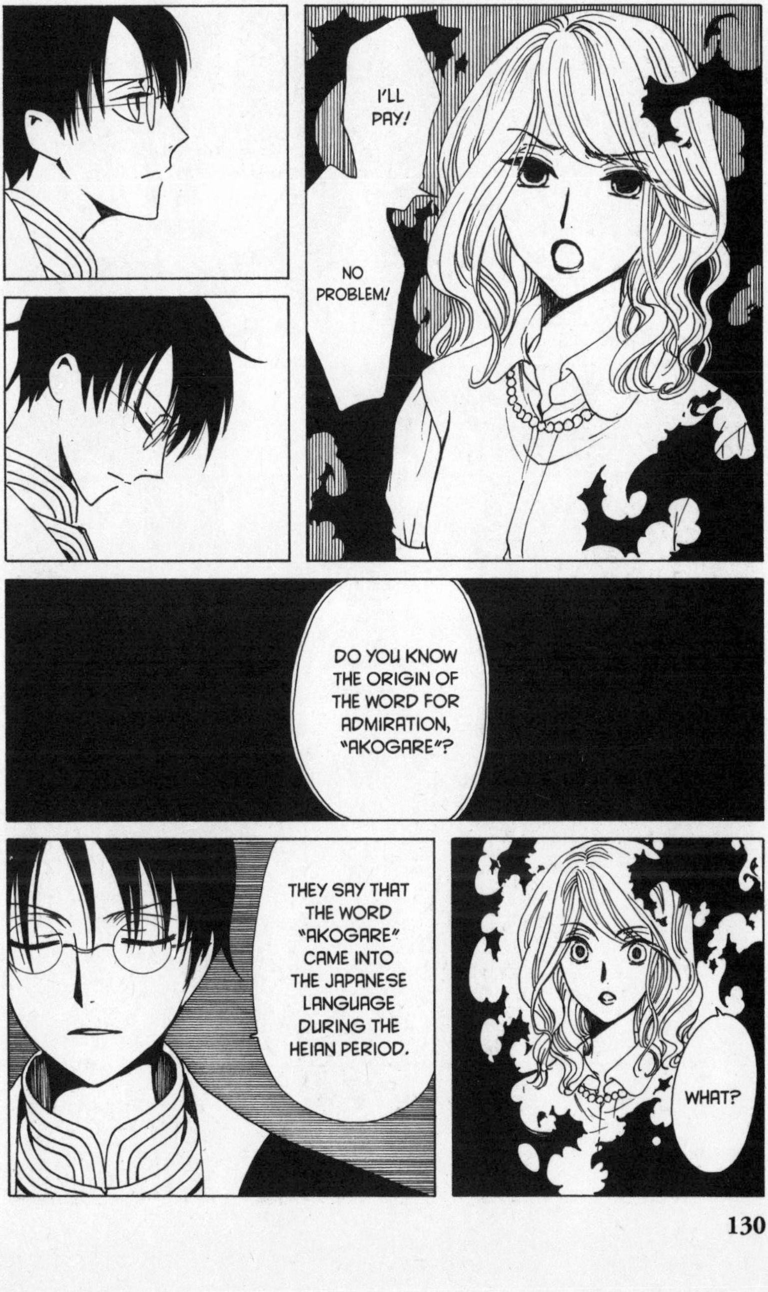
I'LL PAY!
NO PROBLEM!
DO YOU KNOW THE ORIGIN OF THE WORD FOR ADMIRATION, "AKOGARE"?
WHAT?
THEY SAY THAT THE WORD "AKOGARE" CAME INTO THE JAPANESE LANGUAGE DURING THE HEIAN PERIOD.

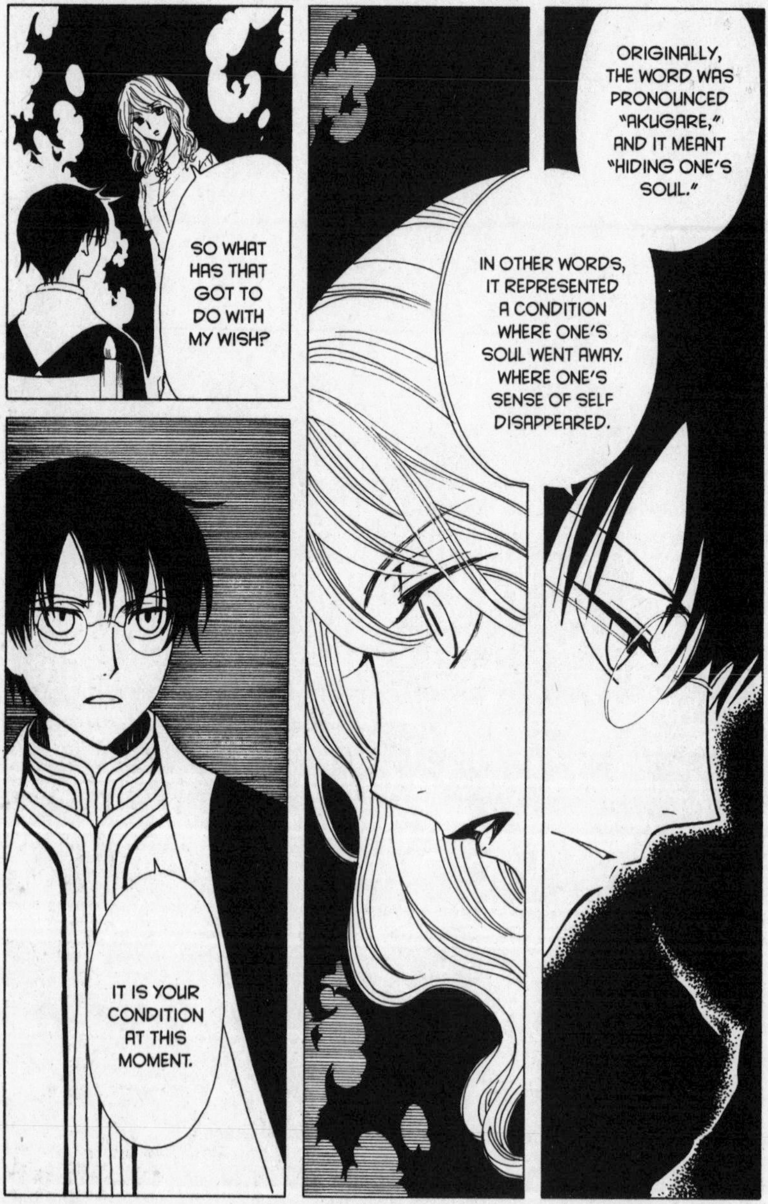
ORIGINALLY, THE WORD WAS PRONOUNCED "AKUGARE," AND IT MEANT "HIDING ONE'S SOUL."
IN OTHER WORDS, IT REPRESENTED A CONDITION WHERE ONE'S SOUL WENT AWAY. WHERE ONE'S SENSE OF SELF DISAPPEARED.
SO WHAT HAS THAT GOT TO DO WITH MY WISH?
IT IS YOUR CONDITION AT THIS MOMENT.

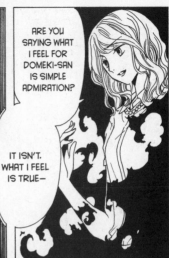

ARE YOU SAYING WHAT I FEEL FOR DOMEKI-SAN IS SIMPLE ADMIRATION?
IT ISN'T. WHAT I FEEL IS TRUE—
NO.
I'M SAYING THAT YOUR SOUL IS PRESENTLY COMPLETELY HIDDEN.
EH...?
RIGHT NOW. WHERE ARE YOU?
HUH?
WHERE ELSE? RIGHT IN FRONT OF YOU!

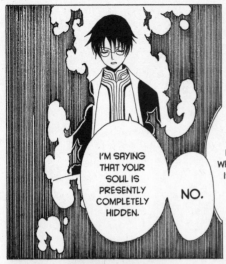

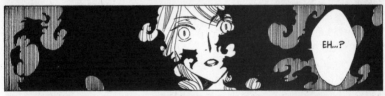

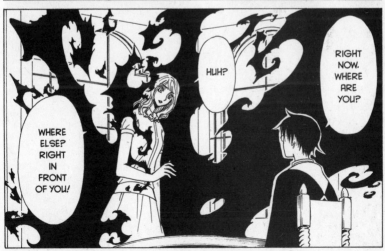

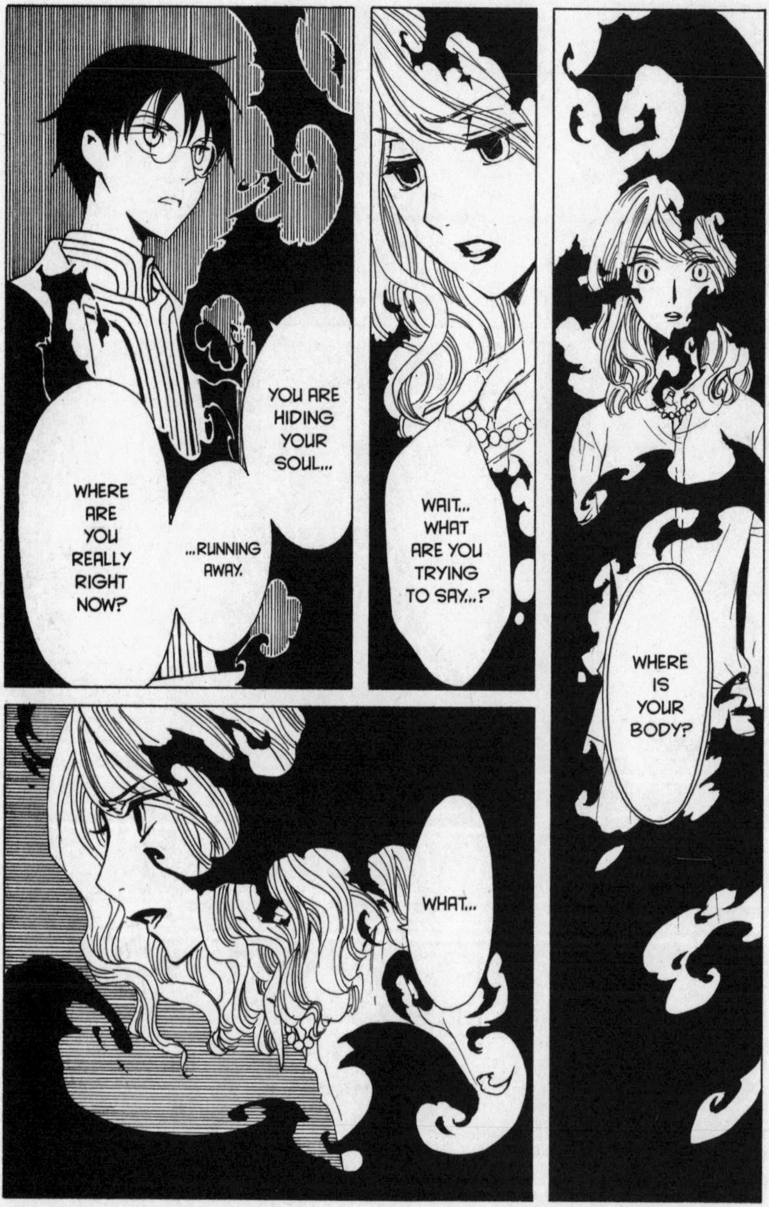
WHERE IS YOUR BODY?
WAIT... WHAT ARE YOU TRYING TO SAY...?
YOU ARE HIDING YOUR SOUL...
...RUNNING AWAY.
WHERE ARE YOU REALLY RIGHT NOW?
WHAT...

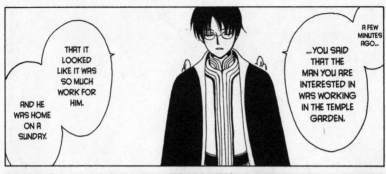

...YOU SAID THAT THE MAN YOU ARE INTERESTED IN WAS WORKING IN THE TEMPLE GARDEN.

THAT IT LOOKED LIKE IT WAS SO MUCH WORK FOR HIM.

AND HE WAS HOME ON A SUNDAY.

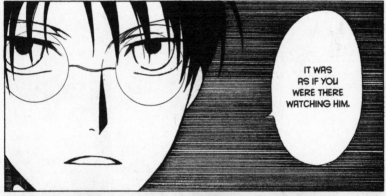

IT WAS AS IF YOU WERE THERE WATCHING HIM.

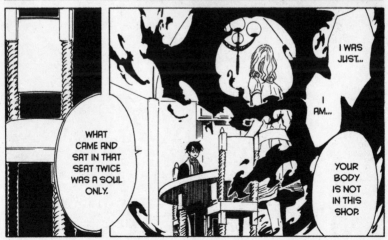

I WAS JUST...

I AM...

YOUR BODY IS NOT IN THIS SHOP.

WHAT CAME AND SAT IN THAT SEAT TWICE WAS A SOUL ONLY.

134

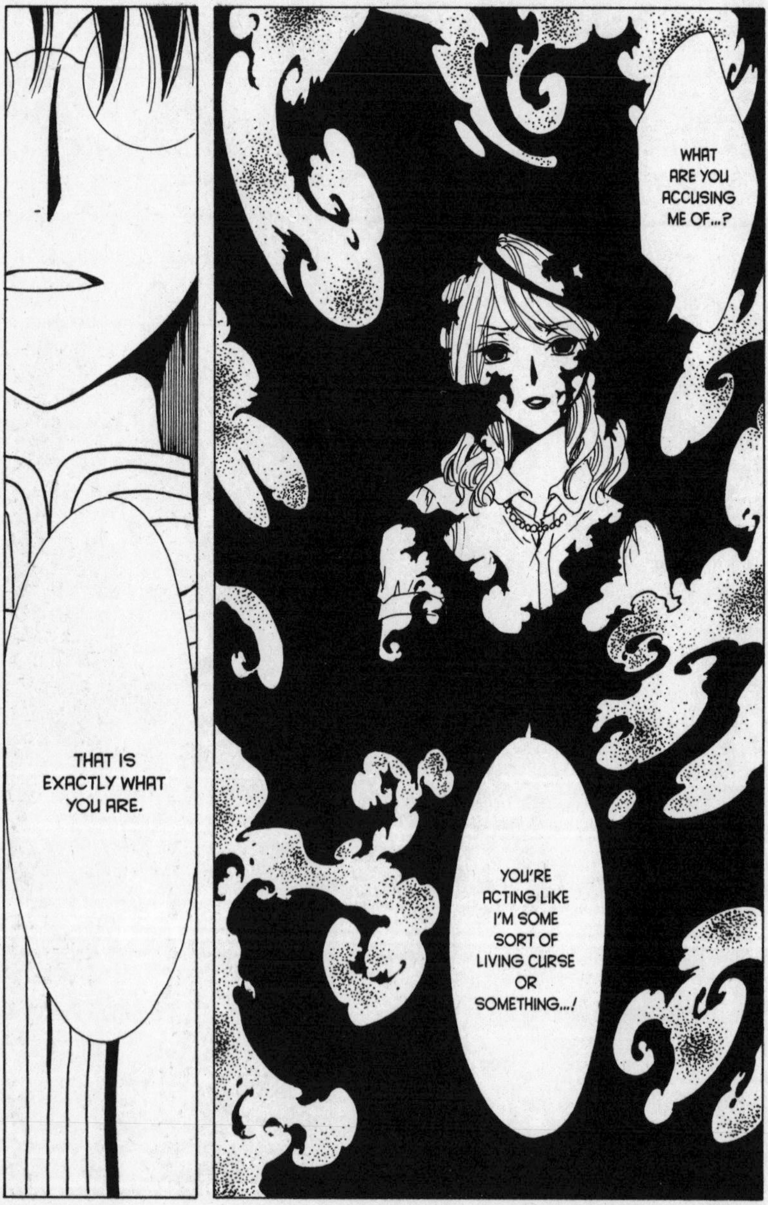
WHAT ARE YOU ACCUSING ME OF...?
YOU'RE ACTING LIKE I'M SOME SORT OF LIVING CURSE OR SOMETHING...!
THAT IS EXACTLY WHAT YOU ARE.

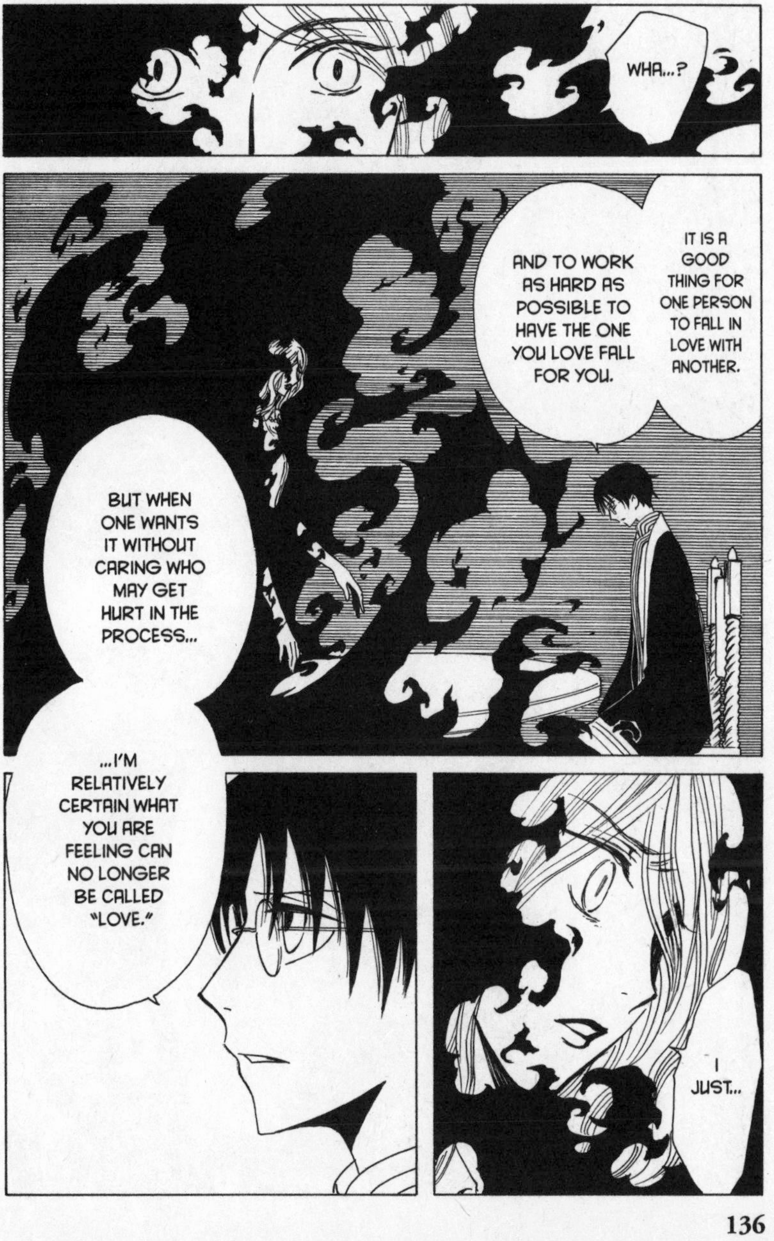
WHA...?
IT IS A GOOD THING FOR ONE PERSON TO FALL IN LOVE WITH ANOTHER.
AND TO WORK AS HARD AS POSSIBLE TO HAVE THE ONE YOU LOVE FALL FOR YOU.
BUT WHEN ONE WANTS IT WITHOUT CARING WHO MAY GET HURT IN THE PROCESS...
...I'M RELATIVELY CERTAIN WHAT YOU ARE FEELING CAN NO LONGER BE CALLED "LOVE."
I JUST...

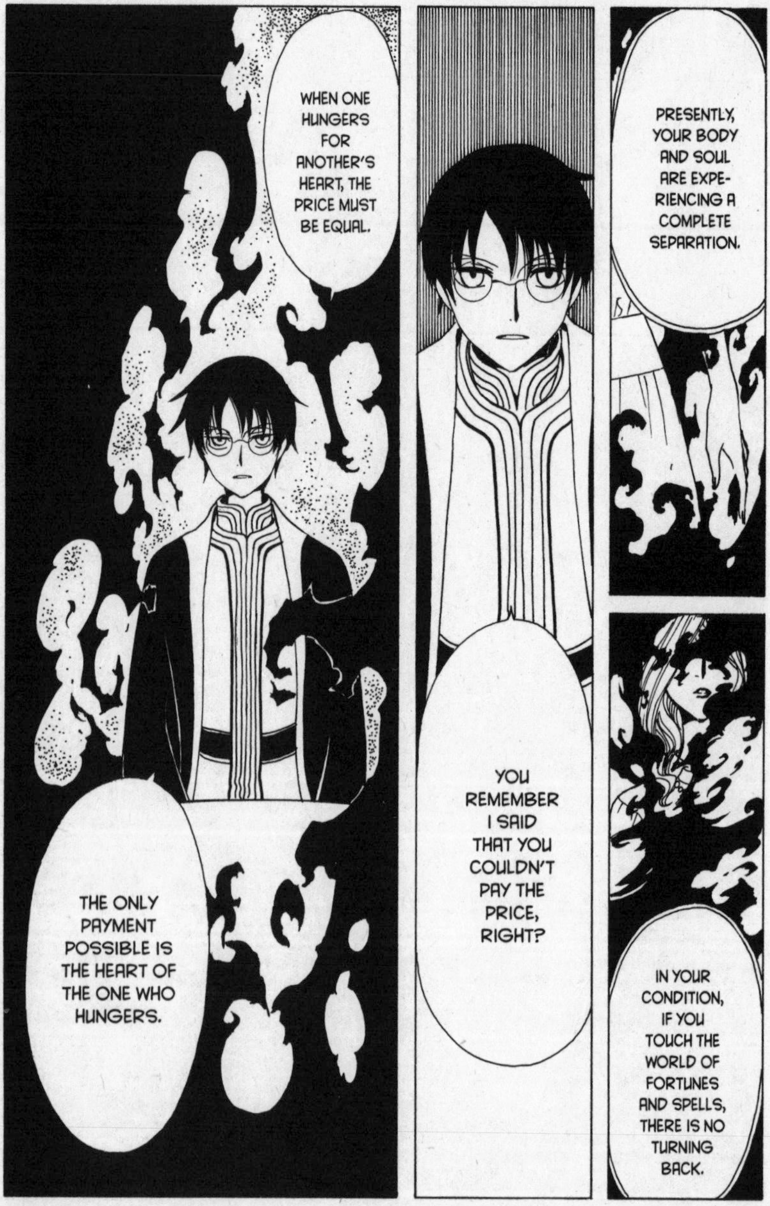
PRESENTLY, YOUR BODY AND SOUL ARE EXPE-RIENCING A COMPLETE SEPARATION.
IN YOUR CONDITION, IF YOU TOUCH THE WORLD OF FORTUNES AND SPELLS, THERE IS NO TURNING BACK.
YOU REMEMBER I SAID THAT YOU COULDN'T PAY THE PRICE, RIGHT?
WHEN ONE HUNGERS FOR ANOTHER'S HEART, THE PRICE MUST BE EQUAL.
THE ONLY PAYMENT POSSIBLE IS THE HEART OF THE ONE WHO HUNGERS.

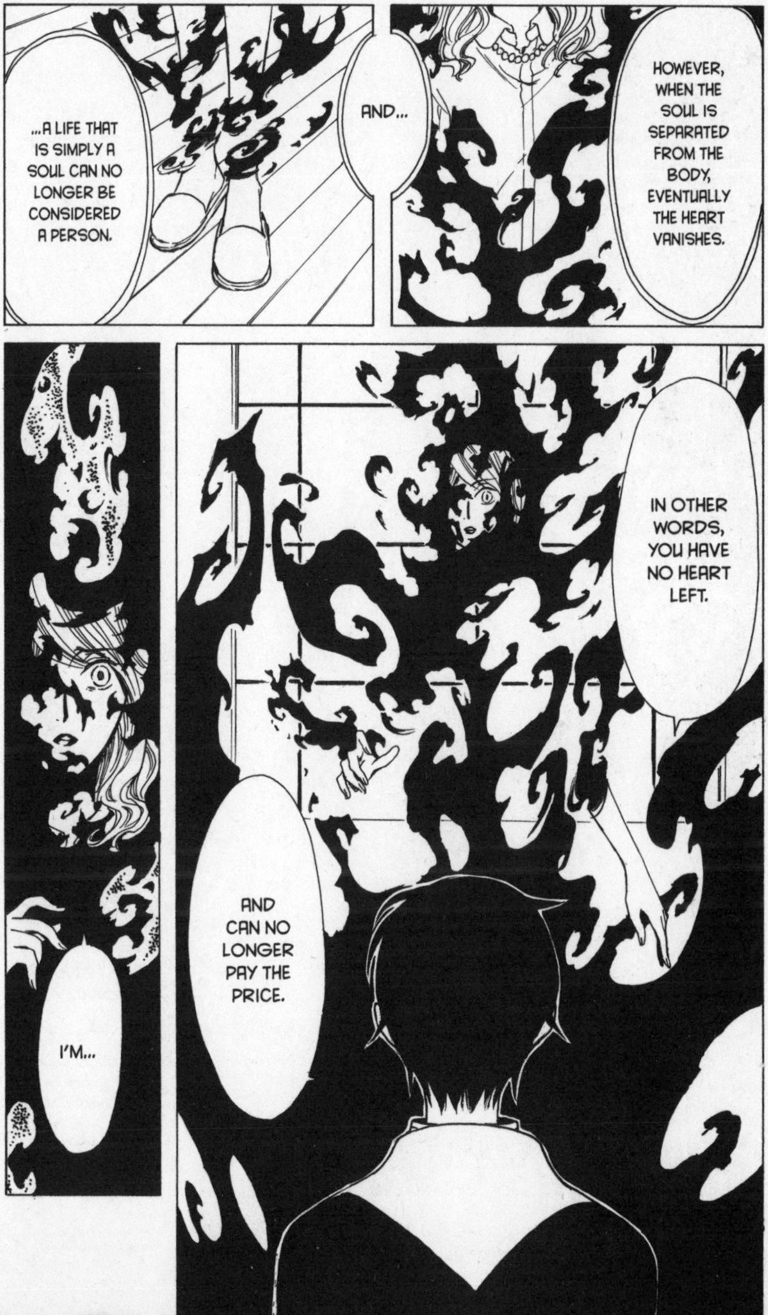
HOWEVER, WHEN THE SOUL IS SEPARATED FROM THE BODY, EVENTUALLY THE HEART VANISHES.
AND...
...A LIFE THAT IS SIMPLY A SOUL CAN NO LONGER BE CONSIDERED A PERSON.
IN OTHER WORDS, YOU HAVE NO HEART LEFT.
AND CAN NO LONGER PAY THE PRICE.
I'M...

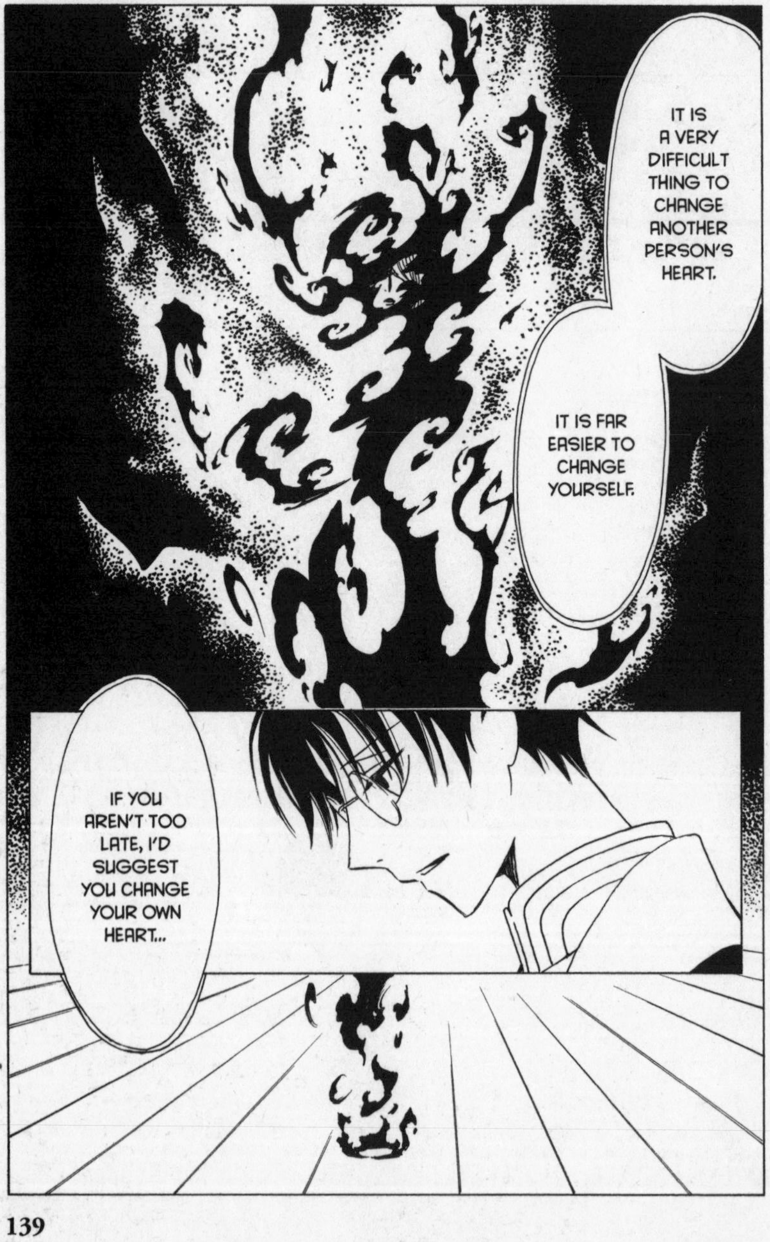
IT IS A VERY DIFFICULT THING TO CHANGE ANOTHER PERSON'S HEART.
IT IS FAR EASIER TO CHANGE YOURSELF.
IF YOU AREN'T TOO LATE, I'D SUGGEST YOU CHANGE YOUR OWN HEART...

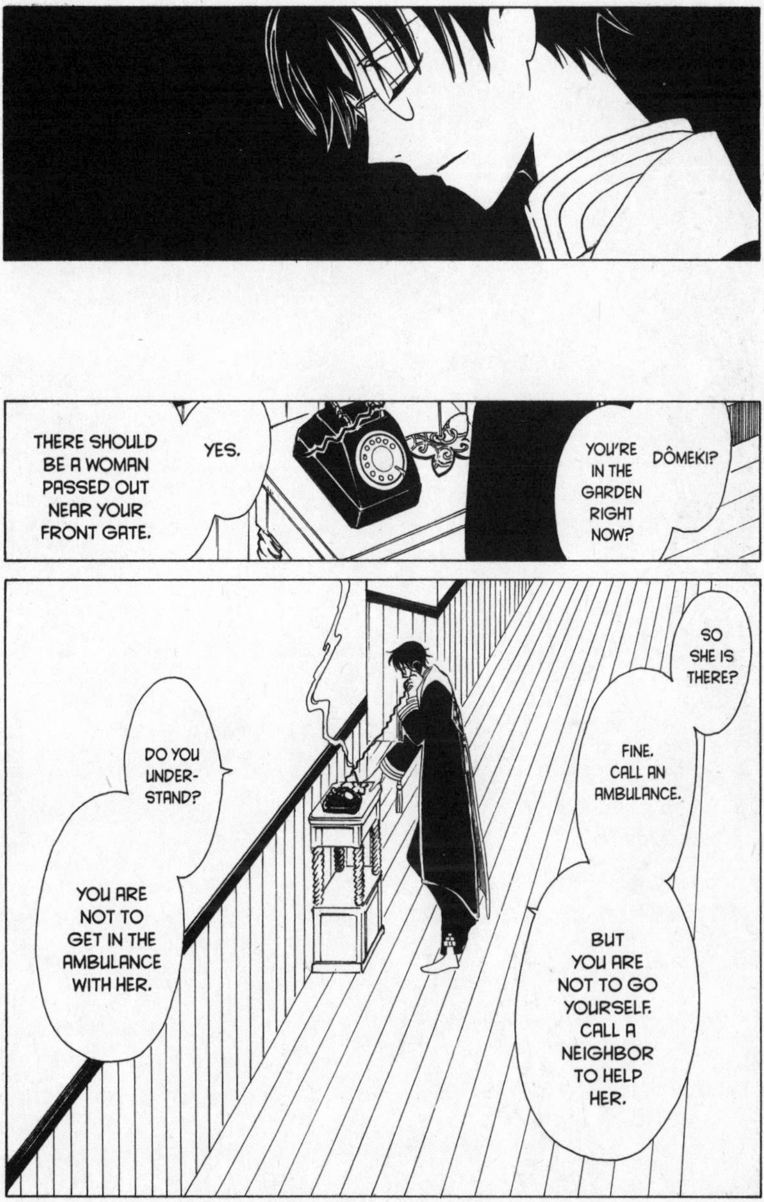
DÔMEKI?
YOU'RE IN THE GARDEN RIGHT NOW?
YES.
THERE SHOULD BE A WOMAN PASSED OUT NEAR YOUR FRONT GATE.
SO SHE IS THERE?
FINE. CALL AN AMBULANCE.
BUT YOU ARE NOT TO GO YOURSELF. CALL A NEIGHBOR TO HELP HER.
DO YOU UNDER-STAND?
YOU ARE NOT TO GET IN THE AMBULANCE WITH HER.

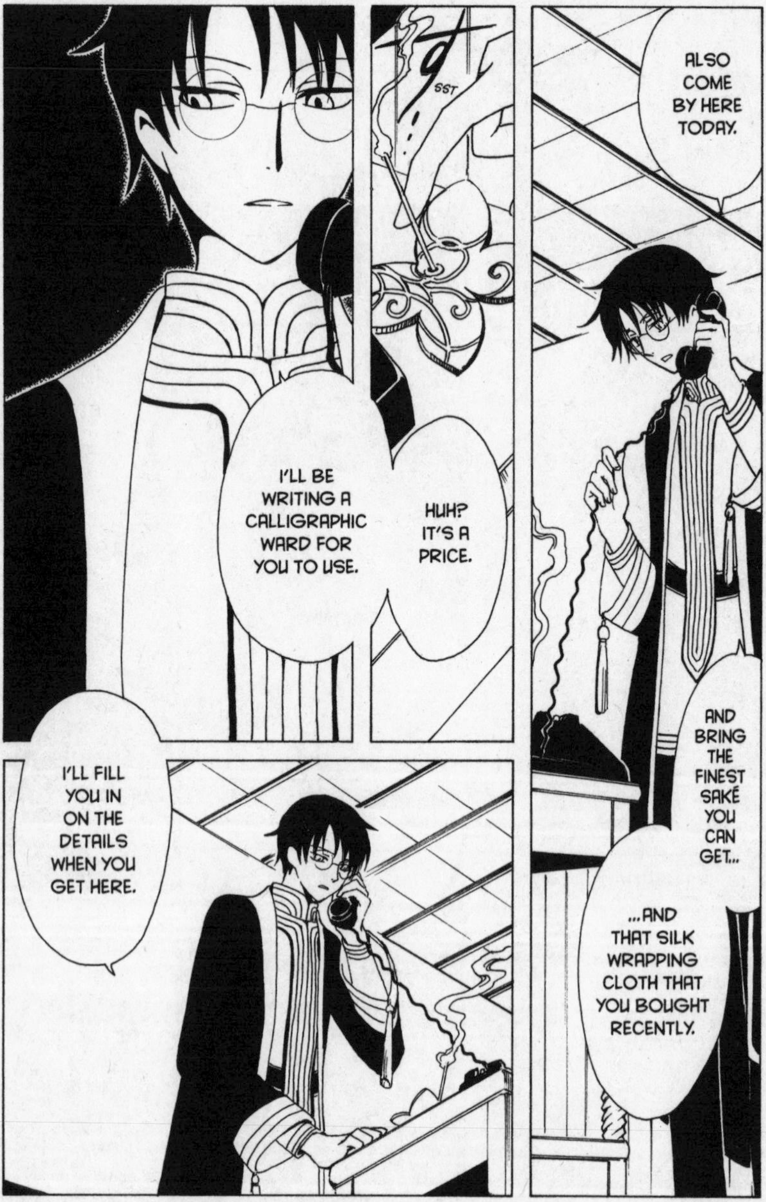
ALSO COME BY HERE TODAY.
AND BRING THE FINEST SAKÉ YOU CAN GET...
...AND THAT SILK WRAPPING CLOTH THAT YOU BOUGHT RECENTLY.
す
SST
HUH? IT'S A PRICE.
I'LL BE WRITING A CALLIGRAPHIC WARD FOR YOU TO USE.
I'LL FILL YOU IN ON THE DETAILS WHEN YOU GET HERE.

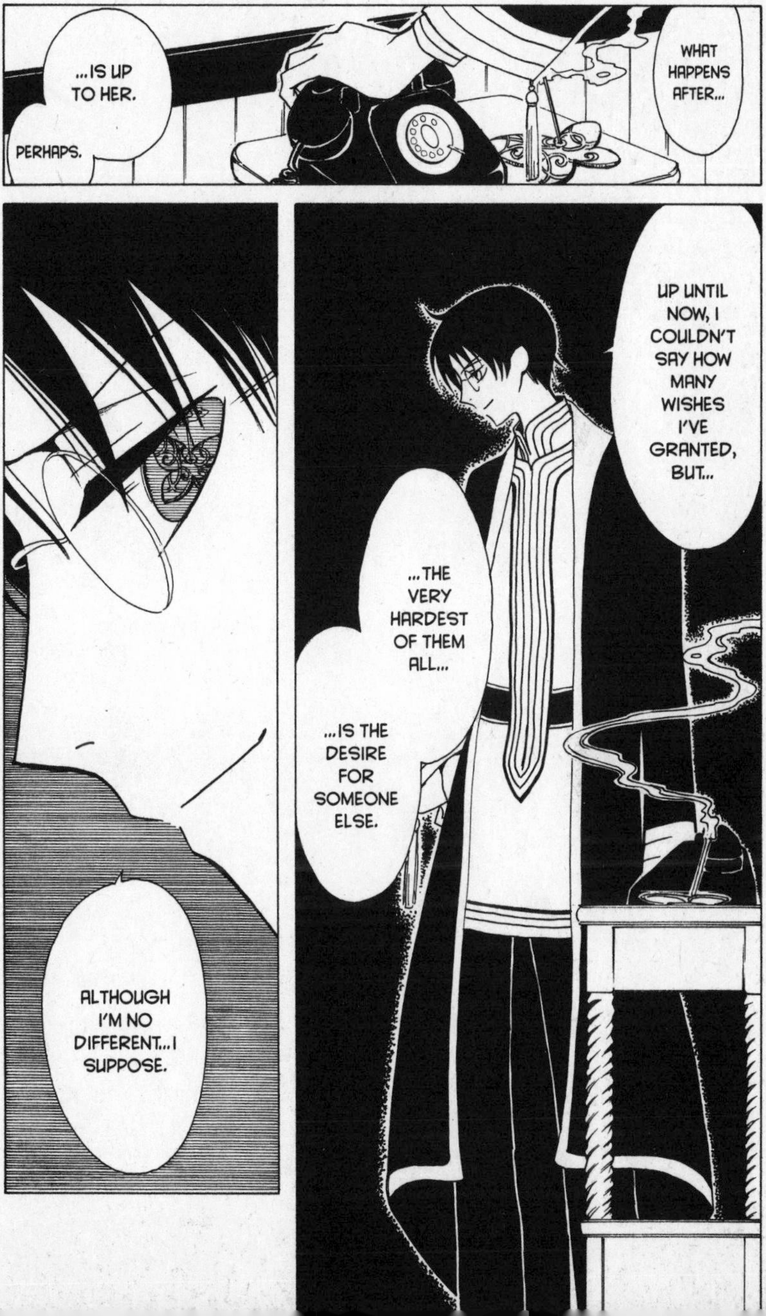
WHAT HAPPENS AFTER...
...IS UP TO HER.
PERHAPS.
UP UNTIL NOW, I COULDN'T SAY HOW MANY WISHES I'VE GRANTED, BUT...
...THE VERY HARDEST OF THEM ALL...
...IS THE DESIRE FOR SOMEONE ELSE.
ALTHOUGH I'M NO DIFFERENT...I SUPPOSE.

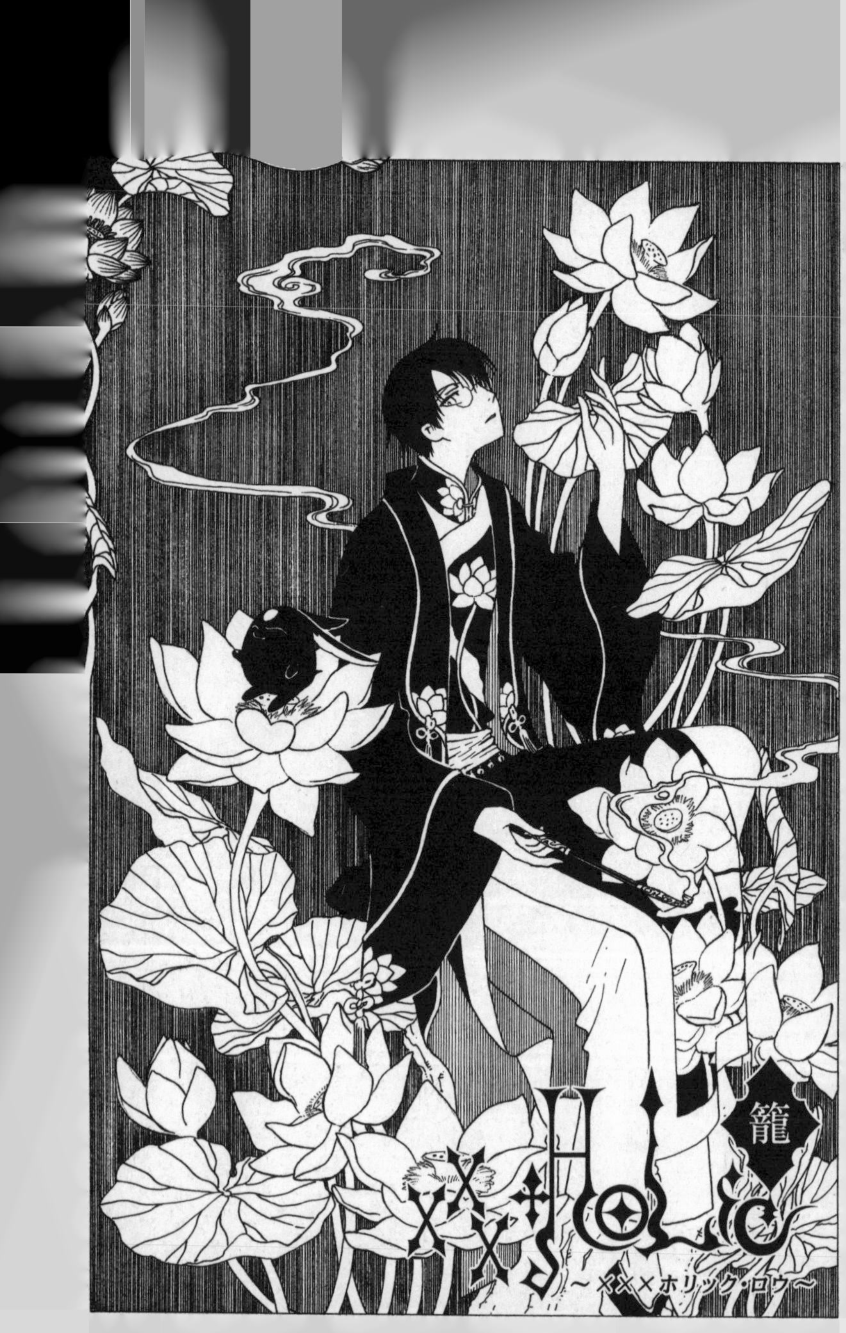
籠
xxxHOLiC
〜×××ホリック・ロウ〜

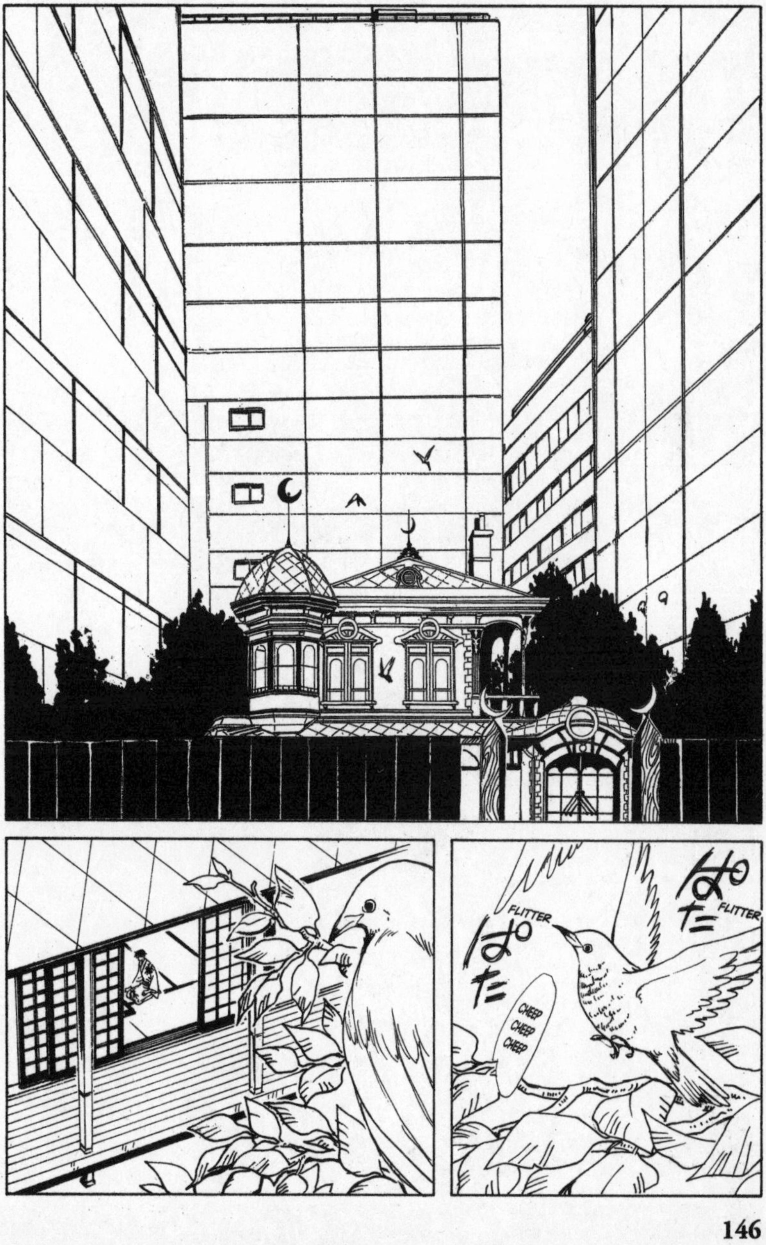

ぱた
FLITTER
ぱた
FLITTER
CHEEP CHEEP CHEEP

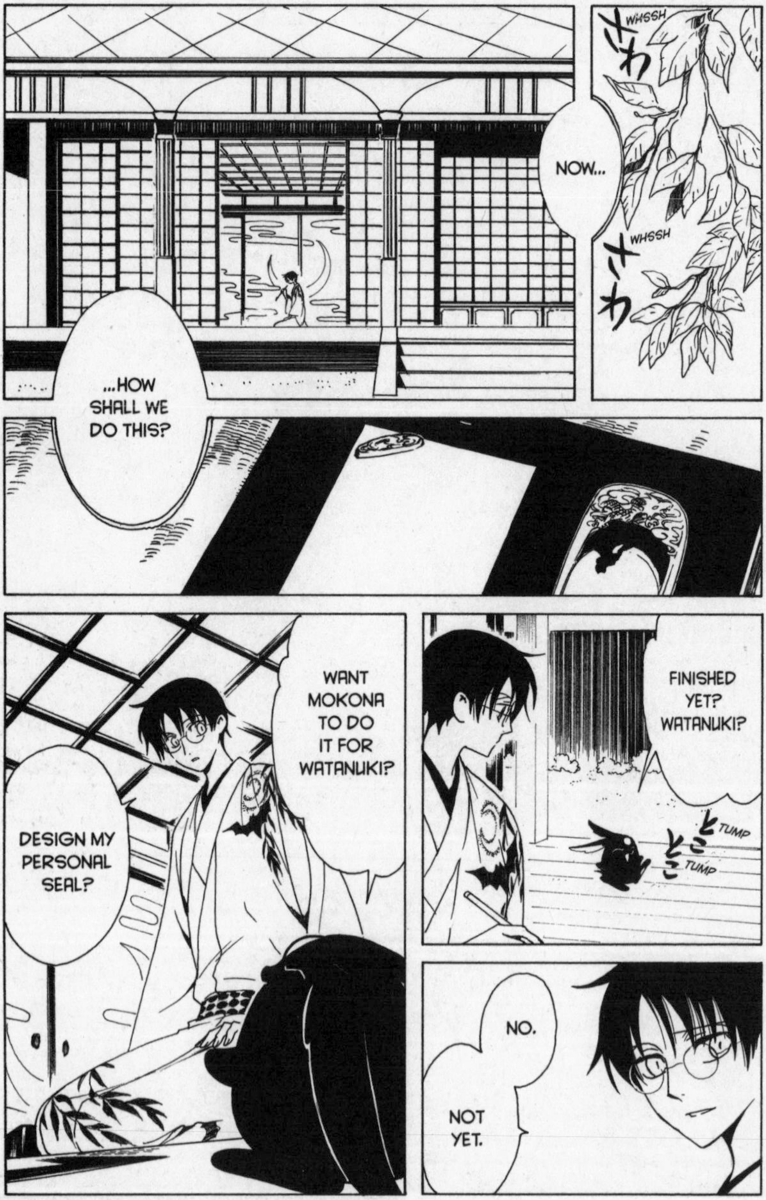
さわ WHSSH
NOW...
さわ WHSSH
...HOW SHALL WE DO THIS?
FINISHED YET? WATANUKI?
とこ TUMP
とこ TUMP
NO.
NOT YET.
WANT MOKONA TO DO IT FOR WATANUKI?
DESIGN MY PERSONAL SEAL?

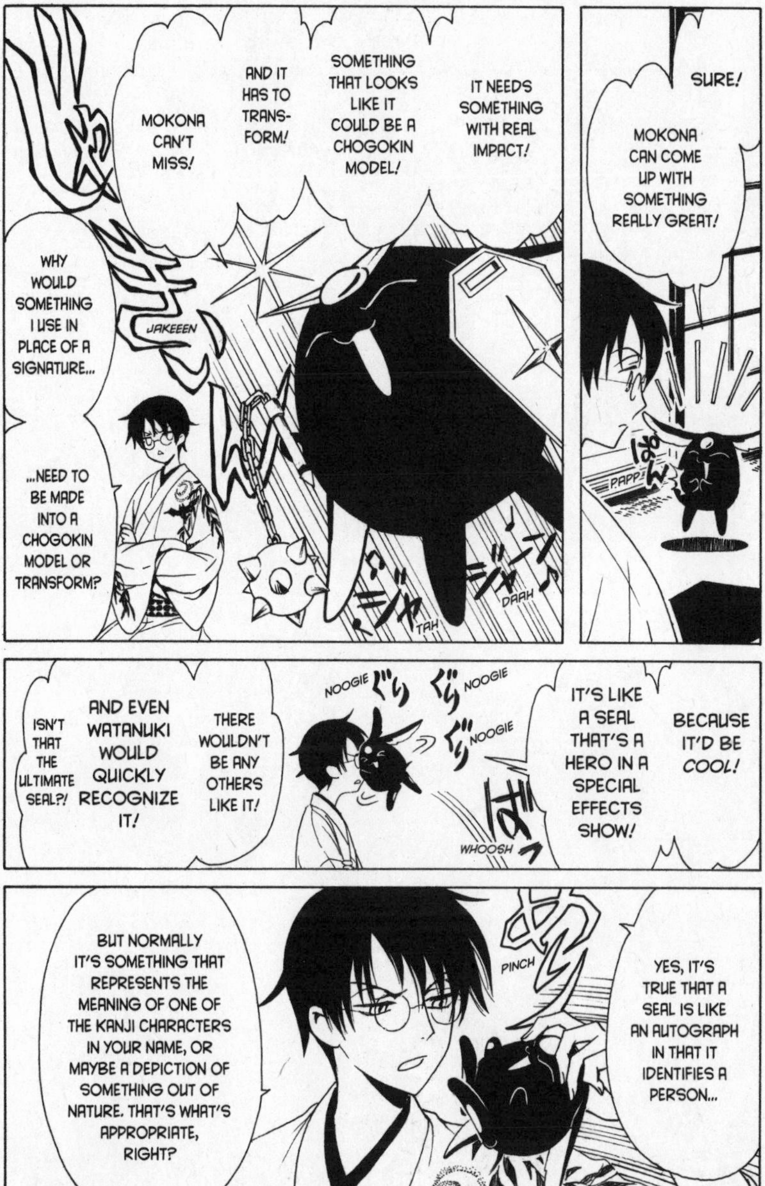
SURE!
MOKONA CAN COME UP WITH SOMETHING REALLY GREAT!
PAPP
IT NEEDS SOMETHING WITH REAL IMPACT!
SOMETHING THAT LOOKS LIKE IT COULD BE A CHOGOKIN MODEL!
AND IT HAS TO TRANS-FORM!
MOKONA CAN'T MISS!
JAKEEEN
DAAH
TAH
WHY WOULD SOMETHING I USE IN PLACE OF A SIGNATURE...
...NEED TO BE MADE INTO A CHOGOKIN MODEL OR TRANSFORM?
BECAUSE IT'D BE COOL!
IT'S LIKE A SEAL THAT'S A HERO IN A SPECIAL EFFECTS SHOW!
WHOOSH
NOOGIE
NOOGIE
NOOGIE
THERE WOULDN'T BE ANY OTHERS LIKE IT!
AND EVEN WATANUKI WOULD QUICKLY RECOGNIZE IT!
ISN'T THAT THE ULTIMATE SEAL?!
YES, IT'S TRUE THAT A SEAL IS LIKE AN AUTOGRAPH IN THAT IT IDENTIFIES A PERSON...
PINCH
BUT NORMALLY IT'S SOMETHING THAT REPRESENTS THE MEANING OF ONE OF THE KANJI CHARACTERS IN YOUR NAME, OR MAYBE A DEPICTION OF SOMETHING OUT OF NATURE. THAT'S WHAT'S APPROPRIATE, RIGHT?

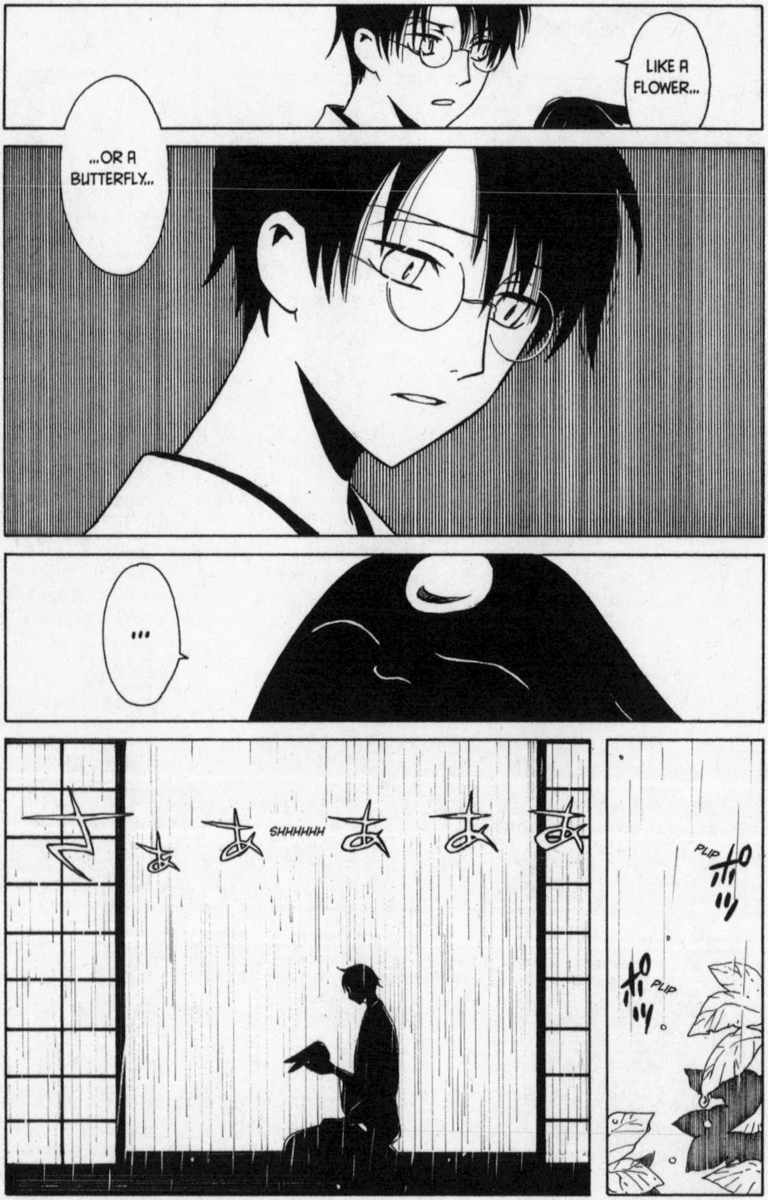
LIKE A FLOWER...
...OR A BUTTERFLY...
...
SHHHHHH
PLIP
PLIP

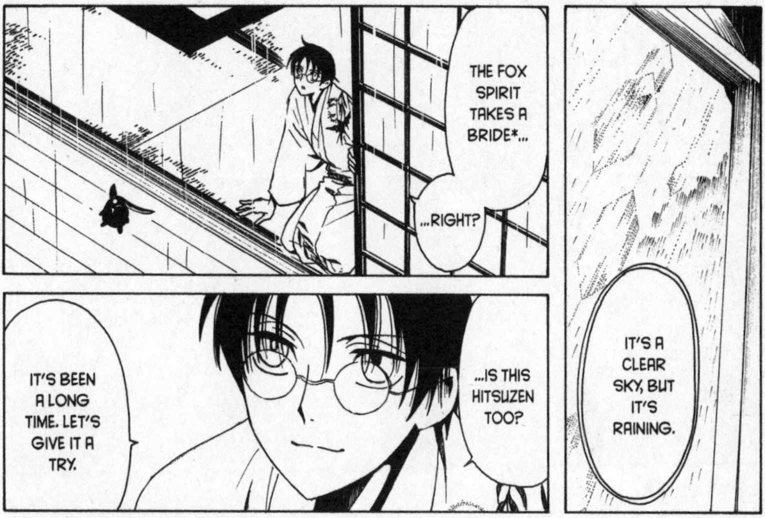
IT'S A CLEAR SKY, BUT IT'S RAINING.
THE FOX SPIRIT TAKES A BRIDE*...
...RIGHT?
...IS THIS HITSUZEN TOO?
IT'S BEEN A LONG TIME. LET'S GIVE IT A TRY.

*THE JAPANESE PHRASE FOR A SUNSHOWER.

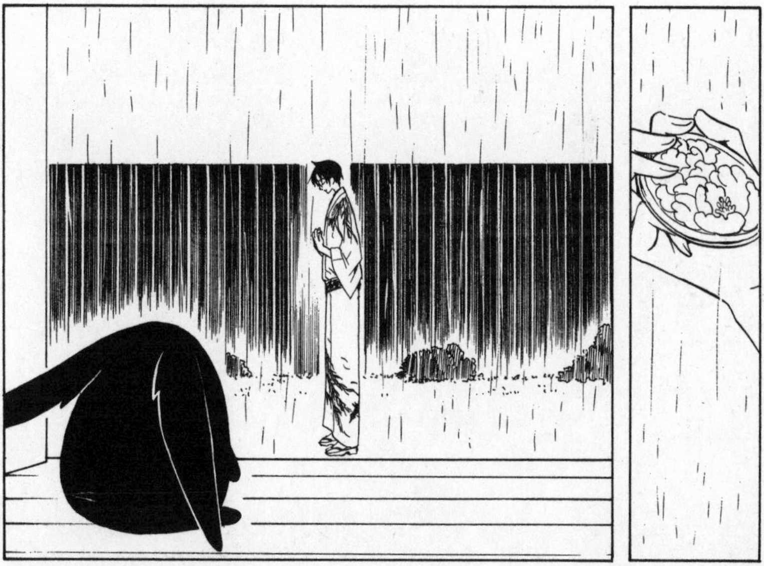

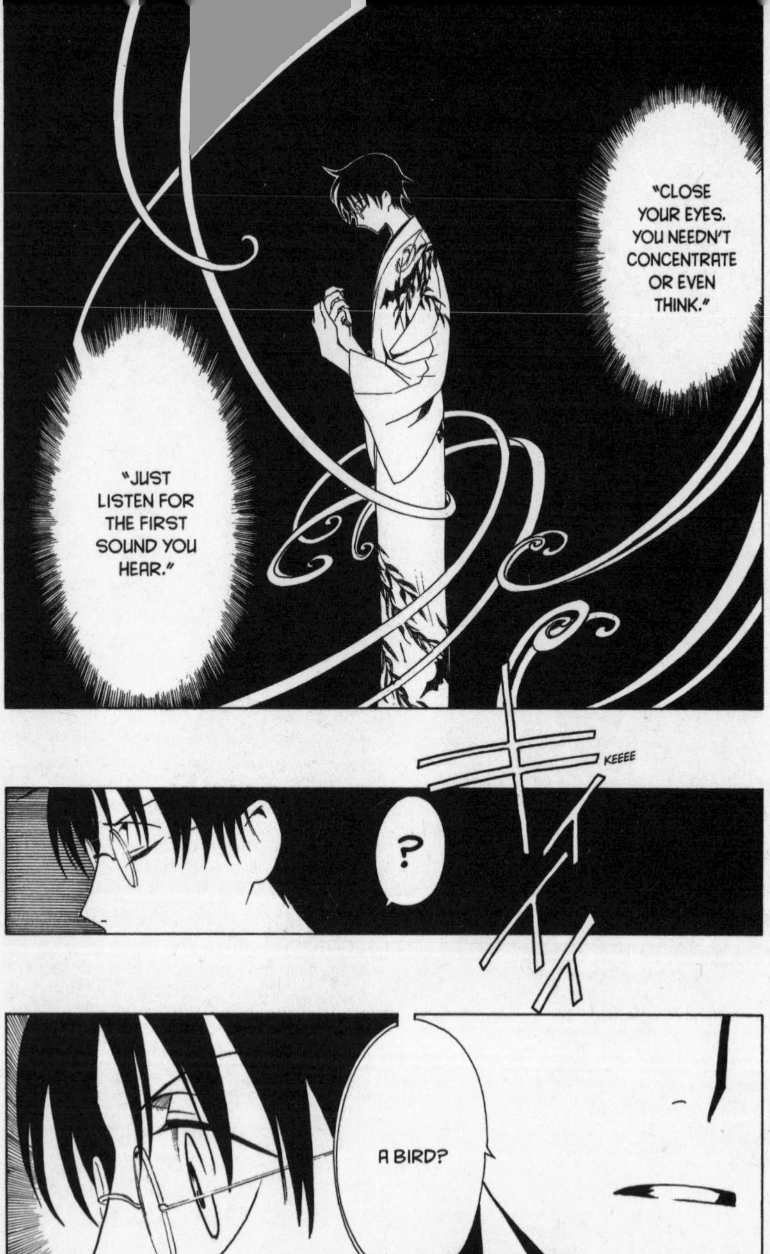
"CLOSE YOUR EYES. YOU NEEDN'T CONCENTRATE OR EVEN THINK."
"JUST LISTEN FOR THE FIRST SOUND YOU HEAR."
KEEEE
?
A BIRD?

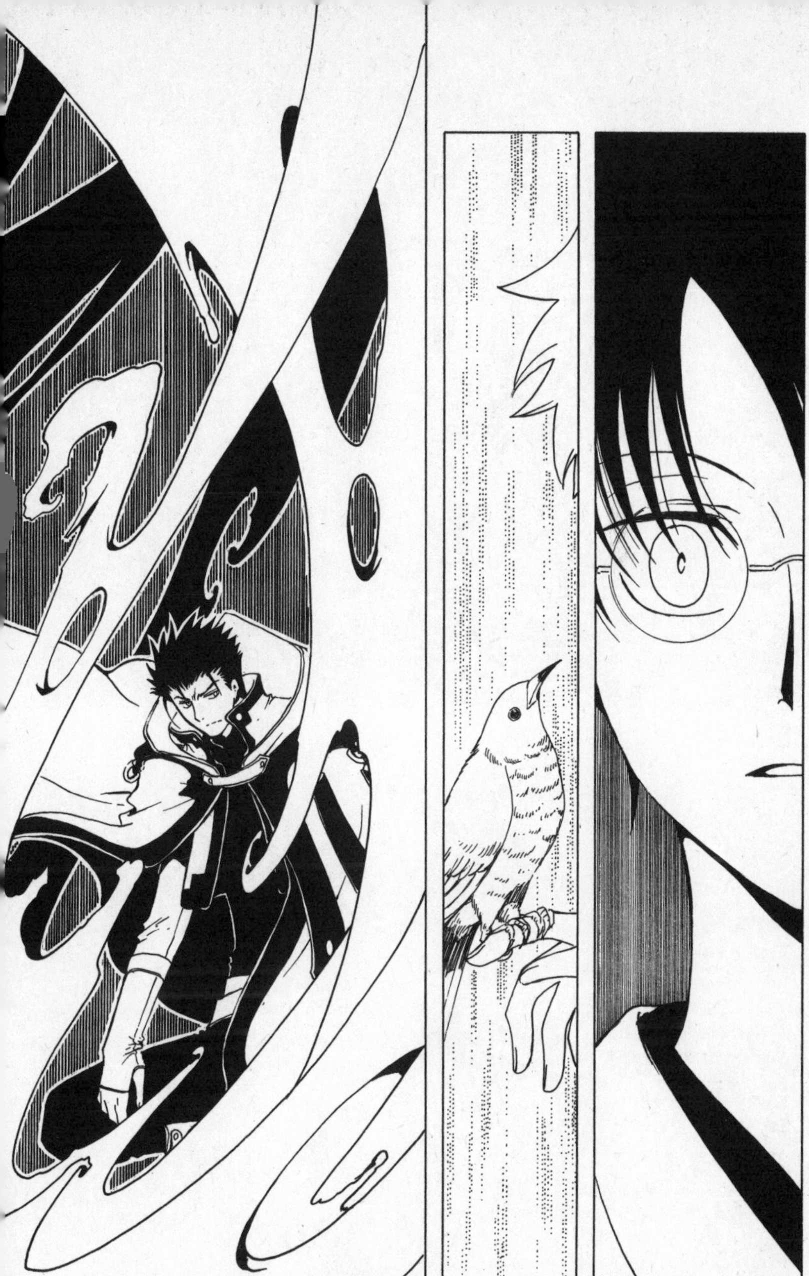

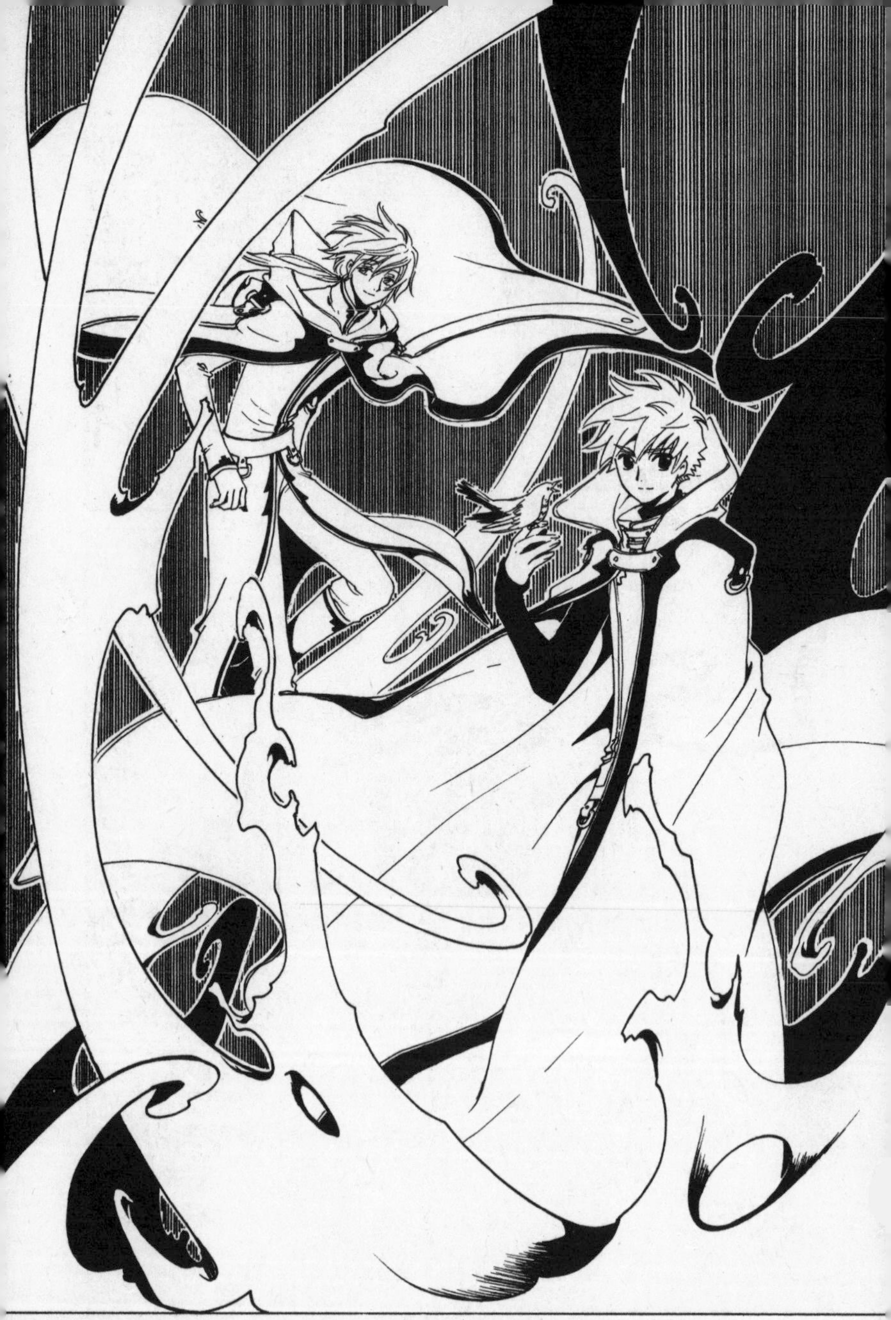

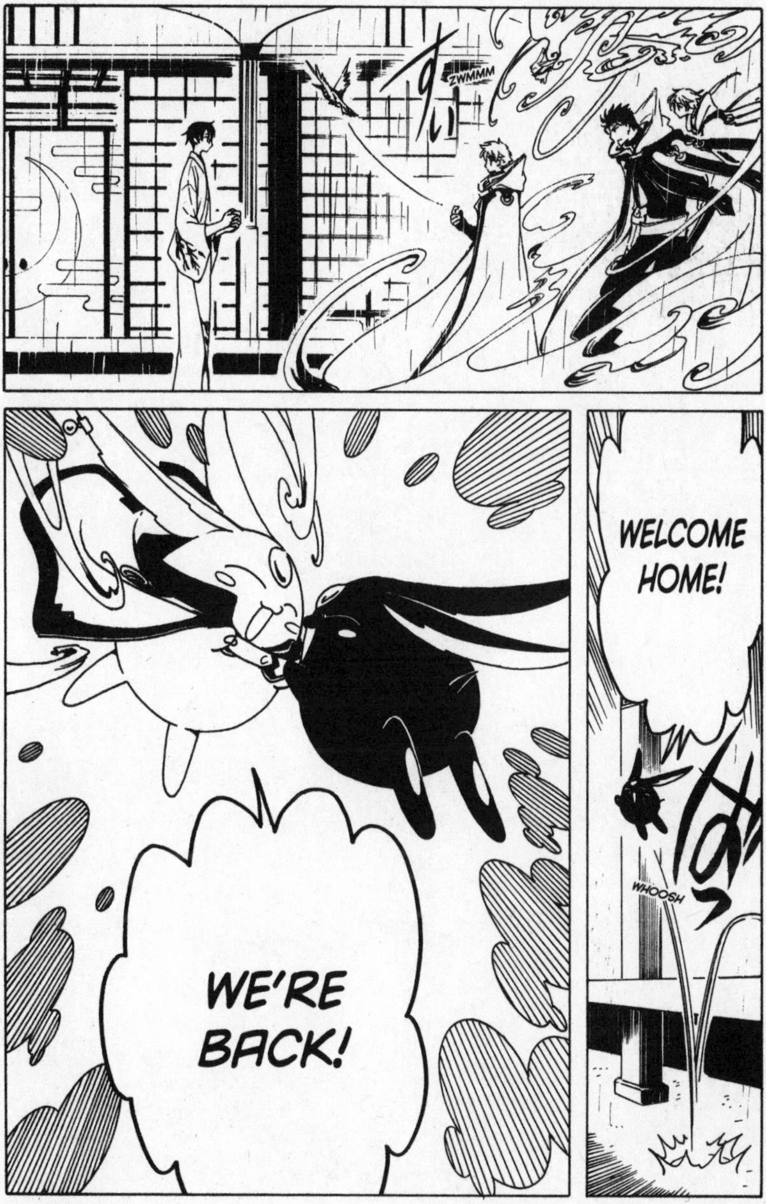
ZWMMM
WELCOME HOME!
WHOOSH
WE'RE BACK!

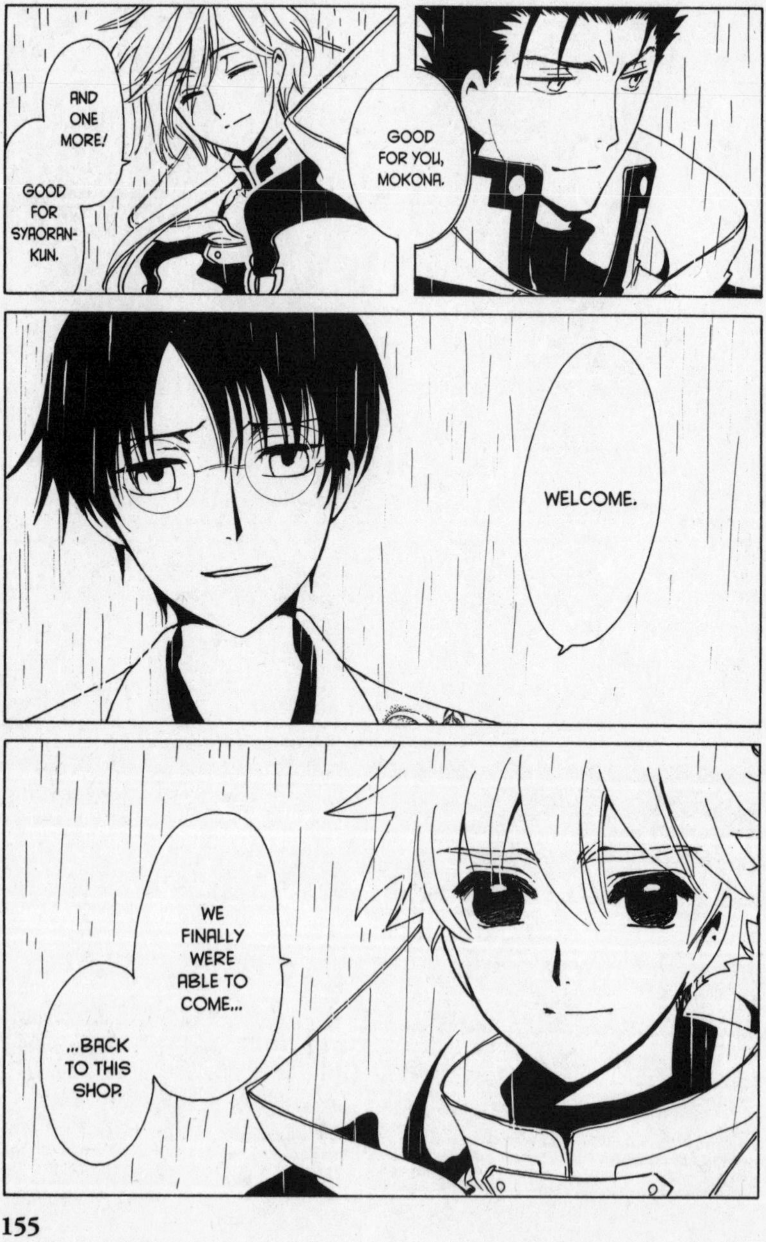
GOOD FOR YOU, MOKONA.
AND ONE MORE!
GOOD FOR SYAORAN-KUN.
WELCOME.
WE FINALLY WERE ABLE TO COME...
...BACK TO THIS SHOP.

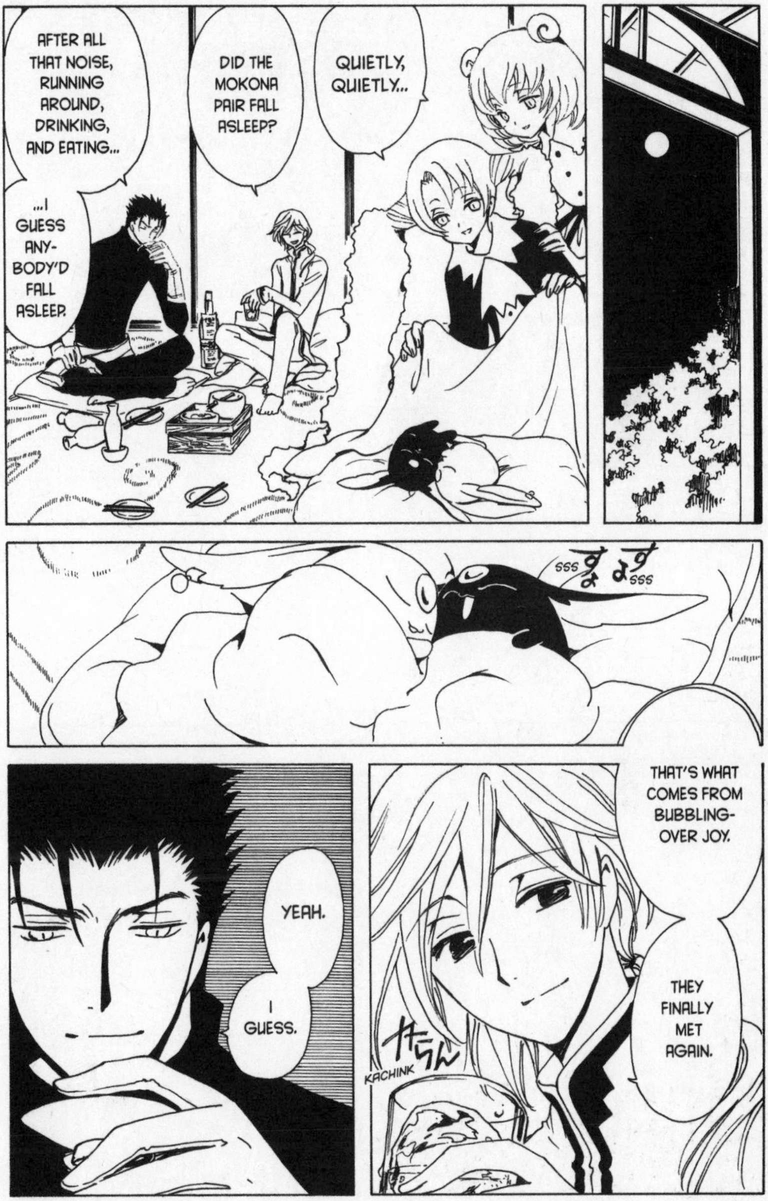
QUIETLY, QUIETLY...
DID THE MOKONA PAIR FALL ASLEEP?
AFTER ALL THAT NOISE, RUNNING AROUND, DRINKING, AND EATING...
...I GUESS ANYBODY'D FALL ASLEEP.
SSS
SSS
THAT'S WHAT COMES FROM BUBBLING-OVER JOY.
THEY FINALLY MET AGAIN.
KACHINK
YEAH.
I GUESS.

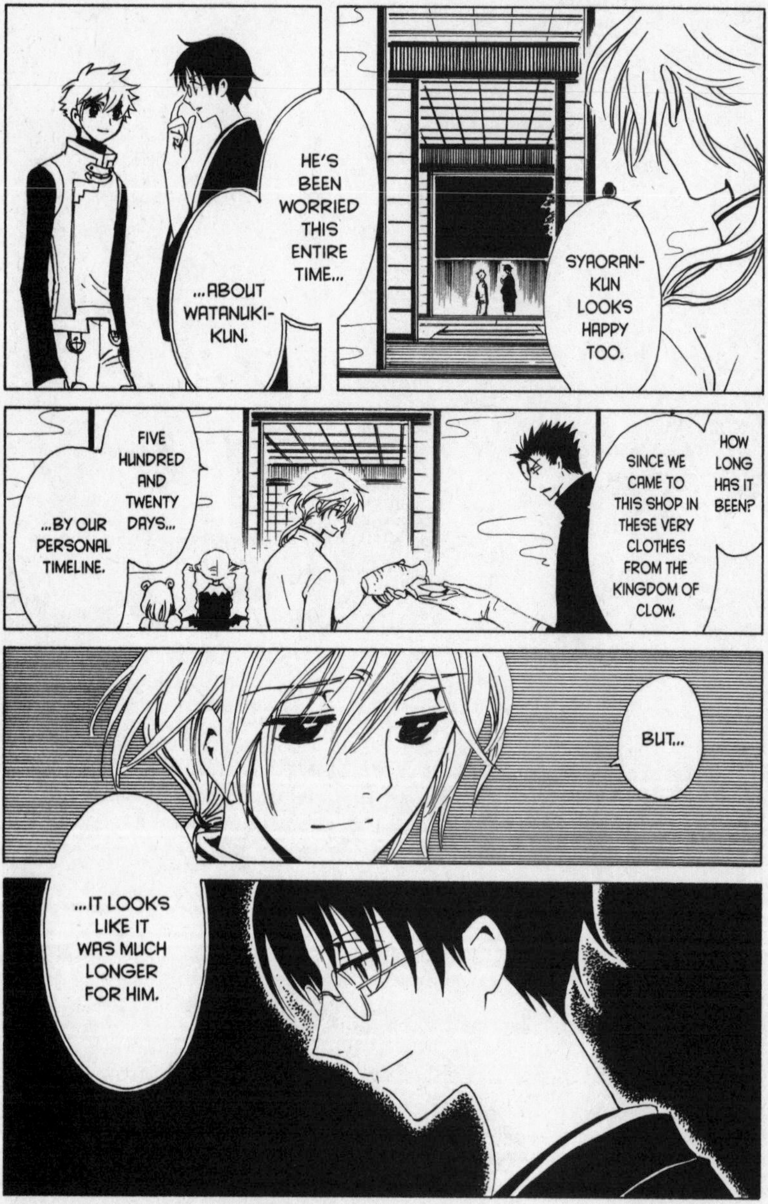
SYAORAN-KUN LOOKS HAPPY TOO.
HE'S BEEN WORRIED THIS ENTIRE TIME...
...ABOUT WATANUKI-KUN.
HOW LONG HAS IT BEEN?
SINCE WE CAME TO THIS SHOP IN THESE VERY CLOTHES FROM THE KINGDOM OF CLOW.
FIVE HUNDRED AND TWENTY DAYS...
...BY OUR PERSONAL TIMELINE.
BUT...
...IT LOOKS LIKE IT WAS MUCH LONGER FOR HIM.

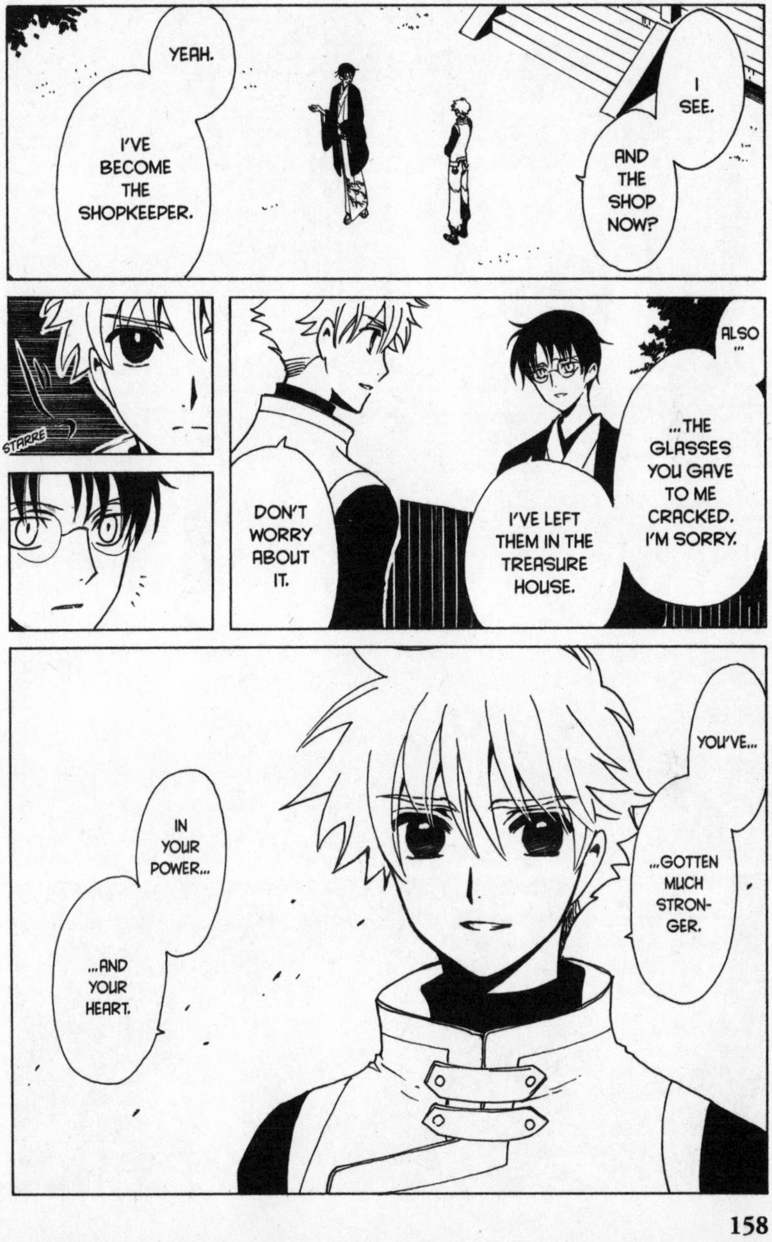
I SEE.
AND THE SHOP NOW?
YEAH.
I'VE BECOME THE SHOPKEEPER.
ALSO...
...THE GLASSES YOU GAVE TO ME CRACKED. I'M SORRY.
I'VE LEFT THEM IN THE TREASURE HOUSE.
DON'T WORRY ABOUT IT.
STARRE
YOU'VE...
...GOTTEN MUCH STRONGER.
IN YOUR POWER...
...AND YOUR HEART.

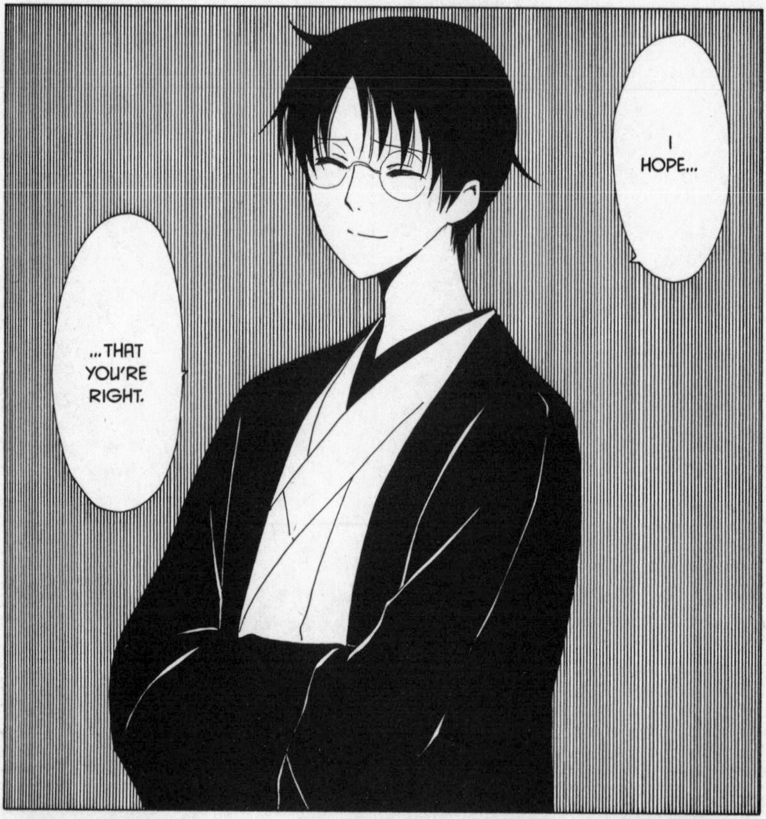
I HOPE...
...THAT YOU'RE RIGHT.

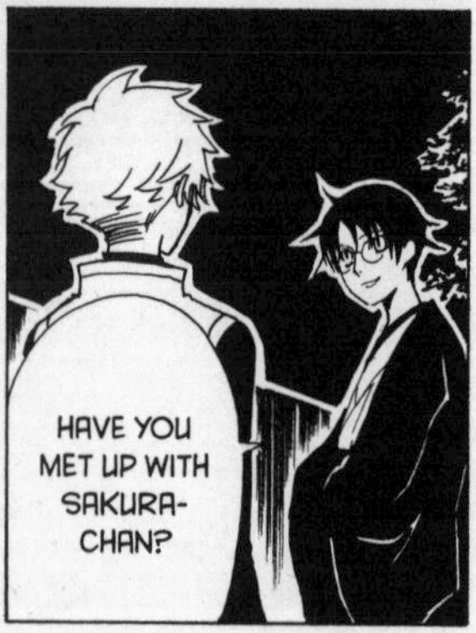
HAVE YOU MET UP WITH SAKURA-CHAN?

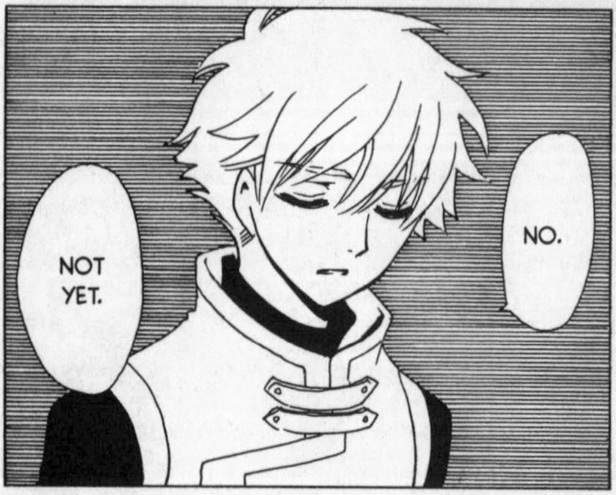
NO.
NOT YET.

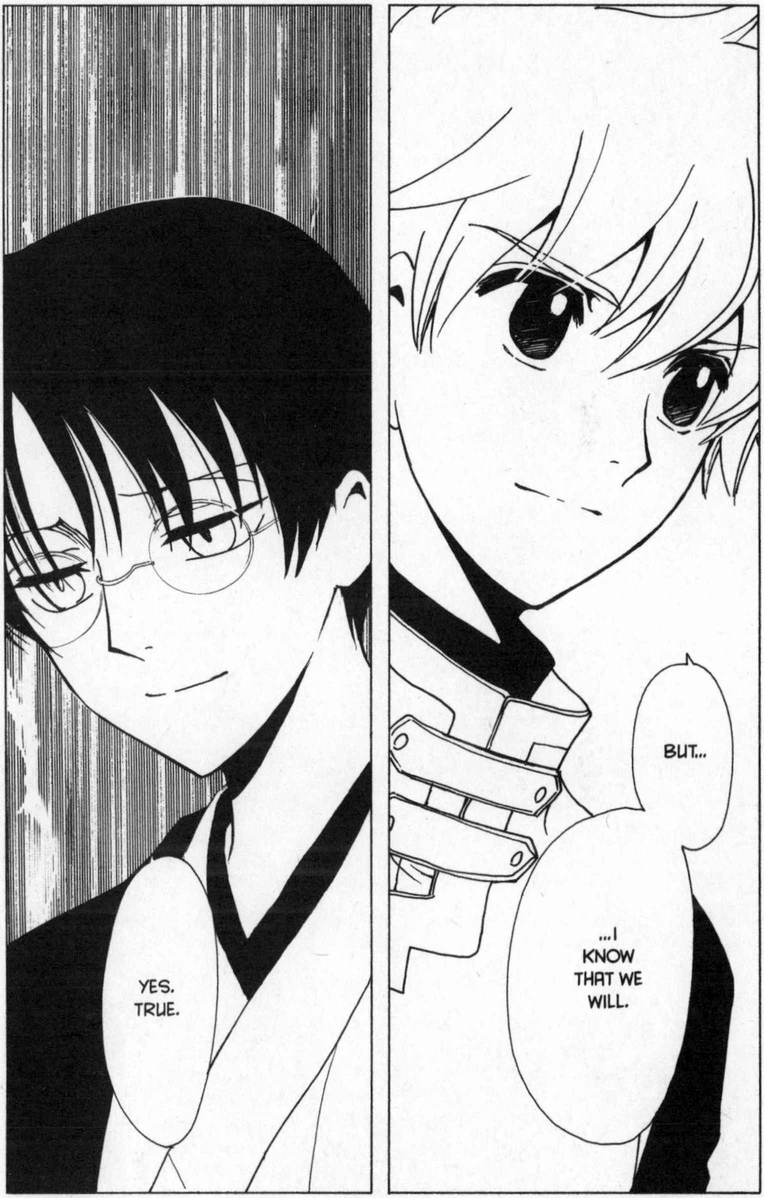
BUT...
...I KNOW THAT WE WILL.
YES. TRUE.

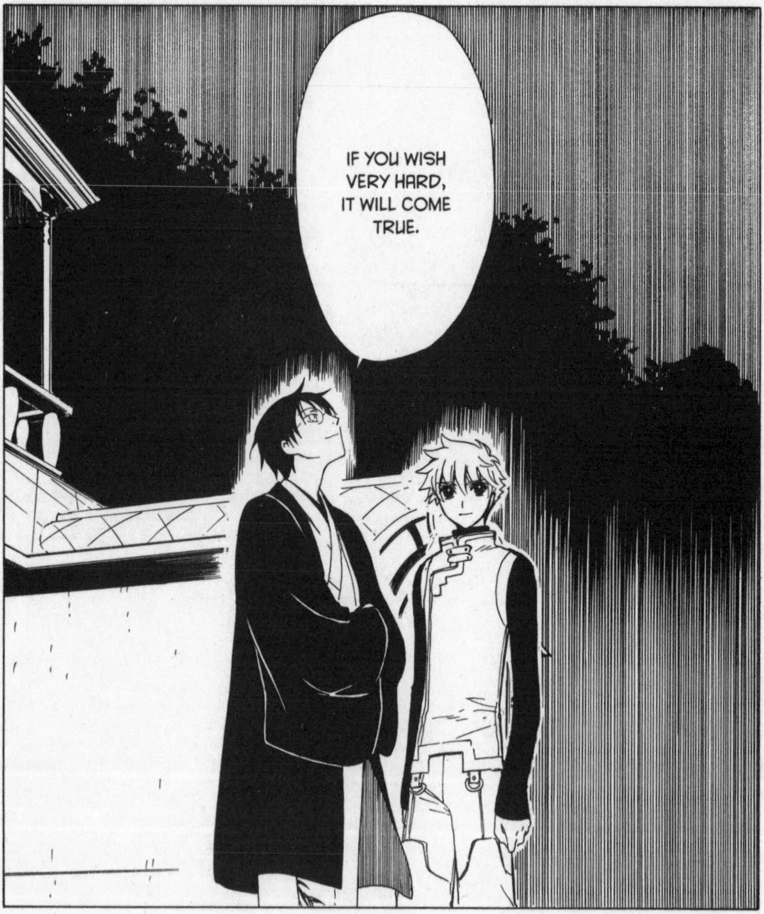
IF YOU WISH VERY HARD, IT WILL COME TRUE.

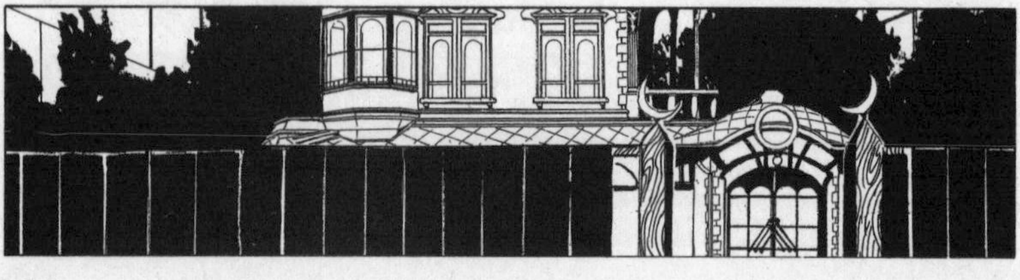

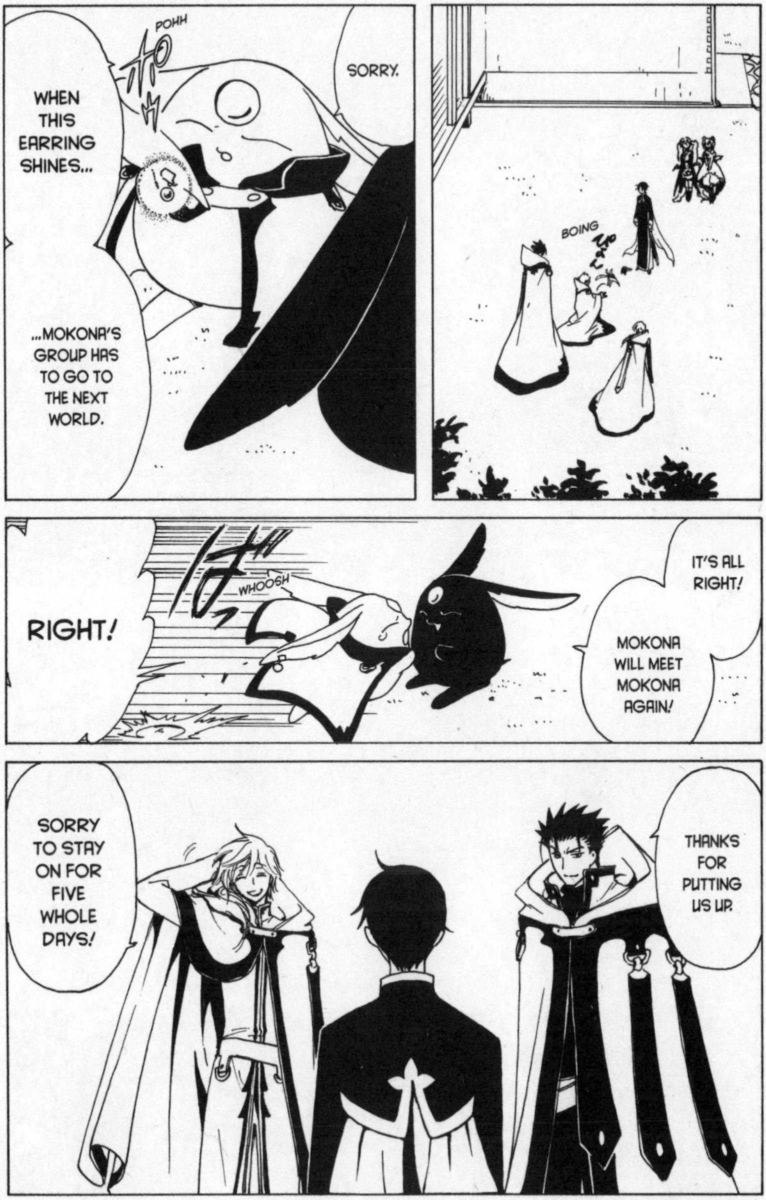
BOING
SORRY.
POHH
WHEN THIS EARRING SHINES...
...MOKONA'S GROUP HAS TO GO TO THE NEXT WORLD.
IT'S ALL RIGHT!
MOKONA WILL MEET MOKONA AGAIN!
WHOOSH
RIGHT!
THANKS FOR PUTTING US UP.
SORRY TO STAY ON FOR FIVE WHOLE DAYS!

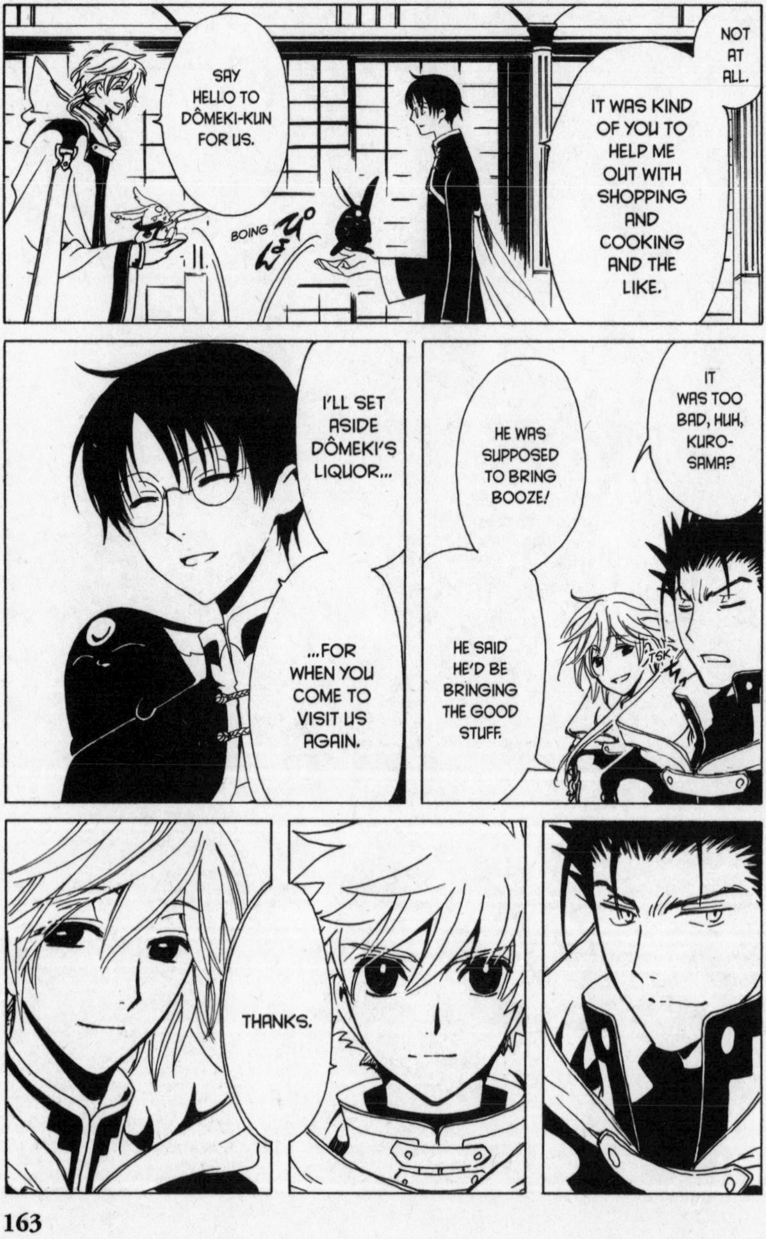
NOT AT ALL.
IT WAS KIND OF YOU TO HELP ME OUT WITH SHOPPING AND COOKING AND THE LIKE.
SAY HELLO TO DÔMEKI-KUN FOR US.
BOING
IT WAS TOO BAD, HUH, KURO-SAMA?
HE WAS SUPPOSED TO BRING BOOZE!
TSK
HE SAID HE'D BE BRINGING THE GOOD STUFF.
I'LL SET ASIDE DÔMEKI'S LIQUOR...
...FOR WHEN YOU COME TO VISIT US AGAIN.
THANKS.

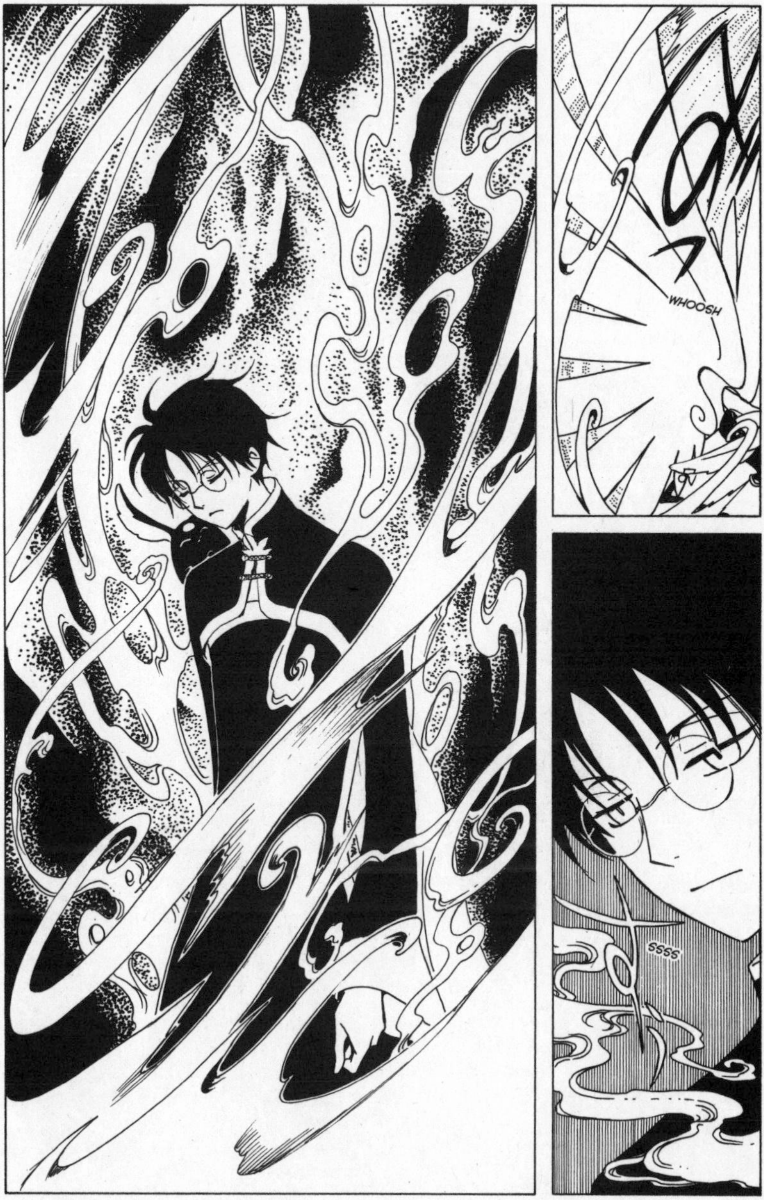
WHOOSH
SSSS

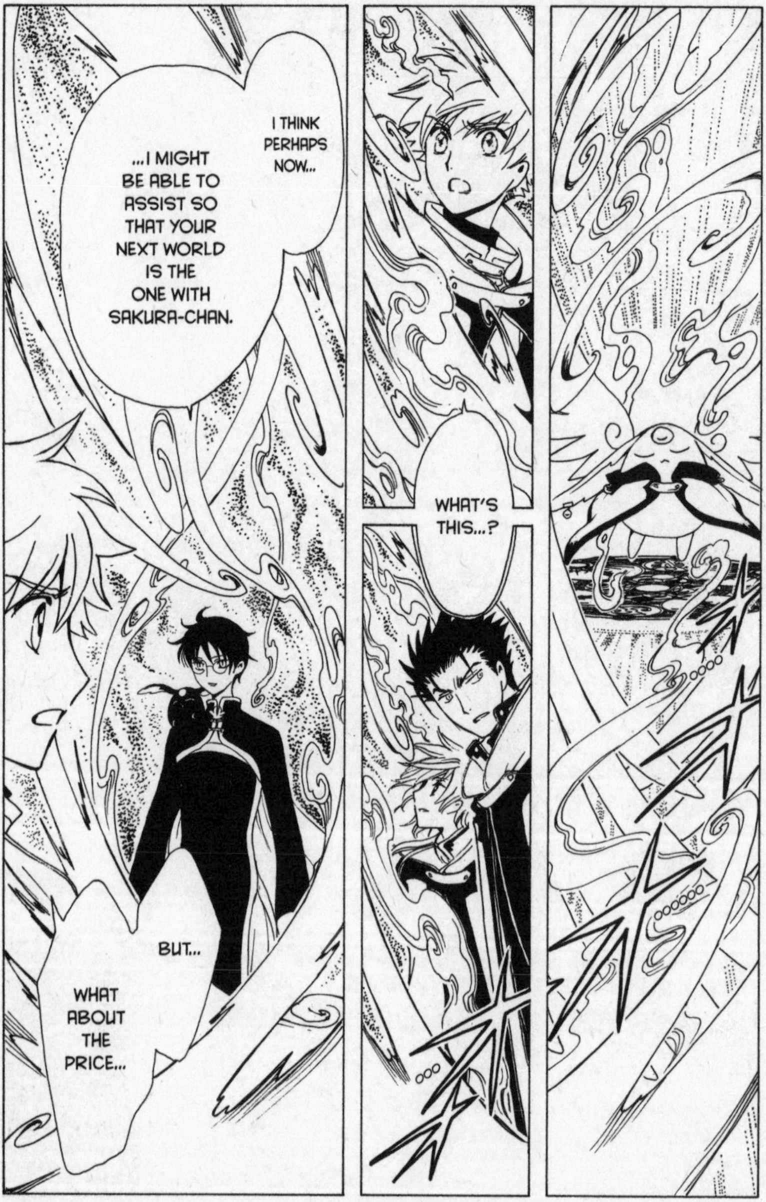
WHAT'S THIS...?
I THINK PERHAPS NOW...
...I MIGHT BE ABLE TO ASSIST SO THAT YOUR NEXT WORLD IS THE ONE WITH SAKURA-CHAN.
BUT...
WHAT ABOUT THE PRICE...

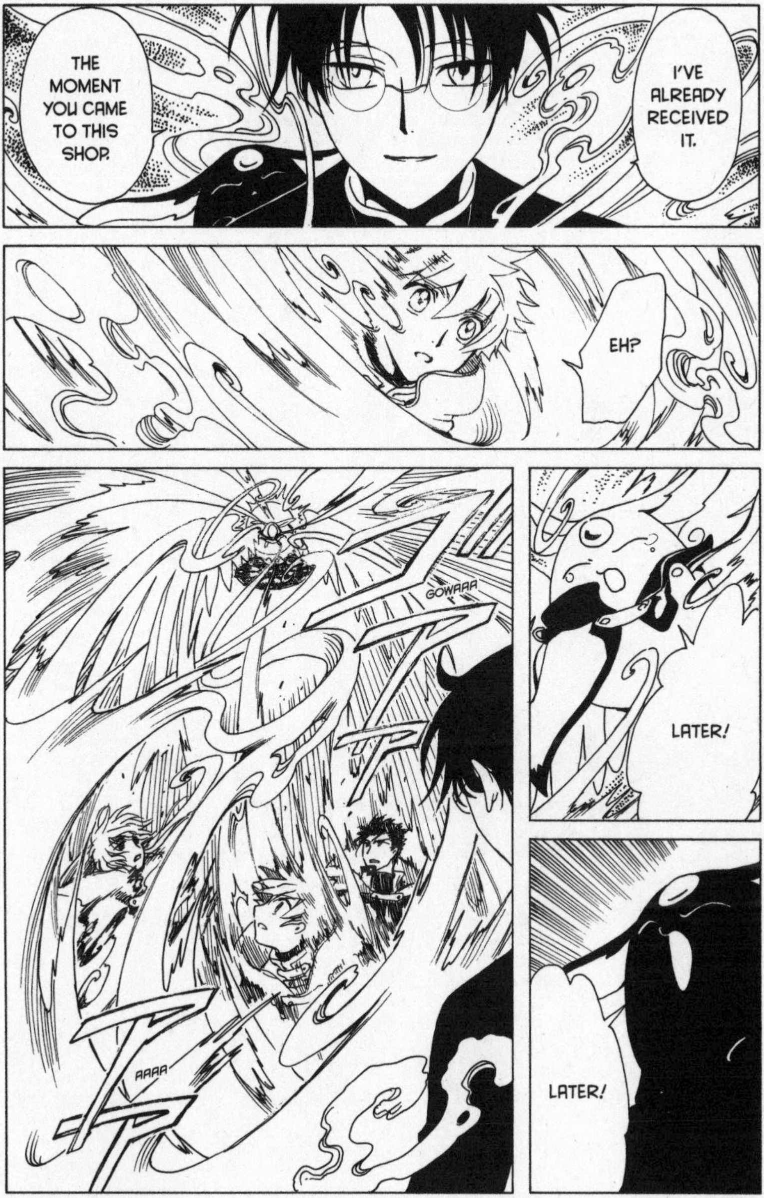
I'VE ALREADY RECEIVED IT.
THE MOMENT YOU CAME TO THIS SHOP.
EH?
LATER!
LATER!
GOWAAA
AAAA

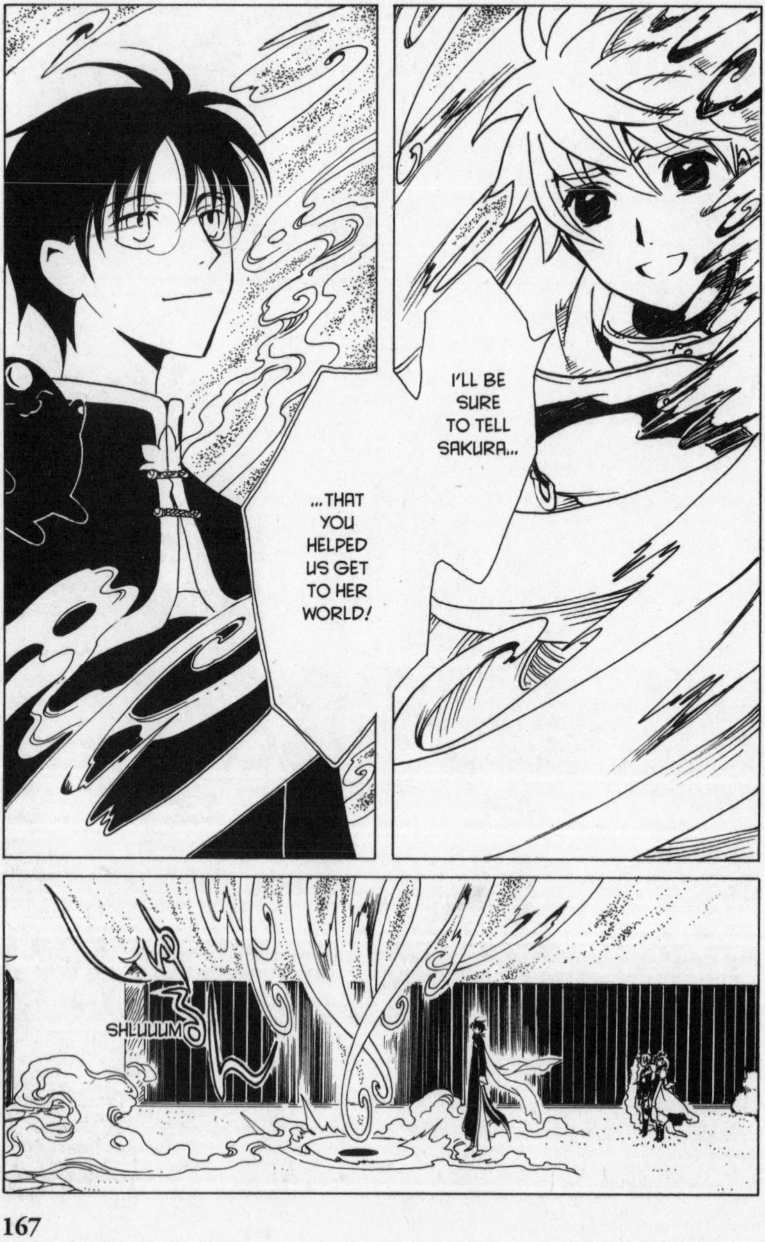
I'LL BE SURE TO TELL SAKURA...
...THAT YOU HELPED US GET TO HER WORLD!
SHLUUUM

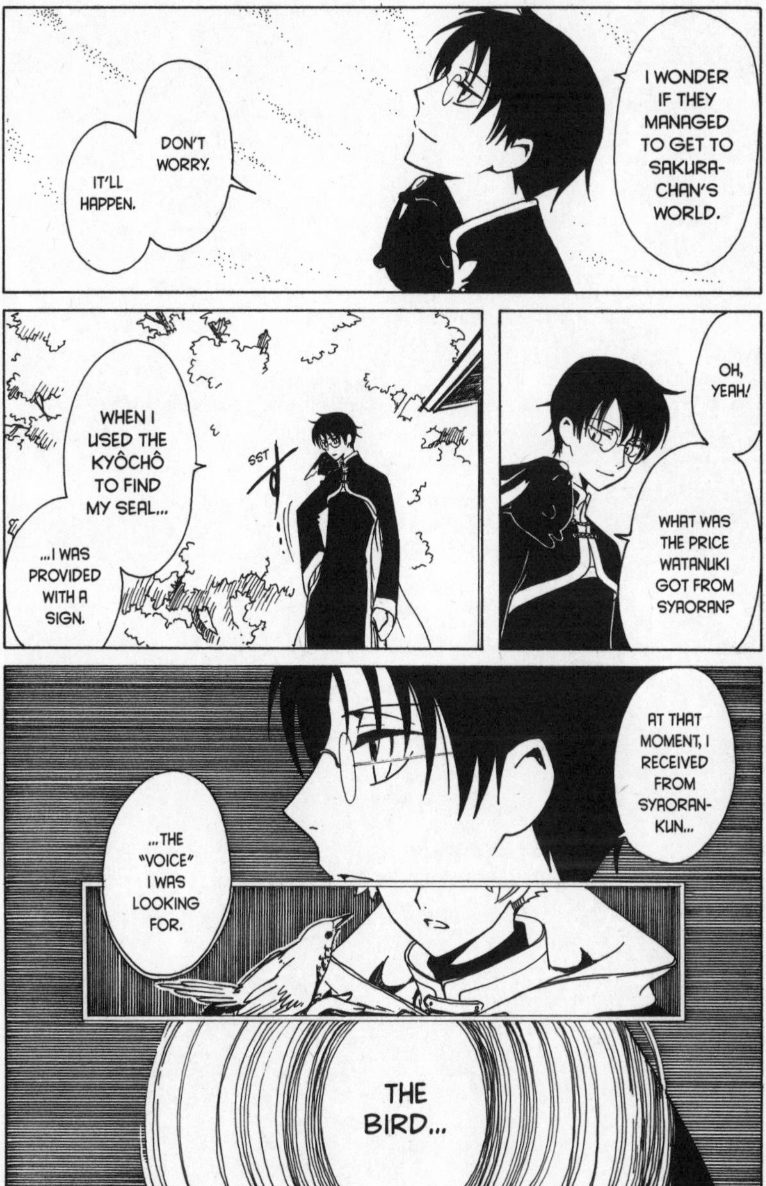
I WONDER IF THEY MANAGED TO GET TO SAKURA-CHAN'S WORLD.
DON'T WORRY. IT'LL HAPPEN.
OH, YEAH!
WHAT WAS THE PRICE WATANUKI GOT FROM SYAORAN?
SST
WHEN I USED THE KYÔCHÔ TO FIND MY SEAL...
...I WAS PROVIDED WITH A SIGN.
AT THAT MOMENT, I RECEIVED FROM SYAORAN-KUN...
...THE "VOICE" I WAS LOOKING FOR.
THE BIRD...

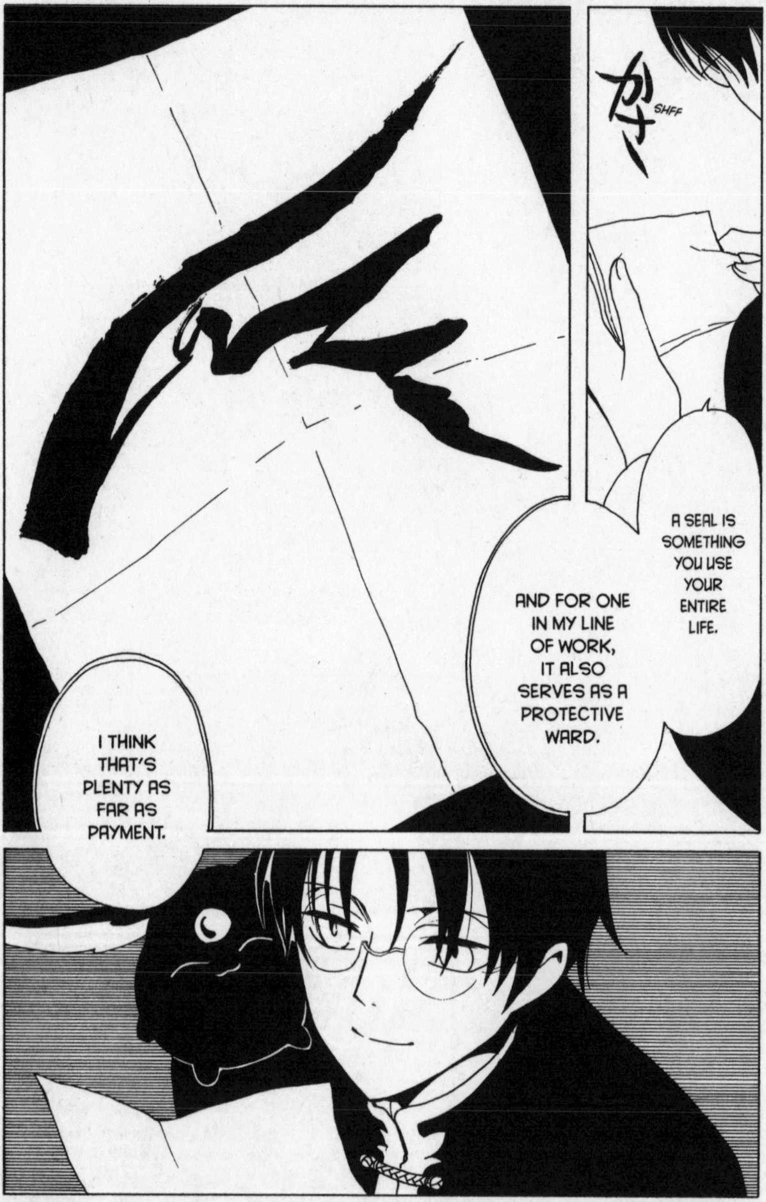
SHFF
A SEAL IS SOMETHING YOU USE YOUR ENTIRE LIFE.
AND FOR ONE IN MY LINE OF WORK, IT ALSO SERVES AS A PROTECTIVE WARD.
I THINK THAT'S PLENTY AS FAR AS PAYMENT.

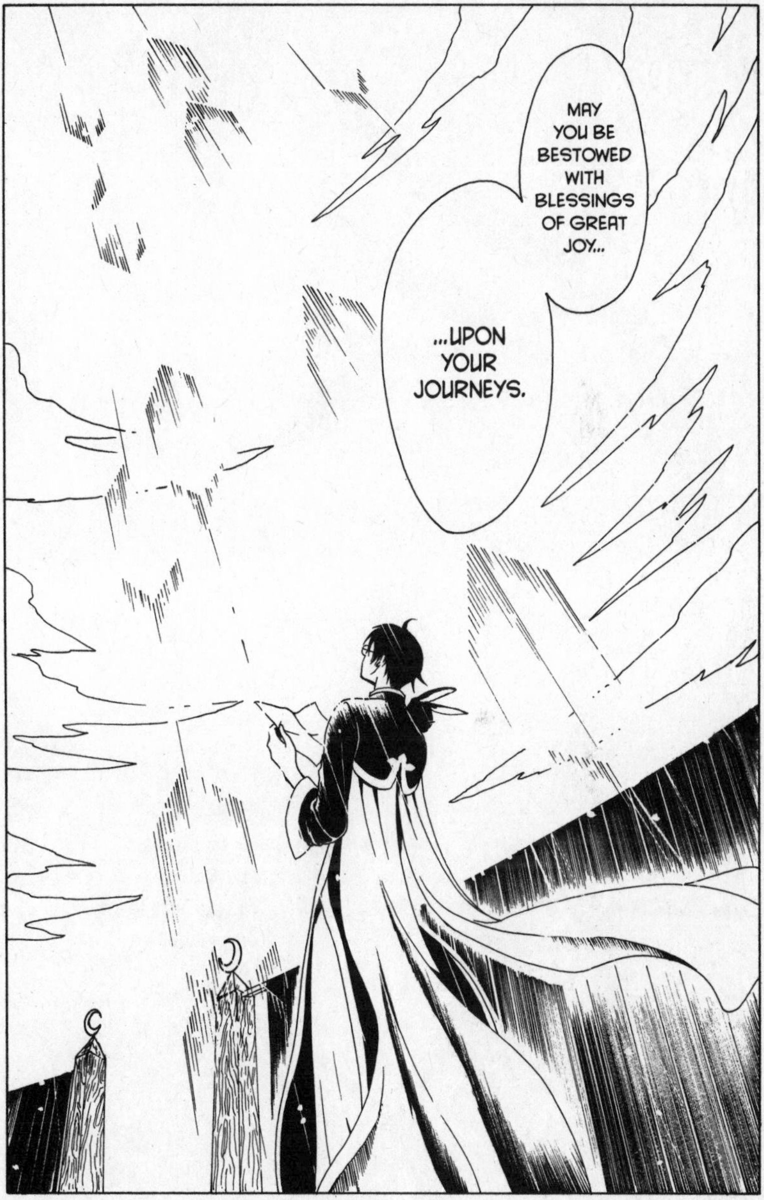
MAY YOU BE BESTOWED WITH BLESSINGS OF GREAT JOY...
...UPON YOUR JOURNEYS.

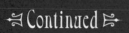
Continued

SO FOR NOW, CROSS THE BRIDGE AND WAIT...

Translation Notes

Japanese is a tricky language for most Westerners, and translation is often more art than science. For your edification and reading pleasure, here are notes on some of the places where we could have gone in a different direction or where a Japanese cultural reference is used.

Chapter titles, the kanji for Rô

The kanji Rô in this incarnation of xxxHOLiC can also be pronounced *kago*, meaning a cage or basket, an enclosed area which prevents escape.

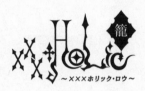

Page 6, *Hakusai*

Hakusai, also called Chinese cabbage, is a leafy vegetable that is often used in dishes such as soups, nabe, and other hot foods. It is usually planted in the autumn and harvested during the onset of winter.

Page 8, Forgive my poor performance

The standard phrase at the end of the meal, *gochisô-sama deshita* means, "It was a feast." But it is unseemly for a host to compliment himself, so a standard response is *osomatsu-sama*, which means, "please forgive my shoddy work."

ぺこり
BOW
FORGIVE MY POOR PERFOR-MANCE.

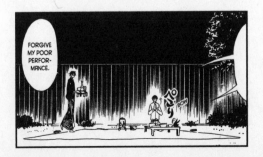

Page 8, *Junmai, Ginjô*

The better saké brewers start with rice which has been "polished" (milled) to remove the outer layers of the grain. The higher the percentage that is polished away, the higher quality the saké. Junmai polishes away 30 percent of the rice grain. Ginjô polishes away 40 percent.

Page 9, *Daiginjô* (saké)

Daiginjô uses rice that has been polished to 50 percent of its size and is considered one of the highest grades of saké available.

Page 16, *Umeboshi*

Umeboshi (literally, "dried ume fruit") is a pickled fruit that is a relative of the apricot (despite commonly being called a pickled plum). See more on this in the notes in Volume 15.

Page 19, *Ofukuwake*

Ofukuwake is the sharing with others of something given to you, sharing one's own bounty with others. Although the concept is common in Japan, the word itself is only rarely used.

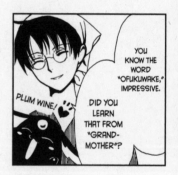

PLUM WINE!

YOU KNOW THE WORD "OFUKUWAKE," IMPRESSIVE.

DID YOU LEARN THAT FROM "GRAND-MOTHER"?

Page 25, Demon bride

As described in the notes for Volume 17, a "demon bride" is an overbearing wife, as made popular in a blog-cum-TV drama, Oniyome-Nikki (Demon Bride Diary).

Page 28, Driver's license

In the United States, a driver's license obtained in one's teen years is almost considered a rite of passage, but in Japan with its readily available, safe public transportation and high cost of driver's training, many go their whole lives without getting a driver's license.

Page 30, *Isshôbin*

As mentioned in the notes of Volume 15, the *isshôbin* is a huge 1.8-liter bottle of saké.

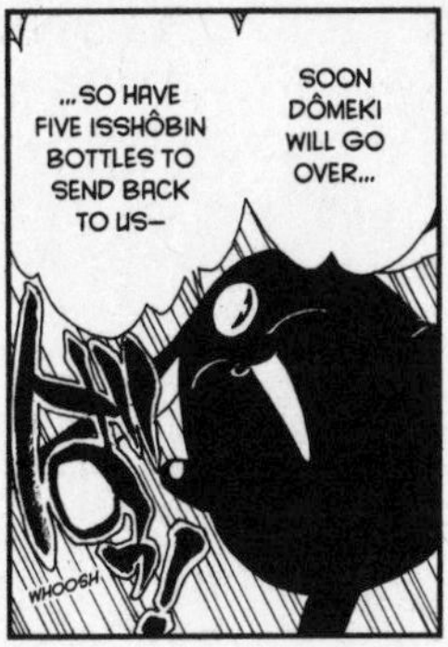
SOON DÔMEKI WILL GO OVER...
...SO HAVE FIVE ISSHÔBIN BOTTLES TO SEND BACK TO US—
WHOOSH

Page 60, *Miki*

Miki or *omiki* is an offering of saké to the gods in the Shinto religion as a part of the food offerings called *shinsen*. Generally, the *miki* is offered to the shrine or as a part of the ceremony, and when the ceremony is complete, the saké is poured and split among the participants. In a sense it is like drinking with the god.

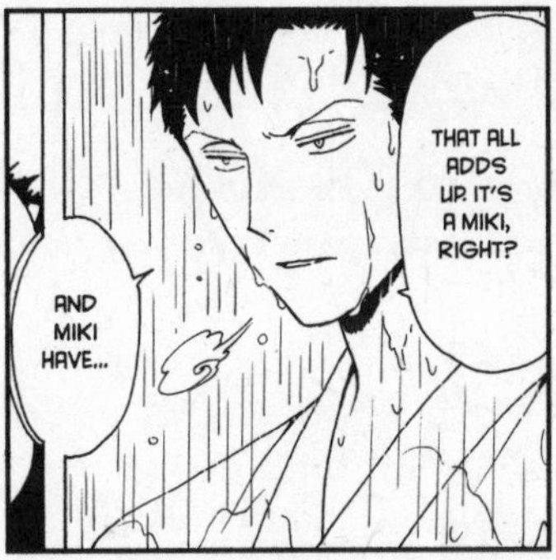
THAT ALL ADDS UP. IT'S A MIKI, RIGHT?
AND MIKI HAVE...

Page 92, Pipe tray

A traditional pipe tray was a box with a metal portion (sometimes stone) for ashes, a place to rest the pipe, a handle, and a drawer for keeping extra tobacco and other accessories.

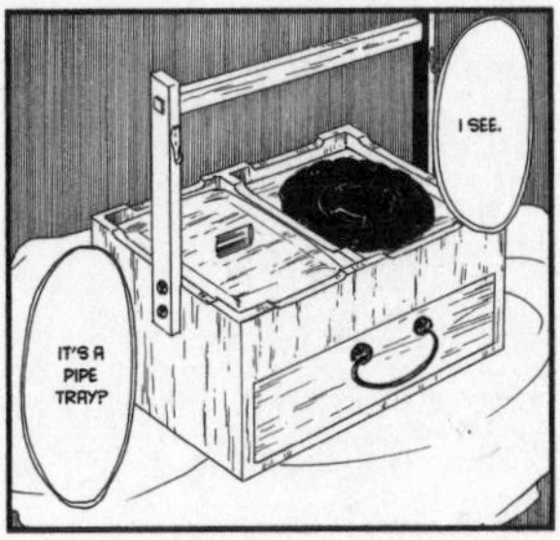
I SEE.
IT'S A PIPE TRAY?

Page 103, Those clothes (*yukata*)

Kimihiro is wearing a kimono specifically made for summer wear. A *yukata* is made of a cool, comfortable cotton and is usually festooned with decorative designs. It certainly is cooler than most other clothes, but in the hot, humid Japanese summer, light clothes alone will not help cool one off. See more information on *yukata* in the notes for Vol. 2.

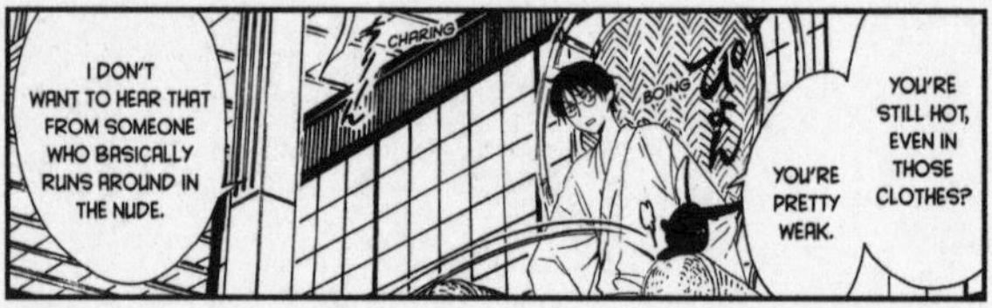
YOU'RE STILL HOT, EVEN IN THOSE CLOTHES?
YOU'RE PRETTY WEAK.
BOING
CHARING
I DON'T WANT TO HEAR THAT FROM SOMEONE WHO BASICALLY RUNS AROUND IN THE NUDE.

Page 130, Heian period

The Heian period (generally considered to be the years between 794–1185) is when the capital of Japan moved from Nara to Heian-kyô, present-day Kyoto.

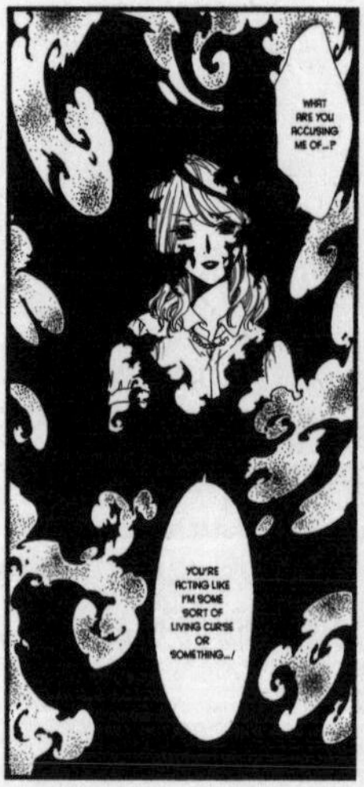
WHAT ARE YOU ACCUSING ME OF...?
YOU'RE ACTING LIKE I'M SOME SORT OF LIVING CURSE OR SOMETHING...!

Page 135, Living curse

The Japanese word *iki-ryô* is made up of words meaning "a living haunting." It is when a person, usually a jilted lover, sends hateful thoughts toward his or her ex, causing bad luck and other effects.

Page 141, Silk wrapping cloth

A *fukusa* is a specialized cloth that has two purposes. The first is to wrap gifts. Originally gifts were given on stylized wooden trays and covered with a *fukusa* cloth decorated with a theme appropriate to the gift. Today it is often used to wrap gifts of money. The second purpose of a *fukusa* is to purify bowls and utensils used in a tea ceremony. The *fukusa* cloth can itself be a very expensive item.

Page 148, Chogokin model

Chogokin is a line of die-cast metal toys that started with Go Nagai's classic giant robot series *Mazinger Z* and grew in the '70s into a franchise for die-cast giant robot models. In the '80s, PVC and other materials replaced metal, but the Chogokin label never fully disappeared. In the '90s and early 2000s, the focus changed to high-quality collectors items. Even now, the name invokes style and quality.

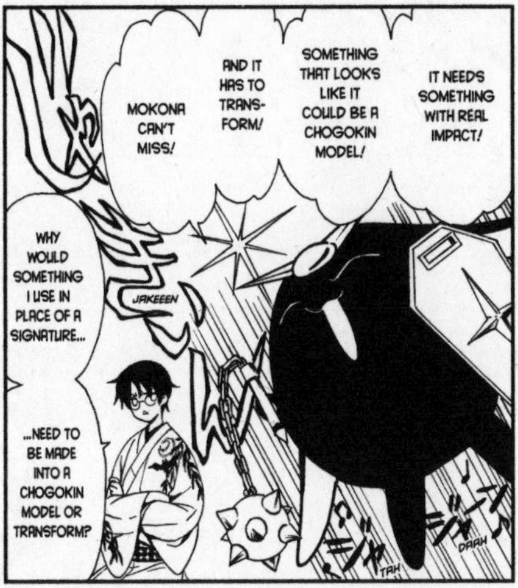
IT NEEDS SOMETHING WITH REAL IMPACT!
SOMETHING THAT LOOKS LIKE IT COULD BE A CHOGOKIN MODEL!
AND IT HAS TO TRANS-FORM!
MOKONA CAN'T MISS!
JAKEEEN
WHY WOULD SOMETHING I USE IN PLACE OF A SIGNATURE...
...NEED TO BE MADE INTO A CHOGOKIN MODEL OR TRANSFORM?
DAAH
TAH

Page 148, Special effects show

The word *tokusatsu* means "special picture," but it really is referring to the special effects that go along with such live-action television shows as *Ultraman, Kamen Rider,* and the *sentai* (battle squad) shows that are the basis for the Power Ranger series.

Contents

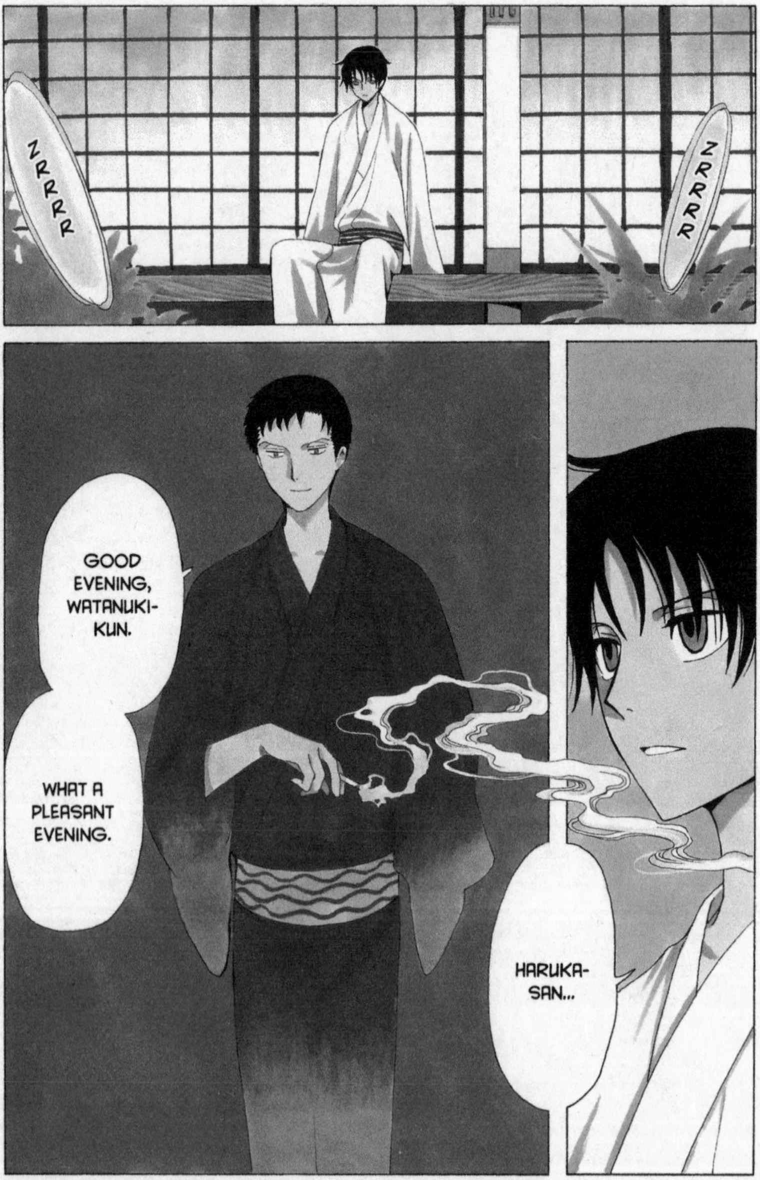
ZRRRR
ZRRRR
HARUKA-SAN...
GOOD EVENING, WATANUKI-KUN.
WHAT A PLEASANT EVENING.

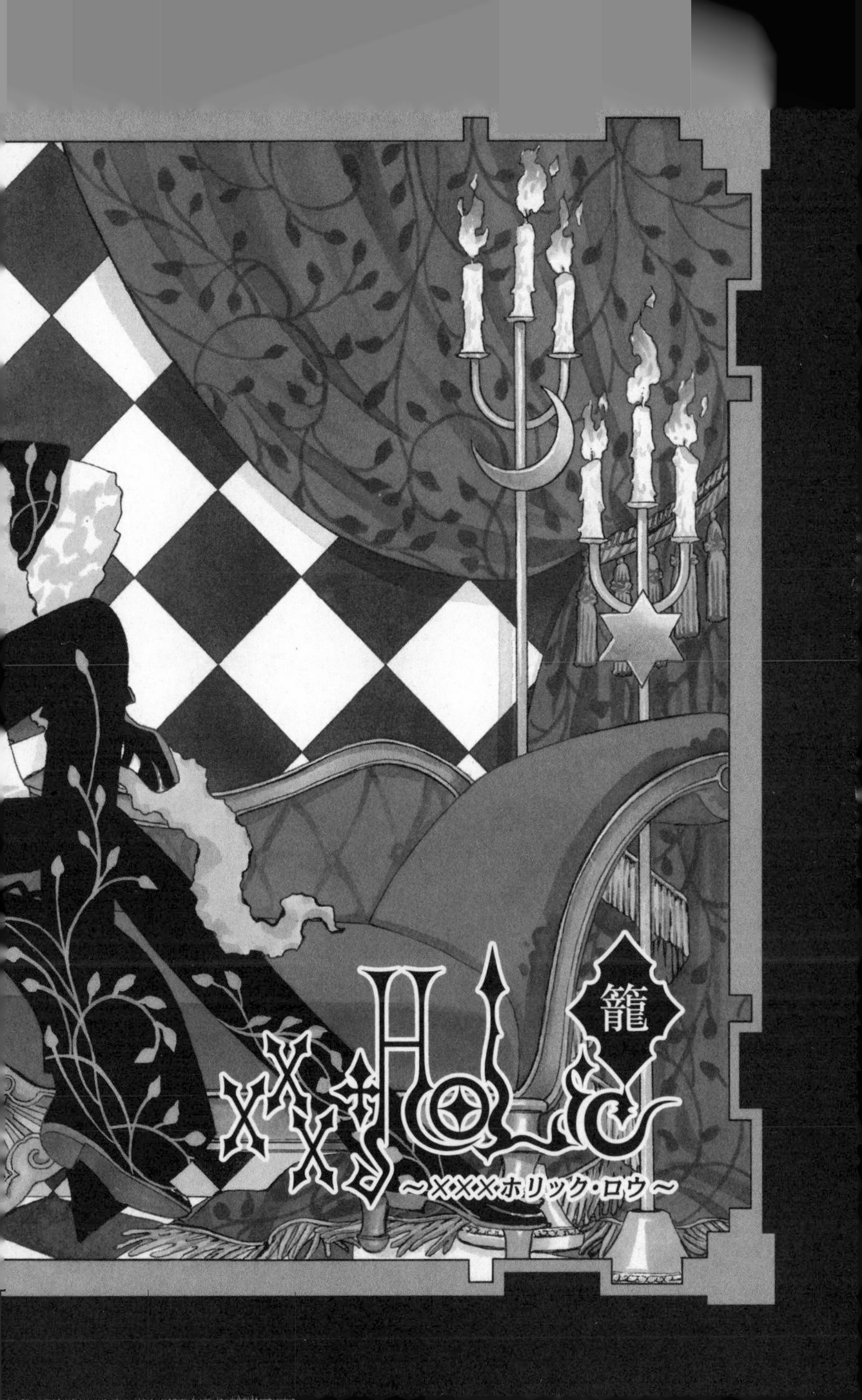
xxxHOLiC
籠
～×××ホリック・ロウ～

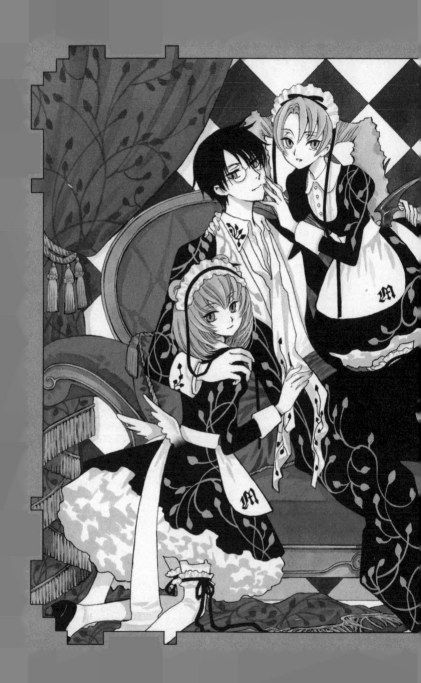

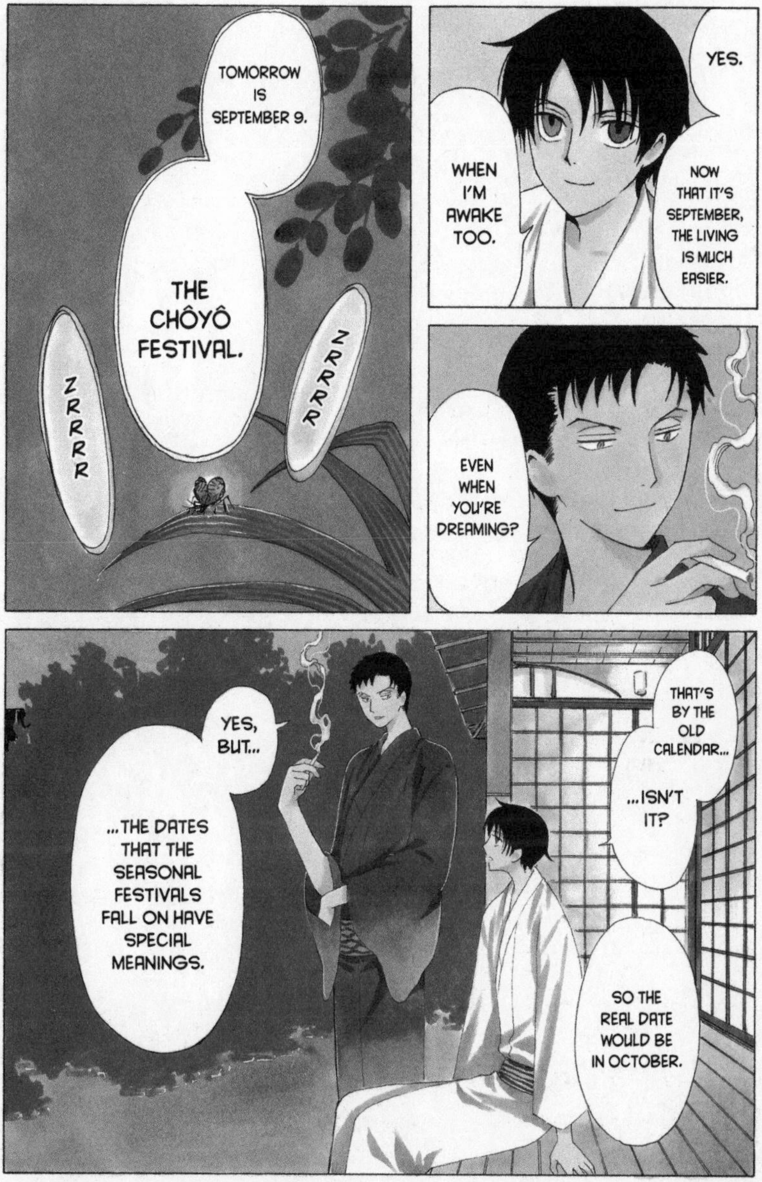
YES.
NOW THAT IT'S SEPTEMBER, THE LIVING IS MUCH EASIER.
WHEN I'M AWAKE TOO.
EVEN WHEN YOU'RE DREAMING?
TOMORROW IS SEPTEMBER 9.
THE CHÔYÔ FESTIVAL.
ZRRRR
ZRRRR
THAT'S BY THE OLD CALENDAR...
...ISN'T IT?
SO THE REAL DATE WOULD BE IN OCTOBER.
YES, BUT...
...THE DATES THAT THE SEASONAL FESTIVALS FALL ON HAVE SPECIAL MEANINGS.

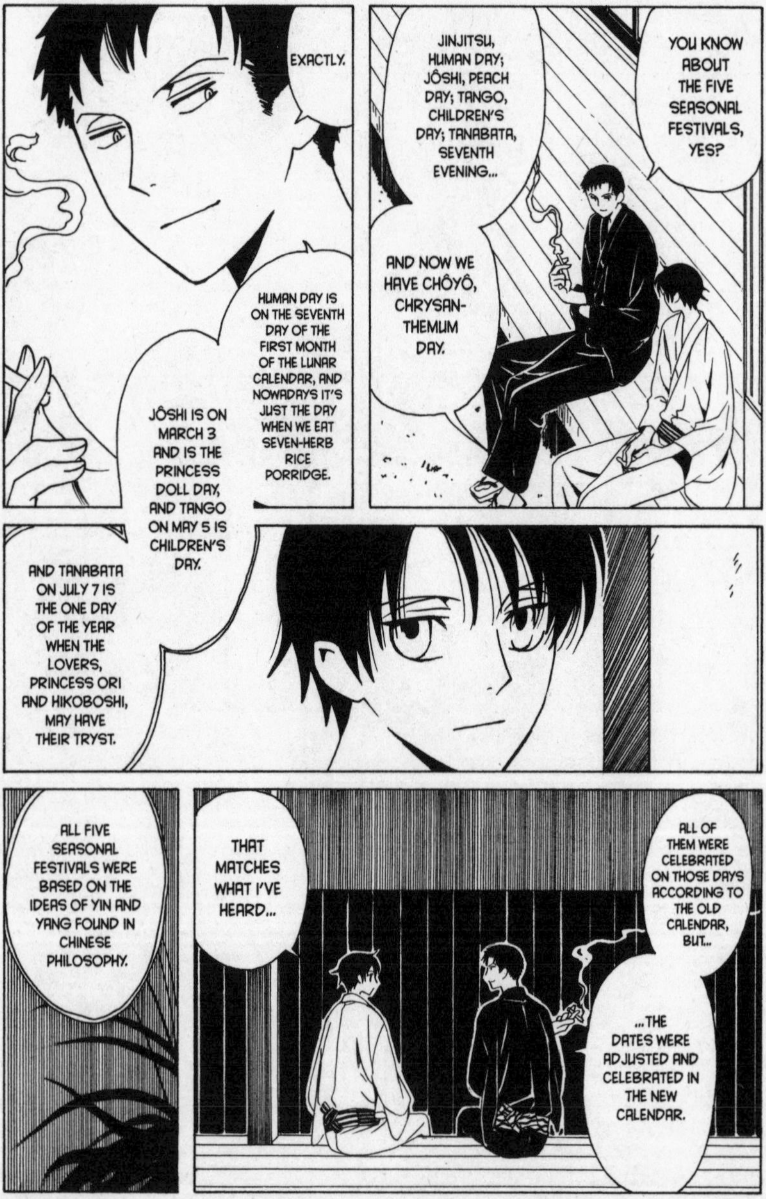
YOU KNOW ABOUT THE FIVE SEASONAL FESTIVALS, YES?
JINJITSU, HUMAN DAY; JÔSHI, PEACH DAY; TANGO, CHILDREN'S DAY; TANABATA, SEVENTH EVENING...
AND NOW WE HAVE CHÔYÔ, CHRYSANTHEMUM DAY.
EXACTLY.
HUMAN DAY IS ON THE SEVENTH DAY OF THE FIRST MONTH OF THE LUNAR CALENDAR, AND NOWADAYS IT'S JUST THE DAY WHEN WE EAT SEVEN-HERB RICE PORRIDGE.
JÔSHI IS ON MARCH 3 AND IS THE PRINCESS DOLL DAY, AND TANGO ON MAY 5 IS CHILDREN'S DAY.
AND TANABATA ON JULY 7 IS THE ONE DAY OF THE YEAR WHEN THE LOVERS, PRINCESS ORI AND HIKOBOSHI, MAY HAVE THEIR TRYST.
ALL OF THEM WERE CELEBRATED ON THOSE DAYS ACCORDING TO THE OLD CALENDAR, BUT...
...THE DATES WERE ADJUSTED AND CELEBRATED IN THE NEW CALENDAR.
THAT MATCHES WHAT I'VE HEARD...
ALL FIVE SEASONAL FESTIVALS WERE BASED ON THE IDEAS OF YIN AND YANG FOUND IN CHINESE PHILOSOPHY.

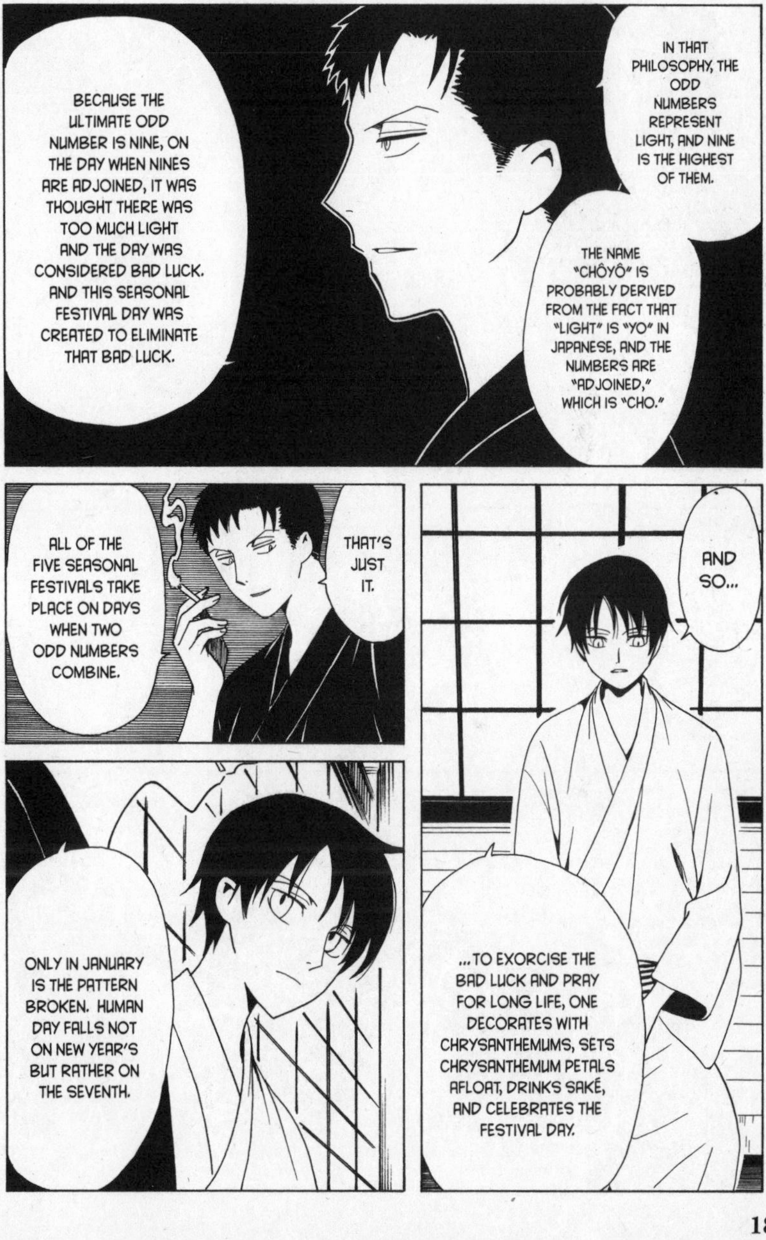
IN THAT PHILOSOPHY, THE ODD NUMBERS REPRESENT LIGHT, AND NINE IS THE HIGHEST OF THEM.
BECAUSE THE ULTIMATE ODD NUMBER IS NINE, ON THE DAY WHEN NINES ARE ADJOINED, IT WAS THOUGHT THERE WAS TOO MUCH LIGHT AND THE DAY WAS CONSIDERED BAD LUCK. AND THIS SEASONAL FESTIVAL DAY WAS CREATED TO ELIMINATE THAT BAD LUCK.
THE NAME "CHÔYÔ" IS PROBABLY DERIVED FROM THE FACT THAT "LIGHT" IS "YO" IN JAPANESE, AND THE NUMBERS ARE "ADJOINED," WHICH IS "CHO."
AND SO...
...TO EXORCISE THE BAD LUCK AND PRAY FOR LONG LIFE, ONE DECORATES WITH CHRYSANTHEMUMS, SETS CHRYSANTHEMUM PETALS AFLOAT, DRINKS SAKÉ, AND CELEBRATES THE FESTIVAL DAY.
THAT'S JUST IT.
ALL OF THE FIVE SEASONAL FESTIVALS TAKE PLACE ON DAYS WHEN TWO ODD NUMBERS COMBINE.
ONLY IN JANUARY IS THE PATTERN BROKEN. HUMAN DAY FALLS NOT ON NEW YEAR'S BUT RATHER ON THE SEVENTH.

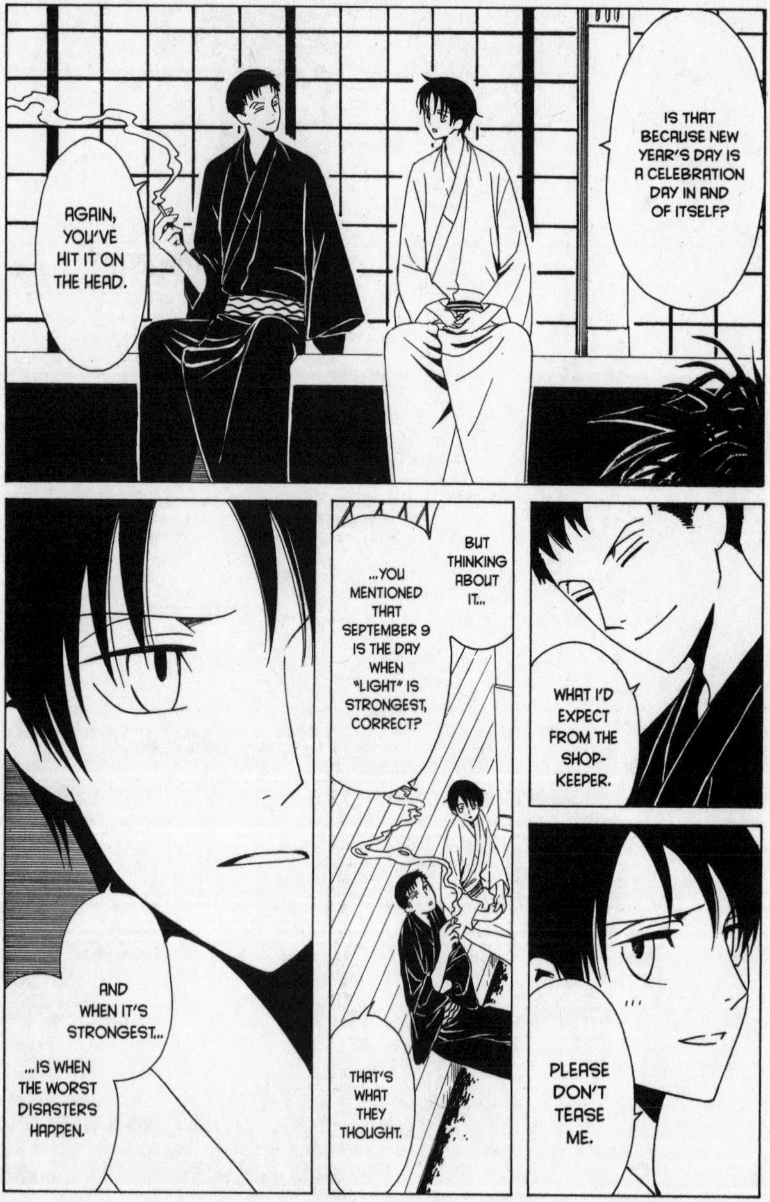
IS THAT BECAUSE NEW YEAR'S DAY IS A CELEBRATION DAY IN AND OF ITSELF?
AGAIN, YOU'VE HIT IT ON THE HEAD.
WHAT I'D EXPECT FROM THE SHOP-KEEPER.
PLEASE DON'T TEASE ME.
BUT THINKING ABOUT IT...
...YOU MENTIONED THAT SEPTEMBER 9 IS THE DAY WHEN "LIGHT" IS STRONGEST, CORRECT?
THAT'S WHAT THEY THOUGHT.
AND WHEN IT'S STRONGEST...
...IS WHEN THE WORST DISASTERS HAPPEN.

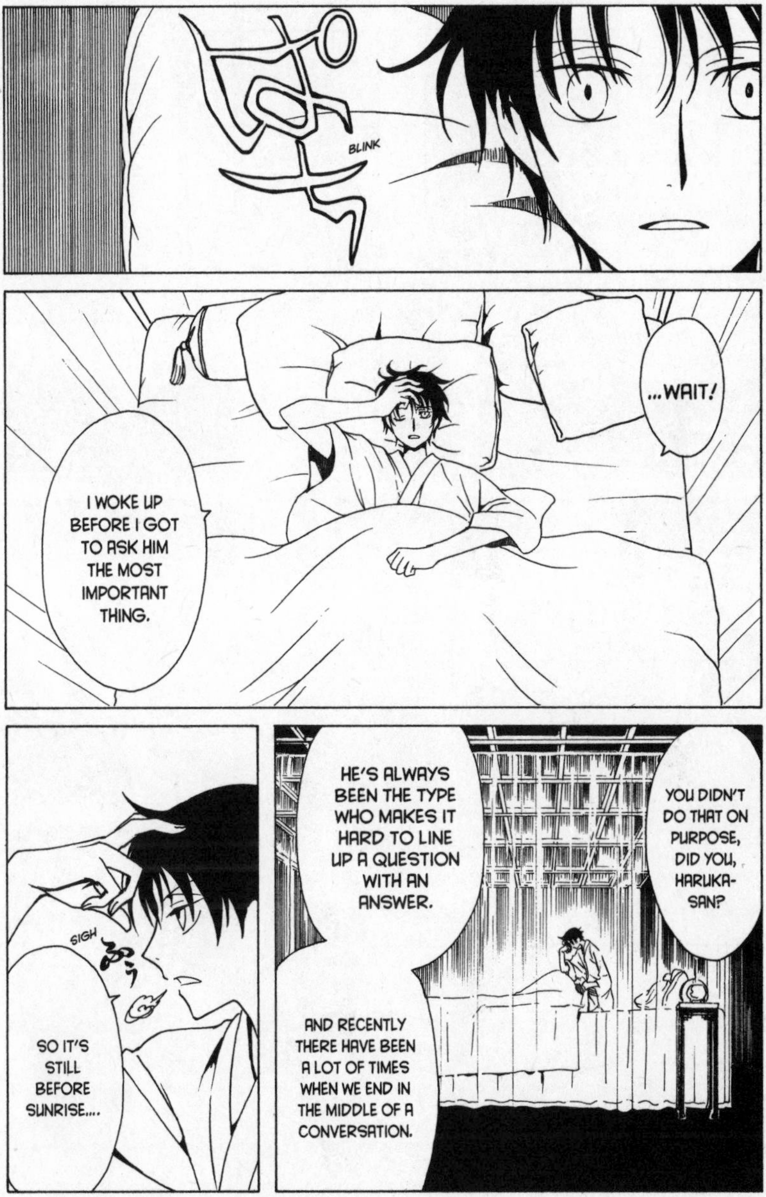
BLINK
...WAIT!
I WOKE UP BEFORE I GOT TO ASK HIM THE MOST IMPORTANT THING.
YOU DIDN'T DO THAT ON PURPOSE, DID YOU, HARUKA-SAN?
HE'S ALWAYS BEEN THE TYPE WHO MAKES IT HARD TO LINE UP A QUESTION WITH AN ANSWER.
AND RECENTLY THERE HAVE BEEN A LOT OF TIMES WHEN WE END IN THE MIDDLE OF A CONVERSATION.
SIGH
SO IT'S STILL BEFORE SUNRISE....

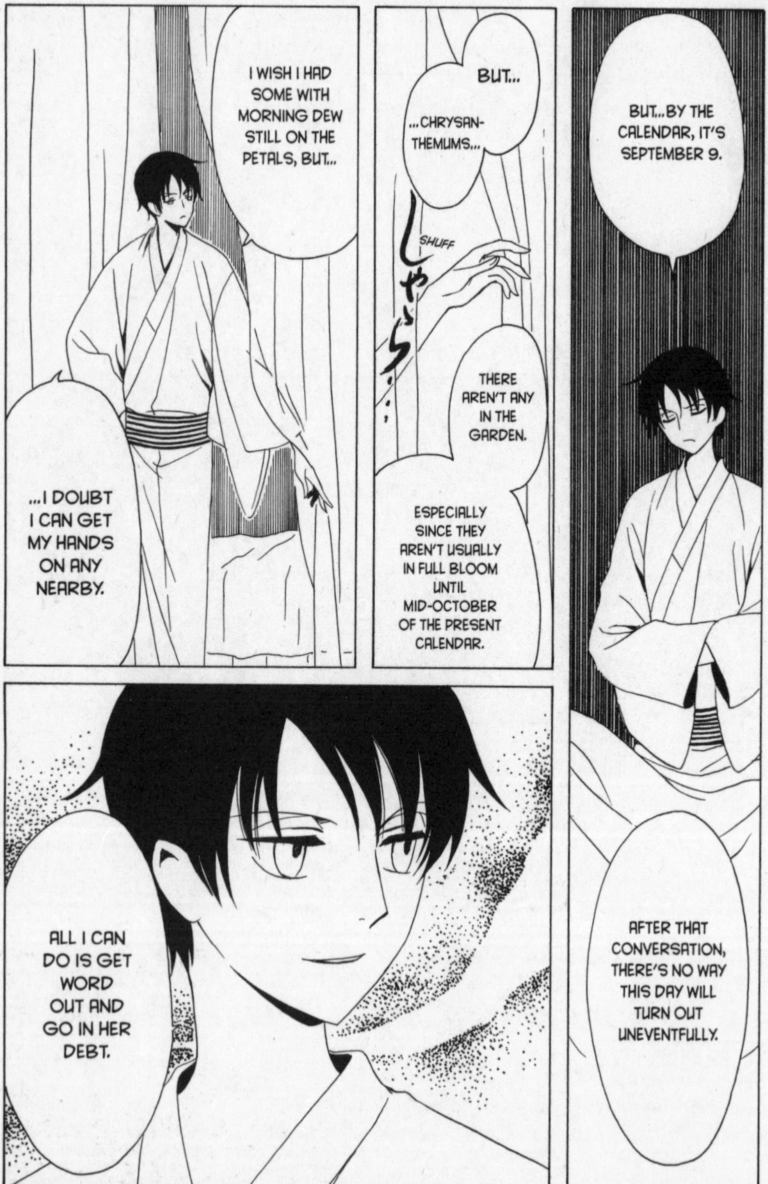
BUT...BY THE CALENDAR, IT'S SEPTEMBER 9.
AFTER THAT CONVERSATION, THERE'S NO WAY THIS DAY WILL TURN OUT UNEVENTFULLY.
BUT...
...CHRYSAN-THEMUMS...
しゃらら
SHUFF
THERE AREN'T ANY IN THE GARDEN.
ESPECIALLY SINCE THEY AREN'T USUALLY IN FULL BLOOM UNTIL MID-OCTOBER OF THE PRESENT CALENDAR.
I WISH I HAD SOME WITH MORNING DEW STILL ON THE PETALS, BUT...
...I DOUBT I CAN GET MY HANDS ON ANY NEARBY.
ALL I CAN DO IS GET WORD OUT AND GO IN HER DEBT.

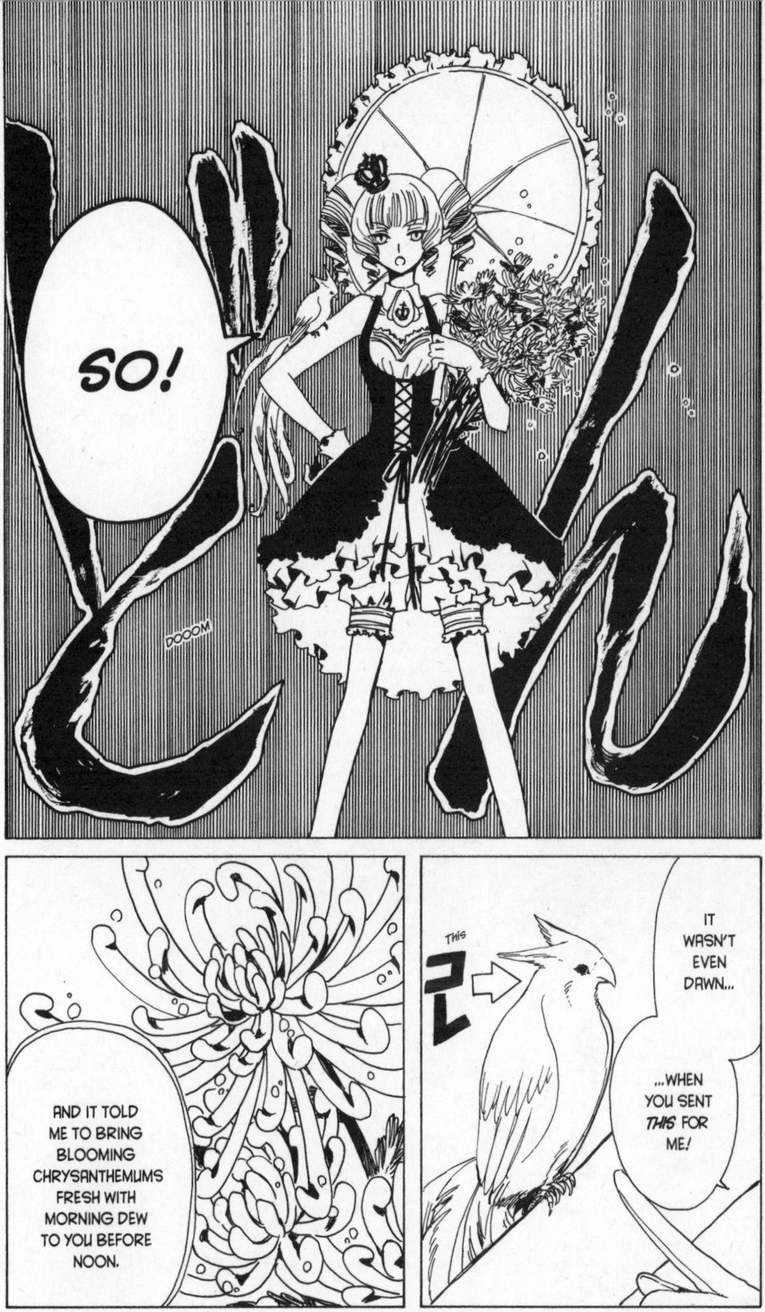
SO!
DOOOM
IT WASN'T EVEN DAWN...
THIS
...WHEN YOU SENT *THIS* FOR ME!
AND IT TOLD ME TO BRING BLOOMING CHRYSANTHEMUMS FRESH WITH MORNING DEW TO YOU BEFORE NOON.

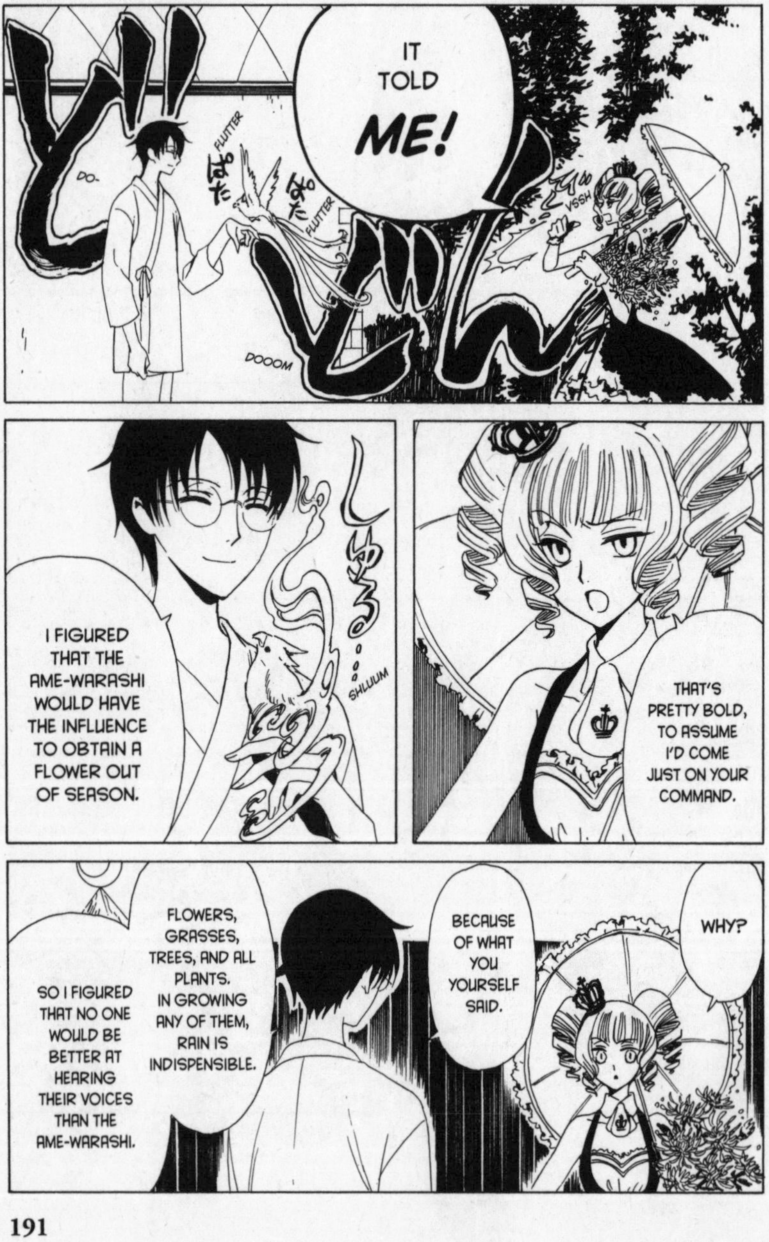
VSSH
IT TOLD ME!
FLUTTER
FLUTTER
DO-
DOOOM
THAT'S PRETTY BOLD, TO ASSUME I'D COME JUST ON YOUR COMMAND.
SHLUUM
I FIGURED THAT THE AME-WARASHI WOULD HAVE THE INFLUENCE TO OBTAIN A FLOWER OUT OF SEASON.
WHY?
BECAUSE OF WHAT YOU YOURSELF SAID.
FLOWERS, GRASSES, TREES, AND ALL PLANTS. IN GROWING ANY OF THEM, RAIN IS INDISPENSIBLE.
SO I FIGURED THAT NO ONE WOULD BE BETTER AT HEARING THEIR VOICES THAN THE AME-WARASHI.

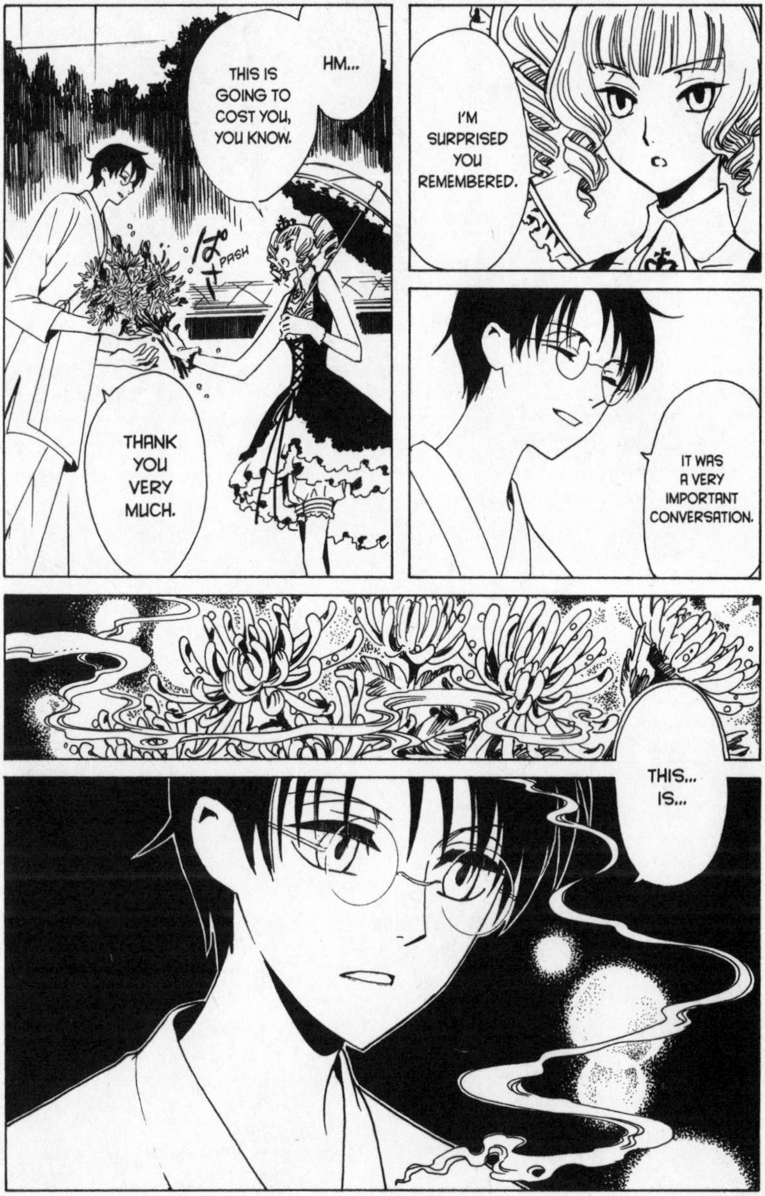
I'M SURPRISED YOU REMEMBERED.
IT WAS A VERY IMPORTANT CONVERSATION.
HM... THIS IS GOING TO COST YOU, YOU KNOW.
ぱさ PASH
THANK YOU VERY MUCH.
THIS... IS...

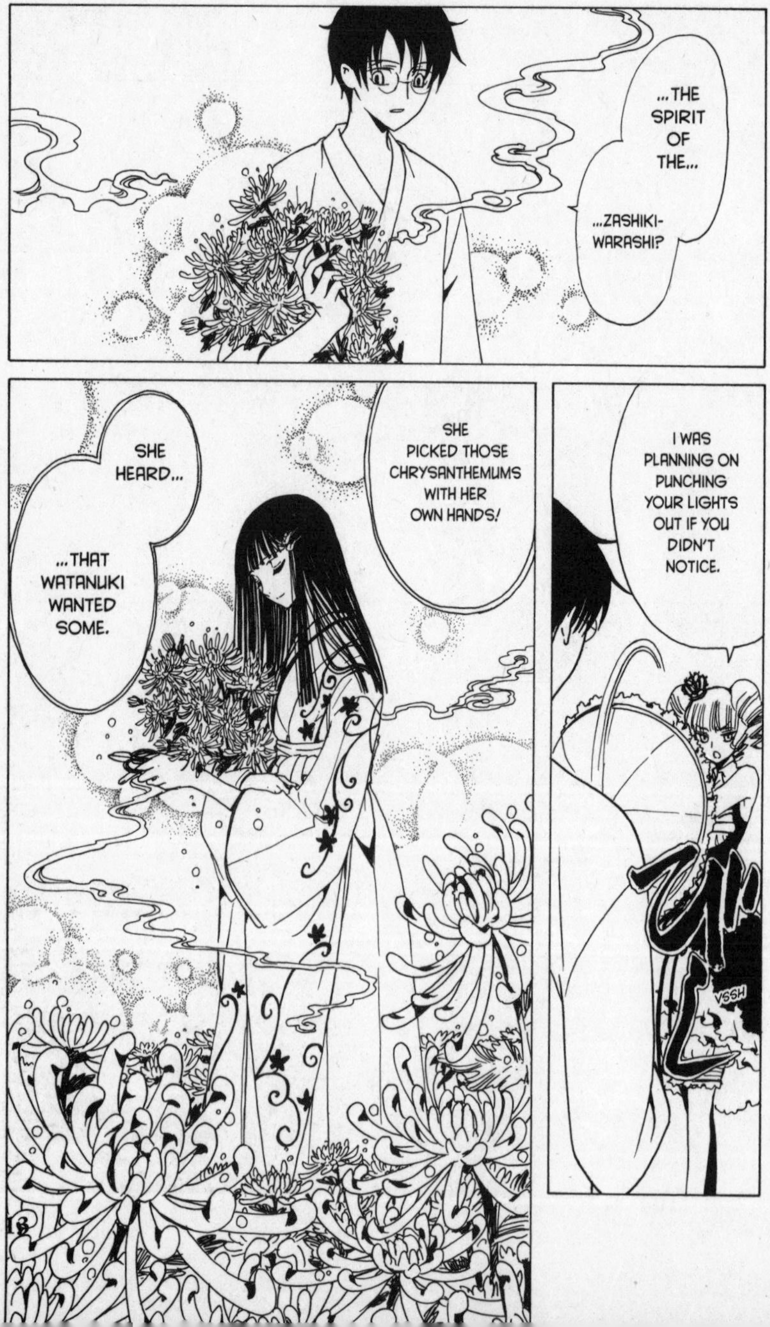
...THE SPIRIT OF THE...
...ZASHIKI-WARASHI?
I WAS PLANNING ON PUNCHING YOUR LIGHTS OUT IF YOU DIDN'T NOTICE.
VSSH
SHE PICKED THOSE CHRYSANTHEMUMS WITH HER OWN HANDS!
SHE HEARD...
...THAT WATANUKI WANTED SOME.

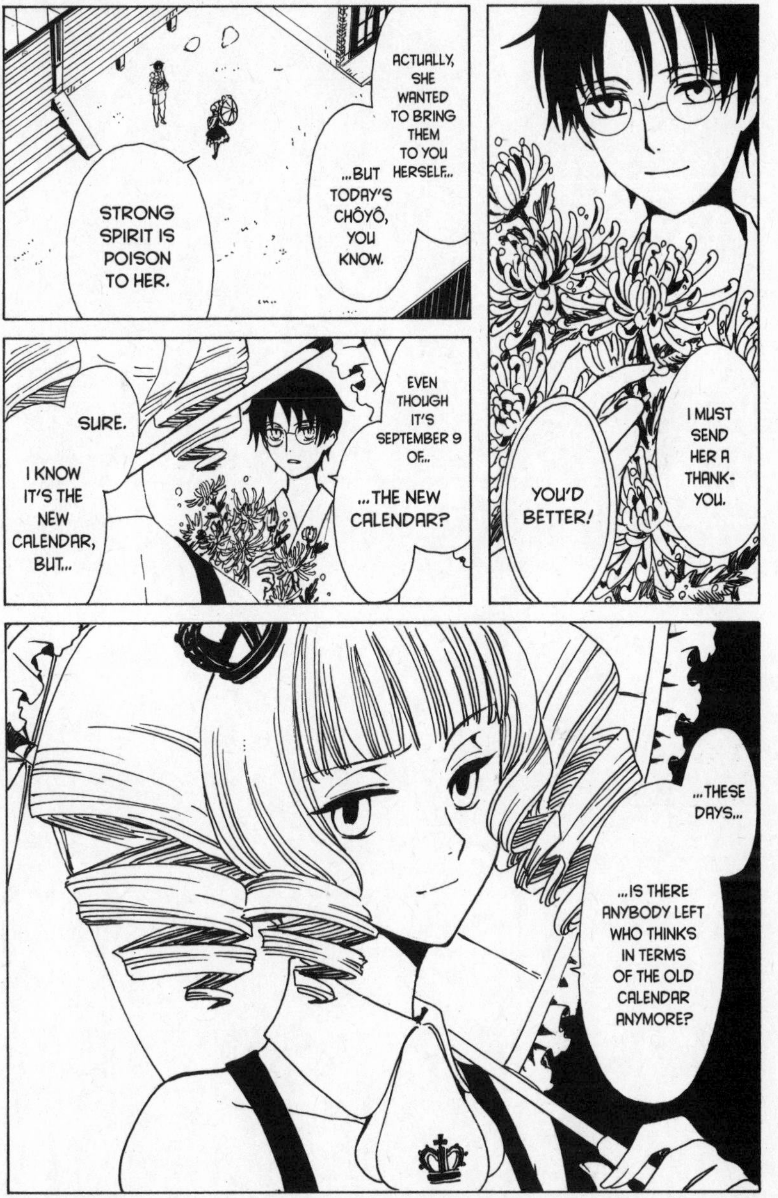
I MUST SEND HER A THANK-YOU.
YOU'D BETTER!
ACTUALLY, SHE WANTED TO BRING THEM TO YOU HERSELF...
...BUT TODAY'S CHÔYÔ, YOU KNOW.
STRONG SPIRIT IS POISON TO HER.
EVEN THOUGH IT'S SEPTEMBER 9 OF...
...THE NEW CALENDAR?
SURE.
I KNOW IT'S THE NEW CALENDAR, BUT...
...THESE DAYS...
...IS THERE ANYBODY LEFT WHO THINKS IN TERMS OF THE OLD CALENDAR ANYMORE?

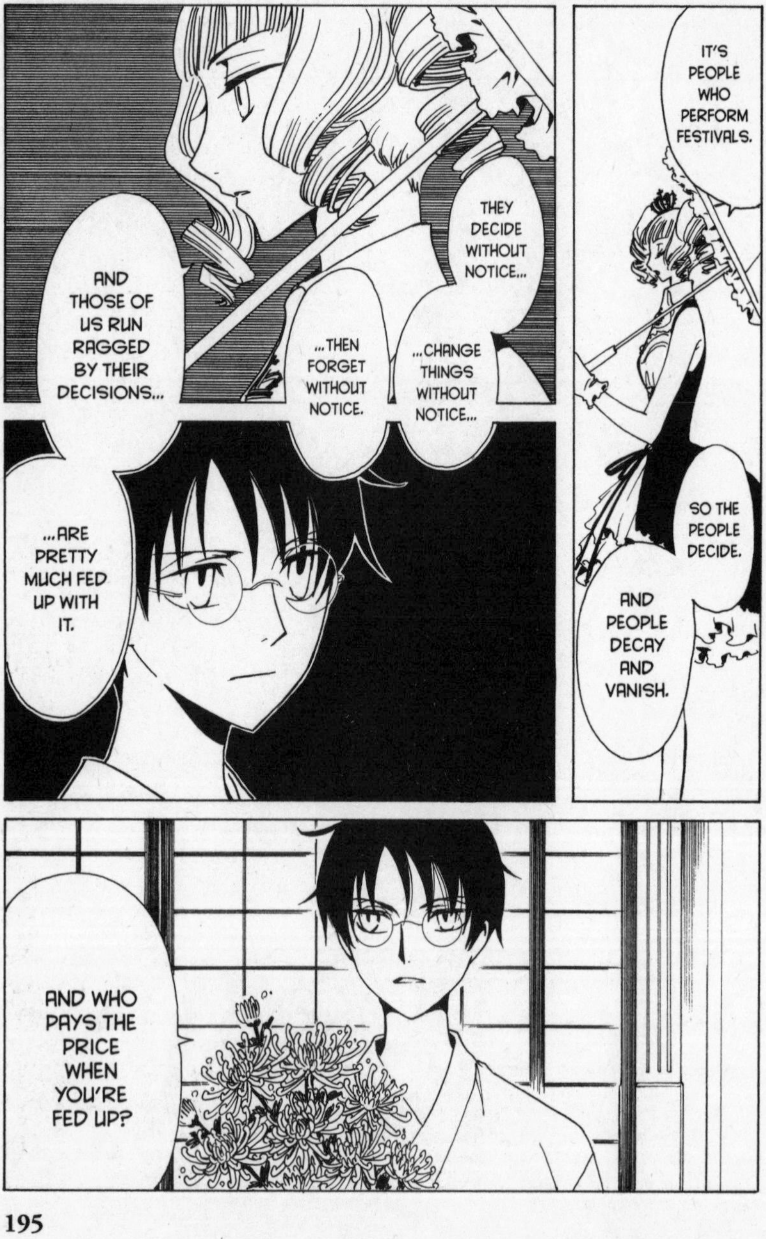
IT'S PEOPLE WHO PERFORM FESTIVALS.
SO THE PEOPLE DECIDE.
AND PEOPLE DECAY AND VANISH.
THEY DECIDE WITHOUT NOTICE...
...CHANGE THINGS WITHOUT NOTICE...
...THEN FORGET WITHOUT NOTICE.
AND THOSE OF US RUN RAGGED BY THEIR DECISIONS...
...ARE PRETTY MUCH FED UP WITH IT.
AND WHO PAYS THE PRICE WHEN YOU'RE FED UP?

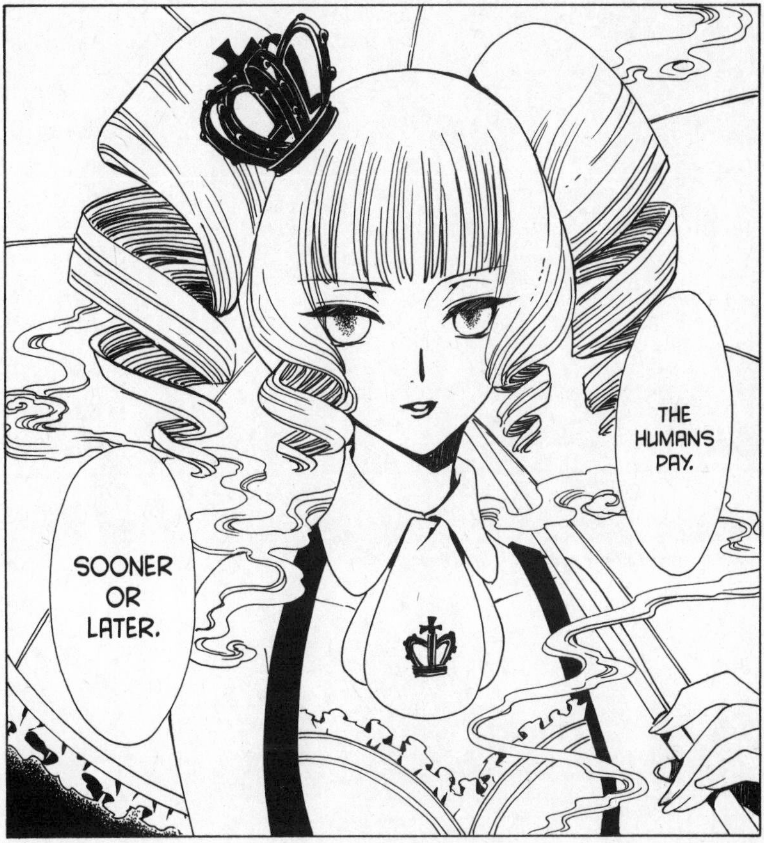
THE HUMANS PAY.
SOONER OR LATER.

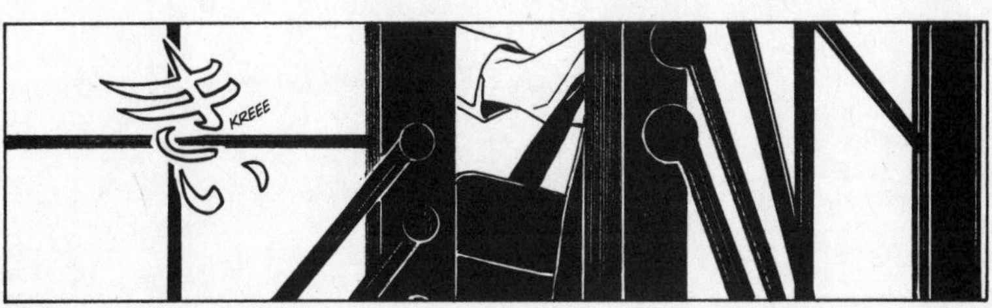
KREEE

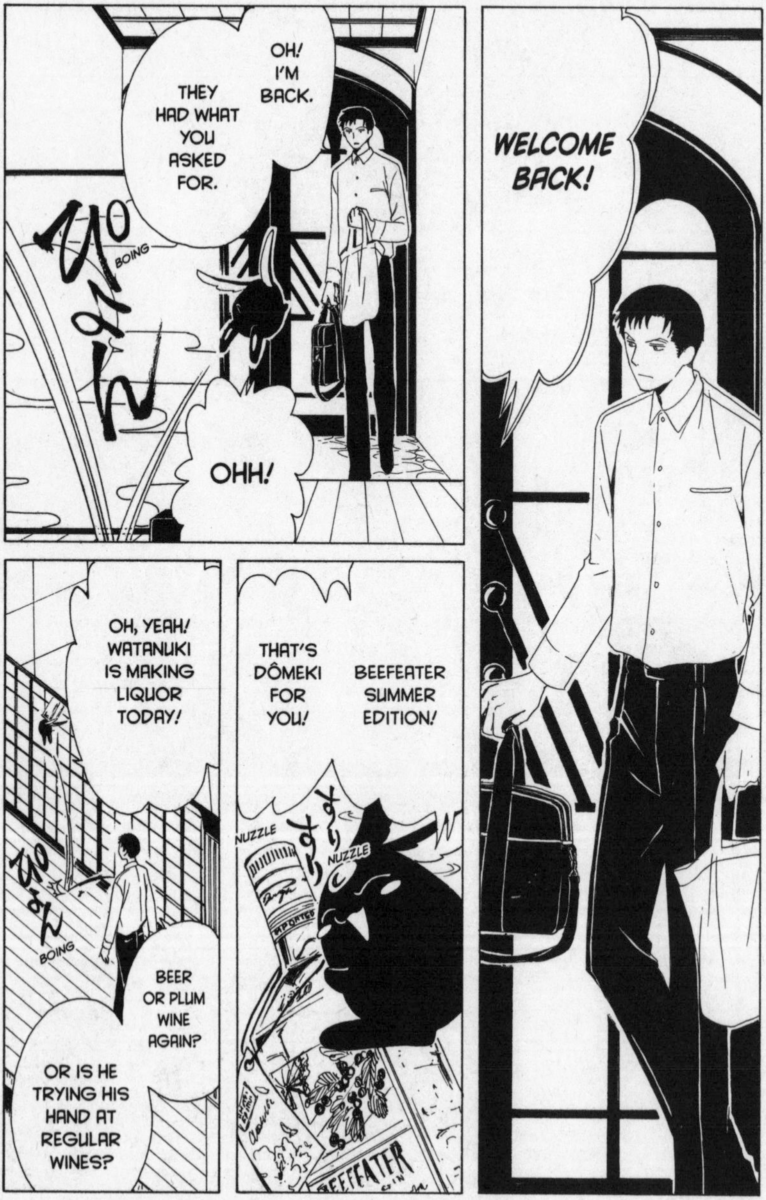

WELCOME BACK!
OH! I'M BACK.
THEY HAD WHAT YOU ASKED FOR.
BOING
OHH!
BEEFEATER SUMMER EDITION!
THAT'S DÔMEKI FOR YOU!
NUZZLE
NUZZLE
OH, YEAH! WATANUKI IS MAKING LIQUOR TODAY!
BOING
BEER OR PLUM WINE AGAIN?
OR IS HE TRYING HIS HAND AT REGULAR WINES?

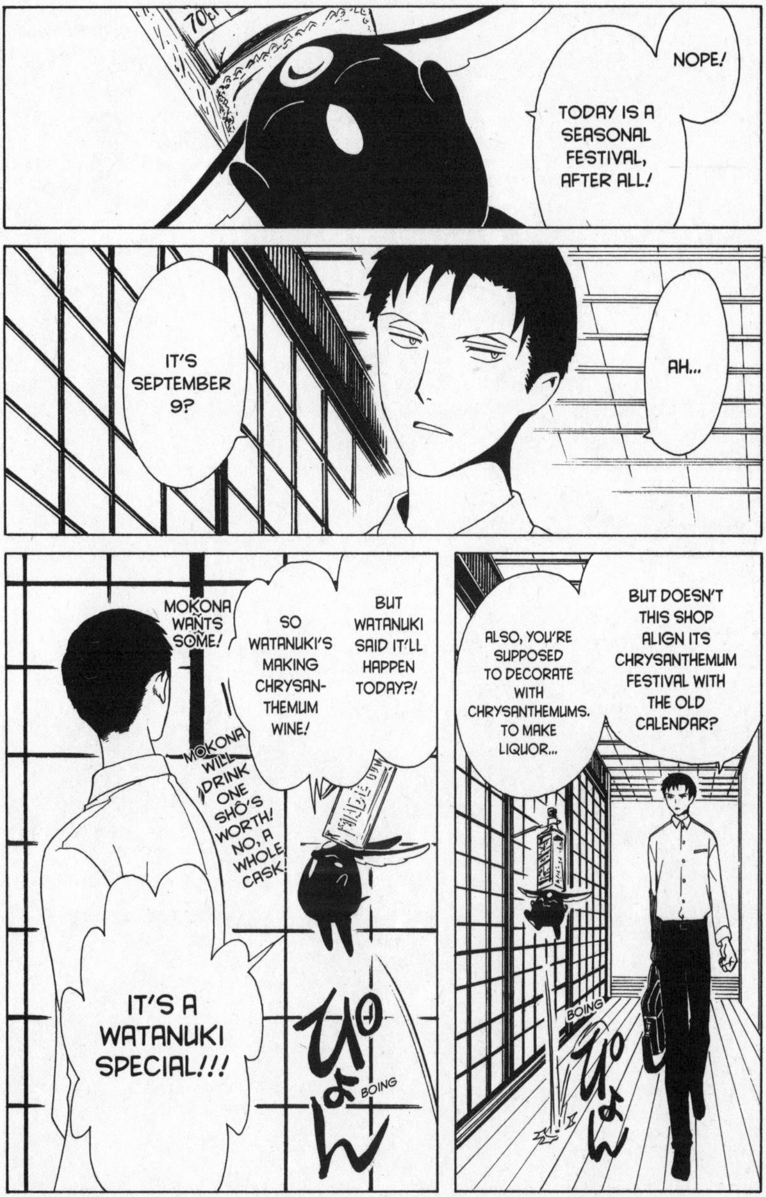
NOPE!
TODAY IS A SEASONAL FESTIVAL, AFTER ALL!
AH...
IT'S SEPTEMBER 9?
BUT DOESN'T THIS SHOP ALIGN ITS CHRYSANTHEMUM FESTIVAL WITH THE OLD CALENDAR?
ALSO, YOU'RE SUPPOSED TO DECORATE WITH CHRYSANTHEMUMS. TO MAKE LIQUOR...
BOING
ぴょん
BUT WATANUKI SAID IT'LL HAPPEN TODAY?!
SO WATANUKI'S MAKING CHRYSAN-THEMUM WINE!
MOKONA WANTS SOME!
MOKONA WILL DRINK ONE SHÔ'S WORTH! NO, A WHOLE CASK!
ぴょん
BOING
IT'S A WATANUKI SPECIAL!!!

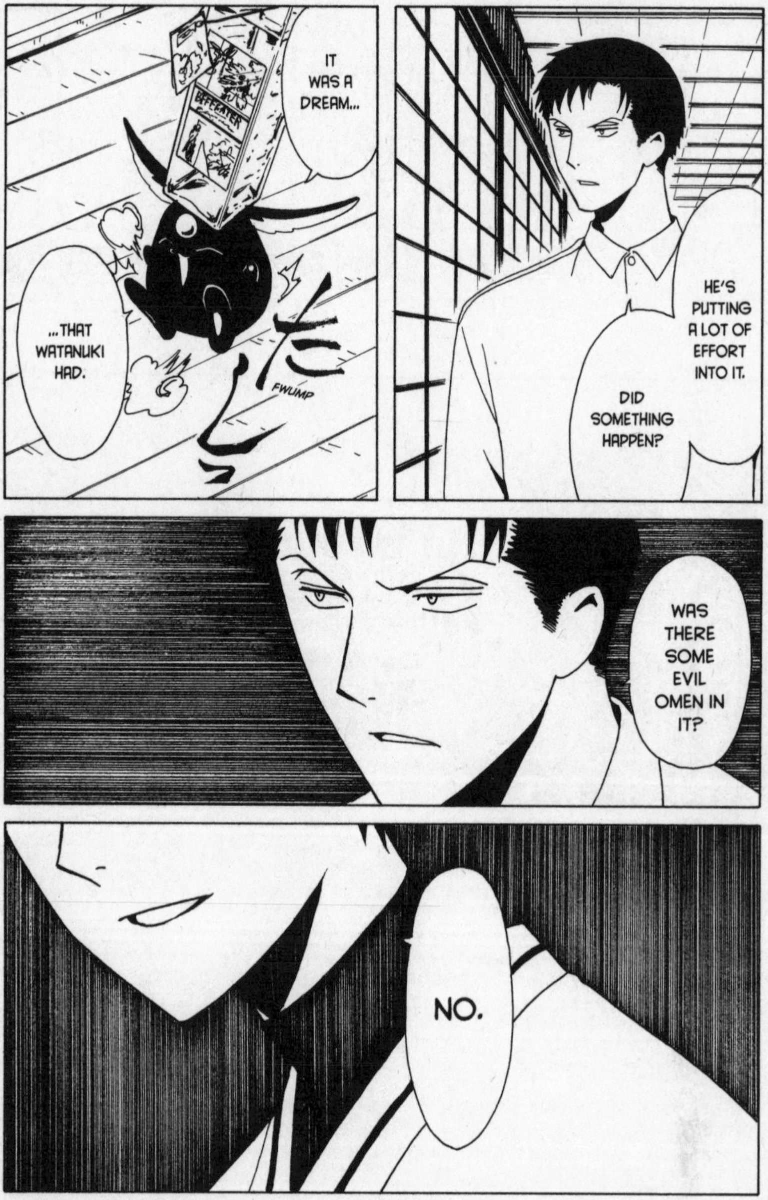
HE'S PUTTING A LOT OF EFFORT INTO IT.
DID SOMETHING HAPPEN?
IT WAS A DREAM...
...THAT WATANUKI HAD.
FWUMP
WAS THERE SOME EVIL OMEN IN IT?
NO.

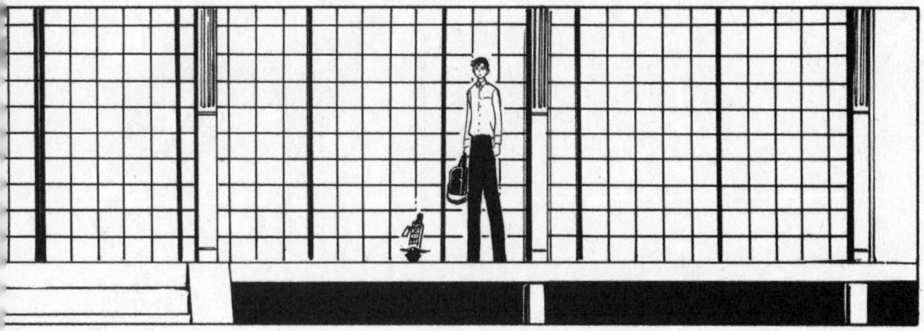
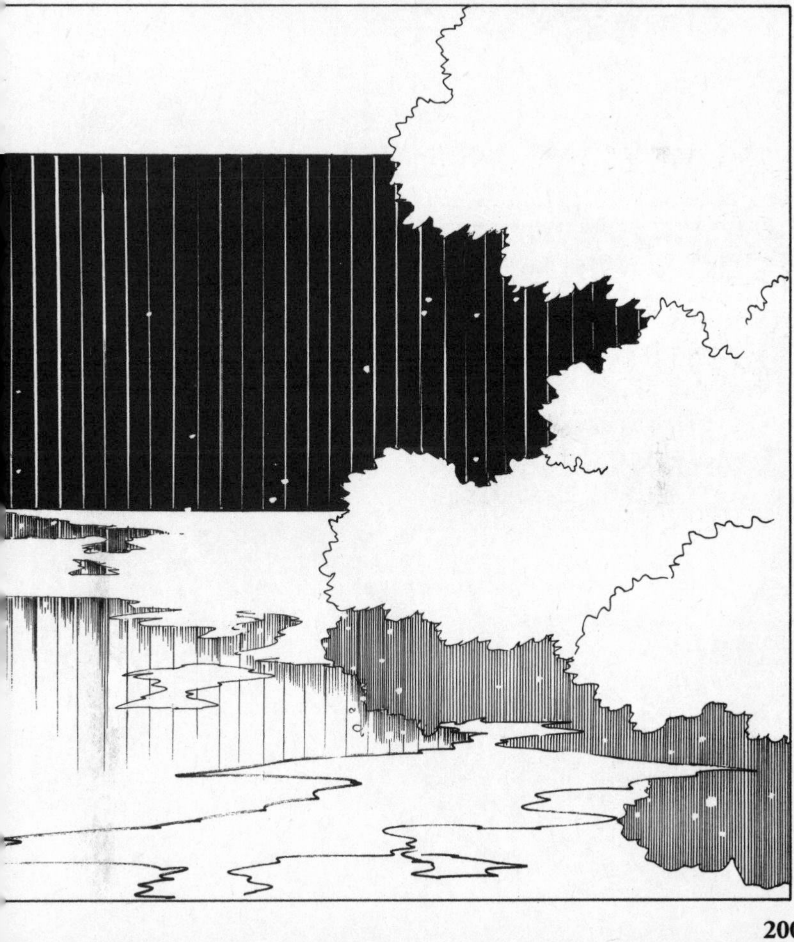

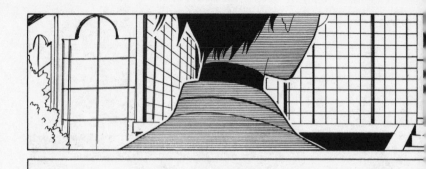

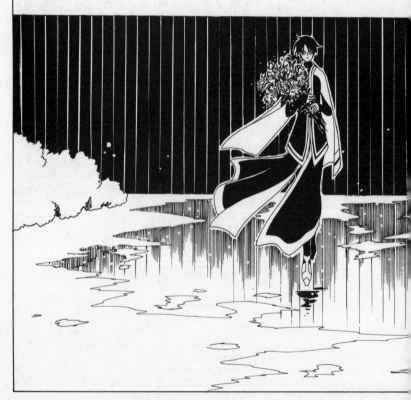

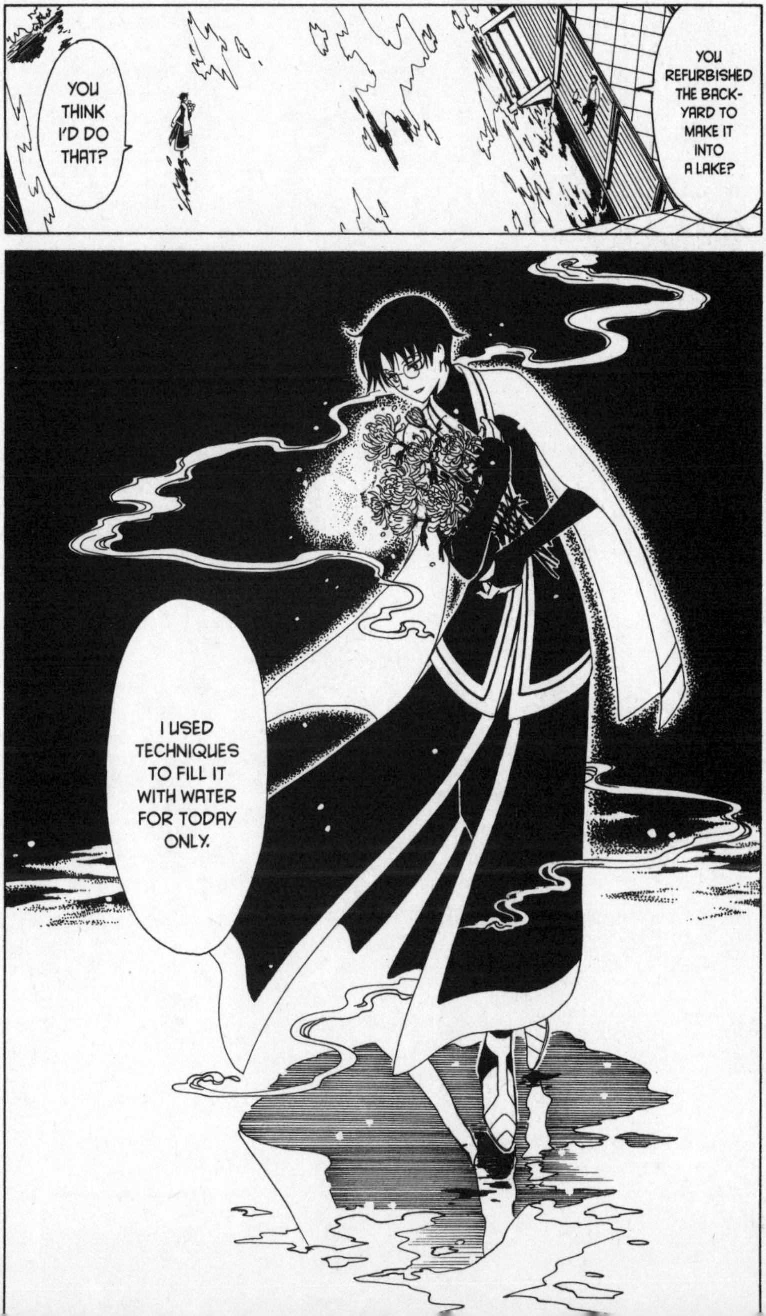
YOU REFURBISHED THE BACK-YARD TO MAKE IT INTO A LAKE?
YOU THINK I'D DO THAT?
I USED TECHNIQUES TO FILL IT WITH WATER FOR TODAY ONLY.

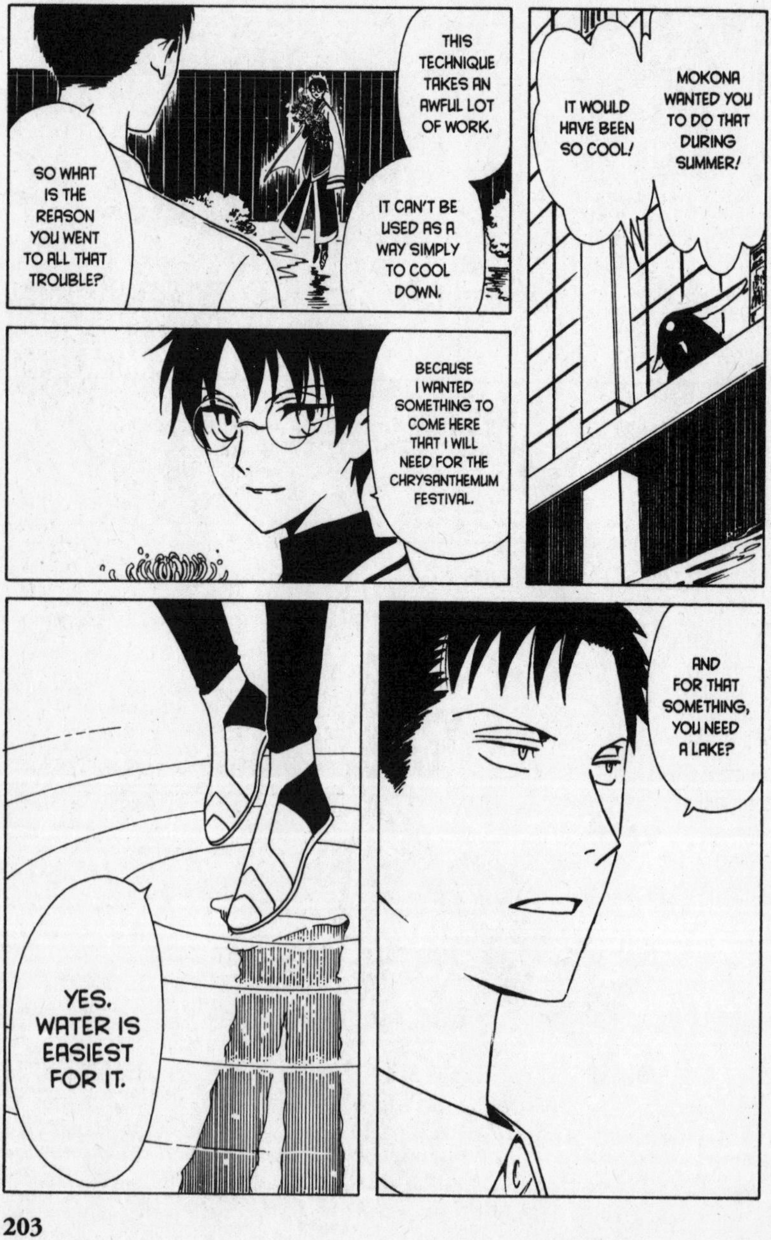
MOKONA WANTED YOU TO DO THAT DURING SUMMER!
IT WOULD HAVE BEEN SO COOL!
THIS TECHNIQUE TAKES AN AWFUL LOT OF WORK.
IT CAN'T BE USED AS A WAY SIMPLY TO COOL DOWN.
SO WHAT IS THE REASON YOU WENT TO ALL THAT TROUBLE?
BECAUSE I WANTED SOMETHING TO COME HERE THAT I WILL NEED FOR THE CHRYSANTHEMUM FESTIVAL.
AND FOR THAT SOMETHING, YOU NEED A LAKE?
YES. WATER IS EASIEST FOR IT.

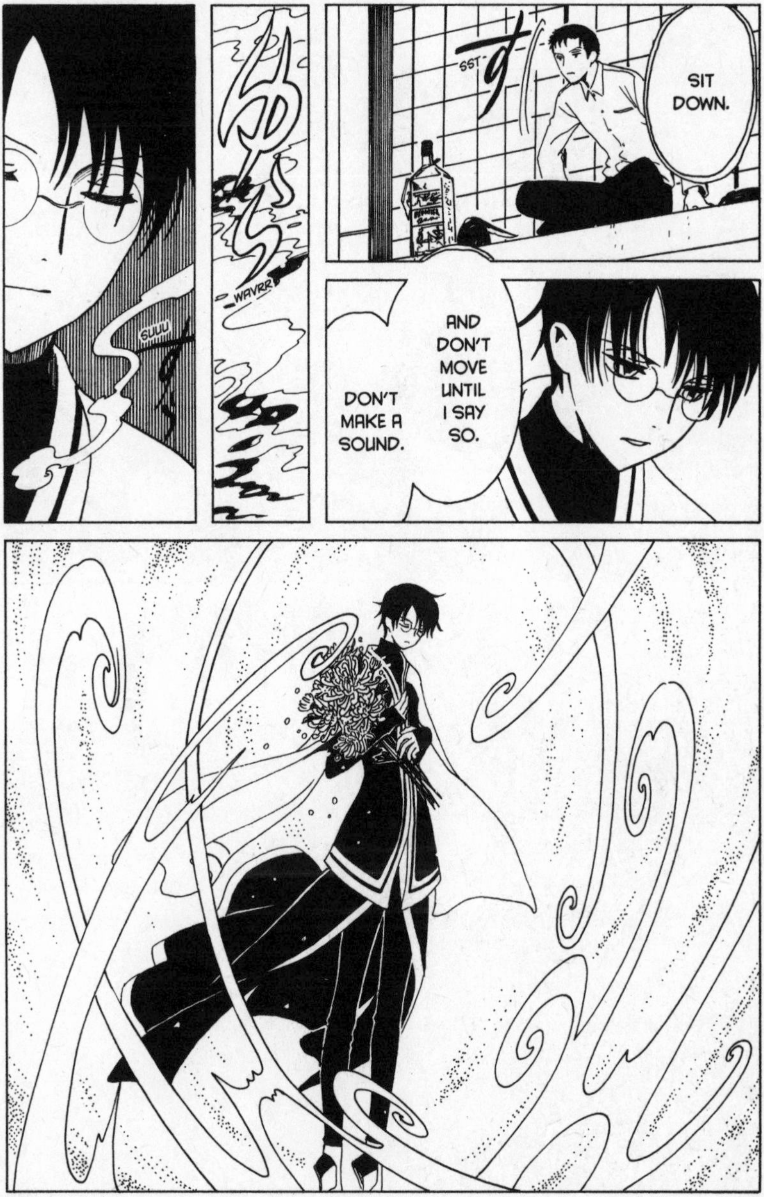
SIT DOWN.
SST
AND DON'T MOVE UNTIL I SAY SO.
DON'T MAKE A SOUND.
WAVRR
SUUU

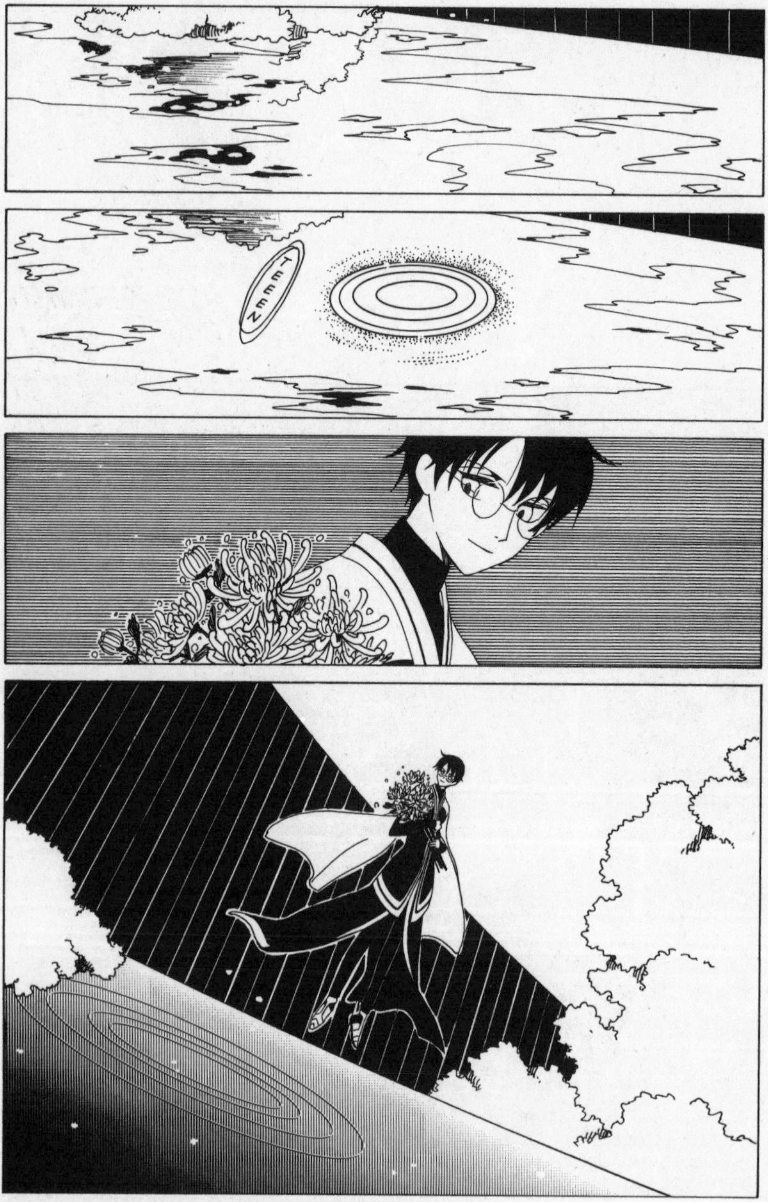
TEEEN

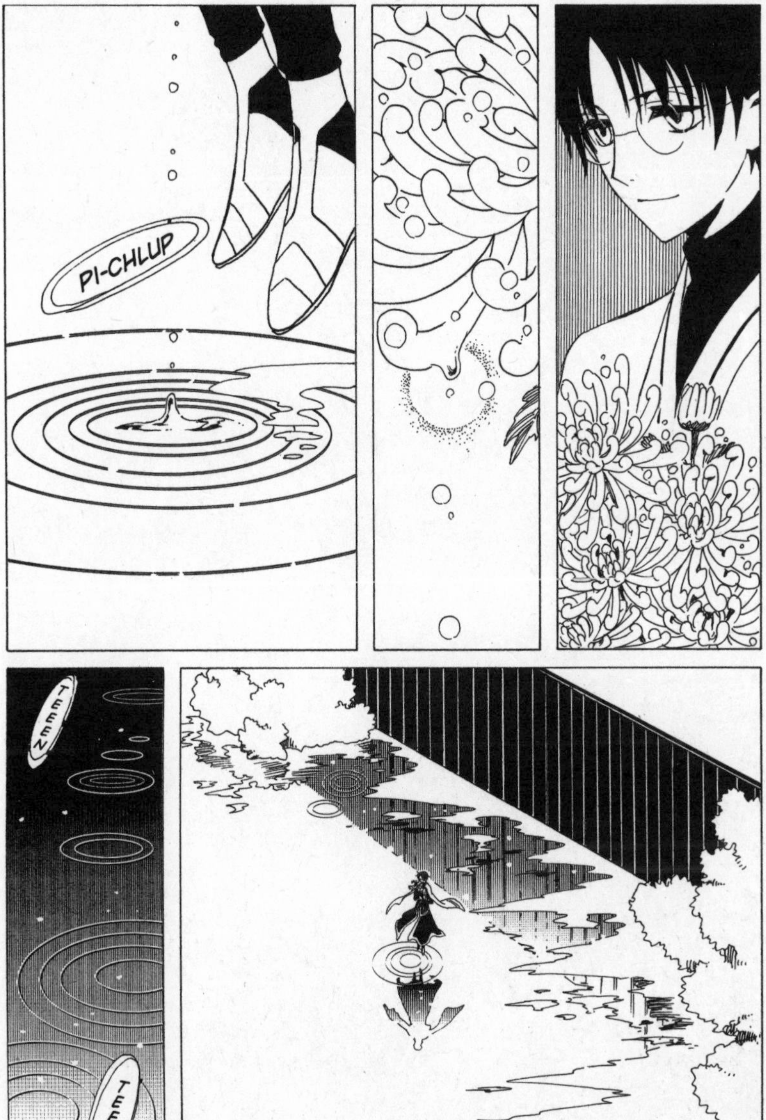
PI-CHLUP
TEEEN
TEEEN

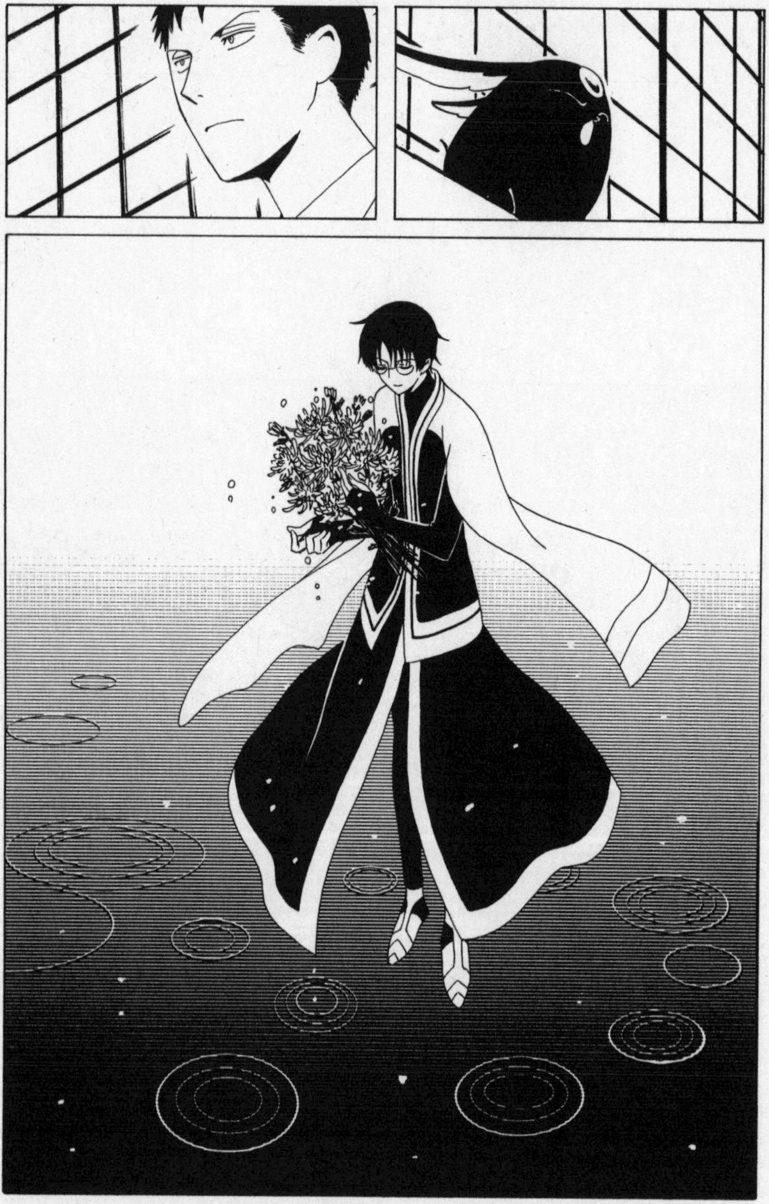

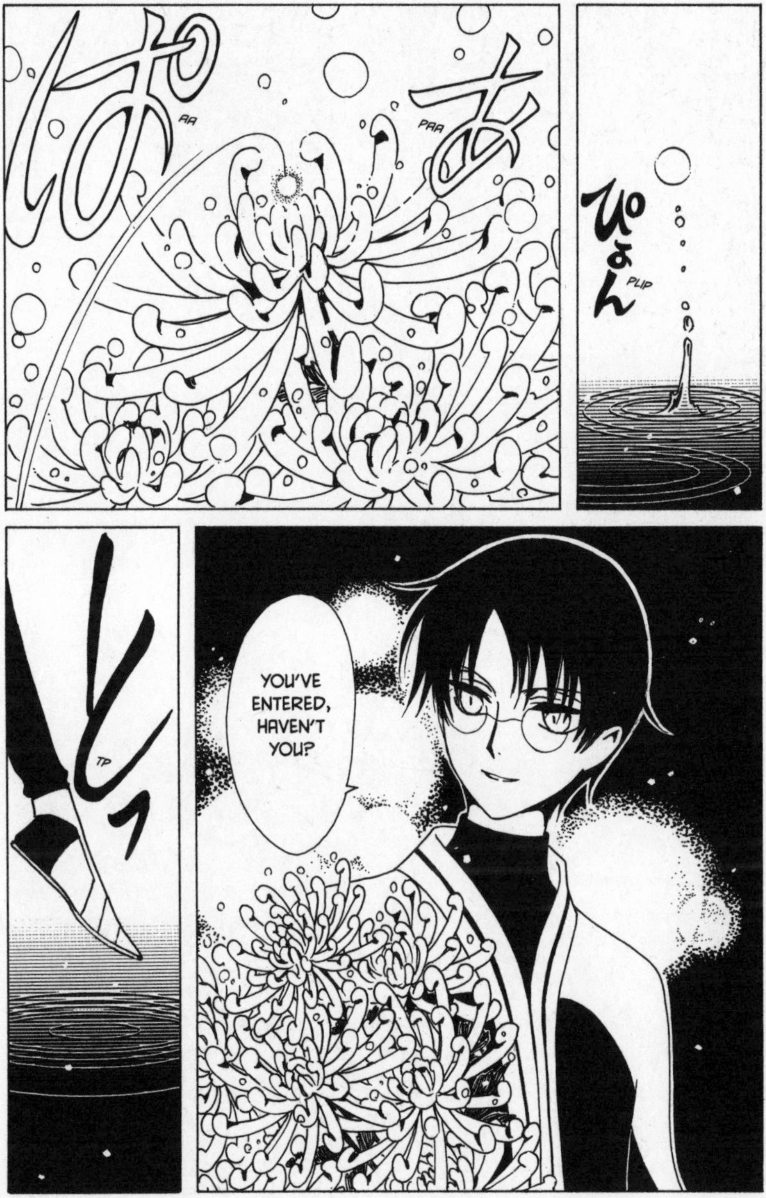
ぴょん
PLIP
ぱあ
PAA
YOU'VE ENTERED, HAVEN'T YOU?
とっ
TP

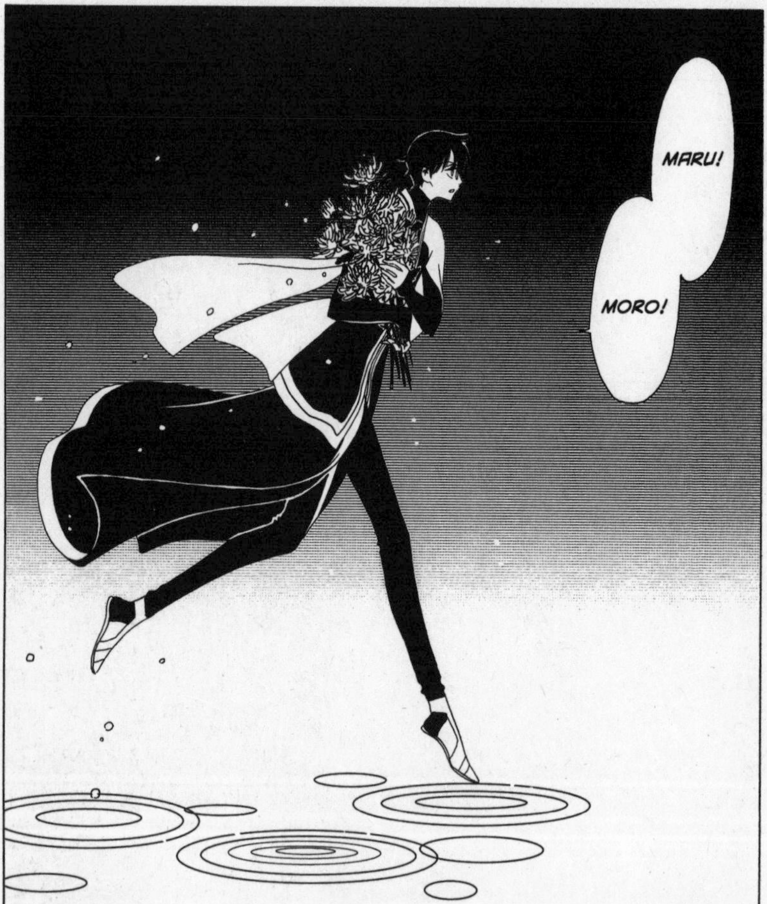
MARU!
MORO!

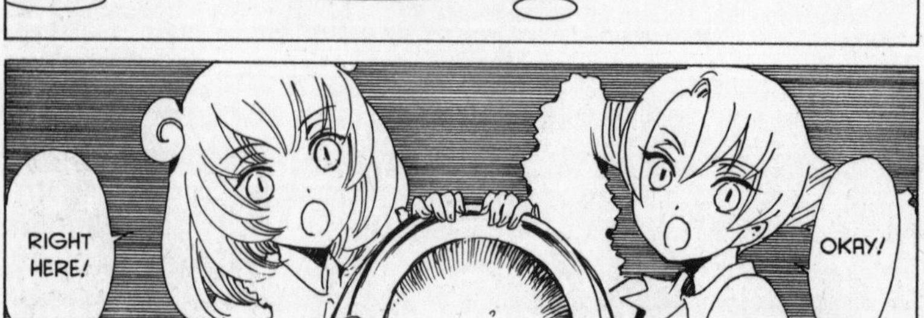
OKAY!
RIGHT HERE!

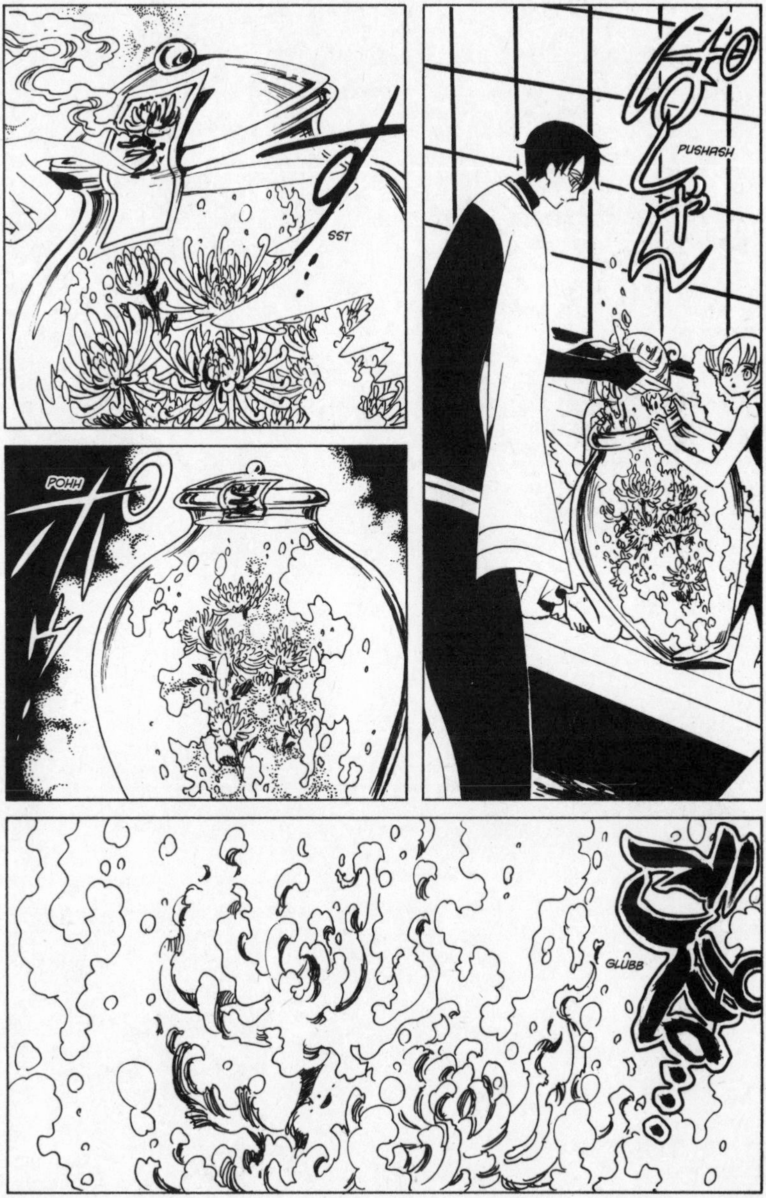
ぱしゃん
PUSHASH
す
SST
POHH
GLUBB

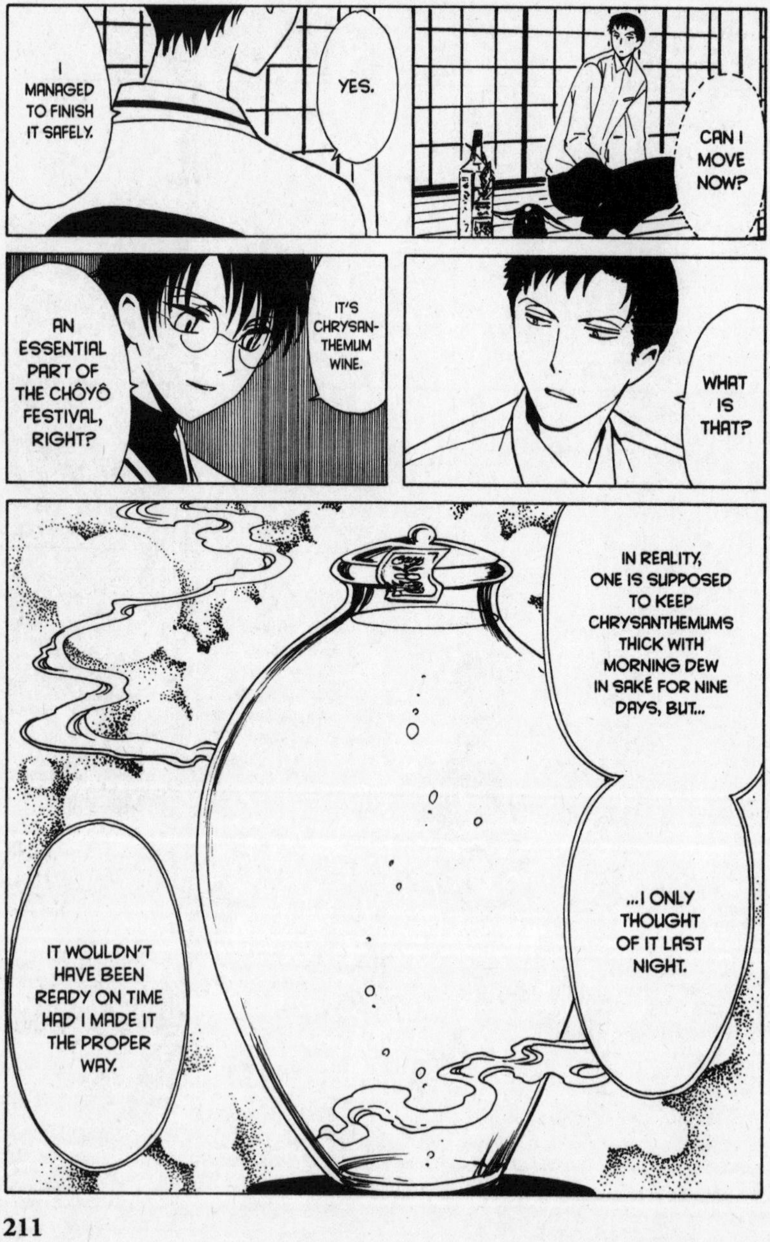
CAN I MOVE NOW?
YES.
I MANAGED TO FINISH IT SAFELY.
WHAT IS THAT?
IT'S CHRYSANTHEMUM WINE.
AN ESSENTIAL PART OF THE CHÔYÔ FESTIVAL, RIGHT?
IN REALITY, ONE IS SUPPOSED TO KEEP CHRYSANTHEMUMS THICK WITH MORNING DEW IN SAKÉ FOR NINE DAYS, BUT...
...I ONLY THOUGHT OF IT LAST NIGHT.
IT WOULDN'T HAVE BEEN READY ON TIME HAD I MADE IT THE PROPER WAY.

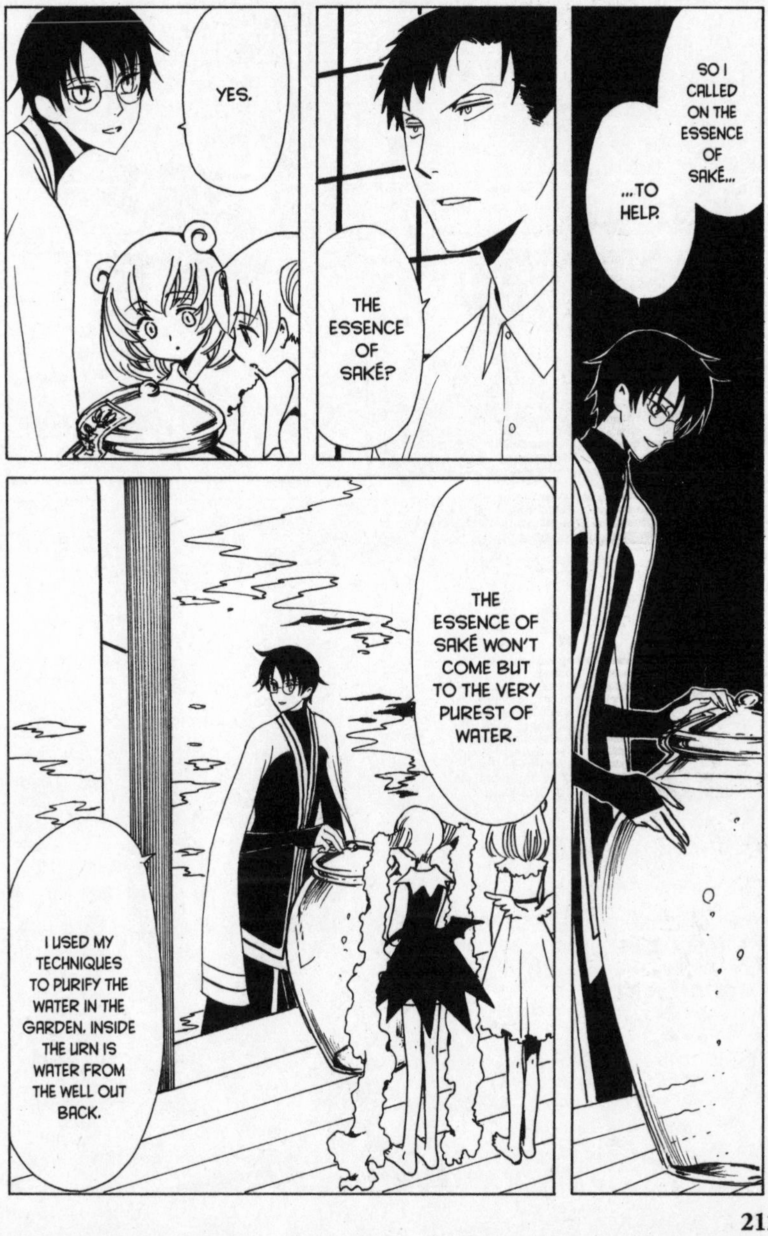
SO I CALLED ON THE ESSENCE OF SAKÉ...
...TO HELP.
THE ESSENCE OF SAKÉ?
YES.
THE ESSENCE OF SAKÉ WON'T COME BUT TO THE VERY PUREST OF WATER.
I USED MY TECHNIQUES TO PURIFY THE WATER IN THE GARDEN. INSIDE THE URN IS WATER FROM THE WELL OUT BACK.

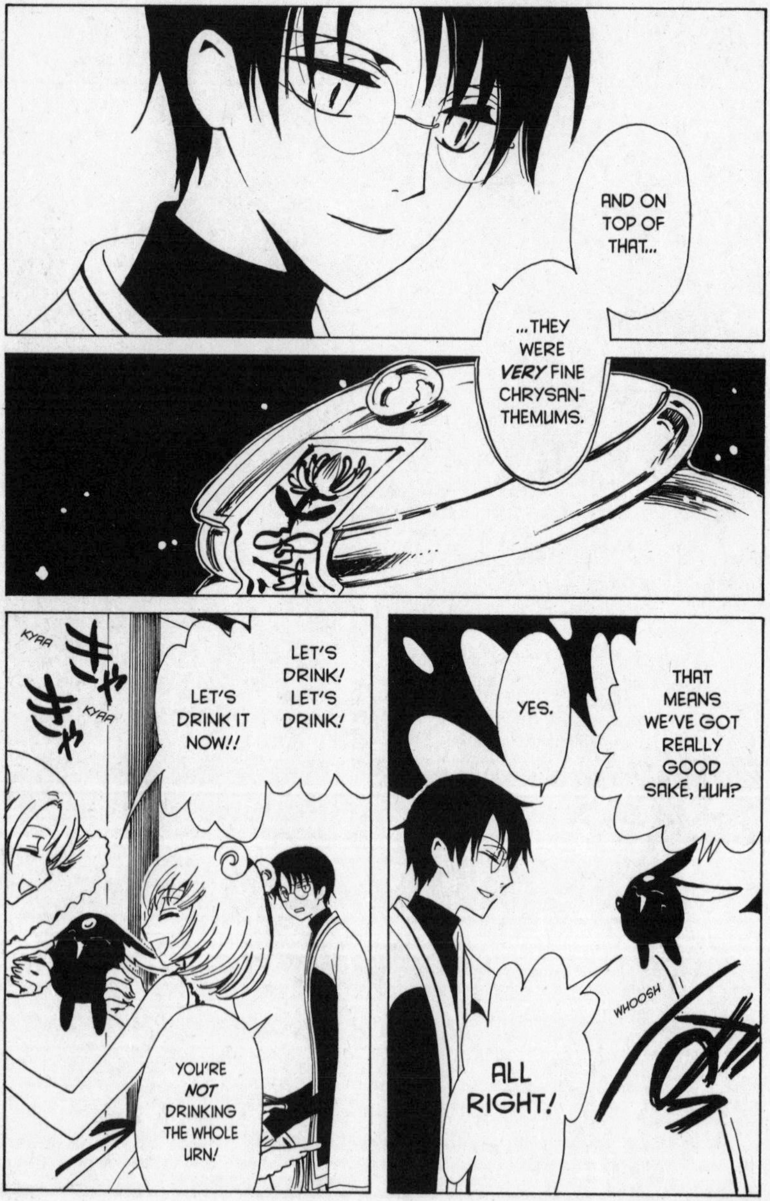
AND ON TOP OF THAT...
...THEY WERE *VERY* FINE CHRYSANTHEMUMS.
THAT MEANS WE'VE GOT REALLY GOOD SAKÉ, HUH?
YES.
WHOOSH
ALL RIGHT!
LET'S DRINK! LET'S DRINK!
LET'S DRINK IT NOW!!
KYAA
KYAA
YOU'RE *NOT* DRINKING THE WHOLE URN!

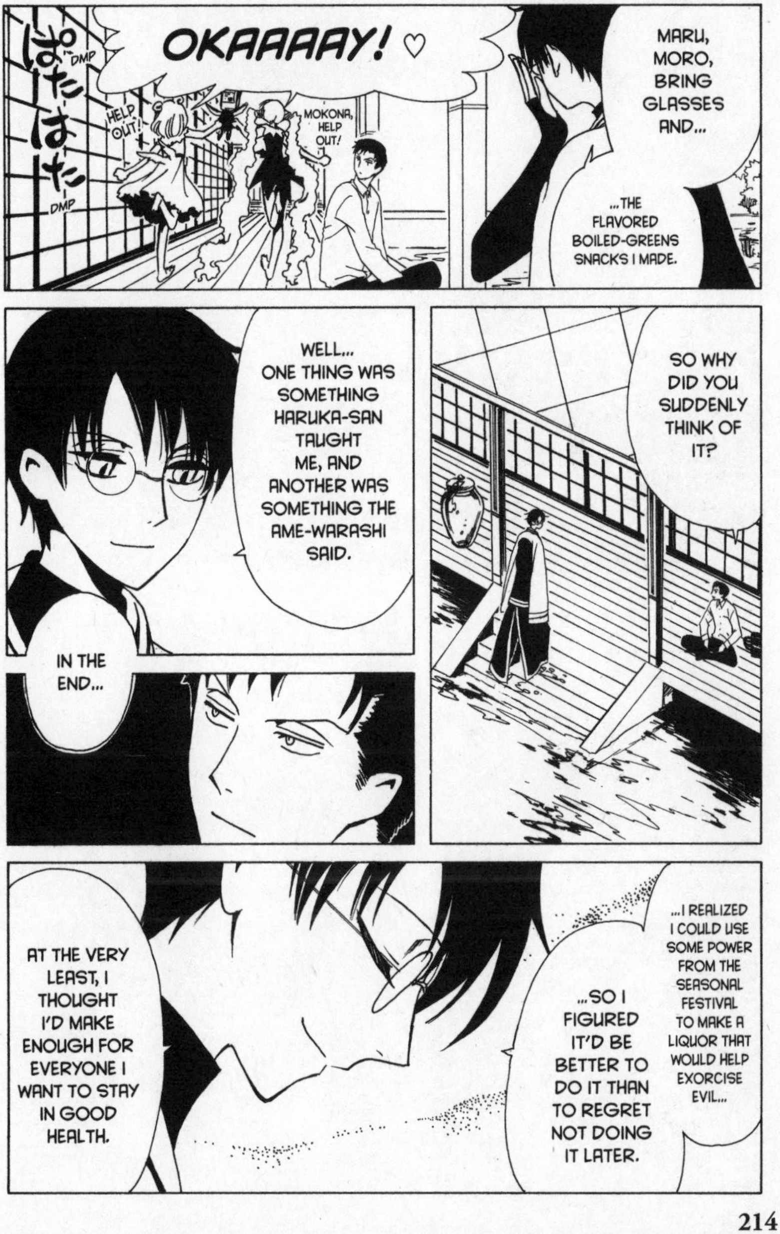
MARU, MORO, BRING GLASSES AND...
...THE FLAVORED BOILED-GREENS SNACKS I MADE.
OKAAAAY! ♡
MOKONA, HELP OUT!
HELP OUT!
ぱたぱた DMP DMP
SO WHY DID YOU SUDDENLY THINK OF IT?
WELL... ONE THING WAS SOMETHING HARUKA-SAN TAUGHT ME, AND ANOTHER WAS SOMETHING THE AME-WARASHI SAID.
IN THE END...
...I REALIZED I COULD USE SOME POWER FROM THE SEASONAL FESTIVAL TO MAKE A LIQUOR THAT WOULD HELP EXORCISE EVIL...
...SO I FIGURED IT'D BE BETTER TO DO IT THAN TO REGRET NOT DOING IT LATER.
AT THE VERY LEAST, I THOUGHT I'D MAKE ENOUGH FOR EVERYONE I WANT TO STAY IN GOOD HEALTH.

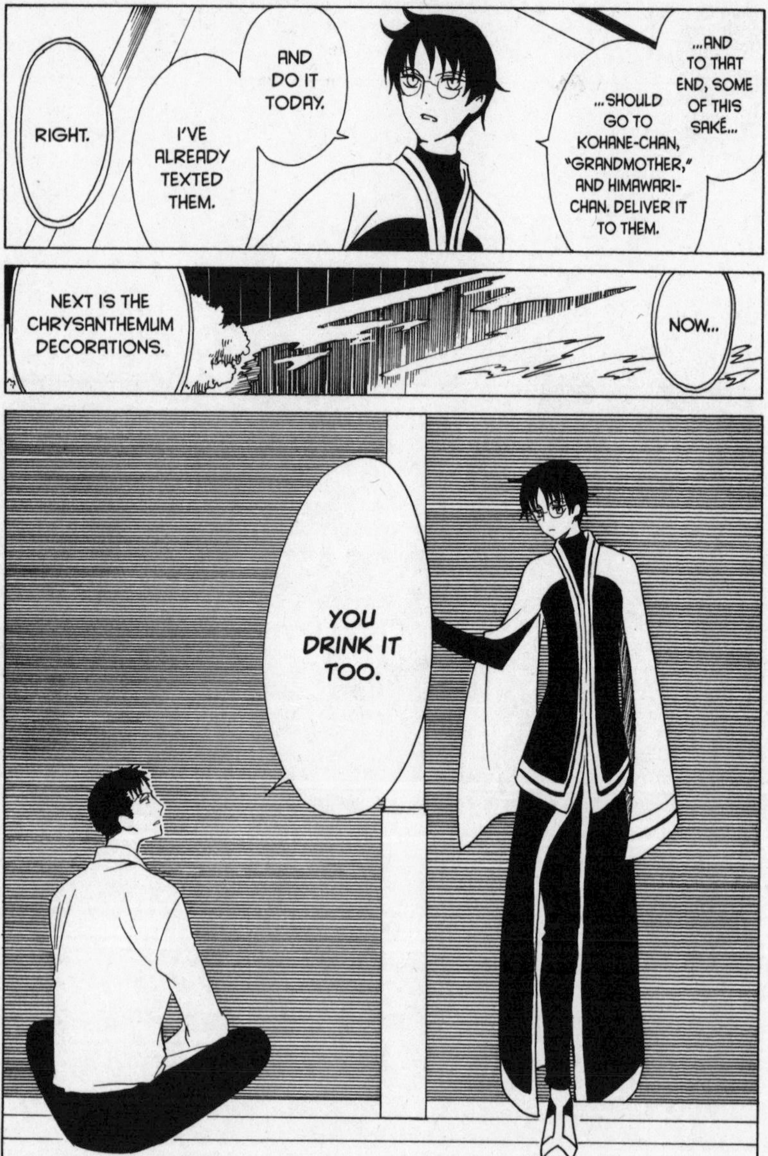
...AND TO THAT END, SOME OF THIS SAKÉ...
...SHOULD GO TO KOHANE-CHAN, "GRANDMOTHER," AND HIMAWARI-CHAN. DELIVER IT TO THEM.
AND DO IT TODAY.
I'VE ALREADY TEXTED THEM.
RIGHT.
NOW...
NEXT IS THE CHRYSANTHEMUM DECORATIONS.
YOU DRINK IT TOO.

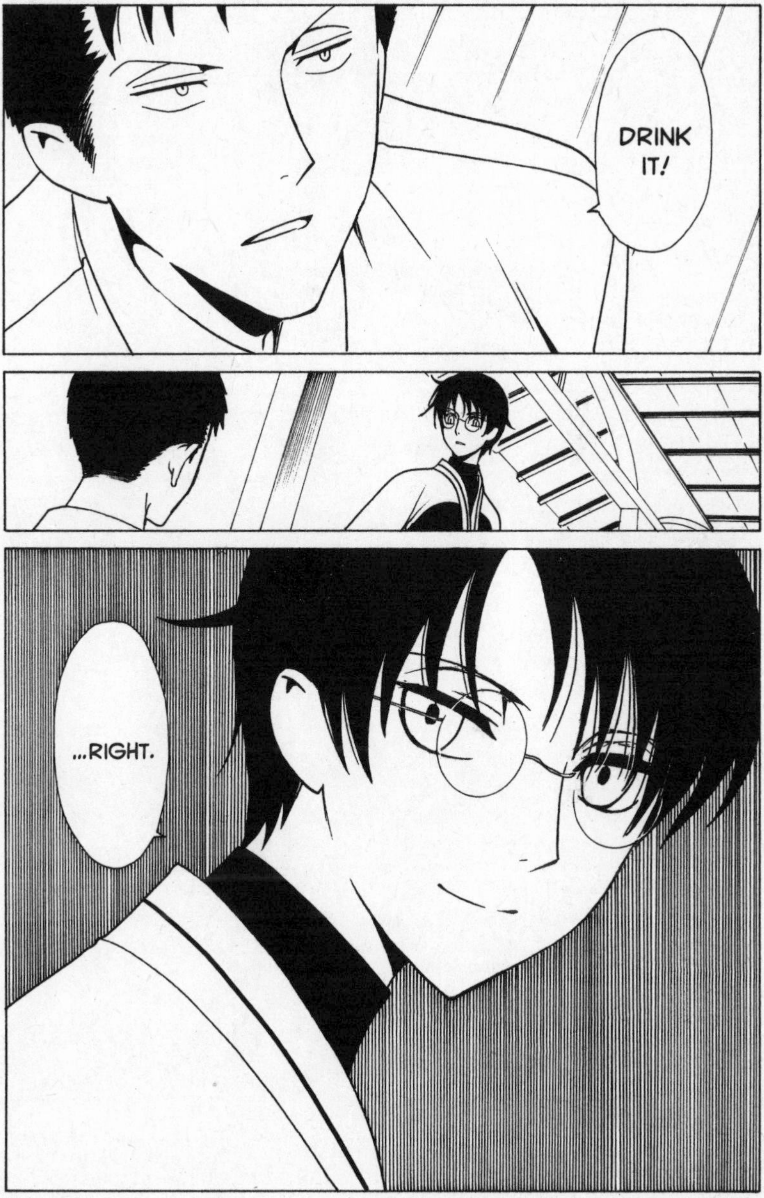
DRINK IT!
...RIGHT.

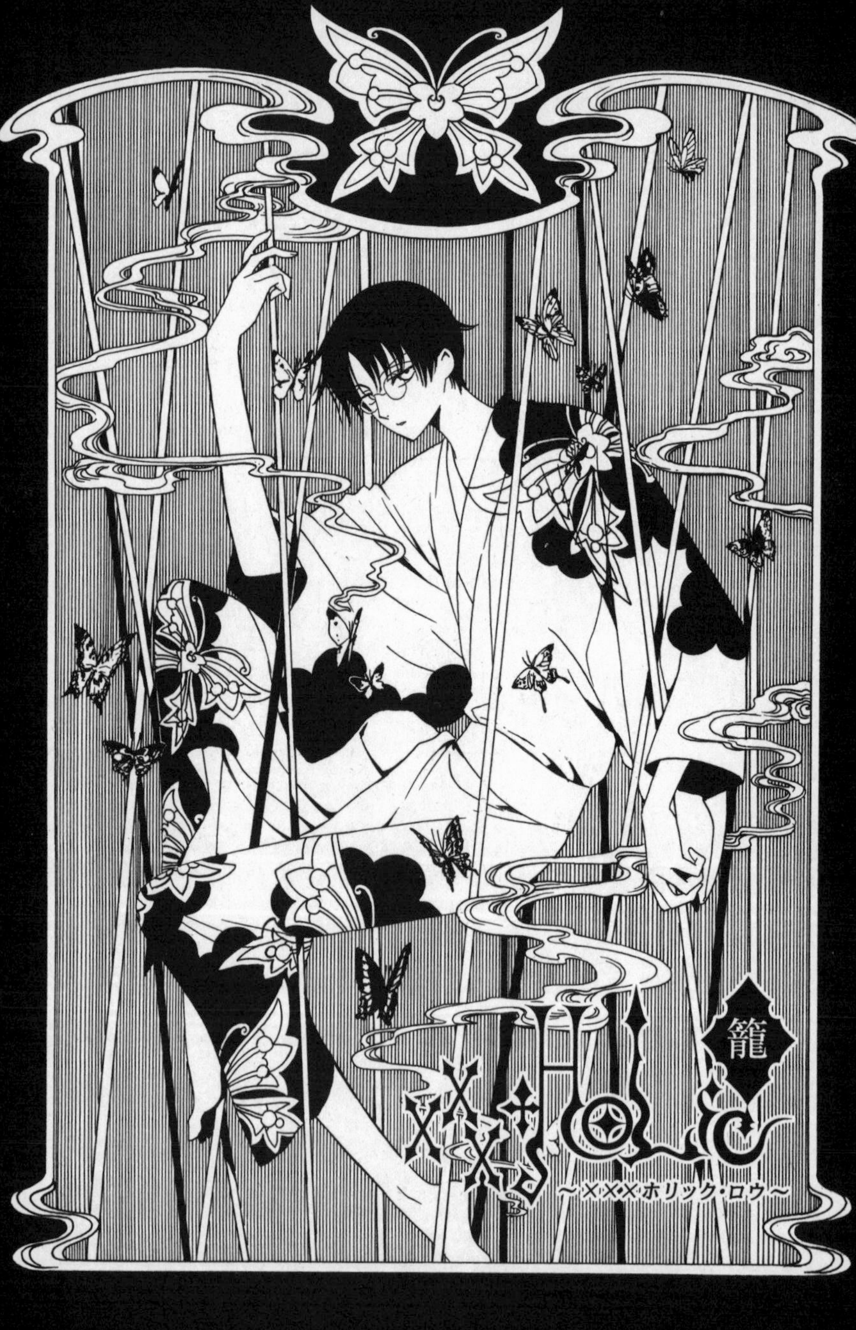
籠
xxxHOLiC
〜×××ホリック・ロウ〜

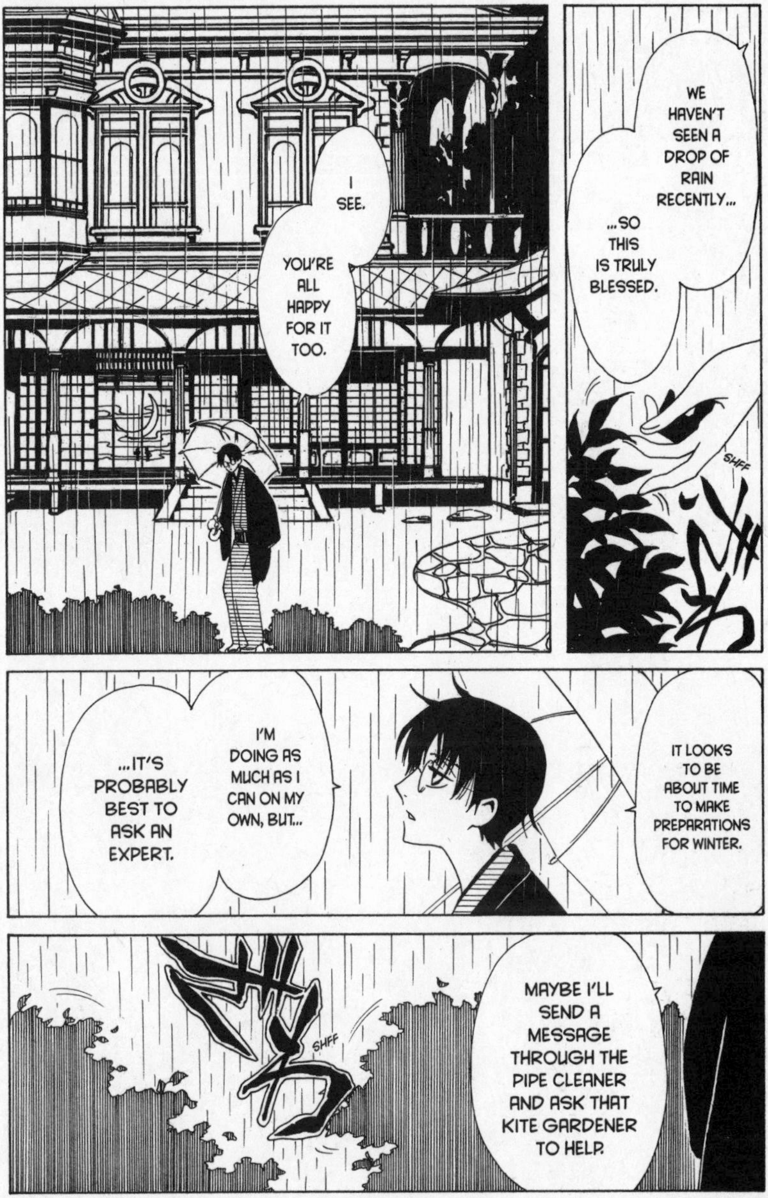
WE HAVEN'T SEEN A DROP OF RAIN RECENTLY...
...SO THIS IS TRULY BLESSED.
SHFF
I SEE.
YOU'RE ALL HAPPY FOR IT TOO.
IT LOOKS TO BE ABOUT TIME TO MAKE PREPARATIONS FOR WINTER.
I'M DOING AS MUCH AS I CAN ON MY OWN, BUT...
...IT'S PROBABLY BEST TO ASK AN EXPERT.
MAYBE I'LL SEND A MESSAGE THROUGH THE PIPE CLEANER AND ASK THAT KITE GARDENER TO HELP.
SHFF

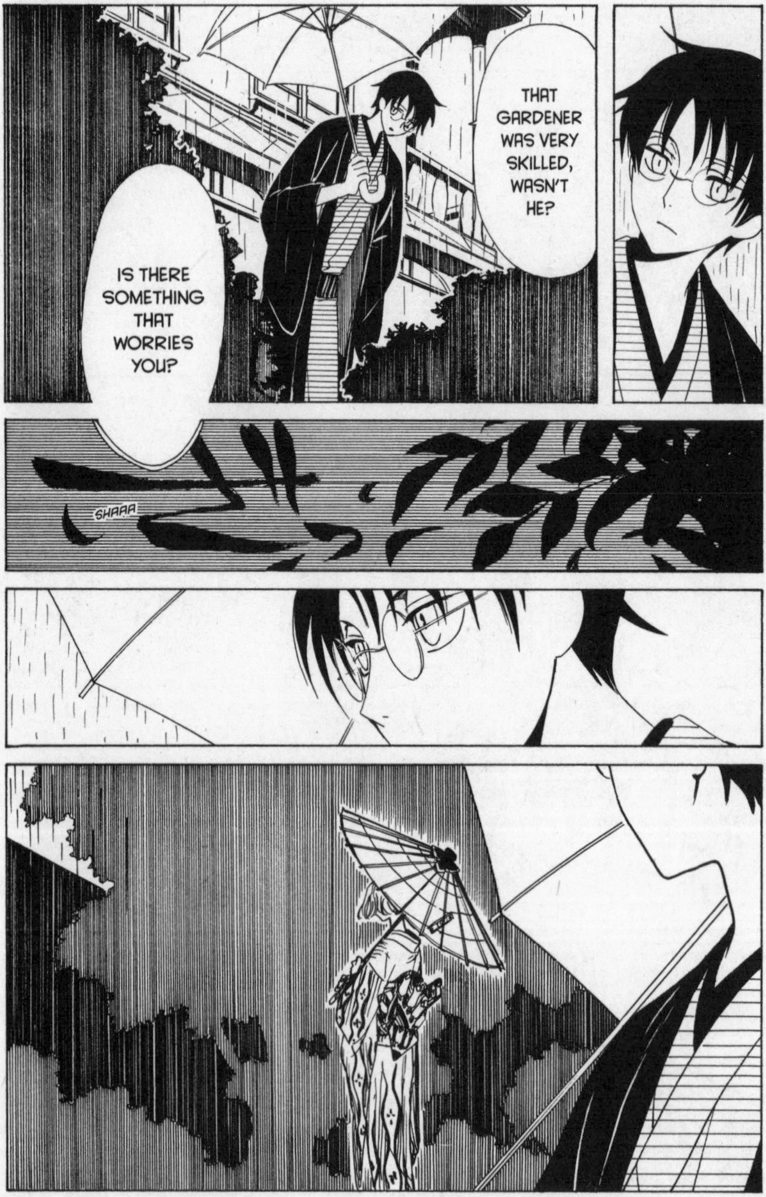
THAT GARDENER WAS VERY SKILLED, WASN'T HE?
IS THERE SOMETHING THAT WORRIES YOU?
SHAAA

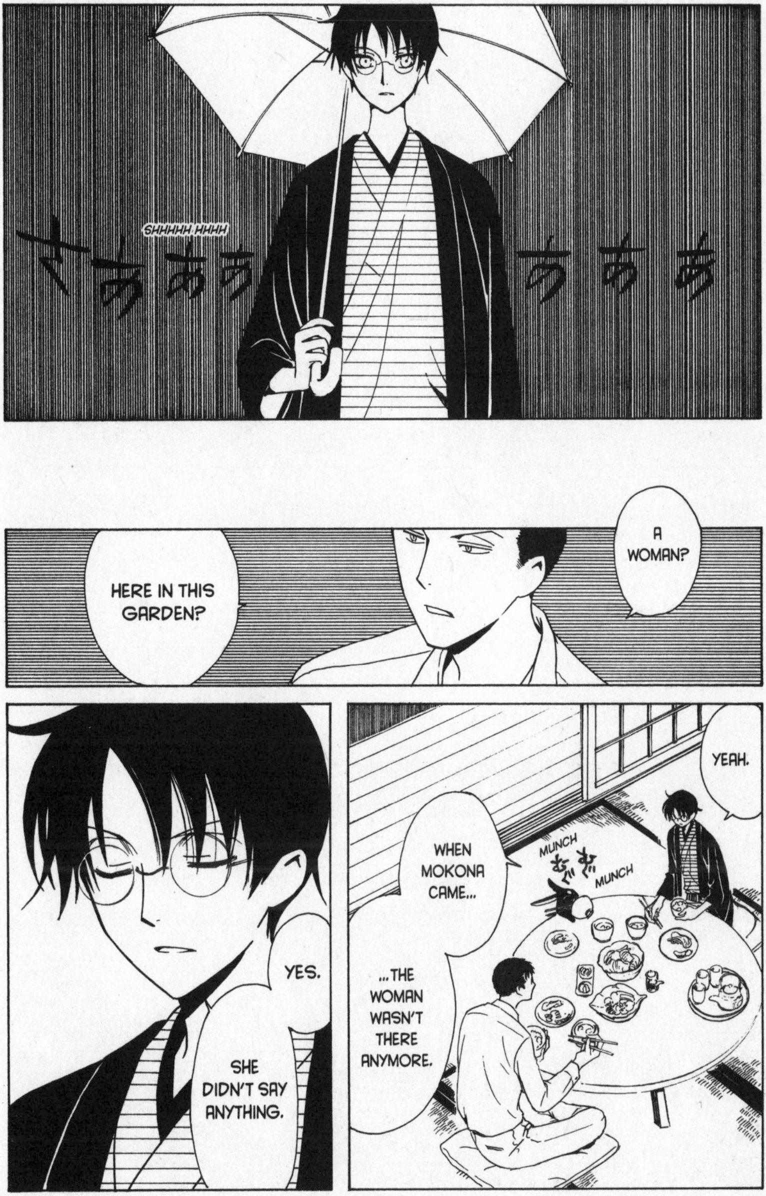
SHHHHH HHHH
A WOMAN?
HERE IN THIS GARDEN?
YEAH.
WHEN MOKONA CAME...
MUNCH
MUNCH
...THE WOMAN WASN'T THERE ANYMORE.
YES.
SHE DIDN'T SAY ANYTHING.

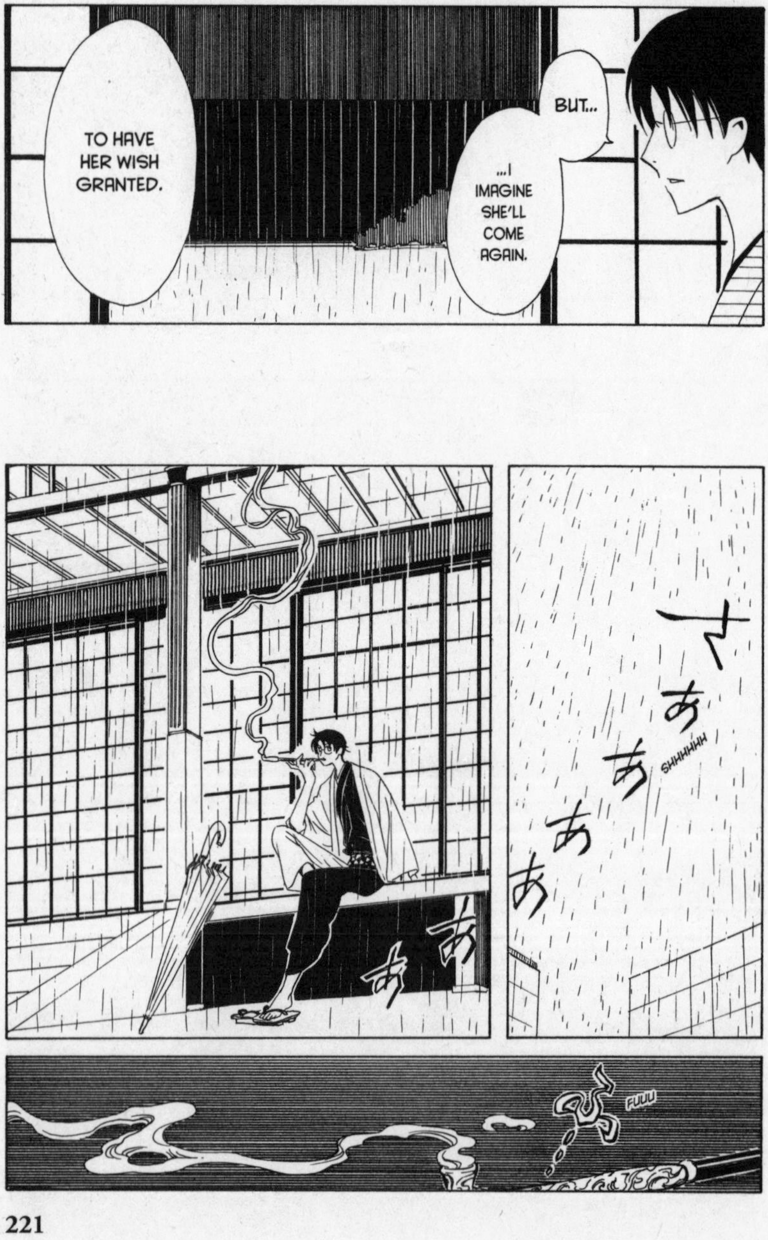
BUT...
...I IMAGINE SHE'LL COME AGAIN.
TO HAVE HER WISH GRANTED.
さああああ
SHHHHHH
ああ
ふ
FUUU

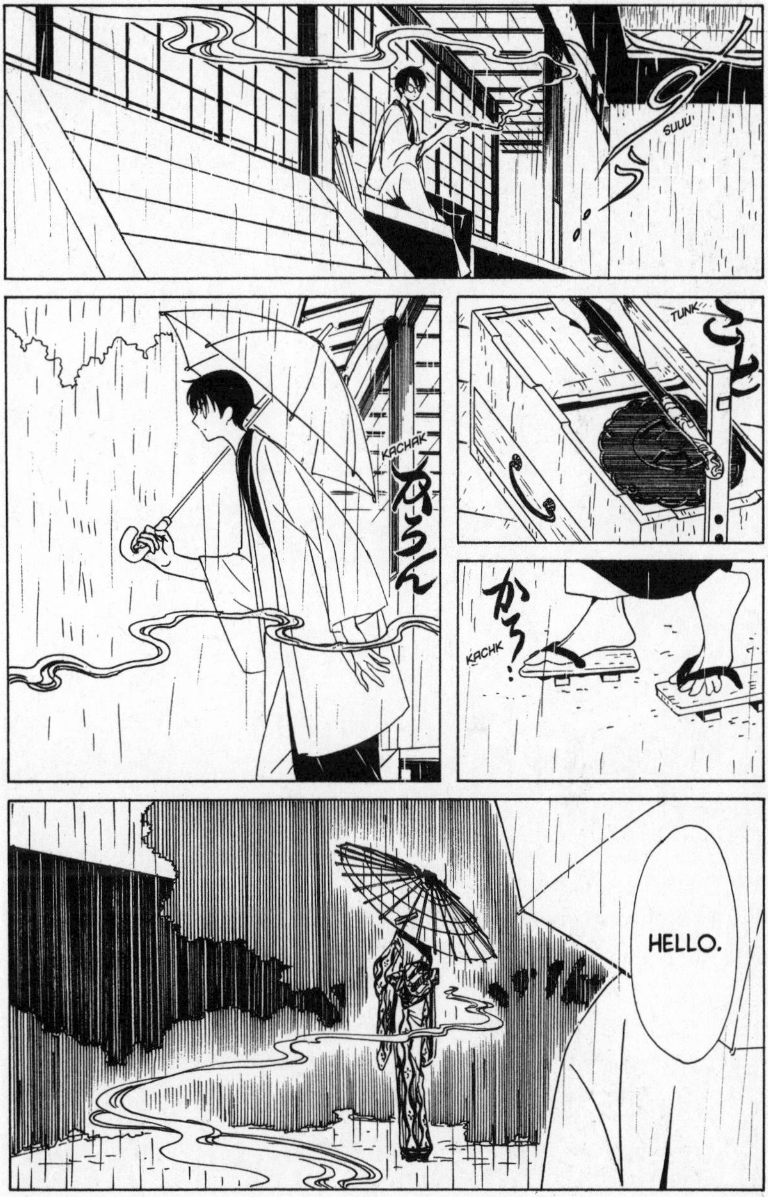
SUUU
TUNK
KACHK
KACHAK
HELLO.

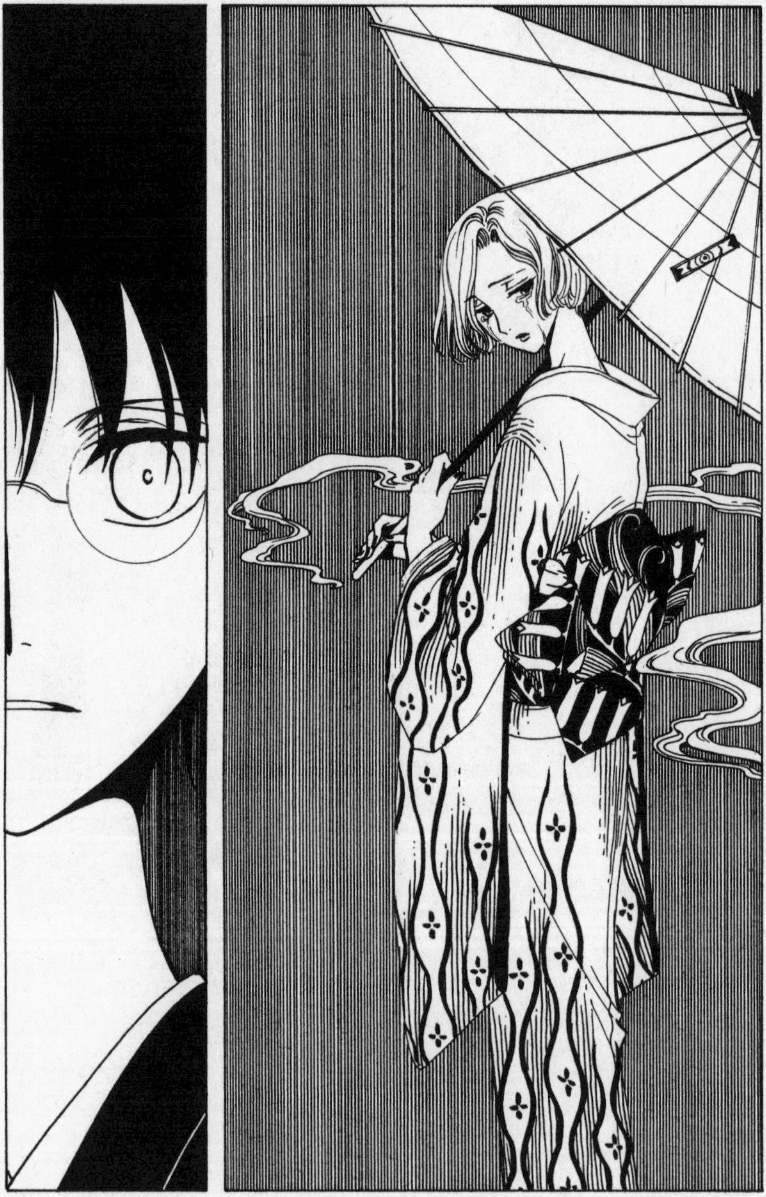

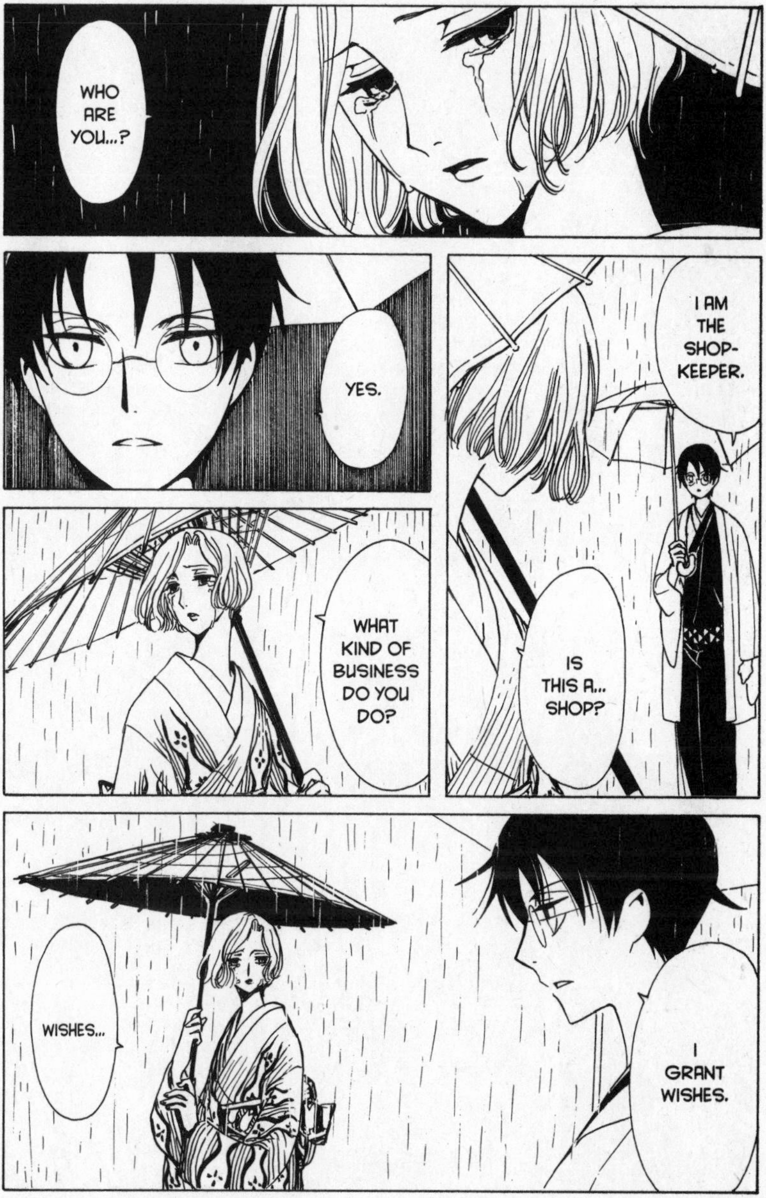
WHO ARE YOU...?
I AM THE SHOP-KEEPER.
IS THIS A... SHOP?
YES.
WHAT KIND OF BUSINESS DO YOU DO?
I GRANT WISHES.
WISHES...

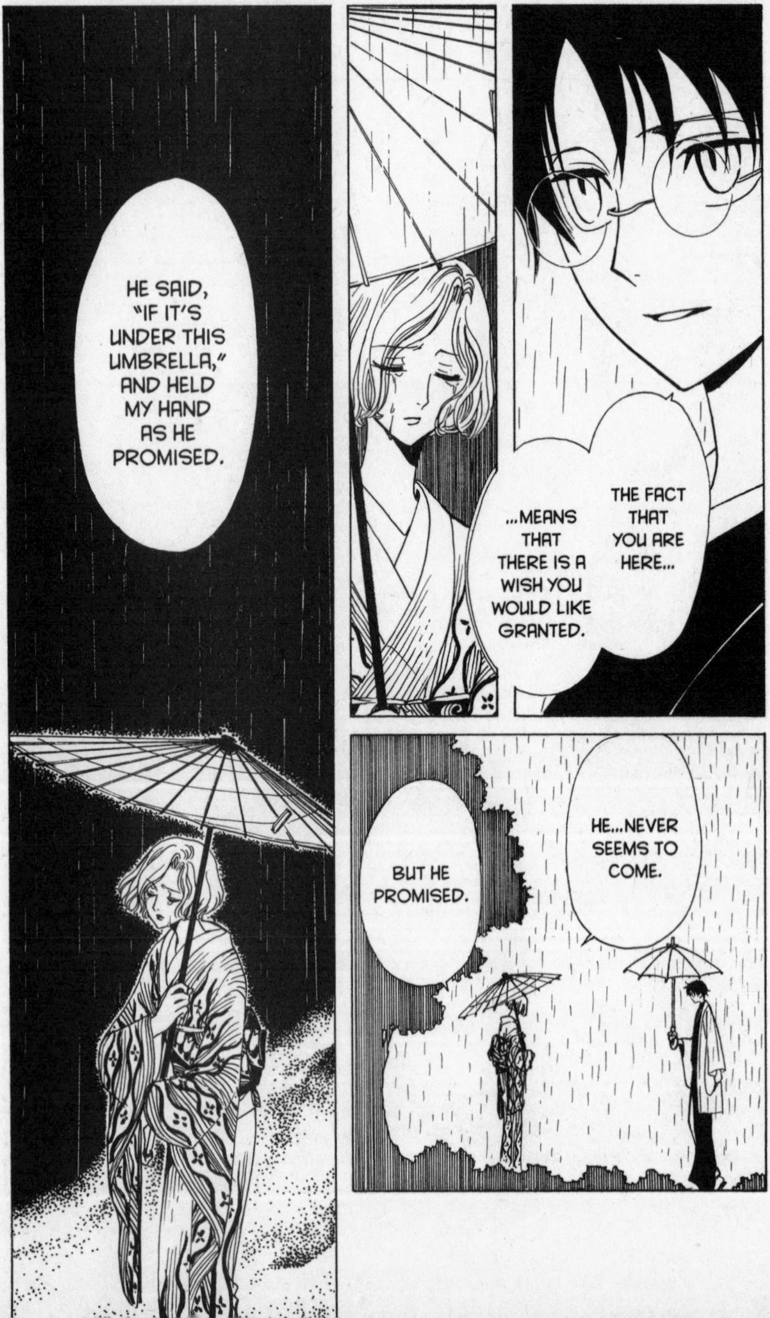
THE FACT THAT YOU ARE HERE...
...MEANS THAT THERE IS A WISH YOU WOULD LIKE GRANTED.
HE...NEVER SEEMS TO COME.
BUT HE PROMISED.
HE SAID, "IF IT'S UNDER THIS UMBRELLA," AND HELD MY HAND AS HE PROMISED.

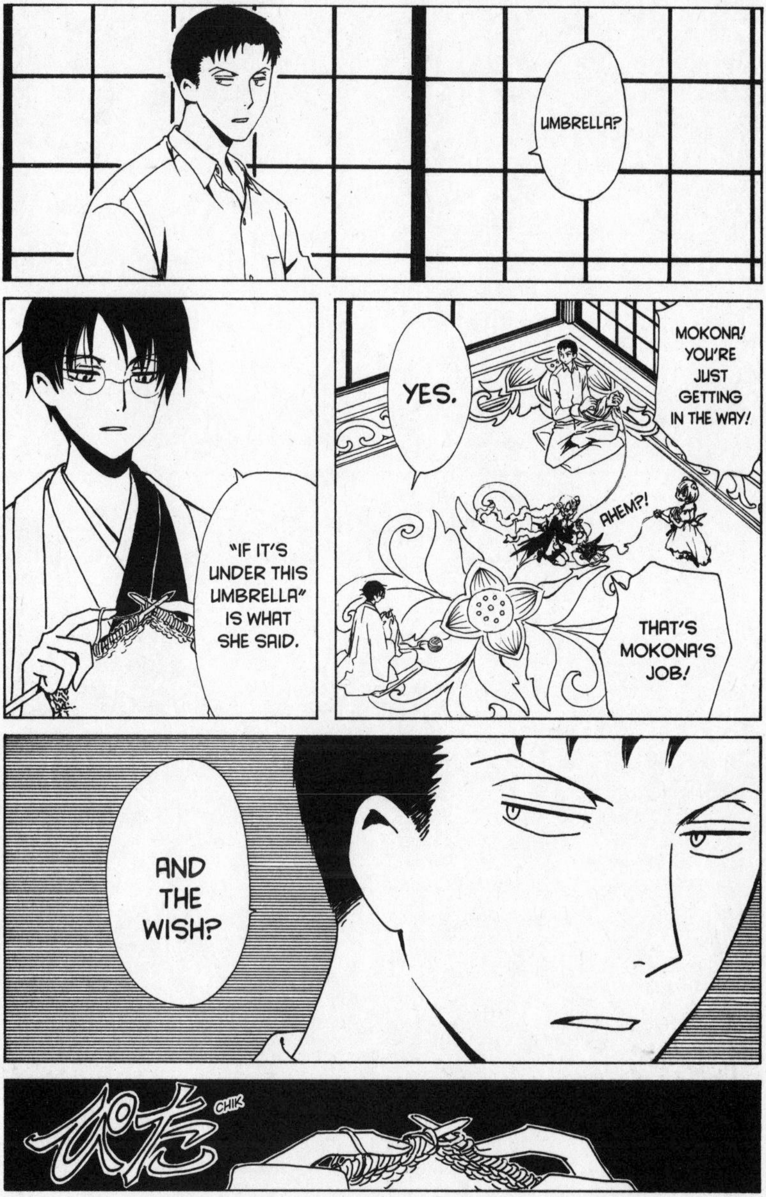
UMBRELLA?
MOKONA! YOU'RE JUST GETTING IN THE WAY!
YES.
AHEM?!
THAT'S MOKONA'S JOB!
"IF IT'S UNDER THIS UMBRELLA" IS WHAT SHE SAID.
AND THE WISH?
ぴた
CHIK

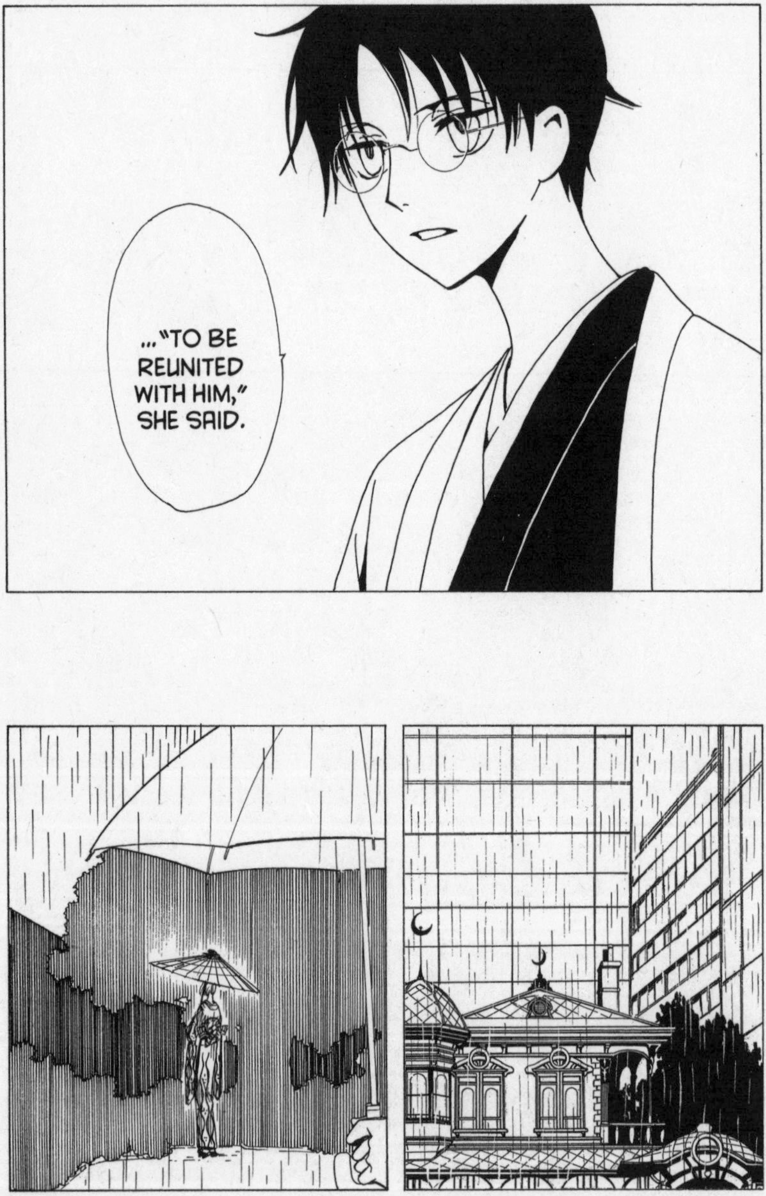
..."TO BE REUNITED WITH HIM," SHE SAID.

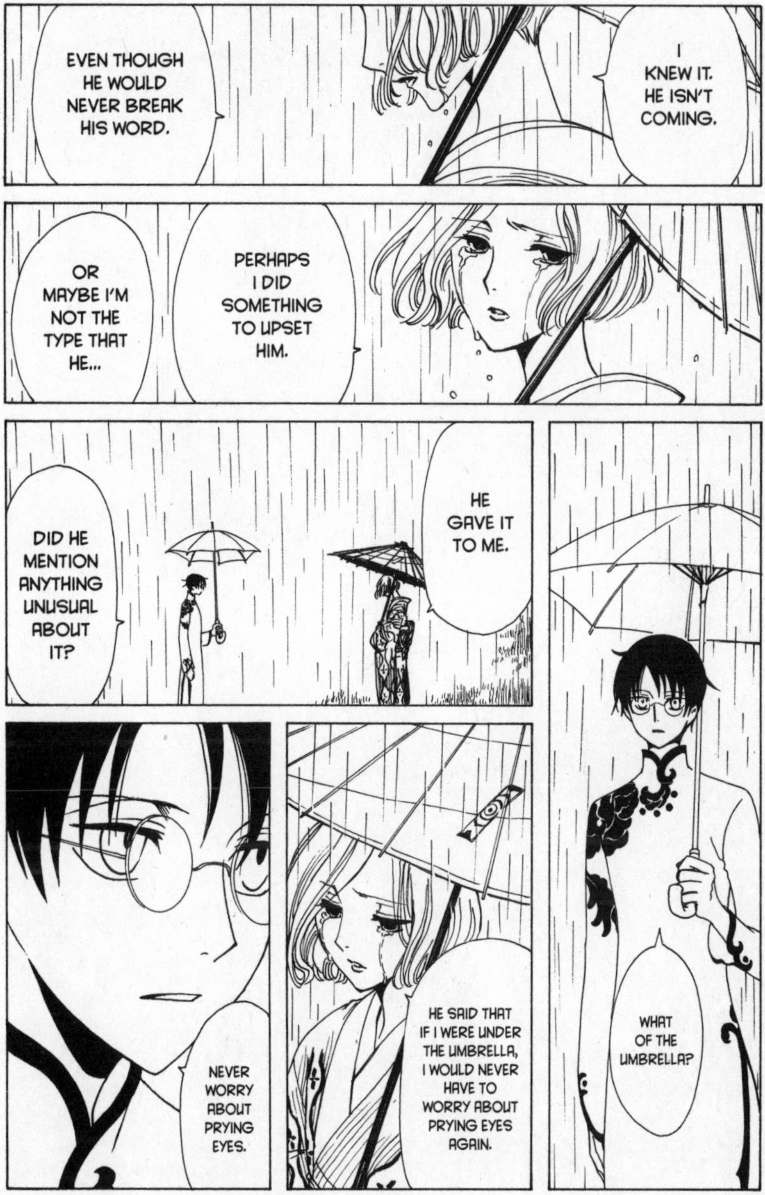
I KNEW IT. HE ISN'T COMING.
EVEN THOUGH HE WOULD NEVER BREAK HIS WORD.
PERHAPS I DID SOMETHING TO UPSET HIM.
OR MAYBE I'M NOT THE TYPE THAT HE...
WHAT OF THE UMBRELLA?
HE GAVE IT TO ME.
DID HE MENTION ANYTHING UNUSUAL ABOUT IT?
HE SAID THAT IF I WERE UNDER THE UMBRELLA, I WOULD NEVER HAVE TO WORRY ABOUT PRYING EYES AGAIN.
NEVER WORRY ABOUT PRYING EYES.

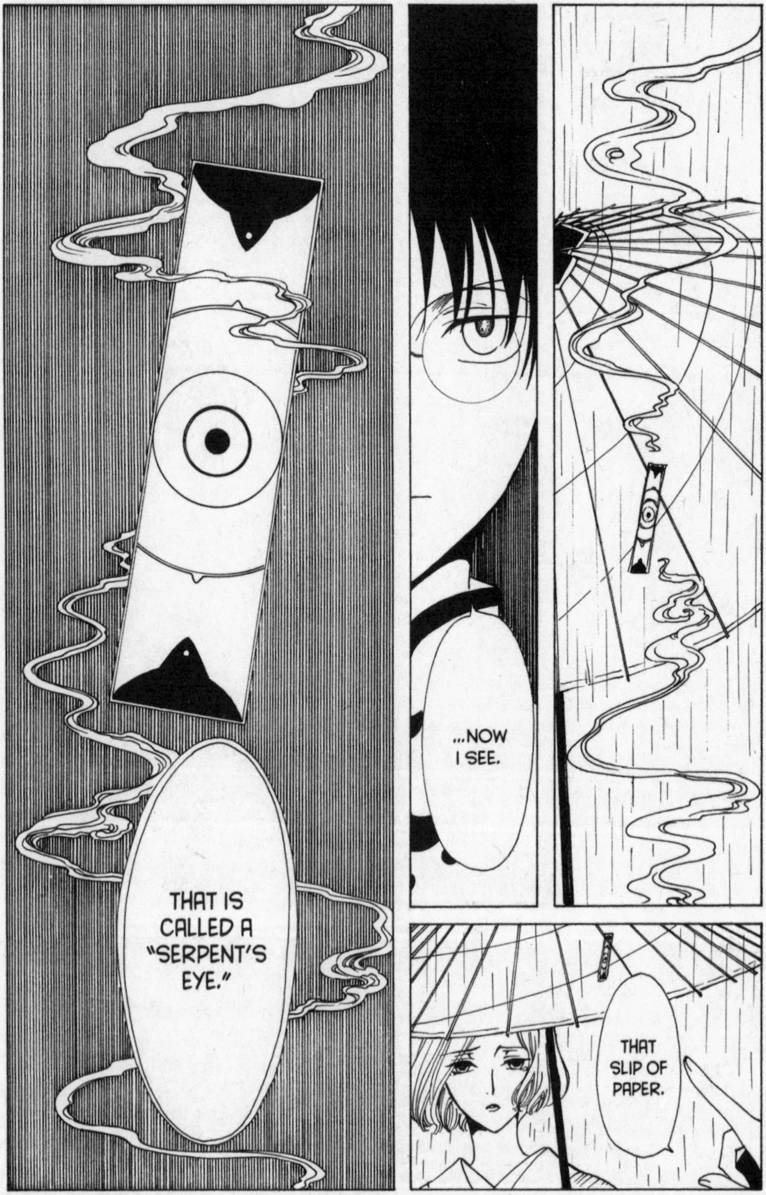
...NOW I SEE.
THAT SLIP OF PAPER.
THAT IS CALLED A "SERPENT'S EYE."

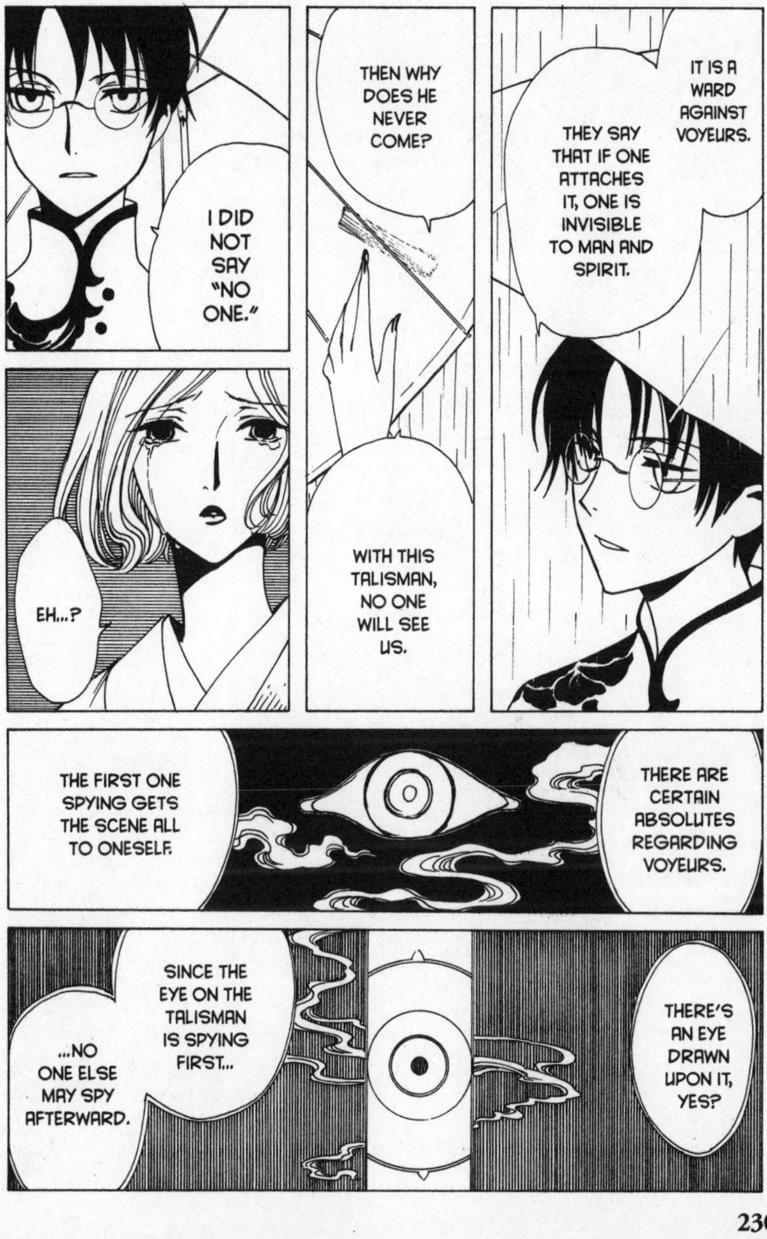
IT IS A WARD AGAINST VOYEURS.
THEY SAY THAT IF ONE ATTACHES IT, ONE IS INVISIBLE TO MAN AND SPIRIT.
THEN WHY DOES HE NEVER COME?
WITH THIS TALISMAN, NO ONE WILL SEE US.
I DID NOT SAY "NO ONE."
EH...?
THERE ARE CERTAIN ABSOLUTES REGARDING VOYEURS.
THE FIRST ONE SPYING GETS THE SCENE ALL TO ONESELF.
THERE'S AN EYE DRAWN UPON IT, YES?
SINCE THE EYE ON THE TALISMAN IS SPYING FIRST...
...NO ONE ELSE MAY SPY AFTERWARD.

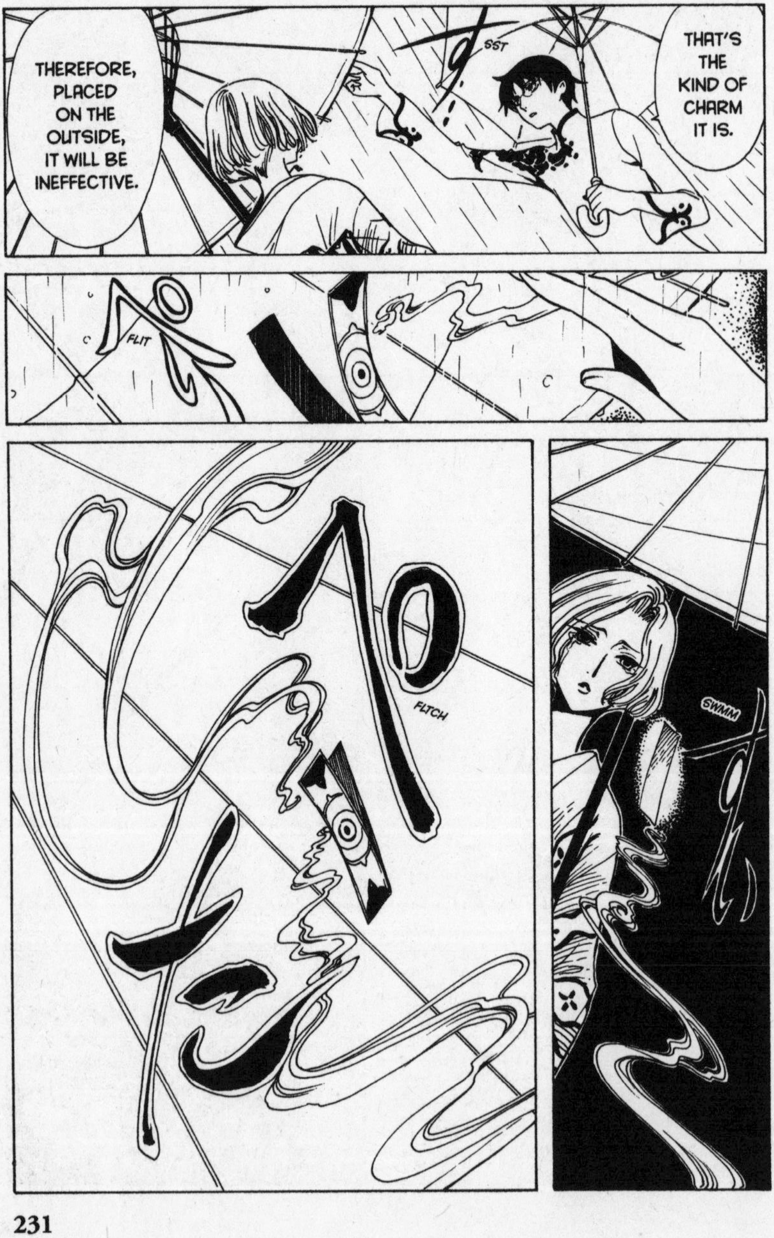
THAT'S THE KIND OF CHARM IT IS.
SST
THEREFORE, PLACED ON THE OUTSIDE, IT WILL BE INEFFECTIVE.
FLIT
SWMM
FLTCH

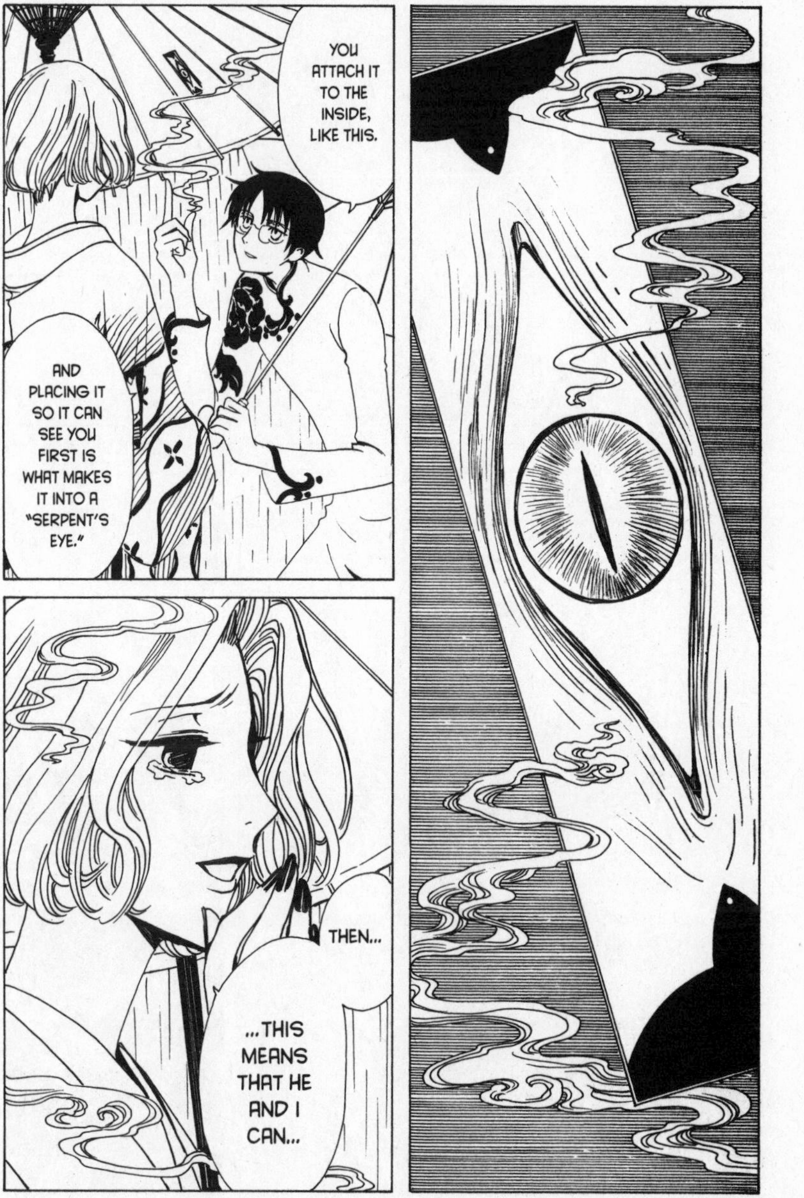
YOU ATTACH IT TO THE INSIDE, LIKE THIS.
AND PLACING IT SO IT CAN SEE YOU FIRST IS WHAT MAKES IT INTO A "SERPENT'S EYE."
THEN...
...THIS MEANS THAT HE AND I CAN...

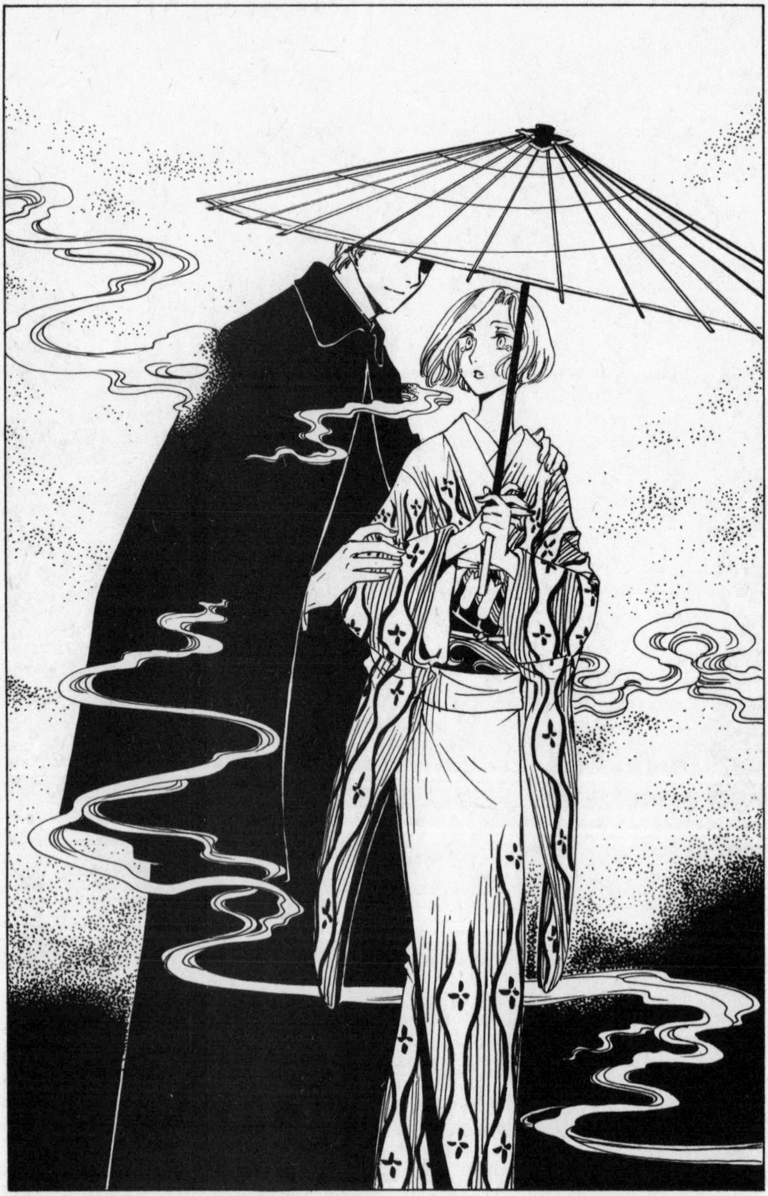

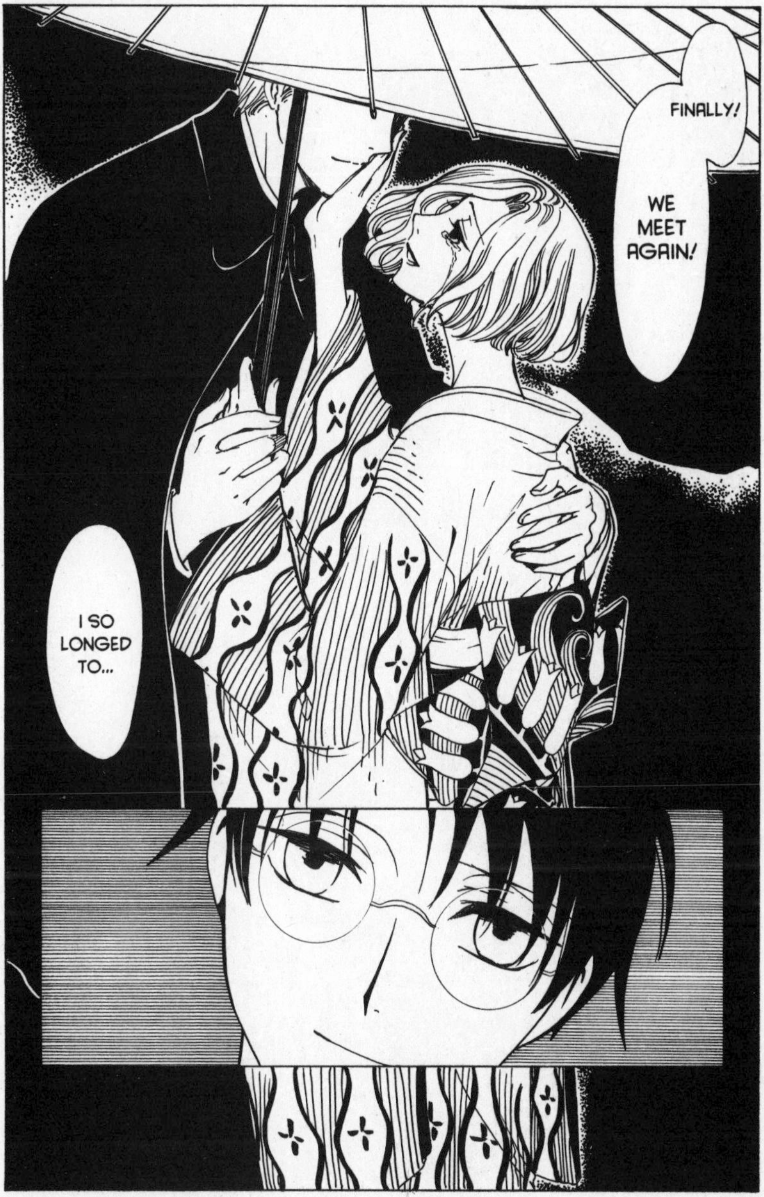
FINALLY!
WE MEET AGAIN!
I SO LONGED TO...

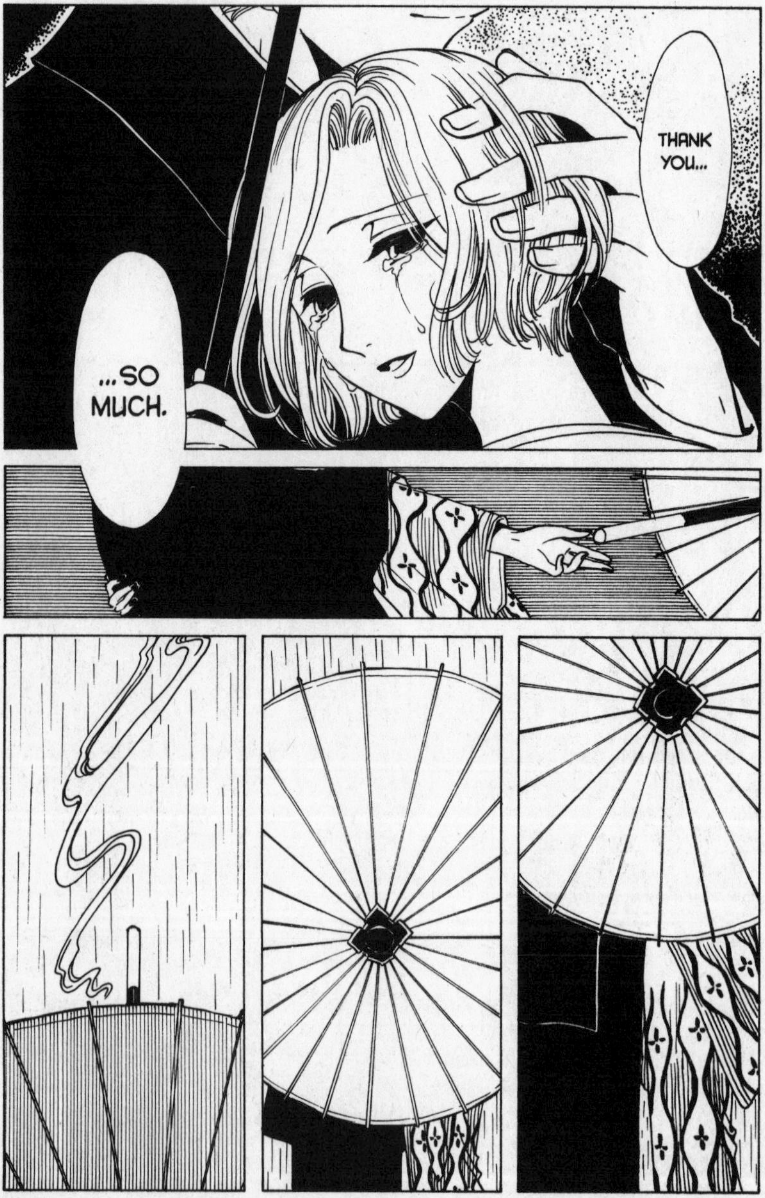
THANK YOU...
...SO MUCH.

...I WISH YOU HAPPINESS AT YOUR DESTINATION.
SO...
...THAT'S THE PAYMENT?
WHOOSH
YES.

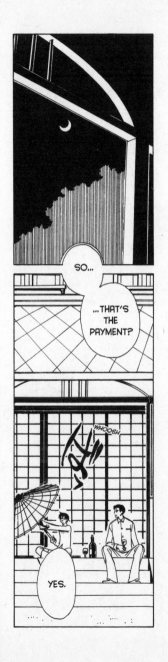

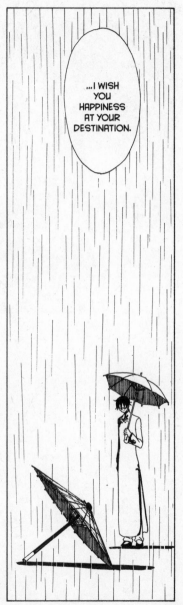

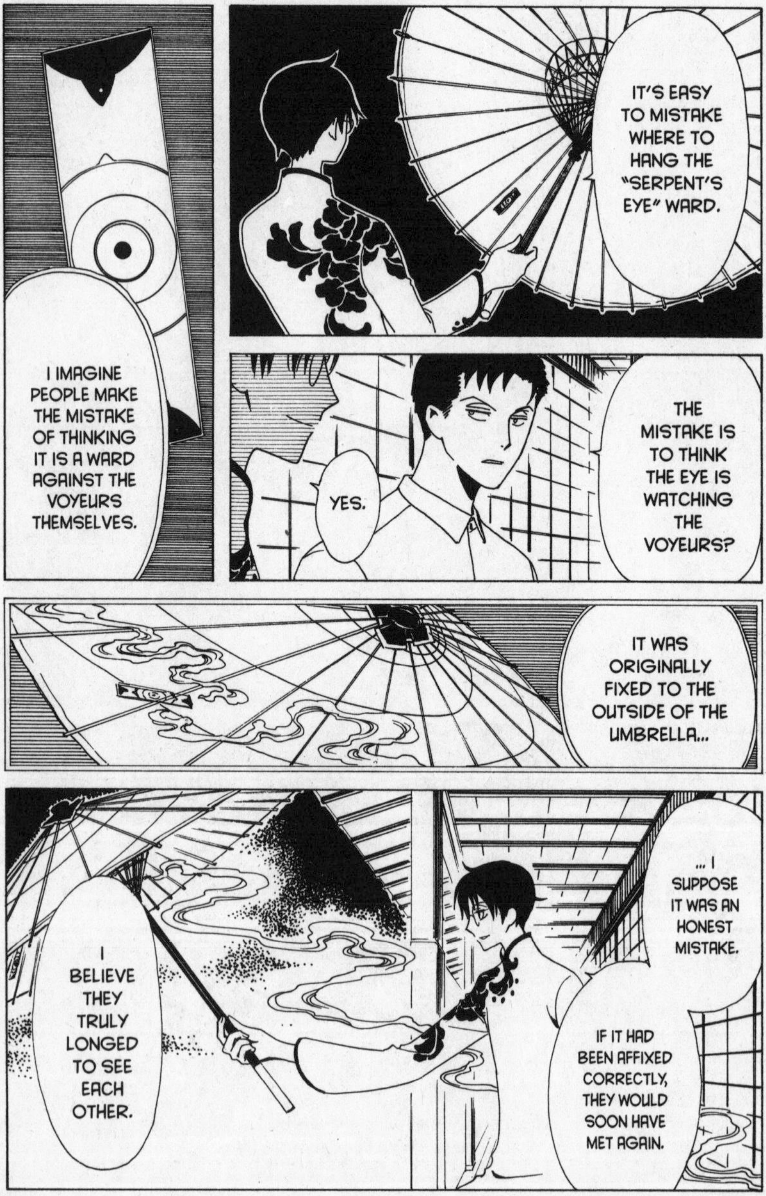
IT'S EASY TO MISTAKE WHERE TO HANG THE "SERPENT'S EYE" WARD.
THE MISTAKE IS TO THINK THE EYE IS WATCHING THE VOYEURS?
YES.
I IMAGINE PEOPLE MAKE THE MISTAKE OF THINKING IT IS A WARD AGAINST THE VOYEURS THEMSELVES.
IT WAS ORIGINALLY FIXED TO THE OUTSIDE OF THE UMBRELLA...
...I SUPPOSE IT WAS AN HONEST MISTAKE.
IF IT HAD BEEN AFFIXED CORRECTLY, THEY WOULD SOON HAVE MET AGAIN.
I BELIEVE THEY TRULY LONGED TO SEE EACH OTHER.

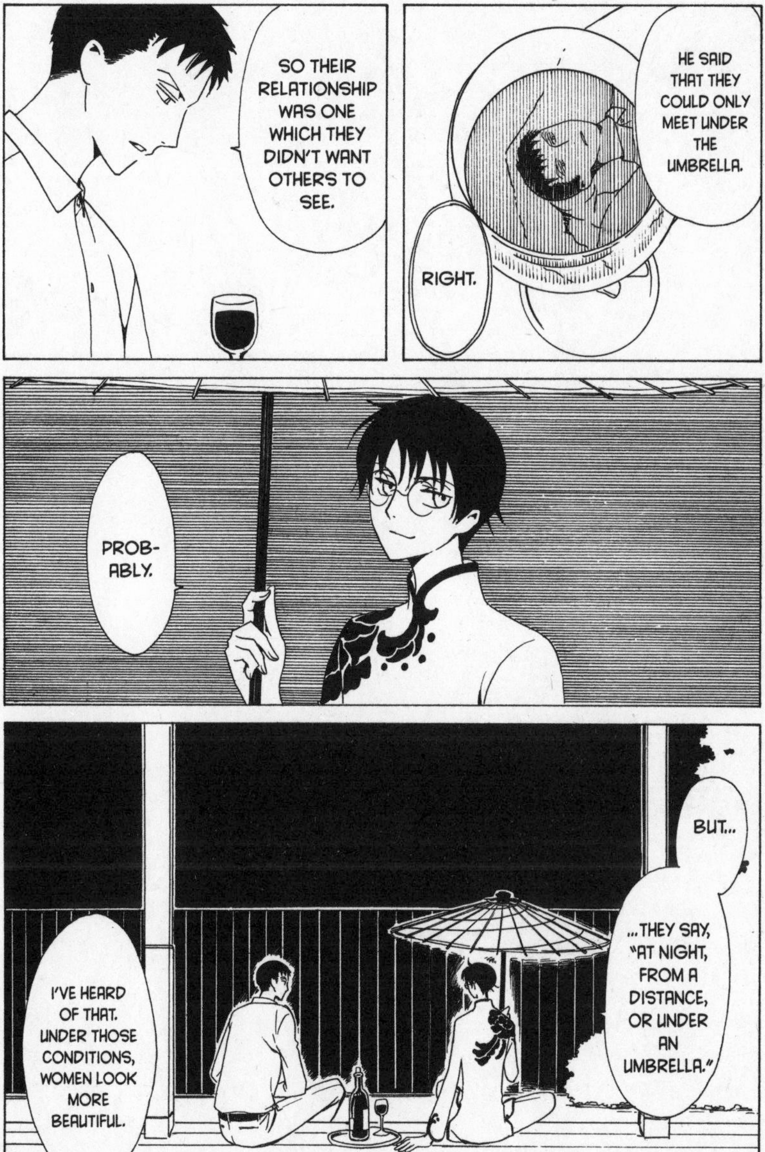
HE SAID THAT THEY COULD ONLY MEET UNDER THE UMBRELLA.
RIGHT.
SO THEIR RELATIONSHIP WAS ONE WHICH THEY DIDN'T WANT OTHERS TO SEE.
PROB-ABLY.
BUT...
...THEY SAY, "AT NIGHT, FROM A DISTANCE, OR UNDER AN UMBRELLA."
I'VE HEARD OF THAT. UNDER THOSE CONDITIONS, WOMEN LOOK MORE BEAUTIFUL.

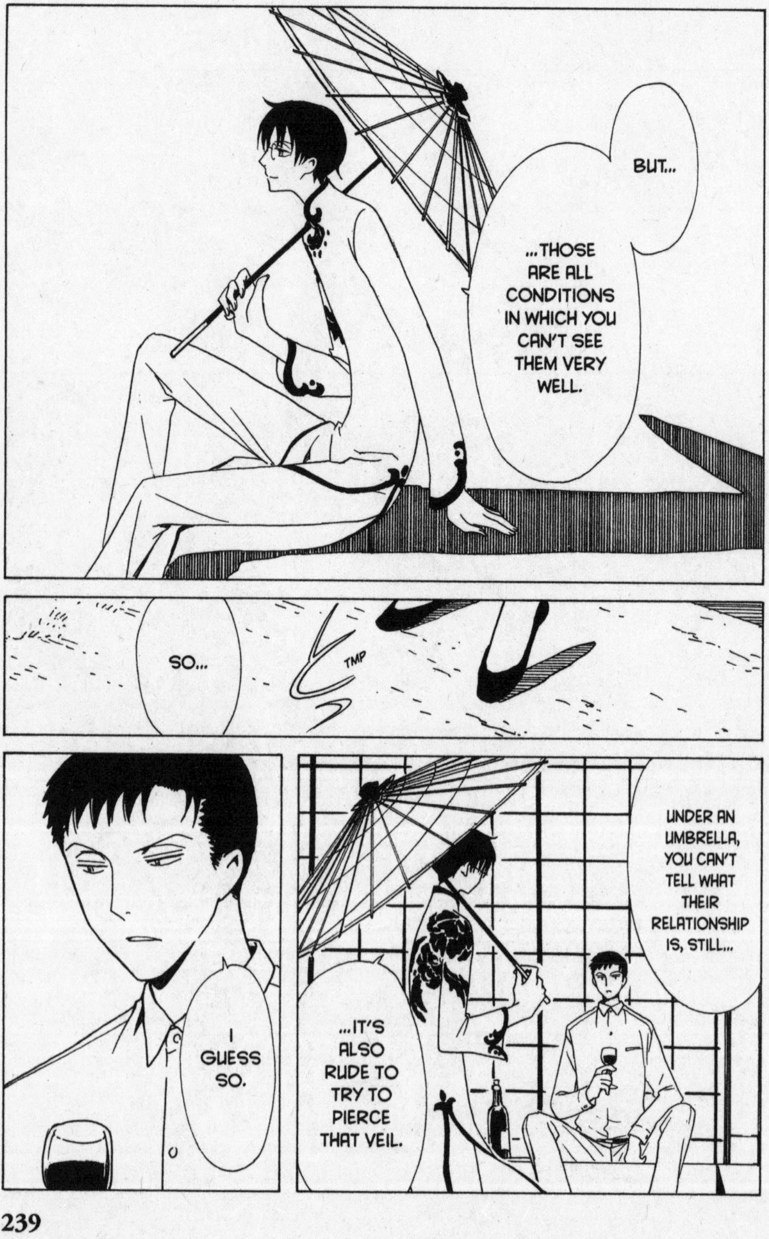
BUT...
...THOSE ARE ALL CONDITIONS IN WHICH YOU CAN'T SEE THEM VERY WELL.
TMP
SO...
UNDER AN UMBRELLA, YOU CAN'T TELL WHAT THEIR RELATIONSHIP IS, STILL...
...IT'S ALSO RUDE TO TRY TO PIERCE THAT VEIL.
I GUESS SO.

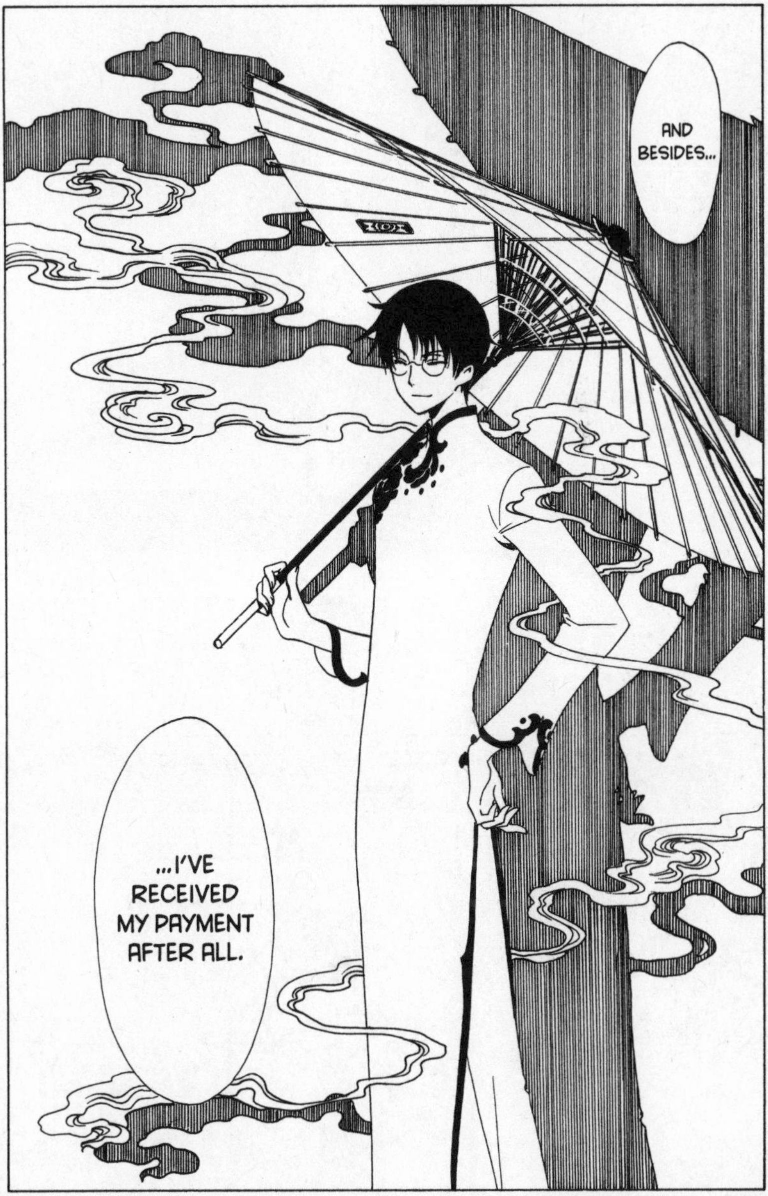
AND BESIDES...
...I'VE RECEIVED MY PAYMENT AFTER ALL.

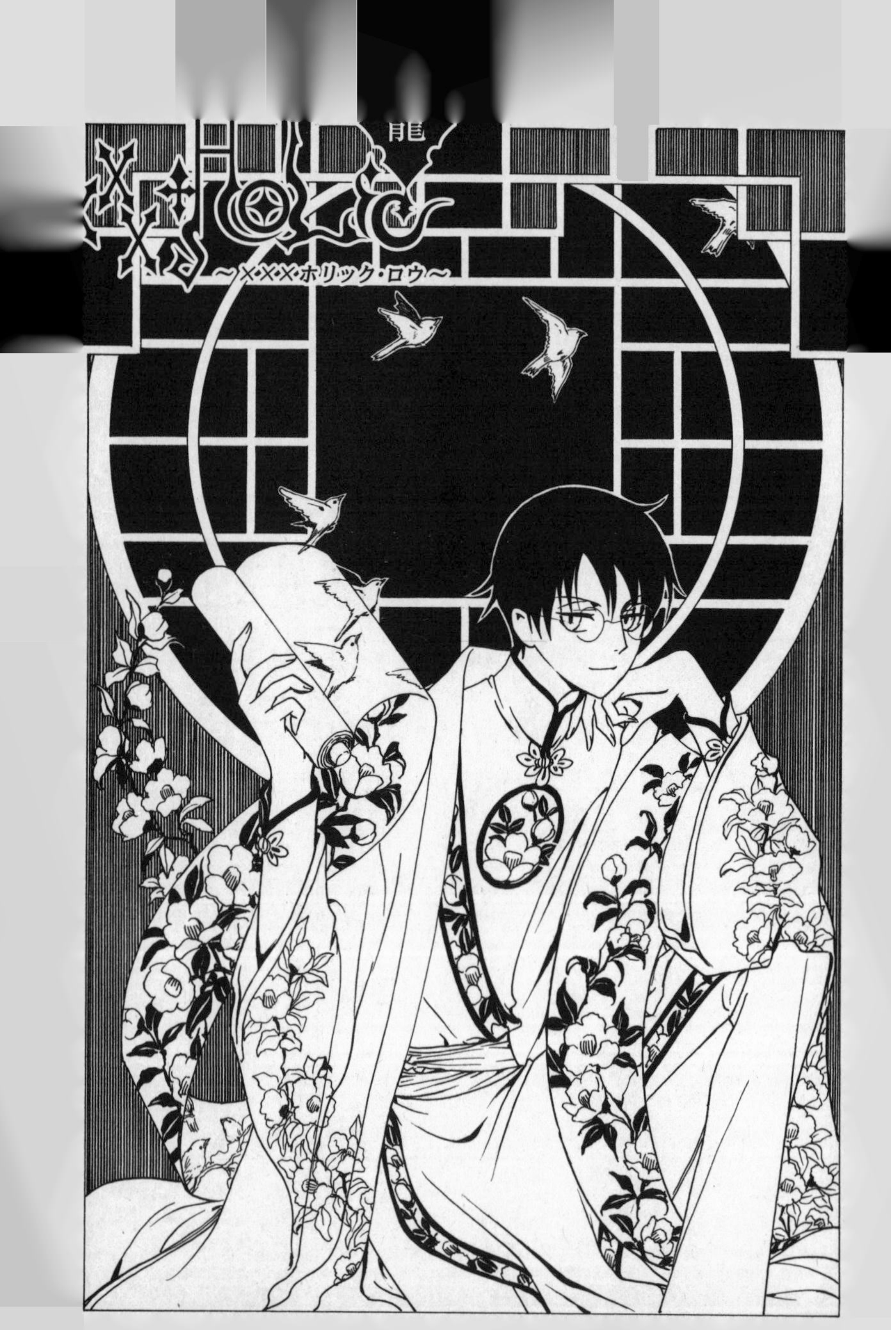
xxxHOLiC
~×××ホリック・ロウ~

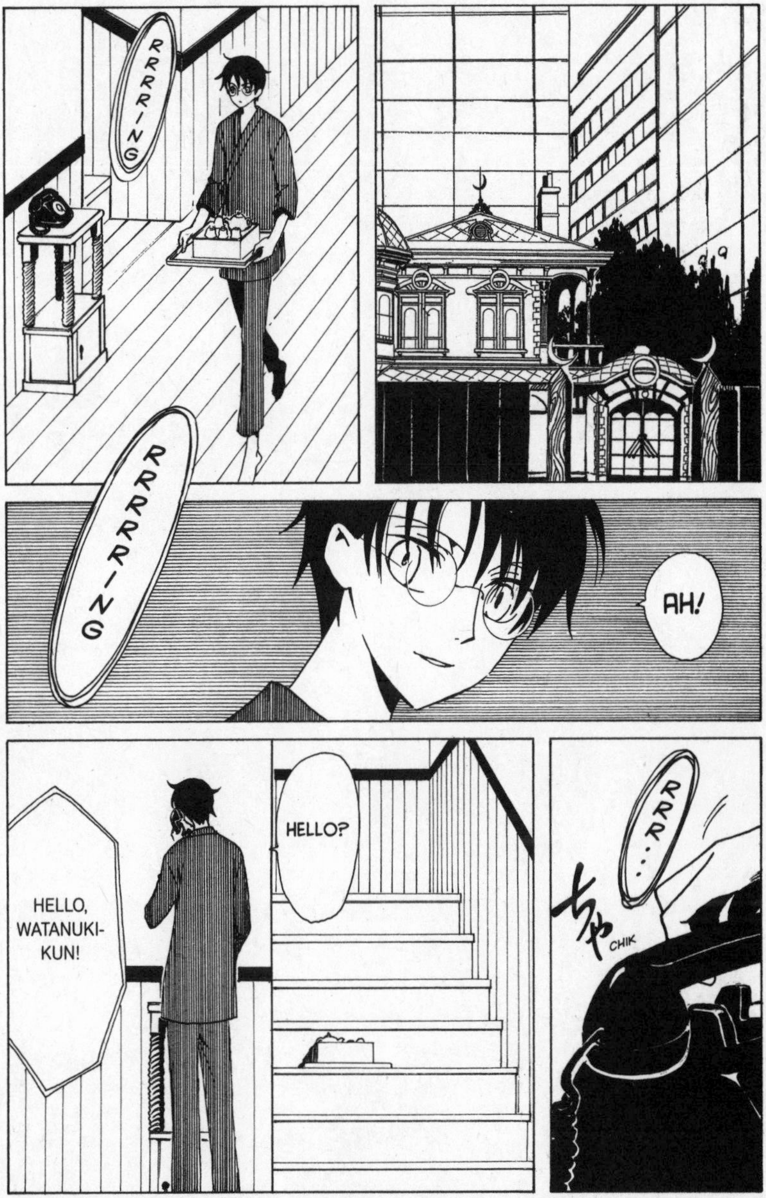
RRRRING
RRRRRING
AH!
RRR...
ちゃ CHIK
HELLO?
HELLO, WATANUKI-KUN!

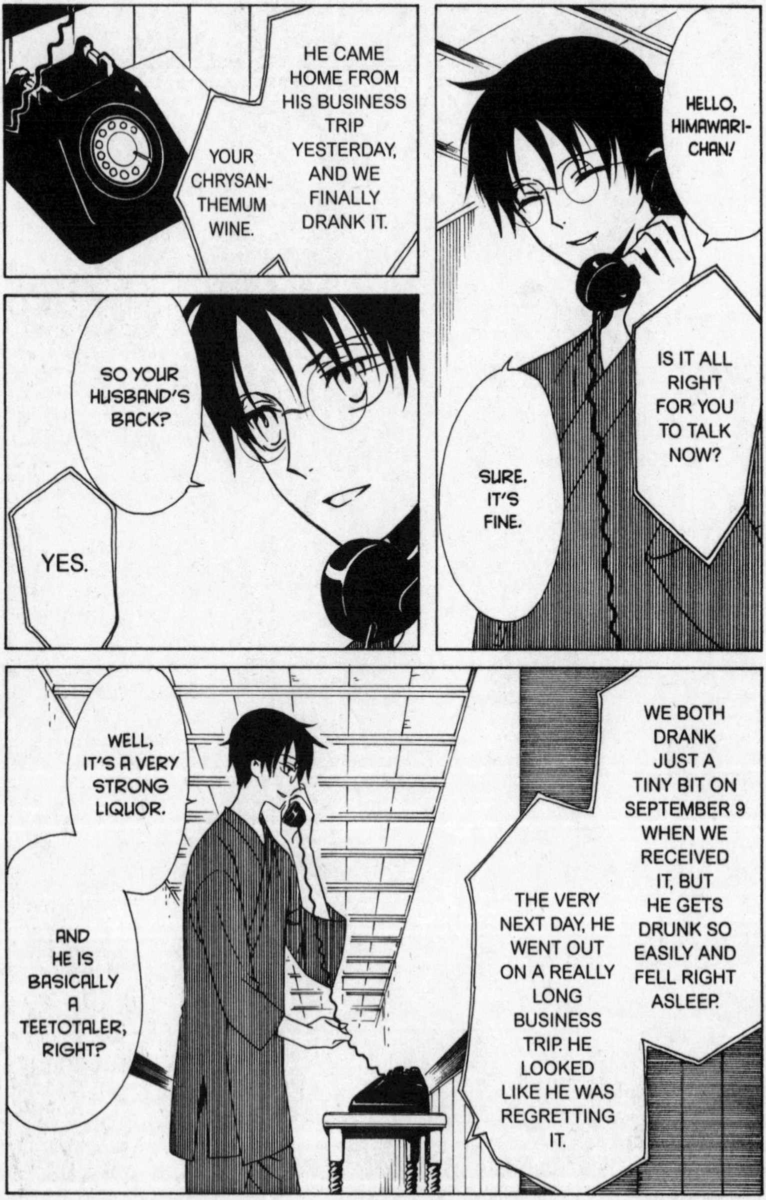
HELLO, HIMAWARI-CHAN!
IS IT ALL RIGHT FOR YOU TO TALK NOW?
SURE. IT'S FINE.
HE CAME HOME FROM HIS BUSINESS TRIP YESTERDAY, AND WE FINALLY DRANK IT.
YOUR CHRYSAN-THEMUM WINE.
SO YOUR HUSBAND'S BACK?
YES.
WE BOTH DRANK JUST A TINY BIT ON SEPTEMBER 9 WHEN WE RECEIVED IT, BUT HE GETS DRUNK SO EASILY AND FELL RIGHT ASLEEP.
THE VERY NEXT DAY, HE WENT OUT ON A REALLY LONG BUSINESS TRIP. HE LOOKED LIKE HE WAS REGRETTING IT.
WELL, IT'S A VERY STRONG LIQUOR.
AND HE IS BASICALLY A TEETOTALER, RIGHT?

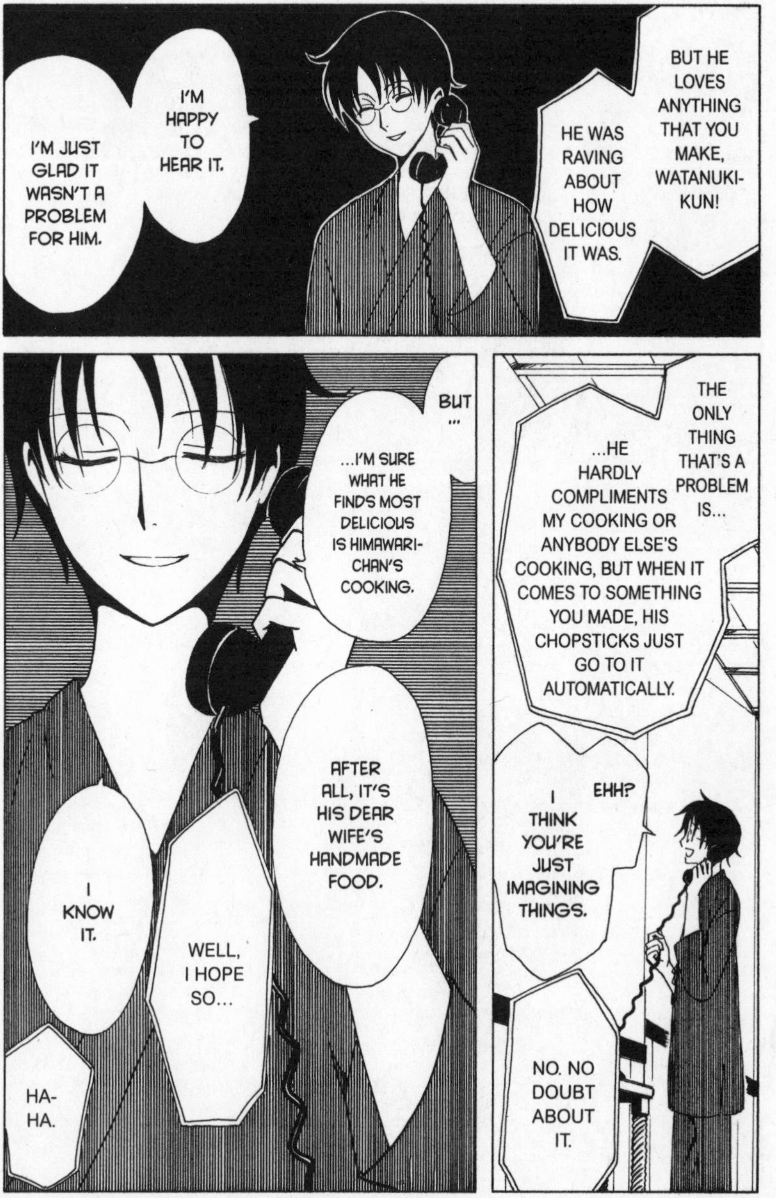
BUT HE LOVES ANYTHING THAT YOU MAKE, WATANUKI-KUN!
HE WAS RAVING ABOUT HOW DELICIOUS IT WAS.
I'M HAPPY TO HEAR IT.
I'M JUST GLAD IT WASN'T A PROBLEM FOR HIM.
THE ONLY THING THAT'S A PROBLEM IS...
...HE HARDLY COMPLIMENTS MY COOKING OR ANYBODY ELSE'S COOKING, BUT WHEN IT COMES TO SOMETHING YOU MADE, HIS CHOPSTICKS JUST GO TO IT AUTOMATICALLY.
EHH?
I THINK YOU'RE JUST IMAGINING THINGS.
NO. NO DOUBT ABOUT IT.
BUT ...
...I'M SURE WHAT HE FINDS MOST DELICIOUS IS HIMAWARI-CHAN'S COOKING.
AFTER ALL, IT'S HIS DEAR WIFE'S HANDMADE FOOD.
WELL, I HOPE SO...
I KNOW IT.
HA-HA.

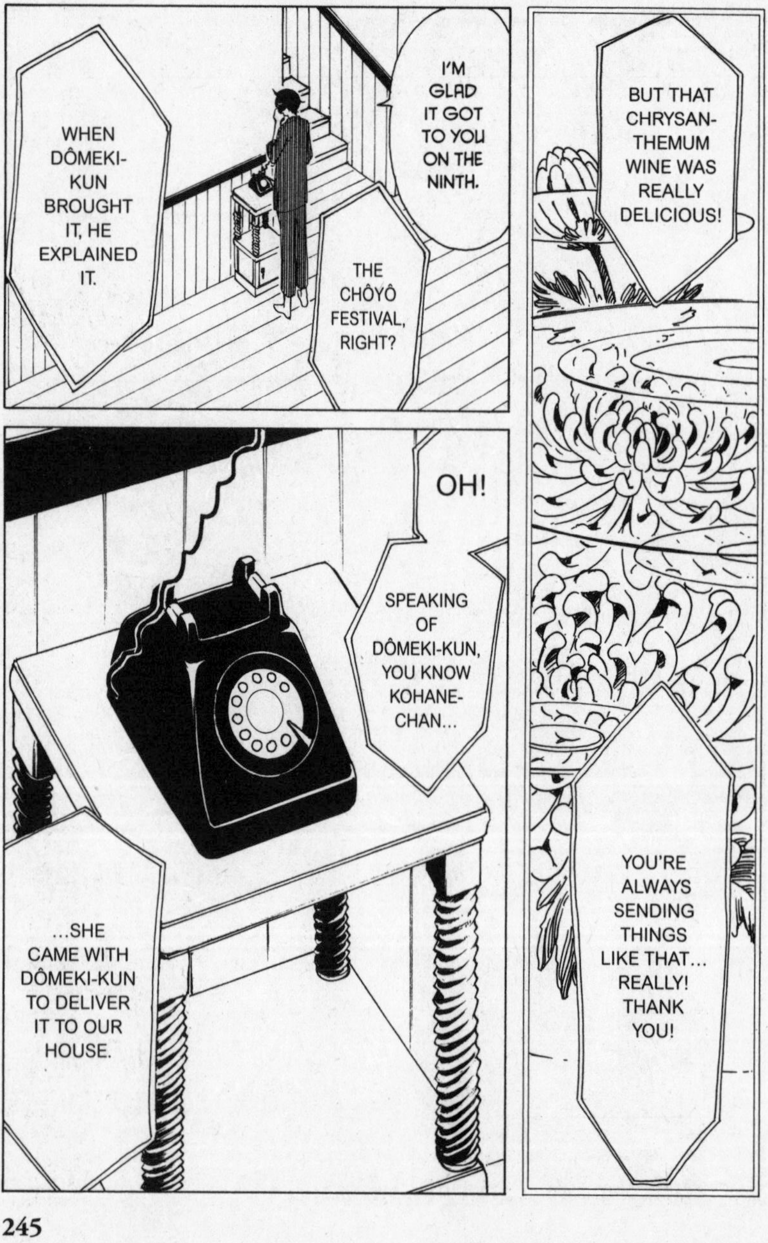
BUT THAT CHRYSAN-THEMUM WINE WAS REALLY DELICIOUS!
YOU'RE ALWAYS SENDING THINGS LIKE THAT... REALLY! THANK YOU!
I'M GLAD IT GOT TO YOU ON THE NINTH.
THE CHÔYÔ FESTIVAL, RIGHT?
WHEN DÔMEKI-KUN BROUGHT IT, HE EXPLAINED IT.
OH!
SPEAKING OF DÔMEKI-KUN, YOU KNOW KOHANE-CHAN...
...SHE CAME WITH DÔMEKI-KUN TO DELIVER IT TO OUR HOUSE.

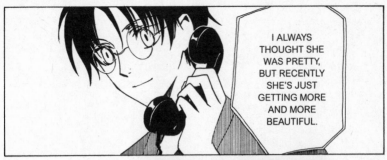

I ALWAYS THOUGHT SHE WAS PRETTY, BUT RECENTLY SHE'S JUST GETTING MORE AND MORE BEAUTIFUL.

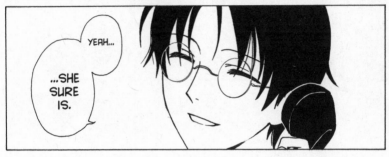

YEAH...

...SHE SURE IS.

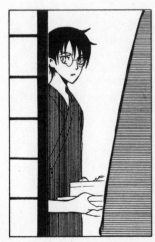

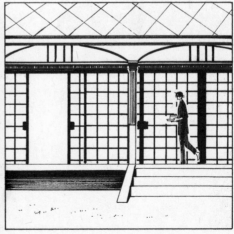

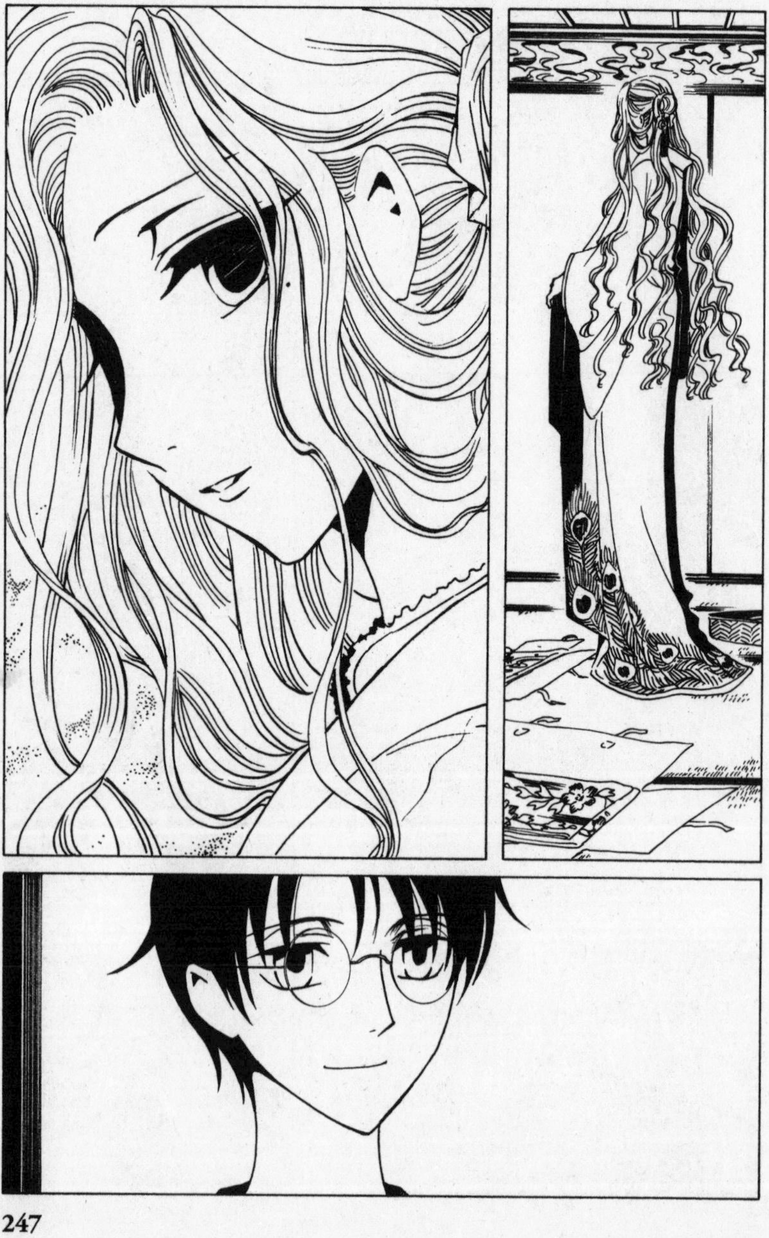

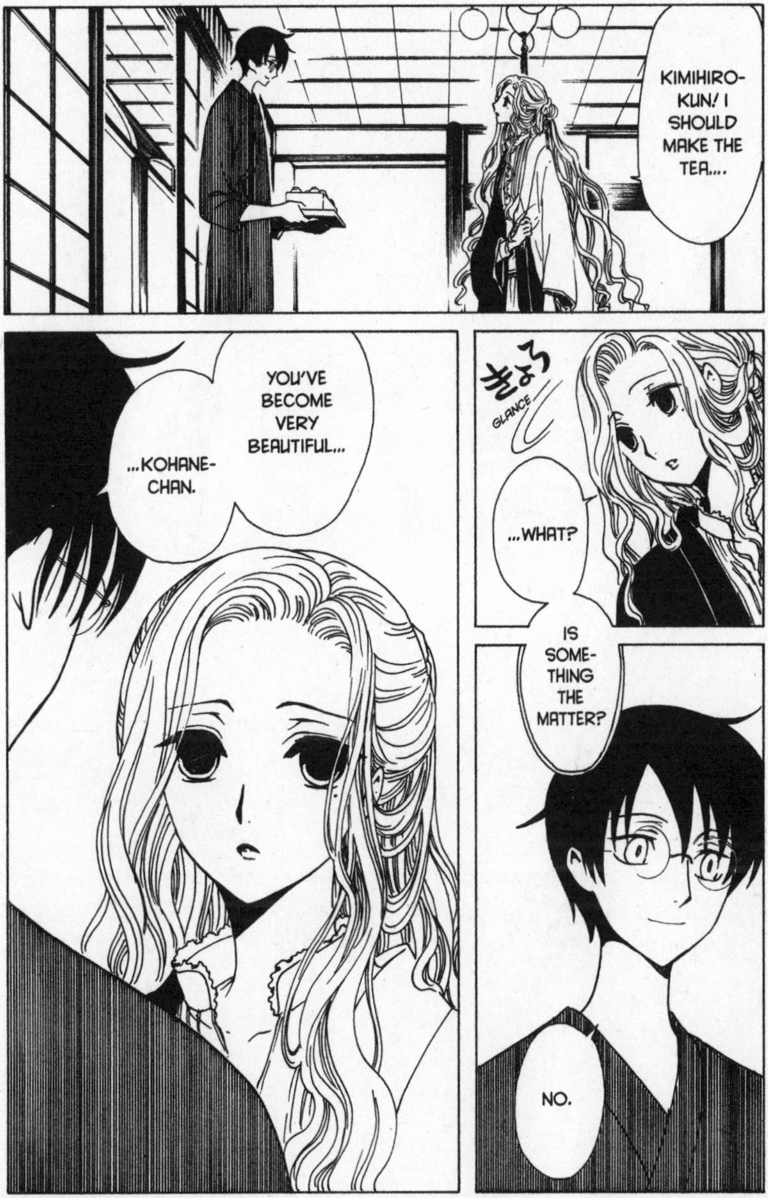
KIMIHIRO-KUN! I SHOULD MAKE THE TEA....
きょろ
GLANCE
...WHAT?
IS SOMETHING THE MATTER?
NO.
YOU'VE BECOME VERY BEAUTIFUL...
...KOHANE-CHAN.

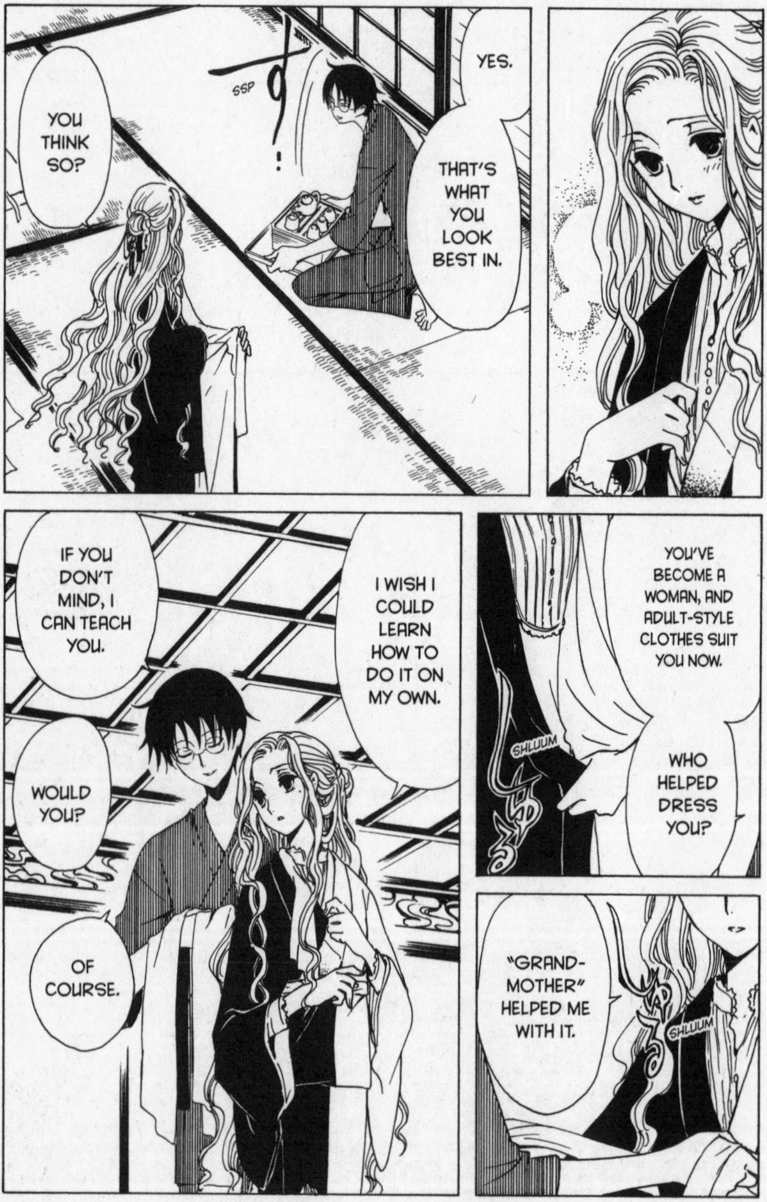
YES.
THAT'S WHAT YOU LOOK BEST IN.
SSP
YOU THINK SO?
YOU'VE BECOME A WOMAN, AND ADULT-STYLE CLOTHES SUIT YOU NOW.
SHLUUM
WHO HELPED DRESS YOU?
SHLUUM
"GRAND-MOTHER" HELPED ME WITH IT.
I WISH I COULD LEARN HOW TO DO IT ON MY OWN.
IF YOU DON'T MIND, I CAN TEACH YOU.
WOULD YOU?
OF COURSE.

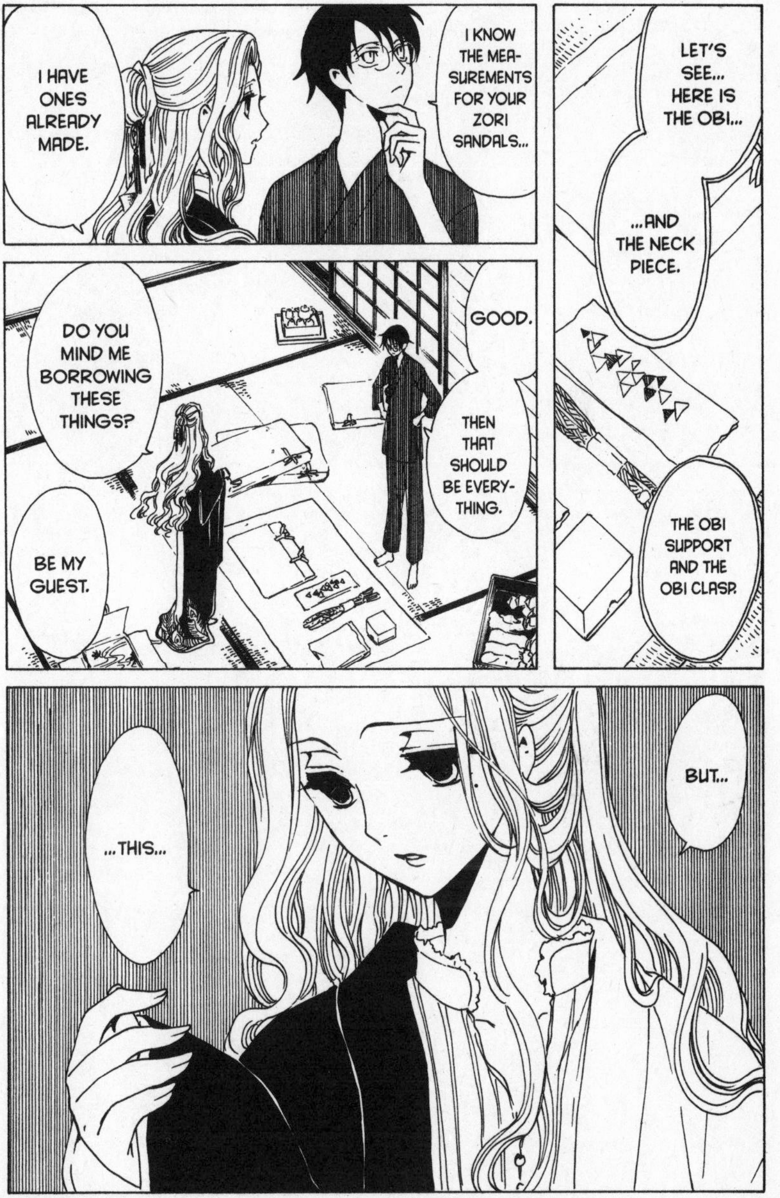
LET'S SEE... HERE IS THE OBI...
...AND THE NECK PIECE.
THE OBI SUPPORT AND THE OBI CLASP.
I KNOW THE MEA-SUREMENTS FOR YOUR ZORI SANDALS...
I HAVE ONES ALREADY MADE.
GOOD.
THEN THAT SHOULD BE EVERY-THING.
DO YOU MIND ME BORROWING THESE THINGS?
BE MY GUEST.
BUT...
...THIS...

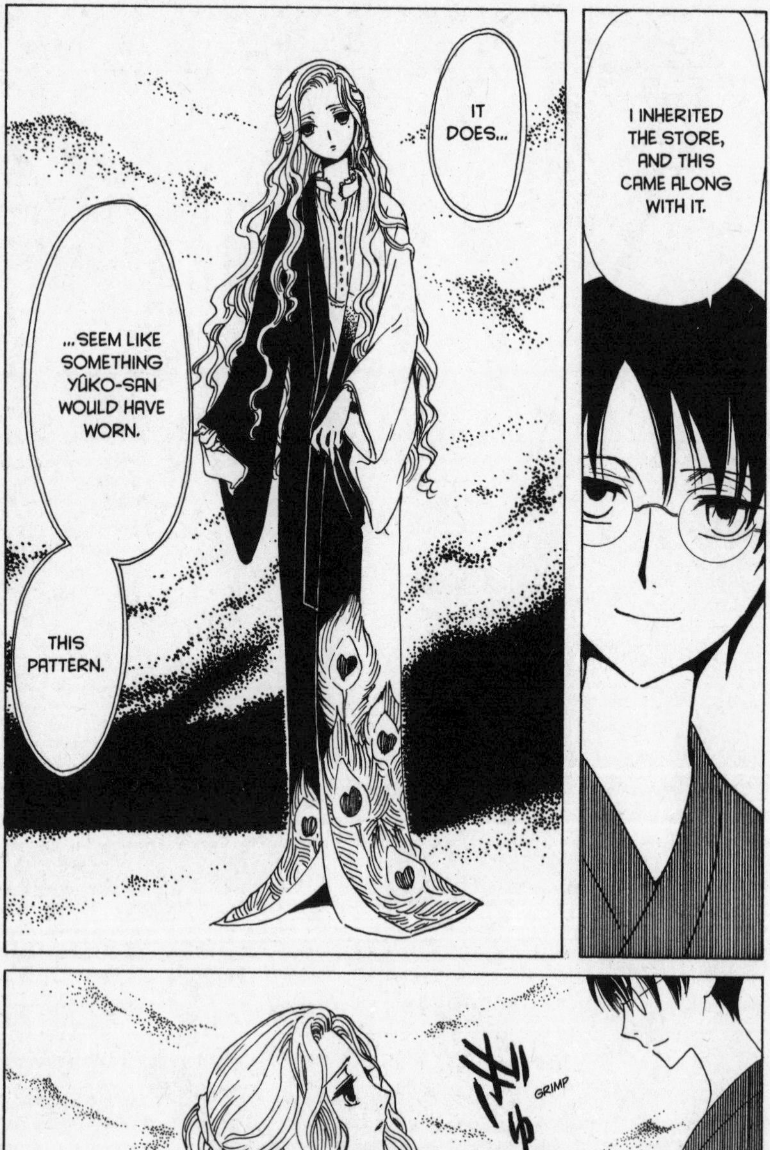
I INHERITED THE STORE, AND THIS CAME ALONG WITH IT.
IT DOES...
...SEEM LIKE SOMETHING YÛKO-SAN WOULD HAVE WORN.
THIS PATTERN.
GRIMP

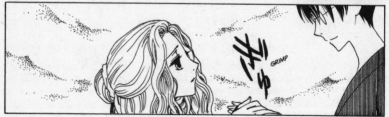

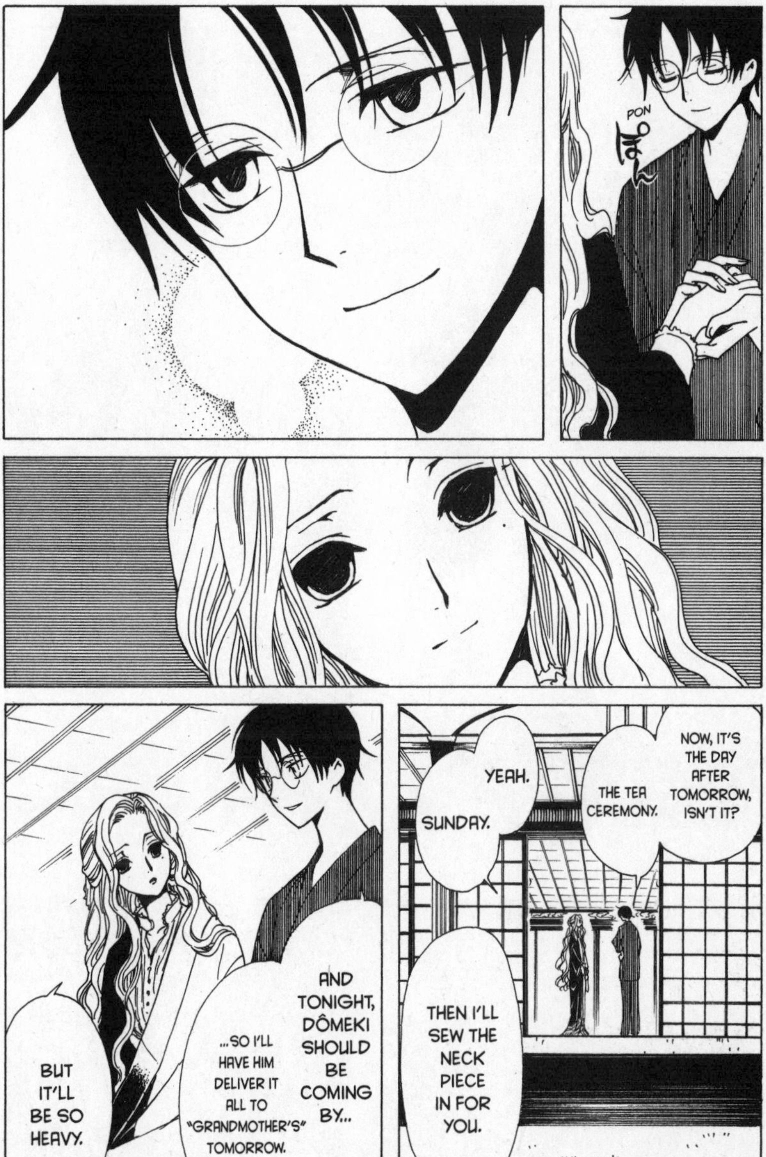
PON
ぽん
NOW, IT'S THE DAY AFTER TOMORROW, ISN'T IT?
THE TEA CEREMONY.
YEAH.
SUNDAY.
THEN I'LL SEW THE NECK PIECE IN FOR YOU.
AND TONIGHT, DÔMEKI SHOULD BE COMING BY...
...SO I'LL HAVE HIM DELIVER IT ALL TO "GRANDMOTHER'S" TOMORROW.
BUT IT'LL BE SO HEAVY.

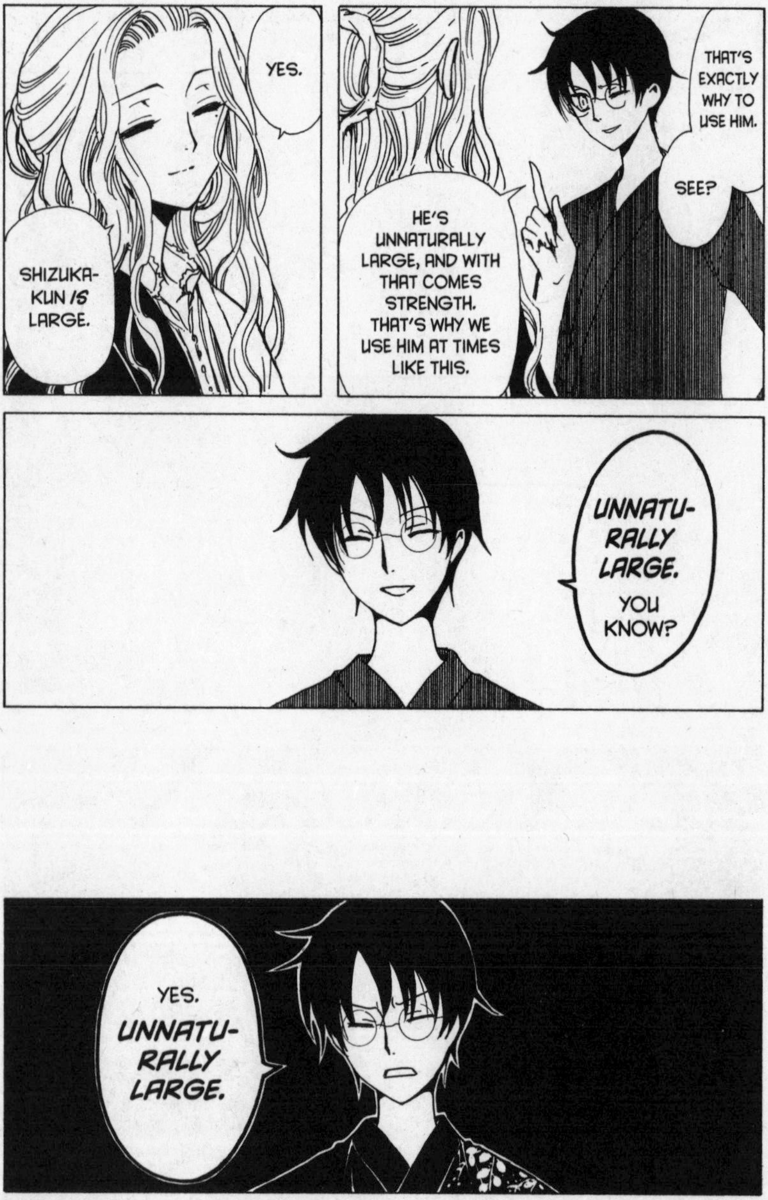
THAT'S EXACTLY WHY TO USE HIM.
SEE?
HE'S UNNATURALLY LARGE, AND WITH THAT COMES STRENGTH. THAT'S WHY WE USE HIM AT TIMES LIKE THIS.
YES.
SHIZUKA-KUN *IS* LARGE.
UNNATURALLY LARGE. YOU KNOW?
YES. *UNNATURALLY LARGE.*

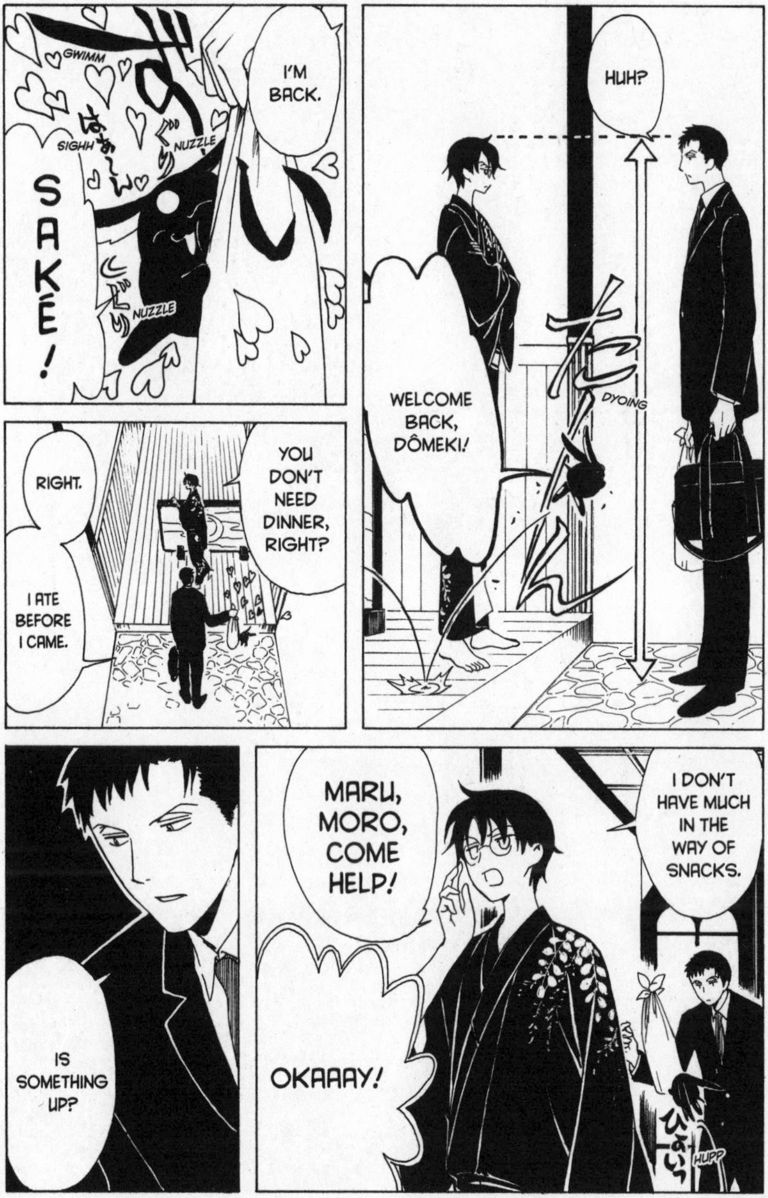
HUH?
WELCOME BACK, DÔMEKI!
DYOING
I'M BACK.
GWIMM
SIGHH
NUZZLE
SAKÉ!
NUZZLE
YOU DON'T NEED DINNER, RIGHT?
RIGHT.
I ATE BEFORE I CAME.
I DON'T HAVE MUCH IN THE WAY OF SNACKS.
MARU, MORO, COME HELP!
OKAAAY!
HUPP
IS SOMETHING UP?

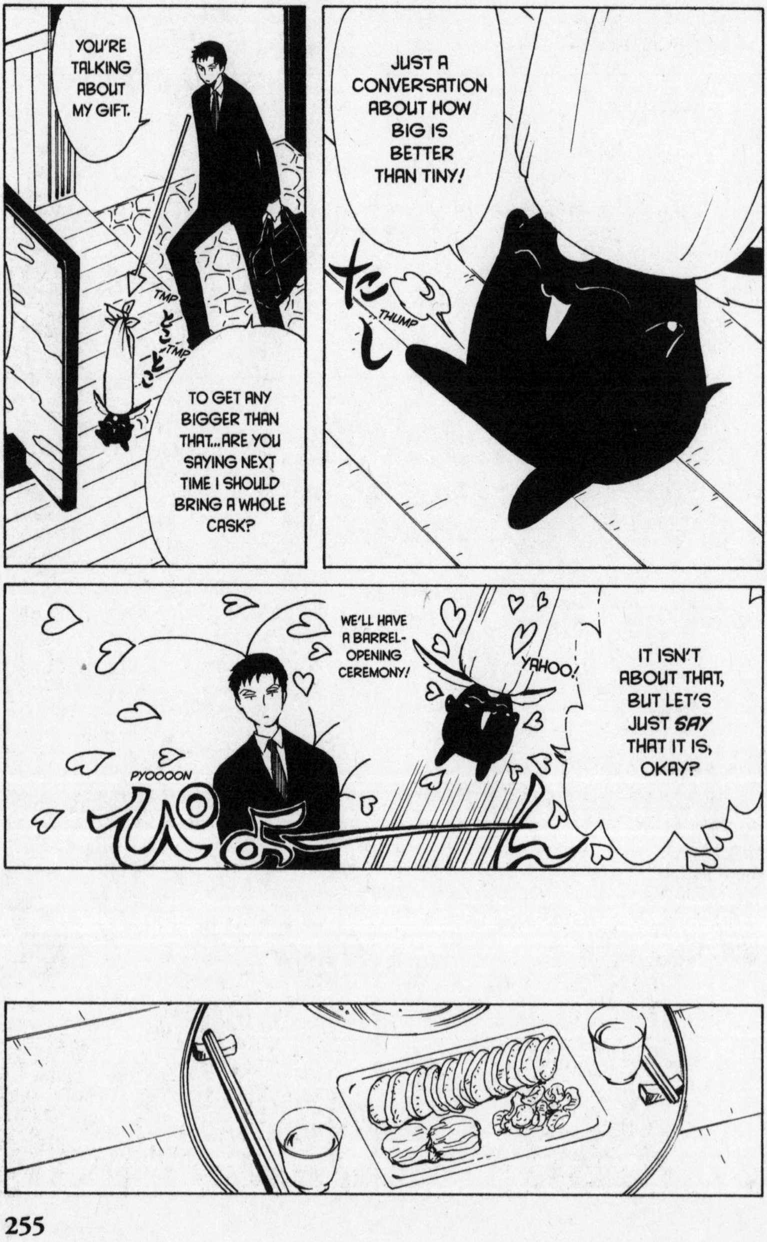
JUST A CONVERSATION ABOUT HOW BIG IS BETTER THAN TINY!
たし
THUMP
YOU'RE TALKING ABOUT MY GIFT.
とことこ
TMP TMP
TO GET ANY BIGGER THAN THAT...ARE YOU SAYING NEXT TIME I SHOULD BRING A WHOLE CASK?
IT ISN'T ABOUT THAT, BUT LET'S JUST SAY THAT IT IS, OKAY?
YAHOO!
WE'LL HAVE A BARREL-OPENING CEREMONY!
ぴょーん
PYOOOON

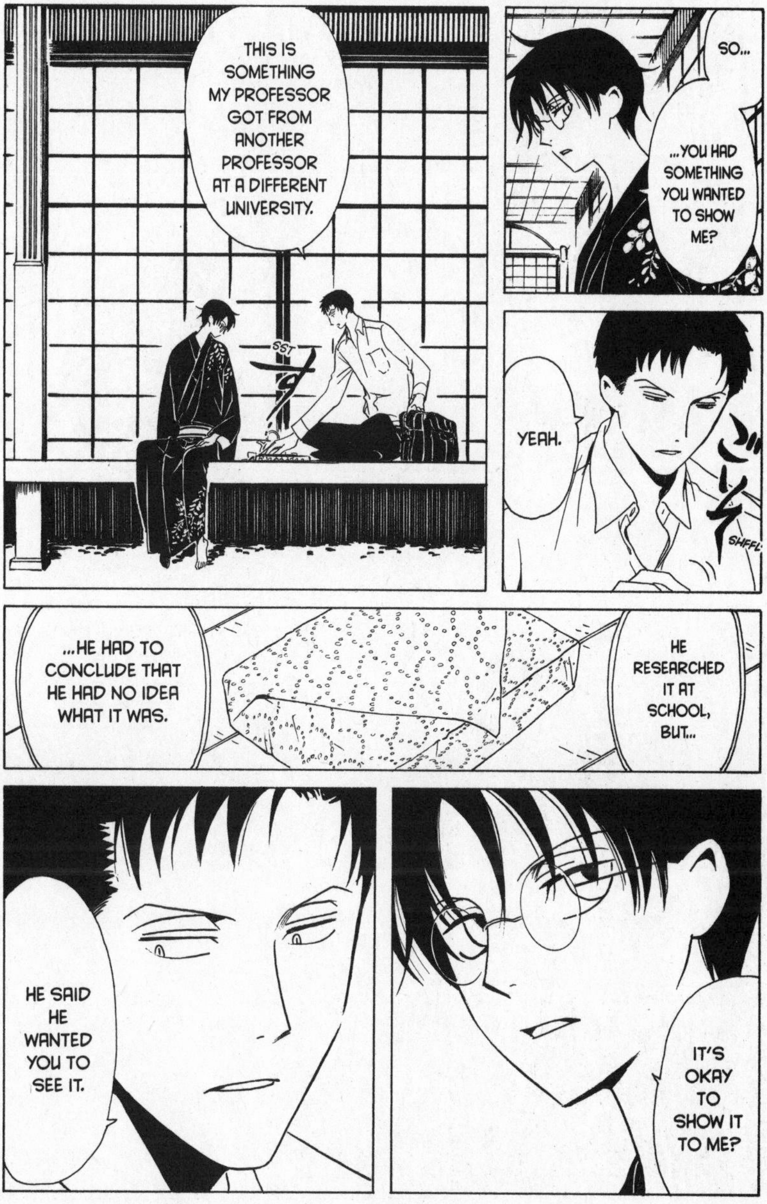
SO...
...YOU HAD SOMETHING YOU WANTED TO SHOW ME?
YEAH.
SHFFL
THIS IS SOMETHING MY PROFESSOR GOT FROM ANOTHER PROFESSOR AT A DIFFERENT UNIVERSITY.
SST
HE RESEARCHED IT AT SCHOOL, BUT...
...HE HAD TO CONCLUDE THAT HE HAD NO IDEA WHAT IT WAS.
IT'S OKAY TO SHOW IT TO ME?
HE SAID HE WANTED YOU TO SEE IT.

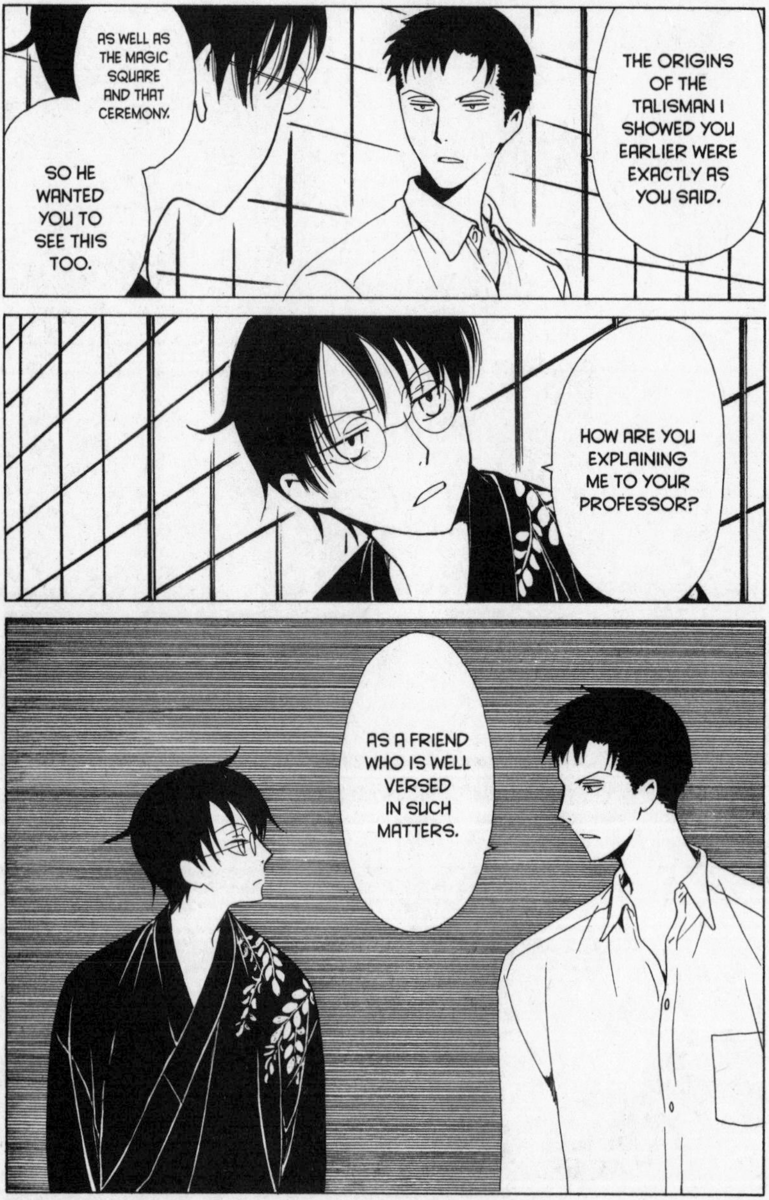
THE ORIGINS OF THE TALISMAN I SHOWED YOU EARLIER WERE EXACTLY AS YOU SAID.
AS WELL AS THE MAGIC SQUARE AND THAT CEREMONY.
SO HE WANTED YOU TO SEE THIS TOO.
HOW ARE YOU EXPLAINING ME TO YOUR PROFESSOR?
AS A FRIEND WHO IS WELL VERSED IN SUCH MATTERS.

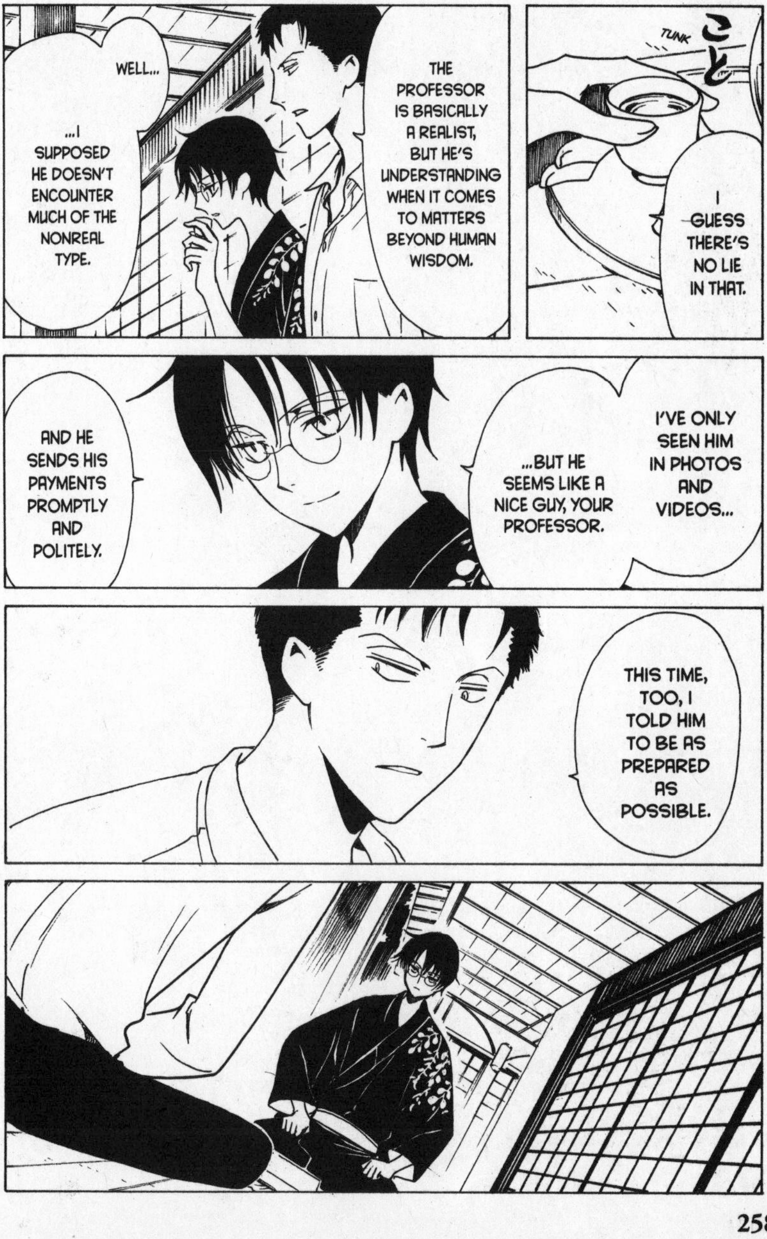
TUNK
こと
I GUESS THERE'S NO LIE IN THAT.
THE PROFESSOR IS BASICALLY A REALIST, BUT HE'S UNDERSTANDING WHEN IT COMES TO MATTERS BEYOND HUMAN WISDOM.
WELL...
...I SUPPOSED HE DOESN'T ENCOUNTER MUCH OF THE NONREAL TYPE.
I'VE ONLY SEEN HIM IN PHOTOS AND VIDEOS...
...BUT HE SEEMS LIKE A NICE GUY, YOUR PROFESSOR.
AND HE SENDS HIS PAYMENTS PROMPTLY AND POLITELY.
THIS TIME, TOO, I TOLD HIM TO BE AS PREPARED AS POSSIBLE.

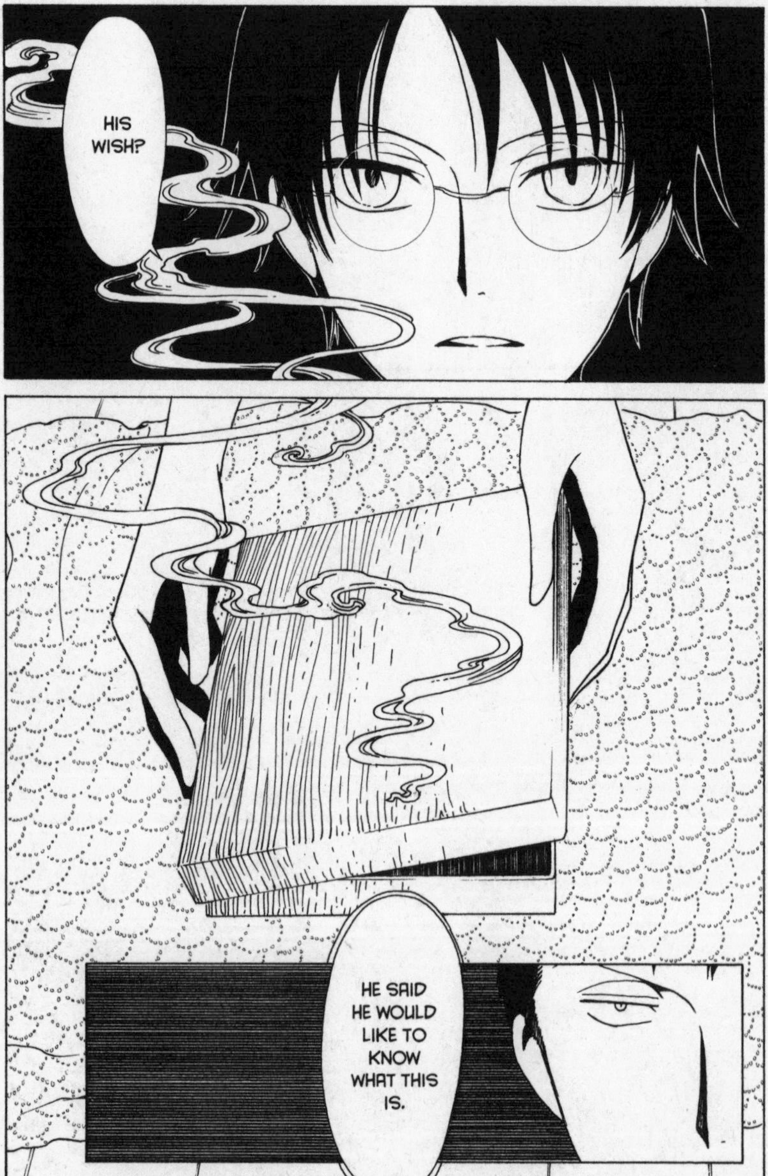
HIS WISH?
HE SAID HE WOULD LIKE TO KNOW WHAT THIS IS.

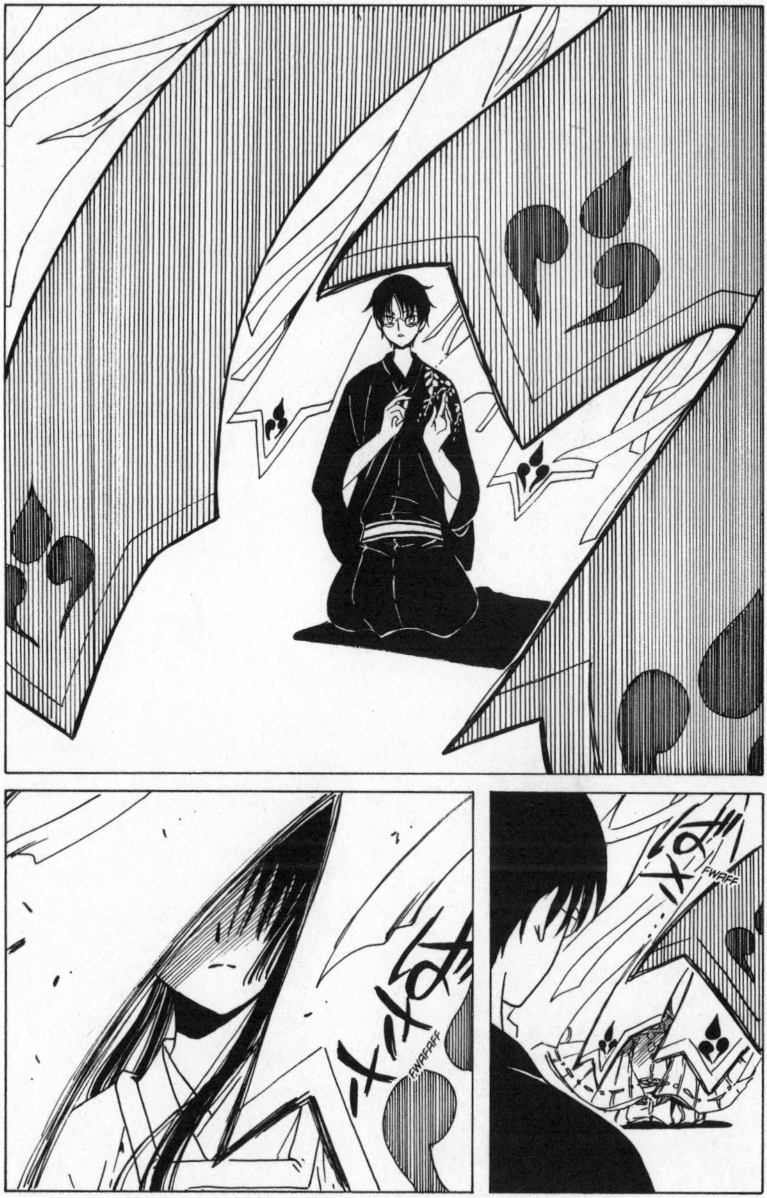
FWAFF
FWAFAFF

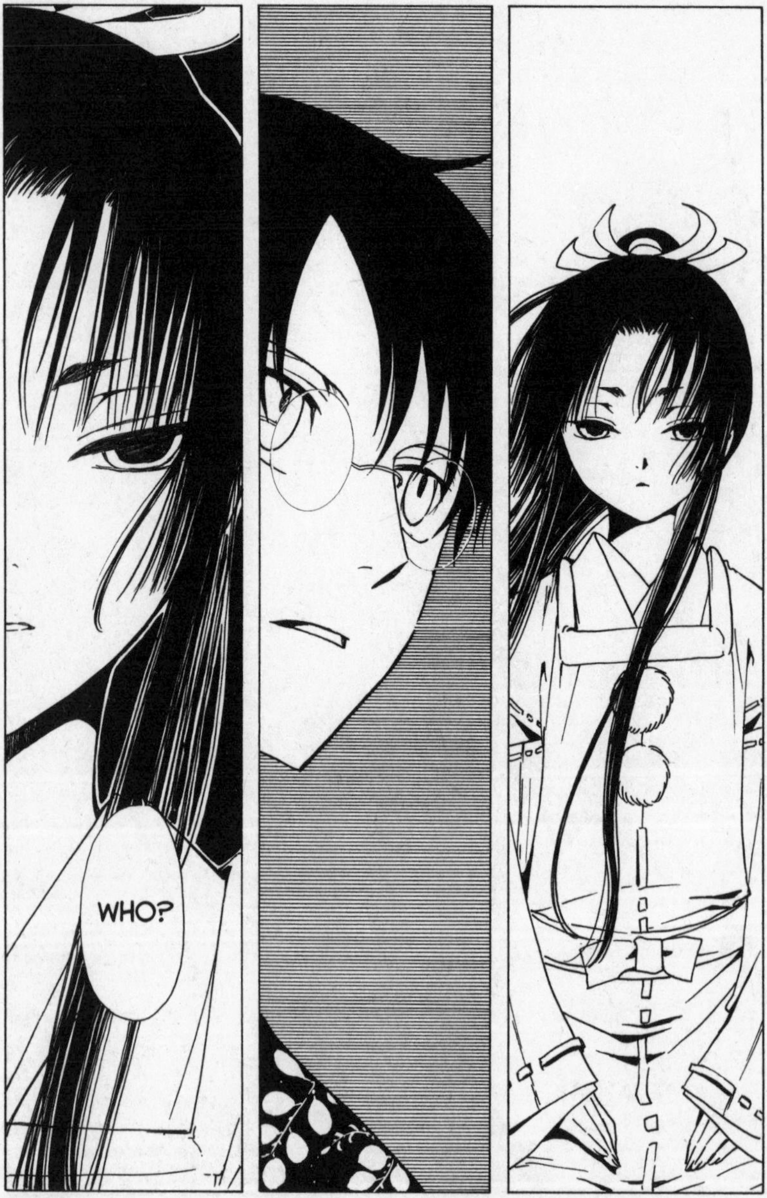
WHO?

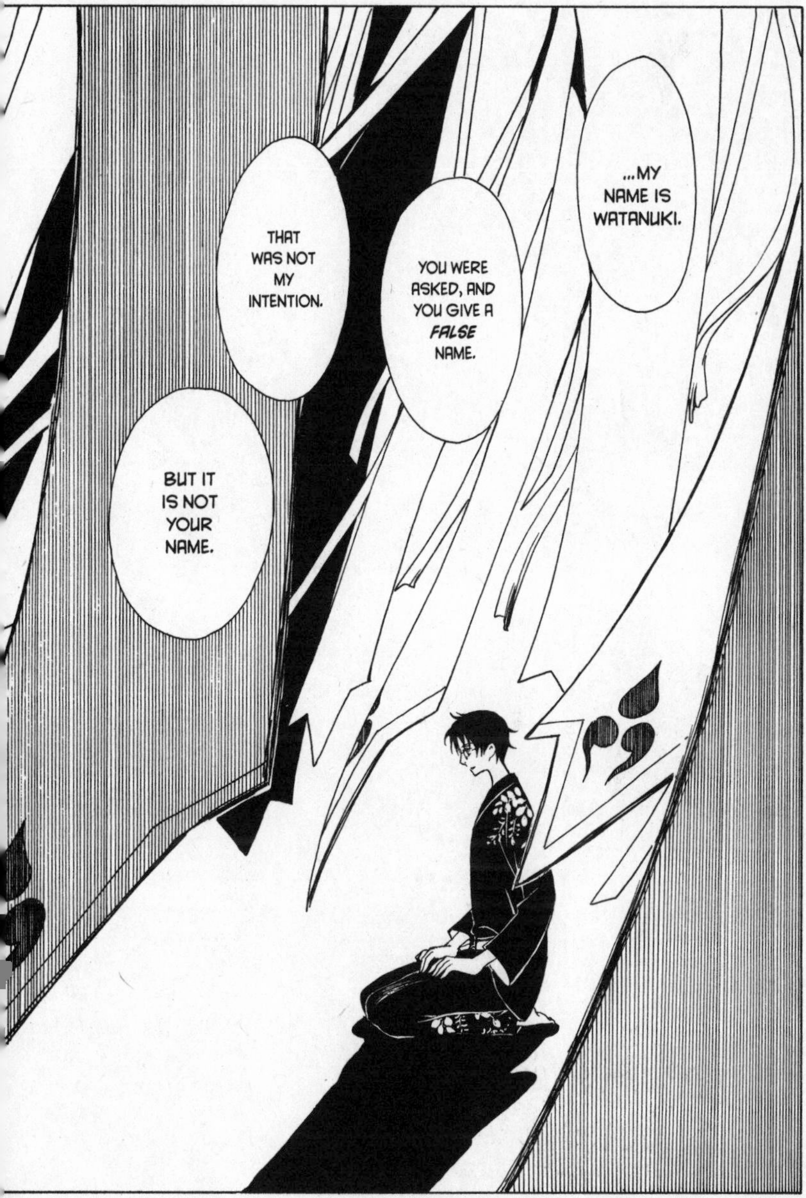
...MY NAME IS WATANUKI.
YOU WERE ASKED, AND YOU GIVE A *FALSE* NAME.
THAT WAS NOT MY INTENTION.
BUT IT IS NOT YOUR NAME.

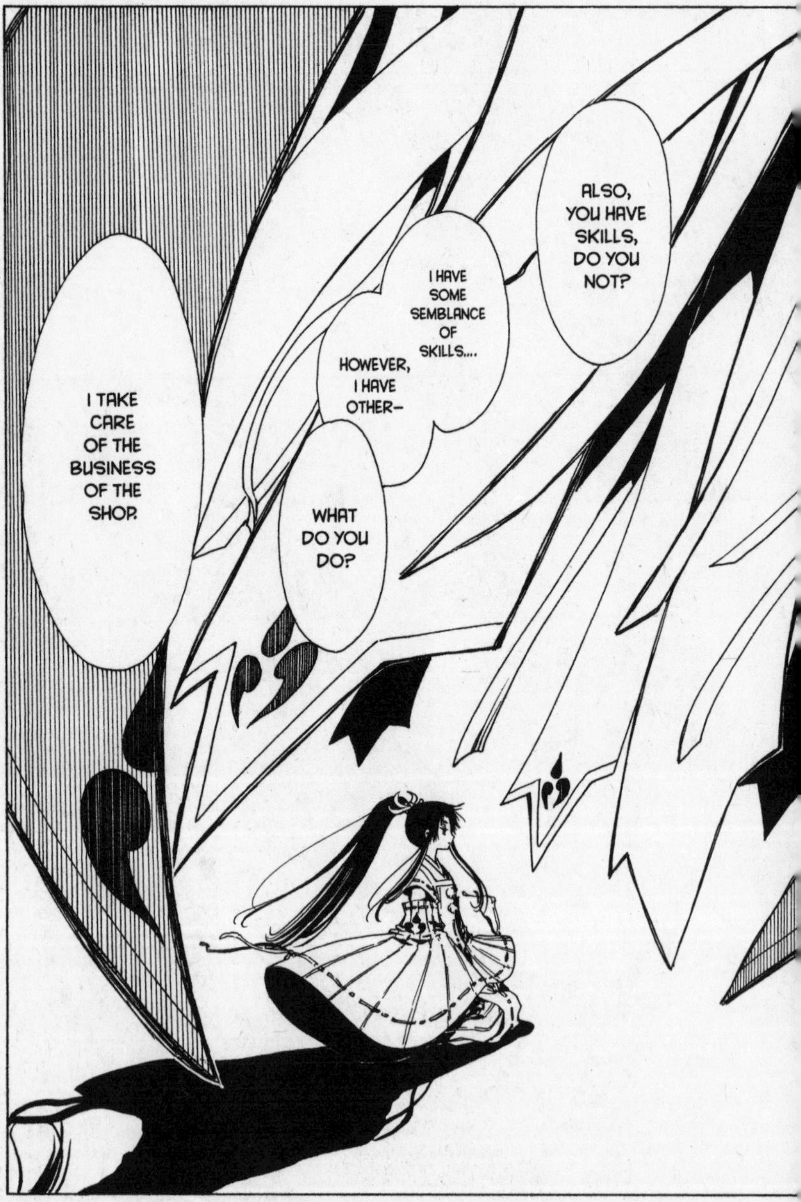
ALSO, YOU HAVE SKILLS, DO YOU NOT?
I HAVE SOME SEMBLANCE OF SKILLS....
HOWEVER, I HAVE OTHER-
WHAT DO YOU DO?
I TAKE CARE OF THE BUSINESS OF THE SHOP.

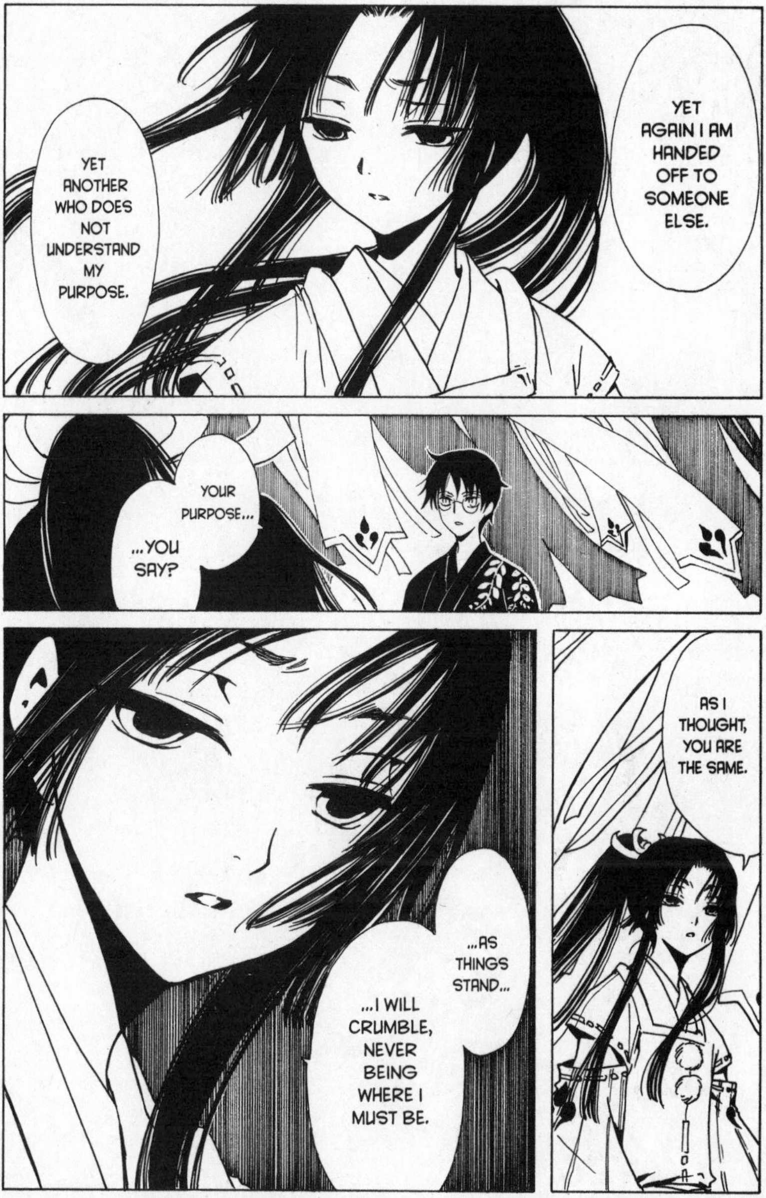
YET AGAIN I AM HANDED OFF TO SOMEONE ELSE.
YET ANOTHER WHO DOES NOT UNDERSTAND MY PURPOSE.
YOUR PURPOSE...
...YOU SAY?
AS I THOUGHT, YOU ARE THE SAME.
...AS THINGS STAND...
...I WILL CRUMBLE, NEVER BEING WHERE I MUST BE.

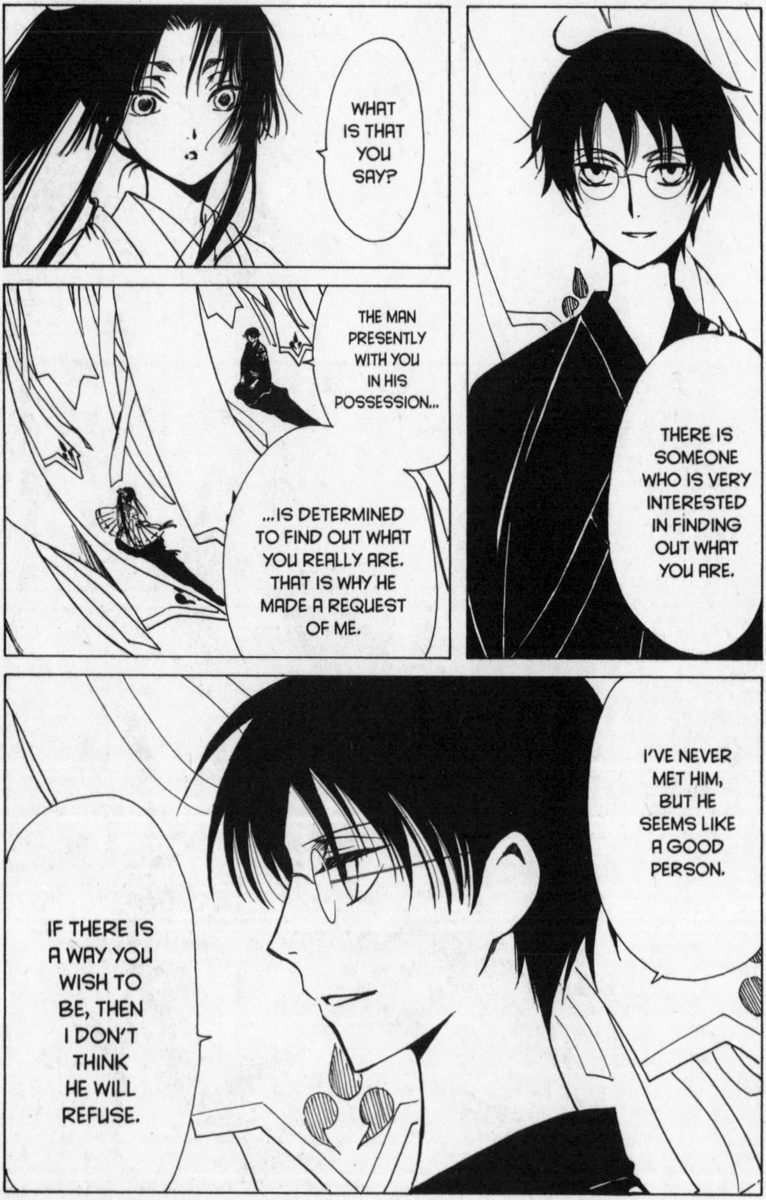
THERE IS SOMEONE WHO IS VERY INTERESTED IN FINDING OUT WHAT YOU ARE.
WHAT IS THAT YOU SAY?
THE MAN PRESENTLY WITH YOU IN HIS POSSESSION...
...IS DETERMINED TO FIND OUT WHAT YOU REALLY ARE. THAT IS WHY HE MADE A REQUEST OF ME.
I'VE NEVER MET HIM, BUT HE SEEMS LIKE A GOOD PERSON.
IF THERE IS A WAY YOU WISH TO BE, THEN I DON'T THINK HE WILL REFUSE.

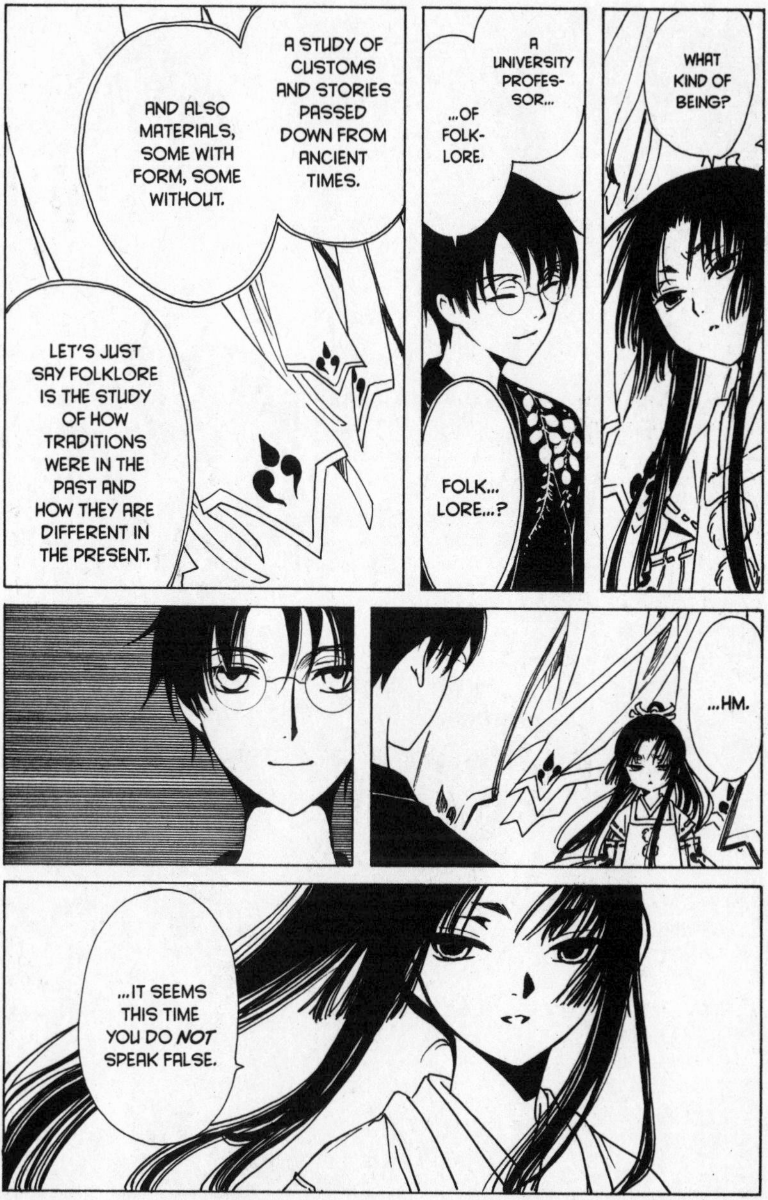
WHAT KIND OF BEING?
A UNIVERSITY PROFES-SOR...
...OF FOLK-LORE.
FOLK... LORE...?
A STUDY OF CUSTOMS AND STORIES PASSED DOWN FROM ANCIENT TIMES.
AND ALSO MATERIALS, SOME WITH FORM, SOME WITHOUT.
LET'S JUST SAY FOLKLORE IS THE STUDY OF HOW TRADITIONS WERE IN THE PAST AND HOW THEY ARE DIFFERENT IN THE PRESENT.
...HM.
...IT SEEMS THIS TIME YOU DO *NOT* SPEAK FALSE.

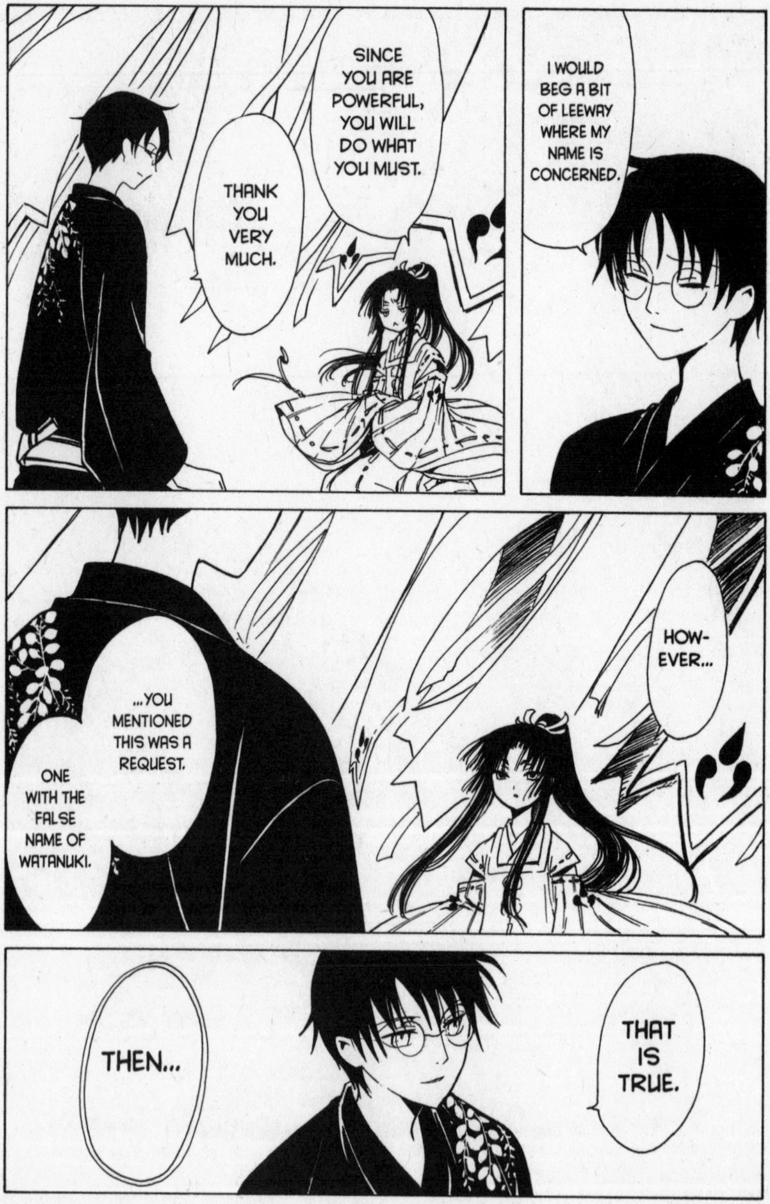
I WOULD BEG A BIT OF LEEWAY WHERE MY NAME IS CONCERNED.
SINCE YOU ARE POWERFUL, YOU WILL DO WHAT YOU MUST.
THANK YOU VERY MUCH.
HOW-EVER...
...YOU MENTIONED THIS WAS A REQUEST.
ONE WITH THE FALSE NAME OF WATANUKI.
THAT IS TRUE.
THEN...

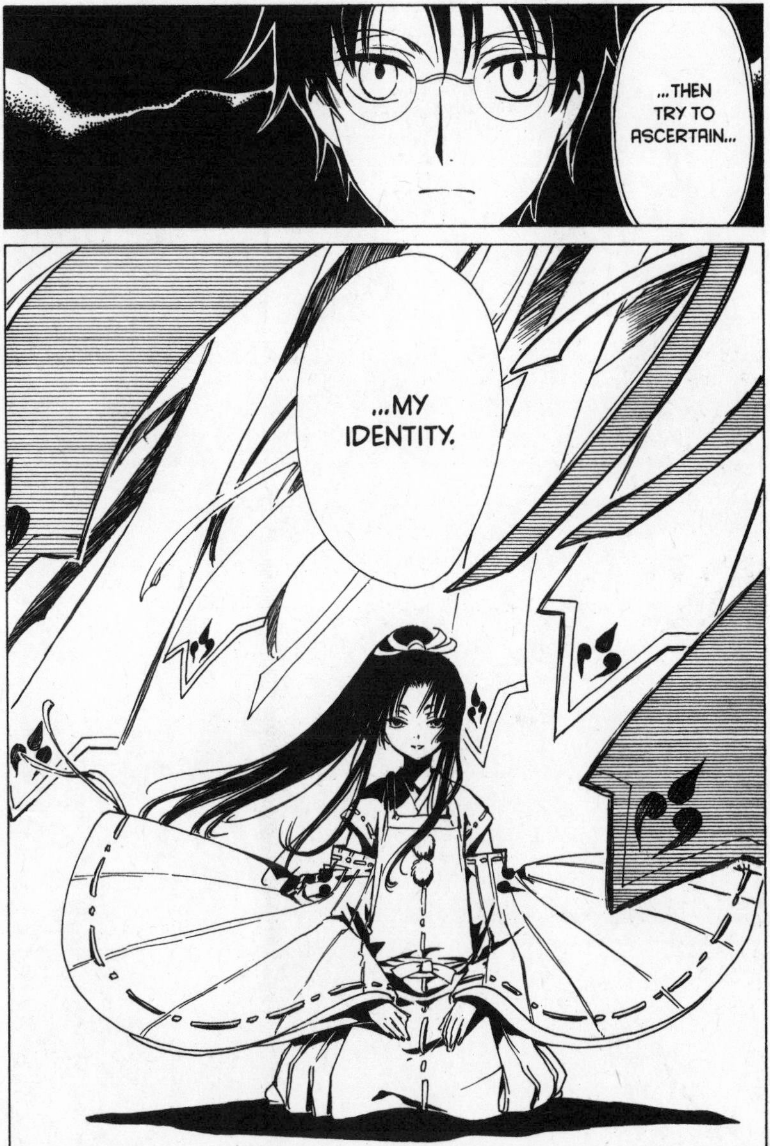
...THEN TRY TO ASCERTAIN...
...MY IDENTITY.

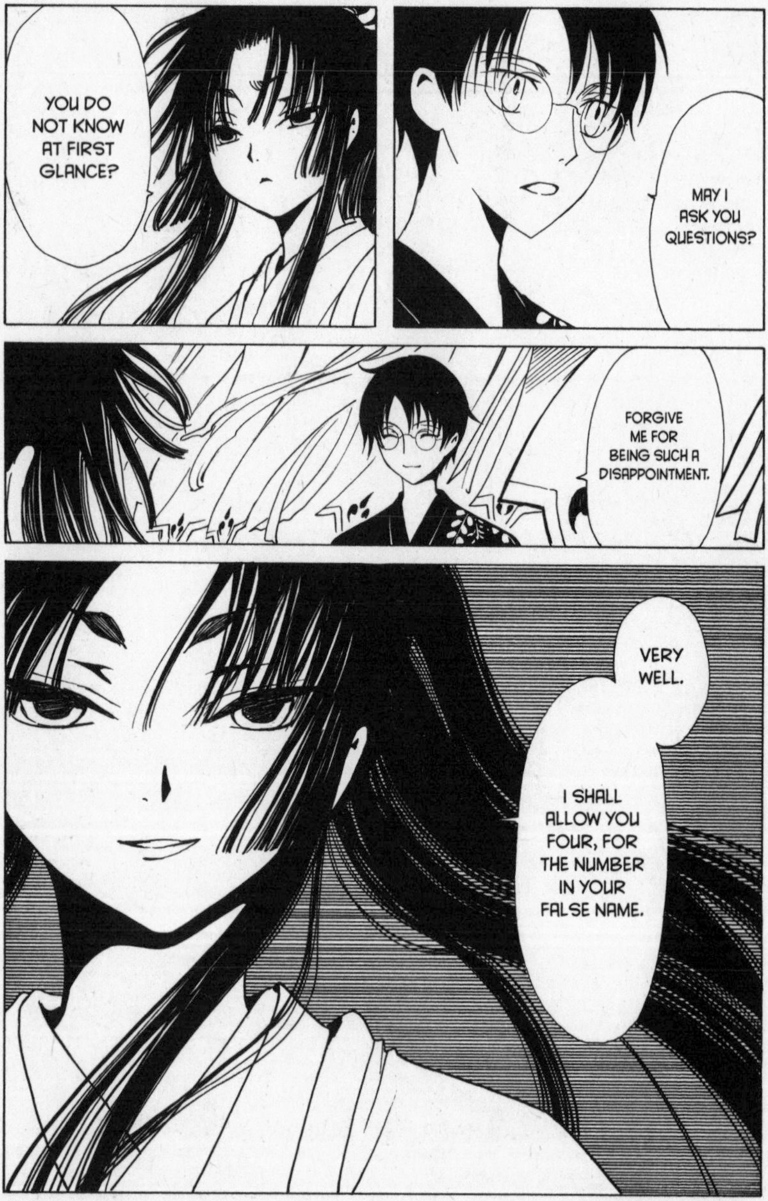
MAY I ASK YOU QUESTIONS?
YOU DO NOT KNOW AT FIRST GLANCE?
FORGIVE ME FOR BEING SUCH A DISAPPOINTMENT.
VERY WELL.
I SHALL ALLOW YOU FOUR, FOR THE NUMBER IN YOUR FALSE NAME.

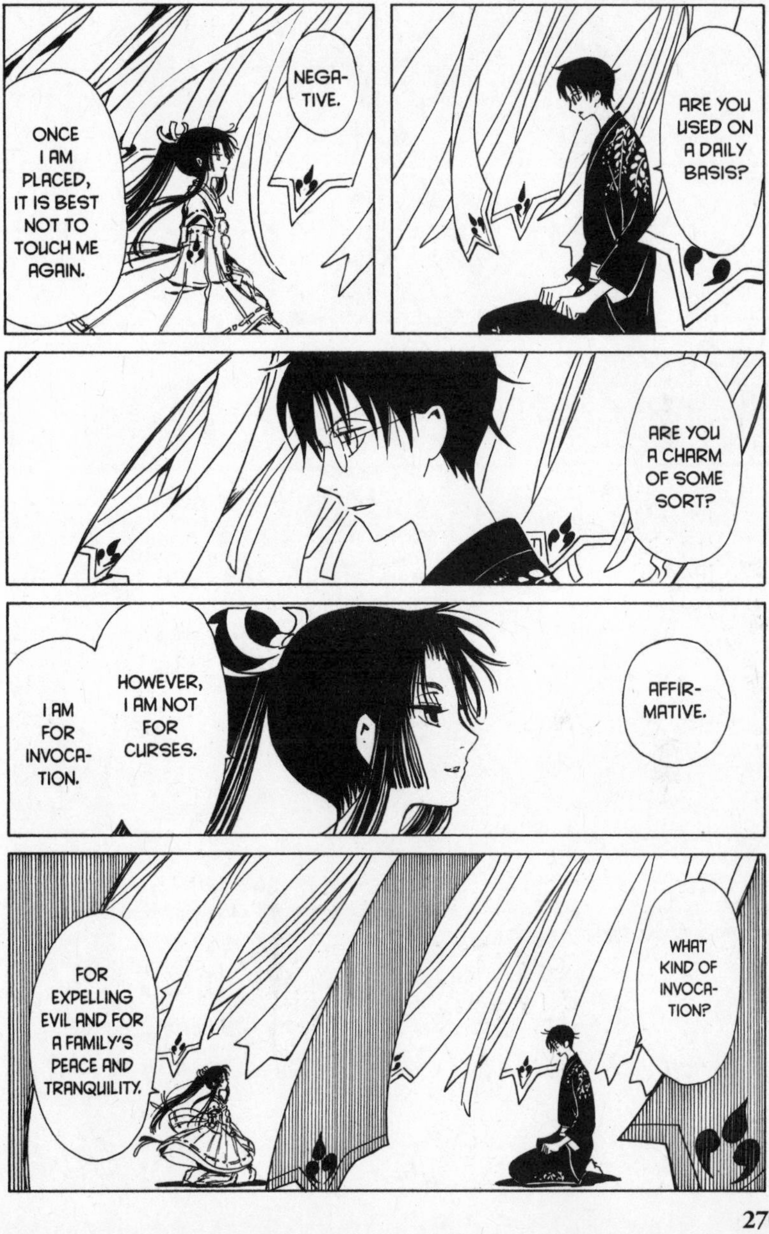
ARE YOU USED ON A DAILY BASIS?
NEGA-TIVE.
ONCE I AM PLACED, IT IS BEST NOT TO TOUCH ME AGAIN.
ARE YOU A CHARM OF SOME SORT?
AFFIR-MATIVE.
HOWEVER, I AM NOT FOR CURSES.
I AM FOR INVOCA-TION.
WHAT KIND OF INVOCA-TION?
FOR EXPELLING EVIL AND FOR A FAMILY'S PEACE AND TRANQUILITY.

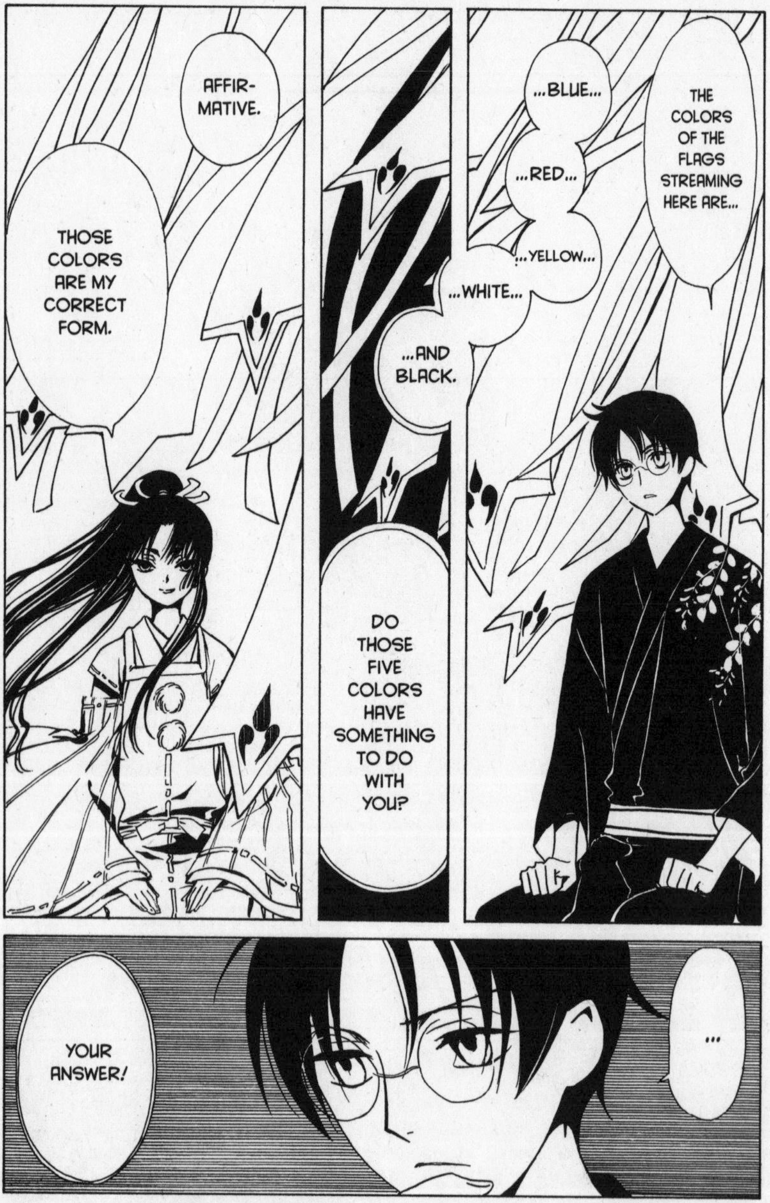
THE COLORS OF THE FLAGS STREAMING HERE ARE...
...BLUE...
...RED...
...YELLOW...
...WHITE...
...AND BLACK.
DO THOSE FIVE COLORS HAVE SOMETHING TO DO WITH YOU?
AFFIR-MATIVE.
THOSE COLORS ARE MY CORRECT FORM.
...
YOUR ANSWER!

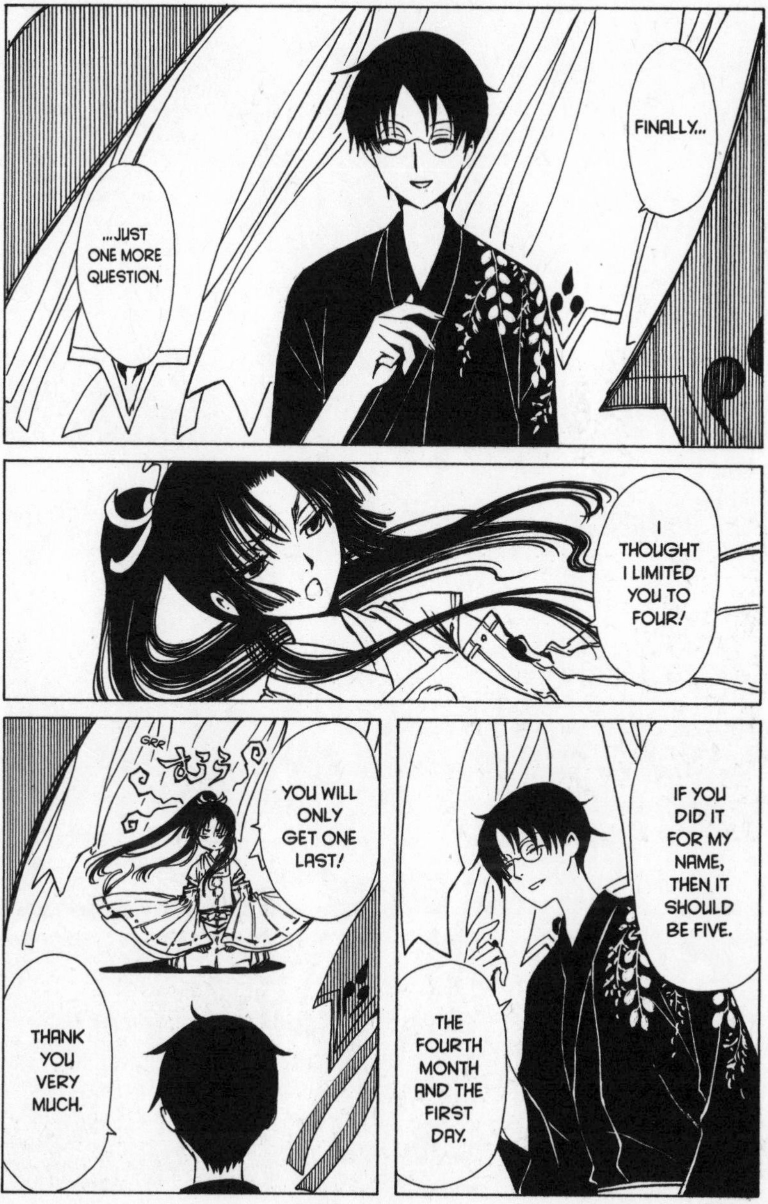
FINALLY...
...JUST ONE MORE QUESTION.
I THOUGHT I LIMITED YOU TO FOUR!
IF YOU DID IT FOR MY NAME, THEN IT SHOULD BE FIVE.
THE FOURTH MONTH AND THE FIRST DAY.
GRR
YOU WILL ONLY GET ONE LAST!
THANK YOU VERY MUCH.

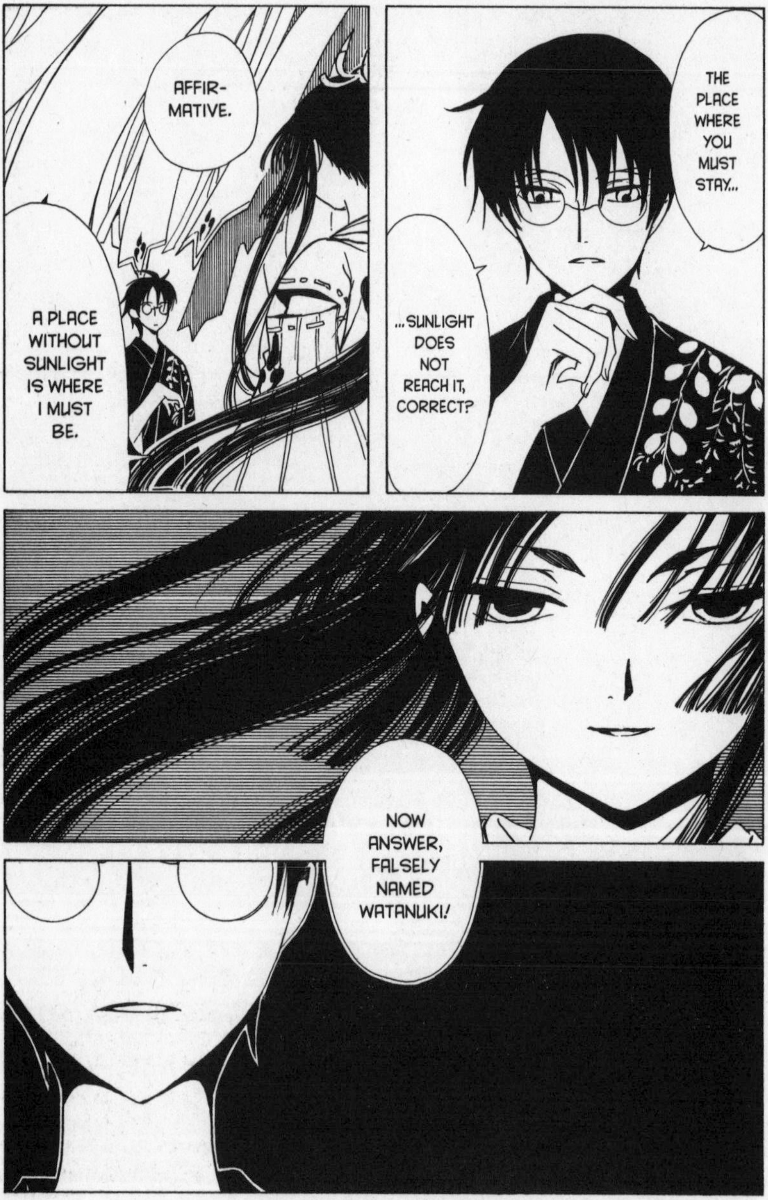
THE PLACE WHERE YOU MUST STAY...
...SUNLIGHT DOES NOT REACH IT, CORRECT?
AFFIR-MATIVE.
A PLACE WITHOUT SUNLIGHT IS WHERE I MUST BE.
NOW ANSWER, FALSELY NAMED WATANUKI!

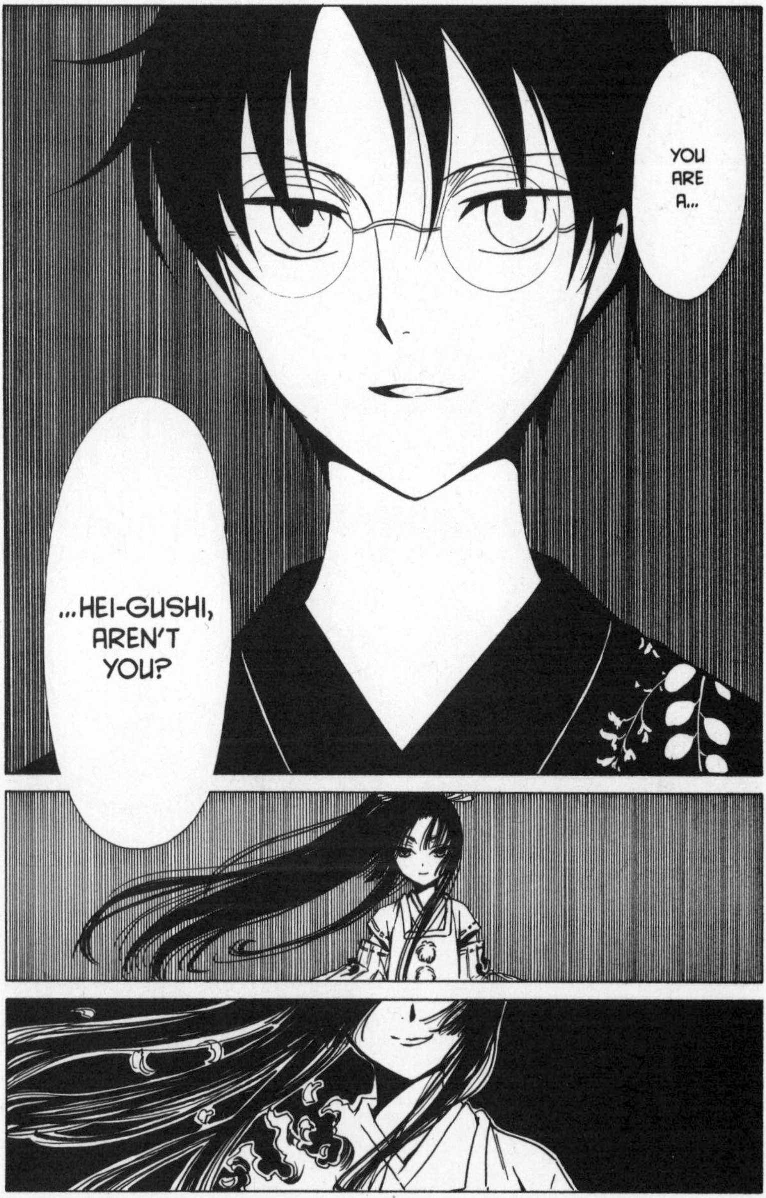
YOU ARE A...
...HEI-GUSHI, AREN'T YOU?

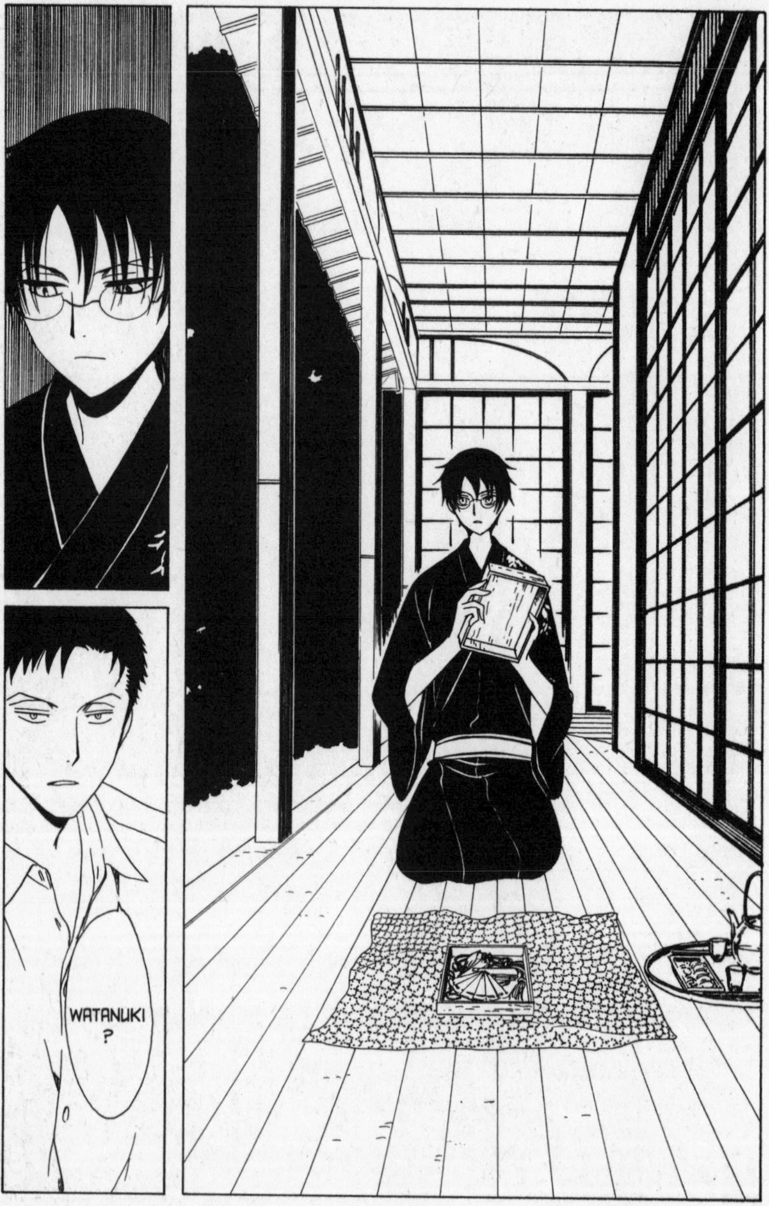
WATANUKI ?

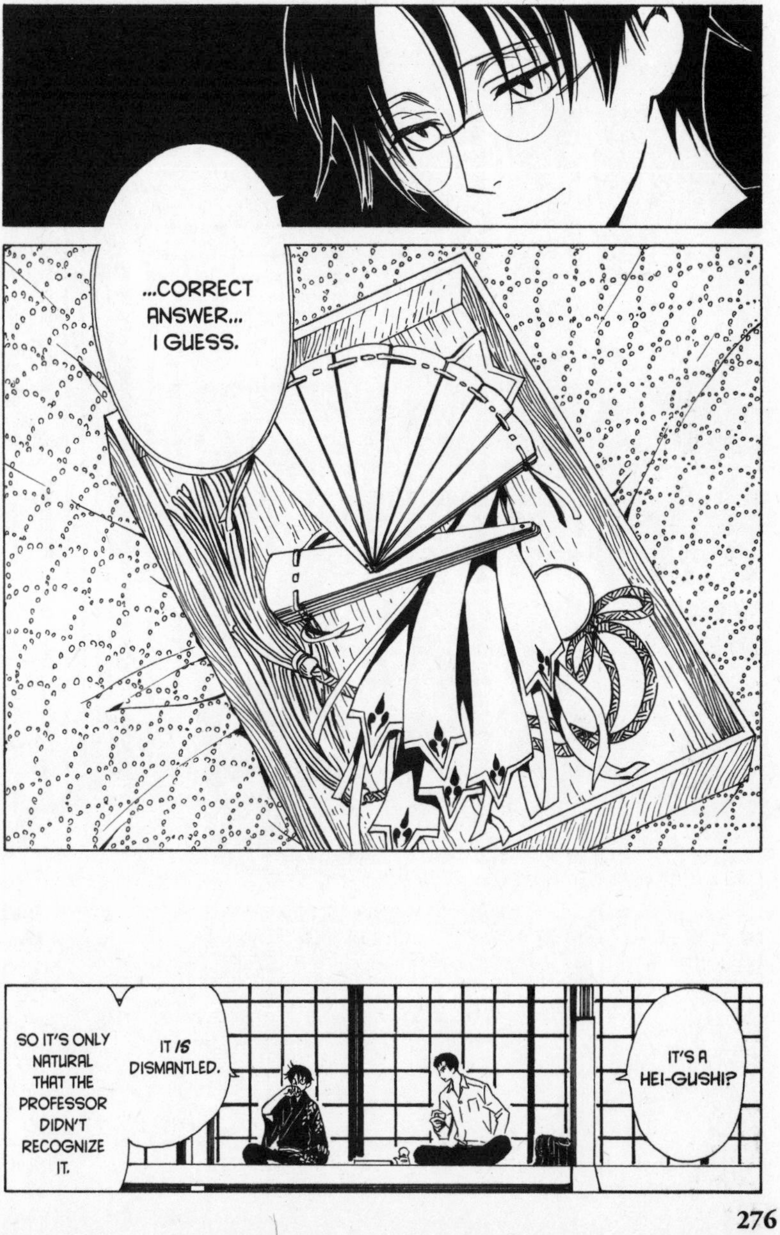
...CORRECT ANSWER... I GUESS.
IT'S A HEI-GUSHI?
IT *IS* DISMANTLED.
SO IT'S ONLY NATURAL THAT THE PROFESSOR DIDN'T RECOGNIZE IT.

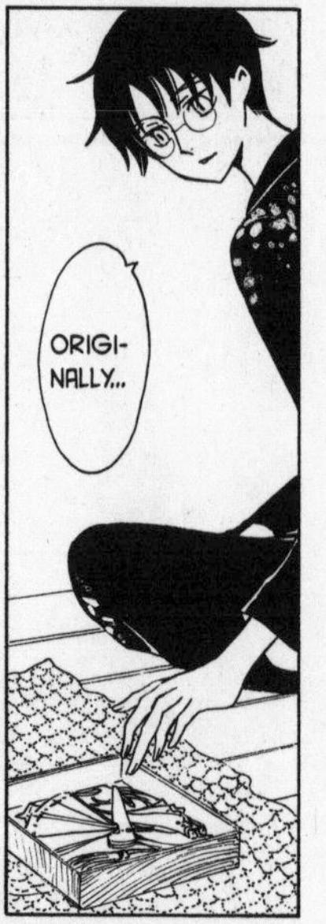
ORIGINALLY...

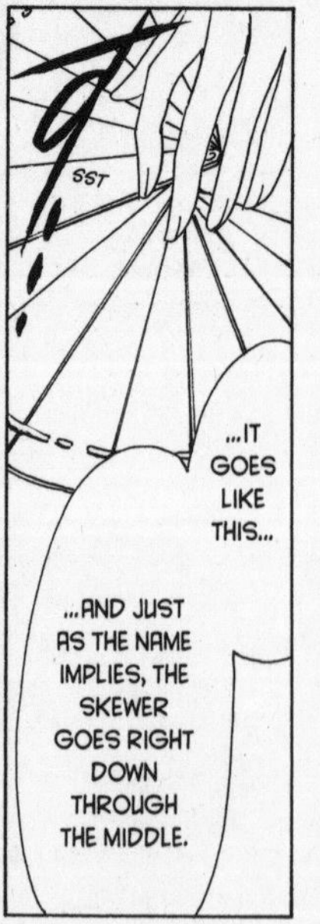
SST
...IT GOES LIKE THIS...
...AND JUST AS THE NAME IMPLIES, THE SKEWER GOES RIGHT DOWN THROUGH THE MIDDLE.

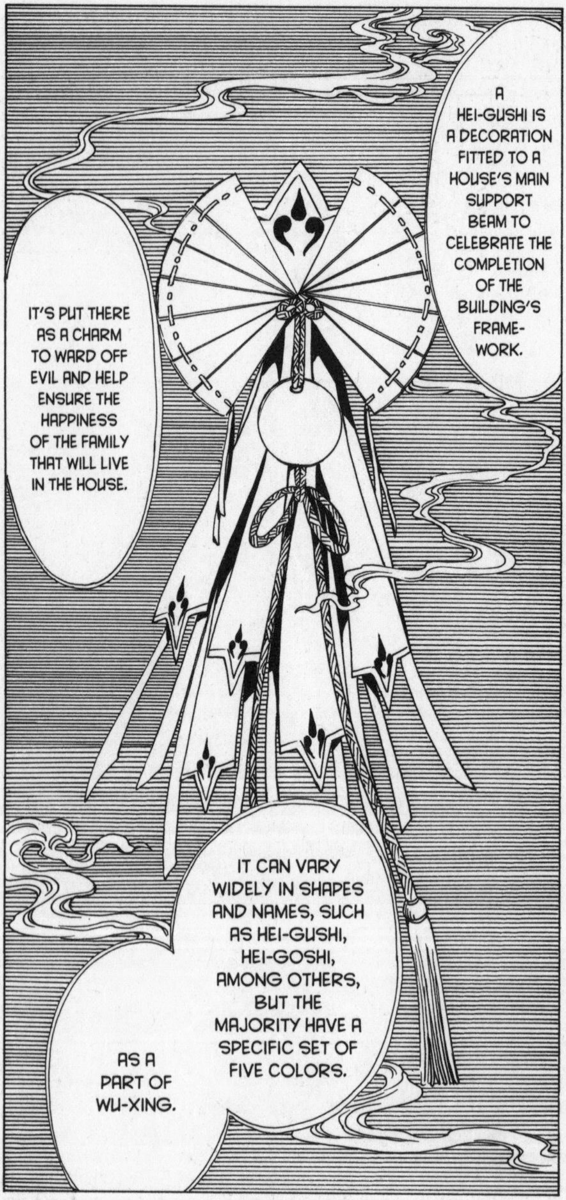
A HEI-GUSHI IS A DECORATION FITTED TO A HOUSE'S MAIN SUPPORT BEAM TO CELEBRATE THE COMPLETION OF THE BUILDING'S FRAMEWORK.
IT'S PUT THERE AS A CHARM TO WARD OFF EVIL AND HELP ENSURE THE HAPPINESS OF THE FAMILY THAT WILL LIVE IN THE HOUSE.
IT CAN VARY WIDELY IN SHAPES AND NAMES, SUCH AS HEI-GUSHI, HEI-GOSHI, AMONG OTHERS, BUT THE MAJORITY HAVE A SPECIFIC SET OF FIVE COLORS.
AS A PART OF WU-XING.

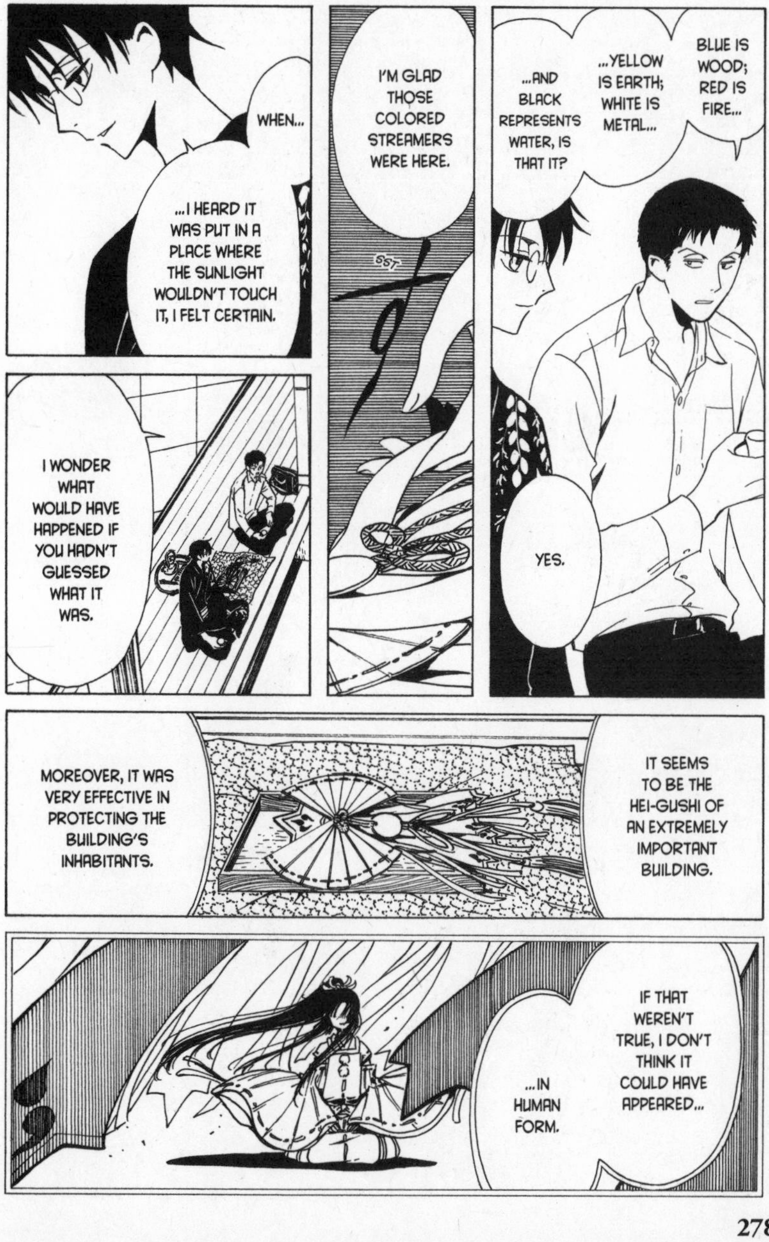
BLUE IS WOOD; RED IS FIRE...
...YELLOW IS EARTH; WHITE IS METAL...
...AND BLACK REPRESENTS WATER, IS THAT IT?
YES.
I'M GLAD THOSE COLORED STREAMERS WERE HERE.
SST
WHEN...
...I HEARD IT WAS PUT IN A PLACE WHERE THE SUNLIGHT WOULDN'T TOUCH IT, I FELT CERTAIN.
I WONDER WHAT WOULD HAVE HAPPENED IF YOU HADN'T GUESSED WHAT IT WAS.
IT SEEMS TO BE THE HEI-GUSHI OF AN EXTREMELY IMPORTANT BUILDING.
MOREOVER, IT WAS VERY EFFECTIVE IN PROTECTING THE BUILDING'S INHABITANTS.
IF THAT WEREN'T TRUE, I DON'T THINK IT COULD HAVE APPEARED...
...IN HUMAN FORM.

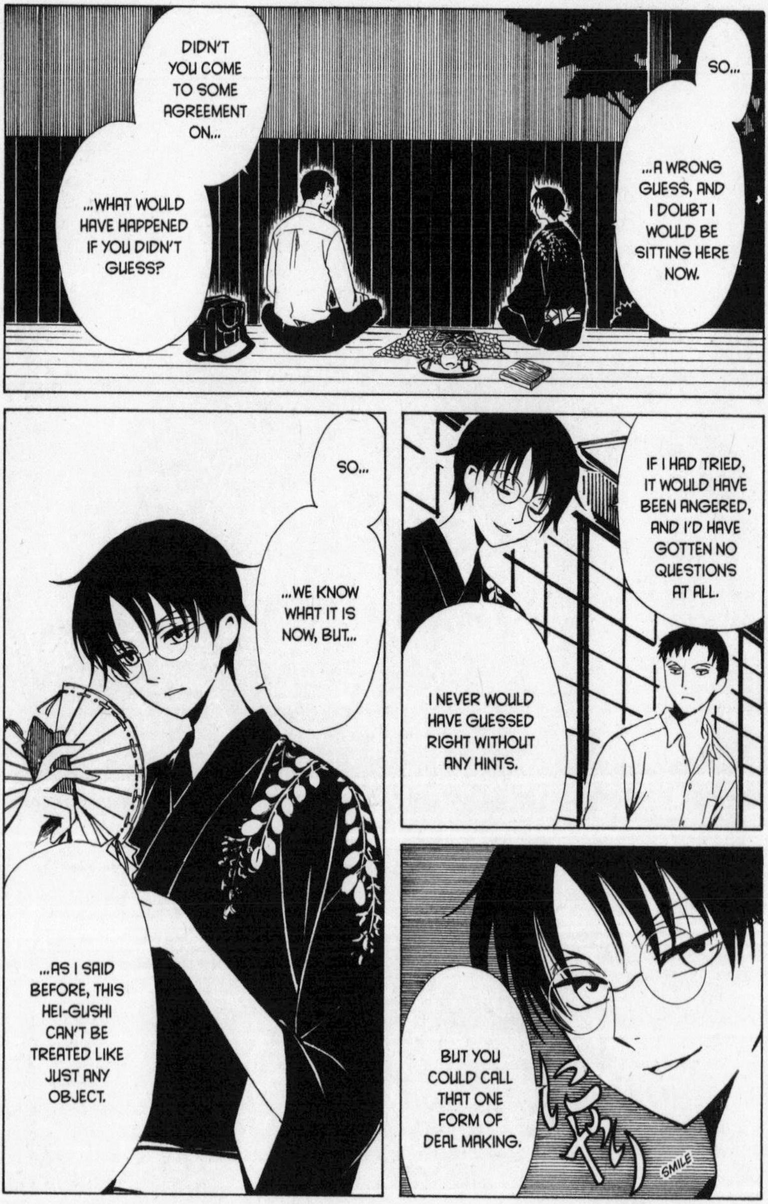
DIDN'T YOU COME TO SOME AGREEMENT ON...
...WHAT WOULD HAVE HAPPENED IF YOU DIDN'T GUESS?
SO...
...A WRONG GUESS, AND I DOUBT I WOULD BE SITTING HERE NOW.
IF I HAD TRIED, IT WOULD HAVE BEEN ANGERED, AND I'D HAVE GOTTEN NO QUESTIONS AT ALL.
I NEVER WOULD HAVE GUESSED RIGHT WITHOUT ANY HINTS.
BUT YOU COULD CALL THAT ONE FORM OF DEAL MAKING.
SMILE
SO...
...WE KNOW WHAT IT IS NOW, BUT...
...AS I SAID BEFORE, THIS HEI-GUSHI CAN'T BE TREATED LIKE JUST ANY OBJECT.

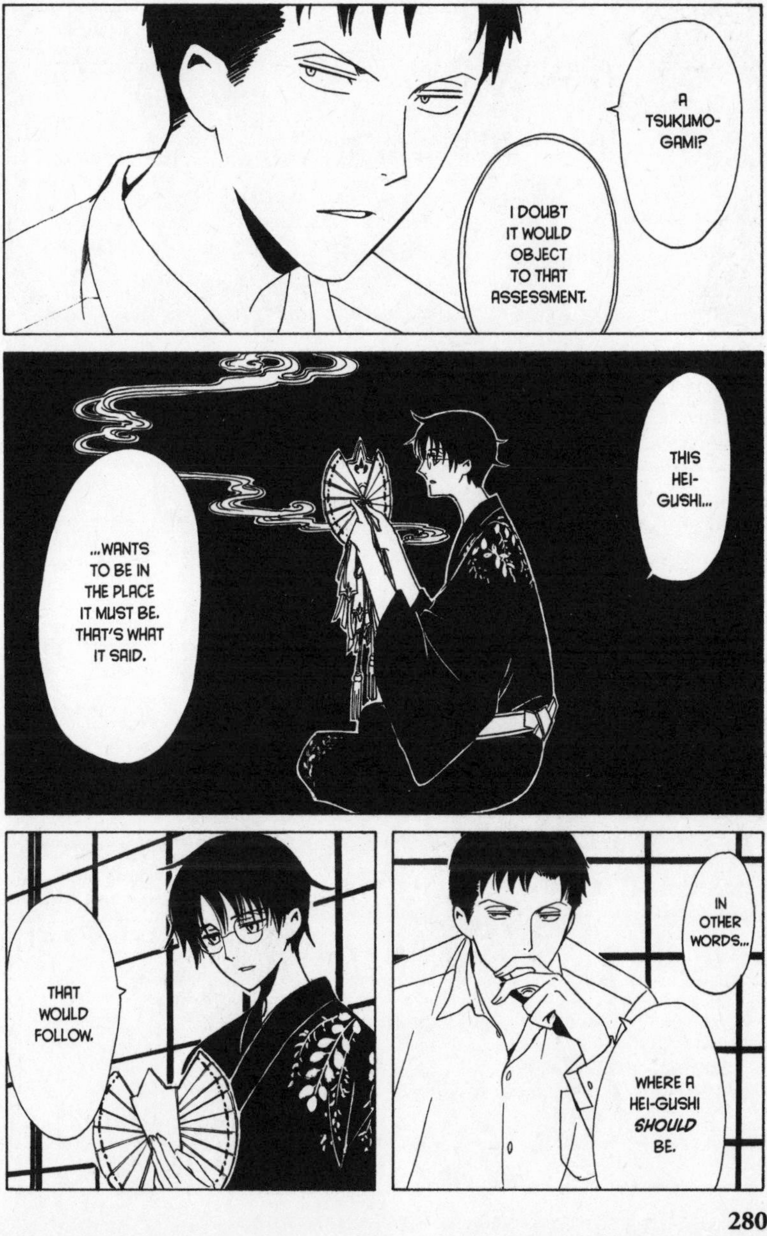
A TSUKUMO-GAMI?
I DOUBT IT WOULD OBJECT TO THAT ASSESSMENT.
THIS HEI-GUSHI...
...WANTS TO BE IN THE PLACE IT MUST BE. THAT'S WHAT IT SAID.
IN OTHER WORDS...
WHERE A HEI-GUSHI *SHOULD* BE.
THAT WOULD FOLLOW.

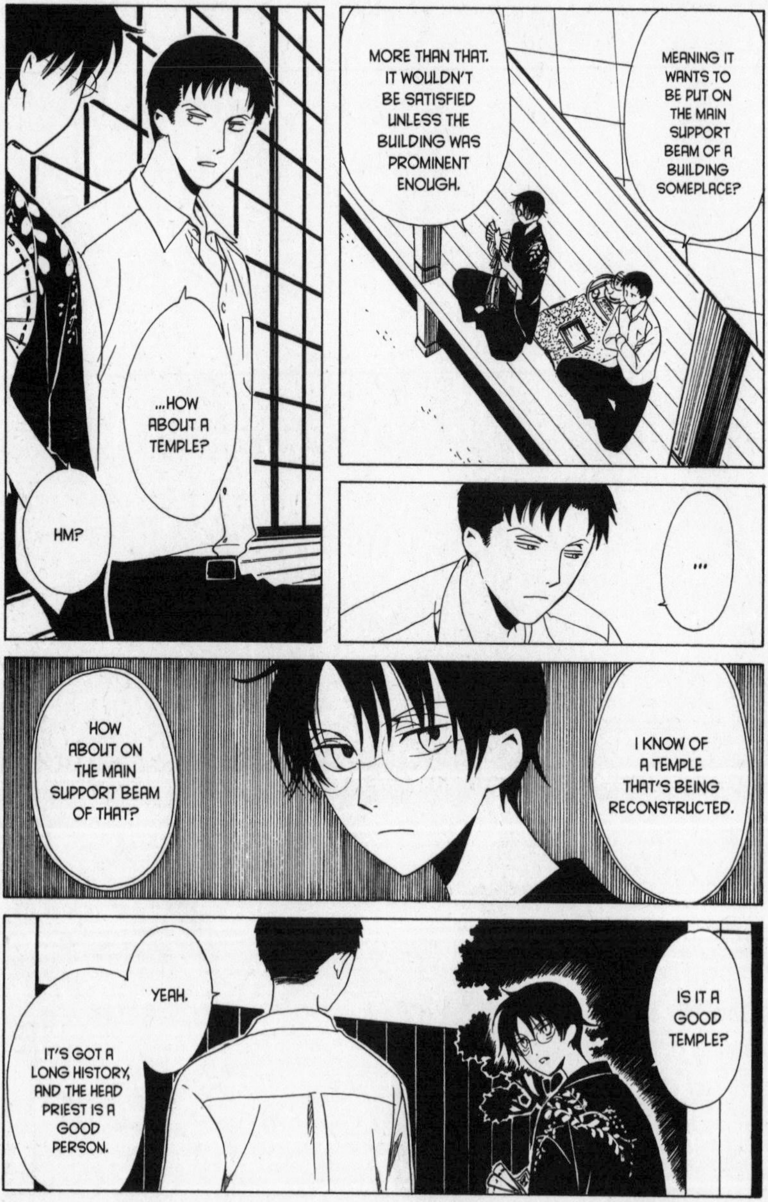
MEANING IT WANTS TO BE PUT ON THE MAIN SUPPORT BEAM OF A BUILDING SOMEPLACE?
MORE THAN THAT. IT WOULDN'T BE SATISFIED UNLESS THE BUILDING WAS PROMINENT ENOUGH.
...
...HOW ABOUT A TEMPLE?
HM?
I KNOW OF A TEMPLE THAT'S BEING RECONSTRUCTED.
HOW ABOUT ON THE MAIN SUPPORT BEAM OF THAT?
IS IT A GOOD TEMPLE?
YEAH.
IT'S GOT A LONG HISTORY, AND THE HEAD PRIEST IS A GOOD PERSON.

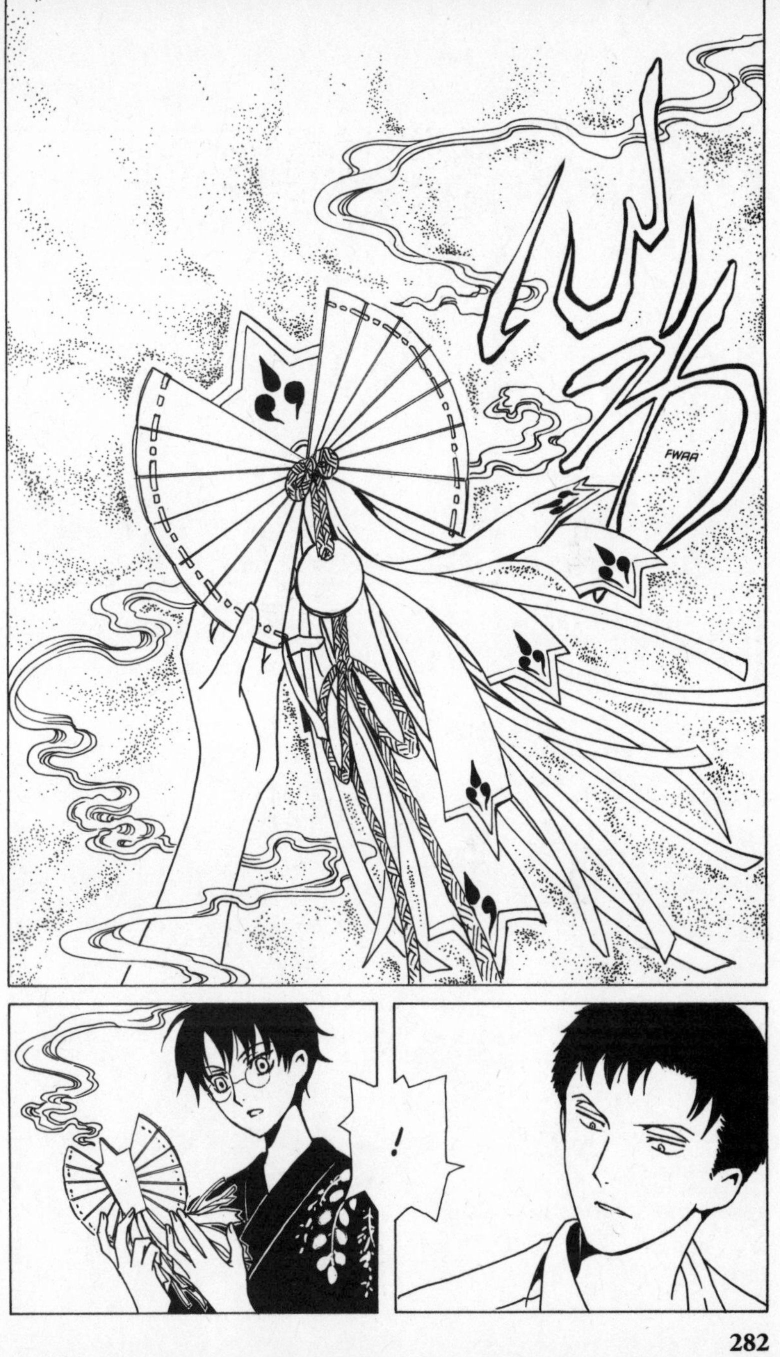
FWAA
!

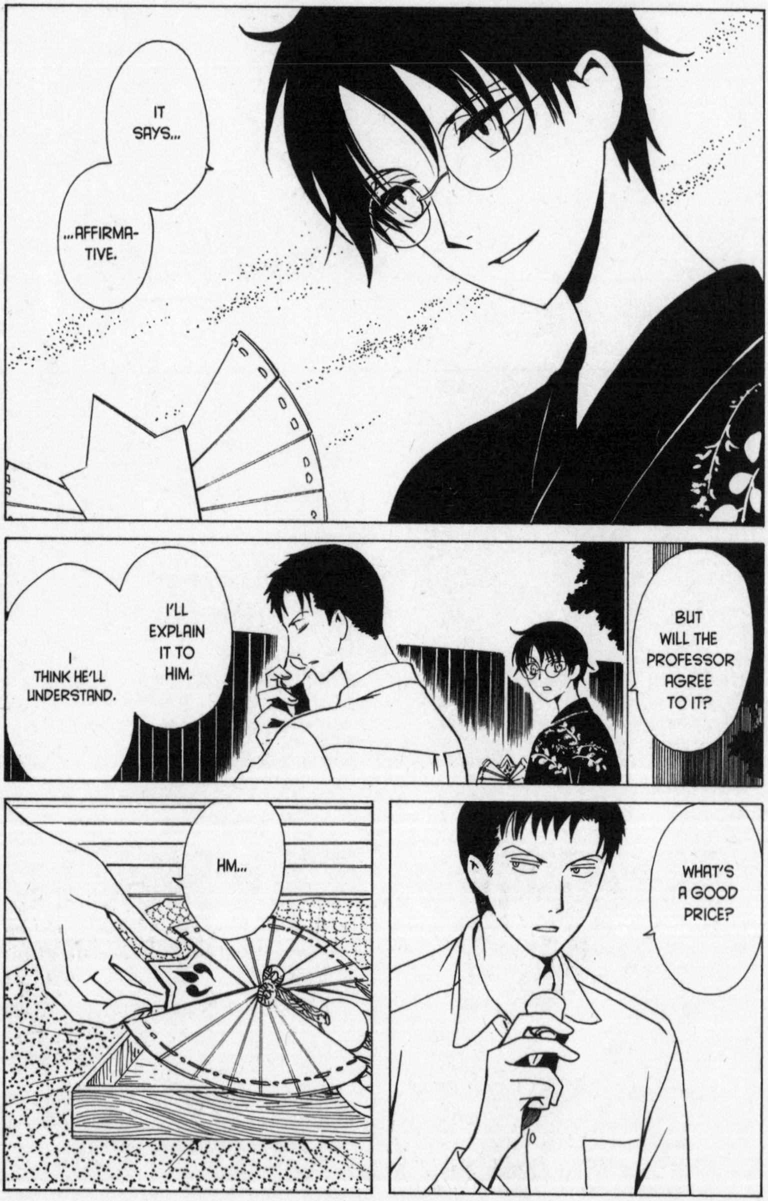
IT SAYS...
...AFFIRMATIVE.
BUT WILL THE PROFESSOR AGREE TO IT?
I'LL EXPLAIN IT TO HIM.
I THINK HE'LL UNDERSTAND.
WHAT'S A GOOD PRICE?
HM...

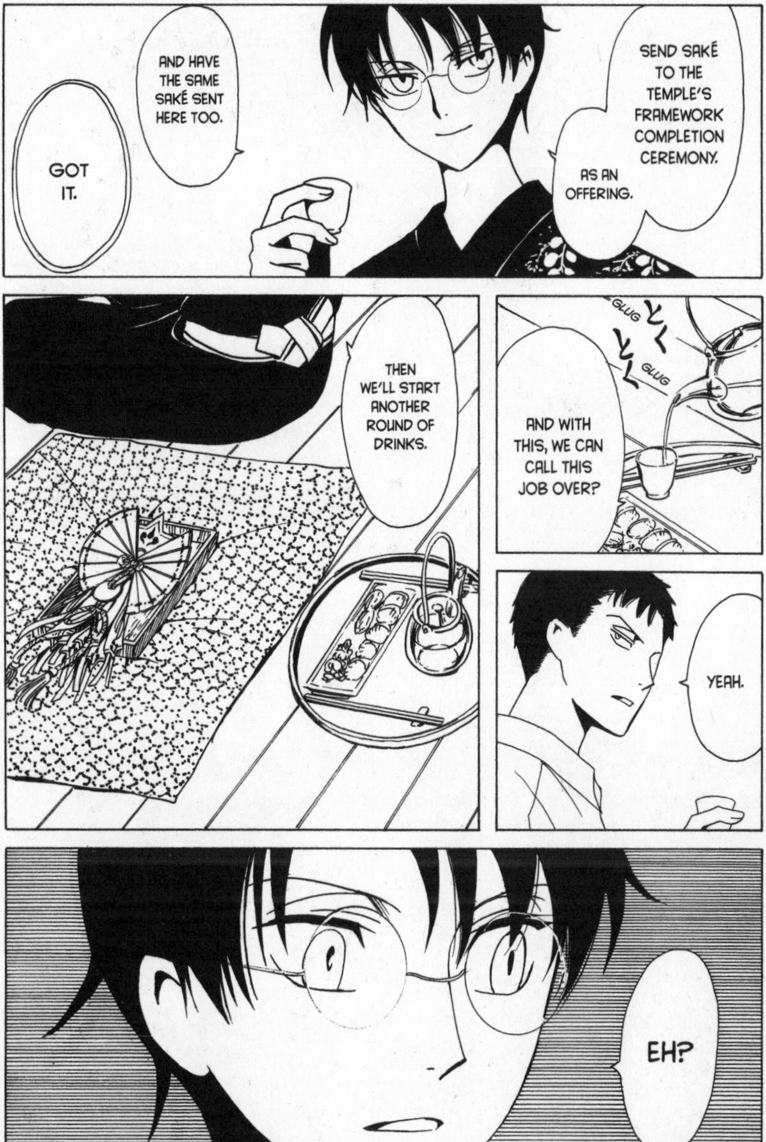
SEND SAKÉ TO THE TEMPLE'S FRAMEWORK COMPLETION CEREMONY.
AS AN OFFERING.
AND HAVE THE SAME SAKÉ SENT HERE TOO.
GOT IT.
GLUG
GLUG
AND WITH THIS, WE CAN CALL THIS JOB OVER?
YEAH.
THEN WE'LL START ANOTHER ROUND OF DRINKS.
EH?

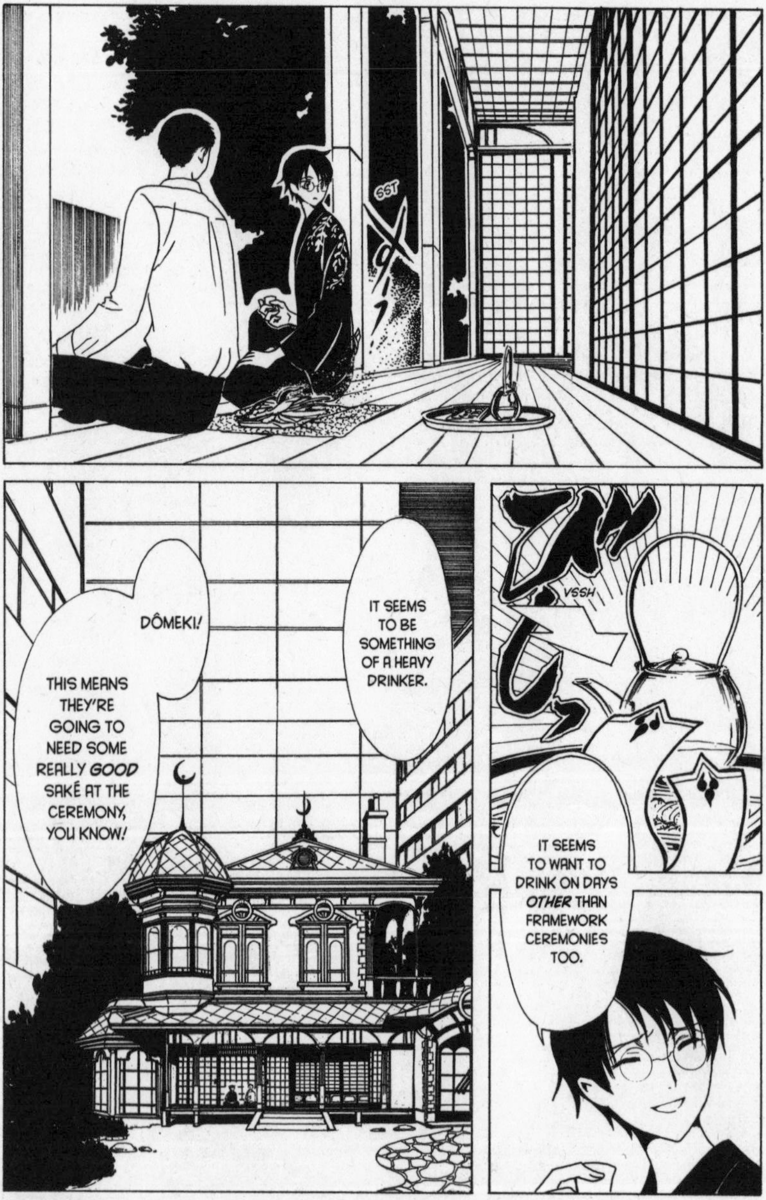
SST
VSSH
IT SEEMS TO WANT TO DRINK ON DAYS *OTHER* THAN FRAMEWORK CEREMONIES TOO.
IT SEEMS TO BE SOMETHING OF A HEAVY DRINKER.
DÔMEKI!
THIS MEANS THEY'RE GOING TO NEED SOME REALLY *GOOD* SAKÉ AT THE CEREMONY, YOU KNOW!

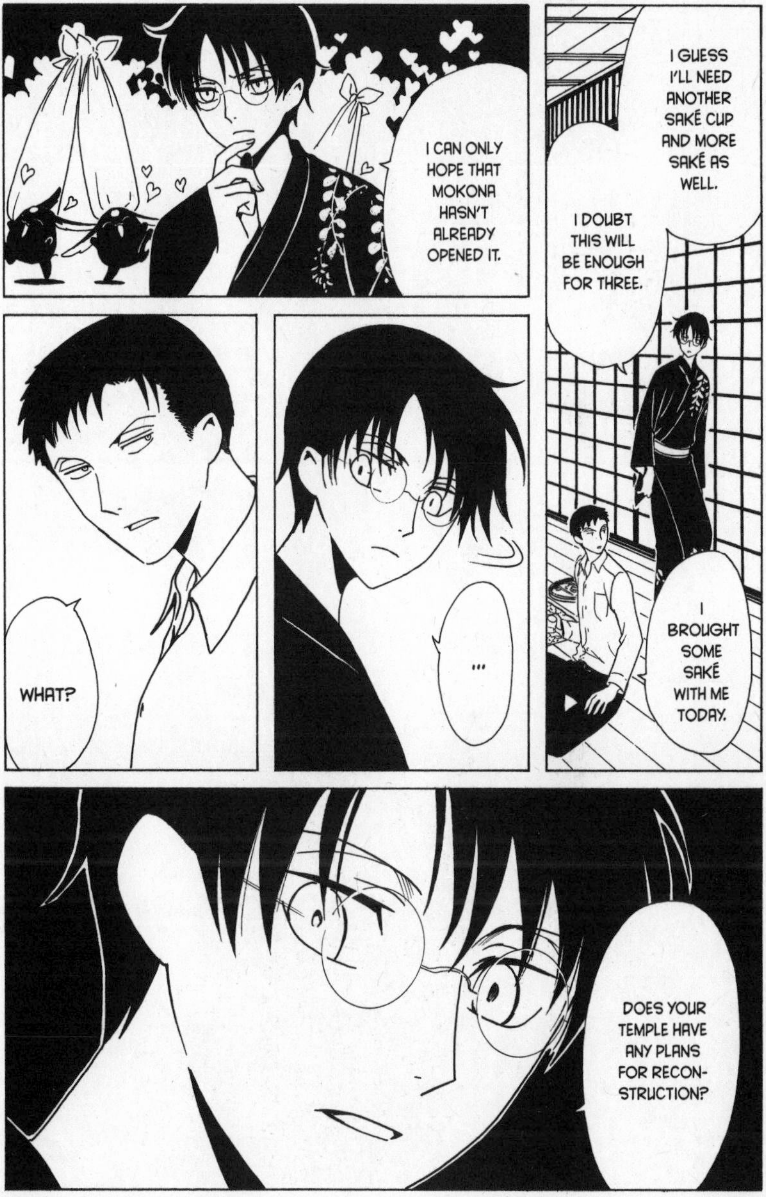
I GUESS I'LL NEED ANOTHER SAKÉ CUP AND MORE SAKÉ AS WELL.
I DOUBT THIS WILL BE ENOUGH FOR THREE.
I BROUGHT SOME SAKÉ WITH ME TODAY.
I CAN ONLY HOPE THAT MOKONA HASN'T ALREADY OPENED IT.
...
WHAT?
DOES YOUR TEMPLE HAVE ANY PLANS FOR RECON-STRUCTION?

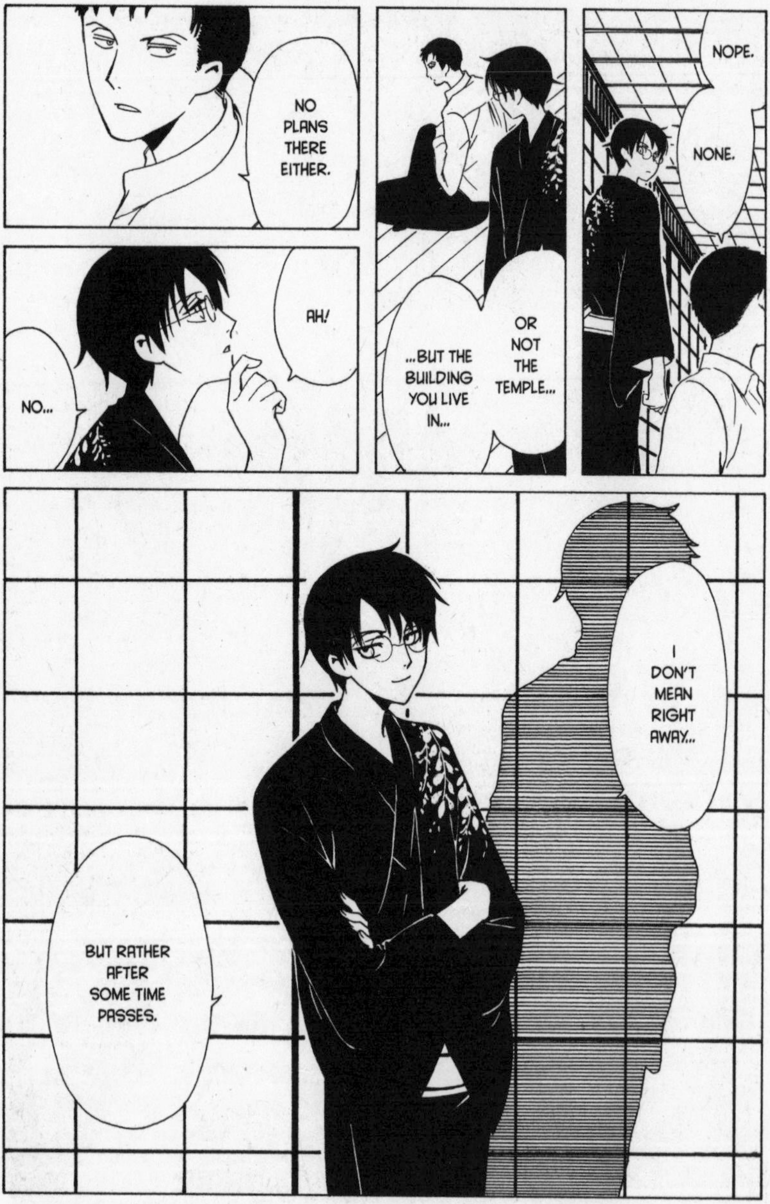
NOPE.
NONE.
OR NOT THE TEMPLE...
...BUT THE BUILDING YOU LIVE IN...
NO PLANS THERE EITHER.
AH!
NO...
I DON'T MEAN RIGHT AWAY...
BUT RATHER AFTER SOME TIME PASSES.

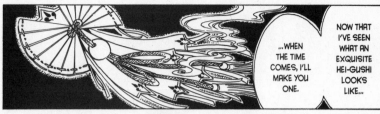

NOW THAT I'VE SEEN WHAT AN EXQUISITE HEI-GUSHI LOOKS LIKE...

...WHEN THE TIME COMES, I'LL MAKE YOU ONE.

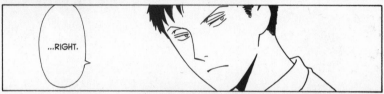

...RIGHT.

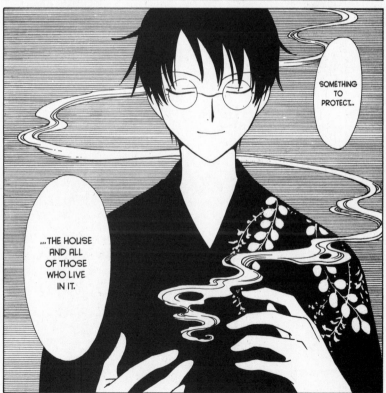

SOMETHING TO PROTECT...

...THE HOUSE AND ALL OF THOSE WHO LIVE IN IT.

288

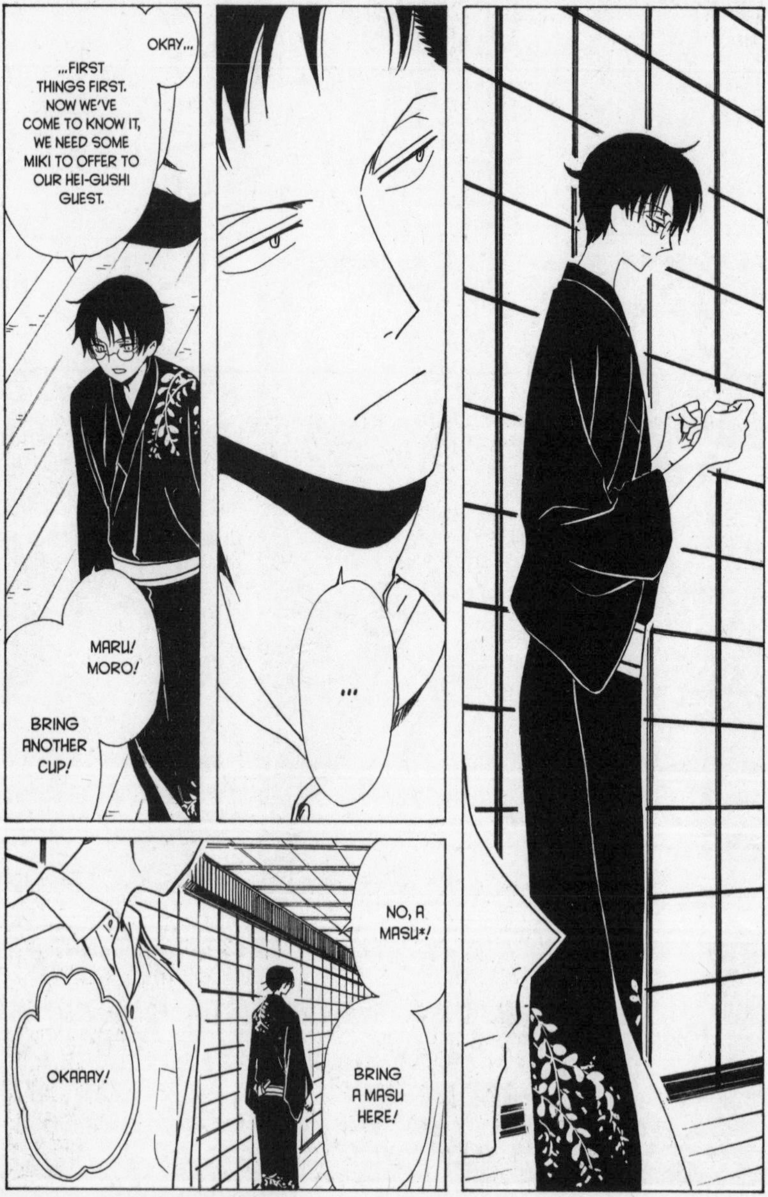
...
OKAY...
...FIRST THINGS FIRST. NOW WE'VE COME TO KNOW IT, WE NEED SOME MIKI TO OFFER TO OUR HEI-GUSHI GUEST.
MARU! MORO!
BRING ANOTHER CUP!
NO, A MASU*!
BRING A MASU HERE!
OKAAAY!

*MASU = 5-LITER MEASURING CUP

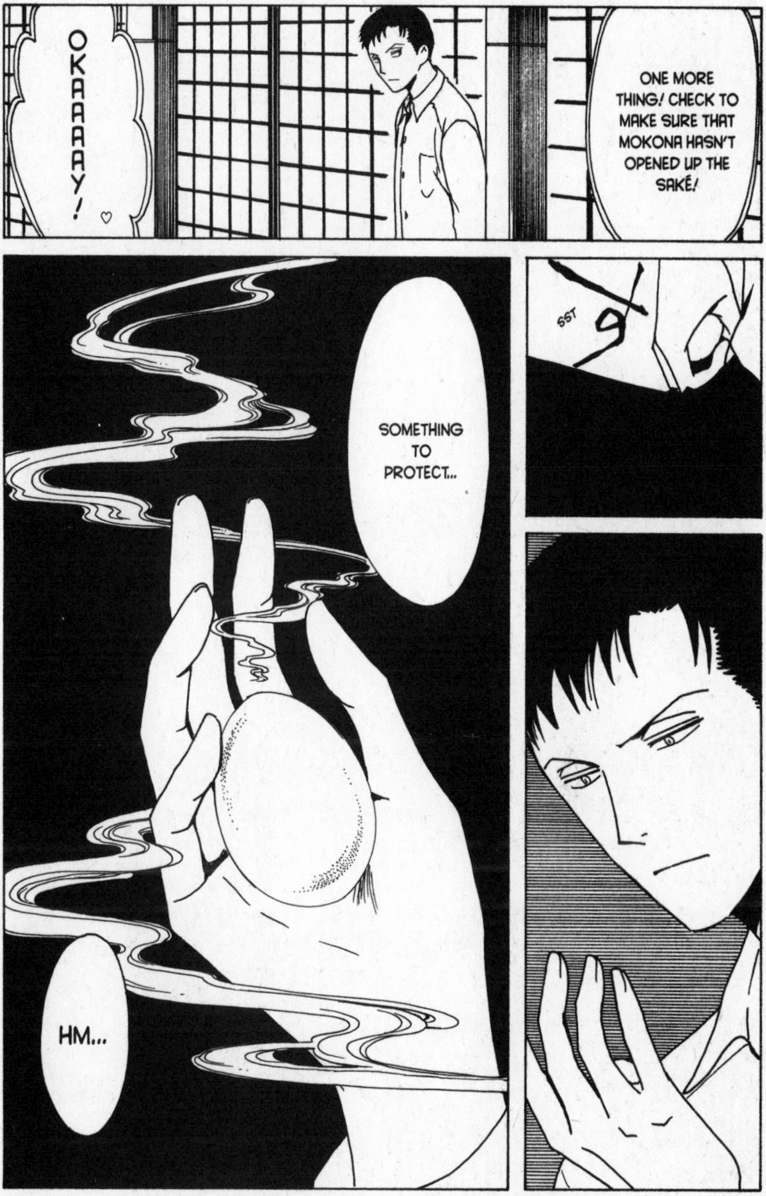
ONE MORE THING! CHECK TO MAKE SURE THAT MOKONA HASN'T OPENED UP THE SAKÉ!
OKAAAAAY! ♡
SST
SOMETHING TO PROTECT...
HM...

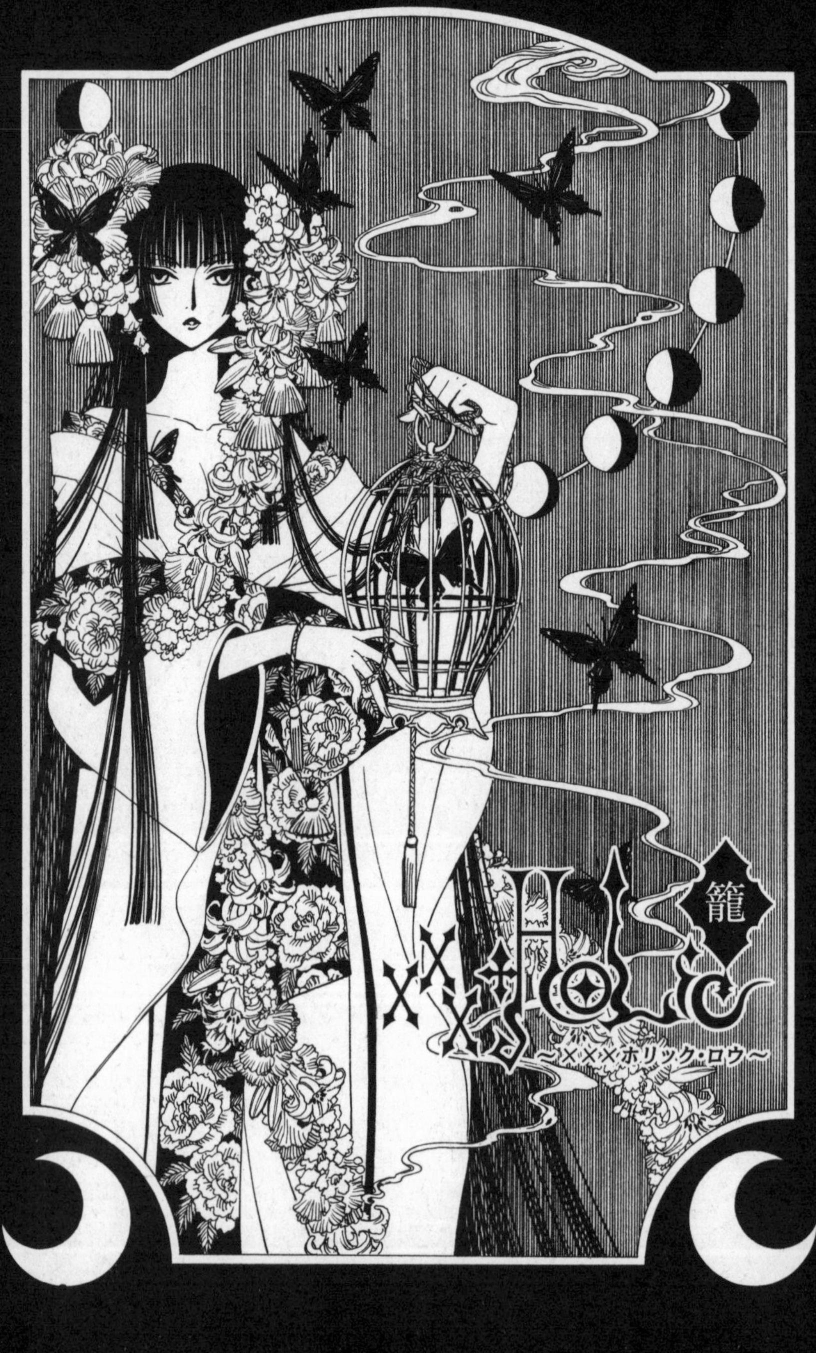

籠
xxxHolic
～×××ホリック・ロウ～

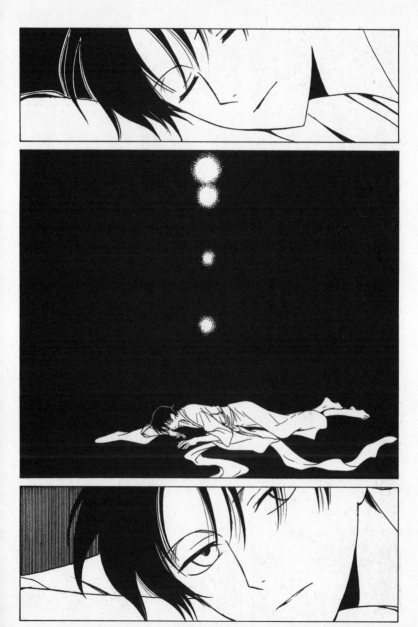

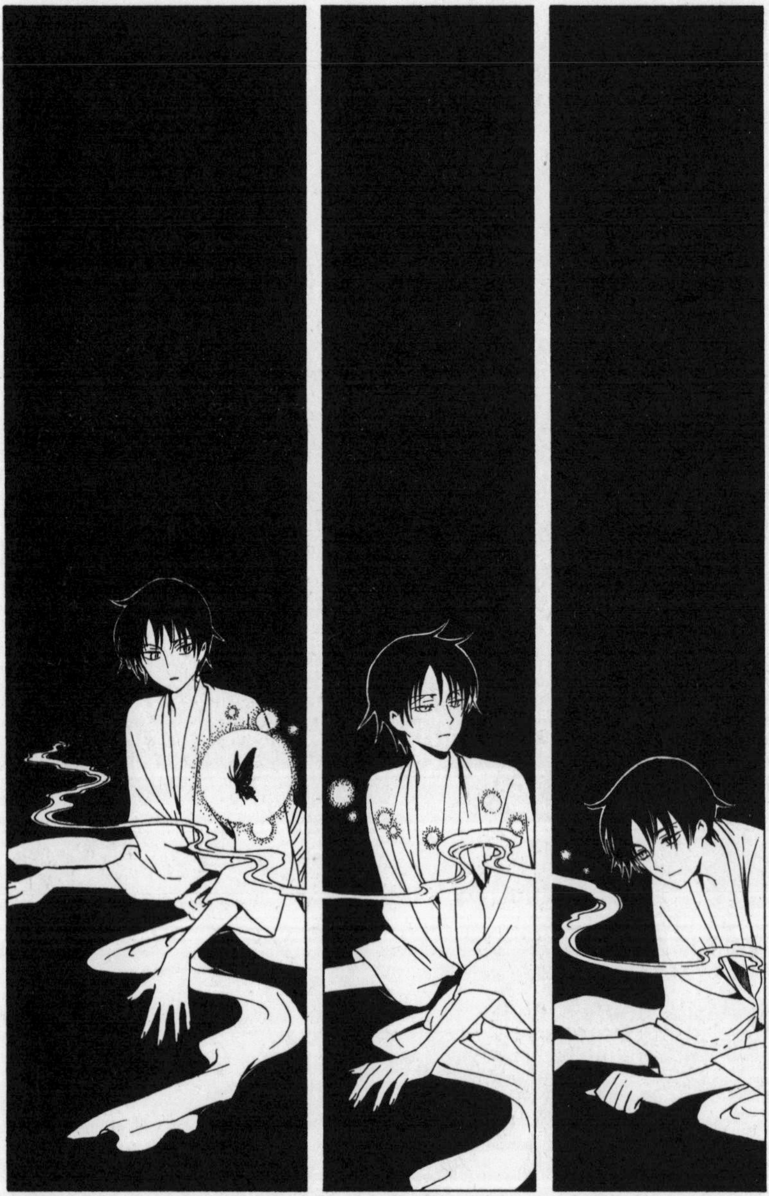

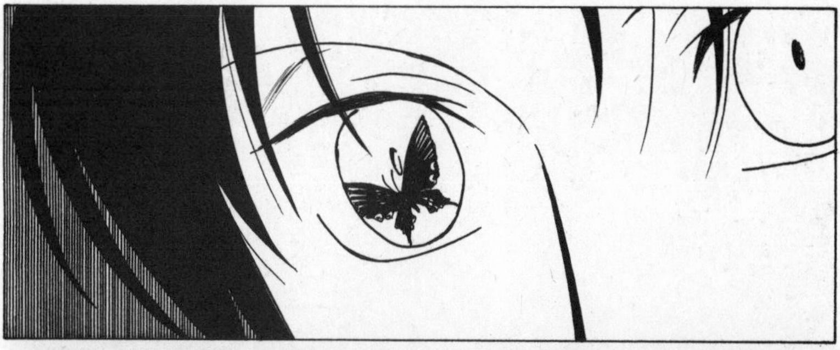

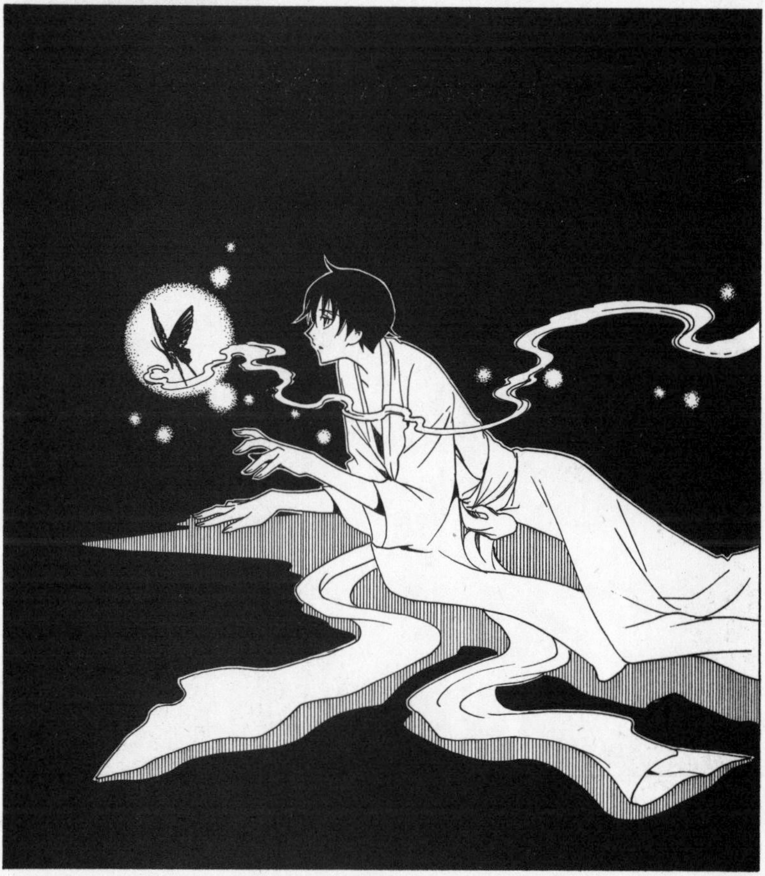

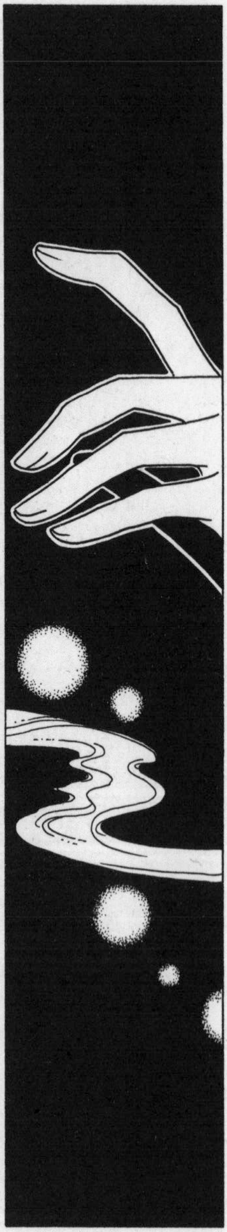

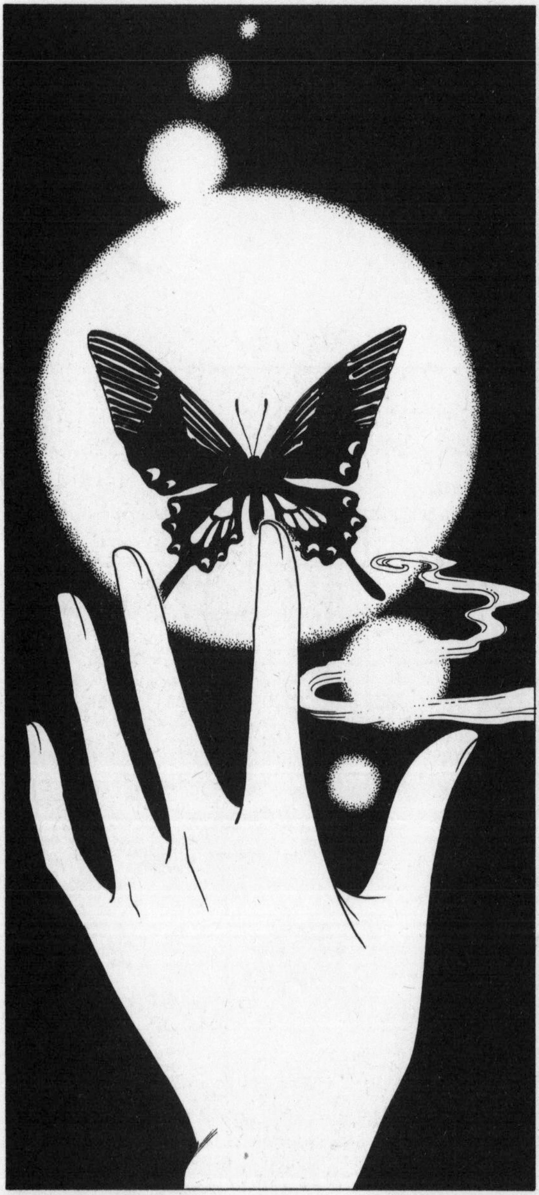

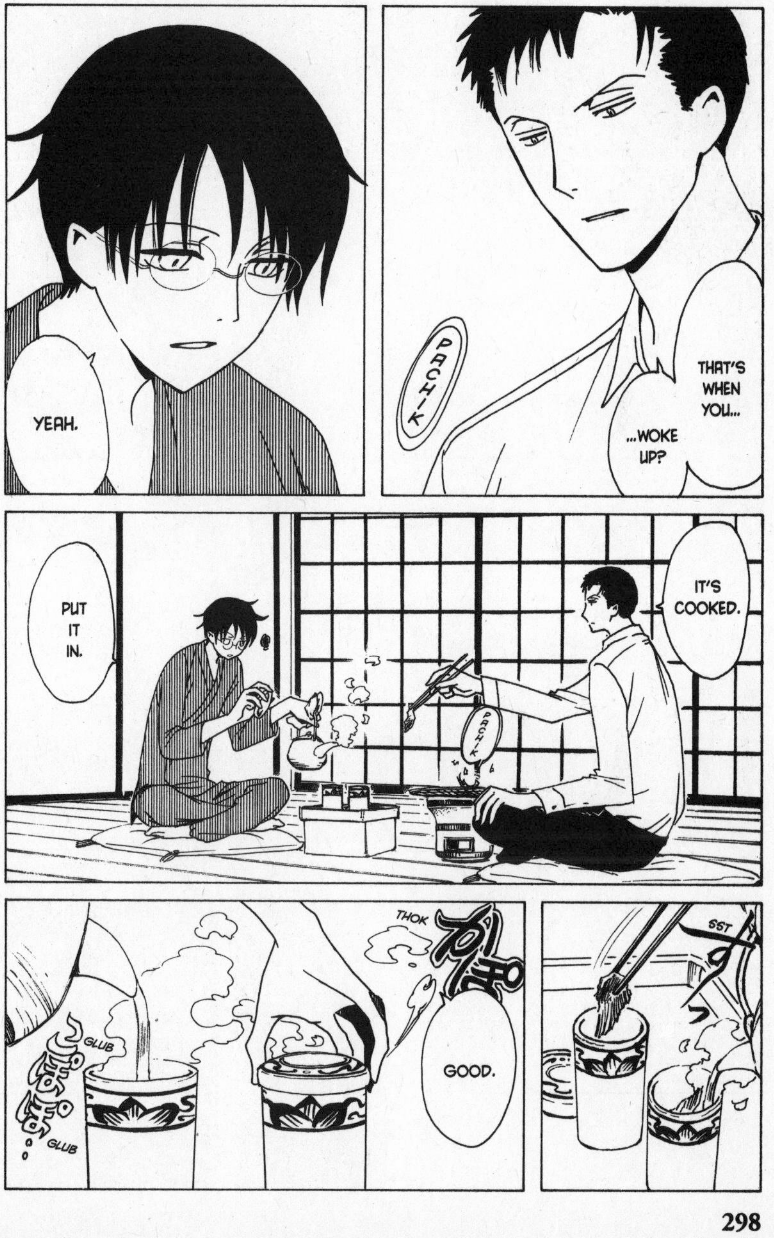
THAT'S WHEN YOU...
...WOKE UP?
PACHIK
YEAH.
IT'S COOKED.
PACHIK
PUT IT IN.
SST
THOK
GOOD.
GLUB
GLUB

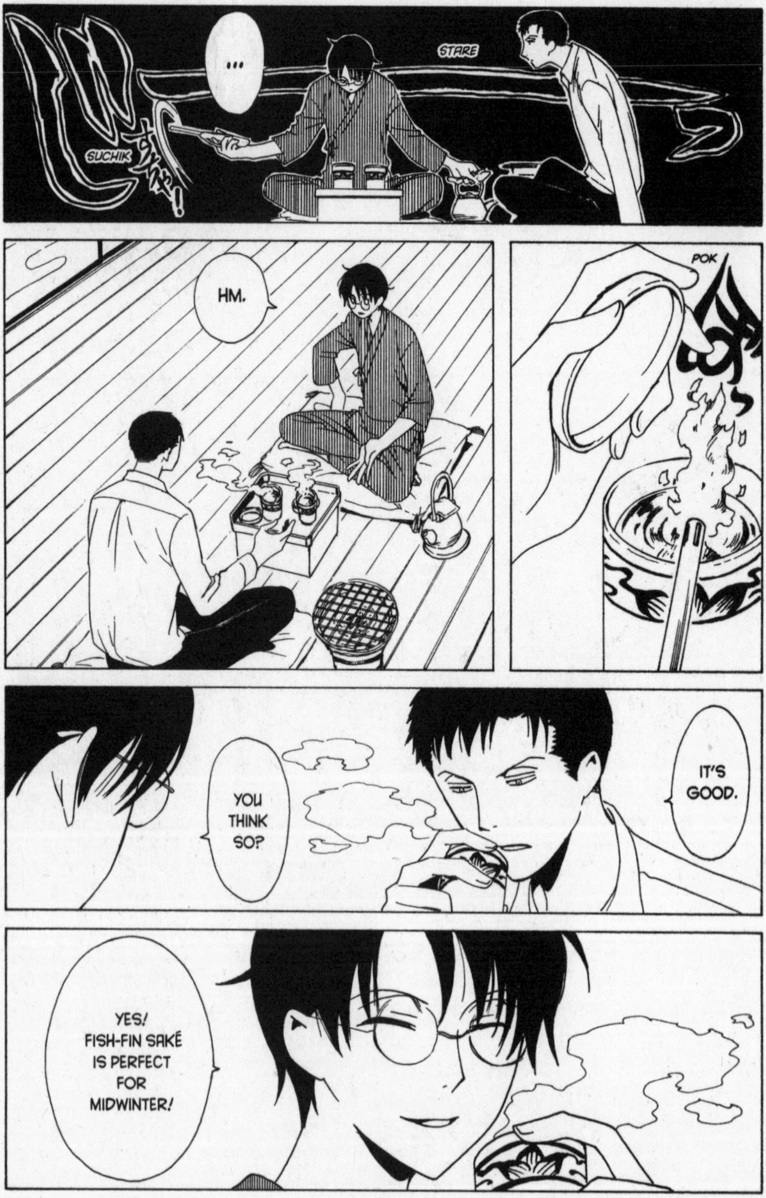
STARE
...
SUCHIK
すちゃ!
POK
HM.
IT'S GOOD.
YOU THINK SO?
YES! FISH-FIN SAKÉ IS PERFECT FOR MIDWINTER!

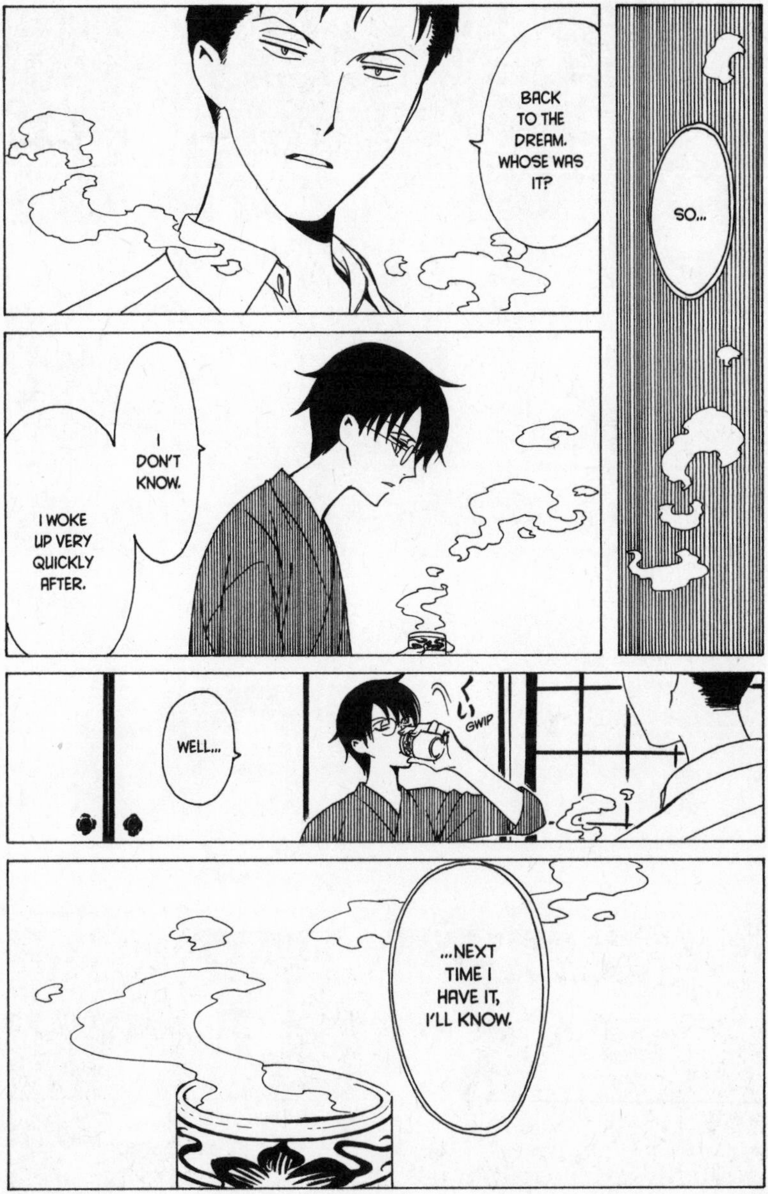
SO...
BACK TO THE DREAM. WHOSE WAS IT?
I DON'T KNOW.
I WOKE UP VERY QUICKLY AFTER.
GWIP
WELL...
...NEXT TIME I HAVE IT, I'LL KNOW.

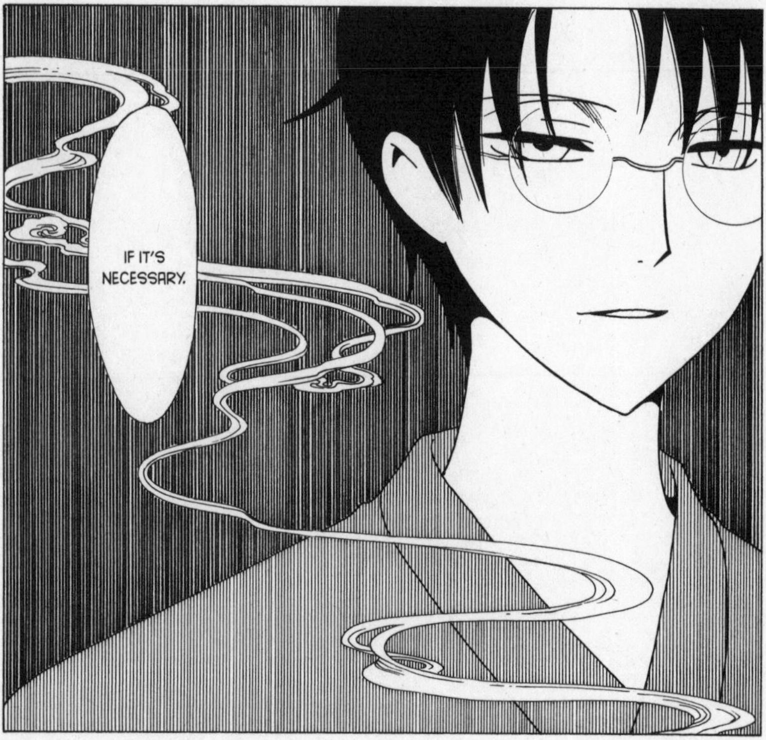
IF IT'S NECESSARY.
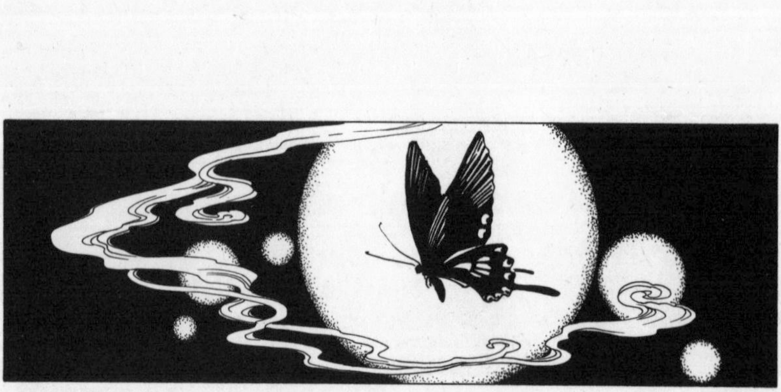

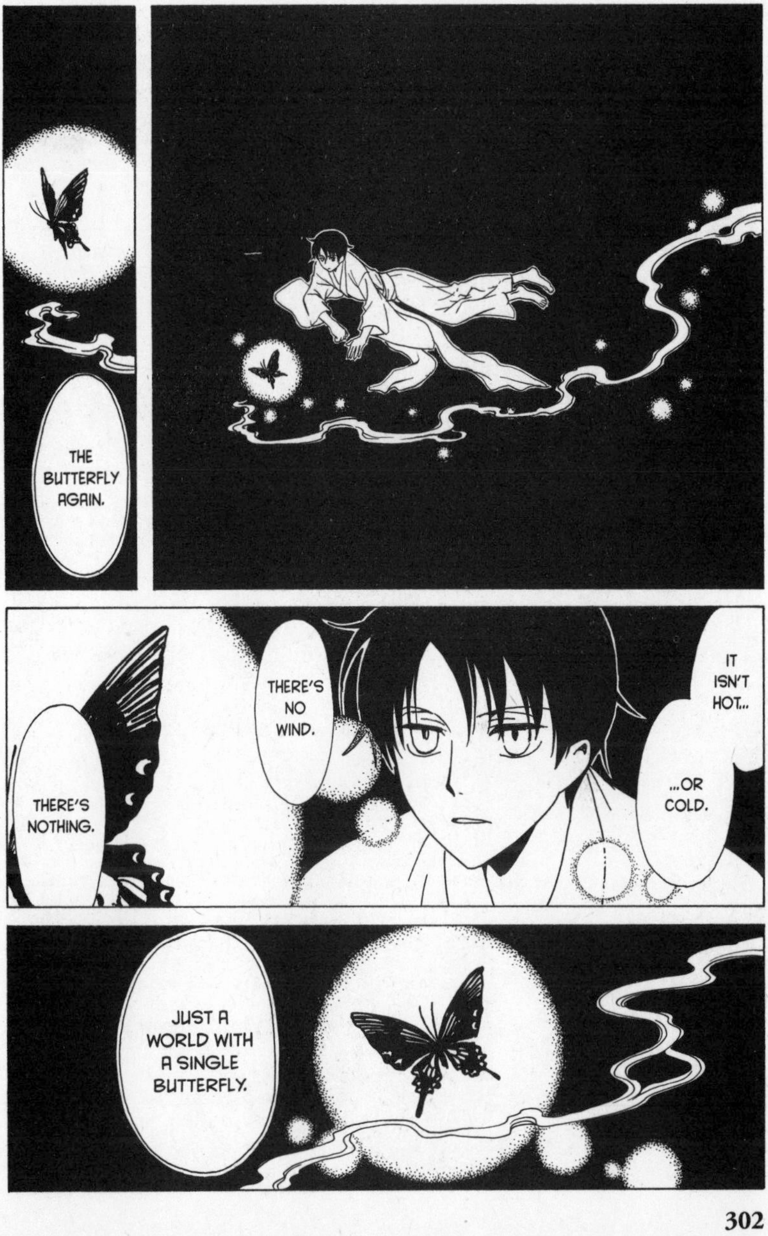
THE BUTTERFLY AGAIN.
IT ISN'T HOT...
...OR COLD.
THERE'S NO WIND.
THERE'S NOTHING.
JUST A WORLD WITH A SINGLE BUTTERFLY.

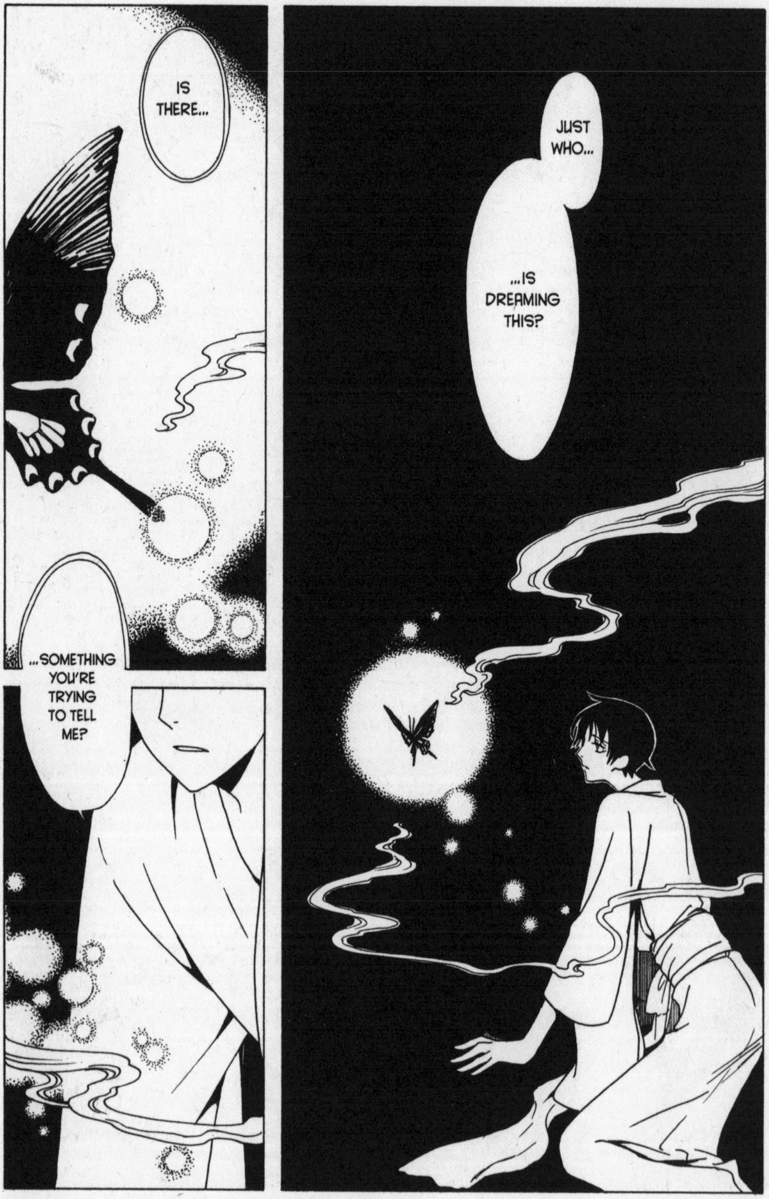
JUST WHO...
...IS DREAMING THIS?
IS THERE...
...SOMETHING YOU'RE TRYING TO TELL ME?

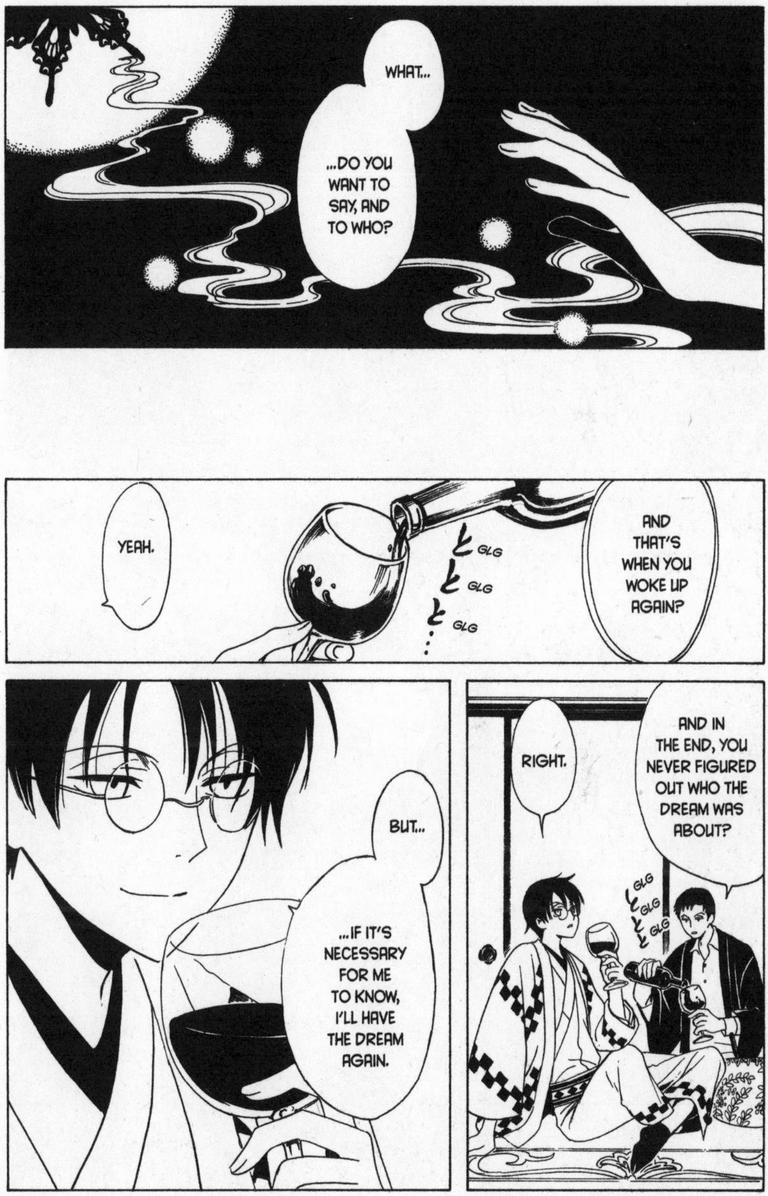
WHAT...
...DO YOU WANT TO SAY, AND TO WHO?
AND THAT'S WHEN YOU WOKE UP AGAIN?
と GLG
と GLG
と GLG
YEAH.
AND IN THE END, YOU NEVER FIGURED OUT WHO THE DREAM WAS ABOUT?
RIGHT.
と GLG
と GLG
と GLG
BUT...
...IF IT'S NECESSARY FOR ME TO KNOW, I'LL HAVE THE DREAM AGAIN.

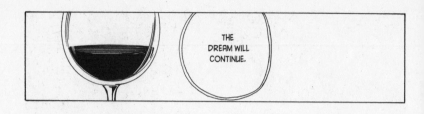

THE DREAM WILL CONTINUE.

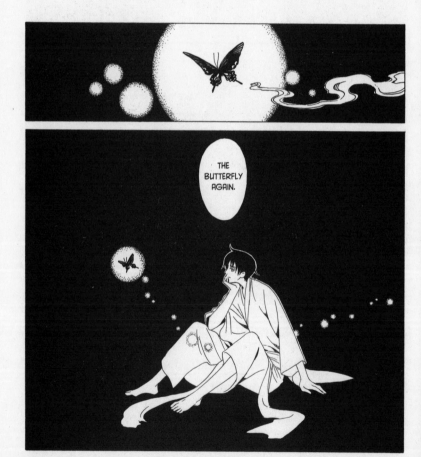

THE BUTTERFLY AGAIN.

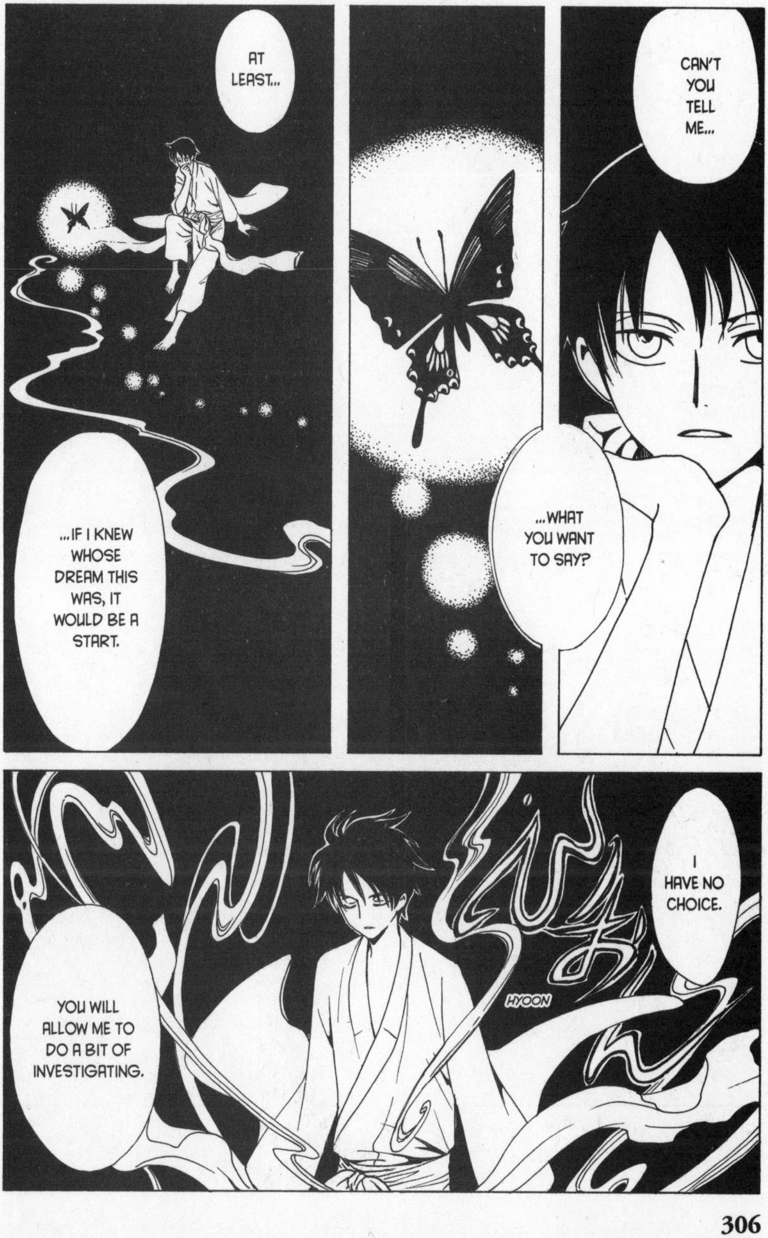
CAN'T YOU TELL ME...
...WHAT YOU WANT TO SAY?
AT LEAST...
...IF I KNEW WHOSE DREAM THIS WAS, IT WOULD BE A START.
I HAVE NO CHOICE.
HYOON
YOU WILL ALLOW ME TO DO A BIT OF INVESTIGATING.

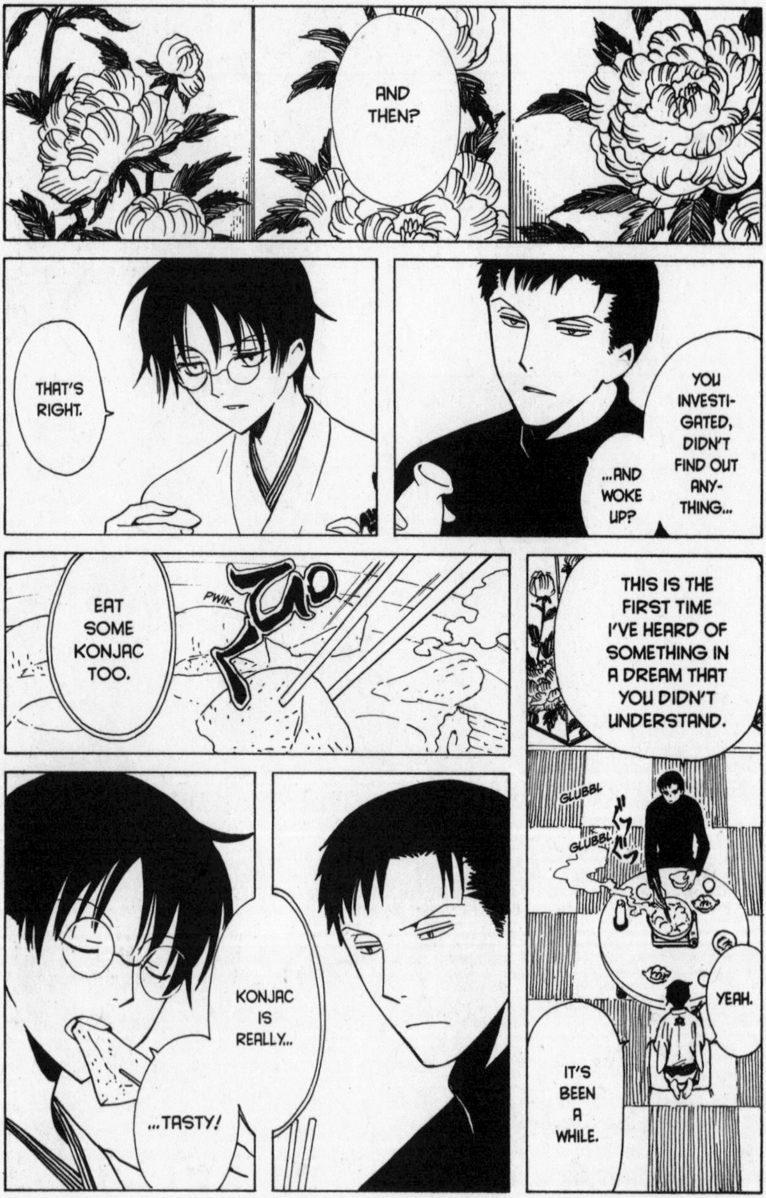
AND THEN?
YOU INVESTIGATED, DIDN'T FIND OUT ANYTHING...
...AND WOKE UP?
THAT'S RIGHT.
THIS IS THE FIRST TIME I'VE HEARD OF SOMETHING IN A DREAM THAT YOU DIDN'T UNDERSTAND.
GLUBBL
GLUBBL
YEAH.
IT'S BEEN A WHILE.
EAT SOME KONJAC TOO.
PWIK
KONJAC IS REALLY...
...TASTY!

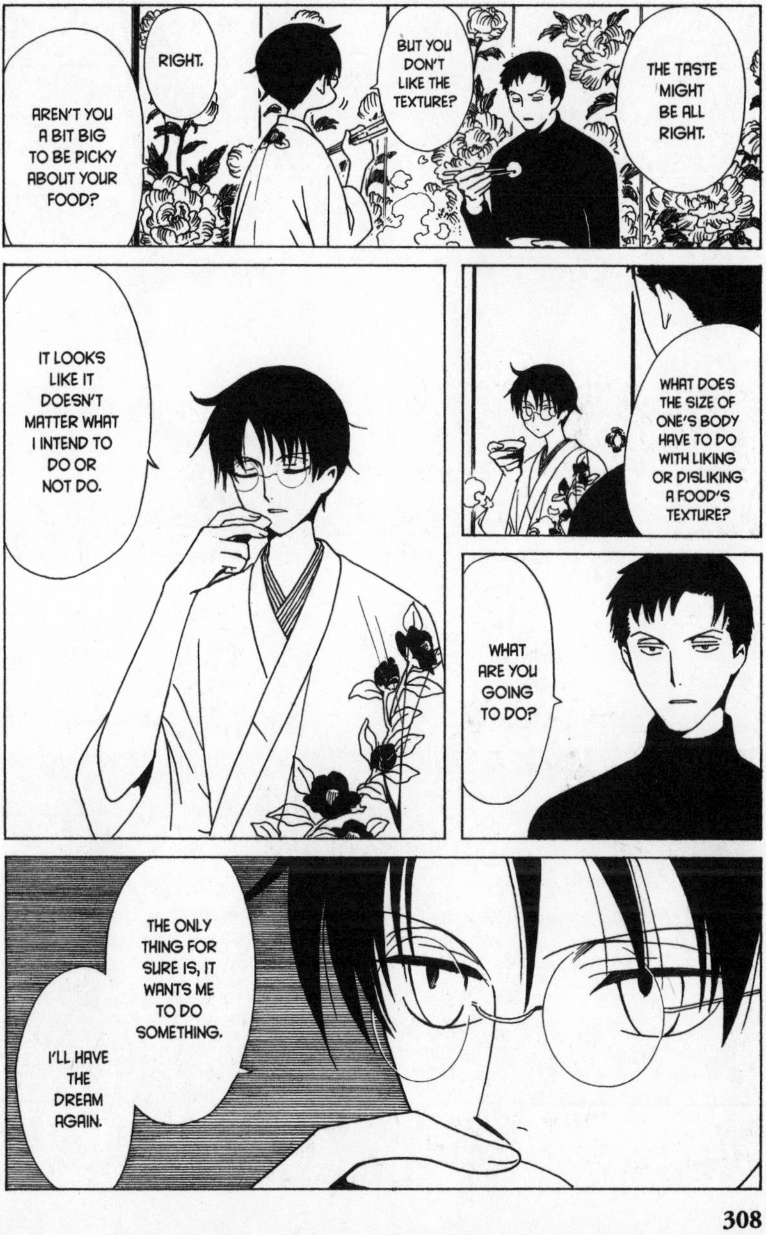
THE TASTE MIGHT BE ALL RIGHT.
BUT YOU DON'T LIKE THE TEXTURE?
RIGHT.
AREN'T YOU A BIT BIG TO BE PICKY ABOUT YOUR FOOD?
WHAT DOES THE SIZE OF ONE'S BODY HAVE TO DO WITH LIKING OR DISLIKING A FOOD'S TEXTURE?
WHAT ARE YOU GOING TO DO?
IT LOOKS LIKE IT DOESN'T MATTER WHAT I INTEND TO DO OR NOT DO.
THE ONLY THING FOR SURE IS, IT WANTS ME TO DO SOMETHING.
I'LL HAVE THE DREAM AGAIN.

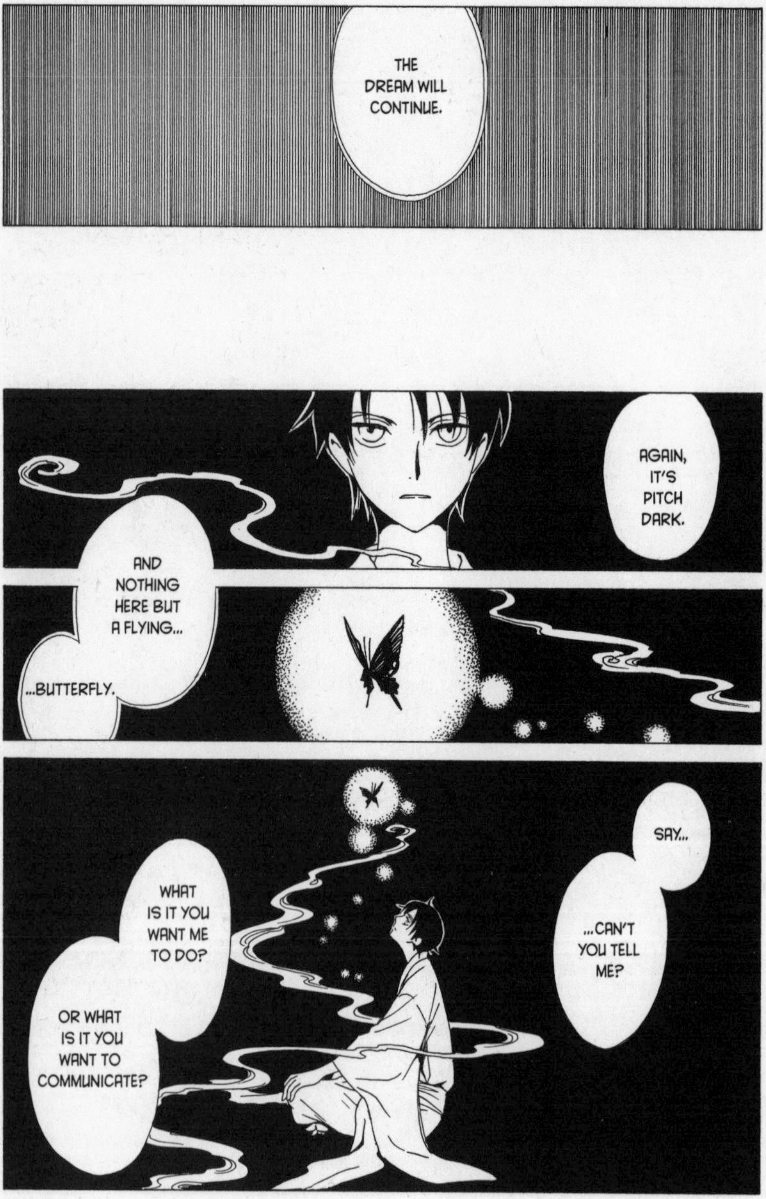
THE DREAM WILL CONTINUE.
AGAIN, IT'S PITCH DARK.
AND NOTHING HERE BUT A FLYING...
...BUTTERFLY.
SAY...
...CAN'T YOU TELL ME?
WHAT IS IT YOU WANT ME TO DO?
OR WHAT IS IT YOU WANT TO COMMUNICATE?

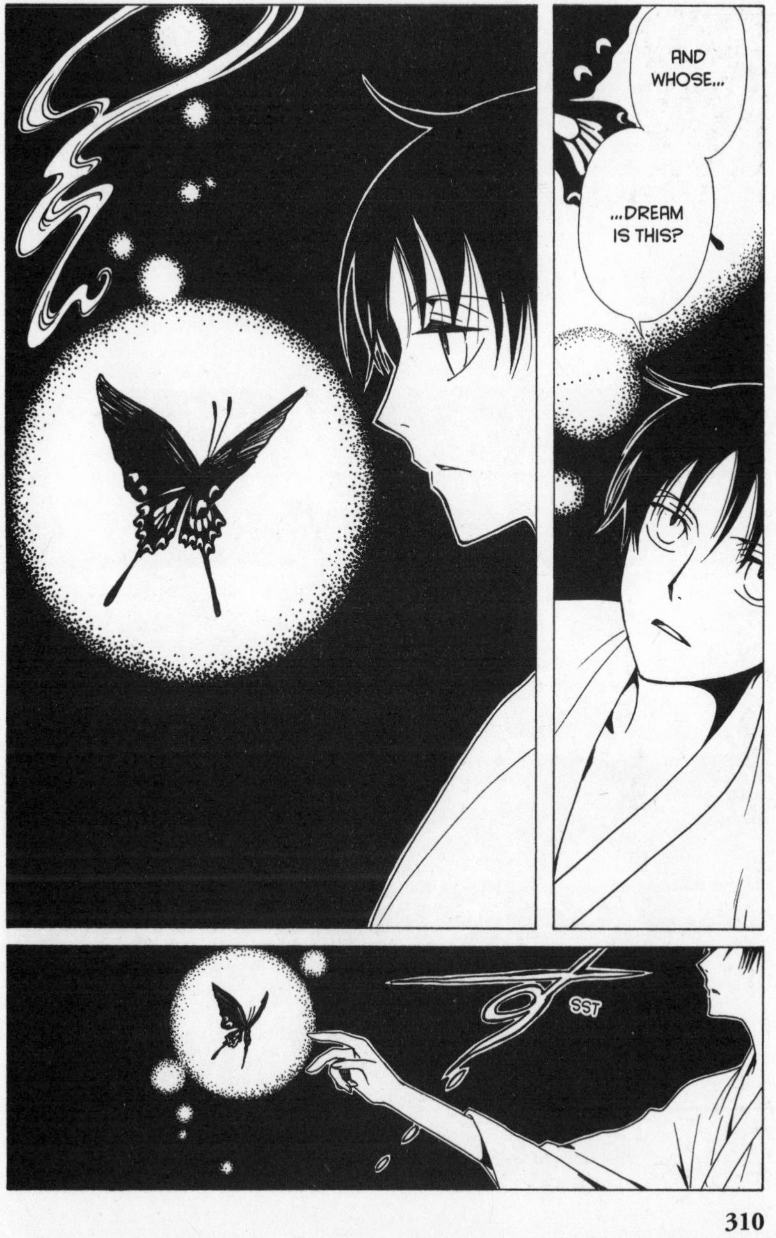
AND WHOSE...
...DREAM IS THIS?
SST

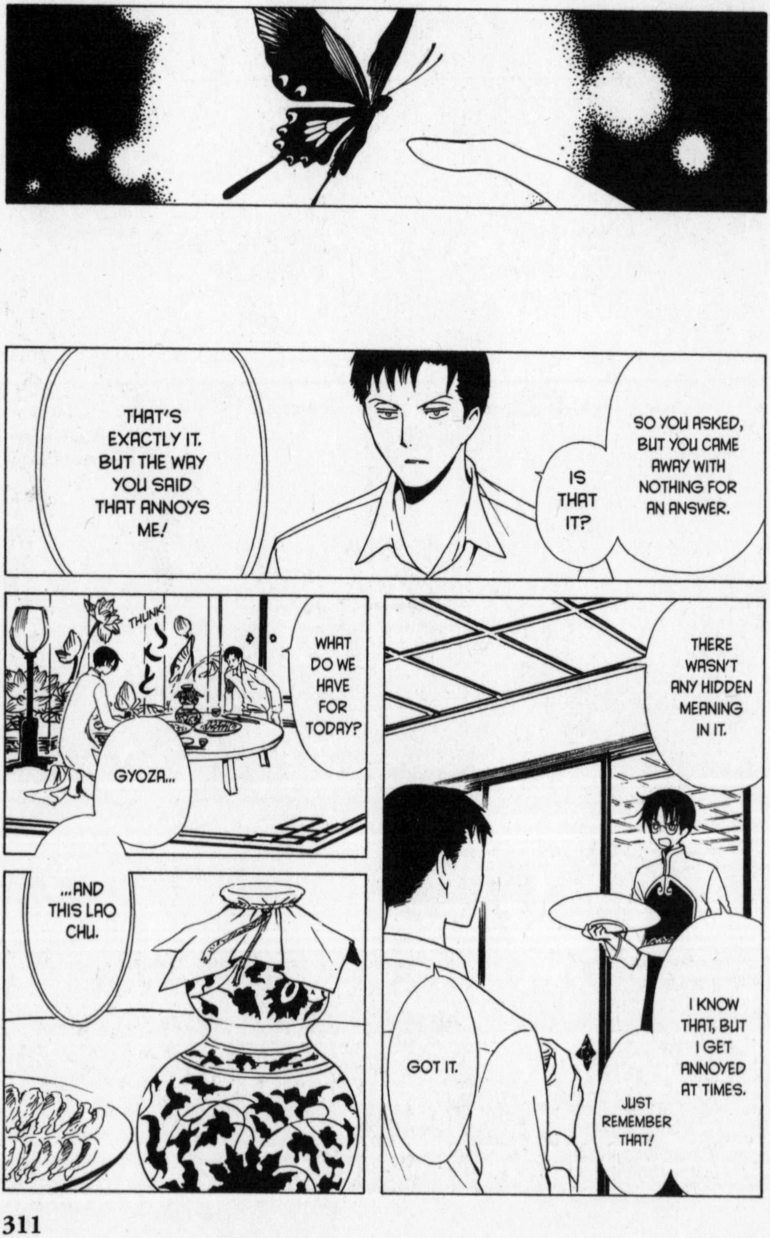
SO YOU ASKED, BUT YOU CAME AWAY WITH NOTHING FOR AN ANSWER.
IS THAT IT?
THAT'S EXACTLY IT. BUT THE WAY YOU SAID THAT ANNOYS ME!
THERE WASN'T ANY HIDDEN MEANING IN IT.
I KNOW THAT, BUT I GET ANNOYED AT TIMES.
JUST REMEMBER THAT!
GOT IT.
THUNK!
WHAT DO WE HAVE FOR TODAY?
GYOZA...
...AND THIS LAO CHU.

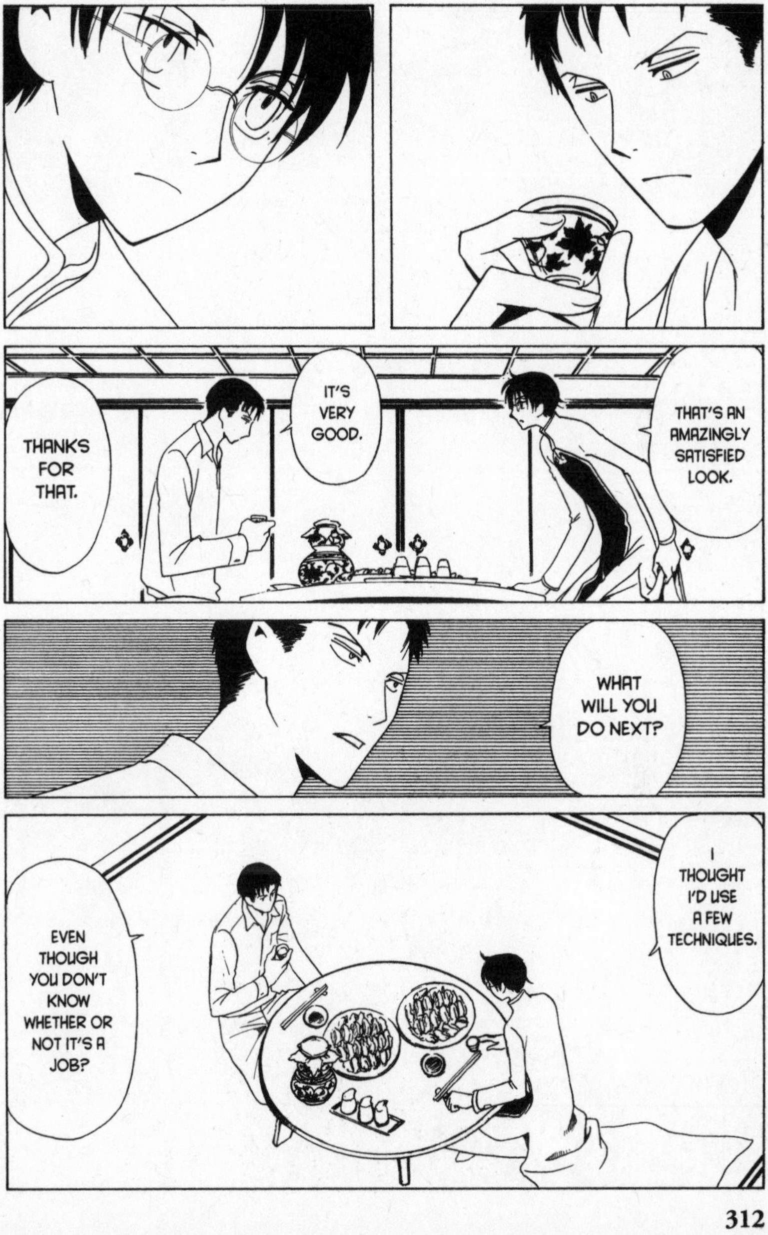
THAT'S AN AMAZINGLY SATISFIED LOOK.
IT'S VERY GOOD.
THANKS FOR THAT.
WHAT WILL YOU DO NEXT?
I THOUGHT I'D USE A FEW TECHNIQUES.
EVEN THOUGH YOU DON'T KNOW WHETHER OR NOT IT'S A JOB?

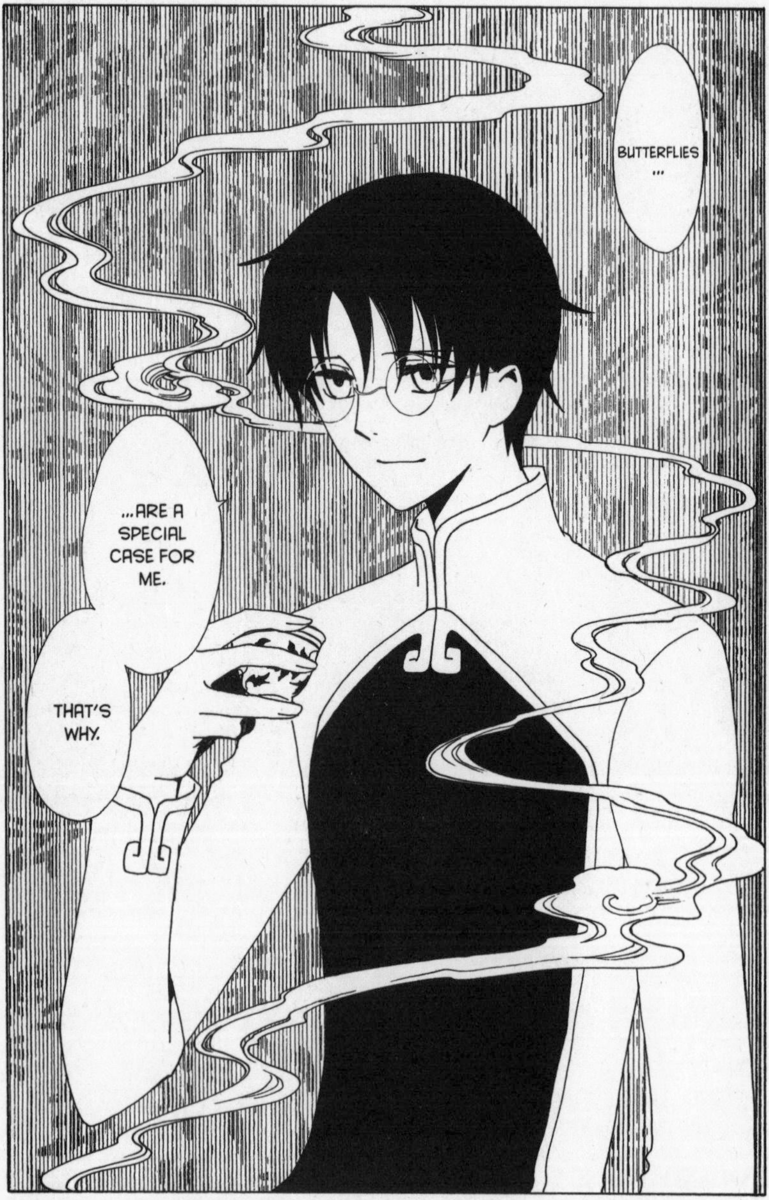
BUTTERFLIES ...
...ARE A SPECIAL CASE FOR ME.
THAT'S WHY.

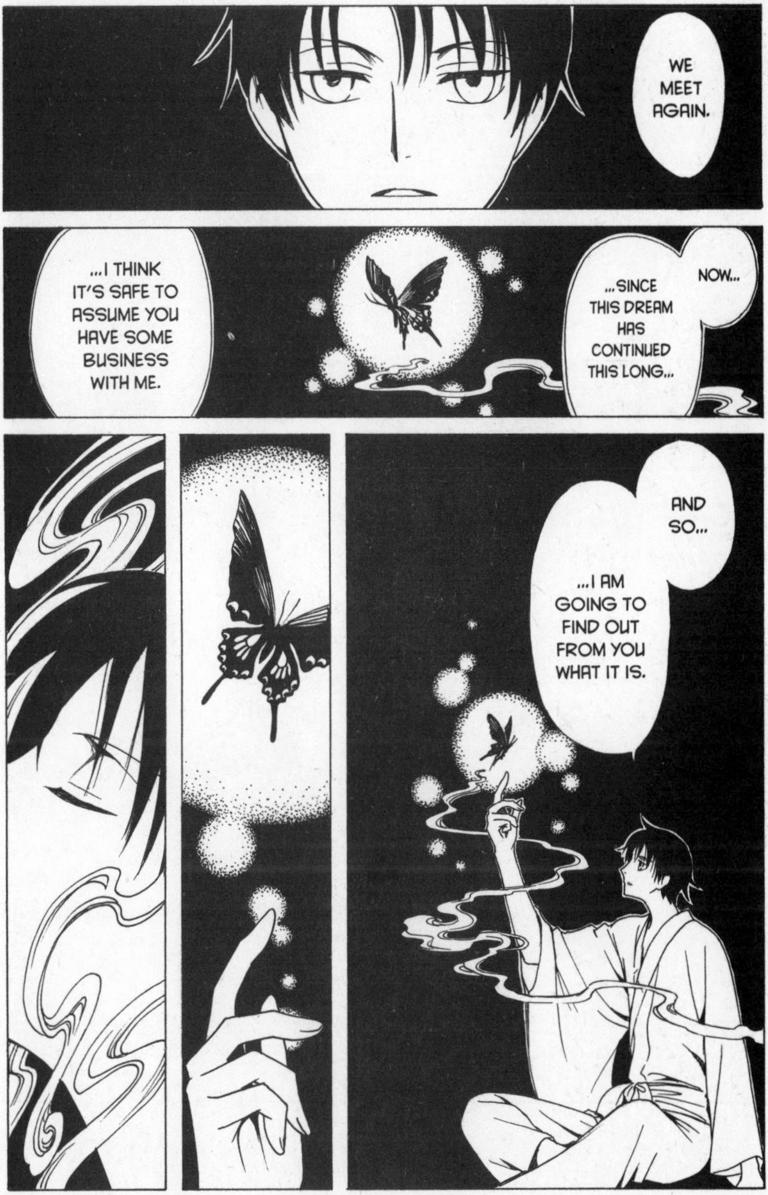
WE MEET AGAIN.
NOW...
...SINCE THIS DREAM HAS CONTINUED THIS LONG...
...I THINK IT'S SAFE TO ASSUME YOU HAVE SOME BUSINESS WITH ME.
AND SO...
...I AM GOING TO FIND OUT FROM YOU WHAT IT IS.

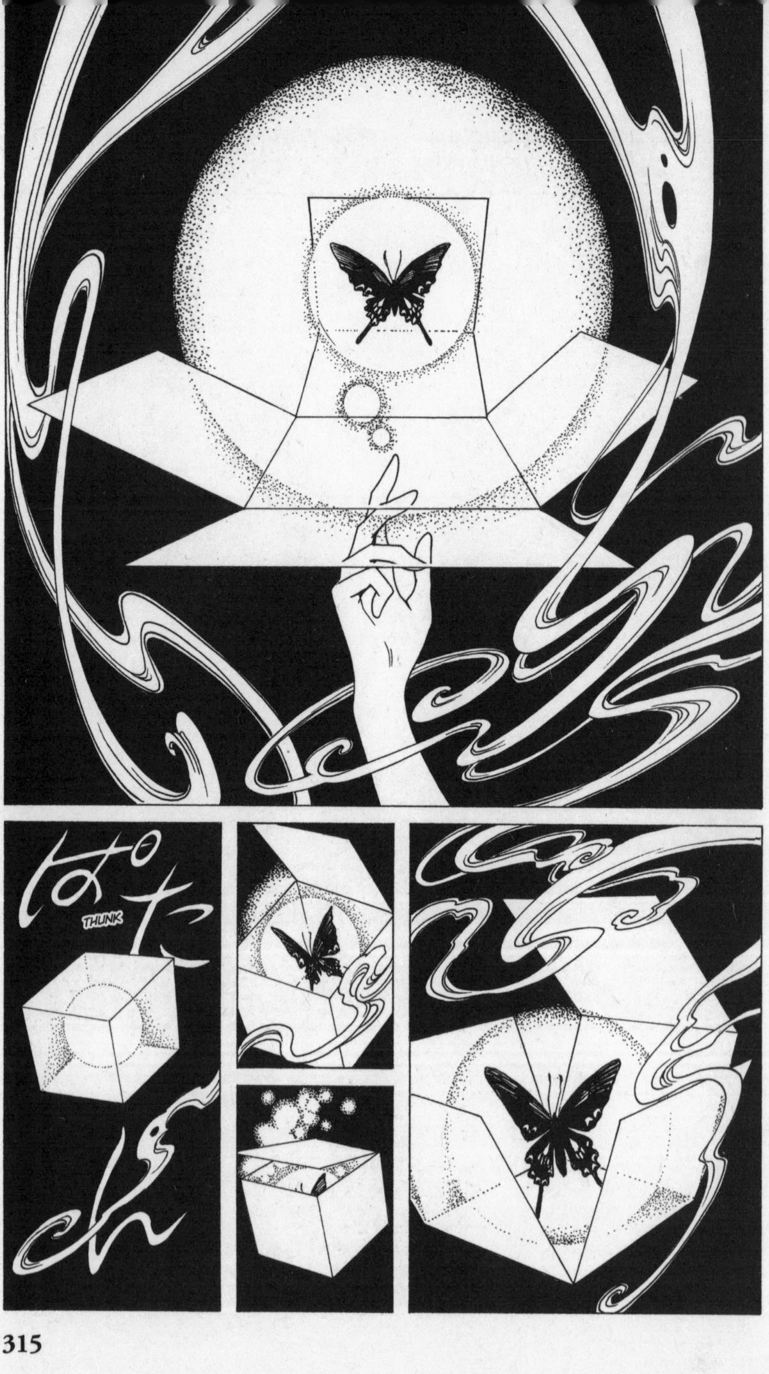
ぱた
THUNK

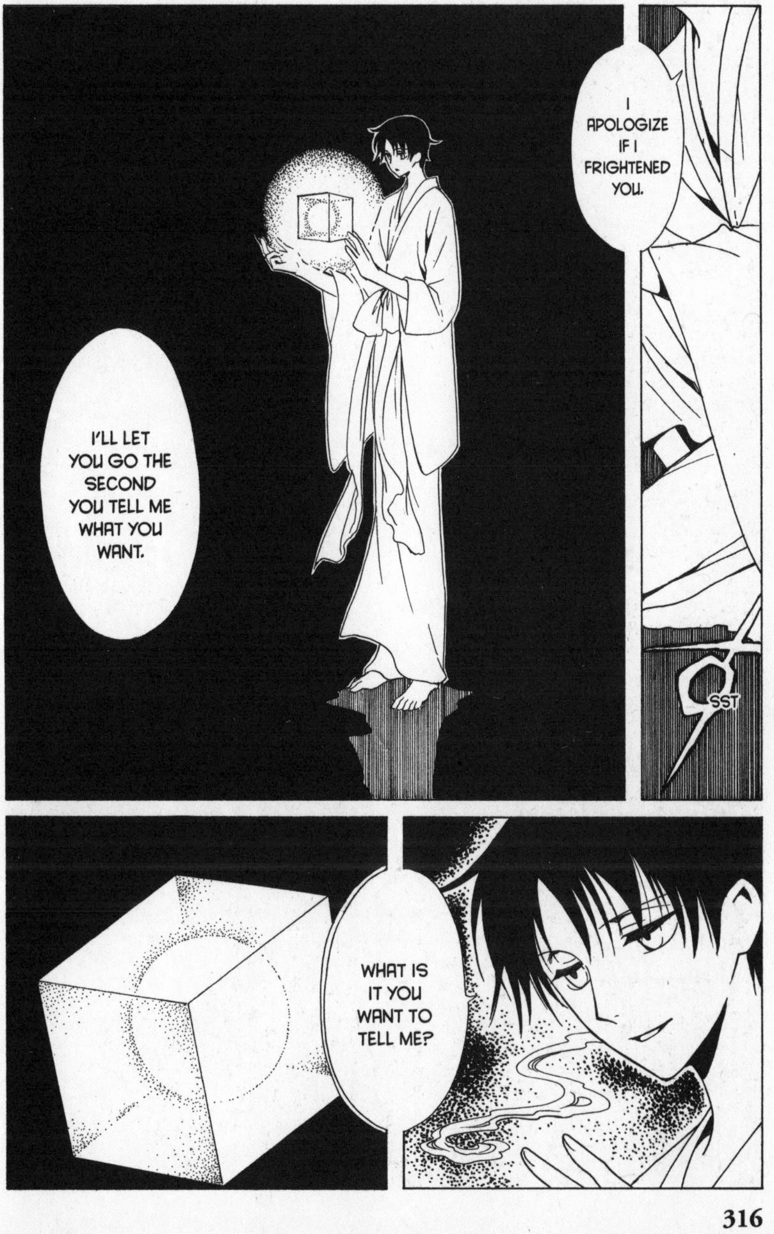
I APOLOGIZE IF I FRIGHTENED YOU.
SST
I'LL LET YOU GO THE SECOND YOU TELL ME WHAT YOU WANT.
WHAT IS IT YOU WANT TO TELL ME?

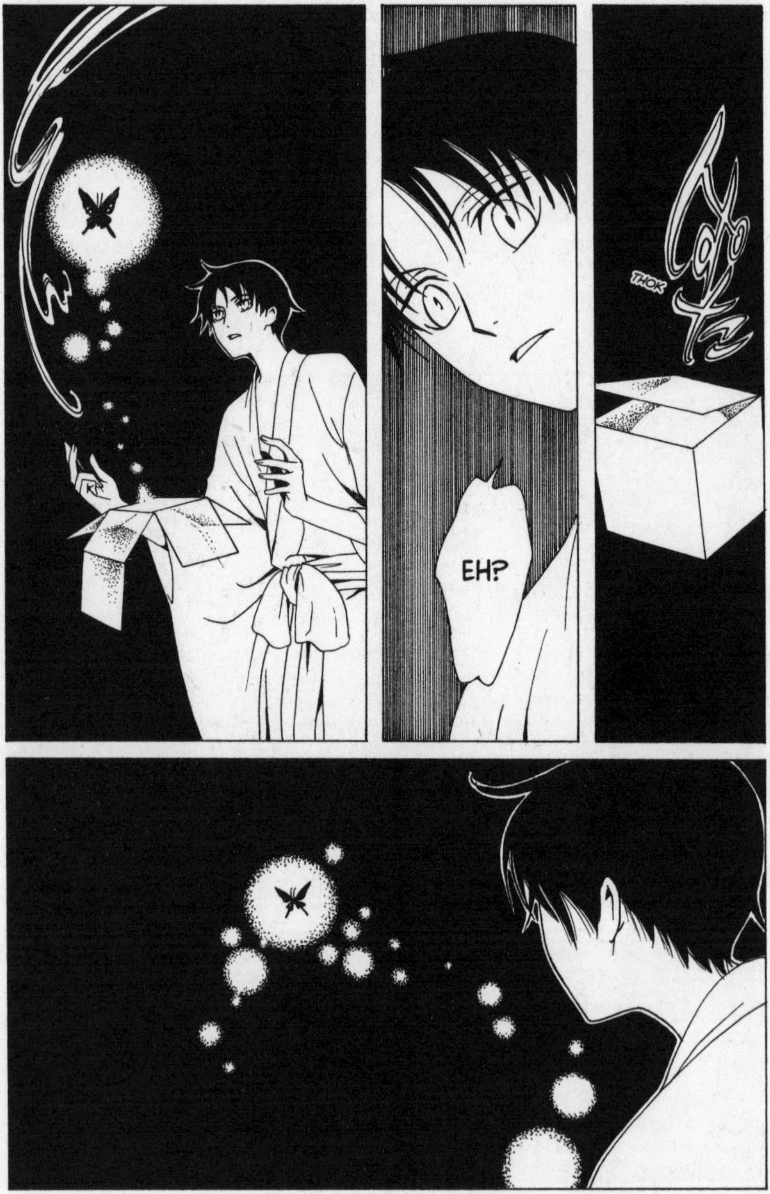
THOK
EH?

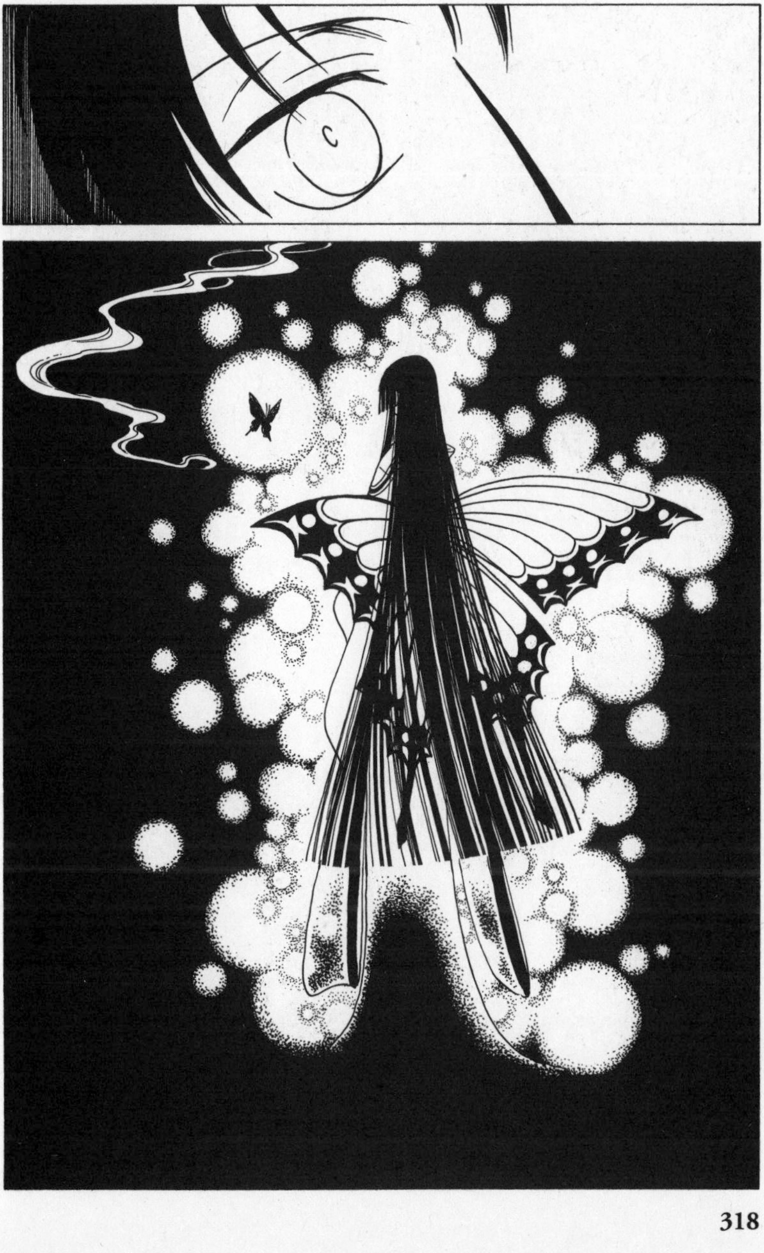

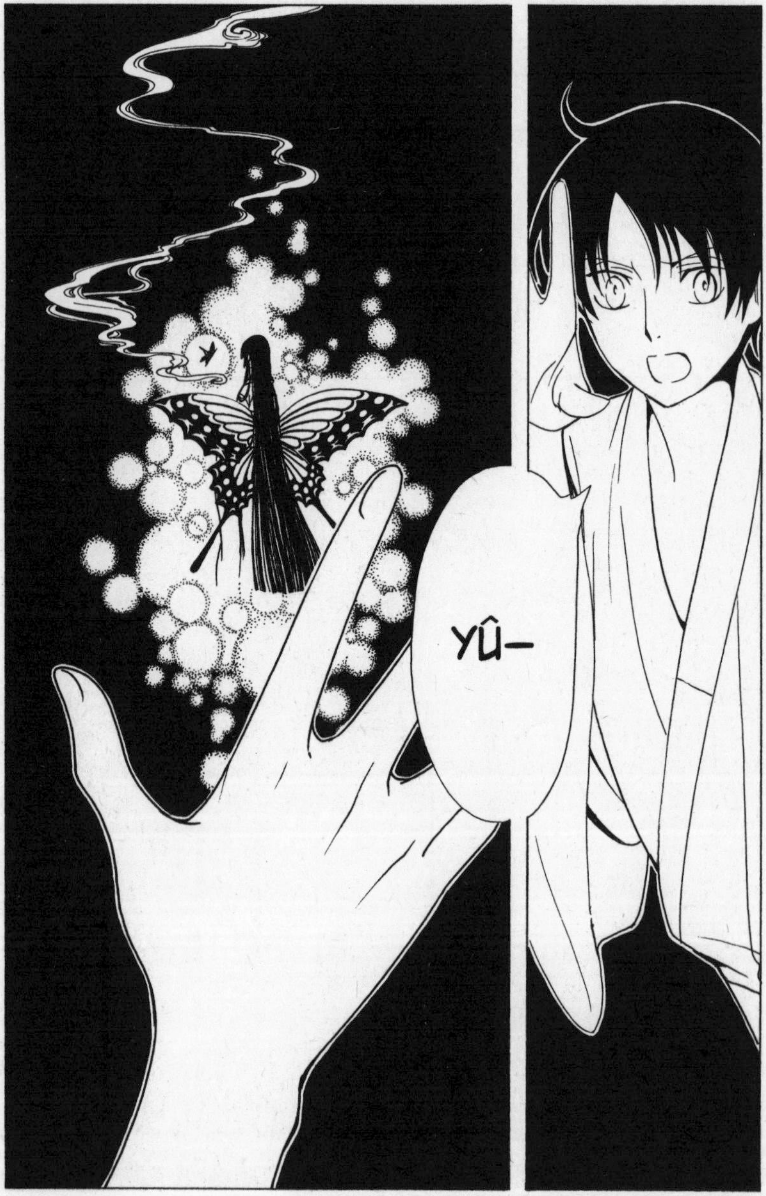
YÛ—

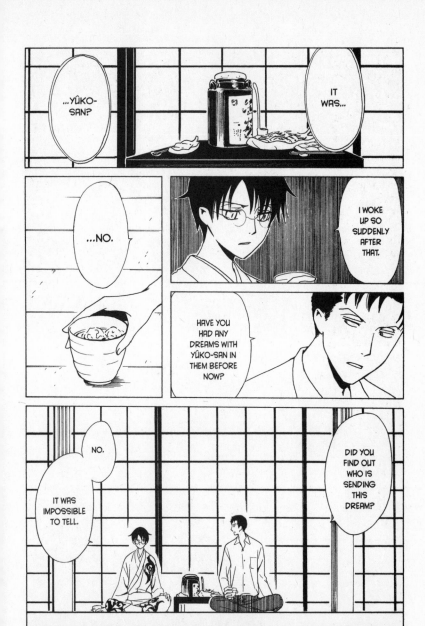

IT WAS...
...YÛKO-SAN?
I WOKE UP SO SUDDENLY AFTER THAT.
HAVE YOU HAD ANY DREAMS WITH YÛKO-SAN IN THEM BEFORE NOW?
...NO.
DID YOU FIND OUT WHO IS SENDING THIS DREAM?
NO.
IT WAS IMPOSSIBLE TO TELL.

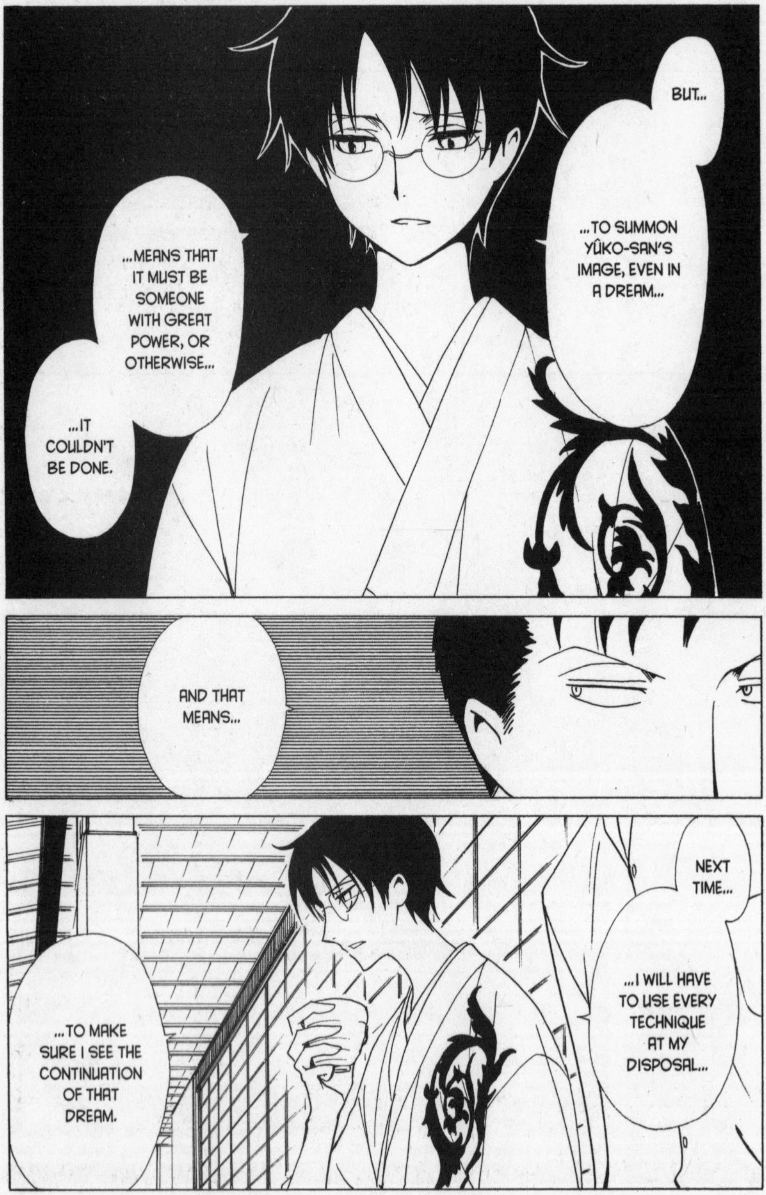
BUT...
...TO SUMMON YÛKO-SAN'S IMAGE, EVEN IN A DREAM...
...MEANS THAT IT MUST BE SOMEONE WITH GREAT POWER, OR OTHERWISE...
...IT COULDN'T BE DONE.
AND THAT MEANS...
NEXT TIME...
...I WILL HAVE TO USE EVERY TECHNIQUE AT MY DISPOSAL...
...TO MAKE SURE I SEE THE CONTINUATION OF THAT DREAM.

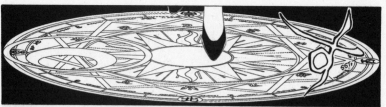

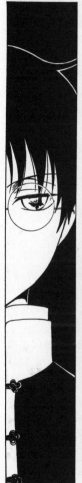

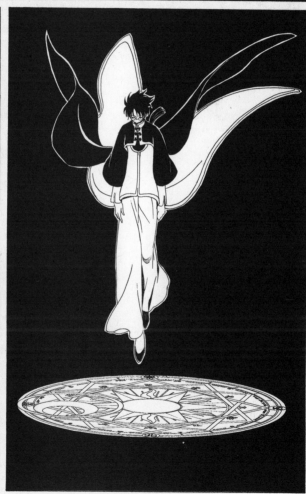

322

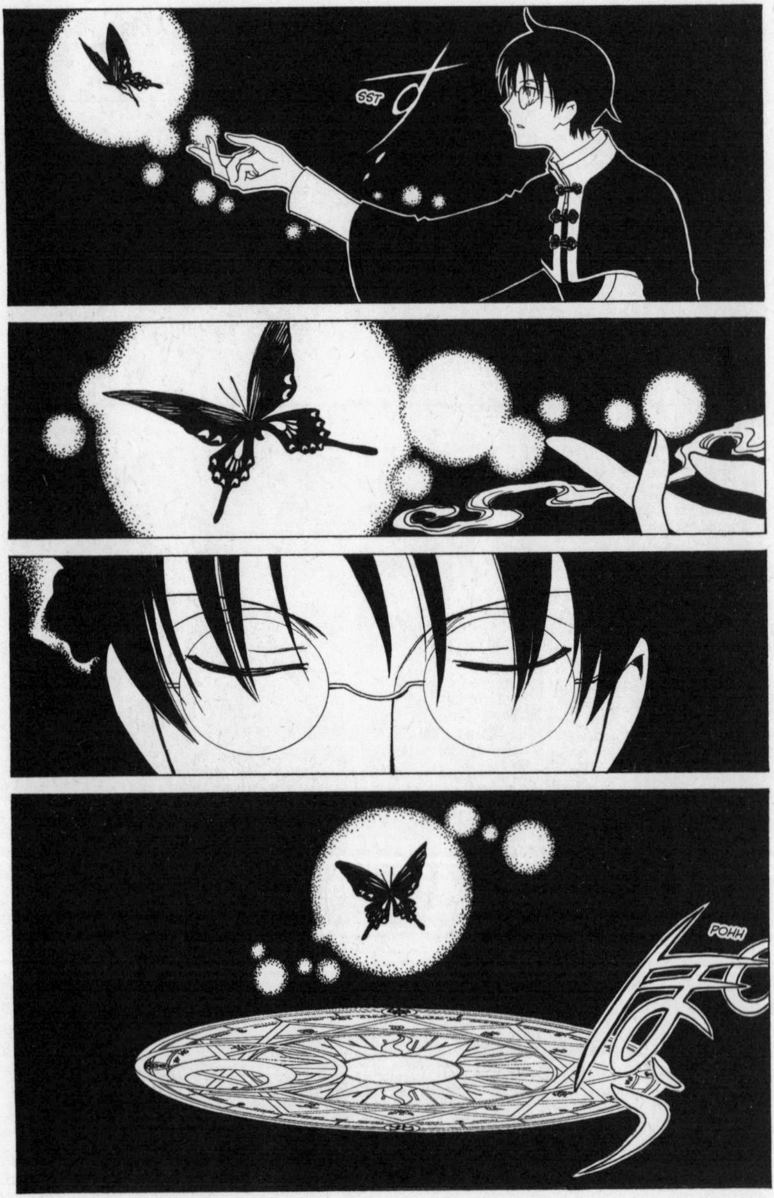
SST
POHH

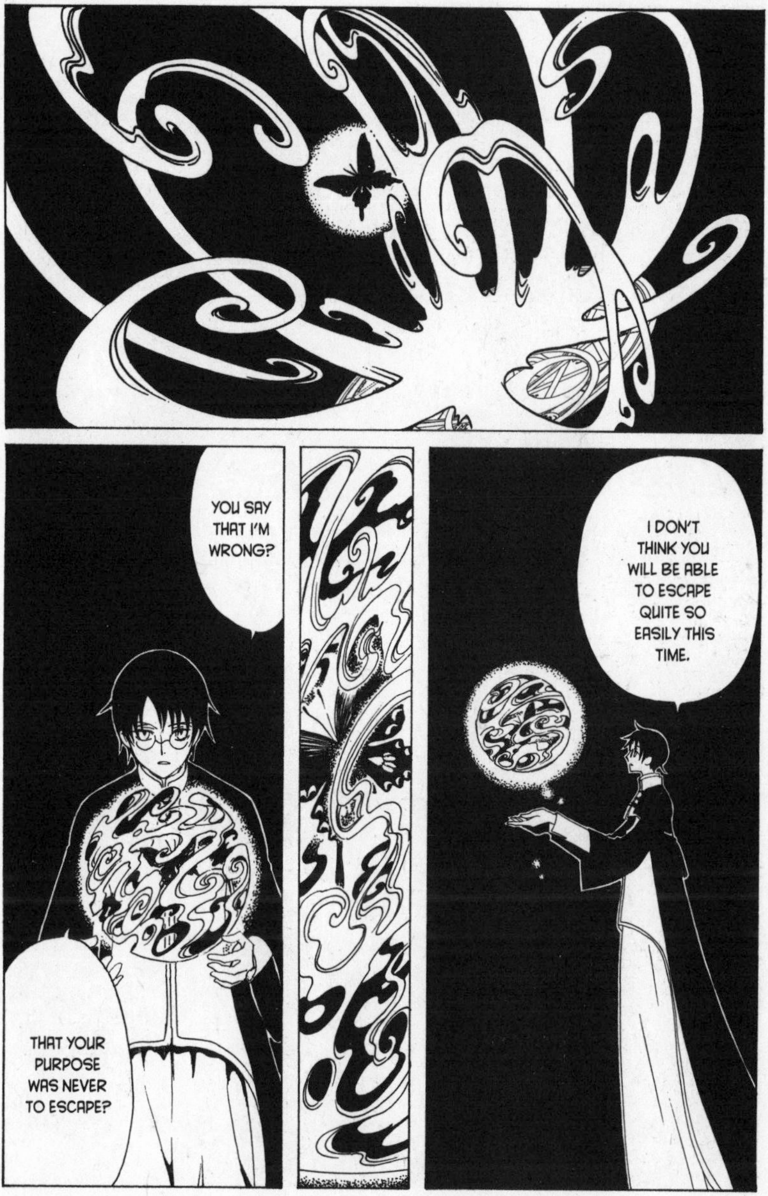
I DON'T THINK YOU WILL BE ABLE TO ESCAPE QUITE SO EASILY THIS TIME.
YOU SAY THAT I'M WRONG?
THAT YOUR PURPOSE WAS NEVER TO ESCAPE?

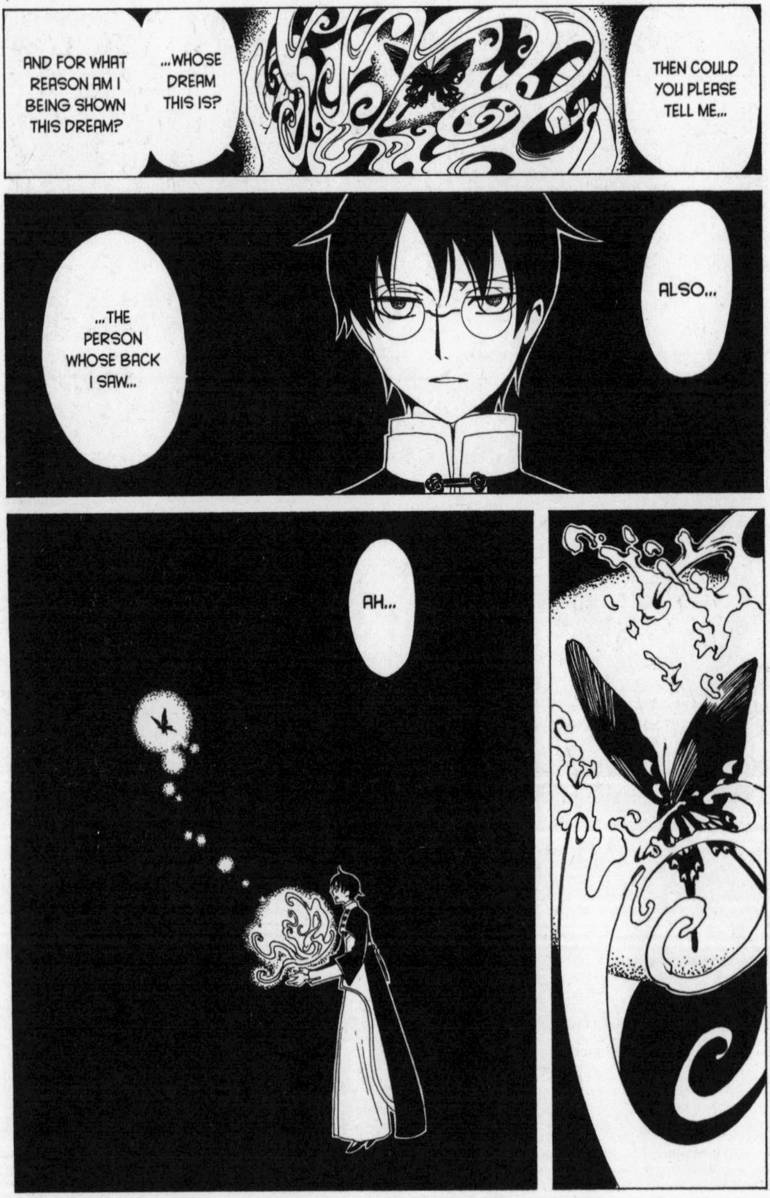
THEN COULD YOU PLEASE TELL ME...
...WHOSE DREAM THIS IS?
AND FOR WHAT REASON AM I BEING SHOWN THIS DREAM?
ALSO...
...THE PERSON WHOSE BACK I SAW...
AH...

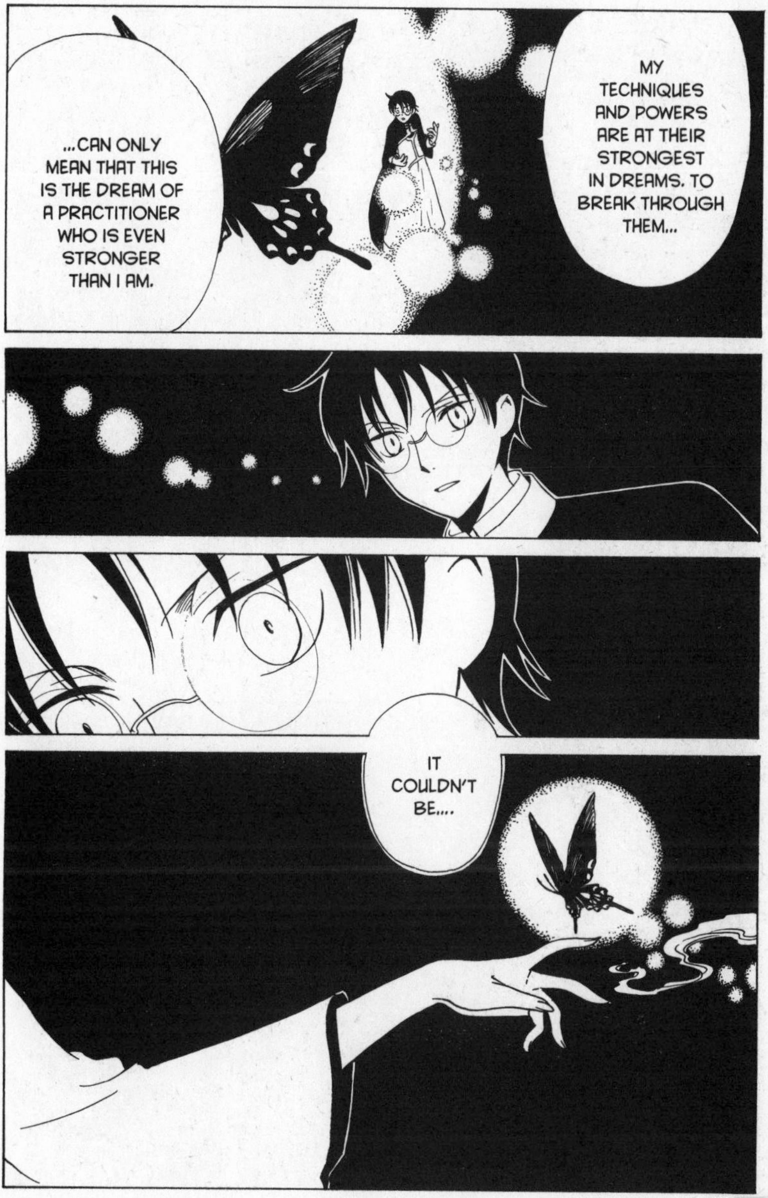
MY TECHNIQUES AND POWERS ARE AT THEIR STRONGEST IN DREAMS. TO BREAK THROUGH THEM...
...CAN ONLY MEAN THAT THIS IS THE DREAM OF A PRACTITIONER WHO IS EVEN STRONGER THAN I AM.
IT COULDN'T BE....

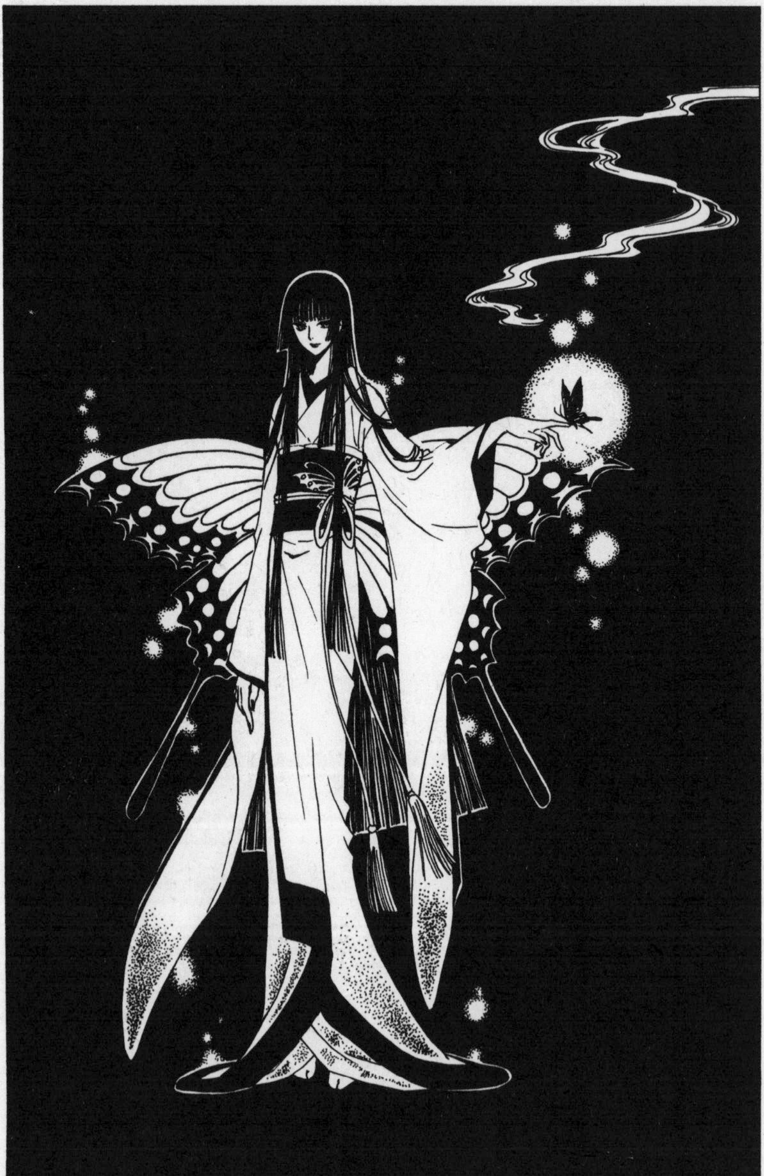

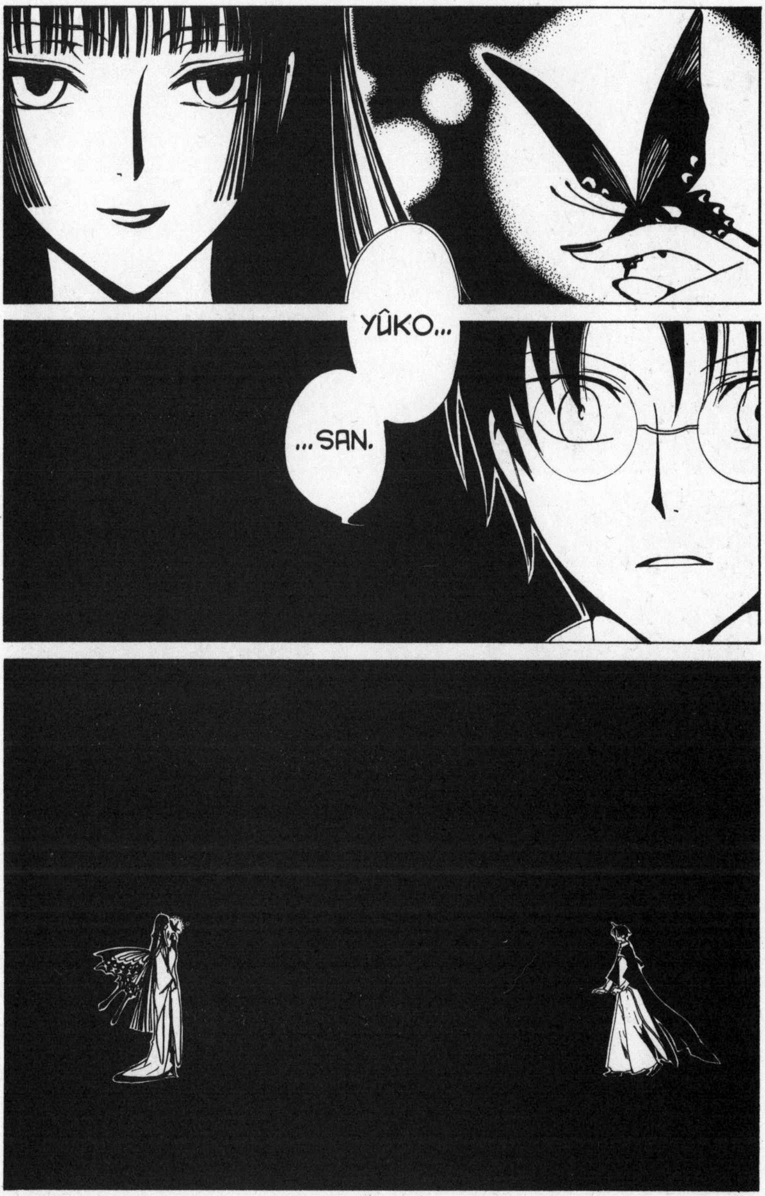
YÛKO...
...SAN.

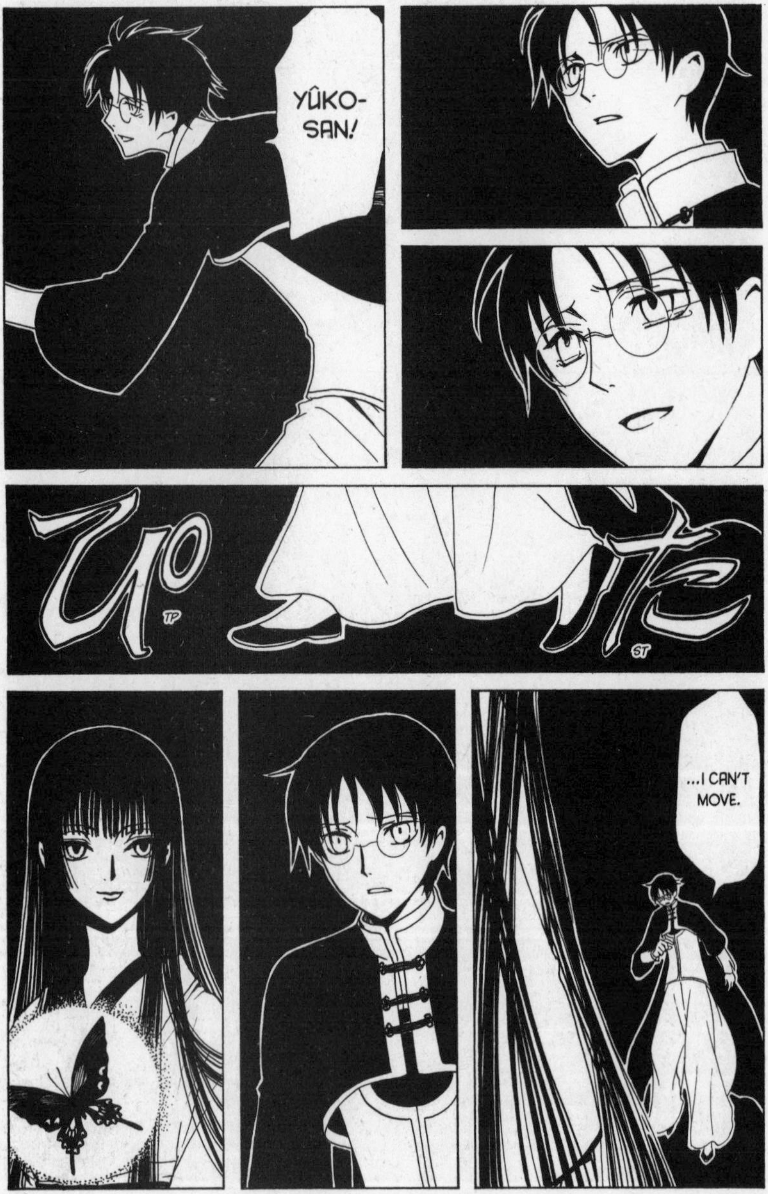
YÛKO-SAN!
ぴ
TP
た
ST
...I CAN'T MOVE.

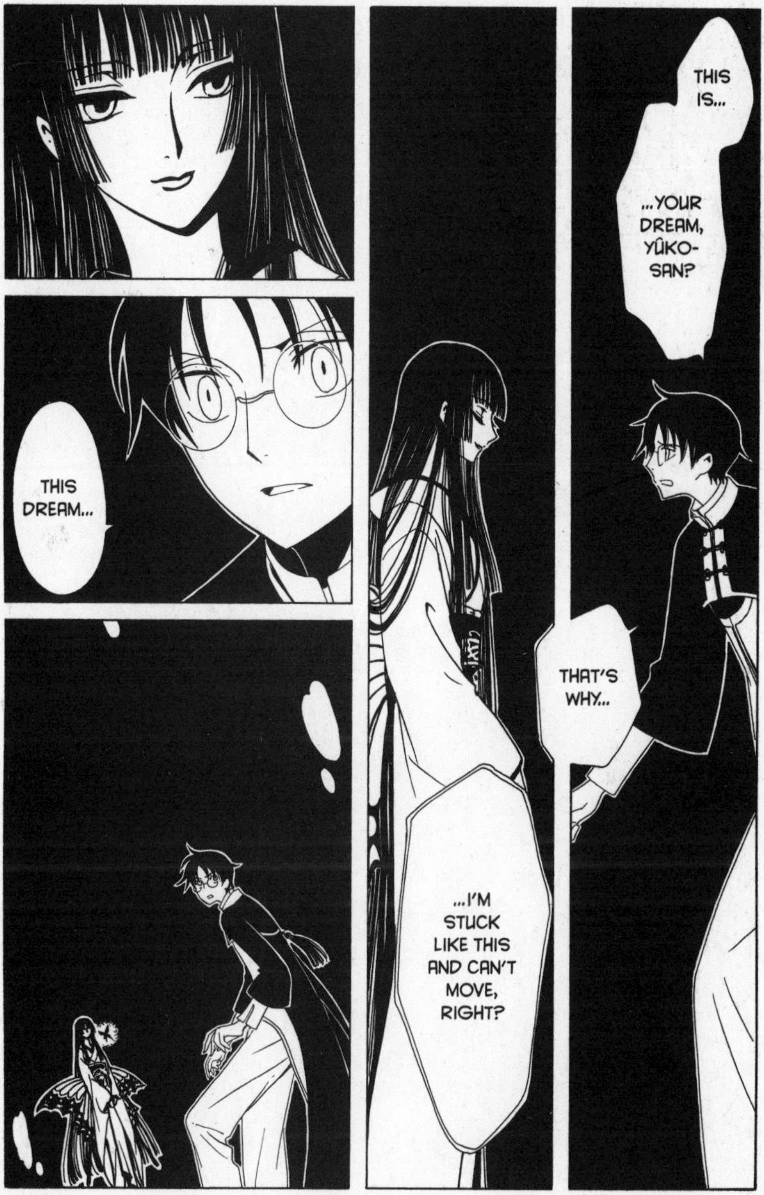
THIS IS...
...YOUR DREAM, YÛKO-SAN?
THAT'S WHY...
...I'M STUCK LIKE THIS AND CAN'T MOVE, RIGHT?
THIS DREAM...

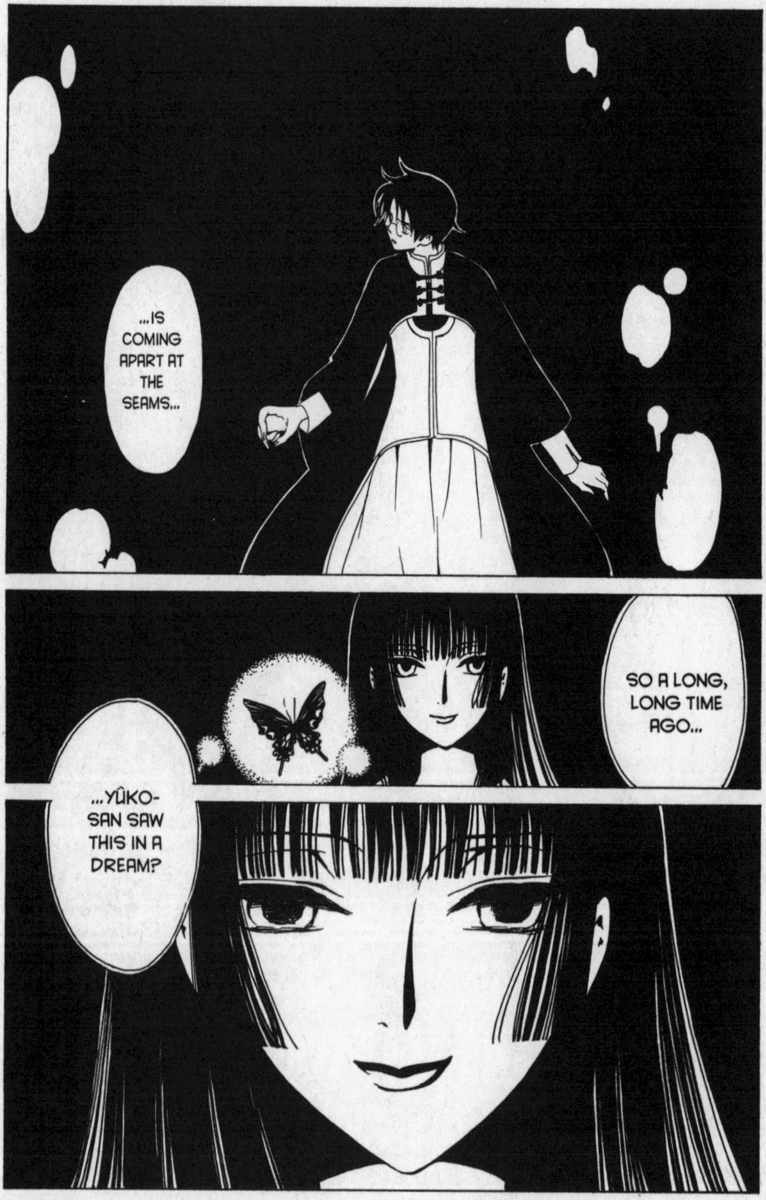
...IS COMING APART AT THE SEAMS...
SO A LONG, LONG TIME AGO...
...YÛKO-SAN SAW THIS IN A DREAM?

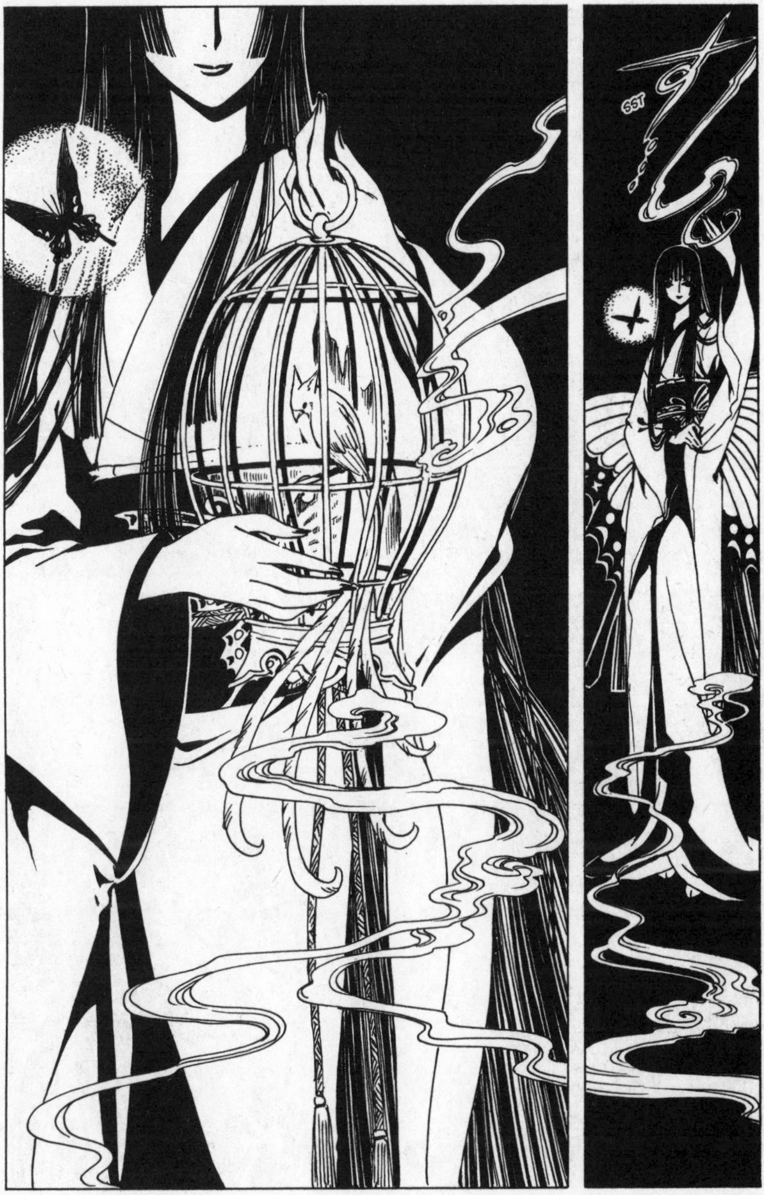
SST

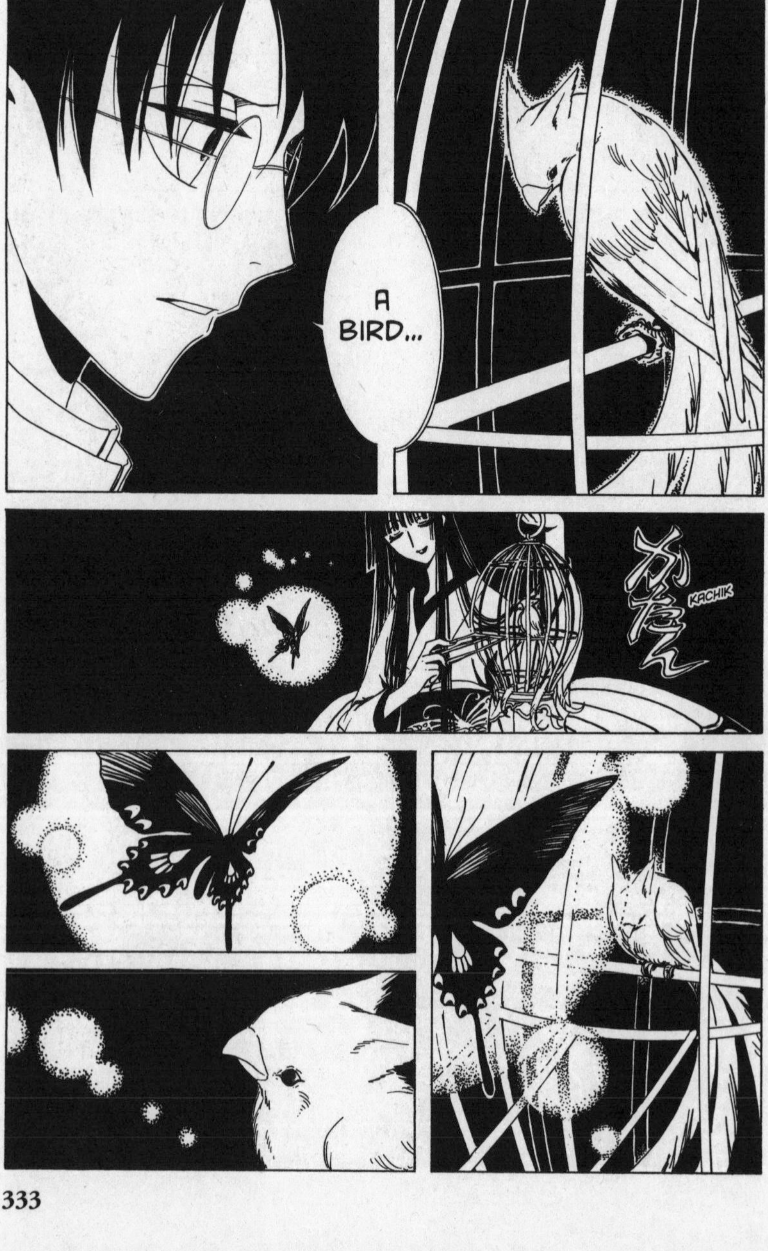
A BIRD...
かたん
KACHIK

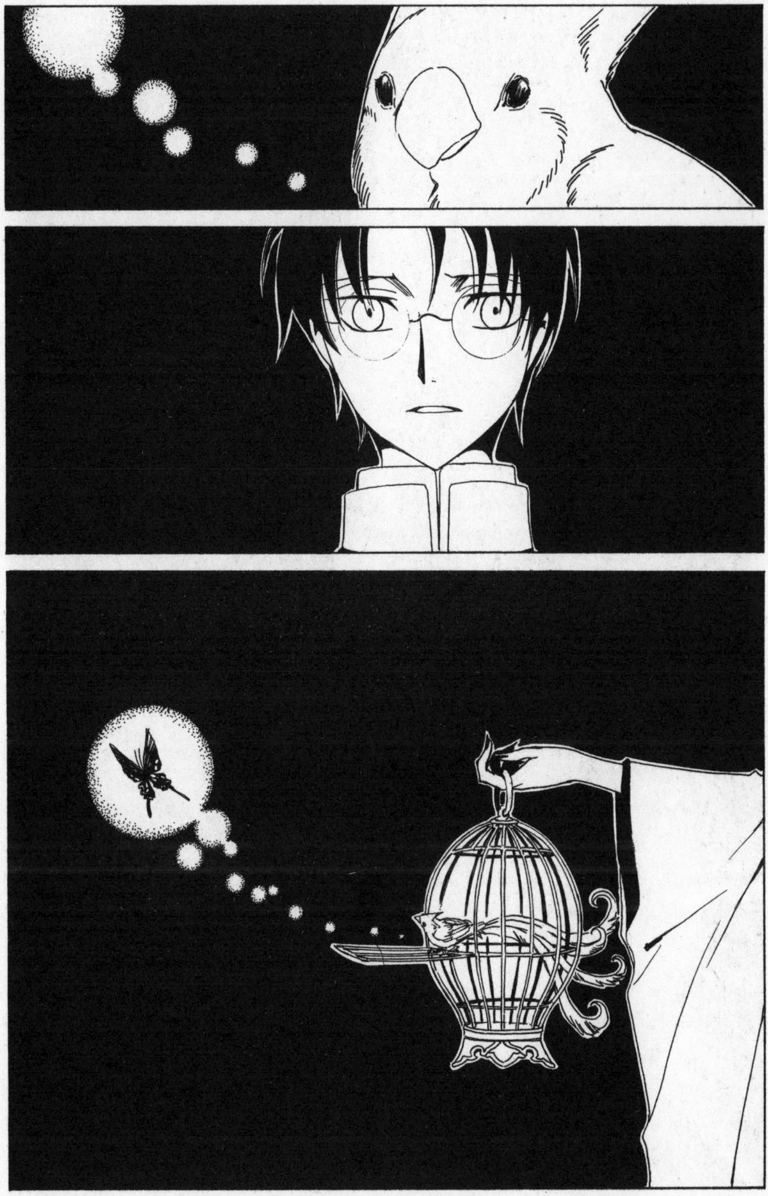

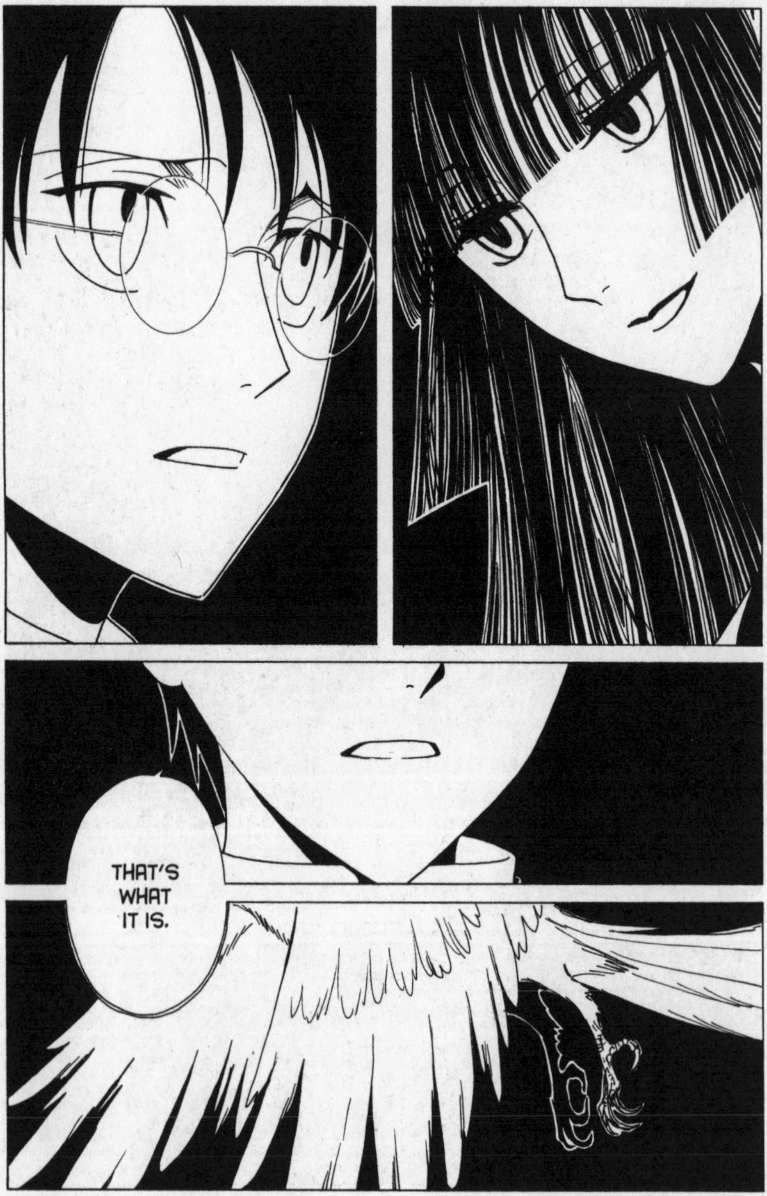
THAT'S WHAT IT IS.

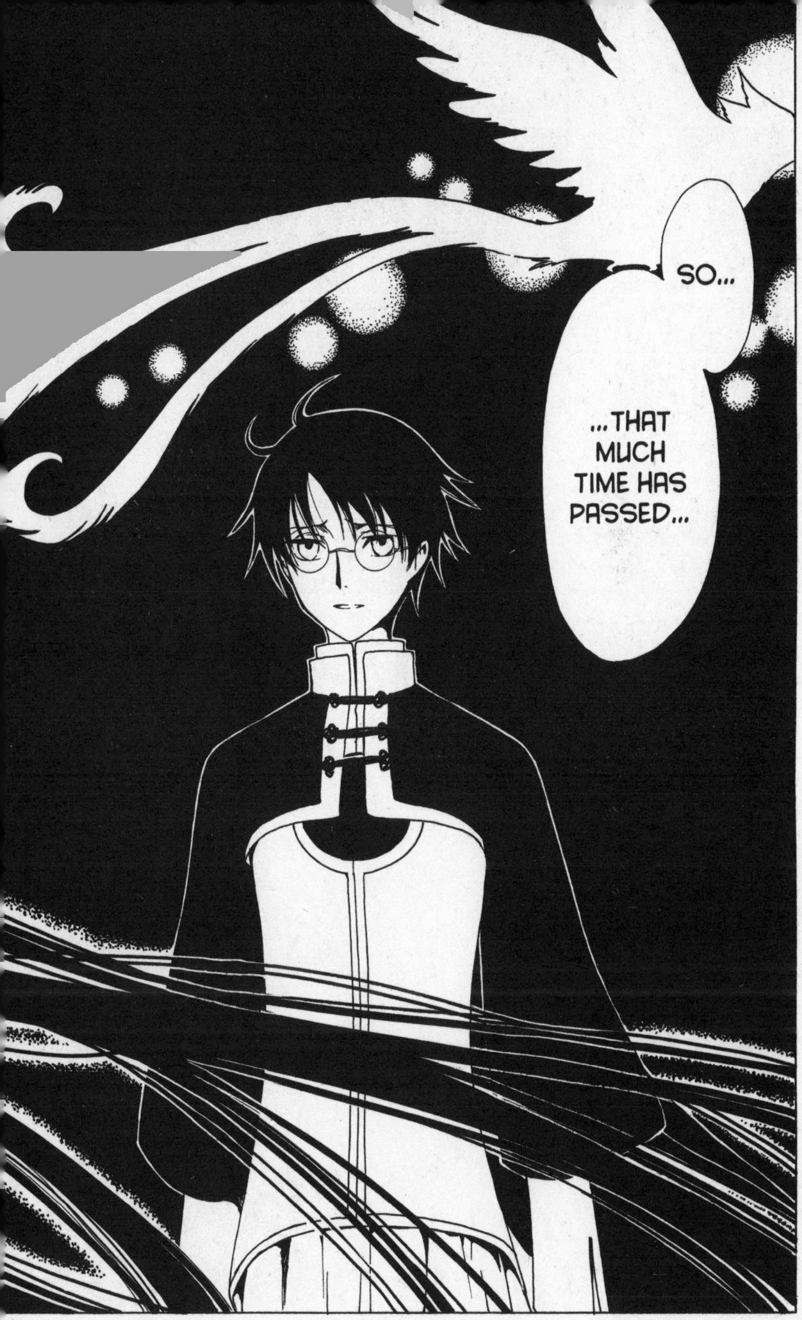
SO...
...THAT MUCH TIME HAS PASSED...

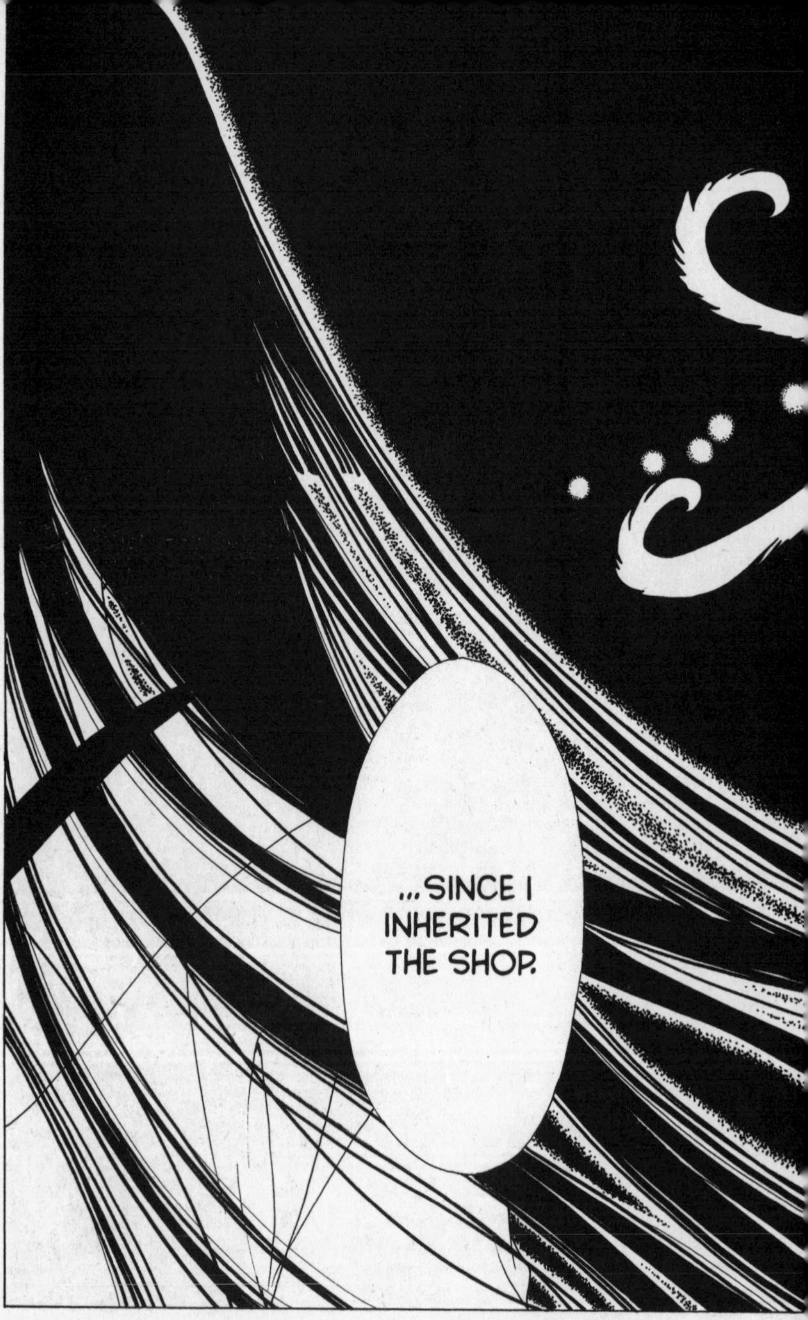
...SINCE I INHERITED THE SHOP.

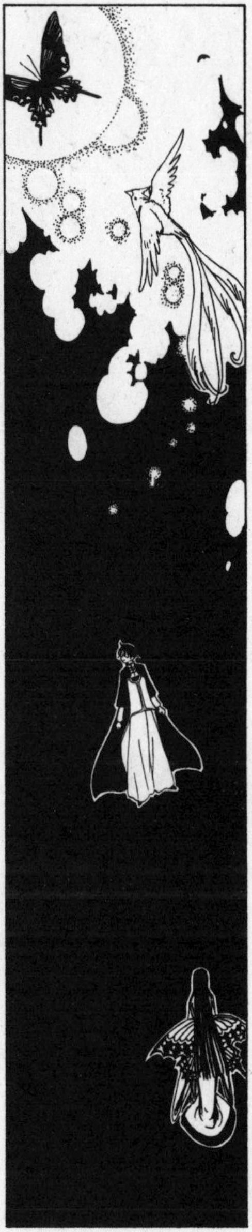

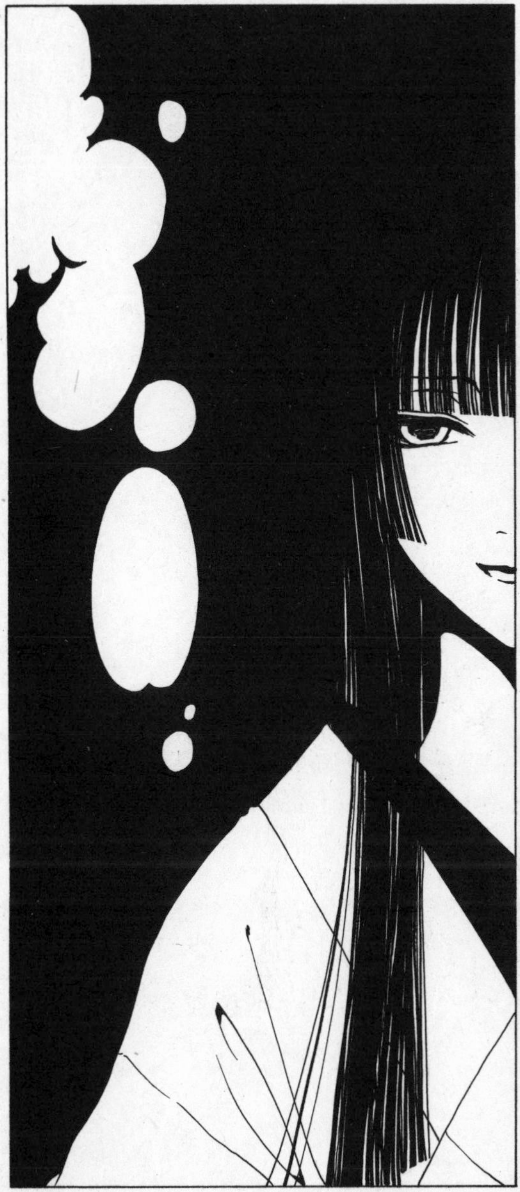

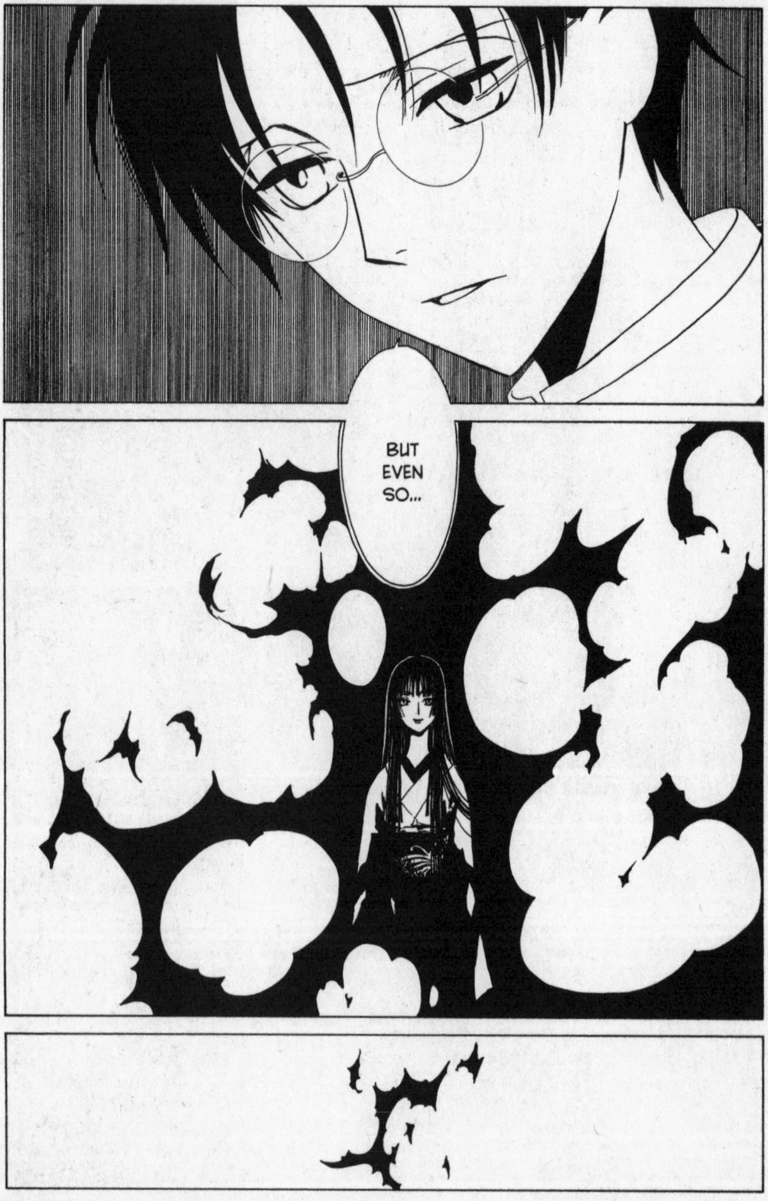
BUT EVEN SO...

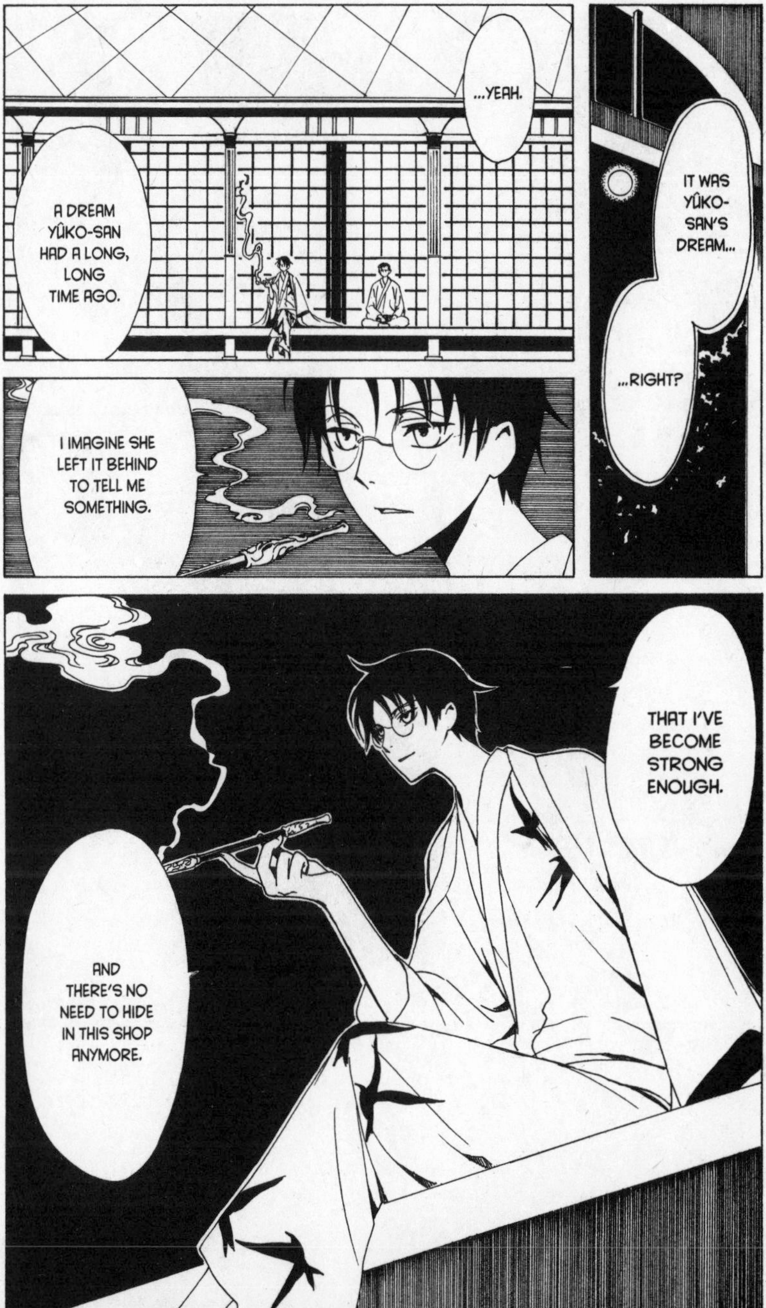
IT WAS YÛKO-SAN'S DREAM...
...RIGHT?
...YEAH.
A DREAM YÛKO-SAN HAD A LONG, LONG TIME AGO.
I IMAGINE SHE LEFT IT BEHIND TO TELL ME SOMETHING.
THAT I'VE BECOME STRONG ENOUGH.
AND THERE'S NO NEED TO HIDE IN THIS SHOP ANYMORE.

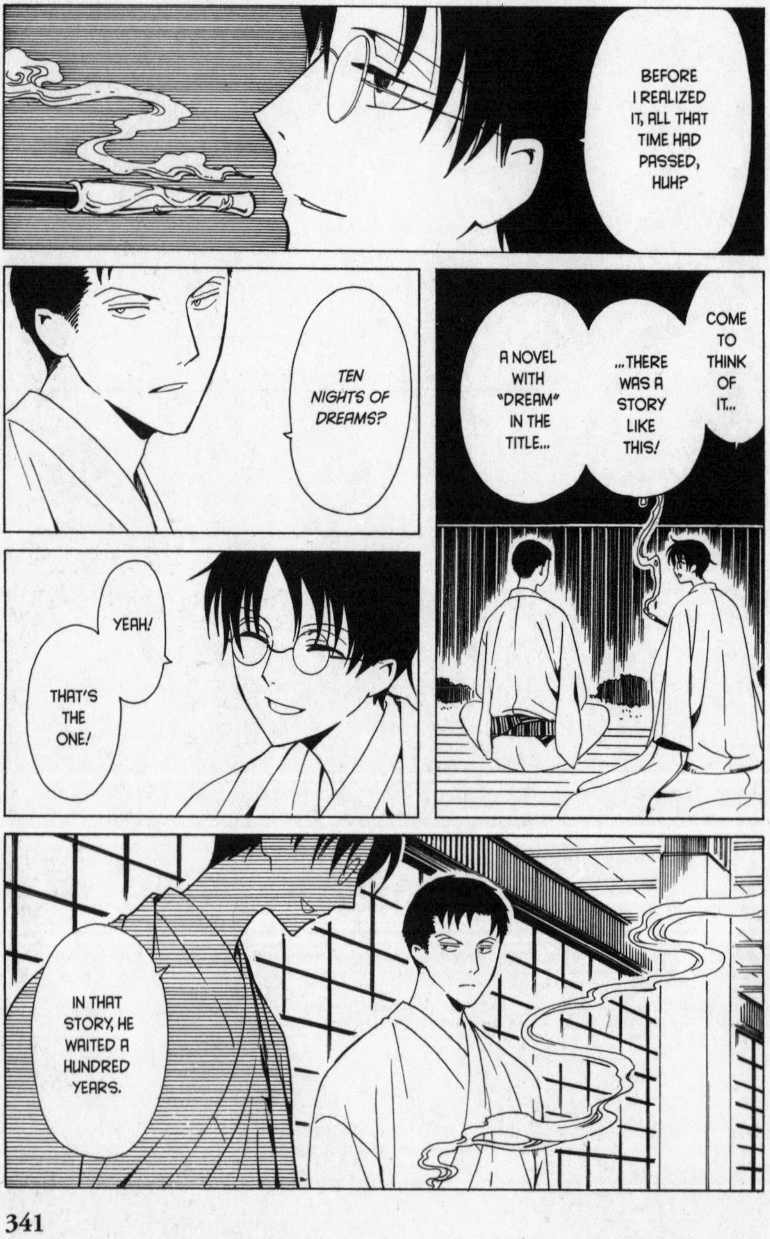
BEFORE I REALIZED IT, ALL THAT TIME HAD PASSED, HUH?
COME TO THINK OF IT...
...THERE WAS A STORY LIKE THIS!
A NOVEL WITH "DREAM" IN THE TITLE...
TEN NIGHTS OF DREAMS?
YEAH!
THAT'S THE ONE!
IN THAT STORY, HE WAITED A HUNDRED YEARS.

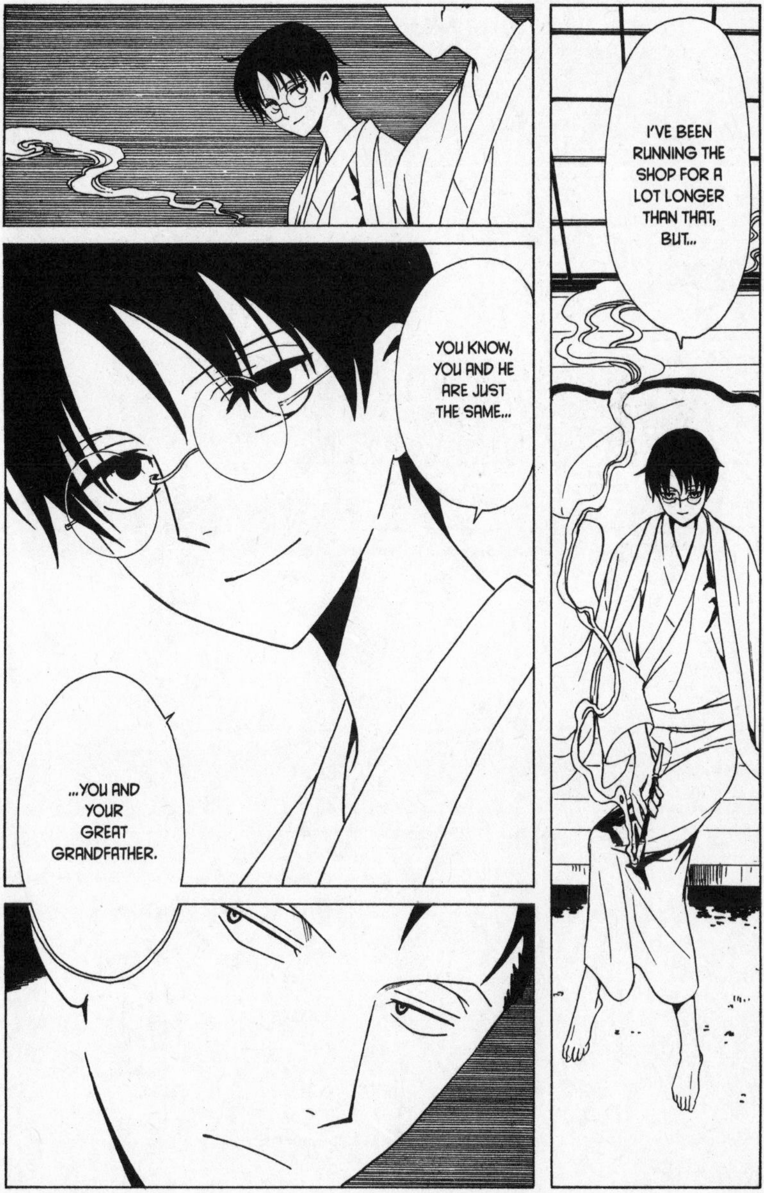
I'VE BEEN RUNNING THE SHOP FOR A LOT LONGER THAN THAT, BUT...
YOU KNOW, YOU AND HE ARE JUST THE SAME...
...YOU AND YOUR GREAT GRANDFATHER.

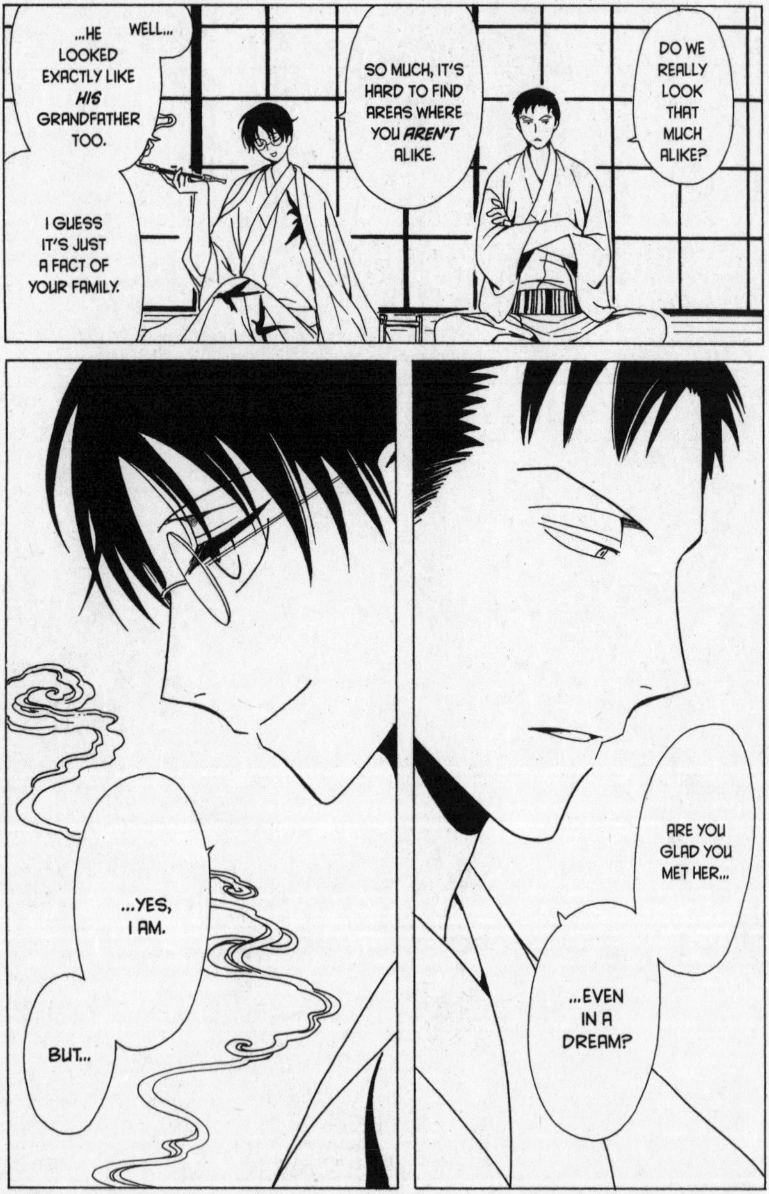
DO WE REALLY LOOK THAT MUCH ALIKE?
SO MUCH, IT'S HARD TO FIND AREAS WHERE YOU AREN'T ALIKE.
WELL...
...HE LOOKED EXACTLY LIKE HIS GRANDFATHER TOO.
I GUESS IT'S JUST A FACT OF YOUR FAMILY.
ARE YOU GLAD YOU MET HER...
...EVEN IN A DREAM?
...YES, I AM.
BUT...

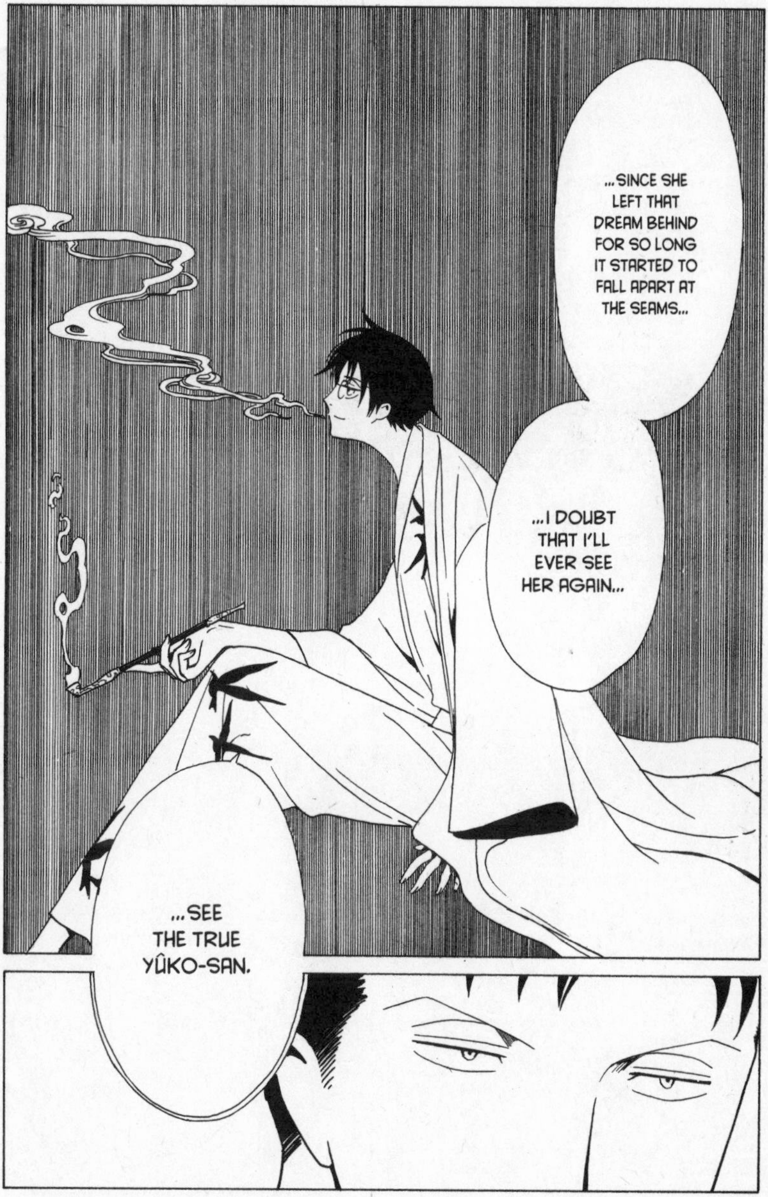
...SINCE SHE LEFT THAT DREAM BEHIND FOR SO LONG IT STARTED TO FALL APART AT THE SEAMS...
...I DOUBT THAT I'LL EVER SEE HER AGAIN...
...SEE THE TRUE YÛKO-SAN.

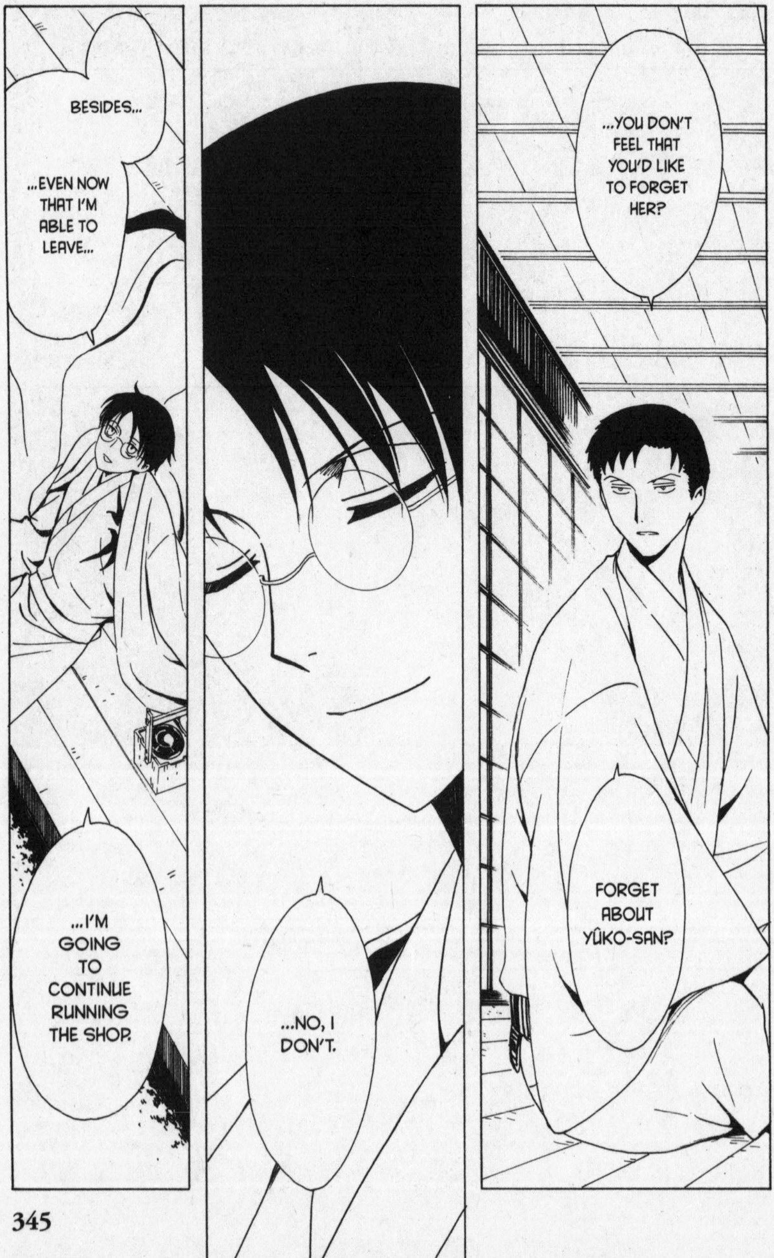
...YOU DON'T FEEL THAT YOU'D LIKE TO FORGET HER?
FORGET ABOUT YÛKO-SAN?
...NO, I DON'T.
BESIDES...
...EVEN NOW THAT I'M ABLE TO LEAVE...
...I'M GOING TO CONTINUE RUNNING THE SHOP.

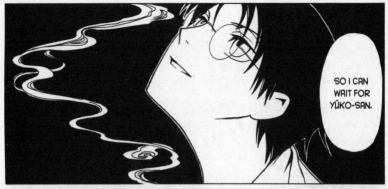

SO I CAN WAIT FOR YÛKO-SAN.
...IS THAT RIGHT?
NOW, DO YOU WANT A DRINK?
YEAH.
SST
I'LL HAVE WHISKEY...
...ON THE ROCKS.
GOT IT.

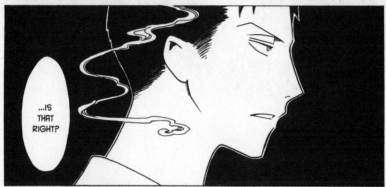

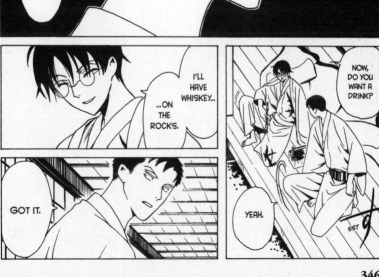

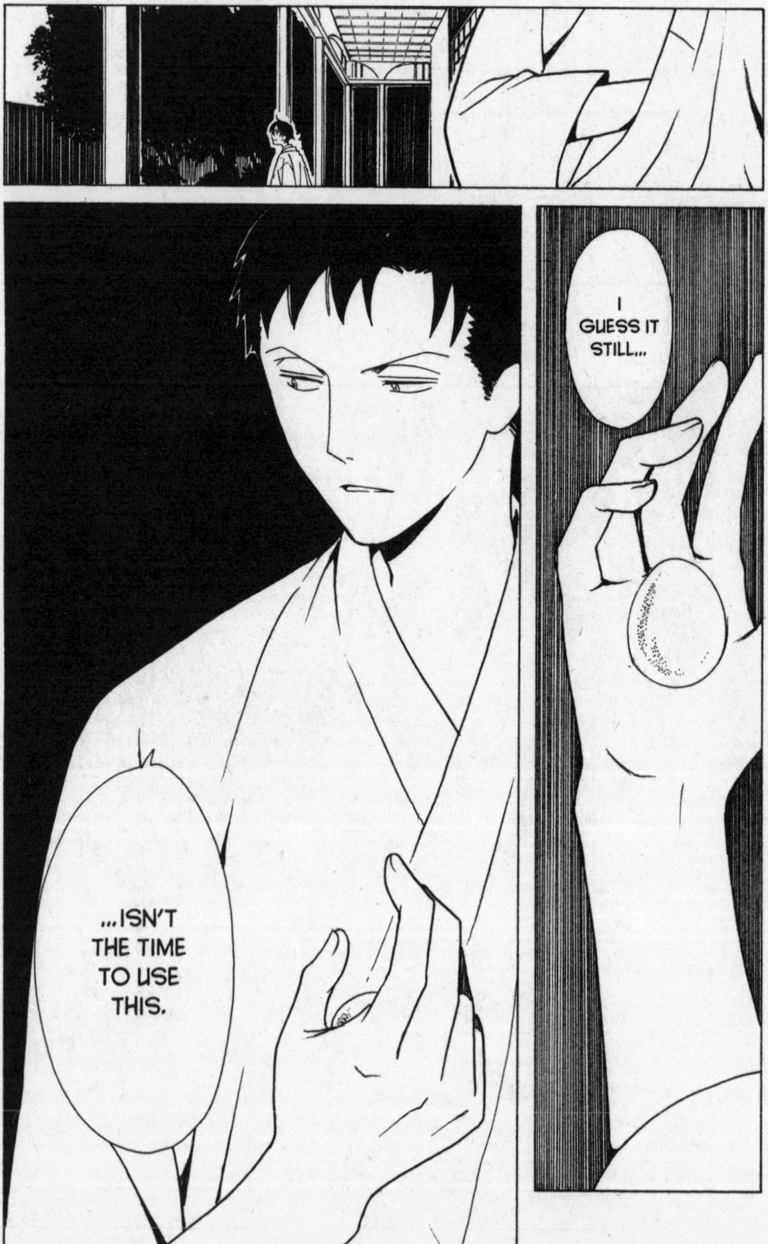
I GUESS IT STILL...
...ISN'T THE TIME TO USE THIS.

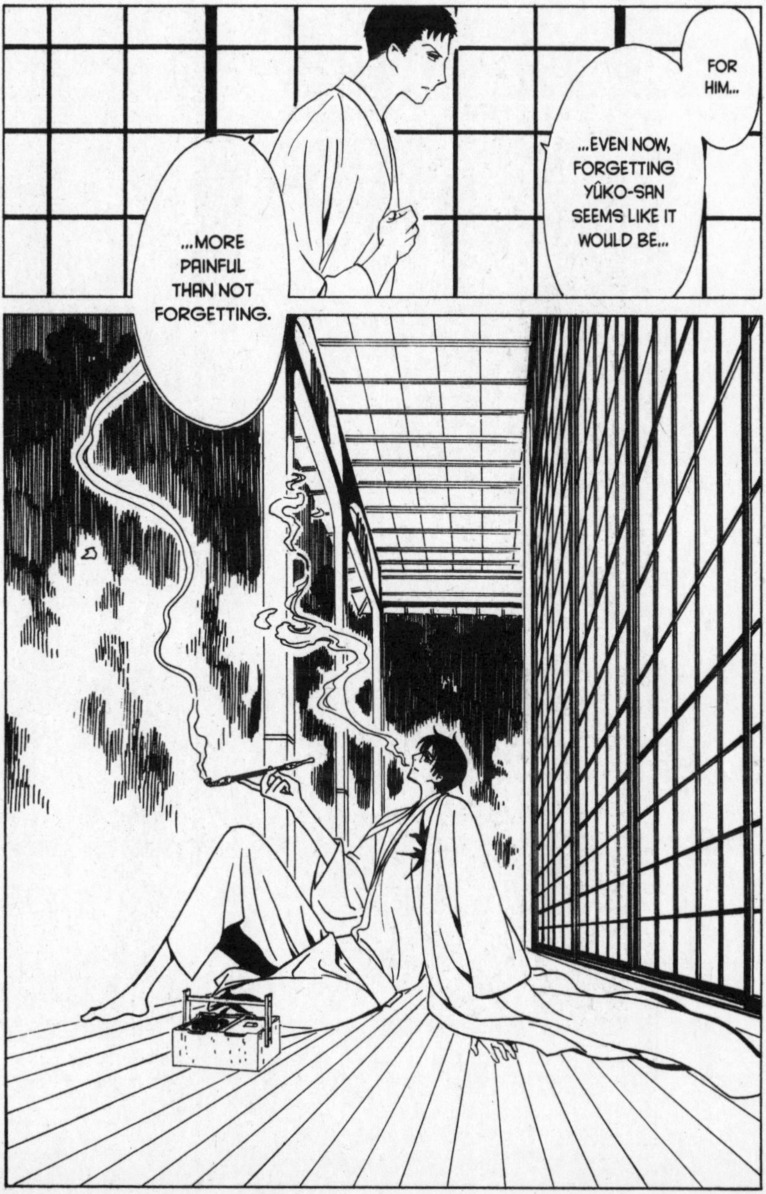
FOR HIM...
...EVEN NOW, FORGETTING YÛKO-SAN SEEMS LIKE IT WOULD BE...
...MORE PAINFUL THAN NOT FORGETTING.

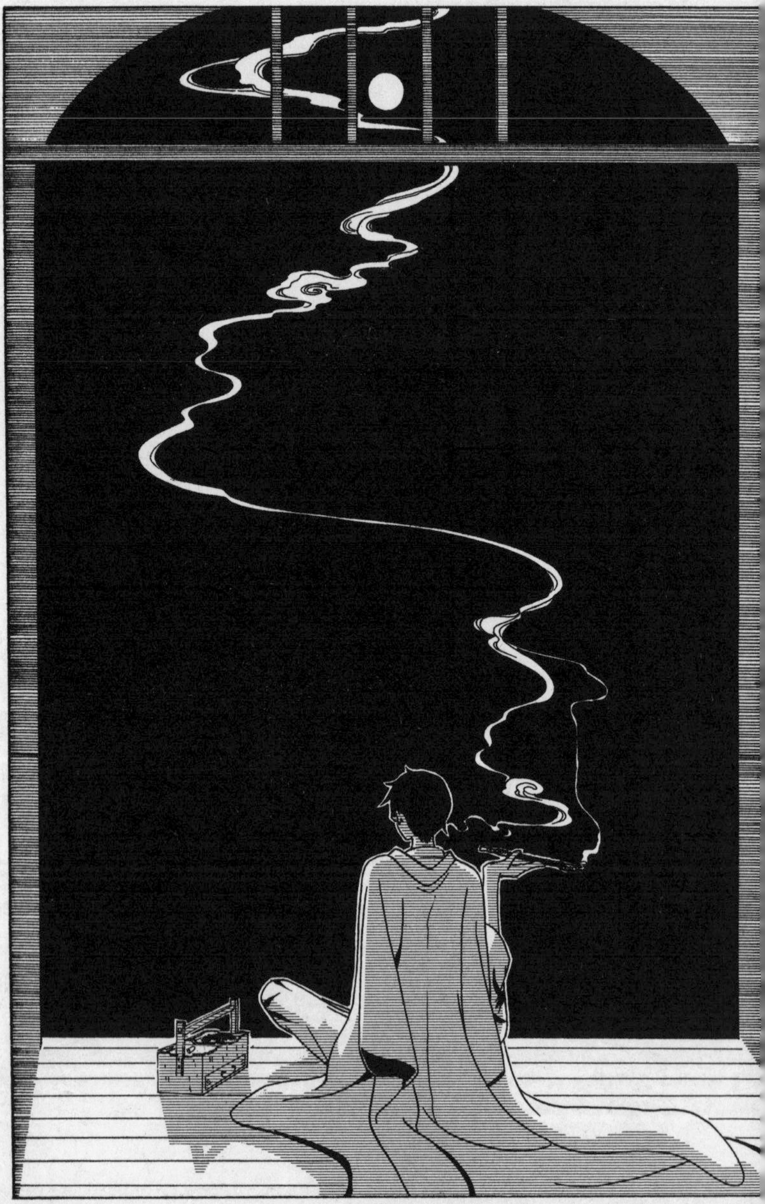

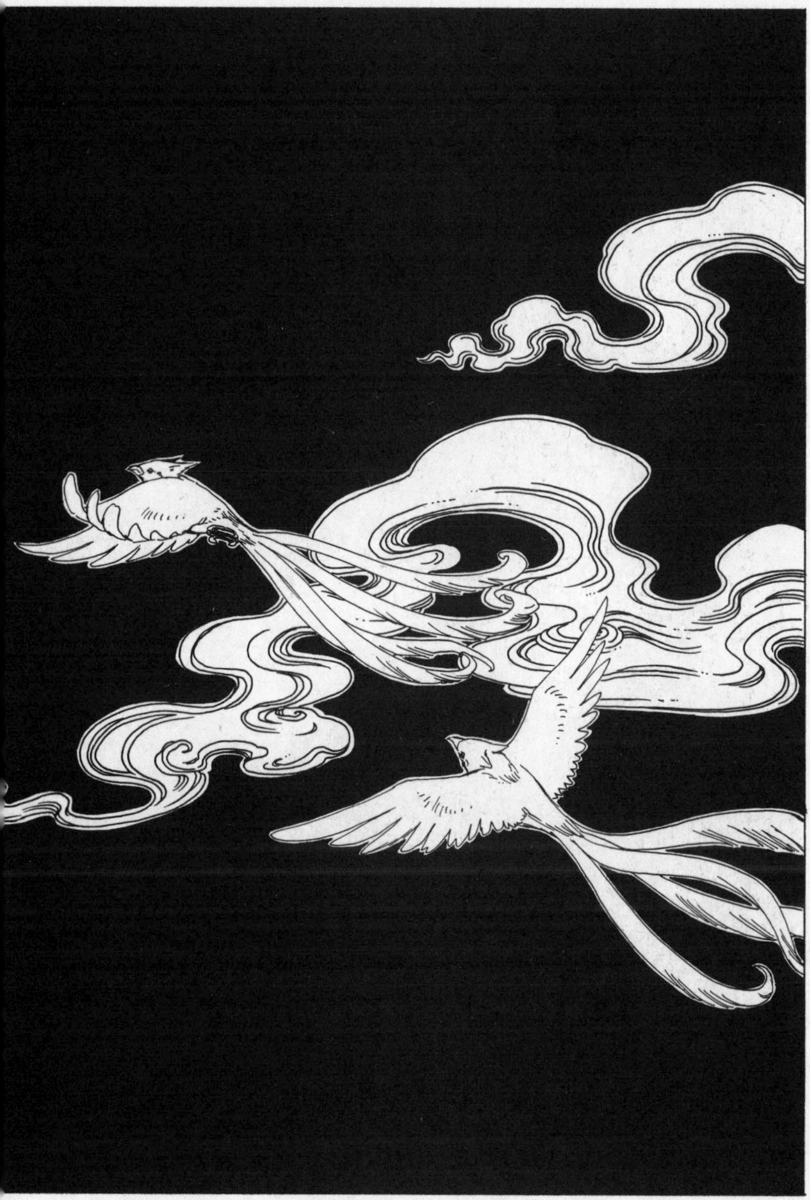

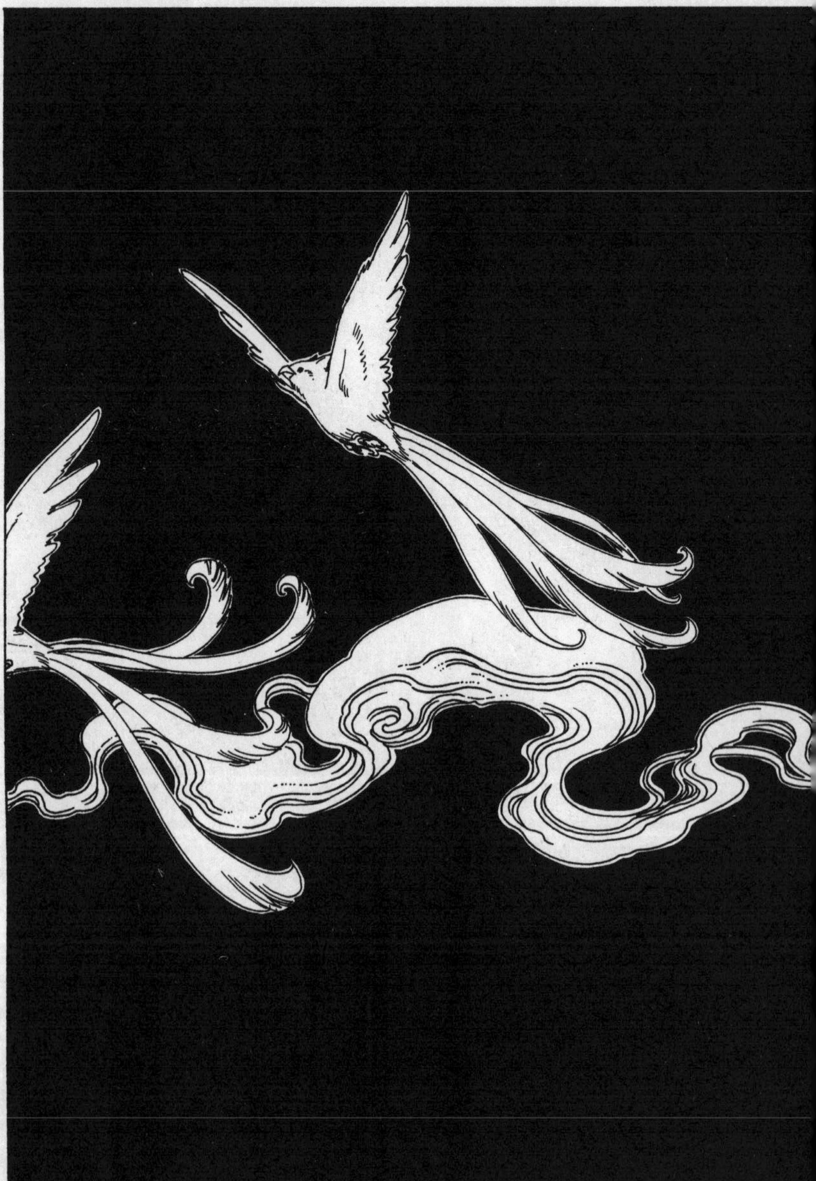

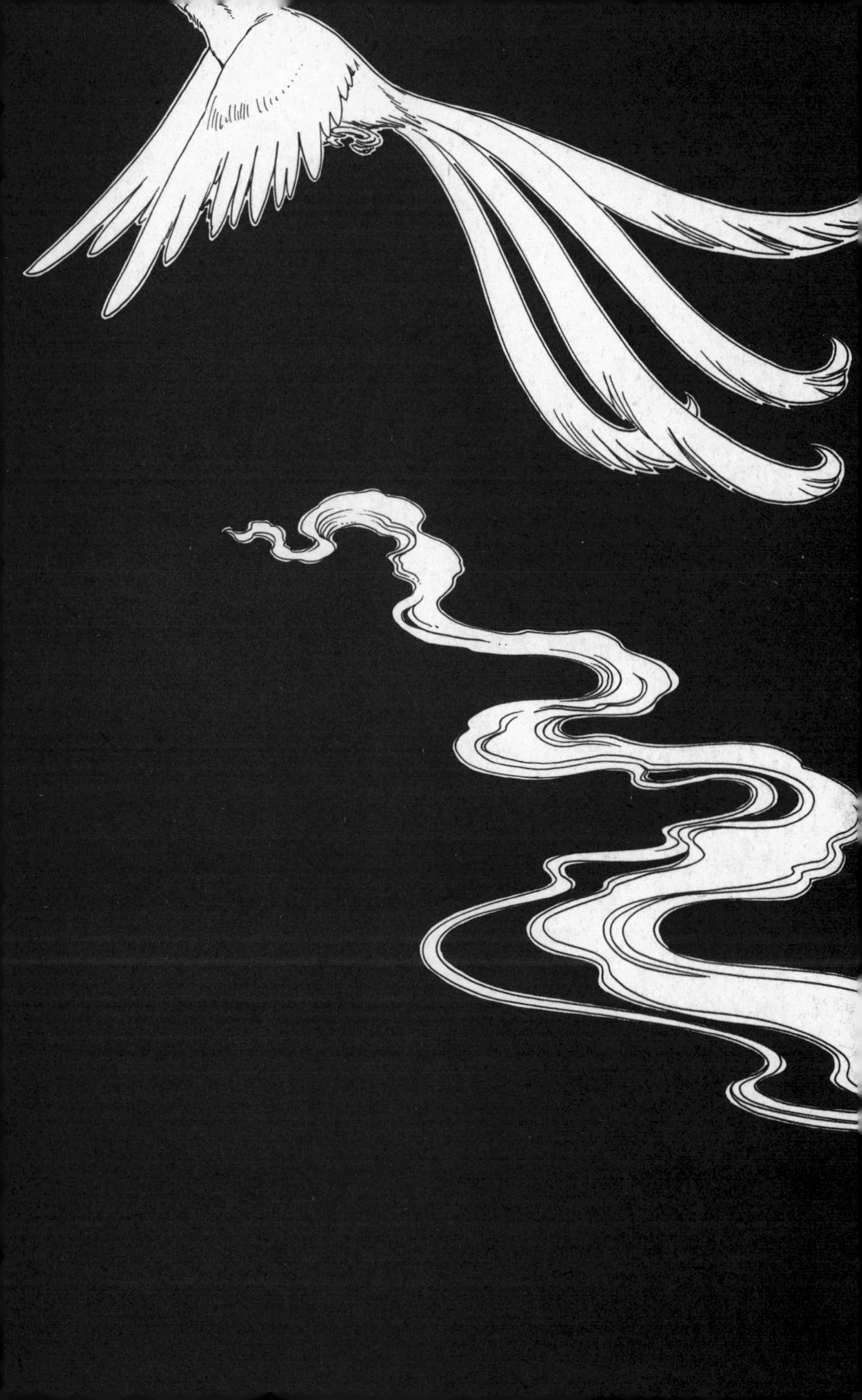

About the Creators

CLAMP is a group of four women who have become the most popular manga artists in America—Nanase Ohkawa, Mokona, Satsuki Igarashi, and Tsubaki Nekoi. They started out as *doujinshi* (fan comics) creators, but their skill and craft brought them to the attention of publishers very quickly. Their first work from a major publisher was RG Veda, but their first mass success was with Magic Knight Rayearth. From there, they went on to write many series, including Cardcaptor Sakura and Chobits, two of the most popular manga in the United States. Like many Japanese manga artists, they prefer to avoid the spotlight, and little is known about them personally.

Translation Notes

Japanese is a tricky language for most Westerners, and translation is often more art than science. For your edification and reading pleasure, here are notes on some of the places where we could have gone in a different direction or where a Japanese cultural reference is used.

Chapter titles, the kanji for Rô

The kanji Rô in this incarnation of xxxHOLiC can also be pronounced *kago*, meaning "a cage" or "a basket," an enclosed area that prevents escape.

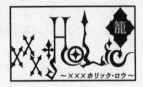

Page 185, Yin and yang and Japanese festivals

Unlike Western dualism, which concentrates on concepts of light versus dark, the Chinese philosophy of yin and yang concentrates on the balance of opposing forces. In other words, a balance of light and dark is preferred, and too much of either extreme is considered bad. Therefore, even though 9 is a "light" number, and September 9 therefore a combination of light numbers, this abundance of light is an ominous thing that throws off the balance of light and dark. The festivals are religious services to help restore the balance.

ALL OF THEM WERE CELEBRATED ON THOSE DAYS ACCORDING TO THE OLD CALENDAR, BUT...
...THE DATES WERE ADJUSTED AND CELEBRATED IN THE NEW CALENDAR.
...THAT MATCHES WHAT I'VE HEARD.
ALL FIVE SEASONAL FESTIVALS WERE BASED ON THE IDEAS OF YIN AND YANG FOUND IN CHINESE PHILOSOPHY.

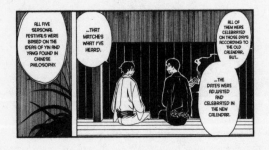

Page 185, Human Day

The first seven days of the year were designated as days honoring particular animals: chicken, dog, boar, sheep, cow, horse, and human. In ancient Japan, Human Day was one day of the year in which the authorities could not execute convicts.

Page 238, "At night, from a distance, or under an umbrella"

This is a phrase translated literally from the Japanese. All the possible English translations of phrases like this came out sounding sarcastic, along the lines of "beer goggles" rather than the more romantic way the Japanese think of this phrase.

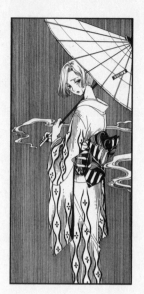

Page 247, Obi

Obi means "belt," but an obi for a kimono is an elaborate, wide silk wrap that is often tied in a complicated bow in back.

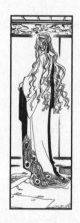

Page 257, Magic square

They say that two thousand years ago, the Chinese had developed what we now call the 3x3 magic square—essentially a tic-tac-toe—style square, in each box of which is placed a number. To make it a magic square, all rows, columns, and diagonals add up to the same numerical sum. In ancient China, these were used for casting fortunes and other occult purposes.

Page 257, Ceremony

In Japanese, the word is more vague. Jutsu-shiki is simply a method of performing a technique. For example, a wedding ceremony is a jutsu-shiki for a marriage. In magic, this may refer to words and actions performed while casting a spell. Since Watanuki's "techniques" are very similar to magical rites, the word "ceremony" seemed to be more appropriate.

Page 277, "as the name implies" The word *kushi* (by linguistic rules, changes to *gushi* under certain circumstances) means "skewer," as in a thin, pointed wooden stick or a long, thin, sharp piece of metal. The *kushi* becomes the backbone of the decoration.

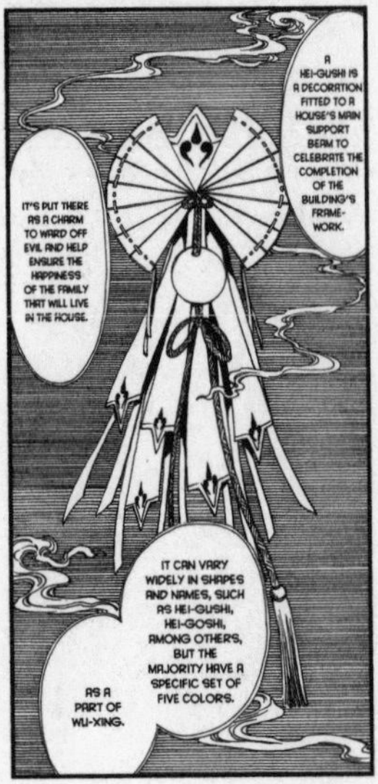
A HEI-GUSHI IS A DECORATION FITTED TO A HOUSE'S MAIN SUPPORT BEAM TO CELEBRATE THE COMPLETION OF THE BUILDING'S FRAME-WORK.
IT'S PUT THERE AS A CHARM TO WARD OFF EVIL AND HELP ENSURE THE HAPPINESS OF THE FAMILY THAT WILL LIVE IN THE HOUSE.
IT CAN VARY WIDELY IN SHAPES AND NAMES, SUCH AS HEI-GUSHI, HEI-GOSHI, AMONG OTHERS, BUT THE MAJORITY HAVE A SPECIFIC SET OF FIVE COLORS.
AS A PART OF WU-XING.

Page 277, Wu-xing-ism

The Chinese doctrine of the five elements—wood, fire, earth, metal, and water—is used in many different areas of Chinese thought, from fortune-telling to traditional medicine. It can be used to determine personality types in love fortunes, but it is also used as a mnemonic device to aid in learning traditional Chinese sciences.

Page 280, Tsukumo-gami

It's said that if tools are well used for a hundred years, they attain a soul of their own and become Tsukumo-gami. According to ancient Japanese legends and folktales, Tsukumo-gami are self-aware and may become vengeful if they are simply discarded after their century of faithful use.

Page 289, Miki

As explained in the notes of Volume 18, miki is saké that is offered up to Shinto gods.

Page 307, Konjac

Konjac (spelled *konnyaku* in Japanese) is a low-calorie jellylike dish made from the konjac potato. It is usually flavored with miso or other sauces.

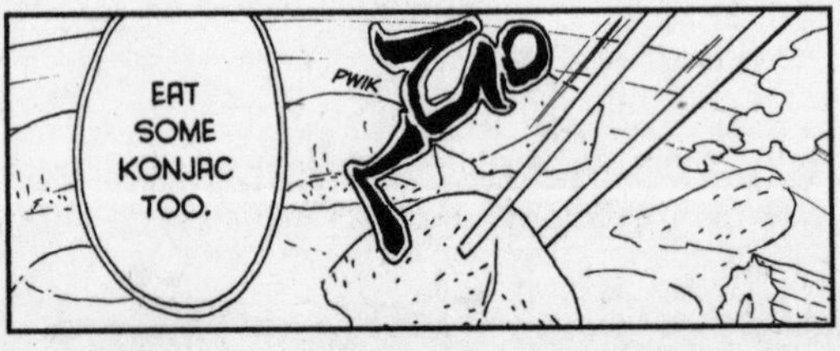
PWIK
EAT SOME KONJAC TOO.

Page 311, Gyoza and Lao Chu

Gyoza (called "pot stickers" in the West) is a Chinese dish that has become very popular in Japan. To go with the Chinese dish is a Chinese drink, Lao Chu, which is a rice-based liquor that can range from a light reddish color to a deep, dark brown.

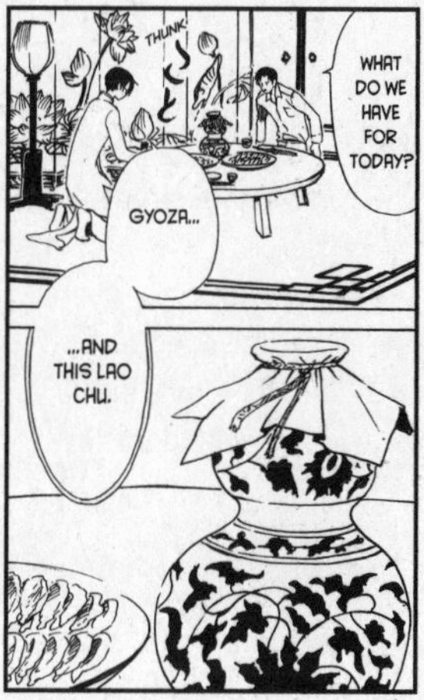
WHAT DO WE HAVE FOR TODAY?
THUNK!
GYOZA...
...AND THIS LAO CHU.

Page 341, *Ten Nights of Dreams*

Natsume Soseki is perhaps the most famous Japanese short-story writer, and his stories "Kokoro" and "I Am a Cat" are reputed to capture the Japanese soul. While writing fiction in installments for a newspaper, he wrote *Ten Nights of Dreams*, ten short shorts that describe various dreams. In the first dream, the protagonist agrees to sit waiting on the grave of the woman he loves for a hundred years. He waits for what seems to be an eternity until one day a white lily sprouts from the grave. When he comes to understand that the lily is what he has been waiting for, he also realizes that a hundred years have passed.

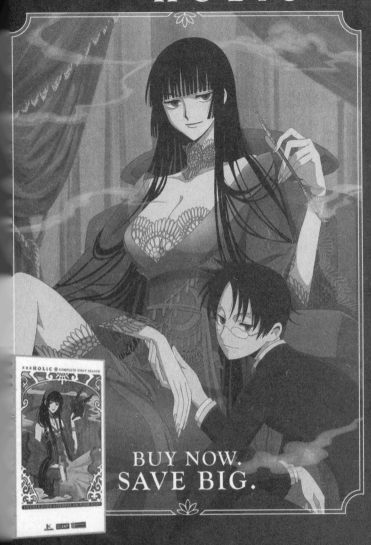

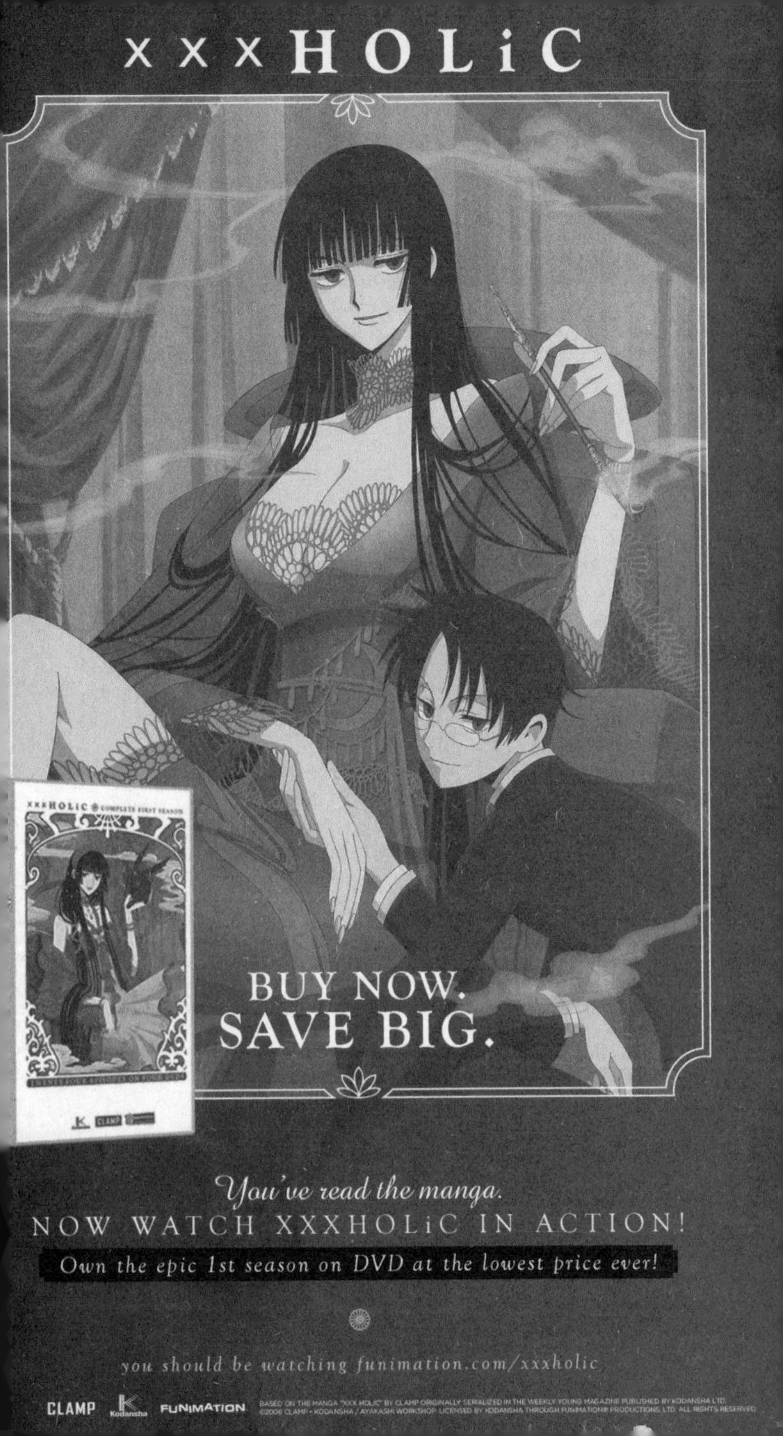

STOP!

[STOP!]

You're going the wrong way!

Manga is a completely different type of reading experience.

To start at the *beginning,* go to the *end*!

That's right! Authentic manga is read the traditional Japanese way—from right to left. Exactly the *opposite* of how American books are read. It's easy to follow: Just go to the other end of the book, and read each page—and each panel—from right side to left side, starting at the top right. Now you're experiencing manga as it was meant to be!